MOOD & ANXIETY DISORDERS

MOOD & ANXIETY DISORDERS

A. John Rush, editor

Professor and Vice-Chairman for Research
Betty Jo Hay Distinguished Chair in Mental Health
Rosewood Corporation Chair in Biomedical Science
The University of Texas
Southwestern Medical Center
Dallas, Texas

With 42 contributors

Williams & Wilkins

A WAVERLY COMPANY

BALTIMORE • PHILADELPHIA • LONDON • PARIS • BANGKOK
BUENOS AIRES • HONG KONG • MUNICH • SYDNEY • TOKYO • WROCLAW

Developed by **Current Science, Inc.**
Philadelphia

Current Science, Inc.
400 Market Street, Suite 700
Philadelphia, PA 19106

Managing Editor:	**Crystal G. Norris**
Developmental Editor:	**Elizabeth Rexon**
Editorial Assistant:	**Michelle Paolucci**
Art Director:	**Paul Fennessy**
Interior Design and Layout:	**Patrick Ward**
Cover Design:	**Christine Keller**
Illustration Director:	**Ann Saydlowski**
Illustrator:	**Lisa Weischedel**
Production:	**Lori Holland**
Indexing:	**Ann Cassar**

ISBN: 0-683-30516-6

ISSN:1083–9402

Every effort has been made to ensure that the drug dosage schedules within this text are accurate and conform to standards at the time of publication. However, as treatment recommendations vary in the light of continuing research and clinical experience, the reader is advised to verify drug dosage schedules herein with information found on product information sheets. This is especially true in cases of new or infrequently used drugs.

Printed in the United States by Edwards Brothers
5 4 3 2 1

DISTRIBUTED WORLDWIDE BY WILLIAMS & WILKINS

Contributors

Robert Abrams, MD
Department of Psychiatry
Payne Whitney Clinic
New York Hospital-Cornell Medical Center
New York, New York

George Alexopoulos, MD
Professor of Psychiatry
Department of Psychiatry
Cornell University Medical College
Director, Specialized Services Division
New York Hospital-Cornell Medical Center
Westchester Division
White Plains, New York

Roseanne Armitage, BSc, MA, PhD
Associate Professor
Department of Psychiatry
University of Texas Southwestern
    Medical Center
Director, Sleep Study Unit
Dallas, Texas

Mark S. Bauer, MD
Associate Professor
Department of Psychiatry and
    Human Behavior
Brown University
Chief, Mental Health and Behavioral
    Sciences Service
Providence Veteran's Administration
    Medical Center
Providence, Rhode Island

Charles L. Bowden, MD
Professor
Department of Psychiatry
The University of Texas Health Science Center
San Antonio, Texas

John F. Clarkin, PhD
Professor of Clinical Psychology
Department of Psychiatry
Cornell Medical College
New York Hospital-Cornell Medical Center
Westchester Division
White Plains, New York

C. Munro Cullum, PhD
Associate Professor
Department of Psychiatry and Neurology
University of Texas Southwestern
    Medical Center
Dallas, Texas

Kirk D. Denicoff, MD
National Institute of Mental Health
National Institutes of Health
Bethesda, Maryland

Roberto A. Dominguez, MD
Professor
Department of Psychiatry and
    Behavioral Sciences
University of Miami School of Medicine
Director, Adult Outpatient Services
Jackson Memorial Hospital
Miami, Florida

Graham J. Emslie, MD
Departments of Psychiatry and Psychology
University of Texas Southwestern
    Medical Center
Children's Medical Center of Dallas
Dallas, Texas

Brenda Erickson, MD
Assistant Professor
Department of Psychiatry
University of Nevada
Reno, Nevada

Maurizio Fava, MD
Associate Professor
Department of Psychiatry
Harvard Medical School
Massachusetts General Hospital
Boston, Massachusetts

Mark A. Frye, MD
Biological Psychiatry Branch
National Institute of Mental Health
National Institutes of Health
Bethesda, Maryland

Mark S. George, MD
Associate Professor
Departments of Psychiatry, Radiology,
    and Neurology
Medical University of South Carolina
Charleston, South Carolina

Anne T. Harvey, PhD
Psychiatric Research Institute
Wichita, Kansas

Robert Hoffmann, PhD
Research Associate
Department of Psychiatry
University of Texas Southwestern
    Medical Center
Dallas, Texas

Carroll W. Hughes, PhD
Professor
Department of Psychiatry
University of Texas Southwestern
    Medical Center
Dallas, Texas
Director of Psychology
Terrell State Hospital
Terrell, Texas

Wayne Katon, MD
Professor
Department of Psychiatry
University of Washington Medical School
Chief of Psychiatric Services
University Hospital
Seattle, Washington

Ira Katz, MD
Sleep and Chronobiology Center
University of Pittsburgh Medical Center
Pittsburgh, Pennsylvania

Terence A. Ketter, MD
Department of Psychiatry and
    Behavioral Science
Stanford University School of Medicine
Stanford, California

Tim A. Kimbrell, MD
Biological Psychiatry Branch
National Institute of Mental Health
National Institutes of Health
Bethesda, Maryland

Laura H. Lacritz, PhD
Assistant Professor
Department of Psychiatry
Neuropsychology Lab
University of Texas Southwestern
    Medical Center
Dallas, Texas

Gabriele S. Leverich, MSW, LCSW
Biological Psychiatry Branch
National Institute of Mental Health
National Institutes of Health
Bethesda, Maryland

Wilson McDermut, PhD
Department of Psychiatry
Rhode Island Hospital
Providence, Rhode Island

Benoit H. Mulsant, MD
Associate Professor of Psychiatry
Department of Psychiatry
University of Pittsburgh School of Medicine
Western Psychiatric Institute and Clinic
Pittsburgh, Pennsylvania

Robert M. Post, MD
Chief, Biological Psychiatry Branch
National Institute of Mental Health
National Institutes of Health
Bethesda, Maryland

Sheldon H. Preskorn, MD
Professor and Vice Chairman
Department of Psychiatry
University of Kansas School of Medicine
Director, Psychiatric Research Institute
Via Christi Medical Center
Wichita, Kansas

Joan Prudic, MD
Assistant Professor of Clinical Psychiatry
Department of Psychiatry
Columbia University
New York State Psychiatric Institute
New York, New York

Charles F. Reynolds III, MD
Professor of Psychiatry and Neuroscience
Department of Psychiatry
University of Pittsburgh School of Medicine
Western Psychiatric Institute and Clinic
Pittsburgh, Pennsylvania

Jerrold F. Rosenbaum, MD
Associate Professor
Department of Psychiatry
Harvard Medical School
Clinical Psychopharmacology Unit
Massachusetts General Hospital
Boston, Massachusetts

Harold A. Sackeim, PhD
Professor
Departments of Psychiatry and Radiology
Columbia University
Chief, Department of Biological Psychiatry
New York State Psychiatric Institute
New York, New York

Herbert C. Schulberg, PhD
Professor
Departments of Psychiatry, Psychology,
    and Medicine
University of Pittsburgh School of Medicine
Western Psychiatric Institute and Clinic
Pittsburgh, Pennsylvania

M. Tracie Shea, PhD
Associate Professor
Department of Psychiatry and
    Human Behavior
Brown University
Posttraumatic Stress Disorders Clinic
Veteran's Administration Medical Center
Providence, Rhode Island

M. Katherine Shear, MD
Associate Professor
Department of Psychiatry
University of Pittsburgh School of Medicine
Anxiety Disorders Prevention Program
Pittsburgh, Pennsylvania

Mark A. Smith, MD, PhD
CNS Diseases Research
DuPont Merck Pharmaceutical Company
Wilmington, Delaware

Andrew M. Speer, MD
Senior Staff Fellow
Biological Psychiatry Branch
National Institute of Mental Health
National Institutes of Health
Bethesda, Maryland

Christina Stanga, MD
Department of Psychiatry
University of Kansas School of Medicine
Wichita Psychiatric Consultants
Wichita, Kansas

Susan R.B. Weiss, PhD
Biological Psychiatry Branch
National Institute of Mental Health
National Institutes of Health
Bethesda, Maryland

Joel Yager, MD
Professor and Vice Chair for Education
Department of Psychiatry
University of New Mexico School of Medicine
Albuquerque, New Mexico

Kimberly A. Yonkers, MD
Assistant Professor
Departments of Psychiatry and Obstetrics
    and Gynecology
University of Texas Southwestern
    Medical Center
Dallas, Texas

Mark Zimmerman, MD
Associate Professor of Psychiatry
Department of Psychiatry
Brown University School of Medicine
Rhode Island Hospital
Providence, Rhode Island

Caron Zlotnick, PhD
Assistant Professor
Department of Psychiatry and Human
    Behavior
Brown University
Butler Hospital
Women and Infants' Hospital
Providence, Rhode Island

Preface

On a daily basis, psychiatric, mental health, and primary care practitioners are confronted with patients with mood, anxiety, eating, and personality disorders. These conditions are both common, disabling, and associated with a disproportionate amount of general medical and mental health care services due in part to the chronic and recurrent nature of these conditions, especially if left partially treated or untreated. In addition, it is well established for mood disorders, and likely for other mental illnesses, that they worsen the prognosis for co-occurring general medical conditions and increase the patient's focus on their somatic well being, causing them to seek general medical care for somatic complaints that are, in fact, a part of their mental illness.

The good news is that our available treatment armamentaria for effectively intervening in these conditions have grown remarkably over the past two decades. Not only have psychopharmacologic advances provided new, safer, and better tolerated medicines, but psychotherapeutic investigations have revealed that time-limited, disorder-targeted psychotherapies are highly effective for selected mood, anxiety, and eating disorders.

Supplementing these advances in treatment, research has begun to reveal a far more specific and discerning picture of the neural mechanisms and physiologic factors that underlie these conditions. This more basic neurobiologic understanding sets the stage for more efficient orchestration of available treatments, as well as subsequent innovations in the development of new treatments.

This book provides practitioners with critical information on the diagnosis, treatment, and basic biology of mood and anxiety disorders in primary care and mental health settings. Dr. George and coworkers bring us up to date with regard to the fundamental neural mechanisms underlying mood disorders, and Dr. Post and coworkers discuss the relevance of the kindling model for understanding the course of these illnesses. Further biologic underpinnings are discussed by Drs. Armitage and Hoffmann in their chapter on the sleep physiology of major mood disorders.

The nuances of treatment for major depressive and dysthymic disorder are presented by Drs. Fava and Rosenbaum. Treatment for bipolar disorder is discussed by Dr. Bowden. Drs. Prudic and Sackeim update our understanding of both the mechanisms and clinical issues in the use of electroconvulsive therapy for mood disorders. Dr. Reynolds and coworkers highlight recent efforts to better define treatments for geriatric mood disorders.

Drs. Preskorn, Harvey, and Stanga provide us with a very readable and clinically useful update on drug interactions and their significance in patient care. Dr. Yonkers provides a most thorough review, as well as practical recommendations for the treatment of premenstrual dysphoric disorder.

We know that the treatment context and comorbidities surrounding mood and anxiety disorders affect outcome. Empirical studies on the treatment of these conditions in the primary care setting are reviewed by Drs. Schulberg, Katon, and Shear. When personality disorders co-occur with mood and anxiety disorders, they affect the management of these patients. Recognition and management of personality disorders in the context of mood disorders, and management of borderline personality disorder are discussed by Drs. Clarkin and Abrams, and Drs. Zlotnick and Shea, respectively.

Dr. Dominguez reviews our knowledge of how to treat obsessive-compulsive disorder, adding critical clinical experiences to his review of the scientific data. Drs. Yager and Erickson discuss the impact of the coexistence of eating disorders and mood disorders and the role of this comorbidity on treatment selection and patient management. Drs. Hughes and Emslie provide a critical review of what we know of the treatment of anxiety disorders in children and adolescents. Drs. McDermut and Zimmerman discuss the degree and nature of the effect of personality disorders on the outcome of treatment for depression.

Finally, mood disorders often co-occur with various general medical conditions. When present, these conditions affect our ability to treat these mood disorders and may demand revision of our treatment strategies and tactics. This issue is discussed by Drs. Lacritz and Cullum with regard to stroke and depression.

This book was designed to be a synthesis of state-of-the-art research and clinical information by experienced practitioners with the aim of improving our ability to select and implement appropriate treatment for individual patients, thereby improving both symptomatic and functional outcomes. I believe readers will find this collection to be of practical clinical benefit, while also providing some intriguing new insights into the etiology and pathobiology of these conditions.

A. John Rush, MD
Dallas, Texas

Contents

CHAPTER 1

Neural Mechanisms of Mood Disorders

Mark S. George, Robert M. Post, Terence A. Ketter, Tim A. Kimbrell, and Andrew M. Speer

Within the past century investigators have realized that mood dysregulation arises from dysfunction within specific regions of the brain. Initially, theories of the regional neurobiology of depression were based on information from brain-injured patients. More recently, animal models of depression, and studies of a host of measures (eg, platelet receptors, cerebrospinal fluid neurotransmitters, neuropeptides and metabolites, electrophysiologic studies of evoked potentials or electroencephalograms, functional neuroimaging) have aided thinking in this area. Psychiatric conditions in general, and mood disorders in particular, challenge researchers and clinicians to simultaneously integrate information from multiple conceptual levels. This chapter reviews several models of mood dysregulation from a theoretical perspective, focusing on the level of regional neuroanatomic defects, while attempting to incorporate information from "above" (ie, more clinical, such as the role of psychologic stress, grief, and loss) and from "below" (ie, more basic, such as pharmacologic information at the level of the synapse and genetic information at the level of the nucleus). Eventually, modern psychiatry must integrate knowledge from these conceptual levels to fully understand the complexity of such neuropsychiatric conditions as "mood disorders."

Historically, clinical depression has been understood at various times as a disorder involving the heart (Aristotle), bodily humors (Galen), the mind in an abstract sense (Freud), or the brain in a global, black-box fashion (behaviorism) (Fig. 1). It is only within the past century that investigators have come to realize that mood dysregulation arises from dysfunction within specific regions of the brain.

Initially, theories of the regional neurobiology of depression were based on information from brain-injured patients, in whom depression arose in the setting of other brain diseases (referred to as *secondary depressions*). More recently, advances in imaging techniques now permit direct examination of the working brain during episodes of clinical depression, permitting more direct testing of hypotheses concerning abnormal neural mechanisms. Studies with these techniques have confirmed and refined earlier models, suggesting that the frontal and temporal lobes, the basal ganglia, the cerebellum, and parts of the limbic system (amygdala and anterior cingulate) behave abnormally in patients with depression or mania.

This chapter reviews several models of mood dysregulation from a theoretical perspective. We also incorporate older lesion and other studies with more recent neuroimaging results to suggest an emerging neuroanatomy of depression.

Mood and other psychiatric disorders challenge us to simultaneously integrate information from multiple conceptual levels to explain and understand these illnesses (Fig. 2). Any model of clinical depression must somehow account for genetic factors, especially for bipolar illnesses, and integrate knowledge about family, cognitive, and pharmacologic therapies.

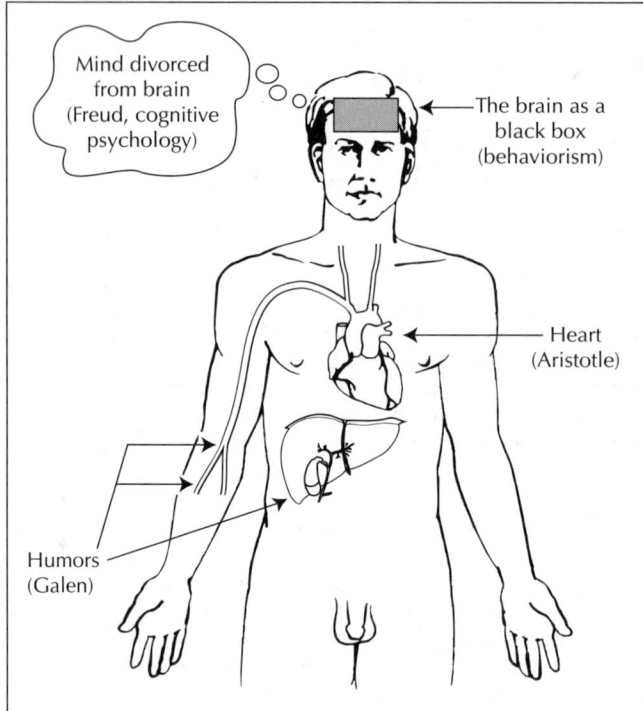

Figure 1. The different historical locations for depression or melancholia. Depression has been viewed only recently as a disease of specific structures within the brain. Information from brain-injured patients and new functional imaging techniques is finally permitting investigation of the neuroanatomy of depression.

This chapter focuses on the level of regional neuroanatomic defects, while attempting to incorporate information from "above" and from "below." The distinction between overt brain structural abnormalities and brain dysfunction is critical in conceptualizing mood dysregulation.

Problems in behavior (or function) could exist in the setting of grossly normal structure. Visually apparent structural abnormalities are generally absent in primary mood disorders. Thus, mood disorders, much like primary generalized epilepsy, are neuropsychiatric diseases with abnormal brain function, despite grossly normal structure. Just as the EEG has helped to legitimize the disease of epilepsy [1,2], functional-imaging tools (single photon emission computed tomography [SPECT], positron emission tomography [PET], and functional magnetic resonance imaging [fMRI]) are now affirming the neurologic basis for mood disorders despite normal structure.

Organizational Models and Frameworks

Where in the brain does abnormal mood regulation (*eg,* depression or mania) reside? Depression, a disease of and about the brain [3–8], also has profound effects throughout the body. Numerous studies have now found abnormalities in the hypothalamopituitary–adrenal (HPA) axis in clinically depressed subjects [9]. MRI studies have found that the adrenal glands in depressed subjects are larger than in nondepressed controls, perhaps owing to persistent HPA axis overactivity [10]. It is clear that the primary defect in some forms of clinical depression resides outside of the brain, and that the central nervous system (CNS) effects are secondary (*eg*, endocrinopathies of the thyroid, adrenal, and parathyroid glands, with their consequent levels of thyroid hormone, cortisol, or calcitonin, respectively) [8,11].

Whether mood dysregulation arises from primary defects in regional brain function or secondary effects orchestrated by the CNS, which regions are involved? Considerable evidence implicates selected limbic structures (especially the amygdala, anterior cingulate, and prefrontal cortical structures). Some have argued that mood dysregulation occurs as a result of changes in individual discrete brain structures (*eg*, the left amygdala), but more commonly researchers have proposed that coordinated regional brain systems (*ie*, networks) participate in regulating emotion [12–17]. Several of these systems or approaches are discussed below.

Concept of the limbic system

MacLean's concept of the triune brain, and also the limbic system [18], is an attractive heuristic way to organize our thinking about the neural mechanisms of depression [19–22]. The triune brain consists of three concentric brain systems, physically layered on top of each other, with each successive layer representing an evolutionary advance. Each advance simultaneously allows new behaviors, while recapitulating older ones. The human brain can be thought of as representing a composite of three brains in one (*ie*, the triune brain). The deepest layer, found in reptiles, is the reptilian brain or basal ganglia

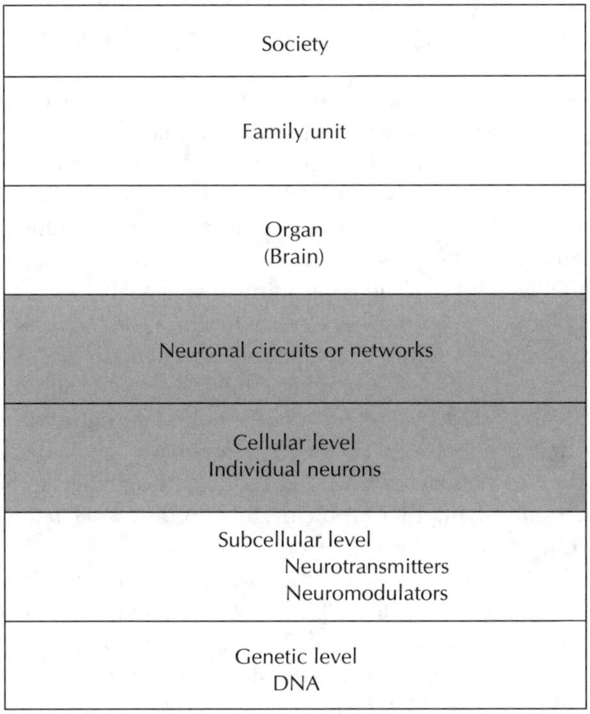

Society
Family unit
Organ (Brain)
Neuronal circuits or networks
Cellular level Individual neurons
Subcellular level Neurotransmitters Neuromodulators
Genetic level DNA

Figure 2. Biosocial levels of understanding mood disorders. Similar to other neuropsychiatric disorders, the study of mood disorders requires the integration of information from several different levels of the biopsychosocial spectrum. The *shaded areas* indicate that this paper, and functional neuroimaging data in general, give information at the level of the organ (brain) or networks within the brain.

(olfactory tubercle, nucleus accumbens, caudate, putamen, and globus pallidus). This largely motor-focused brain allows simple actions (alertness, eating, procreating) in pre-programmed rigid routines, which lack flexibility and emotion. The next layer (paleo-mammalian) arose with early mammals and corresponds to the great limbic lobe of Broca and connected brain stem structures. This extension is only rudimentary in reptiles and birds. The final part of the human triune brain is the neomammalian brain, com-prising the neocortex and connected brain stem structures. These structures are thought to have an important part in organizing behaviors that are unique to mammals, such as bonding, caring for young, and play.

This heuristic scheme involves the notion of the recapitulation of function within the brain. Thus, affect or mood regulation is represented in all three components of the tri-une brain, and the triune brain concept would be consistent with the idea that direct damage to some reptilian brain structures (eg, the caudate) are associated with defects in affective recognition or mood regulation. More importantly, damage to the early mam-malian brain (limbic system) would more likely derange affective regulation. Mammals, in contrast with lizards, engage in three family-related behaviors—nursing and parental care, vocal communication with offspring, and play [23]. Thus, phylogenetically, the newly emergent limbic system would be more important in producing and regulating these characteristic mammalian behaviors that involve recognizing and displaying affect to build social relationships. Finally, direct damage to the neocortex, greatly expanded in humans, might also disrupt mood, largely through interruption of frontal cortical regulation of the limbic and reptilian brains.

The triune brain model is consistent with experimental data implicating numerous structures in mood regulation; from basal ganglia and limbic system to the cortex. (For further reading see MacLean [20,21]).

Evidence for limbic system dysregulation in mood disorders comes from neuropsy-chologic, imaging, ablation, and stimulation studies in humans and other species [24–26]. Clinical studies by Penfield and Perot [27] revealed that stimulation of limbic structures in patients produced a gamut of emotional reactions. Stimulation [24–26,28,29] and abla-tion studies have established that the limbic system plays a critical role in modulating and controlling affect (ie, the external displays of emotion such as smiling, frowning, scream-ing). Similarly, our laboratory (initially at NIMH and continuing now at MUSC) has used a variety of neuropsychologic and pharmacologic probes to elicit limbic activity in patients suffering from clinical depression. Depressed subjects had defects in recognizing the affect displayed on human faces, and they performed in a manner similar to right brain–dam-aged control groups [30]. Using ^{15}O-labeled PET scans, facial emotion recognition was mediated bilaterally by the prefrontal and temporal cortex (anterior as well as medial) in healthy control subjects [31]. Depressed patients performing the same task failed to acti-vate right mesial temporal structures, implying that limbic dysfunction is associated with this affective recognition defect [32]. We and others have also demonstrated that the cin-gulate gyrus activates when healthy subjects perform a complex task requiring inhibition of a competing overlearned response (the Stroop task) [33], but depressed subjects per-forming the same task did not activate the cingulate, but rather activated the left dorsolat-eral prefrontal and bilateral visual cortices (George et al., Unpublished abstract).

Initial work with quantitative EEG [34], and later with ^{15}O-labeled PET scans [34–37] has demonstrated that the affective responses induced by intravenous procaine occur in conjunction with increased activity in anterior paralimbic structures. Interestingly, although there are some differences in regional brain activity depending on affective response to the drug (left amygdala deactivation with euphoria and activation with anxiety), other anterior paralimbic structures are generally and nonspecifically activated despite different phenomenologic responses [35]. The anterior limbic system activates following procaine administration, irrespective of whether or not one is anxious, sad, or euphoric, which confirms that the limbic system controls and regulates affect [18]. However, the same dose of procaine given to medication-free depressed individuals results in a markedly diminished limbic activation [38]. Similar methods [39] have shown that depressed subjects also have blunted limbic responses to amphetamine challenge. Thus, neuropsychologic, functional-imaging, ablation, and stimulation studies provide support for the notion of the limbic system as a functioning, integrated system that regulates normal and pathologic mood.

Frontal–subcortical circuits

An additional conceptualization of the structures involved in clinical depression involves the interconnections of subcortical structures putatively linked to emotional modulation with the cortex, especially the prefrontal cortex. Alexander *et al.* [40] highlighted the concept of at least five important basal ganglia–thalamocortical loops involving the prefrontal lobes (Fig. 3). Each segregated and parallel loop includes a separate part of the prefrontal cortex. These five circuits have been designated *motor, oculomotor, dorsolateral prefrontal* (DLPFC), *lateral orbitofrontal*, and *anterior cingulate*. The elements of each circuit include discrete, nonoverlapping parts of the striatum, globus pallidus, substantia nigra, thalamus, and cortex. Each circuit receives multiple corticostriate inputs from various frontal lobe regions involved in specific tasks. For example, the oculomotor circuit receives input from three separate areas of the frontal lobe, all known to involve eye movements. Thus, these discrete circuits take neuroanatomically distinct frontal lobe areas and combine them into functional working units or circuits. Some researchers have sought to use this framework to explain how prefrontal lobe pathology might result in the symptoms of clinical depression [41,42]. This organizational system posits multiple, noncontiguous areas within the frontal lobes that participate in producing the same behavior (*eg,* motor movement).

Certain clinical syndromes could result from damage anywhere within the circuit, either at the level of the frontal lobes, or subcortically, in the basal ganglia or thalamus. For example, damage to the orbitofrontal circuit results in disinhibition, irritability, and decreased sensitivity to social clues (seen in mania and hypomania). Anterior cingulate (medial frontal) damage produces apathy and reduced motivation (commonly seen in depression). In its most severe form, this damage results in akinetic mutism. Dorsolateral prefrontal damage results in a dementia syndrome with problems in set-shifting and deficits in learning and word list generation. Some have linked dorsolateral prefrontal damage as a potential problem in patients with schizophrenia [43–45]. Many of the symptoms and phenomenology of clinical depression can thus be loosely mapped onto these circuits. Given the symptomatic presentations of depression, one might infer that the lateral orbitofrontal, the anterior cingulate, and to a lesser extent, the dorsolateral prefrontal circuits are probably involved—a finding supported by a recent PET study [46] that "psychomotor retardation" correlated with decreased left DLPFC activity.

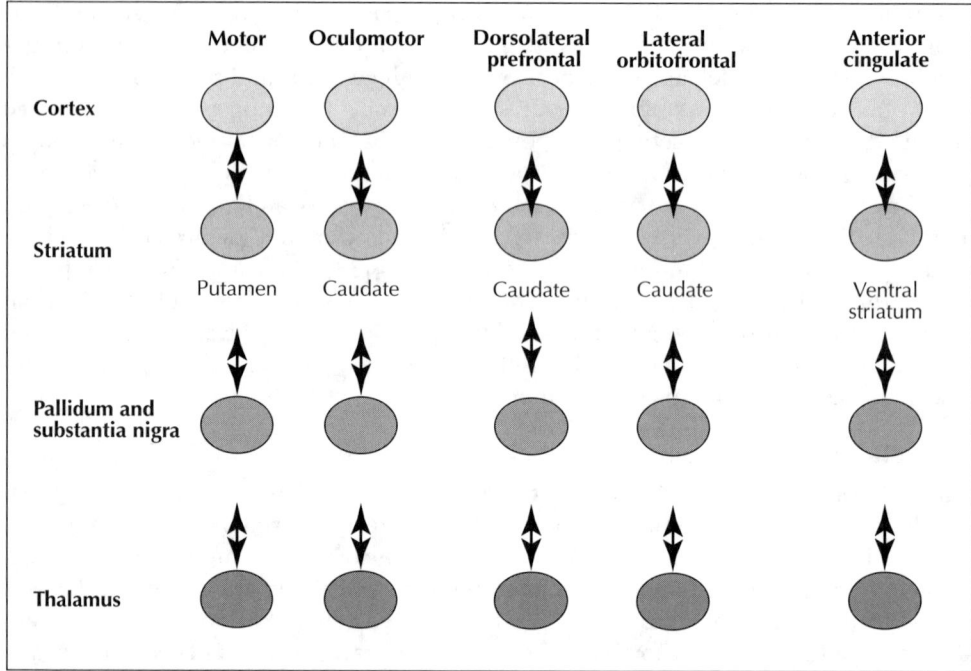

Figure 3. The five known basal ganglia–thalamo–frontal cortex loops demonstrated by Alexander *et al.* [40]. This figure illustrates another way of organizing thinking about the brain basis of mood regulation. Each circuit exists discretely, separately, and in parallel, although there is crosstalk, especially at the subcortical levels. Each circuit combines neuroanatomically separate regions in the frontal lobes into functioning networks controlling specific behaviors. These circuits thus bridge through and connect the three brain layers described by MacLean.

Valence or hemispheric laterality theories

Another hypothesis of neural mechanisms of mood regulation postulates that the left hemisphere mediates positive emotions (*eg,* happiness), whereas the right mediates negative emotions (anger, fear, disgust, anxiety, sadness [47–50]). One's mood state at any given time reflects the relative balance of these two hemispheres. Temporarily or permanently disabling one hemisphere allows the other to act in an unbalanced manner. Using the Wada test [51], separately anesthetizing each hemisphere, observers have noted that sadness and catastrophic reactions are associated with left hemisphere deactivation, whereas right hemisphere deactivation is associated with happy or euphoric responses [46].

Furthermore, numerous studies demonstrate the crucial role of the right brain in both understanding and expressing emotion. The left side of the face (controlled by the right hemisphere) is more expressive of emotion than the right [49]. Verbal and visual stimuli with an emotional content are better processed by the right hemisphere [50]. For example, in a recent PET study, we demonstrated that the right hemisphere is activated when listening to speech for the emotional tone (or prosody), rather than for the content of the words themselves [52].

In a recent attempt to directly test the valence theory of mood, we employed a new technology known as rapid transcranial magnetic stimulation (rTMS) to temporarily excite (and then inhibit) prefrontal cortex and observe the effects on mood. When using rTMS over the right or left prefrontal cortex on different days, in 10 adult, healthy volunteers, we found left prefrontal stimulation associated with increased self-rated sadness, whereas right stimulation caused increased happiness [53]. This study confirmed and extended work by Pascual-Leone *et al.* [54].

Other studies are also consistent with the valence theory of mood. Some PET and SPECT studies have demonstrated that clinically depressed subjects have abnormal prefrontal function, more commonly on the left than on the right [16,55–60]. Several studies of poststroke patients have found that damage to the left prefrontal cortex greatly increases the likelihood of a poststroke depression [61–63]. In addition, depressed compared with nondepressed patients with multiple sclerosis (MS) have more white matter lesions on the left side [64]. These findings are also consistent with sad, crying reactions to left-sided Wada or speech arrest testing in epileptic patients [65,66]. Also in line with the findings in this study, damage to the right hemisphere, especially the right prefrontal or temporal cortex, has been linked to primary or secondary mania [17,67–69].

Finally, in a series of studies, Davidson *et al.* [70] found that asymmetries in prefrontal EEG activity (alpha power) correspond with different selection of happy versus sad items. Healthy subjects with more left frontal activation (increased left activity, relatively decreased right) endorse happy and euphoric items, whereas right activation (and left deactivation) corresponds to endorsement of sad items. Depressed subjects, consistent with other functional-imaging studies and the foregoing valence or laterality model, had more left frontal hypoactivation than controls.

Although the valence hypothesis is supported by many studies, several reports reveal results inconsistent with this theory [71,72] (for a critical review *see* Sackheim [73]), and only a weak plurality of functional-imaging studies of mood disordered patients support lateralized dysfunction. In contrast with the valence theory of mood, at least two PET studies in healthy volunteers have now demonstrated that there is *increased* left orbitofrontal and left prefrontal activity during states of transient sadness [74,75]. Further work is necessary to refine this theory of differential hemispheric contribution to mood.

It may be that, in fact, there is a difference in hemispheric contribution or regulation of mood, but that this also depends on differential activity within the hemispheres, the limbic system, and other subcortical structures. Conversely, it is possible that the limbic system, acting in an integrated way and spanning the two hemispheres, moderates or enhances this differential cortical regulation, producing and amplifying noise that confuses findings to date. It may also be that just as the laterality of handedness does not always follow a rule, there may be individual subjects who are lateralized to a lesser degree, or even differently, than the majority of individuals.

Pharmacologic models: serotonin, dopamine, norepinephrine

Antidepressant medications that affect norepinephrine, serotonin, or perhaps dopamine now effectively treat most individuals suffering from clinical depression. In addition, lithium, carbamazepine, and valproate have been effective in controlling mood dysregulation [76–80]. Comprehensive models of the regional neurobiology of disordered mood regulation must somehow integrate this important information.

Serotonin-, dopamine-, and norepinephrine-containing neurons richly connect with many of the limbic and prefrontal sites previously discussed. Although these cell bodies arise in deep brain nuclei, they project into limbic and neocortical areas, thereby bridging and spanning the triune brains. Presumably, treatment with medications that alter transmission of serotonin, dopamine, or norepinephrine causes changes in activity in the regions to which these neurons project. Unfortunately, there are as yet only a few studies linking changes in functional imaging with changes in regional neurotransmitter function [81].

A recent study by Bremner *et al.* [81] is one of the first to use this new paradigm of combining functional neuroimaging with pharmacology. They scanned remitted depressed subjects with [18F]fluorodeoxyglucose (FDG)-labeled PET scans before and after administering a tryptophan depletion diet, which caused some subjects to re-experience their depressive symptoms. Those who relapsed during tryptophan depletion had higher activity in their cingulate gyrus at rest (before tryptophan depletion), and had decreased prefrontal activity during symptomatic relapse. This implies a potential coupling of the prefrontal hypoactivity with changes in serotonin.

Specific Structures Implicated in Mood Regulation

In addition to the systems and models previously reviewed, several distinct brain regions appear to be especially important in regulating mood. Evidence for their involvement is presented here by structure.

Prefrontal cortex

The prefrontal cortex is significantly connected to many brain regions and is uniquely situated to simultaneously control motor behavior, interpret the significance of sensory input from several different modalities, and then set the internal state of arousal and tone through connections with limbic and neuroendocrine regions.

However, localization of specific behaviors to frontal lobe subregions is difficult because discrete frontal lobe regions often participate together to produce or modulate behavior through basal ganglia–thalamocortical loops, and most pathologic processes affecting the frontal lobes are not anatomically discrete or precise.

Lesion studies

Animal and human cases of frontal lobe damage demonstrate a wide range of possible responses to frontal lobe disruption. The literature in this area is highly controversial and inconsistent, clouded by the issues mentioned previously concerning the exact location of the lesion and the extent of premorbid brain changes [82]. It appears that in some individuals, possibly depending on which regions within the frontal lobes are damaged and whether there is premorbid brain damage, specific behavioral sequelae result. For example, *orbitofrontal leukotomies* were frequently reported to produce euphoria and disinhibition and, therefore, were used in catatonically depressed subjects [83]. More anterior leukotomies, involving the frontal convexity, produced flattening of affect and, thus, were used in agitated or manic patients [84]. However, these findings were by no means consistent, and in other studies and in other individuals, removal of large parts of the prefrontal cortex has virtually no effect on day-to-day behavior. In at least some persons there are resultant mood changes (euphoria, irritability, emotional indifference) and character changes (lack of initiative, boastfulness) [85]. Thus, damage to the prefrontal lobes is perhaps necessary to produce distinct behavioral syndromes, but mere damage alone is not always sufficient. An irritative lesion, such as a seizure discharge, may be more disruptive and harder to compensate than ablative lesions. Clearly, multiple other factors, some possibly relating to the frontal lobes' governance over or interconnection with limbic structures, are also important in producing the behavior.

A common clinical axiom is that after prefrontal lobe damage the premorbid personality coarsens [82,86]. Accordingly, if a patient is fretful and anxious to begin with, prefrontal damage often makes this worse. Similarly, a jocular individual may become disinhibited and intrusive after frontal lobe damage. Regardless of the species, prefrontal ablation often does not qualitatively change premorbid behaviors; rather, prior behaviors are accentuated [87,88]. Conceivably, regions in the prefrontal lobes may regulate or govern, in some way, the primitive unmodulated behaviors (drives or natural tendencies) that are ingrained in subcortical structures and the limbic system. Removal of this highest-level integrative or modulatory function of the prefrontal lobes may unleash more primitive limbic-mediated behaviors. In psychodynamic terms, the prefrontal cortex may thus play the dual roles of the ego and superego, whereas deeper structures (limbic and basal ganglia) are more representative of the id. Following this line of thinking, some signs and symptoms of depression (appetite, sleep disturbance) might result not from direct prefrontal dysfunction, but from the lack of frontal governance over, or integration of, other temporal, limbic, or hypothalamic activity. For example, mania might thus be due to a lack of control over amygdala or other limbic output, rather than a direct product of prefrontal dysfunction.

Livingston [89] described two separate, but parallel, frontal–limbic–hypothalamic–midbrain circuits for emotional control, similar to those described earlier by Alexander *et al.* [40]. The medial frontal–cingulate–hippocampus circuit was thought to be more important in regulating depression, whereas the lateral orbital frontal–temporal–amygdala circuit was more committed to governing anxiety and manic symptoms. Blumer and Benson [90] reasoned similarly when they described two distinct syndromes following frontal damage. One syndrome, which they called *pseudodepression*, featured apathy, unconcern, and lack of drive, and resulted from lesions in the medial frontal lobes and cingulate cortex. The other syndrome consisted of *disinhibition*, including facetiousness, sexual disinhibition, and lack of empathy. This occurred more frequently after orbital frontal injury. These behaviors can and do, in fact, result from frontal lobe damage. However, because of the difficulties noted earlier, the correlation of specific behaviors with specific subareas within the frontal lobes is less tenable and unlikely to be proved by individual case studies.

Anatomic studies

The original studies of the structural anatomy of patients with affective illness were largely unremarkable [91–93]. Recently, however, well-designed studies using advanced imaging techniques have found differences involving the prefrontal lobes and neighboring regions in depressed subjects compared with controls. Several investigators have found an increase in ventricular size in patients with recurrent mood disorders compared with age-matched controls [94,95]. The interpretation of these studies is unclear, as numerous pathophysiologic processes may result in ventricular enlargement. However, atrophy of periventricular white matter regions, including the frontal lobes, is one possible mechanism. This formulation is interesting in light of recent work by Coffey *et al.* [96], who used MRI scans to investigate 48 inpatients with severe depression and compared them with 76 healthy controls. Depressed patients had a 7% smaller mean total frontal lobe volume than controls.

Structural MRI has also been used in at least two other studies implicating frontal lobe dysfunction in depression. Rangel-Guerra *et al.* [97] used MRI to examine bipolar affective disorder subjects (BPAD) and found increased T_1 values in frontal and temporal white matter, which normalized with lithium therapy. The significance of increased T_1 values is unclear, but possibly reflects shifts in water distribution which, in turn, may represent changes in metabolism. Dolan *et al.* [98] examined 14 medicated patients with BPAD, 10 medicated patients with unipolar depression, and 10 controls. Interestingly, they also found increases in T_1 signal intensity in the frontal white matter. However, this was true of only unipolar depressed subjects compared with controls. It is unclear whether these results represent a change in brain structure, function, or both.

Secondary depression

Other studies indicate that frontal involvement of other CNS diseases can increase the probability of developing secondary depression. Robinson *et al.* [61–63,67] have demonstrated that ischemic damage to the left frontal cortex greatly increases the chance of developing poststroke depression (Fig. 4). However, other investigators have failed to replicate these findings [71,72]. In a similar vein, George *et al.* [64] studied patients with MS using MRI. Patients with both MS and comorbid depression had significantly more plaques in left hemisphere white matter compared with nondepressed subjects with a similarly severe MS disease state. These studies imply that other brain illnesses can precipitate a secondary depression, possibly by damaging left frontal lobe function.

Primary depression

Numerous investigators using PET and SPECT have demonstrated that depressed patients have decreased metabolism or flow in the prefrontal lobes, particularly in the

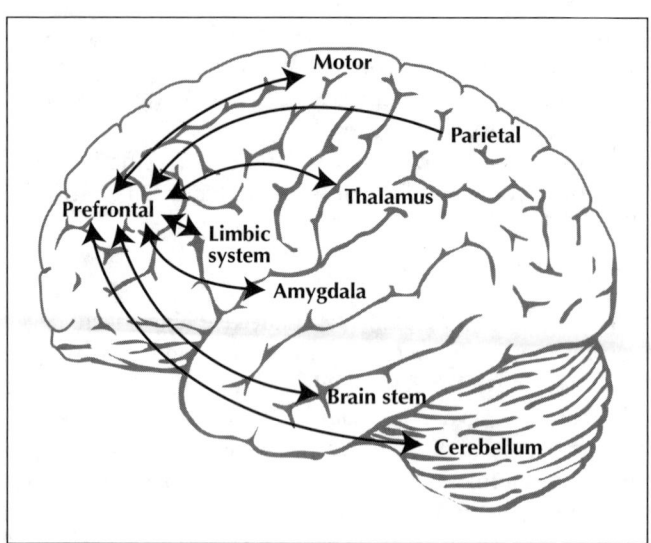

Figure 4. The interconnections of prefrontal cortex. Just as many neurons originating in deep structure project to the frontal cortex, the frontal cortex sends fibers to most other cortical, limbic, and subcortical regions (*arrows*). The prefrontal cortex is thus neuroanatomically situated and connected to have a broad role in integrating cognitive and affective information and to regulate other brain structures.

left anterolateral prefrontal cortex (ALPFC) [16,56,58,60,99–102]. Some, but not all, studies have found a significant negative correlation between Hamilton depression ratings and left prefrontal cortex metabolism; *ie*, the more severe the depression, the lower the left frontal cortex metabolism.

Another interesting link between the prefrontal cortex and mood is suggested by studies examining normal mood states in healthy controls. Pardo *et al.* [74] initially found that left ALPFC activity increases when subjects are asked to think sad thoughts. Work in our own laboratory has demonstrated that the induction of transient sadness (by recalling past events and viewing sad faces) is associated with increased activity in the left anterior cingulate, left medial frontal cortex, and the anterior temporal lobes bilaterally [75]. Thus, two studies have now found increased left prefrontal activity during sadness, which is in contrast with the bulk of studies in depression that have found left prefrontal decreases. These counterintuitive findings suggest a possible relation between the substrates involved in acute sadness or acute complicated grief reactions and the later development of clinical depression. In this situation, an interesting parallel may exist with focal epilepsy.

During an epileptic seizure there is focally increased metabolism at the seizure site that is visible on PET or SPECT scans, whereas after and between the seizures (postictal and interictal) the same regions are hypometabolic. Early episodes of clinical depression are often associated with psychosocial stressors that induce sadness, threats to self-esteem, and one's role in the family social system and hierarchy, whereas later episodes are more autonomous [103–106]. Thus, repeated or prolonged episodes of sadness or grief, with left prefrontal hypermetabolism, might be followed by hypometabolism and a state of clinical depression, much as a hypermetabolic seizure is followed by interictal hypometabolism at the seizure site [107]. This formulation is now being tested with sequential imaging of subjects undergoing a grief reaction, some of whom go on to develop clinical depression.

Prefrontal lobe changes associated with antidepressant treatment response

The mechanism or mechanisms of action of electroconvulsive therapy (ECT) are unknown. However, Sackeim *et al.* [108] have used SPECT to demonstrate that, in some patients, transient changes in prefrontal lobe function following ECT may be crucial to eventual treatment response. They performed SPECT scans before and within an hour after ECT in a group of depressed subjects, and then followed their clinical response. In virtually all subjects, ECT resulted in decreased brain activity in many regions. Interestingly, depressed subjects with the best clinical response to ECT also had the largest decrease in frontal lobe activity immediately after treatment. Put another way, a large transient decrease in frontal lobe activity immediately after ECT was positively correlated with a good clinical response to such therapy. Whether these changes would eventually reverse polarity and be associated with normalization of the prefrontal hypometabolism remains to be fully explored.

In summary, many functional neuroimaging studies have now demonstrated that the prefrontal lobes have abnormalities at rest (or in response to psychologic or pharmacologic challenge) in clinical depression and that abrupt changes in prefrontal activity predicts response to ECT.

The cingulate gyrus

As mentioned earlier in the discussion of the triune brain, the cingulate gyrus is an extension of the limbic system that is present in mammals and not in lower species, such as lizards (Fig. 5) [23,109]. This phylogenetic understanding led to early specula-tion, which has been confirmed in numerous studies, emphasizing the important role of the cingulate in mating and pair-bonding, parenting, and play [110–112]. In addition to these uniquely mammalian behaviors, the cingulate gyrus also appears to be impor-tant in directed attention and choosing the appropriate response in the presence of dis-tractions or competing responses [33,113–115] (*eg*, adding flexibility to the inflexible reptilian brain).

Some studies of depressed studies have found increased cingulate activity at rest, and three studies have shown that patients with baseline cingulate hyperactivity selectively respond to a night of sleep deprivation [116–118]. In depressed subjects with cingulate hyperactivity, a night without sleep reverses the cingulate hyperactivity in concert with an improvement in mood. These studies indicate that, in at least a subset of patients with clinical depression, limbic hyperactivity may be associated with depression and that an antidepressant response to sleep deprivation occurs in association with a normalization of limbic tone.

Three previous imaging studies have established that the standard Stroop task acti-vates the anterior cingulate in healthy controls [33,115,119]. We found that although depressed subjects were nonsignificantly slower than controls during both the standard and the sad Stroop tasks, the anterior cingulate failed to activate when scanned with ^{15}O PET while performing the Stroop. Instead, in depressed patients the left dorsolateral pre-frontal cortex (DLPFC) and visual cortex was activated [33].

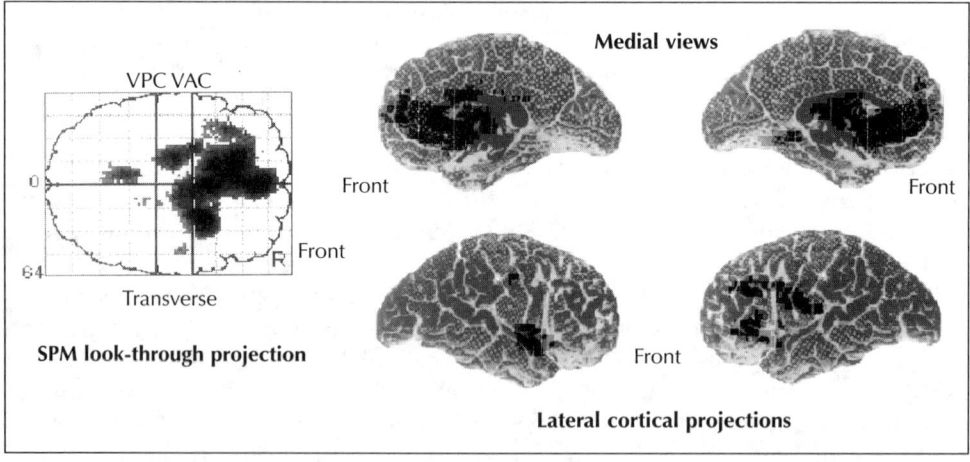

Figure 5. Increases in regional brain activity during transient sadness. The method, used to probe the neural mechanisms involved in regulating emotion, is to induce emotional changes in healthy controls and then image the brain changes (in this case with a ^{15}O-labeled positron emission tomography [PET] scan). The images are a composite from 11 adult women and show that the anterior limbic system and left prefrontal cortex is activated during sadness compared with a neutral emotion. These provide fur-ther evidence for the concept of the limbic system as a generator of mood, with prefrontal modulation. Interestingly, the left prefrontal cortex, which is often hypoactive in clinically depressed subjects, is increased in sadness. Studies are underway to further investigate the relation between brain activity dur-ing stress, grief, and loss, and the evolution in susceptible individuals into episodes of clinical depres-sion. SPM—statistical parametric mapping; VAC—ventral anterior commissure; VPC—ventral posterior commissure.

Amygdala

The amygdala is a collection of nuclei situated within the mesial temporal lobes, with important afferent and efferent connections throughout the rest of the limbic system as well as cortex [120,121]. The role of the amygdala in emotion regulation and recognition has been established by studies using ablation, stimulation, and more recently functional neuroimaging. Although discussed as separate structures, it is important to remember that the amygdala is both internally heterogeneous and a part of a continuous arch involving the septum and the hippocampus, with the amygdala structurally supporting one end and the septum the other.

Historically, the findings of Kluver and Bucy [122] of behavioral changes in animals after amygdala ablation served to support Papez' emerging theory of emotion. After bilateral removal of the temporal lobes in rhesus monkeys (which thus included removing the amygdala), the pair noted the monkeys were more docile and fearless, even to the sound of a hissing snake. Furthermore, the animals had no emotional displays, constantly examined all objects in their environment, and engaged in indiscriminate eating and sexual activity [122]. Stimulation of the amygdala produces a wide range of visceral and viscerosomatic responses [25,123]. With its unique input from multiple sensory areas and direct connections back out to all levels of the cortex, the amygdala likely serves as a quick response route for determining the affective significance of external stimuli. Thus, it probably acts as an important noncortical route for evaluating the external world. In monkeys and humans, the amygdala activates during emotional recognition of faces [124–127].

Recent work has demonstrated the prominent role of the amygdala during states of intense emotion (Fig. 6). Intravenous procaine appears to quickly cause amygdalaloidal changes along with prominent symptoms of anxiety or euphoria. There may be an interesting hemispheric difference in activation of the amygdala, depending on the emotion involved. It appears that the right amygdala activates nonspecifically during a range of emotions (happiness, sadness, anxiety). Three different imaging studies have now found that the left amygdala, however, is activated during sadness or dysphoria, but decreases in activity during happiness or euphoria.

A Tentative Model

As discussed previously, any working model of the regional neurobiologic basis of mood dysregulation must take into account changes at the level of genes, synapses, regional dysfunction, and higher-order cognitive and environmental factors. Although no comprehensive model such as this exists, the important pieces of the puzzle are beginning to reveal themselves. They are as follows:

At the level of the synapse, there is indirect evidence of alterations in function of dopamine, norepinephrine, and serotonin.

At the level of gene transcription, there are clear genetic vulnerabilities, especially in bipolar forms of the illness, as well as epigenetic or experimental effects on gene expression based on stresses and life experiences.

At the level of regional neuroanatomy, damage to or dysfunction of the left prefrontal cortex predisposes to the development of clinical depression. Imaging studies during depression imply that the left prefrontal cortex is hypoactive. Furthermore, damage to the right hemisphere, particularly the right insula and anterior temporal cortex,

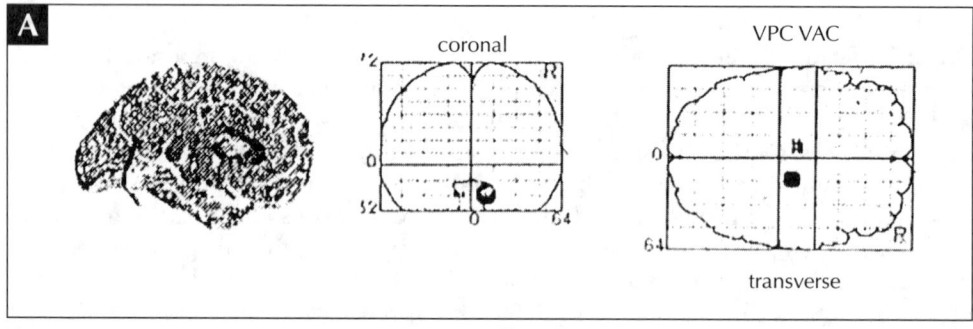

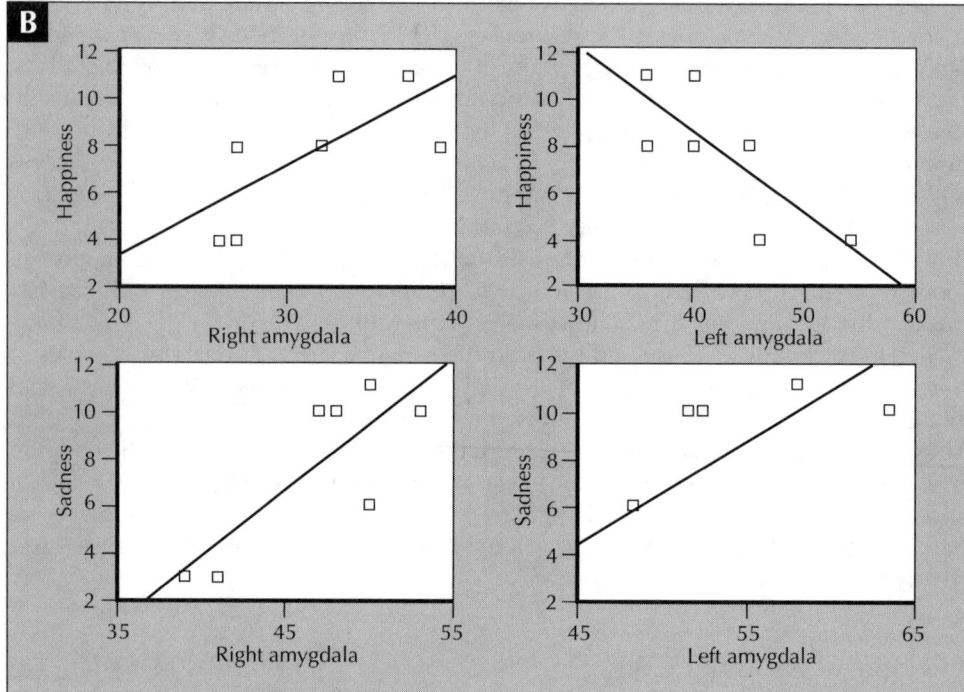

Figure 6. A and **B**, Different right and left amygdala activity during happiness and sadness.

may predispose to the development of mania. Although preliminary, imaging studies during mania have shown decreased right anterior temporal activity; they also show increased right anterior temporal activity during depression in bipolar type I patients [128]. Intriguingly, Ketter *et al.* [129] found that right anterior temporal hyperactivity predicts response to the anticonvulsant and mood-stabilizing drug carbamazepine, whereas hypoactivity, especially prefrontal, is associated with response to nimodipine. Lastly, activation studies in depressed patients have found that the anterior limbic system is blunted in actively depressed subjects. Electroconvulsive therapy and, to some extent, rTMS, appears to work best when applied over the prefrontal regions (left more so than right). Yet in normal volunteers, prefrontal rTMS on the left causes transient sadness and on the right, happiness.

How can one begin to integrate these bits of information at different conceptual levels into a working model of depression? One such attempt supposes that the limbic system is a critical generator and modulator of normal and pathologic degrees of emotion, and that the various phenomenologic correlates are a function not only of which parts of the limbic system are active, but also of their afferent and efferent loops to other parts of neocortex. The prefrontal cortex is presumed to serve a modulating, dampening, and governing role on this limbic activity. Right limbic activity is more associated with anxiety, anger, and sadness, with left limbic activity more involved in positive emotions of happiness and euphoria. The corresponding cortex has a negative feedback to the ipsilateral limbic system (amygdala). Thus, in healthy controls during transient sadness, there would be increased activity in the anterior limbic system and the prefrontal cortex, more in the left than in the right, with left frontal activity representing a brake on left limbic activity, allowing the emotion of sadness. Clinical depression would occur if the governing role of the left prefrontal cortex were lost owing to a stroke or tumor, or to prolonged regulatory dysfunction, as in an unresolved grief reaction. Clinical depression might also arise if the limbic affective drive were intrinsically stronger than the ipsilateral governing prefrontal cortex (as might occur in borderline personality, for example). Finally, prolonged limbic hyperactivity might result in compensatory blunting in some limbic circuits, as several studies now indicate. In mania, there may be a relative loss of right hemispheric cortical governance, leaving right-sided limbic activity unchecked.

There is some evidence for the role of prefrontal or cortical governance of underlying limbic responses. Studies by LeDoux *et al.* [130,131] indicate that, in the presence of cortical lesions, initial stimulus–reward associations formed in the amygdala are resistant to extinction. A functioning cortex is important to change or modify present limbic (here, the amygdala) pathways and responses. Rolls *et al.* [127] have also demonstrated that stimulus–reward associations formed in the amygdala are relatively less flexible than associations formed in the orbital frontal cortex. Thus, with decreased prefrontal cortical activity, limbic structures may be relatively disconnected from the normal cortical modulation. Whereas the prefrontal lobe may permit complex, flexible, and environmentally contingent cognitions, limbic cognitions might be more primitive, preprogrammed, and autonomous. If negative biases toward the self or world were laid down in primitive limbic memories on the basis of early childhood experience, these may come to predominate in the face of decreased prefrontal activity, resulting in clinical depression, with prominent negative ("automatic") thoughts. Cognitive and interpersonal therapy for depression may thus be viewed as a way of rehabilitation, or temporarily substituting for normal, prefrontal governance of limbic tone, allowing more refined rational responses to modulate primitive automatic thoughts.

Conclusions

Obviously, a comprehensive model of the neurobiology of mood dysregulation is still many years away. Nevertheless, there are numerous, although still insufficient, pieces of available data to begin to solve the puzzle. Several key studies need to be performed over the next two decades to test the foregoing model; the results are likely to advance our understanding of the regional brain basis of mood regulation.

First and foremost, more ("resting") functional images of depressed patients need to be performed in large clinical settings to assess the frequency and severity of prefrontal changes and whether these are more common in certain disease (*eg*, unipolar versus bipolar depression) or phenomenologic (anxious versus psychomotorically retarded) subtypes. In conjunction, serial scans throughout a patient's lifetime would greatly advance knowledge about which brain changes are part of the state of depression, and which may represent vulnerability factors to developing depression. Serial images would also help answer the important question of if, and for how long, changes in regional brain function persist following an episode of clinical depression.

It is also possible to begin integrating regional brain activity information with knowledge about underlying pharmacologic mechanisms. This can be done by using sophisticated PET and SPECT ligands, by imaging before and after administering pharmacologic challenges, or by simultaneously measuring cerebrospinal fluid changes and regional brain activity.

Finally, TMS could allow the direct testing of several of these models. This technique allows the noninvasive stimulation (by single pulses) or temporary inhibition (by repeated trains) of the cortex. Current technology limits this to probing only the superficial cortex, but in the future, it may be possible to directly stimulate deeper structures in awake individuals. This tool transcends conventional functional neuroimaging by allowing one not to merely image regional brain changes during different mood states, but to precisely alter regional activity and to observe attendant effects on normal and pathologic mood.

These studies, using the new tools of functional imaging combined with more specific pharmacologic treatments and probes, will undoubtedly greatly advance our understanding in the 21st century of the neural substrate of normal and pathologic mood.

Acknowledgments

We thank Drs. Paul MacLean, Michael Trimble, Charles Kellner, and James Ballenger for discussions about the regional brain basis of mood and for helpful comments about this chapter.

References

1. Temkin O: *The Falling Sickness: A History of Epilepsy From the Greeks to the Beginning of Modern Neurology.* Baltimore: Johns Hopkins Press; 1945.
2. Engel J: *Seizure and Epilepsy.* Philadelphia: FA Davis & Co; 1989.
3. George MS, Ketter TA, Post RM: SPECT and PET imaging in mood disorders. *J Clin Psychiatry* 1993, 54:6–13.
4. George MS, Ketter TA, Post RM: Prefrontal cortex dysfunction in clinical depression. *Depression* 1994, 2:59–72.
5. George MS: An introduction to the emerging neuroanatomy of depression. *Psychiatr Ann* 1994, 24:635–636.
6. Post RM, Weiss SRB, Ketter TA, *et al.*: The temporal lobes and affective disorders. In *The Temporal Lobe and Limbic System: Basic and Clinical Perspectives.* Edited by Bolwig T, Trimble M. London: Wrightson Biomedical Publishing; 1992:247–265.
7. George MS, Ketter TA, Kimbrell TA, Post RM: Brain imaging in mania. In *Mania.* Edited by Goodnick PJ. Washington, DC: American Psychiatric Press; 1997.
8. Post RM, Ballenger JC, eds: *Neurobiology of Mood Disorders.* Baltimore: Williams & Wilkins, 1984.
9. Dolan RJ, Calloway SP, Fonagy P, *et al.*: Life events, depression and hypothalamic–pituitary–adrenal axis function. *Br J Psychiatry* 1985, 147:429–433.

10. Amsterdam JD, Marinelli DL, Arger P, *et al.*: Assessment of adrenal gland volumes by computed tomography in depressed patients and healthy volunteers: a pilot study. *Psychiatric Res* 1987, 21:189–197.

11. Kirkegaard C, Faber J: Altered serum levels of thyroxine, triiodothyronines and diiodothyronines in endogenous depression. *Acta Endocrinol (Copenh)* 1981, 96:199–207.

12. Sackeim HA, Putz E, Vingiano W, *et al.*: Lateralization in the processing of emotionally laden information. I. Normal functioning. *Neuropsychiatry Neuropsychol Behav Neurol* 1988, 1:97–110.

13. Sackeim HA, Prohovnik I, Moeller JR, *et al.*: Regional cerebral blood flow in mood disorders. I. Comparison of major depressives and normal controls at rest. *Arch Gen Psychiatry* 1990, 47:60–70.

14. Sackeim HA, Prohovnik I: Brain imaging studies of depressive disorders. In *The Biology of Depressive Disorders*. Edited by Mann JJ, Kupfer DJ. New York: Plenum Press; 1993.

15. Schwartz JM, Baxter LR, Mazziotta JC, *et al.*: The differential diagnosis of depression: relevance of positron emission tomography studies of cerebral glucose metabolism to the bipolar–unipolar dichotomy. *JAMA* 1987, 258:1368–1374.

16. Baxter LR Jr, Schwartz JM, Phelps ME, *et al.*: Reduction of prefrontal cortex glucose metabolism common to three types of depression. *Arch Gen Psychiatry* 1989, 46:243–250.

17. Baxter LR, Phelps ME, Mazziotta JC, *et al.*: Cerebral metabolic rates for glucose in mood disorders: studies with PET and FDG. *Arch Gen Psychiatry* 1985, 42:441–447.

18. Papez JW: A proposed mechanism of emotion. *Arch Neurol Psychiatry* 1937, 38:725–743.

19. MacLean PD: The limbic system and its hippocampal formation: studies in the animals and their possible application to man. *J Neurosurg* 1954, 11:29–44.

20. MacLean PD: A triune concept of the brain and behavior. In *The Clarence M. Hicks Memorial Lectures, 1969*. Edited by Boag TJ, Campbell D. Toronto: University of Toronto Press; 1973.

21. MacLean PD: *The Triune Brain in Evolution: Role in Paleocerebral Functions*. New York: Plenum Press; 1990.

22. MacLean PD: The limbic brain in relation to the psychoses. In *Physiological Correlates of Emotion*. Edited by Black P. New York: Academic Press; 1970:129–146.

23. MacLean PD: Introduction: perspectives on cingulate cortex in the limbic system. In *Neurobiology of Cingulate Cortex and Limbic Thalamus: A Comprehensive Handbook*. Edited by Vogt BA, Gabriel M. Boston: Birkhauser, 1993:1–19.

24. Stevens JR, Mark VH, Ervin F, *et al.*: Deep temporal stimulation in man. *Arch Neurol* 1969, 21:157.

25. Halgren E, Walter RD, Cherlow DG, *et al.*: Mental phenomena evoked by electrical stimulation of the human hippocampal formation and amygdala. *Brain* 1978, 101:83–117.

26. Heath RG: Pleasure response of human subjects to direct stimulation of the brain: physiologic and psychodynamic considerations. In *The Role of Pleasure in Behavior*. Edited by Heath RG. New York: Paul B. Hoeber; 1964:219–243.

27. Penfield W, Perot P: The brain's record of auditory and visual experience: a final summary and discussion. *Brain* 1963, 86:595–696.

28. Heath RG: Activity of the human brain during emotional thought. In *The Role of Pleasure in Behavior*. Edited by Heath RG. New York: Hoebe, Harper and Row; 1994.

29. Heath RG, Mickle WA: Evaluation of seven years experience with depth electrode studies in human patients. In *Electrical Studies of the Unanesthetized Brain*. Edited by Ramey ER, O'Doherty D. New York: Paul B. Hoeber; 1960:214–247.

30. Rubinow DR, Post RM: Impaired recognition of affect in facial expression in depressed patients. *Biol Psychiatry* 1992, 31:947–953.

31. George MS, Ketter TA, Gill D, *et al.*: Brain regions involved in recognizing facial emotion or identity: an [15]O PET study. *J Neuropsychiatry Clin Neurol* 1993, 5:384–394.

32. George MS, Ketter TA, Gill DS, *et al.*: Blunted CBF with emotion recognition in depression [abstract]. *American Psychiatric Association Annual Meeting New Research Program 1993*. Washington, DC: APA Press; 1993:114–188.

33. George MS, Ketter TA, Parekh PI, *et al.*: Regional brain activity when selecting a response despite interference: an [15]O PET study of the Stroop and an emotional Stroop. *Human Brain Mapping* 1994, 1:194–209.

34. Kellner CH, Post RM, Putnam F, *et al.*: Intravenous procaine as a probe of limbic system activity in psychiatric patients and normal controls. *Biol Psychiatry* 1987, 22:1107–1126.

35. Ketter TA, Andreason PJ, George MS, *et al.*: Paralimbic rCBF increases during procaine-induced psychosensory and emotional experiences [abstract]. *Biol Psychiatry* 1993, 33:66A-107A.

36. Parekh PI, Spencer JW, George MS, *et al.*: Procaine-induced increases in limbic rCBF correlate positively with increases in occipital and temporal EEG fast activity. *Brain Topogr* 1995, 7:209–216.

37. Ketter TA, Andreason PJ, George MS, *et al.*: Anterior paralimbic mediation of procaine-induced emotional and psychosensory experiences. *Arch Gen Psychiatry* 1996, 53:59–61.

38. Ketter TA, Andreason PJ, George MS, *et al.*: Blunted CBF response to procaine in mood disorders [abstract]. *New Res Prog* 1993:134.

39. Trivedi MH, Blackburn T, Lewis S, *et al.*: Effects of amphetamine in major depressive disorder using functional MRI [abstract]. *Biol Psychiatry* 1995, 37:657.

40. Alexander GE, DeLong MR, Strick PL: Parallel organization of functionally segregated circuits linking basal ganglia and cortex. *Annu Rev Neurosci* 1986, 9:357–381.

41. Cummings JL: The neuroanatomy of depression. *J Clin Psychiatry* 1993, 54:14s–20s.

42. Mega MS, Cummings JL: Frontal subcortical circuits and neuropsychiatric disorders. *J Neuropsychiatry Clin Neurosci* 1994, 6:358–370.

43. Weinberger DR, Berman KF, Zec RF: Physiologic dysfunction of dorsolatral prefrontal cortex in schizophrenia: I. Regional cerebral blood flow evidence. *Arch Gen Psychiatry* 1986, 43:114–124.

44. Casey DE: Affective disorders and tardive dyskinesia. *Encephale* 1988, 14:221–226.

45. Weinberger DR, Berman KF, Illowsky BP: Physiological dysfunction of dorsolateral prefrontal cortex in schizophrenia. III. A new cohort and evidence for a monoaminergic mechanism. *Arch Gen Psychiatry* 1988, 45:609–615.

46. Christianson SA, Saisa J, Garvill J, *et al.*: Hemispheric inactivation and mood-state changes. *Brain Cogn* 1993, 23:127–144.

47. Ross ED, Homan RW, Buck R: Differential hemispheric lateralization of primary and social emotions: implications for developing a comprehensive neurology for emotions, repression and the subconscious. *Neuropsychiatry Neuropsychol Behav Neurol* 1994, 7:1–19.

48. Sackeim HA, Greenberg MS, Weiman AL, *et al.*: Hemispheric asymmetry in the expression of positive and negative emotions: neurologic evidence. *Arch Neurol* 1982, 39:210–218.

49. Sackeim HA, Gur RC: Lateral asymmetry in intensity of emotional expression. *Neuropsychologia* 1978, 163:473–481.

50. Sackeim HA, Gur RC, Saucy MC: Emotions are expressed more intensely on the left side of the face. *Science* 1978, 202:434–436.

51. Wada J, Rasmussen T: Intracarotid injection of sodium amytal for the lateralization of cerebral speech dominance: experimental and clinical observations. *J Neurosurgery* 1960, 17:266–282.

52. George MS, Parekh PI, Rosinsky N, *et al.* Understanding emotional prosody activates right hemisphere regions. *Arch Neurol* 1996, 53:665–670.

53. George MS, Wassermann EM, Williams W, *et al.*: Changes in mood and hormone levels after rapid-rate transcranial magnetic stimulation of the prefrontal cortex. *J Neuropsychiatry Clin Neurol* 1996, 8:172–180.

54. Pascual-Leone A, Catala MD, Pascual AP: Lateralized effect of rapid-rate transcranial magnetic stimulation of the prefrontal cortex on mood. *Neurology* 1996, 46:499–502.

55. Drevets WC, Videen TO, Preskorn SH, *et al.*: A functional anatomical study of unipolar depression. *J Neurosci* 1992, 12:3628–3641.

56. Bench CJ, Friston KJ, Brown RG, *et al.*: The anatomy of melancholia: focal abnormalities of cerebral blood flow in major depression. *Psychol Med* 1992, 22:607–615.

57. Mathew RJ, Meyer JS, Francis DJ, *et al.*: Cerebral blood flow in depression. *Am J Psychiatry* 1980, 137:1449–1450.

58. Austin MP, Dougall N, Ross M, *et al.*: Single photon emission tomography with ^{99m}Tc-exametazime in major depression and the pattern of brain activity underlying the psychotic/neurotic continuum. *J Affect Disord* 1992, 26:31–43.

59. Bench CJ, Friston KJ, Brown RG, *et al.* Regional cerebral blood flow in depression measured by positron emission tomography: the relationship with clinical dimensions. *Psychol Med* 1993, 23:579–590.

60. Mayberg HS, Lewis PJ, Regenold W, *et al.*: Paralimbic hypoperfusion in unipolar depression. *J Nucl Med* 1994, 35:929–934.

61. Robinson RG, Szetela B: Mood change following left hemisphere brain injury. *Ann Neurol* 1981, 9:447–453.

62. Robinson RG, Kubos KL, Starr LB, *et al.*: Mood disorders in stroke patients: importance of location of lesion. *Brain* 1984, 107:81–93.

63. Robinson RG, Morris PLP, Fedoroff JP: Depression and cerebrovascular disease. *J Clin Psychiatry* 1990, 51:26–31.

64. George MS, Kellner CH, Bernstein H, *et al.*: An MRI investigation into mood disorders in multiple sclerosis: a pilot study. *J Nerv Ment Dis* 1994, 182:410–412.

65. Pascual-Leone A, Gates JR, Dhuna A: Induction of speech arrest and counting errors with rapid-rate transcranial magnetic stimulation. *Neurology* 1991, 41:697–702.

66. Jennum P, Friberg L, Fuglsang-Frederiksen A, *et al.*: Speech localization using repetitive transcranial magnetic stimulation. *Neurology* 1994, 44:269–273.

67. Robinson RG, Boston JD, Starkstein SE, *et al.*: Comparison of mania and depression after brain injury: causal factors. *Am J Psychiatry* 1988, 145:172–178.

68. Starkstein SE, Pearlson GD, Boston J, *et al.*: Mania after brain injury: a controlled study of causative factors. *Arch Neurol* 1987, 44:1069–1073.

69. Starkstein SE, Fedoroff P, Berthier ML, *et al.*: Manic–depressive and pure manic states after brain lesion. *Biol Psychiatry* 1991, 29:149–158.

70. Davidson RJ: Asymmetric brain function, affective style, and psychpathology: the role of early experience and plasticity. *Dev Psychopathol* 1994, 6:741–758.

71. House A, Dennis M, Warlow C, *et al.*: Mood disorders after stroke and their relation to lesion location. *Brain* 1990, 113:1113–1129.

72. Sharpe M, Hawton K, House A, *et al.*: Mood disorders in long-term survivors of stroke: associations with brain lesion location and volume. *Psychol Med* 1990, 20:815–828.

73. Sackeim HA: Emotion, disorders of mood, and hemispheric functional specialization. In *Psychopathology and the Brain.* Edited by Carroll BJ, Barrett JE. New York: Raven Press; 1991:209–242.

74. Pardo JV, Pardo PJ, Raichle ME: Neural correlates of self-induced dysphoria. *Am J Psychiatry* 1993, 150:713–719.

75. George MS, Ketter TA, Parekh PI, *et al.*: Brain activity during transient sadness and happiness in healthy women. *Am J Psychiatry* 1995, 152:341–351.

76. Ballenger JC, Post RM: Therapeutic effects of carbamazepine in affective illness: a preliminary report. *Commun Psychopharmacol* 1978, 2:159–175.

77. Ballenger JC, Post RM: Carbamazepine in manic–depressive illness: a new treatment. *Am J Psychiatry* 1980, 137:782–790.

78. Post RM, Uhde TW, Ballenger JC, *et al.*: Prophylactic efficacy of carbamazepine in manic–depressive illness. *Am J Psychiatry* 1983, 140:1602–1604.

79. Calabrese JR, Delucchi GA: Phenomenology of rapid cycling manic depression and its treatment with valproate. *J Clin Psychiatry* 1989, 50:30–34.

80. Calabrese JR, Markovitz PJ, Kimmel SE, *et al.*: Spectrum of efficacy of valproate in 78 rapid-cycling bipolar patients. *J Clin Psychopharmacol* 1992, 12:53S–56S.

81. Bremner JD, Innis RB, Salomon RM, *et al.*: PET measurement of cerebral metabolic correlates of depressive relapse. *Arch Gen Psychiatry* 1997, in press.

82. Stuss DT, Benson DF: *The Frontal Lobes.* New York: Raven Press; 1986.

83. Mclardy T, Meyer A: Anatomical correlates of improvement after leucotomy. *J Ment Sci* 1949, 95:182–192.

84. Reitman F: Orbital cortex syndrome following leucotomy. *Am J Psychiatry* 1946, 103:238–241.

85. Ross ED, Rush AJ: Diagnosis and neuroanatomical correlates of depression in brain-damaged patients. *Arch Gen Psychiatry* 1981, 38:1344–1354.

86. Adams RD, Victor M: *Principles of Neurology,* edn 3. New York: McGraw-Hill; 1985.

87. Langworthy OR, Richter CP: Increased spontaneous activity produced by frontal lobes lesions in cats. *Am J Physiol* 1939, 126:158–161.

88. Sato M: Prefrontal cortex and emotional behaviors. *Folia Psychiatr Neurol Jpn* 1971, 25:69–78.

89. Livingston KE: Limbic system dysfunction induced by "kindling": its significance for psychiatry. In *Neurosurgical Treatment in Psychiatry, Pain and Epilepsy.* Edited by Sweet WH, Obrador S, Martin-Rodriguez JG. Baltimore: University Park Press; 1977; 63–75.

90. Blumer D, Benson DF: Personality changes with frontal and temporal lobe lesions. In *Psychiatric Aspects of Neurologic Disease*. Edited by Benson DF, Blumer D. New York: Grune & Stratton; 1975.

91. Schlegel S, Kretzschmar K: Computed tomography in affective disorders. Part II: Brain density. *Biol Psychiatry* 1987, 22:15–23.

92. Schlegel S, Kretzschmar K: Computed tomography in affective disorders. Part I: Ventricular and sulcal measurements. *Biol Psychiatry* 1987, 22:4–14.

93. Schlegel S, Frommberger U, Buller R: Computerized tomography (CT) in affective disorders: relationship with psychopathology. *Psychiatry Res* 1989, 29:271–272.

94. Kellner CH, Rubinow DR, Post RM: Cerebral ventricular size and cognitive impairment in depression. *J Affect Disord* 1986, 10:215–219.

95. Altshuler LL, Conrad A, Hauser P, *et al.*: Reduction of temporal lobe volume in bipolar disorder: a preliminary report of magnetic resonance imaging [letter]. *Arch Gen Psychiatry* 1991, 48:482–483.

96. Coffey CE, Wilkinson WE, Weiner RD, *et al.*: Quantitative cerebral anatomy in depression: a controlled magnetic resonance imaging study. *Arch Gen Psychiatry* 1993, 50:7–16.

97. Rangel-Guerra RA, Perez-Payan H, Minkoff L, *et al.*: Nuclear magnetic resonance in bipolar affective disorders. *AJNR Am J Neuroradiol* 1983, 4:229–231.

98. Dolan RJ, Poynton AM, Bridges PK, *et al.*: Altered magnetic resonance white-matter T_1 values in patients with affective disorder. *Br J Psychiatry* 1990, 157:107–110.

99. Mayberg HS, Starkstein SE, Sadzot B, *et al.*: Selective hypometabolism in the inferior frontal lobe in depressed patients with Parkinson's disease. *Ann Neurol* 1990, 28:57–64.

100. Mayberg HS, Jeffery PJ, Wagner HN, Simpson SG: Regional cerebral blood flow in patients with refractory unipolar depression measured with TC-99m HMPAO SPECT [abstract]. *J Nucl Med* 1991, 32:951.

101. Baxter LR Jr, Phelps ME, Mazziotta JC, *et al.*: Cerebral metabolic rates for glucose in mood disorders: studies with positron emission tomography and fluorodeoxyglucose F 18. *Arch Gen Psychiatry* 1985, 42:441–447.

102. Dolan RJ, Bench CJ, Brown RG, *et al.*: Regional cerebral blood flow abnormalities in depressed patients with cognitive impairment. *J Neurol Neurosurg Psychiatry* 1992, 55:768–773.

103. Paykel ES: Life events and early environment. In *Handbook of Affective Disorders*. Edited by Paykel ES. New York: Churchill Livingstone; 1982:146–161.

104. Paykel ES: Causal relationship between clinical depression and life events. In *Stress and Mental Disorder*. Edited by Barrett JE, Rose RM, Klerman GL. New York: Raven Press; 1979:71–86.

105. Paykel ES: Contribution of life events to causation of psychiatric illness. *Psychol Med* 1978, 8:245–253.

106. Ellicott A, Hammen C, Gitlin M, *et al.*: Life events and the course of bipolar disorder. *Am J Psychiatry* 1990, 147:1194–1198.

107. Shen W, Lee BJ, Park HM, *et al.*: HIPDM-SPECT brain imaging in the presurgical evaluation of patients with intractable seizures. *J Nucl Med* 1990, 31:1280–1284.

108. Sackeim HA, Devanand DP, Prudic J: Medication resistance as a predictor of ECT outcome and relapse [abstract]. *ACNP Abstr Panels Posters* 1992:51.

109. MacLean PD: Culminating developments in the evolution of the limbic system: the thalamocingulate division. In *The Limbic System: Functional Organization and Clinical Disorders*. Edited by Doane BK, Livinston KE. New York: Raven Press; 1986.

110. Slotnick BM: Disturbances of maternal behavior in the rat following lesions of the cingulate cortex. *Behaviour* 1967, 29:204–236.

111. Beyer FC, Agnuiano L, Mena J: Oxytocin release in response to stimulation of cingulate gyrus. *Am J Physiol* 1961, 200:625–627.

112. MacLean PD, Newman JD: Role of midline frontolimbic cortex in production of the isolation call of squirrel monkeys. *Brain Res* 1988, 45:111–123.

113. Pardo JV, Pardo PJ, Janer KW, *et al.*: The anterior cingulate cortex mediates processing selection in the Stroop attentional conflict paradigm. *Proc Natl Acad Sci U S A* 1990, 87:256–259.

114. Paus T, Petrides M, Evans AC, *et al.*: Role of the human anterior cingulate cortex in the control of oculomotor, manual and speech responses: a positron emission tomography study. *J Neurophysiol* 1993, 70:453–469.

115. Bench CJ, Frith CD, Grasby PM, *et al.*: Investigations of the functional anatomy of attention using the Stroop test. *Neuropsychologia* 1993, 31:907–922.

116. Wu JC, Gillin JC, Buchsbaum MS, *et al.*: Effect of sleep deprivation on brain metabolism of depressed patients. *Am J Psychiatry* 1992, 149:538–543.

117. Ebert D, Feistel H, Barocka A: Effects of sleep deprivation on the limbic system and the frontal lobes in affective disorders: a study with Tc-99m-HMPAO SPECT. *Psychiatry Res* 1991, 40:247–251.

118. Ebert D, Feistel H, Barocka A, *et al.*: Increased limbic flow and total sleep deprivation in major depression with melancholia. *Psychiatry Res* 1994, 55:101–109.

119. Pardo JV, Pardo PJ, Janer KW, *et al.*: The anterior cingulate cortex mediates processing selection in the Stroop attentional conflict paradigm. *Proc Natl Acad Sci U S A* 1990, 87:256–259.

120. Aggelton JP (ed.): *The Amygdala.* New York: Wiley-Liss; 1992.

121. Amaral DG, Price JL, Pitkanen A, Carmichael ST: Anatomical organization of the primate amygdaloid complex. In *The Amygdala: Neurobiological Aspects of Emotion, Memory and Mental Dysfunction.* Edited by Aggleton JP. New York: Wiley-Liss; 1992:1–66.

122. Kluver H, Bucy PC: Preliminary analysis of functions of the temporal lobes in monkeys. *Arch Neurol* 1939, 42:979–1000.

123. Ervin FR, Mark VH, Stevens J: Behavioral and affective response to brain stimulation in man. *Procedures of the Annual Meeting of the American Psychopathologists Association* 1969, 58:54–65.

124. Leonard CM, Rolls ET, Wilson FAW, *et al.*: Neurons in the amygdala of the monkey with responses selective for faces. *Behav Brain Res* 1985, 15:159–176.

125. Hasselmo ME, Rolls ET, Baylis GC: The role of expression and identity in the face-selective responses of neurons in the neurons in the temporal visual cortex of the monkey. *Behav Brain Res* 1989, 32:203–218.

126. Rolls ET: Neurons in the cortex of the temporal lobe and in the amygdala of the monkey with responses selective for faces. *Hum Neurobiol* 1984, 3:209–222.

127. Rolls ET: The neural basis of brain stimulation reward. *Progr Neurobiol* 1975, 3:73–110.

128. Ketter TA, George MS, Andreason PJ, *et al.*: CMRglu in unipolar versus bipolar depression [abstract]. *American Psychiatric Association Annual Meeting.* Washington, DC: American Psychiatric Association Press; 1994:172.

129. Ketter TA, George MS, Andreason PJ, *et al.*: Carbamazepine decreases regional cerebral glucose metabolism in affective disorders and has complex relationships with mood states [abstract]. *Neuropsychopharmacology* 1994, 10:83s.

130. Iwata J, LeDoux JE: Dissociation of associative and nonassociative concomitants of classical fear conditioning in the freely behaving rat. *Behav Neurosci* 1988, 102:66–76.

131. LeDoux JE: Emotion. In *Handbook of Physiology.* Edited by Mountcastle VB, Plum F, Geiger SR. Bethesda: American Physiology Society; 1987:419–459.

CHAPTER 2

The Kindling Model: Implications for the Etiology and Treatment of Mood Disorders

Robert M. Post, Susan R.B. Weiss, Terence A. Ketter,
Kirk D. Denicoff, Mark S. George, Mark A. Frye,
Mark A. Smith, and Gabriele S. Leverich

Aspects of the phenomenology, progression in clinical course, and pharmacology of mood disorders show a parallelism with the progressive evolution of kindling. These include, in a general pattern over successive episodes, the progression from minor to major episodes; a decreased "well interval;" episodes that are initially triggered but then emerge spontaneously; a pattern of increasing treatment resistance; and a pharmacology that differs as a function of stage of illness evolution. Using this indirect, nonbehaviorally nonhomologous model allows one to conceptualize the impact of stressors and episodes of affective illness at the level of gene expression as well as in relation to drug tolerance and illness recurrence. The concept also suggests that cyclicity could emerge out of the balance of changes in the ratio of pathophysiologic versus adaptive factors in gene transcription. A variety of treatment implications that are derived from this model, such as the importance of early and sustained intervention, can be specifically tested in the clinic.

Until recently, most neurobiologic theories of the affective disorders have focused on neural mechanisms involved in single acute illness episodes. This was particularly true of the original catecholamine hypothesis for depression, which suggested that catecholamine levels decrease in depression and increase in mania. However, the serotonergic deficit or "permissive" hypothesis, which is based on deficient serotonergic tone, suggested a longer-lasting vulnerability to recurrence.

Given the emerging evidence that affective illness tends to be not only recurrent but also progressive [1,2], it is prudent to focus on those neurobiologic mechanisms that could mediate long-lasting and progressive increases in vulnerability. We have primarily used two different animal models that demonstrate increases in behavioral or neurophysiologic responsivity to the same stimulation over time: 1) behavioral sensitization to the psychomotor stimulant cocaine, and 2) amygdala kindling. Each has its strategic advantages and disadvantages.

Cocaine sensitization is a relevant model for many reasons; there are considerable homologies between cocaine abuse disorders and the affective disorders at multiple levels. Early acute and low-dose cocaine use produces a syndrome that closely parallels episodes of euphoric mania or hypomania [3,4]. With repeated dosing and/or dose escalation, the cocaine-use syndrome begins to mirror aspects of dysphoric mania and, ultimately, may progress to a full-blown schizophreniform-like paranoid psychosis [5–7] akin to stage III mania [8]. Thus, cocaine-use syndromes may be useful for considering the recurrence and progression of manic syndromes. At the same time, cocaine is an interesting model "stressor" [3]. It induces many of the same catecholamine and indolamine changes that are associated with stress and increases a variety of stress hormones and neuropeptides, including corticotropin-releasing hormone (CRH). Convergent with this view is the finding that sensitization (increased responsivity) to cocaine shows cross-sensitization to stresses and vice versa [9–12]. Finally, there is a uniquely high incidence of comorbidity [13,14] of cocaine or related substance abuse and the primary affective disorders, particularly bipolar illness. Kessler *et al.* [15] (unpublished data) indicate that the incidence of comorbidity of mania and substance abuse is much greater than in any other psychiatric illness, and patients with mania are three times more likely to have multiple comorbidities than those found in all other psychiatric illnesses. Thus, cocaine abuse and affective syndromes may propel one another.

The rationale for the use of the kindling model is less direct than the rationale for studying cocaine sensitization because the physiologic and behavioral endpoints of the kindling model do not mimic those of affective illness. Thus, kindling is a nonhomologous model of the affective disorders and, as such, one must be extremely wary in using it to directly predict mechanisms of affective illness. These caveats have been summarized in detail elsewhere [16•]. Nonetheless, we believe there is an overriding applicability in the use of the kindling model, for it helps us consider processes and neurobiologic mechanisms that may underlie the progression of an illness (albeit quite dissimilar from that of the affective disorders) from a minor to a major stage, and from being triggered to occurring spontaneously. In addition, recent evidence in animals suggests that seizure episodes may periodically break through effective pharmacotherapy with the mood-stabilizing anticonvulsants carbamazepine and valproate. Because tolerance is increasingly recognized as a problem in the long-term treatment of bipolar illness, the episodic breakthrough of seizures progressing toward full-blown tolerance (which can be more fully dissected in terms of its molecular mechanisms in the kindling model [17•]) provides an additional rationale for its use.

Indices of Illness Progression

Many different variables in the phenomenology of the affective disorders suggest a progression and sensitization over time. Kraepelin [18] described two major pieces of evidence in his earliest works: 1) there was a tendency for increased rapidity of cycling or shorter well intervals between successive episodes of illness, and 2) there was evidence for stress sensitization. Kraepelin noted that early episodes might be associated with an actual, perceived, or threatened loss, but that subsequent episodes ("quite without external occasion") emerged with less provocation, (*ie*, spontaneously). These initial observations have now been replicated by many early observers in the field and by a series of controlled studies using a variety of methodologies, as reviewed elsewhere [2]. Additionally, there is evidence that the severity of episodes may increase over time with minor episodes progressing to more major episodes, as indicated in the work of Angst [19], Kendler *et al.* [20], and Maj *et al.* [21].

In the bipolar illnesses (bipolar and bipolar II), episode patterns may change their frequency or severity characteristics, progressing from isolated, intermittent patterns to more rhythmic and even continuous cycles. Ultimately, illness patterns can progress to ultrarapid cycling, with episodes lasting days to weeks, or ultra-ultrarapid (ultradian) cycling, wherein mood fluctuations can occur more than once every 24 hours [22]. It was originally assumed that 48-hour cycling was the upper limit in bipolar illness, but we have increasingly observed patients with three to five or more dramatic oscillations in mood in one 24-hour period [22]. This phase of ultradian oscillations bears great resemblance to the mathematics of the chaos theory [23]. Lastly, there is emerging evidence that with more frequent episode occurrence, the likelihood of treatment refractoriness increases, as noted in the National Institute of Mental Health (NIMH) collaborative study of Thase [24] in patients with unipolar depression, in whom an approximate 10% risk of refractoriness compounded with each successive episode recurrence. This was also noted in preliminary observations in bipolar illness [25–28]. Consistent with this evidence are the data of Angst [19], indicating that even the second episode of unipolar depression is less responsive to pharmacotherapy than the first, and our own observations of bipolar illness that repeated discontinuations of effective lithium therapy—which result in relapses—may yield patients who are ultimately refractory to previously effective treatments [29–30].

Molecular Mechanisms Involved in Kindling Evolution

If we seek to understand what mechanisms might underlie the tendency for progression in the affective disorders, we can begin by looking at the neurobiologic alterations in kindling for several reasons: 1) greater clarification of the neurobiologic processes involved in kindling than in affective illness at this time, 2) kindling's applicability to the progression from precipitated to spontaneous episodes, 3) kindling's ability to model rhythmic recurrences of the illness, and 4) with the use of kindling, the ability to examine the mechanisms underlying the tendency toward tolerance (when animals are treated with the mood-stabilizing anticonvulsants carbamazepine and valproate).

Amygdala kindling is typically achieved by using once-daily electrical stimulation with 60 Hz for 1 second. This stimulation initially evokes little behavioral reaction, but does evoke afterdischarges from the amygdala that, over days, spread in duration, complexity, and anatomic distribution. The process acquires such neuronal strength that a full-blown seizure eventually occurs in response to the same 1-second (previously subthreshold) stimulation. If continued sufficiently, seizures cease to require triggering by electrical stimulation and begin to occur spontaneously. Thus, the kindling process provides an interesting model for conceptualization of the growth of neural memory-like mechanisms as a progression from minor to major and from reactive to spontaneous changes in behavior and physiological processes [31–33•].

Many of the neurobiologic mechanisms of kindling evolution are beginning to be clarified. It is clear that, as in many other models of long-term memory [34], alterations in protein synthesis and gene expression are required for kindling evolution. There is increasing recognition that brain stimulation leads not only to short-term adaptations but also to long-term modifications of synaptic strength by the induction of immediate early genes (IEGs) and their subsequent downstream effects on late effector genes (LEGs) and other neural processes affected by such transcriptional regulation.

Figure 1 illustrates how neurotransmitter and receptor first-messenger signals may not only activate the classic second-messenger systems of calcium, cyclic-AMP (cAMP), and phosphatidylinositol (PI) turnover and their subsequent effects on protein kinases but also induce a third wave of messengers in the form of IEGs or transcriptional regulators. The messenger RNAs (mRNAs) for these factors are briefly induced, and then migrate to the

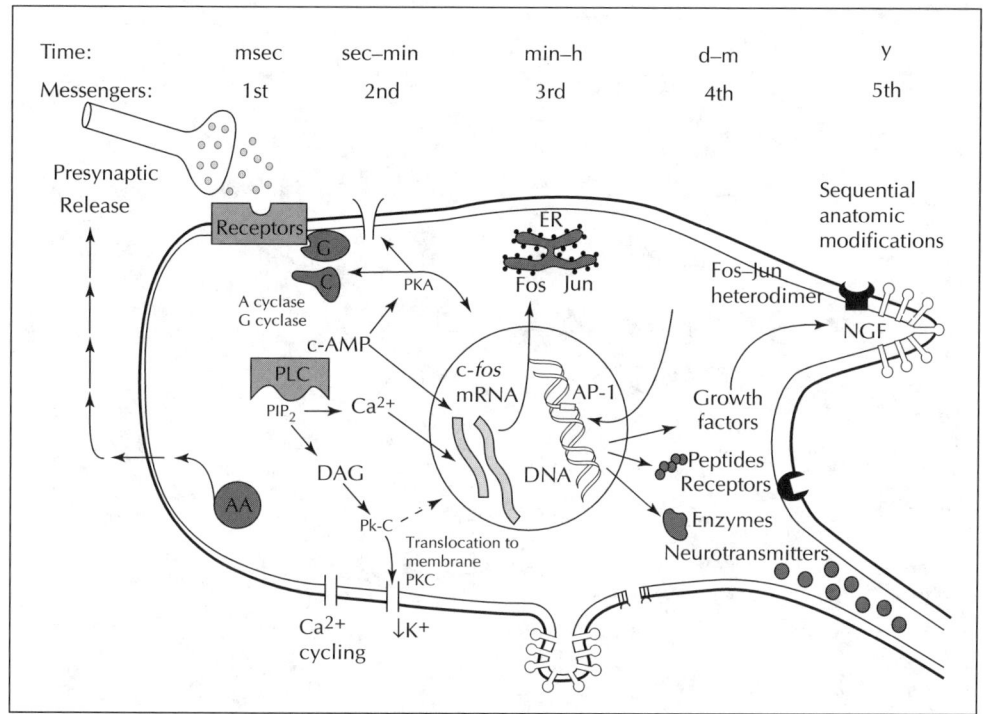

Figure 1. Neural mechanisms of synaptic plasticity, short- and long-term memory. Transient synaptic events induced by external stimuli can exert longer-lasting effects on neural excitability and the microstructure of the brain by a cascade of effects involving alterations in gene transcription. Neurotransmitters activate receptors and second-messenger systems, which then induce immediate early genes such as c-*fos* and c-*jun*. Fos and Jun proteins are synthesized on the endoplasmic reticulum and then bind to DNA to further alter transcription of late effector genes and other regulatory factors, the effects of which could last for months to years. *Arrows* indicate direction and sequence of reactions. AA—amino acid; A cyclase—adenylate cyclase; C—catalytic subunit; cAMP—cyclic AMP; DAG—diacylglycerol; ER—endoplasmic reticulum; G—G protein; G cyclase—guanylate cyclase; NGF—nerve growth factor; PIP_2—phosphatidylinositol-4,5-biphosphate; PKA—protein kinase A; PKC—protein kinase C; PLC—phospholipase C.

endoplasmic reticulum, where their respective proteins are synthesized; these proteins then combine to further alter DNA transcriptional regulation by binding to specific DNA sites on promoter regions of different genes encoding growth factors, enzymes, receptors, neural cell adhesion molecules (N-CAMS), neuropeptides, and other regulatory factors (Fig. 1).

Some of the neurobiologic and anatomic consequences of this cascade of effects on gene expression are illustrated in Figure 2. The dentate granule cell (the first step in the hippocampal–trisynaptic circuit and thought to be critically involved in the acquisition of short- and long-term memory) undergoes dramatic changes in gene expression. Not only are Fos and a variety of other transcriptional regulators induced but the cell remarkably changes its neurotransmitter and receptor machinery, as evidenced by changes in mRNAs for both excitatory and inhibitory regulators in the cell. There is an increase in the entire benzodiazepine–gamma-aminobutyric acid (GABA)—chloride channel complex that might limit the spread of seizures. Anticonvulsant neuropeptides are induced, including

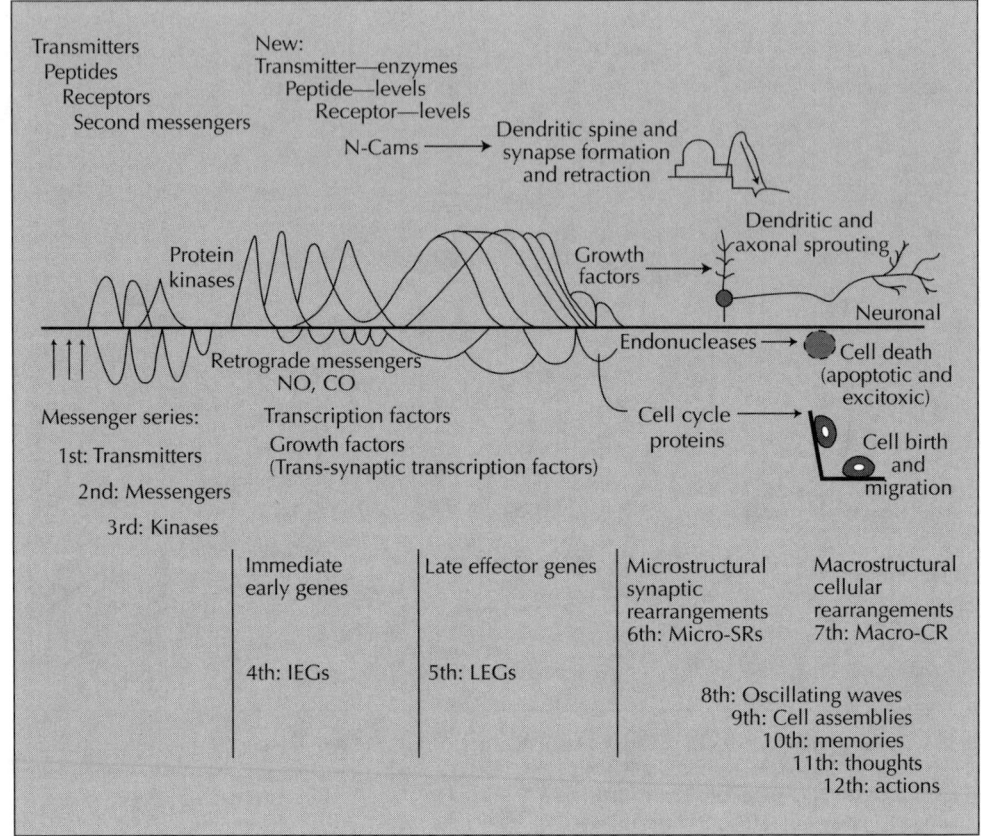

Figure 2. Remodeling the central nervous system based on experience. This figure suggests that environmental stimulation can engage mechanisms capable of changing the connectivity of the brain on a structural basis, including cell sprouting and even cell death. These synaptic changes may ultimately be reflected in larger functional units (eighth and ninth messengers) that encode thoughts, memories, and preparation for action. CR—cellular rearrangements; IEG—immediate early genes; LEG—late effector genes; SR—synaptic rearrangements.

TRH and neuropeptide Y (NPY), as well as growth factors: brain-derived neurotrophic factor (BDNF), which is increased; and neurotrophin-3 (NT3), which is decreased.

Some of these changes may be involved in reprogramming of the dentate granule cell for dendritic sprouting into the supragranular layer, and axonal sprouting into the CA3 pyramidal neurons (the second step in the trisynaptic hippocampal circuit). The CA3 pyramidal cells then, through their Schaeffer collaterals, synapse with the dendrites of the CA1 pyramidal cells and represent the most-studied site of long-term potentiation (LTP), which is N-methyl-D-aspartate (NMDA) receptor-dependent.

Sutula *et al.* [35] also observed a loss of hilar cells in direct proportion to the number of amygdala-kindled stimulations. Recently, Zhang *et al.* [36], in our laboratory, demonstrated that *bax* and other genes involved in preprogrammed cell death or apoptotic programs are also induced with kindled seizures. Taken together, these data emphasize the remarkable synaptic plasticity of this one region of the hippocampus in response to repeated stimulation of the brain. Not only is there dramatic change and reprogramming of the cellular biochemistry but also a change in the structure of the brain itself, perhaps mediated by neurotrophic factors involving both sprouting (readily observed microscopically with Timms stain) and cell loss which, in view of a lack of association with gliosis, may be apoptotic rather than excitotoxic and necrotic.

To the extent that kindling is an excellent model of neuronal memory, as originally argued by Goddard and Douglas [37], with parallels to recurrent posttraumatic stress disorder (PTSD) [38] and affective illness evolution, the data suggest the possibility that experientially triggered neuropsychiatric illnesses might also be associated with biochemical and microstructural alterations in brain. These data are convergent with the recent demonstration by four different groups of decreased hippocampal volume in patients suffering from PTSD (Gurvits *et al.*, Yehuda *et al.*, and Stein *et al.*, Papers presented at the Annual Meeting of the American Psychiatric Association, 1995) [39]. These findings mirror the original observations of Sapolsky and Plotsky [40], in rodents, that chronic severe stresses or high-dose glucocorticoid treatment could be associated not only with decrements in hippocampal glucocorticoid receptors but also with cell loss.

One is now in a position to conceptualize how the central nervous system (CNS) can be remodeled based on experience as derived from the known literature on kindling, cocaine sensitization, stress sensitization, and the emerging literature on less pathologic types of experience, such as learning and memory [34, 41–43], nonetheless, recognizing the important differences between not only cocaine sensitization and electrophysiologic kindling but also stress sensitization. Weiss *et al.* [17●] demonstrated that the neurotrophic factor BDNF is increased and NT3 is decreased with kindling; however, the opposite effect occurs with stress [44]. Moreover, the stress-induced changes in growth factors can be prevented by prolonged administration of antidepressants [45]. Thus, long-term treatment with antidepressant drugs may not only exert prophylactic effects in terms of episode suppression but may also directly prevent some of the neurobiologic adaptations that accumulate as added illness vulnerability factors.

We are not arguing for a direct modeling of stress sensitization by kindling. Instead, we suggest that kindling can provide a structure for assessing the longitudinal evolution and spatiotemporal cascade of effects that might be induced in a parallel fashion, yet involve different time courses, neural substrates, and even different directions of change in IEG and neurotrophic regulation and their downstream consequences for cellular function. Given these strongly restated caveats [16●], one can, nevertheless, begin to conceptualize how such micro- and macrostructural rearrangements of synaptic and neural pathways in substrates modified by kindling and experience can accumulate, increasing behavioral and physiologic responsivity by the recruitment of wider neural networks, and potentially generating oscillating neuronal changes, similar to those induced in development [46,47]. The formation of multiple cell assemblies as postulated by Hebb [48] and Pribram [49], therefore, could be involved in the generation of long-term stable memories, as well as their translation into thoughts and actions at the highest levels of integration in the CNS.

Experiential Genetic Effects on the Recurrent Affective Disorders

Given that related spatiotemporal cascades of effects could occur in response to stresses, and that neurobiologic alterations are associated with affective episodes, one can now schematize a roughly parallel set of events that could occur in the affective disorders (Fig. 3). We reemphasize that we are essentially taking the vulnerability mediated by genetic inheritance as presumptive (*see* line "a" in Fig. 3). Depending on genetic vulnerability, there could be increased or decreased potential for affective disorders. However, we are not focusing on the relative importance of this variable, because it has received much attention elsewhere, but rather on the other set of potential environmental and experiential effects on gene expression and how these plastic processes could leave relatively long-term vulnerability traces in affective episodes and their recurrence. In Figure 3 (*see* **b.1**) we are postulating that early stresses and losses that , as in kindling, are insufficient initially to produce a full-blown episode, on repetition (at **b.2**) may acquire sufficient strength to precipitate a full-blown depressive state.

Neuropeptides

Once a full-blown depressive episode occurs, it is associated with a reprogramming of neural systems as well as multiple neurotransmitter and endocrine abnormalities (*eg*, increases in CRH and TRH and decreases in SRIF [50–52] (*see* Fig. 3). We are postulating that this state and its neurobiologic concomitants leave not only cognitive and memory scars for subsequent depressions (such as in kindling, potentially progressing toward spontaneity) but also that some of the abnormalities in the affective disorders (*eg*, the CRH increases) can induce their own cascade of effects on gene expression (*see* **c.1** and **c.2**, Fig. 3). For example, Clark *et al.* [53] observed that intracerebroventricular administration of CRH to rats induces the IEG *c-fos* in the piriform cortex and other structures intimately linked to memory [54,55]. Moreover, the downstream consequences of CRH

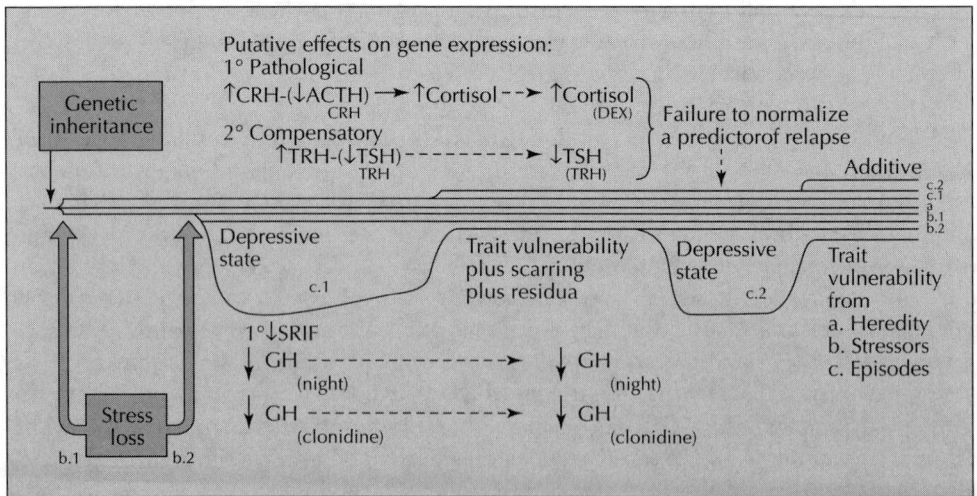

Figure 3. Accumulated experiential genetic vulnerability in recurrent affective illness. Initial stressors that might not be sufficient to trigger the full neurobiologic concomitants of a depressive episode (*State*), nonetheless, may leave behind biologic (*Trait*) vulnerabilities to further alterations. The state of depression with its associated peptide and hormonal increases (**top**) and decreases (**bottom**) may then leave behind additional trait vulnerabilities and residua, propelling the illness to episode recurrence and automaticity. ACTH—adrenocorticotropin; GH—growth hormone; SRIF—somatostatin; TRH—thyrotropin-releasing hormone; TSH—thyroid-stimulating hormone.

hypersecretion (*ie*, increases in glucocorticoids) are themselves also transcriptionally active. Multiple investigators have reported that glucocorticoids are able to inhibit *fos* induction and vice versa. Similarly, the effect of increased TRH on thyroid hormone secretion (T_3) can have transcriptionally activating effects at the T_3 receptor. Although the glucocorticoid receptor is found in cytoplasm and is blocked from migration into the nucleus by heat-shock proteins, the thyroid hormone receptor is located directly in the nucleus.

Thus, there is a set of rich and complicated possibilities for how the neurochemistry of affective episodes could affect gene expression and leave behind either added trait vulnerabilities or residual scarring, as schematically illustrated in Figure 3 by the increased width of the vulnerability line between episodes. We already know that with clinical recovery but failure to normalize either abnormal escape from dexamethasone suppression or a blunted thyroid-stimulating hormone (TSH) response to TRH, depressed patients are at extremely high risk for relapse [54,56]. If sufficient numbers of depressive episodes have occurred, relatively minor stresses may be capable of triggering a depressive state; or, depression may occur spontaneously, as reported in many instances of "endogenous" depression. As illustrated in Figure 3, it is postulated that accumulating depressive episodes would also lead to additive changes in alterations in gene expression, leaving increased trait vulnerability based on 1) heredity, 2) accumulation of stresses, 3) episodes themselves, and perhaps even 4) covert interepisode disease progression.

It is now possible to envision how these kinds of biochemical and neurophysiologic changes could be translated into regional physiologic and anatomic changes imaged in the nervous system. This series of events could lead to transient state-dependent frontal hypometabolism and limbic dysregulation, either hyper- or hypometabolism, as have been found in basal studies and in response to neuropsychologic and pharmacological probes (*see* the article by George *et al.* [pp. 1–21]). The size of the pituitary gland and its adrenal target could also be systematically increased [50], on the basis of concurrent endocrine and neurotrophic induction. The changes in the neuropeptide environments can also be directly assessed from studies of cerebrospinal fluid (CSF) metabolites. However, recent studies indicate that regulation of TRH in the hypothalamic–pituitary–thyroid axis is very different from that of the limbic TRH axis [57], for example, and it is this latter substrate that has been most closely linked to alterations in psychomotor activity, cognition, and affect [58].

Thus, we are left with a further caveat that the endocrine window into the brain may give not only a poor or distorted view of cerebral structures, but in some instances, may be regulated in an opposite fashion and appear more like an opposing mirror than a translucent window [57]. This differential impact of stress and affective episodes on different elements of the neural axis, nonetheless, would have important effects on the pathophysiology of the illness. Endocrine dysfunction and effects on cytokines, which may be regulated opposite those in other parts of the CNS, nonetheless, could feed back and exert powerful regulatory effects on these other substrates as well.

Types and Effects of Stressors

Although we have simplified the concept of stressor for ease and clarity of discussion in the foregoing, one cannot overemphasize that the quality, quantity, intensity, duration, patterning, and degree of control over the stressor, as well as a variety of other variables, could greatly affect the downstream consequences. Brown *et al.* [59] emphasized the necessity for a "matching event" to occur in the stress reexperience, an event that occurs when additional risk factors exist, such as lack of social support, or the threat of loss and abandonment. If the event is similar to events experienced early in life, such as the loss of a parent, it might be associated with a greater effect than the occurrence of a different type of event with, perhaps, equal intensity, but does not represent accumulation of the particular individual's vulnerable "memory trace." Given the single induction of a stressor of sufficient meaning or magnitude, or the recurrence of a mediating stressor, a full-blown state of depression occurs.

The types of stresses that are threats to self-esteem and the ability to function in a social context appear much more likely to precipitate affective episodes, compared with those stresses that are a threat to the physical integrity of the self, which tend to precipitate PTSD. We have described in more detail the possible direct relations to PTSD of both the stress sensitization and kindling models for the long-term imprinting of emotional and ideatic memory (Yehuda *et al.*, Paper presented at the Annual Meeting of the American Psychiatric Association, 1995). Combining both kindling and sensitization concepts might allow one to account for both the long-term consequences of single trauma (as in stress sensitization) and repeated traumas and the ability to trigger flashbacks, first in a precipitated and then in a more generalized or autonomous fashion (as in kindling).

Similarly, we have considered how the cocaine sensitization and kindling processes could help conceptualize the development of cocaine-use syndrome and related panic attacks that then go on to occur autonomously, (ie, even after cocaine use has been discontinued [60–62]). In addition to the influence of quality, intensity, duration, and patterning of the stressor, the degree of threat involved, and the ability to exert control, the developmental phase or critical period in which the trauma occurs may also be crucial to the eventual outcome. The elegant studies of Sapolsky and Plotsky [40], McEwen [63], Plotsky and Meaney [64], and Pihoker *et al.* [65] revealed that trauma in infancy can lead to apparently life-long changes in endocrine setpoints and neural function.

Effects of Comorbid Factors on Gene Expression

With this viewpoint, one begins to have a very different neurobiologic perspective on comorbidity in the affective disorders. If one considers the frequent comorbidity of mania with cocaine abuse disorders [13,14], one then is in the position to posit the triple vulnerability of stress sensitization, episode sensitization, and cocaine sensitization, with the latter able to dramatically affect gene expression. There is considerable evidence from animal studies that prolonged cocaine administration reprograms the direct striatal pathway for increased activation and is associated with increases in c-*fos* through dopamine-1 (D_1) receptors [66–70] and increases in dynorphin [71–73] and substance P [74] in GABAergic neurons. The reprogramming of this pathway could account for the increasing propensity for cocaine-induced dysphoria, with habitual administration, as dynorphin is a dysphorogenic and psychotomimetic peptide. If maternal cocaine abuse were occurring during neonatal development (with the pregnant mother indirectly infusing the fetus with cocaine), further developmental lesions could occur. This type of early cocaine exposure causes a variety of physical developmental delays in head circumference, increased risks for perinatal morbidity and mortality, and sudden infant death syndrome, as well as cocaine-related seizure disorders, hyperactivity, and learning disabilities [75]. Although some of these apparently have been confounded with a variety of other events (comorbid alcohol abuse and nutritional and prenatal care), recent data from Koren [76] and more controlled studies in pregnant laboratory animals have begun to suggest that any of these may be occurring independently of these confounds and may be attributable, at least in part, to a separate neurotoxic effect of cocaine.

Moreover, given that cocaine administration produces dysphoric-like manias, mania could be precipitated in an individual not so otherwise predisposed, or bipolar illness could be exacerbated in individuals already predisposed. Mania is associated with increased drug-seeking behavior, thus primary affective illness would appear capable of increasing the propensity for comorbid substance abuse. Each comorbid condition has a potential additional influence on gene expression and could add vulnerability toward further episodes and refractoriness, as shown in Figure 3 for stressors.

A variety of factors have been suggested in the literature as potentially prognostic of a more difficult course of illness or relative treatment refractoriness. Each of these elements would be capable of influencing gene expression in a negative way, possibly exacerbating the course of illness and its loss of pharmacologic responsivity. We hypothesize that each of these cumulative factors might be capable of conferring added effects on gene expression, compared with patients not sharing these factors, and that the sum total of these factors might have substantial prognostic influence. Moreover, the multiple consequences on gene expression might present identifiable neurobiologic markers with either neuroimaging or direct assessment from CSF or blood tests.

Illness Progression and the Development of Cyclicity and Tolerance

The patient history illustrated in Figure 4 demonstrates many of the patterns of illness progression described by Kraepelin [18]. This patient (in her mid-30s) showed a pattern of intermittent, isolated affective episodes, with 1- to 2-year well intervals between major depressions. However, following electroconvulsant therapy (ECT) treatment of a major depressive episode, with concurrent lithium and antidepressant medications, she began a continuous rhythmic pattern of illness that resulted in a series of depressive hospitalizations and increasing rapidity of cycling, despite several additional brief courses of ECT with lithium, antidepressant, and thyroid augmentation. In her NIMH hospitalization (1985) she demonstrated ultradian cycling frequencies that were only partially responsive to carbamazepine, but disappeared completely with the addition of lithium, which had previously been ineffective with a variety of other treatments. After approximately 3 years of complete remission (1986 to 1989) she began to show increasingly frequent and severe depressive breakthroughs, in an apparent tolerance pattern, and failed to respond to a variety of augmenting strategies and a switch from carbamazepine to valproate.

This patient's rapid and ultrarapid cycling did not respond well to lithium. It is apparent from the kindling model that different phases of the development of kindling are differentially responsive to pharmacologic interventions [1]. This is perhaps now more easily and readily comprehensible, given the previous discussion that increasing and differential neural substrates are sequentially activated as kindling progresses and evolves. The kindling model helps formulate the prediction of a change in pharmacologic responsivity as a function of development phase or course in manic–depressive illness (Fig. 5). In

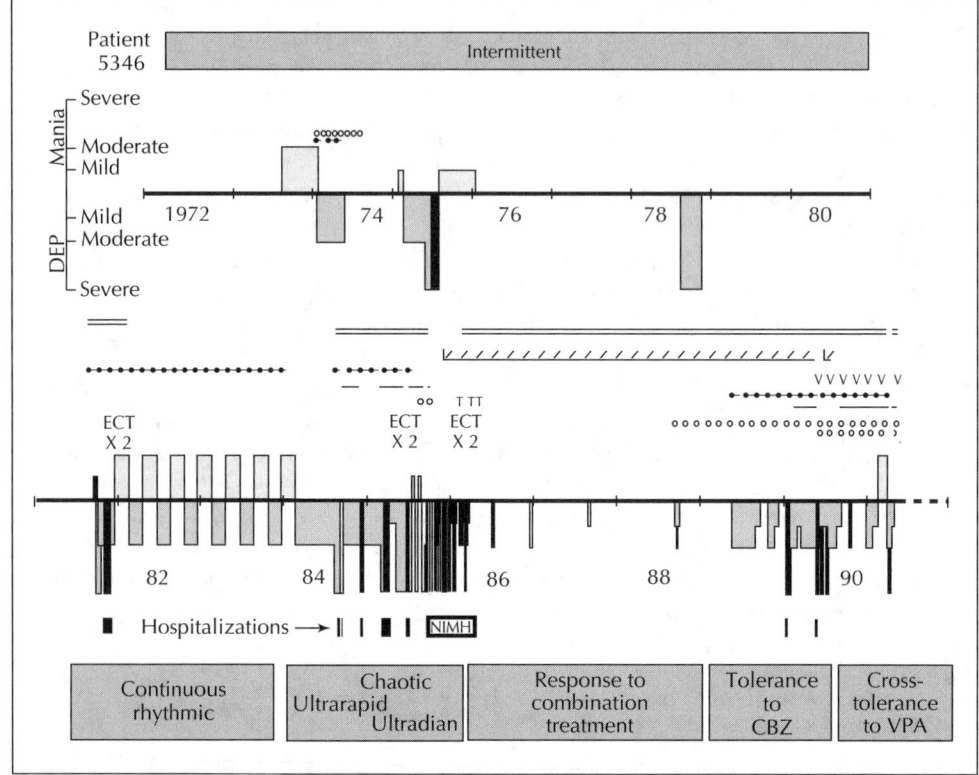

Figure 4. Phases in evolution and treatment response in a woman with bipolar II illness. Lithium is indicated by *parallel lines*. CBZ—carbamazepine; ECT—electroconvulsant therapy; VPA—valproate.

particular, the late spontaneous and rapid-cycling phases may require the multiple mood stabilizers carbamazepine or valproate, in combination with lithium, in combination with each other, or in at least one instance, all three in combination. In other patients who have progressed to ultra-ultrarapid or ultradian cycling, we have also observed response to the dihydropyridine calcium channel blockers nimodipine and isradipine [77], although not necessarily to the more traditional calcium channel blocker verapamil.

Thus, the patient illustrated in Figure 4 benefitted from the combination of lithium and carbamazepine when lithium alone and in combination with other antidepressants had been ineffective. In a more systematic, randomized, controlled trial of an intended 1-year regimen of lithium or carbamazepine, a crossover to the other drug in the second year, and a third year on the combination, rapid-cycling patients did rather uniformly poorly on monotherapy with either agent, but showed a more adequate rate of improvement on the combination, with 51.8% of the patients rated as responders by the Clinical Global Impressions (CGI) scale (Denicoff *et al.*, Unpublished data).

Tolerance to the anticonvulsants

The kindling model and the patient's response (*see* Fig. 4) to the mood-stabilizing anticonvulsants carbamazepine and valproate allow us to explore the phenomenon of tol-

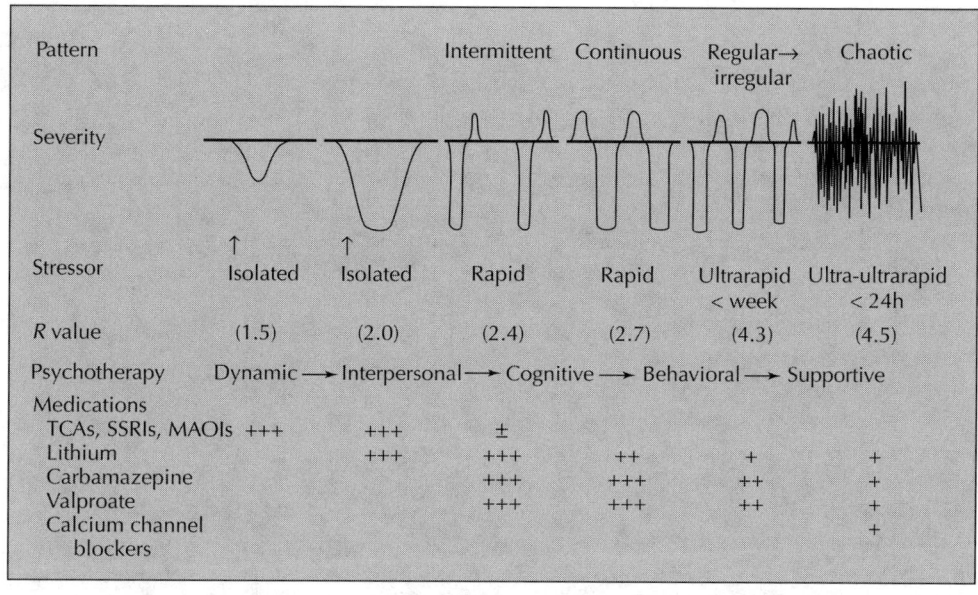

Figure 5. Phases in evolution of mood cycling and their potential relation to response. The progression of bipolar illness from stress-precipitated intermittent episodes of depression to autonomous rapid cycling, and finally to chaotic ultradian cycling, is illustrated. As the illness evolves to greater severity, optimal treatment strategies may also be changing, reflecting alterations in the underlying pathophysiology of the disease. MAOI—monoamine oxidase inhibitor; SSRI—serotonin-specific reuptake inhibitor; TCA—tricyclic antidepressant.

erance development. In the completed phase of kindled seizures, wherein daily stimulation produces reliable generalized seizures, intervention with these anticonvulsant drugs can produce a period of remission. However, following repeated drug pretreatments, seizures begin to emerge despite this cotreatment. Interestingly, this tolerance is not pharmacokinetic; its development is contingent on the drug's being present during seizure stimulation (pretreatment), because the same doses of drug given after the seizure has occurred do not result in tolerance [17•]. Once animals become tolerant, a period of seizure induction without drug, or even, surprisingly, with continued drug administration but after the seizure has occurred, results in the reversal of tolerance.

Endogenous anticonvulsant adaptation to seizures

Weiss *et al.* [17•] identified a variety of neurobiologic events that occur during seizure development, some of which are likely to be endogenous anticonvulsant adaptations. A period without seizures, paradoxically, results in a decreased anticonvulsant efficacy of carbamazepine or diazepam. This suggests that seizures are inducing endogenous adaptive changes that are important to the anticonvulsant efficacy of these drugs [78] and leads to the conceptualization in Figure 6: a dual set of processes occurs with amygdala-kindled seizures: 1) the longer-lasting primary pathologic process that conveys seizure susceptibility and progression, and 2) a set of more transient, endogenous, adaptive changes represents attempts to reinstate homeostasis and exert endogenous anticonvulsant effects.

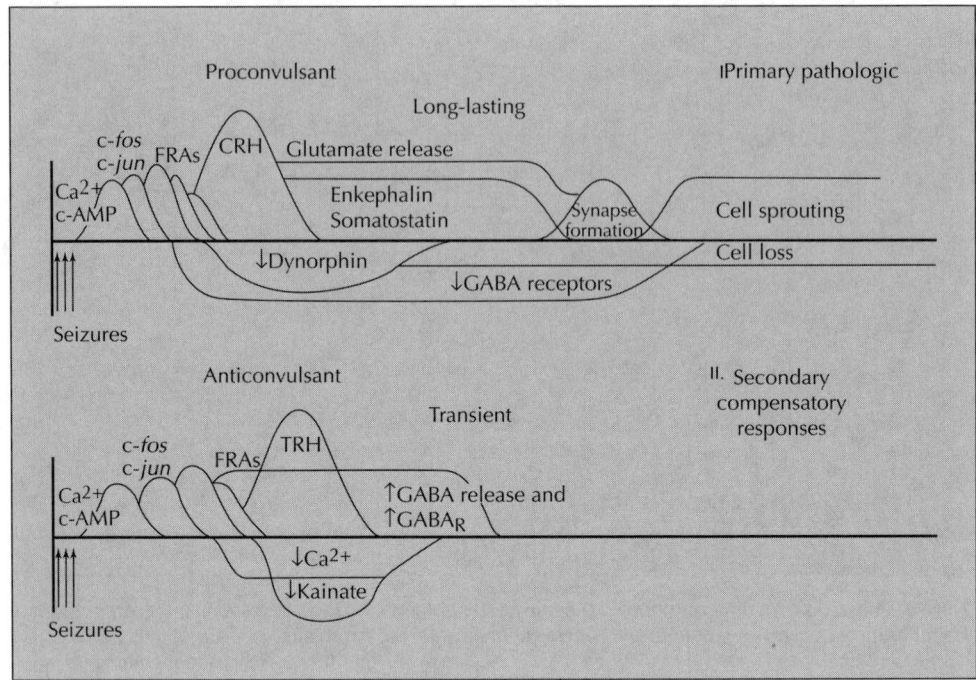

Figure 6. Competing pathologic and adaptive endogenous responses to kindling seizures. Schematic illustration of potential genomic, neurotransmitter, and peptidergic alternations that follow repeated kindled seizures. **Top,** Putative mechanisms related to the primary pathologic drive (*ie,* kindled seizure evolution). **Bottom,** Those thought to be related to the secondary compensatory responses (*ie,* anticonvulsant effects). The *horizontal line* represents time. Sequential transient increases in second messengers and immediate early genes are followed by long-lasting alterations in peptides, neurotransmitters, and receptors or their messenger RNAs (mRNAs), as illustrated *above the line,* whereas decreases are shown *below the line.* Given the potential unfolding of the competing mechanisms in the evolution of seizure disorders, the question arises as to whether parallel opposing processes also occur in the course of affective illness or other psychiatric disorders. Such endogenous adaptive changes may be exploited in the design of new treatment strategies. c-AMP—cyclic-AMP; CRH—corticotropin-releasing hormone; GABA—gamma-aminobutyric acid; TRH—thyrotropin-releasing hormone; FRAs—*fos*-related antigens.

Failure of some adaptations in tolerance

Weiss *et al.* [17•] found that a variety of endogenous adaptive changes that are observed following seizures fail to occur in animals that have been treated with carbamazepine and have become tolerant; these changes include a failure of seizures to induce TRH and NPY mRNA expression and $GABA_A$ receptor upregulation. Clark *et al.* [79] revealed that the failure of $GABA_A$-receptor increases occurs at a specific alpha-4 subunit; in animals that have become tolerant to the anticonvulsant effects of carbamazepine, the mRNA for the alpha-4 subunit fails to increase following seizures, but is induced in kindled animals not tolerant to the drug.

To the extent that TRH, NPY, and $GABA_A$ receptors are major inhibitory and anticonvulsant neuropeptides and receptors, it is possible that the failure of seizures to increase these substances could be related to the loss of anticonvulsant responsivity. This remains to be directly tested and confirmed.

Thyrotropin-releasing hormone

These data, nonetheless, raise the possibility that a similar divergent or opposing set of neurobiologic processes may be occurring in the affective disorders and that, perhaps, one should differentiate between the changes observed in depression that are related to the primary pathophysiology of the illness and those that may be secondary and adaptive (*see* Fig. 3 and 6). We and others have identified sleep deprivation as potentially one of these adaptive processes, because increasing sleep deprivation appears to be associated with at least a transient antidepressant effect in some patients [80]. In the same way, we have wondered whether TRH hypersecretion in depression, evident from increased TRH in CSF and a blunting of the TSH response to TRH in some depressed patients, might be a compensatory process [81]. Both intrathecal and parenteral administration of TRH have recently induced mood elevating and anti-anxiety effects in refractory depressed patients, which would not have been predicted if TRH was part of the primary pathophysiology [81,82]. Whether or not TRH can be "harnessed" for therapeutic purposes remains to be ascertained, but the preliminary data are consistent with the view that TRH could be a positive endogenous antidepressant substance that needs to be facilitated rather than one related to the primary pathophysiology of depression requiring suppression or blockade by therapeutic agents. A direct postulate of the kindling and sensitization perspective, therefore, is that a set of therapeutic agents could be rationally devised that act on some of the processes shown to be abnormal in depression including those that may be secondary and adaptive and in need of enhancement rather than suppression.

Cyclicity as a balance of primary pathophysiology and secondary adaptation

Also, from this perspective, it is possible to conceptualize that illness cyclicity may relate to the balance between primary pathologic and endogenous compensatory factors, assisted by exogenous pharmacotherapeutic agents. Weiss *et al.* [17•] found that when drug effects are in balance with the pathologic driving force of amygdala-kindled seizures, cyclic or oscillatory anticonvulsant responses alternating with periods of seizure breakthroughs occur. Interestingly, individual animals show their own rhythmic patterns of seizure breakthroughs, with an overall tendency to progress toward complete tolerance [83].

Thus, it is possible to speculate that cyclicity could occur in the affective disorders in a similar fashion, during both initial illness development and in relation to intermittent episode breakthroughs of previously effective drug treatment in the tolerance processes (*see* Fig. 4). When seizures do not occur, endogenous adaptive changes begin to dissipate (time-off seizure effect) and the drug can begin to lose anticonvulsant effectiveness (*ie,* tolerance develops). Seizures that occur during drug treatment would not result in the complete reinstitution of drug efficacy, because some of the endogenous adaptive changes would fail to occur. Nonetheless, the breakthrough seizures would be sufficient to induce at least a partial range of neurobiologic adaptations that might be sufficient to renew therapeutic efficacy for a brief period, until these processes are again dissipated and the animal proceeds toward a pattern of complete loss of efficacy.

In the kindled seizure model of cycling, we have been able to decrease the rate of tolerance development by either lowering illness drive, increasing treatment efficacy, or increasing the dose of an effective treatment [17•]. Thus, if an animal begins to show breakthrough seizures on a given dose of valproate associated with tolerance development, the animal can be brought to renewed responsivity with a higher dose of drug. Moreover, a period of discontinuation of medication is sufficient to renew responsivity to both car-bamazepine and valproate, presumably because the seizures occur without concurrent drug administration and the full range of adaptation may be reinduced. In addition, the use of both drugs in combination from the outset results in a much slower emergence of tolerance than with either drug alone at the same threshold dose.

Thus, one is able to postulate a variety of parallel predictions for the course of affec-tive illness based on this nonhomologous preclinical kindling model. A few of these predictions include 1) lower illness drive is likely to result in a more benign course (ill-ness drive may be represented by a combination of genetic and experiential vulnerabil-ities with negative life events, stresses, comorbid medical, neuropsychiatric, substance and physical abuse problems conveying added vulnerability factors); 2) earlier inter-vention in the illness would be more effective than later intervention, (ie, greater num-bers of episodes propel the illness toward spontaneity, faster cycling, and refractoriness); 3) early intervention with high, effective doses may be associated with more positive therapeutic outcome than treating patients with marginally effective doses, attempting drug escalation with each breakthrough [84]; preliminary evidence from our laborato-ry suggests that a descending dosage strategy may also have some therapeutic useful-ness; 4) different drugs may be uniquely effective in different stages and patterns of ill-ness evolution (see Fig. 5); and 5) in a similar fashion, different types of psychothera-pies may be more optimal in different stages of illness evolution with their associated neurobiologic substrates; psychodynamic therapy may have its greatest influence ame-liorating some of the initial effects of stresses, but as the illness evolves and becomes autonomous and relatively independent of these types of stresses as precipitants, other more cognitive, behavioral, and supportive techniques might become more valuable (see Fig. 5). Moreover, as these types of processes begin to enter into the "habit" mem-ory system, as opposed to the one-trial representational memory system in the schema of Mishkin and Appenzeller [85], more formal deconditioning and desensitizing approaches may become increasingly necessary.

Quenching and Its Implications for Therapeutics

So far we have portrayed the kindling and sensitization processes as relatively unidirec-tional and relentlessly progressive, leaving behind relatively permanent neurobiologic memory traces and vulnerability scars (see Fig. 3). However, Weiss [86] in our laborato-ry has recently elucidated a paradigm that not only prevents the development of kin-dling but also reverses its manifestation once fully developed. If amygdala-kindling stim-ulation of 60 Hz for 1 second is followed with repeated, low-frequency stimulation through the same electrode (quenching), the animal does not kindle. Moreover, if a fully kindled animal is given quenching stimulation, 15 minutes daily for 7 days, a long-last-ing anticonvulsant effect is observed [86].

It is of considerable interest that quenching stimulation uses stimulation character-istics that are highly similar to those productive of long-term depression, which is capa-ble of countering long-term potentiation in hippocampal slice preparations. In a similar fashion it appears that the quenching stimulation changes the afterdischarge and seizure threshold in a long-lasting fashion, rendering the animal resistant to seizures, even when it is repeatedly given threshold kindling stimulations after quenching has stopped.

Thus, in an analogous fashion, in the neural systems involved in the affective disorders, one could postulate that some of these apparently permanent increases in vulnerability could be quenched or possibly even reversed. Exactly how one would enter the appropriate neural systems in the most optimal fashion for therapeutic effects remains to be adequately delineated. However, one therapeutic approach is already being explored in clinical populations.

George *et al.* [87] describe a new technique of repeatedly stimulating the brain with repeated transcranial magnetic stimulation (rTMS). They found that rTMS over the left frontal area of brain is associated with antidepressant effects in two of the first six refractory depressed patients studied. In one instance, repeated daily rTMS resulted in complete remission of a patient's depressive symptoms that had been unresponsive to more than 10 previous antidepressant trials. After the patient was discharged, stable for the first time in 3 years, she experienced another severe depression after an interval of 2.5 months. She again returned to the NIMH and was given rTMS at 1-Hz frequency, which was ineffective, but then readily responded to the former stimulation characteristics of 20 Hz for 20 minutes.

These preliminary data are now being followed up by a systematic double-blind randomized study, but they suggest the ability to evoke therapeutic responses in some depressed patients with stimulation of the brain without seizure induction. The ultimate therapeutic efficacy of rTMS and its capability to treat unipolar and bipolar depression on its own, or as an augmenting therapeutic device, remains to be delineated in further clinical studies. Nonetheless, this and related manipulations hold the promise that some aspects of the neural plasticity of the brain can be captured, inducing a sample for therapeutic purposes.

Implications for Prophylaxis

These preclinical vignettes on the possible protective neurobiologic effects of prophylaxis with antidepressants and episode prevention add considerable weight to the already impressive statistically significant evidence for the efficacy of long-term prophylaxis with a variety of antidepressants in the unipolar affective disorders. Davis *et al.* [88] estimates that the P value for statistical significance of antidepressant prophylaxis occurs in the range of 10^{-34}, with an extremely robust effect size. We have observed a clinical course of illness in several unipolar patients that is now consistent with a parallel phenomenon to lithium discontinuation–induced refractoriness [29,30]. In the latter, patients who were initially responsive to lithium–discontinued treatment experienced relapses, and then failed to reresepond on drug rechallenge treatment . This is consistent with the concept that episodes of illness engender neurobiologic alterations in pathophysiologic processes and add to an accumulating vulnerability memory trace. This could then not only propel the illness toward more severe episodes [89] or rapid cycling [18,30] but also to treatment nonresponsiveness [29,30].

This should not be taken, however, as a rationale for not effectively intervening with lithium or some other agent from the outset for fear of engendering such refractoriness. Presumably equal or greater refractoriness would occur in the untreated situation [25–27], and much greater episode-related morbidity would occur as well.

Given all the data, it is possible to view affective illness occurrence and progression as a series of insults affecting gene expression, in a fashion somewhat similar to the multiple somatic mutations that have now been discovered to result in the various stages of cancer progression. In the late stages of malignant cancer progression, it is not only the occurrence of pathologic cell cycle and replicating forces but also the loss of suppressor factors that propel the illness to full malignancy and, finally, to the loss of a variety of constraining factors that allow the cancer to metastasize. Again, it is of interest that these late stages of metastatic cancer are much more prone to rapid development of treatment-resistance, multi-drug resistance, tolerance, and complete drug refractoriness. In the cancer chemotherapies, one uses dramatic interventions in the illness as early as possible in an attempt to engender complete remission. If this is not possible and the illness is encountered in relatively late stages, it might require complex combination therapy; three and sometimes four or five drugs are used in combination, each with different mechanisms of action and additive therapeutic effects, while attempting to keep each drug and the sum of all the drugs below an unacceptable side effects toxicity profile.

Given the preclinical data suggesting combination treatment may be more effective than treatment with a single agent, a variety of clinical therapeutic strategies are immediately suggested. The preliminary data of Denicoff et al. (Unpublished data) and Okuma [90] are consistent with the view that rapid cyclers are relatively poor responders to both lithium and carbamazepine, but do better on the combination. Calabrese et al. [91], McElroy et al. [92], Freeman et al. [93], and Emrich et al. [94] suggest that many patients with rapid-cycling bipolar illness respond to valproate, either alone or in combination with lithium.

The identification of optimal therapeutic strategies for different phases of illness, patterns of illness, and clinical presentations can be ascertained only after appropriate clinical trials. Nevertheless, the empirical database, now bolstered by the sensitization and kindling perspectives discussed herein, strongly support early aggressive prophylactic intervention in the recurrent affective disorders to prevent a malignant transformation of the illness, resulting in cycle acceleration, increasing autonomy, acquisition of comorbidity, potential liabilities of treatment refractoriness, and lethal outcome by suicide, all passed down through generations of offspring. Considerable evidence suggests that lithium may possess antisuicide effects [95]; its use in combination with the mood-stabilizing anticonvulsants, as well as with a variety of other available treatments, including high-potency benzodiazepines and thyroid augmentation strategies, remains to be optimally exploited and explored in clinical trials in patients with bipolar illness. With the equally promising advent of new anticonvulsant agents and their putative ability to exert differential anticonvulsant and potentially mood-stabilizing properties, and with the possibility of regional brain stimulation at subconvulsant intensities with rTMS, a rich agenda of clinical trials is readily constructed.

Conclusions

In this chapter we hope we have illustrated some of the usefulness of theory building in propelling further conceptualizations and specific research questions, even when the model used (ie, kindling of seizures) does not induce behaviors that are directly homologous with the affective disorders. We have purposely chosen models that represent processes that can show increased pathologic responsivity over time, so that some of the potential memorylike mechanisms can be observed and measured in readily accessible neural systems using endpoints such as seizures and behavior. To the extent that these models facilitate the asking of new questions about the course, recurrence, cyclicity, and treatment of bipolar illness and their potential effect on gene expression and to help propel the field to earlier and more effective therapeutic interventions, they will have documented their worth. As preclinical model building progresses, more direct approaches can then take their place.

References and Recommended Reading

Papers of particular interest, published recently, have been highlighted as:
* Of special interest
•• Of outstanding interest

1.   Post RM, Rubinow DR, Ballenger JC: Conditioning and sensitization in the longitudinal course of affective illness. *Br J Psychiatry* 1986, 149:191–201.

2.   Post RM: Transduction of psychosocial stress into the neurobiology of recurrent affective disorder. *Am J Psychiatry* 1992, 149:999–1010.

3.   Post RM: Cocaine psychoses: a continuum model. *Am J Psychiatry* 1975, 131:225–231.

4.   Post RM: Clinical aspects of cocaine: assessment of acute and chronic effects in animals and man. In *Cocaine: Chemical, Biological, Clinical, Social, and Treatment Aspects.* Edited by Mule S. Cleveland: CRC Press; 1976:203–215.

5.   Satel SL, Edell WS: Cocaine-induced paranoia and psychosis proneness. *Am J Psychiatry* 1991, 148:1708–1711.

6.   Satel SL, Southwick SM, Gawin FH: Clinical features of cocaine-induced paranoia. *Am J Psychiatry* 1991, 148:495–498.

7.   Brady KT, Lydiard RB, Malcolm R, Ballenger JC: Cocaine-induced psychosis. *J Clin Psychiatry* 1991, 52:509–512.

8.   Carlson GA, Goodwin FK: The stages of mania: a longitudinal analysis of the manic episode. *Arch Gen Psychiatry* 1973, 28:221–228.

9.   Antelman SM, Eichler AJ, Black CA, Kocan D: Interchangeability of stress and amphetamine in sensitization. *Science* 1980, 207:329–331.

10.   Antelman SM: Stressor-induced sensitization to subsequent stress: implications for the development and treatment of clinical disorders. In *Sensitization in the Nervous System.* Edited by Kalivas PW, Barnes CD. Caldwell NJ: Telford Press; 1988:227–254.

11.   Kalivas PW, Stewart J: Dopamine transmission in the initiation and expression of drug- and stress-induced sensitization of motor activity. *Brain Res Rev* 1991, 16:223–244.

12.   Piazza PV, Deminiere JM, Le Moal M, Simon H: Stress- and pharmacologically-induced behavioral sensitization increases vulnerability to acquisition of amphetamine self-administration. *Brain Res* 1990, 514:22–26.

13.   Regier DA, Farmer ME, Rae DS, *et al.*: Comorbidity of mental disorders with alcohol and other drug abuse. Results from the Epidemiologic Catchment Area (ECA) Study. *JAMA* 1990, 264:2511–2518.

14.   Brady KT, Sonne SC: The relationship between substance abuse and bipolar disorder. *J Clin Psychiatry* 1995, 56(suppl 3):19–24.

15.   Kessler RC, McGonagle KA, Zhao S, *et al.*: Lifetime and 12-month prevalence of DSM-III-R psychiatric disorders in the United States. *Arch Gen Psychiatry* 1994, 51:8–19.

16.•   Weiss SRB, Post RM: Caveats in the use of the kindling model of affective disorders. *J Toxicol Ind Health* 1995, 10:421–447.
Discusses the strengths and limitations of the kindling model as it has been applied to affective illness.

17.•   Weiss SRB, Clark M, Rosen JB, *et al.*: Contingent tolerance to the anticonvulsant effects of carbamazepine: relationship to loss of endogenous adaptive mechanisms. *Brain Res Reviews* 1995, 20:305–325.
Postulates that kindled seizures induce adaptive changes that influence seizure thresholds and potentiate the anticonvulsant effects of exogenously administered drugs such as carbamazepine and diazepam.

18. Kraepelin E: *Manic–depressive insanity and paranoia*. Translated by Barclay RM; edited by Robertson GM. Edinburgh: ES Livingstone; 1921.

19. Angst J: The course of affective disorders. *Psychopathology* 1986, 19(suppl 2):47–52.

20. Kendler KS, Kessler RC, Neale MC, *et al*.: The prediction of major depression in women: toward an integrated etiologic model. *Am J Psychiatry* 1993, 180:1139–1148.

21. Maj M, Veltro F, Pirozzi R, *et al*.: Pattern of recurrence of illness after recovery from an episode of major depression: a prospective study. *Am J Psychiatry* 1992, 149:795–800.

22. Kramlinger KG, Post RM: Ultra-rapid and ultradian cycling in bipolar affective illness. *Br J Psychiatry* 1996, 168:314–323.

23. George MS, Jones M, Post RM, Putnam F, Mikalauskas K, Leverich GS: The longitudinal course of affective illness: a mathematical model involving chaos theory. *Psychiatry Res* 1997, in press.

24. Thase ME: Relapse and recurrence in unipolar major depression: short-term and long-term approaches. *J Clin Psychiatry* 1990, 51:51–57.

25. Winokur G, Coryell W, Keller M, *et al*.: A prospective follow-up of patients with bipolar and primary unipolar affective disorder. *Arch Gen Psychiatry* 1993, 50:457–465.

26. Coryell W, Endicott J, Keller M: Outcome of patients with chronic affective disorder: a five-year follow-up. *Am J Psychiatry* 1990, 147:1627–2633.

27. O'Connell RA, Mayo JA, Flatow L, *et al*.: Outcome of bipolar disorder on longterm treatment with lithium. *Br J Psychiatry* 1991, 159:123–129.

28. Prien RF, Gelenberg AJ: Alternatives to lithium for preventive treatment of bipolar disorder. *Am J Psychiatry* 1989, 146:840–848.

29. Post RM, Leverich GS, Altshuler L, Mikalauskas K: Lithium discontinuation-induced refractoriness: preliminary observations. *Am J Psychiatry* 1992, 149:1727–1729.

30. Post RM, Leverich GS, Pazzaglia PJ, *et al*.: Lithium tolerance and discontinuation as pathways to refractoriness. In *Lithium in Medicine and Biology*. Edited by Birch NJ, Padgham C, Hughes MS. Lancashire, UK: Marius Press; 1993:71–84.

31. Goddard GV, McIntyre DC, Leech CK: A permanent change in brain function resulting from daily electrical stimulation. *Exp Neurol* 1969, 25:295–330.

32. Racine R: Kindling: the first decade. *Neurosurgery* 1978, 3:234–252.

33.• Post RM, Weiss SRB: The neurobiology of treatment-resistant mood disorders. In *Psychopharmacology: The Fourth Generation of Progress*. Edited by Bloom FE, Kupfer DJ. New York: Raven Press; 1995:1155–1170.
Details the putative primary and secondary neurobiologic processes involved in recurrent mood disorder at the level of gene expression and how these may be differentially targeted for therapeutics.

34. Bailey CH, Kandel ER: Structural changes accompanying memory storage. *Ann Rev Physiol* 1993, 55:397–429.

35. Sutula TP, Cavazos JE, Woodard AR: Long-term structural and functional alterations induced in the hippocampus by kindling: Implications for memory dysfunction and the development of epilepsy. *Hippocampus* 1994, 4:254–258.

36. Zhang LX, Zhang L, Smith MA, *et al*.: Ratio of *BCL-2* and *bax* during development and apoptosis of neurons in the CNS [abstract]. *Abstracts of the Society for Neuroscience Meeting* 1995, 21(part 1):559.

37. Goddard GV, Douglas RM: Does the engram of kindling model the engram of normal long term memory. *Can J Neurol Sci* 1975, 2:385–394.

38. Post RM, Weiss SRB, Smith M: Sensitization and kindling: implications for the evolving neural substrate of PTSD. In *Neurobiology and Clinical Consequences of Stress: From Normal Adaptation to PTSD*. Edited by Friedman MJ, Charney DS, Deutch AY. Philadelphia: Lippincott–Raven Publishers; 1995:203–224.

39. Bremner JD, Randall P, Scott TM, *et al*.: MRI-based measurement of hippocampal volume in patients with combat-related posttraumatic stress disorder. *Am J Psychiatry* 1995, 152:973–981.

40. Sapolsky RM, Plotsky PM: Hypercortisolism and its possible neural bases. *Biol Psychiatry* 1990, 27:937–952.

41. Glanzman DL, Kandel ER, Schacher S: Target-dependent structural changes accompanying long-term synaptic facilitation in *Aplysia* neurons. *Science* 1990, 249:799–802.

42. Nelson TJ, Alkon DL: Specific high molecular weight mRNAs induced by associative learning in *Hermissenda*. *Proc Natl Acad Sci U S A* 1990, 87:269–273.

43. Rose SP: How chicks make memories: the cellular cascade from c-*fos* to dendritic remodeling. *Trends Neurosci* 1991, 14:390–397.

44. Smith MA, Makino S, Kvetnansky R, Post RM: Stress and glucocorticoids affect the expression of brain-derived neurotropic factor and neurotrophin-3 mRNAs in the hippocampus. *J Neurosci* 1995, 15:1768–1777.

45. Smith MA, Makino S, Altemus M, *et al.*: Stress and antidepressant differentially regulate neurotrophin-3 mRNA expression in the locus ceruleus. *Proc Natl Acad Sci U S A* 1995, 92:8788–8792.

46. Shatz CJ: Viktor Hamburger Award review. Role for spontaneous neural activity in the patterning of connections between retina and LGN during visual system development. *Int J Dev Neurosci* 1994, 12:531–546.

47. Goodman CS, Shatz CJ: Developmental mechanisms that generate precise patterns of neuronal connectivity. *Cell* 1993, 72 (suppl):77–98.

48. Hebb DO: *The Organization of Behavior: A Neuropsychological Theory.* New York: John Wiley & Sons; 1949.

49. Pribram KH: The neurophysiology of remembering. *Sci Am* 1969, 220:73–86.

50. Nemeroff CB: New vistas in neuropeptide research in neuropsychiatry: focus on corticotropin-releasing factor. *Neuropsychopharmacology* 1992, 6:69–75.

51. Banki CM, Karmacsi L, Bissette G, Nemeroff CB: Cerebrospinal-fluid neuropeptides: a biochemical subgrouping approach. *Neuropsychobiology* 1992, 26:37–42.

52. Rubinow DR: Cerebrospinal fluid somatostatin and psychiatric illness. *Biol Psychiatry* 1986, 21:341–365.

53. Clark M, Post RM, Weiss SRB, *et al.*: Regional expression of c-fos mRNA in rat brain during the evolution of amygdala-kindled seizures. *Mol Brain Res* 1991, 11:55–64.

54. Zola-Morgan S, Squire LR, Clower RP, Rempel NL: Damage to the perirhinal cortex exacerbates memory impairment following lesions to the hippocampal formation. *J Neurosci* 1993, 13:251–265.

55. Murray EA, Gaffan D: Removal of the amygdala plus subjacent cortex disrupts the retention of both intramodal and crossmodal associative memories in monkeys. *Behav Neurosci* 1994, 108:494–500.

56. Arana GW, Baldessarini RJ, Ornsteen M: The dexamethasone suppression test for diagnosis and prognosis in psychiatry [commentary and review]. *Arch Gen Psychiatry* 1985, 42:1193–1204.

57. Rosen JB, Kim SY, Post RM: Differential regional and time course increases in thyrotropin-releasing hormone, neuropeptide Y and enkephalin mRNAs following an amygdala kindled seizure. *Brain Res Mol Brain Res* 1994, 27:71–80.

58. Winokur A: Thyroid axis and depressive disorders. In *Biology of Depressive Disorders, Part A: A Systems Perspective.* Edited by Mann JJ, Kupfer DJ. New York: Plenum Press; 1993:155.

59. Brown GW, Bifulco A, Harris T, Bridge L: Life stress, chronic subclinical symptoms and vulnerability to clinical depression. *J Affective Disord* 1986, 11:1–19.

60. Post RM, Uhde TW, Joffe RT, Bierer L: Psychiatric manifestations and implications of seizure disorders. In *Medical Mimics of Psychiatric Disorders.* Edited by Extein I, Gold M. Washington, DC: APA Press; 1986:35–91.

61. Post RM, Weiss SRB, Pert A, Uhde TW: Chronic cocaine administration: Sensitization and kindling effects. In *Cocaine: Clinical and Biobehavioral Aspects.* Edited by Raskin A, Fisher S. New York: Oxford University Press; 1987:109–173.

62. Post RM, Weiss SRB, Uhde TW, *et al.*: Implications of cocaine kindling, induction of the proto-oncogene c-*fos* and contingent tolerance. In *Biology of Anxiety Disorders.* Edited by Hoehn-Saric R. Washington DC: APA Press; 1993:121–175.

63. McEwen BS: Corticosteroids and hippocampal plasticity. *Ann N Y Acad Sci* 1994, 746:134–144.

64. Plotsky PM, Meaney MJ: Early, postnatal experience alters hypothalamic corticotropin-releasing factor (CRF) mRNA, median eminence CRF content and stress-induced release in adult rats. *Brain Res Mol Brain Res* 1993, 18:195–200.

65. Pihoker C, Owens MJ, Kuhn CM, Schanberg SM, Nemeroff CB: Maternal separation in neonatal rats elicits activation of the hypothalamic-pituitary-adrenocortical axis: a putative role for corticotropin-releasing factor. *Psychoneuroendocrinology* 1993, 18:485–493.

66. Young ST, Porrino LJ, Iadarola MJ: Cocaine induces striatal c-*fos* immunoreactive proteins via dopaminergic D1 receptors. *Proc Natl Acad Sci U S A* 1991, 88:1291–1295.

67. Cole AJ, Bhat RV, Patt C, *et al.*: D1 dopamine receptor activation of multiple transcription factor genes in rat striatum. *J Neurochem* 1992, 58:1420–1426.

68. Graybiel AM, Moratalla R, Robertson HA: Amphetamine and cocaine induce drug-specific activation of the c-*fos* gene in striosome-matrix compartments and limbic subdivisions of the striatum. *Proc Natl Acad Sci U S A* 1990, 87:6912–6916.

69. Moratalla R, Robertson HA, Graybiel AM: Dynamic regulation of *NGFI-A* (zif268, egr1) gene expression in the striatum. *J Neurosci* 1992, 12:2609–2622.

70. Robertson HA, Peterson MR, Murphy K, Robertson GS: D_1-dopamine receptor agonists selectively activate striatal c-*fos* independent of rotational behaviour. *Brain Res* 1989, 503:346–349.

71. Smiley PL, Johnson M, Bush L, et al.: Effects of cocaine on extrapyramidal and limbic dynorphin systems. *J Pharmacol Exp Ther* 1990, 253:938–943.

72. Johnson M, Bush LG, Gibb JW, Hanson GR: Role of *N*-methyl-D-aspartate (NMDA) receptors in the response of extrapyramidal neurotensin and dynorphin A systems to cocaine and GBR 12909. *Biochem Pharmacol* 1991, 41:649–652.

73. Sivam SP: Cocaine selectively increases striatonigral dynorphin levels by a dopaminergic mechanism. *J Pharamacol Exp Ther* 1989, 250:818–824.

74. Cador M, Rivet JM, Kelley AE, et al.: Substance P, neurotensin and enkephalin injections into the ventral tegmental area: comparative study on dopamine turnover in several forebrain structures. *Brain Res* 1989, 486:357–363.

75. Nulman I, Rovet J, Altmann D, et al.: Neurodevelopment of adopted children exposed in utero to cocaine [see comments]. *Can Med Assoc J* 1994, 151:1591–1597.

76. Koren G: Developmental neurotoxicology of cocaine: methodological issues [abstract]. *Canadian College of Neuropsychopharmacology and Japanese Society of Neuropsychopharmacology* 1995, 3.

77. McDermut W, Pazzaglia PJ, Huggins T, et al.: Use of single case analyses in off-on-off-on trials in affective illness: a demonstration of the efficacy of nimodipine. *Depression* 1995, 2:259–271.

78. Post RM, Weiss SRB: Endogenous biochemical abnormalities in affective illness: therapeutic vs. pathogenic. *Biol Psychiatry* 1992, 32:469–484.

79. Clark M, Massenburg GS, Weiss SRB, Post RM: Analysis of the hippocampal $GABA_A$ receptor system in kindled rats by autoradiographic and in situ hybridization techniques: contingent tolerance to carbamazepine. *Brain Res Mol Brain Res* 1994, 26:309–319.

80. Post RM, Uhde TW, Rubinow DR, Huggins T: Differential time course of antidepressant effects following sleep deprivation, ECT, and carbamazepine: clinical and theoretical implications. *Psychiatry Res* 1987, 22:11–19.

81. Marangell LB, George MS, Callahan AM, et al.: Effects of intrathecal thyrotropin-releasing hormone (TRH) in refractory depressed patients. *Arch Gen Psychiatry* 1996, in press.

82. Callahan AM, Frye MA, Marangell LB, et al.: Comparative antidepressant effects of parenteral and intrathecal thyrotropin-releasing hormone: confounding effects of tolerance and implications for therapeutics. *Biol Psychiatry* 1996, in press.

83. Post RM, Weiss SRB: A speculative model of affective illness cyclicity based on patterns of drug tolerance observed in amygdala-kindled seizures. *Mol Neurobiol* 1996, 12:33 60.

84. Kalynchuk LE, Kim CK, Pinel JPJ, Kippin TE: Effect of an ascending dose regimen on the development of tolerance to the anticonvulsant effect of diazepam. *Behav Neurosci* 1994, 108:213–216.

85. Mishkin M, Appenzeller T: The anatomy of memory. *Sci Am* 1987, 256:80–89.

86. Weiss SRB, Li XL, Rosen JB, et al.: Quenching: inhibition of development and expression of amygdala kindled seizures with low frequency stimulation. *Neuroreport* 1995, 6:2171–2176.

87. George MS, Wassermann EM, Williams WA, et al.: Daily repetitive transcranial magnetic stimulation (rTMS) improves mood in depression. *Neuroreport* 1995, 6:1853–1856.

88. Davis JM, Wang Z, Janicak PG: A quantitative analysis of clinical drug trials for the treatment of affective disorders. *Psychopharmacol Bull* 1993, 29:175–181.

89. Maj M, Pirozzi R, Kemali D: Long-term outcome of lithium prophylaxis in patients initially classified as complete responders. *Psychopharmacology* 1989, 98:535–538.

90. Okuma T: Effects of carbamazepine and lithium on affective disorders. *Neuropsychobiology* 1993, 27: 138–145.

91. Calabrese JR, Woyshville MJ, Kimmel SE, Rapport DJ: Predictors of valproate response in bipolar rapid cycling. *J Clin Psychopharmacology* 1993, 13:280–283.

92. McElroy SL, Keck PE, Jr., Pope HG, Jr., Hudson JI: Valproate in the treatment of rapid-cycling bipolar disorder. *J Clin Psychopharmacol* 1988, 8:275–279.

93. Freeman TW, Clothier JL, Pazzaglia P, et al.: A double-blind comparison of valproate and lithium in the treatment of acute mania. *Am J Psychiatry* 1992, 149:108–111.

94. Emrich HM, Dose M, Von Zerssen D: The use of sodium valproate, carbamazepine and oxcarbazepine in patients with affective disorders. *J Affective Disord* 1985, 8:243–250.

95. Crundwell JK: Lithium and its potential benefit in reducing increased mortality rates due to suicide. *Lithium* 1994, 5:193–204.

CHAPTER 3

Sleep Electrophysiology of Major Depressive Disorders

Roseanne Armitage and Robert Hoffmann

Sleep abnormalities are key features of major depressive disorders (MDD), present in over 80% of patients, and are often the presenting symptoms of depression. Sleep characteristics have been not only useful in differentiating those with mood disorders from healthy control subjects, but also in predicting antidepressant treatment response and as biologic markers of MDD. This chapter describes the methods of recording and analyzing electroencephalograms (EEGs) and summarizes the findings in sleep and wakefulness in patients with MDD. Some speculation is offered on the potential mechanisms underlying EEG pathophysiology in depression.

Electrophysiologic recording is a noninvasive procedure, measuring bioelectric potentials from electrodes affixed to the scalp to record EEG activity, to the outer ridges of the eyes to record electrooculographic (EOG) activity, and to the chin-cheek or submental sites to record electromyographic (EMG) activity. Signals are then amplified several thousand times, and the resulting voltage values are either plotted on polygraphic paper or digitized at a fast-sampling rate through analog-to-digital convert-ers in microcomputers. Once digitized, data may be displayed in analog form on a com-puter monitor (a paperless polygraph system) or processed by computed (time series) EEG-frequency analysis.

Sleep Macroarchitectural Analysis

Standard sleep EEG analysis requires visual scoring of 30-second or 1-minute epochs and assigning a single sleep stage designation based on EEG, EOG, and EMG events. Standardized visual stage scoring identifies six distinct stages: awake, rapid eye move-ment (REM), and stages 1 through 4 of non–rapid eye movement (NREM) sleep [1].

In normal subjects, stage 1 sleep occurs 5 to 10 minutes after lights out and occupies less than 10% of total sleep time. Stage 2 sleep occurs thereafter. About 50% of total sleep time is devoted to stage 2 sleep. Stages 3 and 4 sleep, collectively identified as *deep slow-wave sleep*, largely occur within the first hour of sleep. Slow-wave sleep (SWS) is usu-ally restricted to the first half of the night, making up less than 20% of total sleep. An epoch of stage 4 sleep is shown in Figure 1.

Rapid eye movement sleep is characterized by a pattern of low-voltage, mixed-fre-quency, desynchronous EEG activity, binocularly symmetrical REMs, and inhibition of motor activity (atonia or paralysis of antigravity muscles). Only the diaphragm and extraocular muscles are active in REM sleep. REM sleep has been called *paradoxical* or *active sleep* because the pattern of EEG activity closely resembles that of wakefulness, yet muscles are paralyzed [2]. The first REM sleep period occurs 80 to 120 minutes after

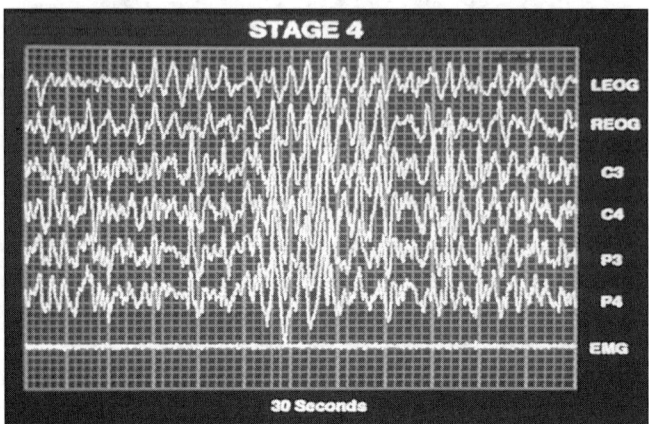

Figure 1. Polygraphic tracings from a 30-second epoch of stage 4 nonrapid eye movement sleep. Tracings are left electrooculogram (LEOG), right electrooculogram (REOG), left central electroencephalograph (EEG [C3]), right central EEG (C4), left parietal EEG (P3), right parietal EEG (P4), and electromyogram (EMG). Note the pattern of slow-rolling eye movements with low-amplitude EEG.

sleep onset and occupies about 20% of total sleep time. Healthy adults have three to five REM periods in a given night, with an average interval of 90 minutes between each REM period. An epoch of REM sleep is shown in Figure 2. Intermittent wakefulness generally contributes 2% to 5% to the total night.

From these stage scores, several sleep parameters can be derived, including (among others) sleep-onset time, latency to the first REM period, percentage of total time spent in each sleep stage, and amount of wakefulness during the night, reflecting sleep efficiency. Collectively, these parameters describe *sleep macroarchitecture*, the global organization of sleep stage characteristics and can be summarized across the night in a hypnogram. Figure 3 shows typical sleep macroarchitecture in a healthy, normal control with commonly reported sleep parameters.

Sleep macroarchitectural findings in depression

Sleep disturbances in patients with MDD are pervasive, with more than 80% of patients reporting sleep difficulties [3]. A recent literature review uncovered more than 1300 studies that have investigated sleep macroarchitecture in patients with MDD. The most common characteristics relative to healthy adults are prolonged sleep onset, short latency to the first REM period (< 65 min), a reduction in SWS, increased light stage 1 sleep, and increased awakenings during the night. The most consistent sleep disturbances in depression involve measures of sleep continuity [3], although short REM latency has been the most widely studied sleep abnormality in patients with MDD. Figure 4 depicts sleep macroarchitecture in a typical symptomatic, unmedicated outpatient with MDD.

Short REM latency appears to differentiate primary from secondary depression [4–8]. Moreover, MDD outpatients with short REM latencies respond better to tricyclic antidepressant therapy than do those with normal REM latency [8,9], and short REM latency may be associated with a greater likelihood of recurrence of depressive symptoms [7] once treatment is stopped. In general, very short REM latency is associated with a more severe clinical course of illness, characterized by more episodes of MDD, with incomplete interepisode recovery [10,11].

Research has also shown that short REM latency characterizes the first-degree relatives of depressed patients, suggesting a genetic modulation of sleep abnormalities

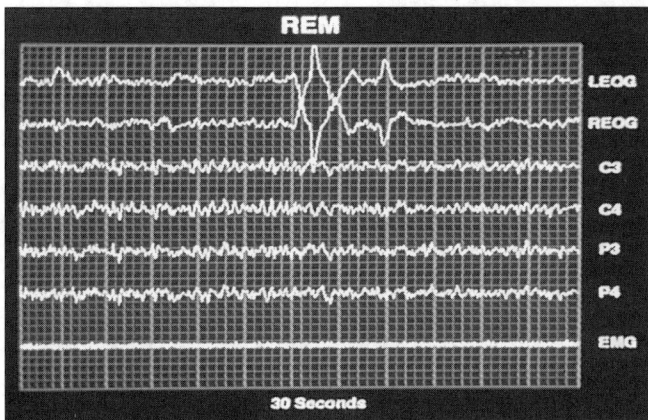

Figure 2. Polygraphic tracings from a 30-second epoch of stage 2 rapid eye movement sleep (REM). Note the low electromyogram (EMG) appearance of REMs and the presence of low-amplitude, higher frequency electroencephalogram (EEG) frequency. LEOG—left electrooculogram; REOG—right electrooculogram; C3—left central EEG; C4—right central EEG; P3—left parietal EEG; P4—right parietal EEG.

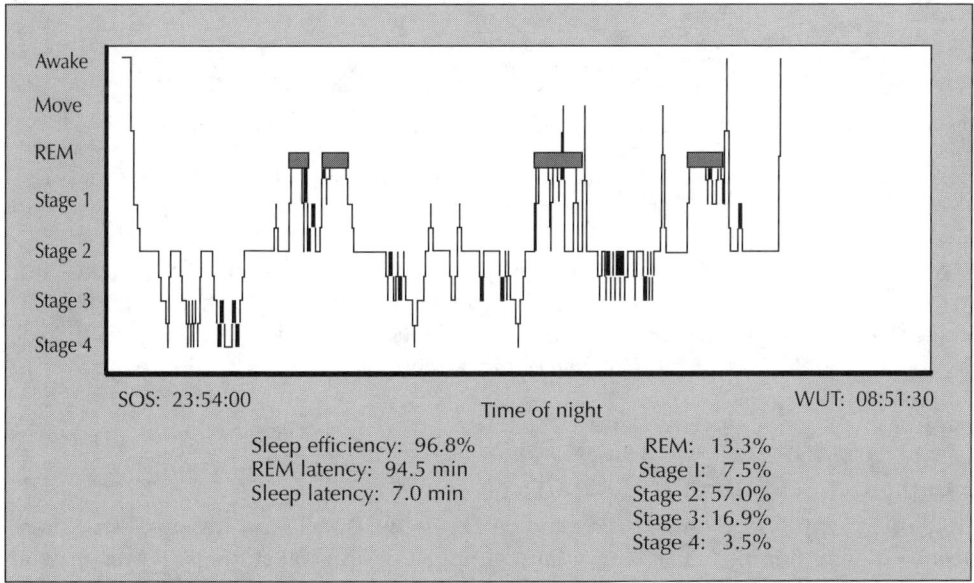

Figure 3. Hypnogram of sleep architecture in a healthy normal control person. Key sleep stage parameters are noted below the hypnogram. Sleep is highly consolidated with few awakenings. Note the predominance of stage 3 and 4 (slow-wave sleep) in the first half of the night. The first rapid eye movement (REM) period (REM latency) occurs 94.5 minutes after sleep onset. Move denotes movement in the sleep record. SOS—sleep onset time; WUT—wake-up time.

[12,13]. In support of this, Lauer *et al.* [14••] have shown that about 18% of never mentally ill individuals who are at risk for depression, based on family history, also show a reduction in SWS and increased REM density, relative to normal controls, but they did not identify REM latency as a potential marker for depression.

However, it is debatable whether the macroarchitectural abnormalities are specific to MDD, because similar sleep disturbances have been reported in other disorder groups. In a recent meta-analysis of published data, Benca *et al.* [15] found that short

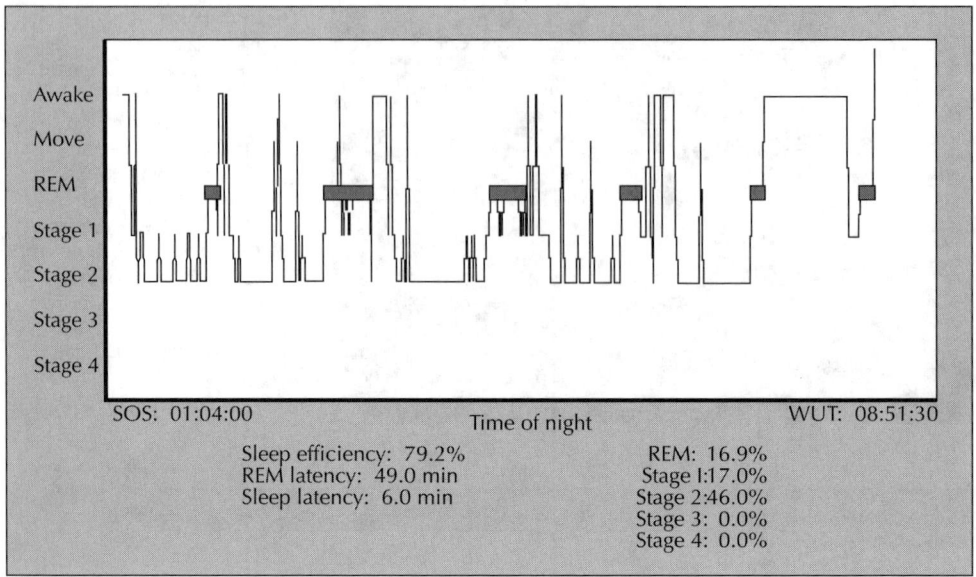

Awake
Move
REM
Stage 1
Stage 2
Stage 3
Stage 4

SOS: 01:04:00   Time of night   WUT: 08:51:30

Sleep efficiency: 79.2%   REM: 16.9%
REM latency: 49.0 min   Stage 1:17.0%
Sleep latency: 6.0 min   Stage 2:46.0%
                                                Stage 3: 0.0%
                                                Stage 4: 0.0%

Figure 4. Hypnogram of sleep architecture in a symptomatic, unmedicated, depressed outpatient. In contrast with the control individual, sleep is highly fragmented in the depressed patient, with multiple awakenings. Rapid eye movement (REM) latency is less than 50 minutes and no slow-wave sleep is present in the record. SOS—sleep onset time; WUT—wake-up time.

REM latency, increased awake time, and reduced SWS are also reported for patients with schizophrenia and obsessive–compulsive disorders. Benca *et al.* [15] concluded that no single sleep parameter reliably differentiates patients with MDD from other psychiatric groups. Although less well studied, sleep microarchitecture has shown more promise in this area.

Sleep Microarchitectural Analyses

Sleep microarchitecture, based on computed EEG frequency algorithms, provides a more detailed description of EEG changes throughout sleep and wakefulness. Power spectral analysis (PSA), based on the fast-Fourier transformation (FFT) and period amplitude analysis (PAA), evaluating the length of time between changes in the EEG, are the two most popular frequency analytic procedures. Both procedures quantify the incidence and amplitude of EEG activity, usually summarized in delta (0.5–4 Hz), theta (4–8 HZ), alpha (8–12 Hz), sigma (12–16 Hz), and beta (16–32 Hz) frequency bands [16••].

Power spectral analysis

Power spectral analysis, based on the FFT, is a frequency-domain approach that evaluates power or energy in discrete frequencies by applying a set of sine and cosine functions to decompose complex EEG waves from 2- to 10-second epochs into reiteratively component frequencies, until all variance is captured. A power value (the square of the magnitude of the FFT), is computed for each sine–cosine fit. The largest power value is presumed to reflect the dominant EEG frequency. The power values are usually then averaged across 30-second or 1-minute epochs [17–19]. Figure 5 illustrates PSA quantification of a single 20-second epoch of sleep EEG, decomposing the EEG signal (*see* Fig. 5A) into its component frequencies (*see* Fig. 5B). The power spectrum can then be plotted across the whole night (Fig. 6). This description summarizes the waxing and waning of EEG frequencies throughout sleep.

An increase in PSA power can reflect an increase in the number of waves in a given frequency, an increase in the amplitude of waves, or both. As such, PSA cannot distinguish between high-amplitude, low-incidence events and low-amplitude, high-incidence events [20,21]. A fundamental assumption of PSA is that the signal is stationary and predictably recurrent [18], although this assumption is rarely tested empirically [17].

Once generated, PSA power values can be evaluated statistically across hours of the night, or by sleep stage. The time course of power spectral changes can be evaluated through regression analyses or through subsequent time series analysis, designed to evaluate rhythms in EEG frequencies across sleep [22–24].

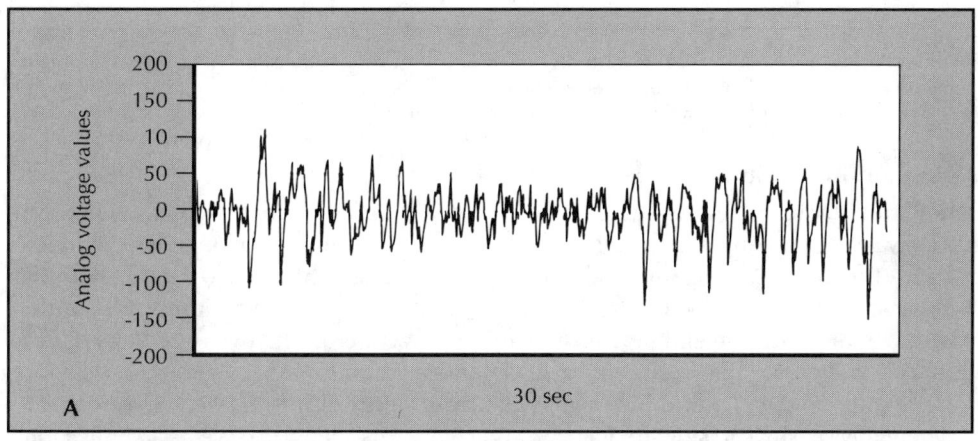

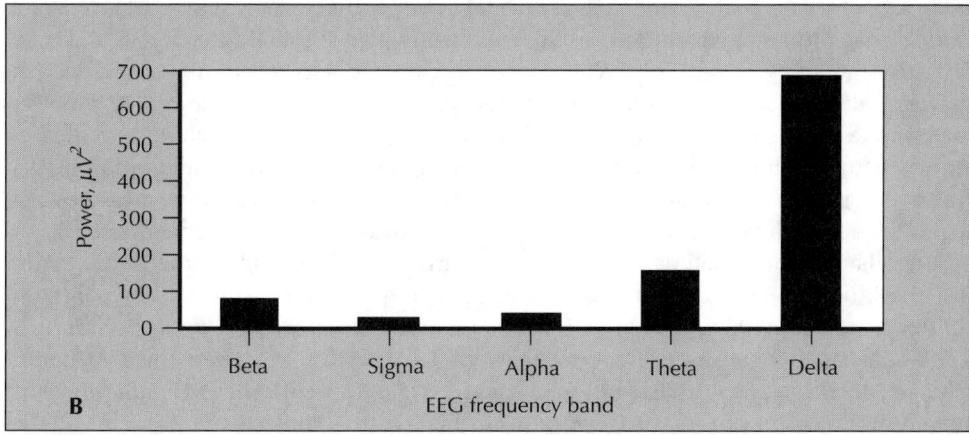

Figure 5. Power spectral analysis (PSA) power values for a 30-second epoch. **A**, Raw electroencephalogram (EEG) tracing from left central (C3) area. **B**, The corresponding PSA power values in the EEG frequency band.

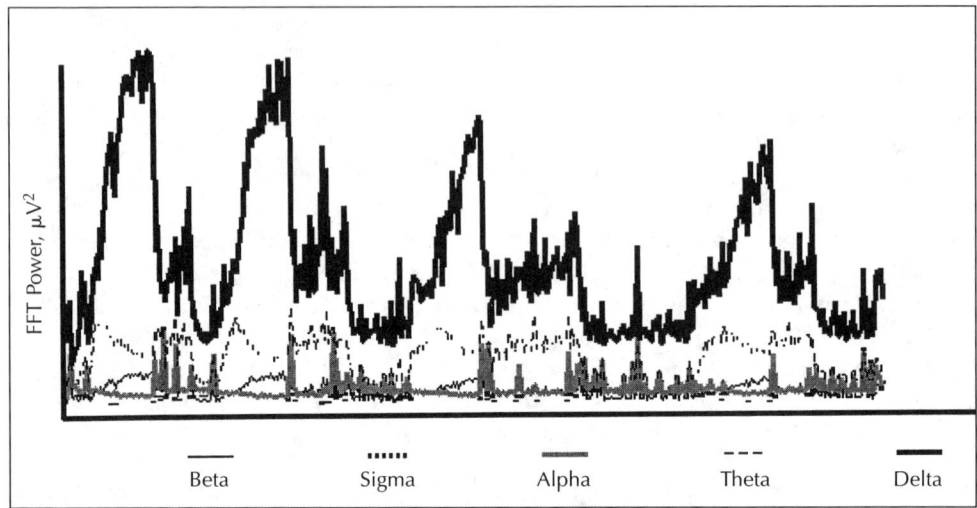

Figure 6. Power spectral analysis spectrum derived through fast-Fourier transformation (FFT) of all-night electroencephalogram, showing the power spectrum of all frequency bands across a full night of sleep. Note the regular waxing and waning of frequencies across the night.

Period amplitude analysis

Period amplitude analysis is a time-domain strategy that evaluates elapsed time between successive voltage changes in the EEG signal, thereby determining the underlying frequency band. The initial PAA algorithm applied to EEG included only a zero-cross analysis that did not adequately describe fast-frequency activity [25]. The PAA algorithms have undergone much modification and now include full-wave zero-cross, half-wave zero-cross, first-derivative, and power analyses of all five EEG frequency bands [16••]. Zero-cross events are polarity shifts in the digitized EEG signal that cross electrical zero (0 V) and, as such, are preferentially sensitive to slow-frequency EEG activity. First-derivative events are inflections in the signal voltage that do not cross zero volts. These events mark instances of zero slope in the signal and are preferentially sensitive to fast-frequency activity. Zero-cross and first-derivative measures reflect wave incidence, whereas PAA power reflects the amplitude (in μV^2) of half-wave zero-crosses in each frequency band. Figure 7 illustrates PAA power analysis of a 30-second epoch in a normal control subject. Note the similarities to the frequency distribution of PSA as shown in Figure 5. Figure 8 shows an all-night plot of PAA power measures in a normal adult. Similarly, zero-cross and first derivative measures can be plotted across the night, to reflect changes in the incidence of EEG frequencies.

Period amplitude analysis data are usually summarized as average time-in-frequency and amplitude in 30-second or 1-minute epochs, and are analyzed in a statistical manner similar to those of PSA data. In addition, our own laboratory uses cross-spectral time series analysis to determine the periodicity of PAA rhythms between the two hemispheres (*interhemispheric coherence*) and within a single hemisphere (*intrahemispheric coherence*), based on our extensive work in normal control subjects [26,27]. This analysis produces a coherence statistic, similar to a Pearson's r^2, that reflects the relative coupling or uncoupling of PAA rhythms [24]. A representation of two EEG measures with high and low coherence is shown in Figure 9.

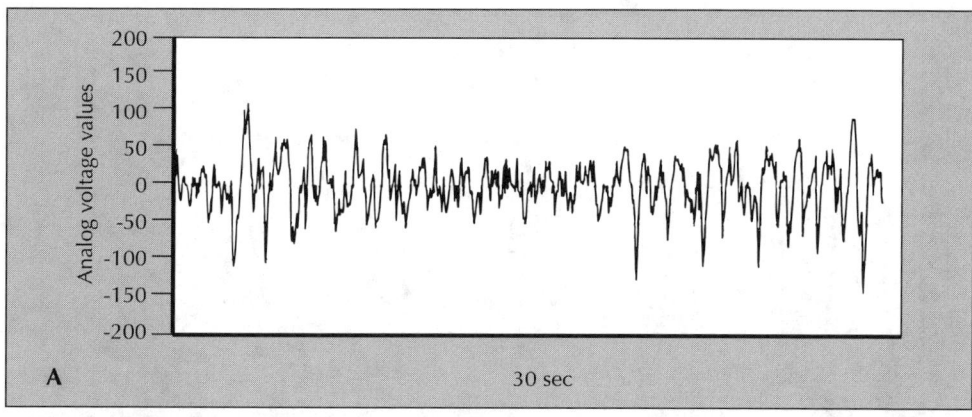

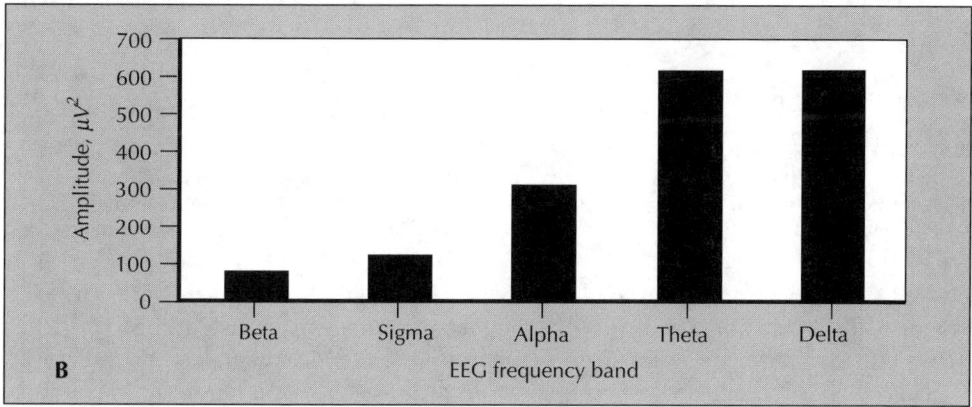

Figure 7. Period amplitude analysis (PAA) power values for the same 30-second epoch of the electroencephalogram (EEG) shown in Figure 5. **A**, A raw electroencephalographic tracing from the left central (C3) area. **B**, The corresponding PAA power values in EEG frequency bands. Note that the PAA detects more sigma, alpha, and theta activity than power spectral analysis of the same epoch. The beta and delta power are equivalent between the two techniques.

There is some controversy over whether PSA or PAA best describes all-night EEG frequency variation, and whether the results from the two analytic procedures are indeed comparable [17,28,29]. Nevertheless there is a growing body of literature on PAA in the study of depression, although it mostly focuses on restricted frequency bands. With this information in mind, we now turn to findings in patients with MDD.

Sleep Microarchitecture in Depression
Power spectral analysis of sleep electroencephalograms in depression
Several studies have investigated PSA of sleep EEG in depression. In one of the earliest studies, delta and alpha power were lower in nine unmedicated, symptomatic, unipolar outpatients with MDD than in healthy normal controls [30]. Using a similar PSA algorithm, however, Mendelson *et al.* [31] could not confirm statistically significant lower delta power in a group of seven bipolar subjects and one unipolar subject. Because the

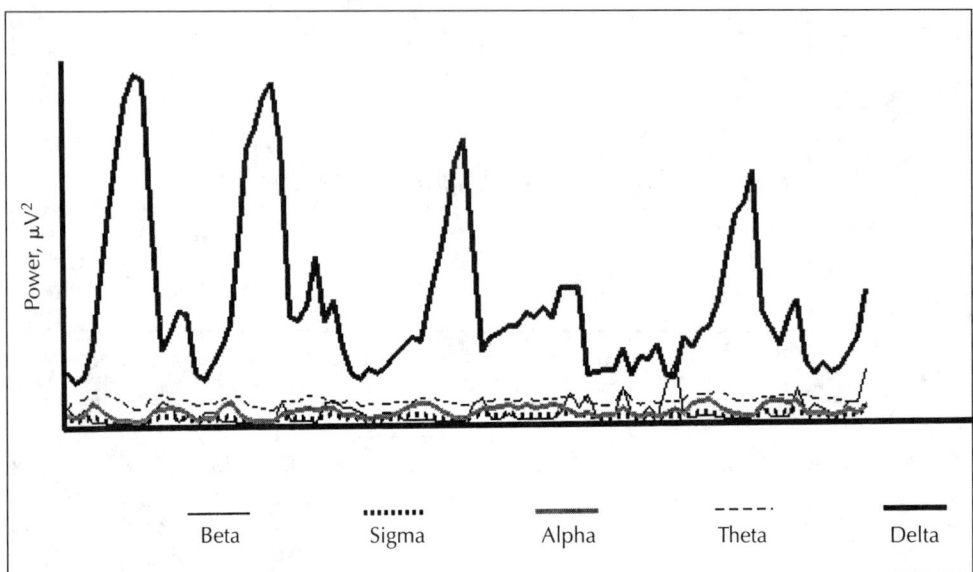

Figure 8. Period amplitude analysis (PAA) power values of all-night electroencephalogram on the same night as Figure 6. Note the high correspondence between PAA and power spectral analysis in quantifying rhythmic electroencephalogram activity. FFT—fast-Fourier transformation.

EEG characteristics of bipolar patients may differ from those observed in unipolar patients with MDD, findings in bipolar patients may not generalize to unipolar patients [16••]. Moreover, delta power for normal controls in Mendelson *et al.*'s [31] study was twice as variable as the depressed group, in contrast with consistent reports of higher variability among patients [16,30,32,33]. Another study [34] confirmed lower delta power in younger (20 to 30 years of age) subjects with MDD, but not in six patients older than 50 years of age [35]. Older patients with MDD showed elevated beta power during sleep, but were indistinguishable from normal controls in lower frequency activity.

Period amplitude analysis of sleep in electroencephalograms in depression

Kupfer *et al.* [36] conducted numerous studies of delta-wave counts based on zero-cross measures from PAA. In one of the earliest of these reports, fewer (high-amplitude) delta waves were found in SWS in 41 unmedicated inpatients with MDD compared with 23 normal controls. In a reanalysis of the same subjects, lower delta counts were reported for subjects with MDD across the whole night, but particularly during the first NREM sleep [37]. In a subsequent comparison with an expanded control group ($n \geq 52$), Kupfer's group [38] confirmed lower delta counts in patients with MDD, but only in the first NREM period. More importantly, there were no differences in awake time between the normal controls and subjects with MDD, indicating that intermittent wakefulness was an unlikely explanation for the lower delta values in subjects with MDD.

Kupfer *et al.* [39] have also suggested that the ratio of delta waves in the first to second NREM period is lower in patients with MDD and that this ratio was related to the course of illness. Patients with higher delta ratios were more likely to remain in clinical remission while they were free of treatment than those with lower delta ratios [39]. A more detailed

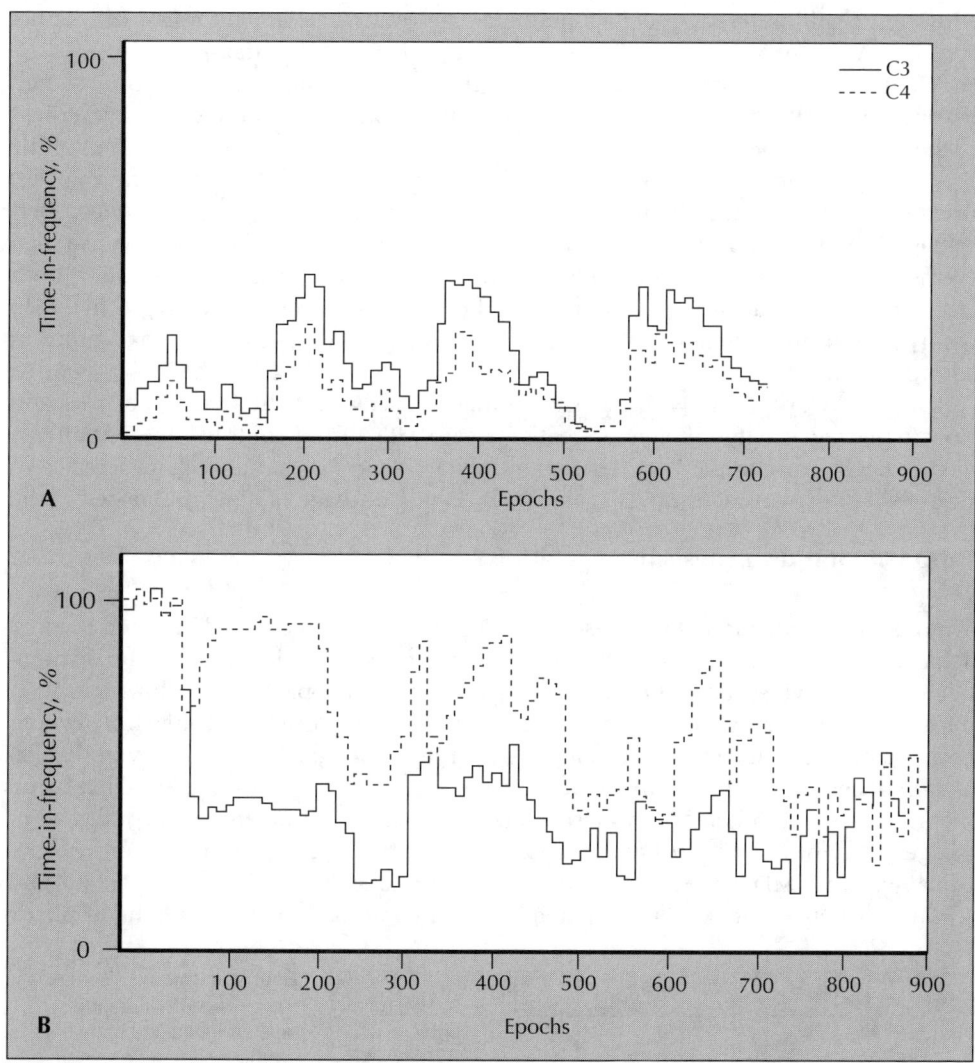

Figure 9. Example of high (**A**) and low (**B**) interhemispheric electroencephalographic coherence throughout sleep. In *panel A*, taken from a normal control individual, changes in left central (C3) and right central (C4) areas are coupled in-phase when coherence is high. In *panel B*, taken from a symptomatic, unmedicated, depressed patient, changes in C3 do not track those observed in C4. Note the inconsistent phase relationship between the two hemispheres.

analysis of delta counts across NREM periods failed to confirm lower delta ratios in patients with MDD [40]. In fact, the normal controls were as likely to show more delta waves in the second NREM period than they were in the first, regardless of whether analyses were restricted to high- or low-amplitude delta waves. It was clear, however, that the *distribution* of delta activity across the night was abnormal in the MDD group, but these abnormalities were not restricted to any NREM period [40]. More recent work supports an abnormal delta distribution among patients with MDD, but it may be only depressed men who show significantly lower delta amplitude than control subjects regardless of whether PSA of PAA is used to quantify EEG (Armitage *et al.*, Unpublished data).

The focus on delta activity in MDD, however, has been a major limitation in quantitative studies. With the exception of two studies [34,35], all of the studies described in the foregoing (including both PSA and PAA) restricted analyses to delta bands alone or to EEG activity below 16 Hz, essentially excluding beta activity from analysis. Because sleep discontinuity, multiple stage transitions, and elevated REM sleep percentages characterize sleep macroarchitecture in patients with MDD, and because such events are associated with abnormalities in faster-frequency activity, evaluating both fast and slow frequencies is essential. Studies that assess fast-frequency activity do report significantly higher beta power among patients with MDD than that found in controls [34].

Our own work, using PAA, has shown that not only do total amounts of fast- and slow-frequency activity differentiate patients with MDD from controls, but that altered distributions in rhythmic beta, theta, and delta activity are striking characteristics of sleep EEG in patients with MDD [16••,32,41,43••](Armitage *et al.*, Unpublished data).

Period amplitude analysis dysregulation
Coherence

Symptomatic, unmedicated subjects with MDD (*n*=9) showed elevated beta and reduced delta activity during sleep when compared with controls [32]. In addition, the distribution of EEG activity is altered in the MDD group, with an apparent breakdown of rhythmicity across frequency bands throughout the night. Intrahemispheric coherence between beta and delta activity was significantly lower in the MDD group, particularly in the regulation of beta and delta activity in the left hemisphere. A trend toward reduced left hemisphere theta–delta coherence was also noted [32]. Reduced coherence was confirmed in a larger group of 12 MDD patients and extended the findings to 12 remitted, unmedicated patients with MDD, reporting significantly lower coherence in both symptomatic and remitted patients with MDD compared with 12 controls. Moreover, interhemispheric

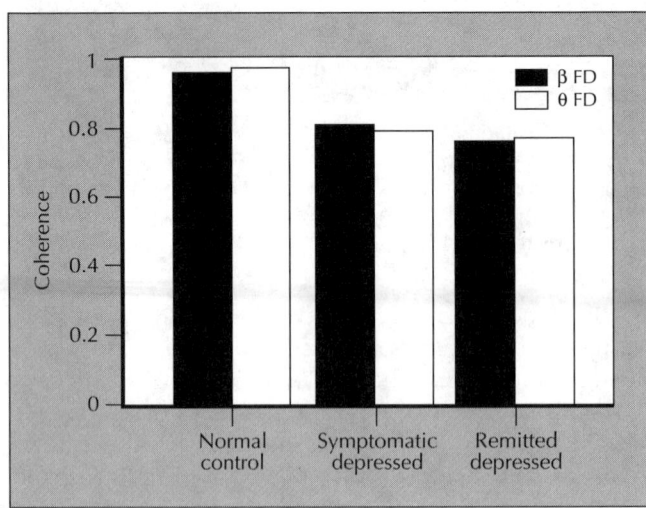

Figure 10. Interhemispheric electroencephalographic beta and theta coherence in symptomatic and remitted depressed patients and healthy normal control groups (*n* = 12 per group). Note that symptomatic and remitted depressed patients do not differ in either beta or theta coherence, but both groups are significantly lower than normal control groups. *Dark bars* denote beta first-derivative (FD), whereas the *light bars* denote theta FD derived from period amplitude analysis.

coherence, reflecting the regulation of beta and theta rhythms between the two sides of the brain, were also lower in the groups with past or present MDD. No differences in coherence were found between symptomatic and MDD patients in remission [33]. These differences are shown in Figure 10.

Both controls and MDD groups showed dominant 90-minute rhythms in each frequency, indicating it was not the loss of rhythmicity itself, but the loss of synchronization between frequency bands that characterized patients with MDD. If a simple phase advance or phase delay had been evident, coherence would not have been lower in the MDD group, although the phase would have been shifted. Moreover, the phase relationship between beta and delta activity was inconsistent in the MDD group, but fixed and regular in the controls. Thus, the data suggest that dysregulation between EEG rhythms characterizes sleep in patients with MDD [32].

Work outside the sleep field has also indicated that interhemispheric relations may be compromised in patients with MDD. A growing body of literature that is based on classic cerebral dominance studies [44], neurophysiologic and neuropsychologic assessment [45], and brain-imaging studies [46] implicated right hemisphere abnormalities in the pathophysiology of MDD.

Interhemispheric sleep electroencephalogram in depression

Hemispheric asymmetries during sleep are minimal in normal controls, about 5% to 10% difference in PAA measures. REM sleep is associated with relative hemispheric balance, whereas SWS is characterized by significantly larger theta and delta asymmetries. Asymmetries in stage 2 sleep are intermediate [41]; however, there is increasing evidence that interhemispheric EEG relations in patients with MDD may not be similar to controls [33,42,43••].

In a more recent study of unmedicated or symptomatic patients with MDD and those in remission, PAA asymmetries in all sleep stages were significantly greater in the MDD groups than in the controls (n=12 per group) [33]. Moreover, REM sleep was associated with significantly more (> 25%) right than left hemisphere beta activity in *all* of the patients with MDD. Less than 2% asymmetry in beta activity was evident in the control group. The pattern of asymmetry across sleep stages also differentiated MDD patients from controls. Depressed patients showed decreasing symmetry from REM to SWS, whereas controls showed the opposite effect. With the exception of delta activity in SWS, none of the control subjects showed asymmetries that were as large as either symptomatic patients or those in remission.

Thus, MDD appears to be characterized by large asymmetries, and these effects appear to persist into clinical remission, suggesting they are "traitlike" features of the illness. This study also confirmed the initial observation that low intrahemispheric coherence [32] characterized MDD and extended the findings to include dysregulation of interhemispheric coherence in both symptomatic and remitted patients with MDD [33].

Gender effects

Measures of EEG coherence and asymmetry may, however, be modulated by gender. In general, the effects of gender are stronger in patients with MDD than those observed in controls [42,43••,47]. Women with MDD show more beta and delta activity than do depressed men.

These findings are in striking contrast to studies of control subjects, in whom the effects of gender are noted primarily in slow- but not fast-frequency bands [48,49]. Moreover, the effects of gender in controls are prevalent only in stage-independent amplitude measures derived from both PSA and PAA. The effects of gender in depressed patients are evident in virtually all frequency bands in both incidence and amplitude measures. These data strongly suggest that women show a greater degree of EEG dysregulation in depression. This greater EEG dysregulation may be related to the increased risk for the development of MDD among women [50,53].

Interpretation of Sleep Abnormalities in Depression

Our own work and studies of neuroendocrine and neurotransmitter regulation point to central nervous system (CNS) dysregulation underlying depression. However, the emphasis on delta frequencies and the macroarchitectural findings in depression has given rise to theories that favor the breakdown of either SWS or REM sleep mechanisms.

Slow-wave sleep dysfunction

In normal controls, slow-wave activity is presumed to show an exponential decay during sleep, followed by a subsequent accumulation of slow-wave pressure during the daytime [54]. This homeostatic "process S" is part of a two-process model of sleep regulation that also includes a sleep-independent circadian dynamic, "process C" [54]. REM sleep is presumed to approximate the level of process C during sleep. It has been suggested that the main dynamic responsible for sleep EEG abnormalities in patients with MDD is a deficiency in SWS pressure, process S [55]. In a slight variation on this theme, Wehr et al. [56,57] have suggested that the oscillator that controls temperature, cortisol secretion, and REM sleep is advanced relative to SWS. They hypothesized that sleep deprivation had antidepressant effects because it shifts REM sleep to a later, less critical phase relative to SWS. This theory has been met with skepticism, however, because sleep deprivation effects on depressed mood are highly controversial [58,59]. Moreover, sleep deprivation effects on quantitative EEG are very similar for MDD patients and controls [59].

The process theory rests on the assumption that SWS is deficient in MDD. Recent data have cast doubt on the reliability of exponential decays in delta activity in controls [60,61], but do not rule out the possibility that MDD is associated with a SWS deficiency. However, van den Hoofdakker and Beersma [59] have shown that the time course and the distribution, but not the total amount, of delta activity differentiate persons with MDD from control subjects. In recent work, delta amplitude was lower in depressed men compared with either controls or women with MDD. Women with MDD did not differ from the controls (Armitage et al., Unpublished data). Thus, gender has a strong and significant influence on delta activity in depression.

Rapid eye movement sleep dysfunction

Depression has also been linked to a disturbance in cholinergic receptor subtypes. The same systems are strongly implicated in the control of REM sleep [62–66]. Evidence for increased cholinergic sensitivity in patients with MDD comes from the effects of cholinergic agonists on mood [67–70]. Moreover, cholinergic agonists, such as arecoline and physostigmine, induce REM sleep macroarchitectural abnormalities that are typically associated with depression [65,71,72]. Cholinergic agonists given to patients with MDD also shorten the latency between successive REM periods [73–75]. Thus, there is strong evidence that depression is associated with cholinergic abnormalities that may result in increased REM pressure [76].

McCarley [65] has aptly pointed out that monoaminergic and cholinergic systems interact to control REM sleep characteristics and potentially depressive symptomatology. Similarly, neurotransmitter systems also interact; thus selectively probing one system, such as serotonin (5-hydroxytryptamine [5-HT]), can have secondary consequences on dopamine (DA) and norepinephrine (NE) regulation, as in SSRI effects on DA motor control [77]. Thus, it seems unlikely that depression is linked exclusively to any one neurotransmitter system. Furthermore, quantitative sleep EEG abnormalities in depression are also unlikely to result from dysfunction of a single neurotransmitter system. Other theories on the mechanisms underlying sleep EEG abnormalities in depression draw on the interaction of neurotransmitters and biologic rhythm control, suggesting depression is more likely to be associated with erratic organization or dysregulation, as discussed later [78]. Waking EEG data are also relevant to the process S theory of depression and should determine whether the build-up of SWS pressure is, in fact, reduced in depressed patients.

Waking electroencephalography in depression

Quantitative EEG analyses have also uncovered abnormalities in patients with MDD during wakefulness, further suggesting that the underlying pathophysiology of MDD is more than a circadian phase shift. There are considerably more studies of quantitative analyses of waking in depression than there are sleep studies, with a substantially longer history. These studies emerged in the 1960s, concomitant with a growing interest in cerebral dominance. Most of the earlier studies reported increased alpha activity in depressed patients [79].

One of the most comprehensive and methodologically advanced studies of waking EEG in depression appeared in 1978. Perris *et al.* [79] suggested that a systemic structural analysis of EEG was more informative in psychiatric patients, focusing on the interrelationships of EEG frequencies and a coherence analysis within and between the two hemispheres. This approach is quite similar to the coherence analysis of PAA data in our own laboratory. These authors reported reduced complexity and coherence in depressed patients with psychomotor retardation compared with high-anxiety depressed patients. Increased beta activity in the right hemisphere was also found in the psychomotor-retarded group.

In a review of more recent waking EEG studies in depression, Pollock and Schneider [80] reported that the most consistent waking EEG abnormality was elevated alpha and beta amplitude among patients with MDD, primarily in frontal and central regions when compared with normal controls. Moreover, alpha abnormalities in depression appeared to be independent of age effects. Two studies have also shown reduced delta activity in patients with MDD [81,82], whereas three studies have reported no difference, or increased delta activity, compared with controls [83–86]. Schaffer *et al.* [86] have also reported that university students with high scores on the Beck Depression Inventory (BDI) had significantly greater frontal alpha activity than those with low BDI scores.

Collectively, the results of these studies directly parallel our own work on sleep EEG, strongly suggesting that the EEG abnormalities observed in the sleep of patients with MDD persist into wakefulness.

The waking EEG literature in patients with MDD is, however, fraught with methodologic difficulties, some of which are also of concern in sleep studies. These include electrode site, failure to evaluate age and gender effects, failure to control cognitive activity during recording, failure to separate bipolar and unipolar patients, lack of control group, patient diagnostic procedures, and confounded medication effects [80,86]. All studies that did control for gender and compared MDD patients with normal controls reported greater asymmetry among patients with MDD, particularly among women [81,86–88]. More importantly, all studies of patients with MDD have identified at least one EEG frequency band that differentiated patients from controls. Moreover, there is also evidence that elevated alpha activity continues to be a characteristic of EEG in patients in remission [89].

With the exception of the early work of Perris et al. [79], EEG studies in depression have not focused on ultradian dysregulation during wakefulness. Thus, it remains unclear whether EEG dysregulation characterizes both sleep and waking EEG activity in depression and to what degree EEG dysregulation is associated with other physiologic abnormalities. Preliminary unpublished data in our own laboratory do suggest that low EEG coherence is also a characteristic of waking EEG in depression. Taken together, the reported sleep and waking EEG abnormalities in patients with MDD suggest that EEG dysregulation is not restricted to the sleep phase of the circadian cycle. The evidence is more in keeping with Siever and Davis' postulation [78] of a more fundamental central nervous dysregulation at the heart of MDD.

Dysregulation in central nervous system

A variety of studies have shown putative circadian rhythm disturbance in core body temperature [90–96], plasma and urinary cortisol [97], prolactin [98], growth hormone [99], melatonin [100], and neuropeptides [101] in MDD patients. Dampened amplitude rhythmicity, rather than a consistent phase advance or delay, is the primary finding in depression (although it is not statistically significant in all studies) [93]. Both the quantitative sleep EEG data and the abnormal displacement of REM sleep point to disruptions in timing in circadian and ultradian rhythms, beyond blunted rhythmicity.

Siever and Davis [78] have clearly argued that a dysregulation hypothesis of depression provides a better fit to sleep, neurotransmitter, and neuroendocrine data, in which dysregulation is the loss of predictive regularity. Simple phase advances or delays are still regular. Dysregulation, on the other hand, would manifest in a breakdown in synchronization of rhythmic events. An oscillation in the phase relationship, fluctuation in the periodicity of rhythms, and low moment-to-moment correlations all meet the Siever and Davis [78] criteria for dysregulation. Dysregulation would account for inconsistencies in published data (eg, a subsensitivity uncovered in one study and a supersensitivity reported in others) [93,102]. In our own work on coherence, the average periodicity of ultradian rhythms in quantitative EEG is twice as variable as that observed in controls, again suggesting loss of predictive regularity. Dysregulation of both EEG (and potentially temperature) are likely to be present throughout sleep and wakefulness. The extensive neuroendocrine work of Holsboer et al. [101] fits nicely with the dysregulation hypothesis of depression. Although the precise mechanisms underlying dysregulation in depression have yet to be uncovered, hypothalamic–limbic dysregulation is clearly implicated [78,93,99,101].

Potential Mechanisms Underlying Electroencephalographic Dysregulation

Because MDD has been associated with abnormalities in both circadian and ultradian rhythms, factors that synchronize the biologic block should impinge on EEG dysregulation. Many hypothalamic peptides, for example, have been implicated in the pathophysiology of MDD [99]. Elevated nocturnal cortisol, high levels of corticotropin-releasing factor, decreased melatonin, and abnormalities in nocturnal temperature rhythms have also been reported in patients with MDD, further implicating the hypothalamic–pituitary–adrenal (HPA) axis in MDD [103]. The suprachiasmatic nucleus (SCN), the circadian rhythm control center, is also located in the hypothalamus. Melatonin- and serotonin-binding sites are present in the SCN [103]. Moreover, ovarian hormones have also been shown to modulate circadian rhythms. β-Estradiol, for example, increases the circadian periodicity of locomotor activity in rats, whereas ovariectomy abolishes locomotor rhythms [104]. Estrogen treatment also alters ultradian rhythms [105]. β-Estradiol also has membrane depolarization effects [106,107]. Progesterone, on the other hand, decreases neuronal discharge by virtue of its antagonistic effects of γ-aminobutyric acid (GABA) neurotransmitters [108,109]. Such effects will have consequences for EEG regulation. Neurohormones may also affect rhythmicity by altering the availability of monoamines, particularly serotonin [110]. Because serotonergic and GABA abnormalities are also present in MDD, these findings may account for the striking gender differences in sleep EEG rhythms in depression and more general sleep abnormalities in patients with MDD.

Evidence also suggests that emotional stimuli in infants elicit hypothalamic activation of corticotropin-releasing factor and corticotropin (ACTH). This link between the limbic system, affect, and higher cortical pathways links the affective symptoms of MDD with EEG dysregulation, regulatory peptides, and hormones in the brain [111]. It does not, however, account for increased EEG asymmetry in patients with MDD. The discovery of serotonergic asymmetries in the brain, in the form of more binding sites in the right than in the left hemisphere, does support a preferential relation between the HPA axis and the right hemisphere [112].

Although highly speculative, these collective findings suggest that it is the organization of brain behavior that underlies the pathophysiology of MDD, rather than a specific neuroanatomic abnormality.

Conclusions

Collectively, studies suggest that dysregulation is a characteristic of EEG activity throughout sleep and wakefulness in patients with MDD. These findings do not support a simple phase shift in circadian rhythms, but argue in favor of a more general breakdown in EEG regulation throughout 24 hours. Moreover, EEG dysregulation persists into clinical remission, suggesting that it is either a scar of previous episodes of depression, or is a true antecedent of the illness. More recent work on those at risk for depression argues that features of both sleep macro- and microarchitectures are indeed potential antecedents of MDD [12,14••] (Armitage *et al.*, Unpublished data).

Future research will undoubtedly shed light on the mechanisms underlying the pathophysiology of MDD, as well as on the clinical relevance and applicability of EEG measurement in the diagnosis, treatment, selection, or prognostication of mood disorders.

References and Recommended Reading

Papers of particular interest, published recently, have been highlighted as:
- •   Of special interest
- ••   Of outstanding interest

1.   Rechtschaffen A, Kales A: *A Manual of Standardized Terminology, Techniques and Scoring System for Sleep Stages of Human Subjects.* National Institute of Health: Washington, DC: US Government Printing Office (Publication 204); 1968.

2.   Carskadon MA, Dement WC: Normal human sleep: an overview. In *Principles and Practice of Sleep Medicine.* Edited by Kryger MH, Roth T, Dement WC. Philadelphia: WB Saunders; 1989:3–13.

3.   Reynolds CF, Kupfer DJ: Sleep research in affective illness: state of the art circa 1987. *Sleep* 1987, 10:199–215.

4.   Coble P, Foster FG, Kupfer DJ: Electroencephalographic sleep diagnosis of primary depression. *Arch Gen Psychiatry* 1976, 33:1124–1127.

5.   Gillin JC, Duncan W, Pettigrew KD, *et al.*: Successful separation of depressed, normal, and insomniac subjects by EEG sleep data. *Arch Gen Psychiatry* 1979, 36:85–90.

6.   Kupfer DJ, Foster FG, Reich L, *et al.*: EEG sleep changes in REM sleep and clinical depression. *Am J Psychiatry* 1976, 133:622–626.

7.   Rush AJ, Giles DE, Roffwarg HP, *et al.*: Sleep EEG and dexamethasone suppression test findings in outpatients with unipolar major depressive disorders. *Biol Psychiatry* 1982, 17:327–340.

8.   Rush AJ, Schlesser MA, Roffwarg HP, *et al.*: Relationship among the TRH, REM latency, and dexamethasone suppression tests: preliminary findings. *J Clin Psychiatry* 1983, 44:23–29.

9.   Rush AJ, Giles DE, Jarrett RJ, *et al.*: Reduced REM latency predicts response to tricyclic medication in depressed outpatients. *Biol Psychiatry* 1989, 26:61–72.

10.   Kupfer DJ, Ehlers CL, Frank E, *et al.*: EEG sleep profiles and recurrent depression. *Biol Psychiatry* 1991, 30:641–655.

11.   Kupfer DJ, Ehlers CL, Frank E, *et al.*: Electroencephalographic sleep studies in depressed patients during long-term recovery. *Psychiatry Res* 1993, 49:121–138.

12.   Giles DE, Biggs MM, Rush AJ, *et al.*: Risk factors in families of unipolar depression: I. Psychiatric illness and reduced REM latency. *J Affect Disord* 1988, 14:51–59.

13.   Giles DE, Kupfer DJ, Roffwarg HP, *et al.*: Polysomnographic parameters in first-degree relatives of unipolar probands. *Psychiatry Res* 1989, 27:127–136.

14.•• Lauer CJ, Schreiber W, Holsboer F, *et al.*: In quest of identifying vulnerability markers for psychiatric disorders by all-night polysomnography. *Arch Gen Psychiatry* 1995, 52:145–153.

15.   Benca RM, Obermeyer WH, Thisted RA, *et al.*: Sleep and psychiatric disorders: a meta-analysis. *Arch Gen Psychiatry* 1992, 49:651–668.

16.•• Armitage R: Microarchitectural findings in sleep EEG in depression: diagnostic implications. *Biol Psychiatry* 1995, 37:72–84.

17.   Armitage R, Hoffmann R, Fitch T, *et al.*: A comparison of period amplitude and power spectral analysis of sleep EEG in normal and depressed outpatients. *Psychiatry Res* 1995, 56:245–256.

18.   Dummermuth G, Molinari L: Spectral analysis of EEG background activity. In *Methods of Analysis of Brain Electrical and Magnetic Signals.* Edited by Gevins AS, Remond A. Amsterdam: Elsevier; 1987:85–130.

19.   Gevins AS: Overview of computer analysis. In *Methods of Analysis of Brain Electrical and Magnetic Signals.* Edited by Gevins AS, Remond A. Amsterdam: Elsevier; 1987:31–83.

20.   Ktonas P: Period-amplitude EEG analysis [editorial comment]. *Sleep* 1987, 10:505–507.

21. Ktonas P, Gosalia A: Spectral analysis vs. period-amplitude analysis of narrowband EEG activity: a comparison based on the sleep delta frequency band. *Sleep* 1981, 4:193–206.

22. Achermann P, Hartmann R, Gunzinger A, *et al*.: All-night sleep EEG and artificial stochastic control signals have similar correlation dimensions. *Electroencephalogr Clin Neurophysiol* 1994, 90:384–387.

23. Dijk D-J, Brunner DP, Borbely AA: Time course of EEG power density during long sleep in humans. *Am J Physiol* 1990, 258:650–661.

24. Gottman J: *Time Series Analysis*. Cambridge: Cambridge University Press; 1981.

25. Saltzberg B, Burch N, McLennan M, *et al*.: A new approach to signal analysis in electroencephalography. *IRE Trans Med Electronics* 1957:24–30.

26. Armitage R, Hoffmann R, Moffitt A: Interhemispheric EEG activity in sleep and wakefulness: individual differences in the basic rest–activity cycle (BRAC). In *The Neuropsychology of Sleep and Dreaming*. Edited by Antrobus JS, Bertini M. Hillsdale, NJ: Lawrence Erlbaum Assoc; 1992:17–45.

27. Klein R, Armitage R: Rhythms in human performance: 1.5 hour oscillations in cognitive style. *Science* 1979, 204:1326–1328.

28. Geering B, Eggimann F, Borbely A: Period-amplitude analysis of the sleep EEG: methodological considerations. *J Sleep Res* 1992, 1(suppl):80.

29. Pigeau R, Hoffmann R, Moffitt A: A multivariate comparison between two EEG analysis techniques: period analysis and fast Fourier transform. *Electroencephalogr Clin Neurophysiol* 1981, 52:656–658.

30. Borbely AA, Tobler I, Loepfe M, *et al*.: All-night spectral analysis of the sleep EEG in untreated depressions and normal controls. *Psychiatry Res* 1984, 12:27–33.

31. Mendelson WB, Sack DA, James SP, *et al*.: Frequency analysis of sleep EEG in depression. *Psychiatry Res* 1987, 21:89–94.

32. Armitage R, Roffwarg HP, Rush AJ, *et al*.: Digital period analysis of sleep EEG in depression. *Biol Psychiatry* 1992, 31:52–68.

33. Armitage R, Roffwarg HP, Rush AJ: Digital period analysis of EEG in depression: periodicity, coherence, and interhemispheric relationships during sleep. *Prog Neuropsychopharmacol Biol Psychiatry* 1993, 17:363–372.

34. Kupfer DJ, Frank E, Ehlers CL: EEG sleep in young depressives: first and second night effects. *Biol Psychiatry* 1989, 25:87–97.

35. Kupfer DJ, Reynolds CF, Ehlers CL: Comparison of EEG sleep measures among depressive subtypes and controls in older individuals. *Psychiatry Res* 1989, 27:13–21.

36. Kupfer DJ, Ulrich RF, Coble PA, *et al*.: Application of automated REM and slow wave sleep analysis: I. normal and depressed subjects. *Psychiatry Res* 1984, 13:325–334.

37. Kupfer DJ, Ulrich RF, Coble PA, *et al*.: Application of an automated REM and slow wave sleep analysis: II. Testing the assumptions of the two-process model of sleep regulation in normal and depressed subjects. *Psychiatry Res* 1984, 13:335–343.

38. Kupfer DJ, Grochocinski VJ, McEachran AB: Relationship of awakening and delta sleep in depression. *Psychiatry Res* 1986, 19:297–304.

39. Kupfer DJ, Frank E, McEachran AB, *et al*.: Delta sleep ratio: a biological correlate of early recurrence in unipolar affective disorder. *Arch Gen Psychiatry* 1990, 47:1100–1105.

40. Armitage R, Calhoun JS, Rush AJ, *et al*.: Comparison of the delta EEG in the first and second non-REM periods in depressed adults and normal controls. *Psychiatry Res* 1992, 41:65–72.

41. Armitage R, Hoffmann R, Loewy D, *et al*.: Variations in period-analyzed EEG asymmetry in REM and NREM sleep. *Psychophysiology* 1989, 26:329–336.

42. Armitage R, Hudson A, Fitch T, *et al*.: Period analysis of sleep onset in depressed outpatients and normal control subjects. In *Sleep Onset: Normal and Abnormal Processes*. Edited by Ogilvie RD, Harsh JR. Washington, DC: American Psychological Association; 1995:185–199.

43.•• Armitage R, Hudson A, Trivedi M, *et al*.: Sex differences in the distribution of EEG frequencies during sleep: depressed outpatients. *J Affect Disord* 1995, 34:121–129.

44. Springer SP, Deutsch G: *Left Brain, Right Brain*. San Francisco: WH Freeman; 1981.

45. Ross E: The aprosodies: functional-anatomical organization of the affective components of language in the right hemisphere. *Arch Neurol* 1981, 20:561–580.

46. Buchsbaum MS, Tang SW, Wu JC, *et al*.: Effects of amoxapine and imipramine on cerebral glucose metabolism assessed by positron emission tomography. *JCP Monogr Ser* 1986, 4:14–17.

47. Reynolds CF, Kupfer DJ, Thase ME, *et al.*: Sleep, gender, and depression: an analysis of gender effects on the electroencephalographic sleep of 302 depressed outpatients. *Biol Psychiatry* 1990, 28:673–684.

48. Armitage R: The distribution of EEG frequencies in REM and NREM sleep stages in healthy young adults. *Sleep* 1995, 18:334–341.

49. Dijk D-J, Beersma DGM, Bloem GM: Sex differences in the sleep EEG of young adults: visual scoring and spectral analysis. *Sleep* 1989, 12:500–507.

50. Heller W: Gender differences in depression: perspectives from neuropsychology. *J Affect Disord* 1993, 29:129–143.

51. Kessler RC, McGonagle KA, Nelson CB, *et al.*: Sex and depression in the National Comorbidity Study. II: Cohort effects. *J Affect Disord* 1994, 30:15–26.

52. Kessler RC, McGonagle KA, Swartz M, *et al.*: Sex and depression in the National Comorbidity Survey. I: Lifetime prevalence, chronicity and recurrence. *J Affect Disord* 1993, 29:85–96.

53. Wiseman MM, Klerman GL: Sex differences in the epidemiology of depression. *Arch Gen Psychiatry* 1977, 34:98–111.

54. Borbely A: A two-process model of sleep regulation. *Hum Neurobiol* 1982, 1:195–204.

55. Borbely AA, Wirz-Justice A: Sleep, sleep deprivation and depression: a hypothesis derived from a model of sleep regulation. *Hum Neurobiol* 1982, 1:205.

56. Wehr TA, Wirz-Justice A: Circadian rhythm mechanisms in affective illness and in antidepressant drug action. *Pharmacopsychiatry* 1982, 15:31–39.

57. Wehr TA, Wirz-Justice A, Goodwin FK, *et al.*: Phase advance of the circadian sleep–wake cycle as an antidepressant. *Science* 1979, 206:710–713.

58. Berger M, Riemann D: REM sleep in depression: an overview. *J Sleep Res* 1993, 2:211–223.

59. van den Hoofdakker RH, Beersma DGM: On the contribution of sleep wake physiology to the explanation and the treatment of depression. *Acta Psychiatr Scand Suppl* 1988, 341:53–72.

60. Armitage R, Roffwarg HP: Distribution of period-analyzed delta activity during sleep. *Sleep* 1992, 15:556–561.

61. Feinberg I: Period/amplitude measures of delta show robust declines across nonrapid eye movement sleep episodes: a comment on Armitage and Roffwarg. *Sleep* 1993, 16:762–763.

62. Jones BE: Basic mechanisms of sleep–wake states. In *Principles and Practice of Sleep Medicine*. Edited by Kryger MH, Roth T, Dement WC. Philadelphia: WB Saunders; 1989:121–138.

63. Jones BE: Paradoxical sleep and its chemical/structural substrates in the brain. *Neuroscience* 1991, 40:637–656.

64. Jones BE: The organization of central cholinergic systems and their functional importance in sleep-waking states. In *Progress in Brain Research*, vol 98. Edited by Cuello AC. Amsterdam: Elsevier Science; 1993:61–71.

65. McCarley RW: REM sleep and depression: common neurobiological control mechanisms. *Am J Psychiatry* 1982, 139:565–570.

66. Siegel JM: Brainstem mechanisms generating REM sleep. In *Principles and Practice of Sleep Medicine*. Edited by Kryger MH, Roth T, Dement WC. Philadelphia: WB Saunders; 1989:104–120.

67. Dubée S: Cholinergic supersensitivity in affective disorders. In *Biology of Depressive Disorders, Part A: A Systems Perspective*. Edited by Mann JJ, Kupfer DJ. New York: Plenum Press; 1993:51–78.

68. Janowsky DS, El-Yousef MK, Davis JM: A cholinergic–adrenergic hypothesis of mania and depression. *Lancet* 1972, 2:632–635.

69. Janowsky DS, Risch SC, Gillin JC: Adrenergic–cholinergic balance and the treatment of affective disorders. *Biol Psychiatry* 1983, 7:297–307.

70. Risch SC: β-Endorphin hypersecretion in depression: possible cholinergic mechanisms. *Biol Psychiatry* 1982, 17:1071–1079.

71. Sitaram N, Gillin JC: Development and use of pharmacological probes of the CNS in man: evidence of cholinergic abnormality in primary affective illness. *Biol Psychiatry* 1980, 15:925–955.

72. Sitaram N, Nurnberger JI, Gershon ES, *et al.*: Cholinergic regulation of mood and REM sleep: potential model and marker of vulnerability to affective disorder. *Am J Psychiatry* 1982, 139:571–576.

73. Gillin JC, Sitaram N, Mendelson WB: Acetylcholine, sleep, and depression. *Hum Neurobiol* 1982, 1:211–219.

74. Gillin JC, Salin-Pascual R, Valezquez-Moctezuma J, *et al.*: Cholinergic receptor subtypes and REM sleep in animals and normal controls. In *Progress in Brain Research*, vol 98. Edited by Cuello AC. Amsterdam: Elsevier Science; 1993:379–387.

75. Riemann D, Berger M: EEG sleep in depression and in remission and the REM sleep response to the cholinergic agonist RS 86. *Neuropsychopharmacology* 1989, 2:145–152.

76. Kupfer DJ: Neurophysiological factors in depression: new perspectives. *Eur Arch Psychiatry Neurol Sci* 1989, 238:251–258.

77. Armitage R, Rush AJ, Trivedi M, *et al.*: The effects of nefazodone on sleep architecture in depression. *Neuropsychopharmacology* 1994, 10:123–127.

78. Siever LJ, Davis KL: Overview: toward a dysregulation hypothesis of depression. *Am J Psychiatry* 1985, 142:1017–1031.

79. Perris C, Monakhov K, von Knorring L, *et al.*: Systemic structural analysis of the electroencephalogram of depressed patients: general principles and preliminary results of an international collaborative study. *Neuropsychobiology* 1978, 4:207–228.

80. Pollock VE, Schneider LS: Quantitative, waking EEG research on depression. *Biol Psychiatry* 1990, 27:757–780.

81. Brenner RP, Ulrich RF, Spiker DG, *et al.*: Computerized EEG spectral analysis in elderly normal, demented and depressed subjects. *Electroencephalogr Clin Neurophysiol* 1986, 64:483–492.

82. John ER, Prichep LS, Fridman J, *et al.*: Neurometrics: computer-assisted differential diagnosis of brain dysfunctions. *Science* 1988, 239:162–169.

83. Kemali D, Vacca L, Marciano F, *et al.*: CEEG findings in schizophrenics, depressives, obsessives, heroin addicts and normals. *Adv Biol Psychiatry* 1981, 6:17–28.

84. Knott VJ, Lapierre YD: Computerized EEG correlates of depression and antidepressant treatment. *Biol Psychiatry* 1987, 11:213–221.

85. Visser SL, van Tilburg W, Hooijer C, *et al.*: Visual evoked potentials (VEPs) in senile dementia (Alzheimer type) and in non-organic behavioral disorders in the elderly: comparison with EEG parameters. *Electroencephalogr Clin Neurophysiol* 1985, 60:115–121.

86. Schaffer CE, Davidson RJ, Saron C: Frontal and parietal electroencephalogram asymmetry in depressed and nondepressed subjects. *Biol Psychiatry* 1983, 18:753–762.

87. Monakhov K, Perris C: Neurophysiological correlates of depressive symptomatology. *Neuropsychobiology* 1980, 6:268–279.

88. Shagass C, Roemer RA, Straumanis JJ: Relationships between psychiatric diagnosis and some quantitative EEG variables. *Arch Gen Psychiatry* 1982, 39:1423–1435.

89. Pollock VE, Schneider LS: Topographic EEG alpha in recovered depressed elderly. *J Abnorm Psychol* 1989, 98:268–273.

90. Avery DH, Wildschiodtz G, Rafaelsen OJ: Nocturnal temperature in affective disorder. *J Affect Disord* 1982, 4:61–71.

91. Avery D, Wildschiodtz G, Rafaelsen O: REM latency and temperature in affective disorder before and after treatment. *Biol Psychiatry* 1982, 17:463–470.

92. Avery DH, Wildschiodtz G, Smallwood RG, *et al.*: REM latency and core temperature relationships in primary depression. *Acta Psychiatr Scand* 1986, 74:269–280.

93. Healy D: Rhythm and blues: neurochemical, neuropharmacological and neuropsychological implications of hypothesis of circadian rhythm dysfunction in affective disorders. *Psychopharmacology* 1987, 93:271–285.

94. Souetre E, Salvati E, Wehr TA, *et al.*: Twenty-four-hour profiles of body temperature and plasma TSH in bipolar patients during depression and during remission and in normal control subjects. *Am J Psychiatry* 1988, 145:1133–1137.

95. Souetre E, Salvati E, Belugou J-L, *et al.*: Circadian rhythms in depression and recovery: evidence for blunted amplitude as the main chronobiological abnormality. *Psychiatry Res* 1989, 28:268–278.

96. Wehr TA, Goodwin FK: Biological rhythms in manic depressive illness. In *Circadian Rhythms in Psychiatry*. Edited by Wehr TA, Goodwin FK. Pacific Grove, CA: Boxwood Press; 1983:129–184.

97. Fullerton D, Wenzel F, Lohernz F, *et al.*: Circadian rhythm of adrenal cortical activity in depression. *Arch Gen Psychiatry* 1968, 19:674–681.

98. Mendelwicz J, van Cauten E, Linkowski P, *et al.*: The 24 hour profile of prolactin in depression. *Life Sci* 1980, 27:2015–2024.

99. Ehlers CL, Kupfer DJ: Hypothalamic peptide modulation of EEG sleep in depression: a further application of the S-process hypothesis. *Biol Psychiatry* 1987, 22:513–517.

100. Claustrat B, Chazot G, Brun J, *et al.*: A chronobiological study of melatonin and cortisol secretion in depressed subjects: plasma melatonin, a biochemical marker in major depression. *Biol Psychiatry* 1984, 19:1215–1217.

101. Holsboer F: Psychiatric implications of altered limbic–hypothalamic–pituitary–adrenocortical activity. *Eur Arch Psychiatry Neurol Sci* 1989, 238:302–322.

102. Risch SC, Janowsky DS: Limbic–hypothalamic–pituitary–adrenal axis dysregulation in melancholia. In *Psychobiological Foundations in Clinical Psychiatry*. Edited by Cavenar JO. Philadelphia: JB Lippincott; 1986:165–178.

103. Wetterberg L, Beck-Friis J, Kjellman BF: Melatonin as a marker for a subgroup of depression in adults. In *Biological Rhythms, Mood Disorders, Light Therapy, and the Pineal Gland*. Edited by Shafii M, Shafii SL. Washington, DC: American Psychiatric Press; 1990:69–95.

104. Takahashi JS, Menaker M: Interaction of estradiol and progesterone: effects on circadian locomotor rhythm of female golden hamsters. *Am J Physiol* 1980, 239:R497–R504.

105. Wollnik F, Dohler KD: Effects of adult or perinatal hormonal environment on ultradian rhythms in locomotor activity of laboratory LEW/Ztm rats. *Physiol Behav* 1986, 38:229–240.

106. McEwen BS: Non-genomic and genomic effects of steroids on neural activity. *Trends Pharmacol Sci* 1991, 12:141–147.

107. Minamik T, Oomura Y, Nabedura J, *et al.*: 17β-Estradiol depolarization of hypothalamic neurons is mediated by cyclic AMP. *Brain Res* 1990, 519:301–307.

108. Majewska MD: Steroids and brain activity: essential dialogue between body and mind. *Biochem Pharmacol* 1987, 36:3781–3788.

109 Majewska MD, Ford-Rice F, Falkay G: Pregnancy-induced alterations of GABA receptor sensitivity in maternal brain: an antecedent of post-partum "blues"? *Brain Res* 1989, 482:397–401.

110. Johnson MD, Crowley WR: Acute effects of estradiol on circulating luteinizing hormone and prolactin concentrations and on serotonin turnover in individual brain nuclei. *Endocr Res* 1983, 113:1935–1941.

111. Schore AN: *Affect Regulation and the Origin of the Self*. Hillsdale, NJ: Lawrence Erlbaum Assoc; 1994.

112. Arato M, Frecska E, Tekes K, *et al.*: Serotonergic interhemispheric asymmetry: gender differences in orbital cortex. *Acta Psychiatr Scand* 1991, 84:110–111.

CHAPTER 4

Treatment of Major Depressive and Dysthymic Disorder

Maurizio Fava and Jerrold F. Rosenbaum

Unipolar depressive disorders, in particular major depressive and dysthymic disorder, are fairly heterogenous. Pharmacotherapy with antidepressants, certain forms of psychotherapy, and electroconvulsive treatment have clearly proven to be efficacious in most types of unipolar depressive disorders. Further characterization of these disorders has suggested that certain treatments may be more effective than are others in specific subtypes. The short-term efficacy of antidepressant treatments has been well established; however, most of the continuation and maintenance studies have focused on the usefulness of drug therapy. This chapter reviews the most common pharmacologic approaches to the treatment of unipolar depressive disorders, with special emphasis on the management of treatment-resistant patients. Finally, the chapter discusses the use of light therapy, electroconvulsive treatment, and certain forms of psychotherapy in the treatment of depressive disorders.

The past focus on efficacy of psychiatric treatments in populations suffering from major depressive disorder in its more severe forms, such as melancholia, has expanded to include treatment of milder forms of mood disorders occurring in the community and in nonpsychiatric hospitals [1]. Multiple drug treatments and psychotherapies are effective in the treatment of unipolar depression. Given the marked heterogeneity of unipolar depressive disorders, however, the demonstration of efficacy in a population sample or a specific subtype does not necessarily imply that the same efficacy is observed in other samples or subtypes.

Major Depressive Disorder and Its Subtypes

All marketed antidepressants, electroconvulsive treatment (ECT), and two specific types of psychotherapy (interpersonal and cognitive) have established efficacy in unipolar major depression [2•]. In addition, some antidepressants and ECT have shown efficacy in particular forms of unipolar depression. Three subtypes may have a distinctive responsiveness to antidepressant treatment: psychotic depression, major depressive disorder with melancholic features, and atypical major depression.

Psychotic depression is represented by a major depressive episode accompanied by either delusions or hallucinations (typically auditory). This subtype, which has the most enduring diagnostic stability across multiple subsequent episodes [3] and relatively poorer outcome after 1 year [4], has a relatively low response rate to treatment with tricyclic antidepressants (TCAs) alone, compared with nonpsychotic depressed patients [5], and a preferential response to treatment with the combination of an antidepressant with an antipsychotic drug, compared with antidepressant alone [6]. The only exception may be amoxapine, a tetracycline antidepressant and a very potent serotonin receptor antagonist, with a neuroleptic as one of its metabolites, which is effective in patients with psychotic depression [7].

Major depressive disorder with melancholic features is a subtype characterized by either lack of reactivity of mood, or loss of pleasure in almost all activities plus three or more of the following: distinct quality of depressed mood, depression regularly worse in the morning, early-morning awakening, marked psychomotor retardation or agitation, significant anorexia or weight loss, and excessive or inappropriate guilt. Tricyclic antidepressants have been traditionally viewed as effective treatments for endogenous or melancholic depression [8]. Although many clinicians believe that non-TCAs are relatively less effective in the treatment of this subtype, a large multicenter study with the selective serotonin-reuptake inhibitor (SSRI) fluoxetine did not support this view (Rosenbaum *et al.*, Paper presented at the American College of Neuropsychopharmacology 32nd Annual Meeting, Maui, 1993).

Atypical major depressive disorder is a subtype characterized by mood reactivity and two or more of the associated features of overeating, hypersomnia, extreme fatigue (leaden paralysis) when depressed, and chronic oversensitivity to rejection. Liebowitz *et al.* [9] found in this subtype a 71% response rate with phenelzine, a 50% response rate with imipramine, and a 28% response rate with placebo. In addition, a study by Pande *et al.* [10] found the SSRI fluoxetine to be at least as effective as the monoamine oxidase inhibitor (MAOI), phenelzine.

Dysthymic Disorder

Several double-blind placebo-controlled studies have shown the superiority of TCAs, MAOIs, and SSRIs over placebo [11–13,14; Fava *et al.*, Paper presented at the 148th Annual Meeting of the American Psychiatric Association, Miami, 1995]. Keller and Shapiro [15] introduced the term *double depression*, a major depressive episode superimposed on dysthymic disorder. In a naturalistic study, the recovery rate from acute depression was 89%, whereas the recovery rate from both acute and chronic depression was 31% [15]. The TCA imipramine and the MAOI phenelzine were superior to placebo in double depression studies [12,16–18].

Minor Depression

Minor depression is defined as depressed mood or markedly diminished interest or pleasure in almost all activities for at least 2 weeks with two or three of the symptoms characteristic of major depression. Effective treatments for unipolar minor depression have been traditionally understudied. Many researchers believed that drug–placebo differences would be difficult to observe in these populations, as Elkin *et al.* [19] failed to show the superiority of drug therapy over placebo in milder forms of depression. However, Stewart *et al.* [18] were able to show a clear superiority of drug therapy over placebo in a large sample of patients with nonmajor depression. Nonmajor depression is the most frequent form of depression in a sample of children [20] and, in adults treated for depression, is as common as major depressive disorder and dysthymia combined [21]. In one study, the response rate for isocarboxazid (58%) was no different from placebo (44%) in Research Diagnostic Criteria (RDC) minor depression [22]; however, Stewart *et al.* [13] conducted a study in minor depression and found that the response rate was 68% with imipramine, 62% with phenelzine, and 36% with placebo, with a statistically significant difference only between imipramine and placebo.

Acute Versus Continuation Versus Maintenance Phases

The treatment of depressive disorders can be classified into three phases: acute therapy, continuation therapy, and maintenance therapy. *Acute therapy* concerns the short-term treatment of the depressive disorder, with the primary goal of symptom reduction, restoration of social and occupational functioning, and relapse prevention. *Continuation therapy* usually is defined as the continued treatment for 5 to 6 months following the disappearance of acute symptoms to maintain control over the episode and further prevent relapses; *maintenance therapy* refers to treatment extending beyond the continuation phase and administered for long periods (months or years) to prevent recurrences.

Acute-phase treatment with medication

The modern era of psychopharmacolgic treatment of depression began in the last 1950s with the almost simultaneous introduction of imipramine and iproniazid—respectively, the prototypic tricyclic antidepressant and MAOI—following serendipitous observations [23]. The success of these two drugs generated enthusiasm for the development of compounds similar in their structure or in their pharmacologic action *in vitro*. Again, one important methodologic issue reviewing the literature on drug treatments of depression is that "depression" represents a heterogeneous group of disorders and that, over the years, the populations included in research studies has varied depending on the operational criteria used to define depression and on the exclusion criteria employed to select more or less "pure" samples of depressed patients. From the literature it is clear that appropriate pharmacotherapy of depression requires adequacy of both dose and duration. Clinicians must be familiar with the established therapeutic doses for antidepressants, while taking into account that all antidepressants have an obligatory latency to efficacy. In fact, few patients respond before 2 to 4 weeks of treatment with a therapeutic dose of TCAs, and many require treatment of 4 to 8 weeks to show significant improvement [24]. Therefore, adequate duration of antidepressant treatment usually involves the administration of adequate doses for at least 8 weeks to estimate full medication benefit.

Tricyclic antidepressants

The TCAs are characterized by a chemical structure with two benzene rings joined through a central seven-member ring. Imipramine was the first compound to be developed. Of the several dozens of tricyclic drugs, only nine are marketed in the United States. These agents are structurally related to each other and share anticholinergic, antihistaminic, and anti-α_1-adrenergic side effects. All TCAs have variable affinity for dopamine muscarinic cholinergic receptors, α_1-adrenoceptors, histamine H_1, dopamine D_2, and serotonin 5-HT_2 receptors [25,26]. *In vitro* studies also have shown that TCAs are norepinephrine, dopamine, and serotonin-uptake inhibitors [27]. The TCAs are dealkylated and oxidized by hepatic microsomal enzymes, followed by conjugation with glucuronic acid. Their side effects are closely related to their chemical structure and their affinity to postsynaptic receptors; during treatment TCAs often cause anticholinergic side effects (dry mouth, constipation, blurred vision), orthostatic hypotension, sedation, and weight gain. Carbohydrate craving and increased appetite are commonly associated with treatment with TCAs and are thought to be related to the histamine H_1 receptor blockade. In fact, a study comparing the incidence of these symptoms with different TCAs found that desipramine, which has only mild affinity for H_1 receptors, was the least likely to induce these symptoms, compared with imipramine, amitriptyline, and doxepin [28]. Tricyclic antidepressants can cause sexual dysfunction, may have significant effects on cardiac conduction, and are contraindicated in the treatment of patients with narrow-angle glaucoma and prostatic hypertrophy; rare adverse events also reported with TCAs are an allergic–obstructive type of jaundice and grand mal seizures [29]. Most of the typical side effects tend to subside after a few weeks for those patients who continue treatment, particularly if dosage escalation has been slow and gradual. In general, the tertiary amine TCAs (those with three methyl groups on the amine side chain; eg, amitriptyline and imipramine) have greater side effect burdens than do the secondary amine TCAs (those with two methyl groups on the side chain; eg, nortriptyline and desipramine). Persistence of bothersome anticholinergic side effects is usually handled by decreasing the dose or by adding cholinergic smooth-muscle stimulants such as bethanecol [30]. An important caution in the use of TCAs with depressed patients is their lethality in overdose. Table 1 lists the TCAs available in the United States, their half-lives, and their starting and therapeutic doses.

Tetracyclic antidepressants

The only tetracyclic (composed of four benzene rings) antidepressant available is maprotiline, which is a derivative of dibenzo(*b,e*)bicyclo (2.2.2.) octadiene and is distinguished from tricyclic antidepressants only by the rigidity of its molecular structure because of its ethylene bridge. Maprotiline has mild affinity for dopamine D_2 and 5-HT_2 receptors, weak affinity for muscarinic cholinergic receptors, and strong affinity for α_1-adrenoceptors and histamine H_1 receptors [25,26]. *In vitro* studies have shown that maprotiline is a strong norepinephrine-uptake inhibitor and weak serotonin-uptake blocker [27]. Table 1 reports maprotiline half-life and its starting and therapeutic doses. The side effects that are reported most frequently are dryness of mouth, tremor, constipation, blurred vision, dizziness, and drowsiness [31]. Although the overall incidence of seizures is low, grand mal seizures have been reported more frequently at normal therapeutic dosages of maprotiline than at such dosages of tricyclic antidepressants [31]. Fatal overdoses with maprotiline have also been reported [31].

Monoamine oxidase inhibitors

Monoamine oxidase inhibitors are an important class of antidepressants that, over the past few years, have been used primarily in the treatment of certain depressive subtypes or as a second, but robust, line of treatment of depression. These antidepressants inhibit the MAO enzymes located in monoamine-containing nerve terminals as well as in the liver and other tissues that metabolize such monoamines as norepinephrine, serotonin, and dopamine. There are two types of MAO isozymes: MAO-A and MAO-B. As Mann *et al.* [32] point out, human brain MAO-A preferentially denatures norepinephrine, serotonin, and, in the cortex, dopamine, whereas MAO-B denatures dopamine and phenylethylamine. These antidepressants are relatively devoid of any postsynaptic receptor affinity. The MAO enzymes also are crucial in inactivating exogenous monoamines arising from foods or the

Table 1. Tricyclic Antidepressants and One Tetracyclic Antidepressant: Their Half-Lives, Dosage Forms, and Dosages

	Half-life, h	Tablets, *mg*	Customary initial dose, *mg/d*	Titrate dose (up to), *mg/d*	Comments
Tricyclic antidepressants					
Amitriptyline	21	10,25,50,75,100,150	25–50	150–300	Not a first-line TCA
Amoxapine	8	50,100,150	50 × 3	200–400	Not a first-line TCA
Clomipramine	20–40	25,50,75	25	150–200	Used for depression with obsessive–compulsive disorder or with anger attacks
Desipramine	21	10,25,50,75,100,150	25–50	150–300	A first-line TCA
Doxepin	17	10,25,50,75,100,150	25–50	150–300	In low doses is a helpful hypnotic
Imipramine	28	10,25,50,75,100,150	25–50	150–300	Established efficacy in treating panic attacks
Nortriptyline	36	10,25,50,75	10–25	50–150	A first-line TCA
Protriptyline	78	5,10	10–15	30–60	Not a first-line TCA
Trimipramine	13	25,50,100	25–50	150–200	In low doses is a helpful hypnotic
Tetracyclic antidepressant					
Maprotiline	43	25,50,75	50–75	150–200	Has 4 benzene rings instead of 3

TCA—tricyclic antidepressant.

action of bacteria in the gut, including the sympathomimetic pressor amine tyramine [29]. The use of MAOIs is therefore associated with a risk of lethal hypertensive crisis related to interactions with drugs or foods containing tyramine [33–35]. There have been reports of hypertensive crisis even with (-)-deprenyl when higher doses have been used [35]. Other rare, but severe, adverse events, such as heat stroke, vascular collapse, or death, may follow interactions with potent serotonergic agents [36]. Two of the three currently marketed MAOIs (phenelzine and tranylcypromine) in the United States are nonselective and inhibit both isozymes. The third marketed MAOI, *L*-deprenyl, preferentially inactivates MAO-B, whereas it has little effect on MAO-A within a dose range of 5–10 mg/d [37]. All of the aforementioned drugs have a prolonged biologic half-life and are considered relatively irreversible MAOIs, in that they exert a persistent inhibitory effect on these isozymes. The normal function of these enzymes is restored only after several drug-free days to allow regeneration of new stores of enzymes. More recently, moclobemide, a newer antidepressant with reversible effects of inhibition of MAO and greatly diminished risk of dietary or other interactions, has become available in Europe and Canada. It is a safe and common practice to wait 2 weeks after discontinuing non-MAOI antidepressants and 5 weeks after discontinuing fluoxetine before starting treatment with nonselective irreversible MAOIs. It is also recommended to wait 2 weeks before starting another antidepressant following discontinuation of an irreversible MAOI. Hepatotoxicity is a rare, but possible, event occurring during the use of MAOIs [29]. Because insomnia is a potential side effect of this class of antidepressants, it is best to administer the last dose in the early afternoon. Other common side effects are sedation, orthostatic hypotension, sexual dysfunction, tremor, dizziness, and agitation [29,38–40]. Despite the apparent lack of affinity for muscarinic cholinergic receptors, such anticholinergic side effects as dry mouth, constipation, and urinary retention may also be observed.

Moclobemide is a benzamide derivative available only in Europe and Canada. It is a short-acting, reversible MAOI preferentially inhibiting MAO-A [41]. Moclobemide, in preclinical experiments, shows neither a toxic effect on the liver nor a significant potentiation of tyramine [42]. Its most frequently observed side effects are dry mouth, somnolence, headache, dizziness, and psychomotor agitation [43]. Although several reports suggest that moclobemide is relatively nontoxic in overdose [44–46], fatal interactions of moclobemide with citalopram and clomipramine, leading to a serotonergic syndrome, have been observed [47]. Table 2 lists the MAOIs that are available in the United States and Canada, their half-lives, and their starting and therapeutic doses. A recent review by Thase *et al.* [48•] concluded that the Food and Drug Administration (FDA)-approved MAOIs (phenelzine, isocarboxazid, and tranylcypromine) treat a somewhat different group of patients than do TCAs and that more severely depressed inpatients may not respond as well to MAOIs as to TCAs.

Selective serotonin-reuptake inhibitors

The relatively recent development of SSRIs has introduced to the world pharmacopoeia a new class of psychotropic compounds with antidepressant activity and an improved side effect profile. These agents are structurally unrelated to TCAs or tetracyclic antidepressants and do not have significant associated anticholinergic, antihistaminic, and anti-α_1-adrenergic effects. The SSRIs have fewer side effects than do TCAs; they do not have significant effects on cardiac conduction and do not tend to cause either weight gain or orthostatic hypotension [49]. They also are safe in overdose. Five drugs of this class (fluoxetine, sertraline, paroxetine, venlafaxine, and fluvoxamine) are available in the United States. Venlafaxine has also been defined as a serotonin-norepinephrine–reuptake inhibitor (SNRI), as this drug and its major metabolite inhibit noradrenergic-firing rates during *in vivo* studies [50,51]. However, venlafaxine's ability to inhibit norepinephrine uptake *in vitro*

Table 2. Monoamine Oxidase Inhibitors: Their Half-Lives, Dosage Form, and Dosages

	Half-life, h	Tablets, mg	Customary initial dose, mg/d	Titrate dose (up to), mg/d
Phenelzine	2.8	15	15 (2–3 ×)	45–90
Isocarboxazid	Production was discontinued		20–30	50
Tranylcypromine	1.5–3	10	20–30	60
(-)-Deprenyl	2	10	20	30–40
Moclobemide	Available only in Canada	150	300	600–1200

is comparable with that of fluoxetine and sertraline [52], and no study has compared ven-lafaxine with other SSRIs in terms of *in vivo* inhibition of noradrenergic-firing rates. As shown in Table 3, when the ability to inhibit uptake of serotonin *in vitro* is compared with the inhibition of norepinephrine uptake *in vitro*, fluvoxamine and sertraline are the most selective, and fluoxetine and venlafaxine the least selective. Similarly, when the ability to inhibit uptake of serotonin *in vitro* is compared with the inhibition of dopamine uptake *in vitro*, fluvoxamine and paroxetine are the most selective, whereas sertraline is the least selective. It is unclear whether relative selectivity is truly an advantage for drugs of this par-ticular class. In addition, *in vitro* uptake inhibition studies do not necessarily reflect *in vivo* potency; for example, Shank *et al.* [54] found that sertraline was 10 times more potent than was fluoxetine *in vitro*, but almost half as potent *in vivo*, using as an animal model the potentiation of (*l*)-5-hydroxytryptophan-induced head twitches in mice.

In terms of safety and tolerability, the more common side effects of the SSRIs are nausea, headache, nervousness, insomnia, diarrhea, dry mouth, somnolence, male sex-ual dysfunction, headache, and vomiting [55–58]. Rash, rarely associated with joint pain and swelling, appears to be the most common potentially serious adverse event with flu-oxetine [58]. Table 4 lists the SSRIs available in the United States, their half-lives, and their starting and therapeutic doses.

Atypical antidepressants

Several agents used in the treatment of depression have chemical structures different from those of TCAs, MAOIs, and SSRIs. These include the antidepressants trazodone, nefazodone, and bupropion, as well as other agents, such as the stimulants dextroam-phetamine and methylphenidate.

Bupropion (2-*tert*butylamino-3'-chlorprophenone hydrochloride) is an aminoketone with almost no affinity for dopamine D_2 receptors, muscarinic cholinergic, and 5-HT_2

Table 3. Selectivity for Inhibition of Serotonin Uptake Versus Either Norepinephrine or Dopamine Uptake in Rat Brain Synaptosomes *In Vitro**

	5-HT/NE ratio	5-HT/DA ratio
SSRI		
Paroxetine	50	2500
Fluvoxamine	167	1669
Sertraline	67	100
Desmethylsertraline	6	6
Fluoxetine	10	200
Norfluoxetine	16.7	50
Venlafaxine	5	143
Tricyclic antidepressant		
Amitriptyline	0.2	100

*Data from Tulloch and Johnson [53] and Bolden-Watson and Richelson [52].
DA—dopamine; 5-HT—serotonin; NE—norepinephrine; SSRI—selective serotonin-reuptake inhibitor.

Table 4. Selective Serotonin-Reuptake Inhibitors: Their Half-Lives, Dosage Form, and Dosages

	Half-life	Tablets, mg	Customary initial dose, mg/d	Titrate dose (up to), mg/d
Fluoxetine	2 d for fluoxetine and 7 d for norfluoxetine	10,20	10–20	40–60
Sertraline	26 h	50,100	50	100,150, or 200
Paroxetine	24 h	10,20,30,40	10–20	40–60
Fluvoxamine	Initial elimination: 2 h 2nd phase: 15 h	50,100	50–100	200
Venlafaxine	4 h	25,37.5,50,75,100	75	350–450

receptors, and very weak affinity for α-adrenoceptors and histamine H_1 receptors [25,26,59]. *In vivo* studies have shown that this antidepressant is a relatively selective dopamine-uptake blocker *in vivo* [60]. Bupropion in plasma is 80% bound to protein and undergoes extensive first-pass metabolism in the liver: four metabolites have been identified, with two of them being active [61,62]. Its most common side effects are agitation, dry mouth, insomnia, headache, nausea, vomiting, constipation, and tremor [63]. Bupropion was approved by the FDA in 1985; just before being marketed, seizures were observed in four of 30 patients in a study of bulimia [64]. Marketing was then delayed and further studies on the incidence of seizures have since established the risk as 0.4% at dosages up to 450 mg/d [65]. The incidence increases almost tenfold at higher doses, so that 450 mg is the maximum recommended daily dose, with 150 mg being the maximum single dose to avoid high peak concentrations of the drug and its metabolites. Only two lethal overdoses with bupropion have been reported, suggesting a relative safety in overdose compared with tricyclic antidepressants [65].

Mirtazepine i (1,2,3,4,10,14b-hexahydro-2-methylpyrazino [2,1-a] pyrido [2,3-c] benzapine) is a piperazino-azepine compound with mild affinity for muscarinic cholinergic and α-1-adrenoceptors and strong affinity for histamine-H_1-receptors. Mirtazepine acts as an antagonist of the central presynaptic α-2-adrenergic inhibitory autoreceptors and heteroreceptors, with a subsequent increase in central noradrenergic and serotonergic activity. Because mirtazepine is a potent antagonist of serotonin 5-HT_2 and 5-HT_3 receptors and has no significant affinity for the serotonin 5-HT_{1A} and 5-HT_{1B} receptors, it has been postulated that the overall central effect of this compound is that of increasing noradrenergic activity and, selectively, serotonergic 5-HT_1 neurotransmission [66]. Mirtazepine in plasma is 85% bound to protein and is extensively metabolized in the liver, with subsequent demethylation and hydroxylation followed by glucuronide conjugation [67]. Its most common side effects are drowsiness, excessive sedation, dry mouth, increased appetite, and weight gain [67]. During the comparative clinical trials of mirtazepine, reversible neutropenias have occurred in 1.9% of mirtazepine-treated patients, 2% of trazodone-treated patients, 1.1% of placebo-treated patients, and 0.4% of amitriptyline-treated patients [67]. Mirtazepine appears to be safe in overdose [68].

Trazodone is a triazolopyridine antidepressant, with low affinity for dopamine D_2 and histamine H_1 receptors, strong affinity for $α_1$-adrenoceptors and 5-HT_2 receptors, and essentially no affinity for muscarinic cholinergic receptors [69]. This antidepressant is a relatively weak norepinephrine-uptake blocker and a mild inhibitor of serotonin uptake *in vitro* [52]. Common side effects are drowsiness, dizziness, headache, nausea, and hypotension, with priapism being an extremely rare, but potentially serious, side effect in men [70]. In a series of 88 reported cases of trazodone overdose, there were no deaths when trazodone was the only substance ingested [71].

Despite the evidence from clinical trials, trazodone has not found acceptance as an antidepressant of efficacy comparable with others, and it is rarely used as a first-line agent for major depressive disorder.

Nefazodone is a phenylpiperazine compound, chemically related to trazodone, but has less α_1-adrenergic blocking properties and seems to cause less sedation and priapism. *In vivo*, it strongly inhibits serotonin uptake and is a strong blocker of 5-HT$_2$ receptors [69,72], with essentially no affinity for muscarinic cholinergic and histamine H$_1$ receptors, strong affinity for α_1-adrenoceptors, and low affinity for D$_2$ receptors [69]. Its most common side effects are headache, dry mouth, and nausea [73].

Dextroamphetamine is a noncatecholamine sympathomimetic amine with central nervous system (CNS) stimulant activity, and methylphenidate (methyl-α-phenyl-2-piperidineacetate hydrochloride) is a CNS stimulant, for which the mode of action is still poorly understood. The most common side effects of these two stimulants are insomnia, nausea, tremor, appetite change, palpitations, blurred vision, dry mouth, constipation, and dizziness [74]. Other reported side effects are blood pressure changes in either direction, dysrhythmias, tachycardia, tremor, and exacerbation of preexisting anxiety [74]. Because the 10 placebo-controlled studies of these two stimulant drugs in primary depression, with one exception, indicated little advantage of drug over placebo [74], stimulants have been primarily used as adjuncts to other treatments in patients with depression.

Table 5 lists the atypical antidepressants available in the United States, their half-lives, and their starting and therapeutic doses.

Acute-phase treatment with psychotherapy

Although many different types of psychotherapy are currently used in the initial treatment of unipolar depressive disorders, controlled data on efficacy are available only for

Table 5. Atypical Antidepressants: Their Half-Lives, Dosage Form, Dosages, and Compound Type

	Half-life, h	Tablets, mg	Customary initial dose, mg/d	Titrate dose (up to), mg/d	Type of compound
Bupropion	Biphasic; β-phase: 8–24	75,100	75–100 × 2	150 × 3	An aminoketone
Mirtazapine	20–40	15,30	15	30–45	A piperazino-azepine
Nefazadone	5	100,150	100 × 2	300–450	A phenylpiperazine
Trazadone	7	50,100,150, 300	50–100	200–600	A triazolopyridine antidepressant
Dextroamphetamine	10	5,10,15	10	40–60	Psychostimulant
Methylphenidate	4	5,10,20	20	90	Psychostimulant

cognitive therapy, behavioral therapy, interpersonal psychotherapy, and brief dynamic psychotherapy. *Cognitive therapy* focuses on identifying and correcting the distorted, negatively biased thinking of the patient and on preventing relapses by identifying and correcting silent assumptions [75]. *Behavioral therapy* of depression, which is based on the social learning theory [76] and on a functional analysis of behavior [77], includes self-control therapy, social skills training, and problem solving. *Interpersonal psychotherapy* is aimed at clarifying and resolving interpersonal difficulties that are thought to be related to depression [23]. Finally, brief *dynamic psychotherapy* focuses on core conflicts that are thought to be causing depressive symptoms [77–79]. The Depression Guideline Panel [80] conducted meta-analyses of the studies concerning the short-term efficacy of these treatments and found an overall efficacy ranging from 46.6% to 55.3% for cognitive, behavioral, and interpersonal psychotherapies, whereas brief dynamic psychotherapy had a much lower efficacy (34.8%).

Acute-phase treatment with electroconvulsive therapy

Side effects, indications, and contraindications for the use of ECT are described elsewhere [81]. The general consensus is that ECT primarily should be used only after adequate antidepressant trials have failed or with patients who have depression marked by delusions, even though ECT has consistently been reported to yield a higher response rate and prompter remission than do antidepressants [81].

Acute-phase treatment with light therapy

Over the past few years, numerous studies have investigated the clinical usefulness of light therapy (phototherapy) in the treatment of depression. This treatment involves exposure of the eyes to light containing very little ultraviolet light. The primary indication for the use of phototherapy has been *seasonal affective disorder* (SAD), a condition characterized by recurrent fall and winter depressions alternating with nondepressed periods in spring and summer [82]. Rosenthal *et al.* [82] pointed out in his review of the literature that all 14 studies using a crossover design had found phototherapy to be more effective than an alternative (control) treatment condition, and that, although there was a consensus that bright light (2500 lux) was superior to dimmer light (≥ 400 lux), optimal timing of light treatment was somewhat more controversial. Even though Kripke [83] and Yerevanian *et al.* [84] have also studied the use of this treatment modality in nonseasonal depressive patients, there is no clear evidence yet for the efficacy of light therapy in this population [2].

Full-spectrum fluorescent light has been the most commonly used source of light, with the light box placed at eye level and an intensity of light of about 2500 lux. The most frequent side effects observed during the course of phototherapy are insomnia, headaches, eyestrain, and irritability [85]. Although the mechanisms of action of phototherapy are still poorly understood, one hypothesis is that its antidepressant effect may be due to the circadian phase–shifting properties of bright light [86].

Treatment-resistant depression

Depressed patients who fail to achieve and sustain euthymia with adequate antidepressant treatment can be considered treatment-resistant. Although clinicians use both psychotherapy and pharmacotherapy to treat these patients, almost all research efforts have focused on pharmacotherapy, with nonresponse always considered in reference to drug treatment. However, no universally accepted definition of treatment-resistant depression exists, in part because of continually evolving standards of adequate antidepressant dose and treatment duration in psychiatric practice [87]. Most clinicians tend to treat patients for 4 to 6 weeks with standard doses of antidepressants before presuming treatment resistance. There are different levels of resistance: some patients show little or no response (nonresponders), whereas others improve, but retain significant symptomatology (partial responders). Between 15% and 30% of depressed patients do not reach a state of well-being and functioning following an initial adequate trial of antidepressant medication. The proportion of treatment-resistant patients is even larger if one includes patients who experience improvement with antidepressant treatment, but suffer from residual symptoms that affect functioning in a wide range of social and occupational roles.

There is some evidence of an association between resistance to treatment and specific comorbid conditions that require specific treatments. Because the efficacy of antidepressants in the treatment of other psychiatric disorders differs across classes, resistance in a depressed patient with comorbid conditions may reflect failure of the selected antidepressant to treat the concurrent disorder. When no class of antidepressant is known to reduce symptoms of the comorbid condition, the use of other psychotropic drugs (*ie*, antianxiety and antipsychotic drugs) with specific efficacy in the treatment of the concurrent disorder is indicated. Comorbid medical conditions can also contribute to treatment resistance. In a study on outcome of psychiatric treatment in the medically ill, only 40% of patients with medical comorbidity responded to antidepressant treatment [88]. Accordingly, clinicians should always consider the possibility of medical comorbidity contributing to resistance in depressed patients and gather a complete medical history before initiating further treatment.

Depressed patients with high anxiety levels may show less response to antidepressants and have a poorer long-term prognosis than do nonanxious depressed patients [89,90], although a recent study failed to support this view [91]. Depressed patients frequently have comorbid personality disorders [92] that may contribute to resistance, depending on the type of antidepressant drug selected as well as on the severity and number of comorbid personality disorders [93]. Finally, clinical studies show that ongoing substance abuse tends to be present in a high proportion of patients who are partial or nonresponding to antidepressant treatment [94], and it is possible that the concomitant mild or moderate use (not abuse) of psychoactive substances, such as alcohol, may have a negative effect on outcome (Worthington *et al.*, Paper presented at the 41st Annual Meeting of the Academy of Psychosomatic Medicine, Phoenix, 1994).

When a depressed patient fails to respond to an antidepressant after an optimized medication trial, one of four treatment strategies are available: augmentation of the failed antidepressant, increasing the dose of the failed antidepressant, combining two classes of antidepressants, or switching to another antidepressant. The following sections review these strategies and some of the studies supporting their use. Alternative strategies are represented by ECT and psychotherapy.

Augmentation strategies

Over the past 30 years, clinicians have been adding a number of different drugs to antidepressants in treatment-resistant patients. The most common augmenting agents probably are lithium and thyroid hormone, although the popularity of adding stimulants is increasing. The strategy of augmentation offers the basic advantage of maintaining continuity of treatment because patients can be kept on the same antidepressant regimen without changes in dosing or switching to different antidepressants. Table 6 lists the augmentation strategies and the starting and therapeutic doses of the augmenting agents.

Lithium augmentation

Johnson [95] reviewed all the case reports, case series, and controlled studies published over 10 years concerning lithium augmentation of TCAs, MAOIs, SSRIs, trazodone, bupropion, and carbamazepine, and concluded that the bulk of the studies support the efficacy of this strategy, particularly with TCAs. The quality and time course of response tend to vary from study to study. A meta-analysis of all available data up to 1991 [96] concluded that the addition of lithium to an ongoing but failed antidepressant trial reduced the odds of remaining ill by between 56% and 95%. As yet, however, only a few controlled reports have focused on lithium augmentation of SSRIs. One group of investigators found that lithium augmentation appeared to be equally effective when added to either desipramine or fluoxetine [97]. We recently have found that lithium augmentation of fluoxetine in patients failing to respond to 8 weeks of treatment with a standard dose of fluoxetine was less effective than was raising the dose among those who partially responded, but as effective as raising the fluoxetine dose, and more effective than adding desipramine among those who did not respond [92].

Traditionally, clinicians tend to aim at therapeutic (0.5–1.2 mEq/L) blood levels of lithium when treating patients with affective disorders. However, researchers have used a very broad range of lithium doses for augmentation of antidepressants. In fact, as pointed out in the review by Johnson [95], several studies and cases series reported successful outcome with low-dose and low lithium blood levels, as well as with blood levels within the traditional therapeutic range. It is apparent that the relevance of lithium dose and blood levels for response to lithium augmentation merits further study [93]. Adverse effects associated with the addition of lithium are those typical of this drug and may include nausea, vomiting, diarrhea, sedation, tremors, polyuria, renal toxicity, hypothyroidism,

Table 6. Augmentation Antidepressant Administration Strategies With Additional Drugs and Suggested Doses

	Starting dose	Therapeutic dose
Lithium	300 mg	600–1200 mg
T_3	25 µg	25–50 µg
T_4	25 µg	50–150 µg
Amantidine	200 mg	400–600 mg
Pergolide	0.05 mg	0.1–5 mg
Bromocriptine	2.5 mg	2.5–10 mg
D-Amphetamine	2.5 mg	5–40 mg
Methylphenidate	5 mg	10–60 mg
Pemoline	18.75 mg	37.5–112.5 mg

T_3—tri-iodothyronine; T_4—thyroxine.

and exacerbation of myoclonus or orthostatic hypotension [29,96]. Clinicians should routinely monitor lithium blood levels, as well as renal and thyroid function. Some investigators have added lithium to an antidepressant after 12 weeks of antidepressant nonresponse [96,98]; however, in actual clinical practice, many physicians would choose to intervene by the 4th to 6th week for patients who show no sign of improvement. Although some patients will respond to lithium augmentation within a few days, others will experience a delay of onset for up to 6 weeks, making it advisable for clinicians to continue at least 4 weeks before abandoning this strategy. It is best to continue to prescribe both the antidepressant and lithium for continuation or maintenance therapy; alternatively, the adjunctive lithium could be discontinued first and restored if symptoms recur [93].

Thyroid augmentation

Earlier reports showed that, when prescribed in addition to an antidepressant, thyroid hormone yielded a faster response in depressed women than did an antidepressant alone [99,100]. Later case reports and series extended these results, suggesting that a broader spectrum of patients benefited from adding thyroid to a failed antidepressant trial [101,102]. Adverse effects associated with the addition of thyroid are typically absent or mild but may include increased anxiety, jitteriness, tachycardia, insomnia, and sweating, with very infrequent occurrence of atrial irritability or high-output cardiac failure [93]. Consequently, clinicians should be cautious when giving thyroid to patients with cardiac insufficiency or to elderly patients.

No guidelines exist for the duration of an adequate initial trial of thyroid augmentation; however, most patients who respond appear to do so within 2 to 3 weeks. A reasonable strategy would be to test whether the augmentation remains necessary for maintaining a response by gradually discontinuing thyroid hormone 6 months after a response to tri-iodothyramine (T_3) or thyroxine (T_4) augmentation. If the patient experiences a relapse during the discontinuation trial, the thyroid adjunct can be reinstated.

Augmentation with dopaminergic agents

There is some evidence that dopaminergic agents, such as bromocriptine, amantadine, and pergolide, may be useful as adjuncts for some depressed patients. Bromocriptine and piribedil are dopamine agonists—used for Parkinson disease—that also appear to have antidepressant properties [103–112]. According to some anecdotal reports, dopaminergic agents seem to be effective within days when added to antidepressants in the treatment of refractory patients [113]. Adverse drug reactions with the use of dopaminergic agents included nausea, headache, dizziness, fatigue, lightheadedness, vomiting, nervousness, insomnia, ataxia, and mania. At higher doses, the use of these drugs has been associated with confusion, delusions, hallucinations, and dyskinesias. Although some clinicians currently employ dopamine agonists as adjuncts to antidepressants, no controlled studies on these agents are yet available. Guidelines for the prescription of dopaminergic agents are based on clinical experience, rather than on controlled trials.

Although stimulants such as amphetamine, methylphenidate, and pemoline have abuse potential in populations of patients with a history of substance abuse, depressed patients have taken these drugs responsibly in stable doses for up to 20 or 30 years [114]. There are no controlled trials on the use of stimulants as depressive adjuncts. Evidence from case reports and series suggests that stimulants are effective in augmenting fluoxetine

[115,116], MAOIs alone, and MAOIs in combination with TCAs [70,117]. The response to the addition of stimulants may be transient, as suggested by a study showing that only 32% of 25 responding patients maintained their improvement [117]. Adverse events with the use of stimulants may include nervousness, anorexia, nausea, weight loss, insomnia, impotence, dizziness, orthostatic hypotension, elevated blood pressure, tachycardia, shakiness, memory difficulties, parkinsonian symptoms, mania, and fatigue. Stimulants may also increase blood levels of other drugs. Extreme caution should be used when stimulants are combined with MAOIs; patients should be instructed about the risk and symptoms of a hypertensive crisis, and stimulants should be added at very low doses with gradual increases. The use of stimulants as adjuncts is best avoided in patients with a recent history of substance abuse or perceived to be at risk for developing drug dependence. Patients should be informed that stimulants are a controlled substance and that they should be taken only as prescribed.

High-dose antidepressants

An alternative approach to augmentation is the use of relatively high doses of antidepressant monotherapy. The MAOIs, TCAs, trazodone, and SSRIs have been safely prescribed in high doses, with significant improvements in patients who had failed to respond to standard doses [118–121]. The only controlled study of high-dose antidepressants found that patients treated with high-dose fluoxetine did significantly better than did patients treated with fluoxetine plus lithium, or than those treated with fluoxetine plus desipramine [92]. Although further controlled studies are necessary to confirm the potential usefulness of this approach, the use of high-dose SSRIs, relatively safer than high-dose TCAs, may serve in treating patients resistant to standard doses. When using high-dose TCAs, clinicians should carefully monitor electrocardiograms (ECGs) and blood levels to minimize the risk of toxicity. No guidelines exist for the adequate duration of a higher-dose antidepressant therapy trial, but 6 weeks is likely to be a sufficient duration. If tolerated, treatment following response can be maintained for 6 to 9 months, followed by a decrease by tapering.

Combined antidepressant treatments

Combination of antidepressants is often useful when depressive symptoms do not improve after treatment with a single antidepressant. For example, when patients do not respond to a TCA alone, the dose of the TCA may be reduced and a standard dosage of an SSRI added. On the other hand, when patients fail to respond to treatment with an SSRI alone, clinicians may initially add TCAs in low doses, from 10 to 25 mg/d, without changing the SSRI dose, and can increase the TCA dose while monitoring the blood levels. The MAOIs have also been combined with TCAs, often by initiating both drugs simultaneously and gradually raising their doses to standard antidepressant levels. For safety, neither SSRIs nor clomipramine should be combined with MAOIs. When buspirone (usually in doses of 10 mg twice a day) is added to an antidepressant, the dose of the antidepressant may remain unchanged. No guidelines exist for the duration of an adequate trial of a combination strategy. Patients who respond have shown initial improvement in a range from 24 hours to several weeks. There are no reports of longitudinal studies or double-blind discontinuation studies of combination strategy responders. To test whether the added antidepressant remains necessary for maintaining a response, a trial discontinuation may be used 6 months or more after a response. If relapse occurs during the discontinuation trial, the combination agent may be reinstated.

Combined antidepressant therapy with MAOIs and TCA was common in the 1960s [123] until rising concern over the safety of this combination led to decreased clinical use [124]. However, the combination of MAOIs and TCAs appears safe if the agents are simultaneously initiated in low doses and increased gradually [125,126]. The combination of MAOIs with imipramine or clomipramine should be avoided, however, because the risk of toxicity is greater [127].

Combining fluoxetine or other SSRIs with a TCA in refractory patients has become increasingly popular [128–131]. However, the only prospective controlled study in patients who had failed to respond to a standard dose of fluoxetine showed that fluoxetine plus desipramine was less effective than was fluoxetine plus lithium in nonresponders and also was less efficacious than was high-dose fluoxetine in patients who were either non- or partial responders [92]. All SSRIs can have drug–drug interactions with the TCAs. However, it is possible to safely administer SSRIs with TCAs if a low dosage of the latter (25–50 mg/d) is used and plasma levels monitored [92].

Buspirone is an azospirodecanedione anxiolytic and a partial $5-HT_{1A}$ agonist that may increase the efficacy of SSRIs in treatment-resistant depression [132–134]. Uncontrolled reports suggest that the addition of buspirone may be helpful in patients not responding to monotherapy with an SSRI [132,134].

Switching strategies

When patients fail to respond to treatment with one antidepressant, a common clinical strategy is to switch antidepressants. Most clinicians believe a switch from one antidepressant class to another yields a greater change of benefit than switching within the same class [87]. Several studies suggest the efficacy of MAOIs [135,136], bupropion [137], and SSRIs [36,138–140; Nierenberg *et al.*, Paper presented at the 146th Annual Meeting of the American Psychiatric Association, San Francisco, 1993] in the treatment of patients who had failed to respond to TCAs. When patients fail to respond to treatment with an antidepressant alone, switching from a TCA to an SSRI, or vice versa, does not typically require washout, but rather, a taper of the first antidepressant and initiation of the second one [93]. To avoid a lapse in treatment, clinicians can start the new drug while tapering the failed agent, although the period of overlap may create drug interaction side effects. When switching to an MAOI, clinicians should wait at least 1 week after discontinuing TCAs (with the exception of protriptyline, which requires 3 weeks of washout) and at least 2 weeks after discontinuing SSRIs (with the exception of fluoxetine, which requires at least 5 weeks of washout) [93]. Clinicians switching from an MAOI to an SSRI or a TCA should wait at least 2 weeks before starting administration of the new antidepressant. When clinicians switch to an antidepressant of the same class, no washout is necessary, except for the change from phenelzine to tranylcypromine, which requires 2 weeks of washout. For patients responding to a switch, the antidepressant may be continued for at least 6 months following response and then gradually discontinued.

Electroconvulsive therapy

Although generally considered as the most potent treatment for depression, limited patient acceptance and administrative obstacles often result in underutilization of ECT.

In view of its safety and efficacy, ECT is a particularly attractive option for any depressed treatment-resistant patient and should be considered a treatment option, rather than a treatment of last resort. A study by Prudic *et al.* [141] found that patients who had previously failed adequate antidepressant pharmacotherapies had a poorer response rate and also a higher relapse rate after ECT treatment than did patients who had not failed an adequate prior antidepressant medication trial.

Psychotherapy

Psychotherapy alone or in combination with pharmacotherapy is also used in refractory depression, but there is as yet only anecdotal evidence supporting this clinical strategy. Psychotherapy is often used in combination with pharmacotherapy in patients with partial response, to address residual symptoms that are not lifted by drug treatment alone [142]. The efficacy, however, of this strategy remains to be demonstrated. There is a great need to conduct systematic studies to evaluate the role of psychotherapy in various depressed populations resistant to treatment.

Continuation-Phase Treatments

In general, most treatments of depression tend to be administered beyond the acute phase to prevent relapse, which is more likely to occur when treatment is discontinued too early. Most of the continuation-phase studies in depression concern the use of pharmacotherapy [143]. Prien and Kupfer [144] reviewed several early investigations on the efficacy of long-term antidepressant drug treatment in depressed patients and concluded that the risk of relapse was approximately 50% when recently improved patients were switched to placebo, as opposed to 20% in patients receiving ongoing treatment with lithium or TCAs. A more recent meta-analysis [145] of studies on the efficacy of long-term antidepressant drug treatment in patients with recurrent major depression found that continuation therapy with antidepressants (amitriptyline and imipramine) was effective. Very little is known about the efficacy of continuation treatment with psychotherapy in unipolar depression.

Maintenance-Phase Treatments

Although long-term psychotherapy is commonly used in psychiatry, no controlled data on its prophylactic efficacy are available. Again, almost all studies focused on pharmacotherapy instead. Both the literature review by Kleinman and Schachter [146] and the meta-analysis by Loonen *et al.* [145] of the studies published between 1974 and 1987 on the efficacy of maintenance antidepressant drug treatment in patients with recurrent major depression, found that there were insufficient data to allow any conclusions about the efficacy of maintenance therapy with antidepressants. However, more recent studies have shown a greater than placebo prophylactic effect for several types of antidepressants, with the combination of pharmacotherapy with psychotherapies, perhaps, being even more promising strategies [143].

Conclusions

In summary, pharmacotherapy is a very effective treatment of unipolar depressive disorders during both the acute and the continuation phase. Several classes of antidepressants are available, with significant differences in side effect profiles and, in some cases, in spectrum of efficacy. Psychotherapy appears to be helpful in the short-term treatment of depressive disorders, with the long-term efficacy remaining to be established. Electroconvulsive therapy also remains a valid and effective treatment for depression, even though its use is most accepted for certain subtypes of depression or for refractory patients. Phototherapy represents a very useful tool in the treatment of SAD; however, its efficacy in nonseasonal depression has not been established. Despite the fact that most patients with depression respond to trials of adequate dose and duration, a substantial minority do not. For these patients, numerous strategies have been developed over the past few years.

Acknowledgments

We thank Rosemarie Mulroy for her technical assistance in the preparation of this chapter.

References and Recommended Reading

Papers of particular interest, published recently, have been highlighted as:
*   Of special interest
••   Of outstanding interest

1.   Snaith RP: The concepts of mild depression. *Br J Psychiatry* 1987, 150:387–393.
2.•   Fava M, Rosenbaum JF: Pharmacotherapy and Somatic Therapies. In *Handbook of Depression.* Edited by Beckham EE, Leber WR. New York: Guilford Publications; 1995.
3.   Coryell W, Winokur G, Shea T, *et al.*: The long-term stability of depressive subtypes. *Am J Psychiatry* 1994, 151:199–204.
4.   Robinson DG, Spiker DG: Delusional depression: a one-year follow-up. *J Affect Disord* 1985, 9:79–83.
5.   Chan CH, Janicak PG, Davis JM, *et al.*: Response to psychotic and nonpsychotic depressed patients to tricyclic antidepressants. *J Clin Psychiatry* 1987, 48:197–200.
6.   Spiker DG, Weiss JC, Dealy RS, *et al.*: The pharmacological treatment of delusional depression. *Am J Psychiatry* 1985, 142:430–436.
7.   Anton RF Jr, Burch EA Jr: A comparison study of amoxapine vs. amitriptyline plus perphenazine in the treatment of psychotic depression. *Am J Psychiatry* 1990, 147:1203–1208.
8.   Raskin A, Crook TH: The endogenous–neurotic distinction as a predictor of response to antidepressant drugs. *Psychol Med* 1976, 6:59–70.
9.   Liebowitz MR, Quitkin FM, Stewart JW, *et al.*: Antidepressant specificity in atypical depression. *Arch Gen Psychiatry* 1988, 45:129–137.
10.   Pande AC, Birkett M, Fechner-Bates S, Haskett RF, Greden JF: Fluoxetine vs. Phenelzine in atypical depression. In press.
11.   Stabl M, Biziere K, Schmid-Burg KW, Amrein R: Review of comparative clinical trials: moclobemide vs tricyclic antidepressant and vs placebo in depressive states. *J Neural Transm* 1989, 28:77–89.
12.   Tyrer P, Seivewright N, Murphy S, *et al.*: The Nottingham study of neurotic disorder: comparison of drug and psychological treatments. *Lancet* 1988, 2:235–240.
13.   Stewart JW, McGrath PJ, Quitkin FM, *et al.*: Relevance of DSM-III depressive subtype and chronicity of antidepressant efficacy in atypical depression. *Arch Gen Psychiatry* 1989, 46:1080–1087.
14.   Hellerstein DJ, Yanowitch P, Rosenthal J, *et al.*: A randomized double-blind study of fluoxetine versus placebo in the treatment of dysthymia. *Am J Psychiatry* 1993, 150:1169–1175.
15.   Keller MB, Shapiro RW: "Double depression": superimposition of acute depressive episodes on chronic depressive disorders. *Am J Psychiatry* 1982, 139:438–442.

16. Kocsis JH, Frances AJ, Mann JJ, *et al.*: Imipramine for the treatment of chronic depression. *Psychopharmacol Bull* 1985, 21:698–700.

17. Kocsis JH, Frances AJ, Voss C, *et al.*: Imipramine treatment for chronic depression. *Arch Gen Psychiatry* 1988, 45:253–257.

18. Stewart JW, McGrath PJ, Quitkin FM: Can mildly depressed outpatients with atypical depression benefit from antidepressants? *Am J Psychiatry* 1992, 149:615–619.

19. Elkin I, Shea MT, Watkins JT, *et al.*: National Institute of Mental Health Treatment of Depression Collaborative Research Program: general effectiveness of treatments. *Arch Gen Psychiatry* 1989, 46:971–982.

20. Kashani JH, McGee RO, Clarkson SE, *et al.*: Depression in a sample of 9-year-old children. Prevalence and associated characteristics. *Arch Gen Psychiatry* 1983, 40:1217–1223.

21. Angst J, Merikangas K, Scheidegger P, Wicki W: Recurrent brief depression: a new subtype of affective disorder. *J Affect Dis* 1990, 19:87–98.

22. Davidson JRT, Giller EL, Zisook S, Overall JE: An efficacy study of isocarboxazid and placebo in depression, and its relationship to depressive nosology. *Arch Gen Psychiatry* 1988, 45:120–127.

23. Klerman GL: Introduction. In *Treatment of Psychiatric Disorders*. [A Task Force Report of the American Psychiatric Association.] Vol. 3. Washington, DC: American Psychiatric Association Press; 1989:1727–1745.

24. Quitkin FM, Rabkin JG, Stewart JW, *et al.*: Study duration in antidepressant research: advantages of a 12-week trial. *J Psychiatr Res* 1986, 20:211–216.

25. Richelson E, Nelson A: Antagonism by antidepressants of neurotransmitter receptors of normal human brain in vitro. *J Pharmacol Exp Ther* 1984, 230:94–102.

26. Wander TJ, Nelson A, Okazaki H, Richelson E: Antagonism by antidepressants of serotonin S-1 and S-2 receptors of normal human brain in vitro. *Eur J Pharmacol* 1986, 132:115–121.

27. Richelson E, Pfenning M: Blockaded by antidepressants and related compounds of biogenic amine uptake into rat brain synaptosomes: Most antidepressants selectively block norepinephrine uptake. *Eur J Pharmacol* 1984, 104:277–286.

28. Yeragani VK, Pohl R, Aleem A, *et al.*: Carbohydrate craving and increased appetite associated with antidepressant therapy. *Can J Psychiatry* 1988, 33:606–610.

29. Baldessarini RJ: *Chemotherapy in Psychiatry*. Cambridge, MA: Harvard University Press; 1985.

30. Pollack MH, Rosenbaum JF: Management of antidepressant-induced side effects: a practical guide for the clinician. *J Clin Psychiatry* 1987, 48:3–8.

31. Pinder RM, Broaden RN, Spite TM, Avery GS: Maprotiline: a review of its pharmacological properties and therapeutic efficacy in mental depressive states. *Drugs* 1977, 13:321–352.

32. Mann JJ, Aarons SF, Frances AJ, Brown RD: Studies of selective and reversible monoamine oxidase inhibitors. *J Clin Psychiatry* 1984, 45(7, sec 2):62–66.

33. McGilchrist JM: Interactions with monoamine oxidase inhibitors. *Br Med J* 1975, 3:591–592.

34. Larsen JK, Rafaelsen OJ: Long-term treatment of depression with isocarboxazide. *Acta Psychiatr Scand* 1980, 62:456–463.

35. McGrath PJ, Stewart JW, Harrison W, *et al.*: A Placebo-controlled trial of L-deprenyl in atypical depression. *Psychopharmacol Bull* 1989, 25:63–67.

36. Beasley CM Jr, Masica DN, Heiligenstein JH, *et al.*: Possible monoamine oxidase inhibitor–serotonin uptake inhibitor interaction: fluoxetine clinical data and preclinical findings. *J Clin Psychopharmacol* 1993, 13:312–320.

37. Knoll J: Deprenyl (selegiline): the history of its development and pharmacological action. *Acta Neurol Scand* 1983, 95:57–80.

38. White K, Razani J, Cadow B, *et al.*: Tranylcypromine vs nortriptyline vs placebo in depressed outpatients: a controlled trial. *Psychopharmacology* 1984, 82:258–262.

39. Ravaris CL, Robinson DS, Ives JO, *et al.*: Phenelzine and amitriptyline in the treatment of depression: a comparison of present and past studies. *Arch Gen Psychiatry* 1980, 37:1075–1080.

40. Mann JJ, Aarons SF, Wilner PJ, *et al.*: A controlled study of the antidepressant efficacy and side-effects of (-)-deprenyl. *Arch Gen Psychiatry* 1989, 46:45–50.

41. Da Prada M, Kettler R, Keller HH, Haefely WE: Neurochemical effects in vitro and in vivo of the antidepressant Ro 11-1163, a specific and short-acting MAO-A inhibitor. *Mod Probl Pharmacopsychiatry* 1983, 19:231–245.

42. Da Prada M, Kettler R, Burkard WP, Haefely WE: Moclobemide, an antidepressant with short-lasting MAO-A inhibition: brain catecholamines and tyramine pressor effects in rats. In *Monoamine Oxidase and Disease Prospects for Therapy with Reversible Inhibitors*. Edited by Dostert P, Benedetti MS, Tipton KF. London: Academic Press; 1984:137.

43. Ucha Udabe R, Marquez CA, Traballi CA, Portes N: Double-blind comparison of moclobemide, imipramine and placebo in depressive patients. *Acta Psychiatr Scand Suppl* 1990, 360:54–56.

44. Heinze G, Sanchez A: Overdose with moclobemide. *J Clin Psychiatry* 1986, 47:438.

45. Moll E, Hetzel W: Moclobemide (Ro 11-1163) safety in depressed patients. *Acta Psychiatr Scand Suppl* 1990, 360:69–70.

46. Myrenfors PG, Eriksson T, Sandstedt CS, Sjöberg G: Moclobemide overdose. *J Int Med* 1993, 233:113–115.

47. Neuvonen PJ, Pohjola-Sintonen S, Tacke U, Vuori E: Five fatal cases of serotonin syndrome after moclobemide–citalopram or moclobemide–clomipramine overdoses. *Lancet* 1993, 342:1419.

48.• Thase ME, Trivedi MH, Rush AJ: MAOIs in the contemporary treatment of depression. *Neuropsychopharmacology* 1995, 12:185–219.

49. Rickels K, Schweizer E: Clinical overview of serotonin reuptake inhibitors. *J Clin Psychiatry* 1990, 51(suppl 12B):9–12.

50. Haskins JT, Moyer JA, Muth EA, Sigg EB: DMA, Wy-45,881 and ciramadol inhibit locus coeruleus neuronal activity. *Eur J Pharmacol* 1985, 115:139–146.

51. Muth EA, Moyer JA, Haskins JT, *et al.*: Biochemical neurophysiologic, and behavioral effects of Wy-45,233 and other identified metabolites of the antidepressant venlafaxine. *Drug Dev Res* 1991, 23:191–199.

52. Bolden-Watson C, Richelson E: Blockade by newly-developed antidepressants of biogenic amine uptake into rat brain synaptosomes. *Life Sci* 1993, 52:1023–1029.

53. Tulloch IF, Johnson AM: The pharmacologic profile of paroxetine, a new selective serotonin reuptake inhibitor. *J Clin Psychiatry* 1992, 53(suppl 2):7–12.

54. Shank RP, Vaught JL, Pelley KA, *et al.*: McN-5652: a highly potent inhibitor of serotonin uptake. *J Pharmacol Exp Ther* 1988, 247:1032–1038.

55. Benfield P, Ward A: Fluvoxamine: a review of its pharmacodynamic and pharmacokinetic properties, and therapeutic efficacy in depressive illness. *Drugs* 1986, 32:313–334.

56. Boyer WF, Blumhardt CL: The safety profile of paroxetine. *J Clin Psychiatry* 1992, 53(suppl 2):61–66.

57. Reimherr FW, Chouinard G, Cohn CK, *et al.*: Antidepressant efficacy of sertraline: a double-blind, placebo- and amitriptyline-controlled, multicenter comparison study in outpatients with major depression. *J Clin Psychiatry* 1990, 51(suppl 12B):18–27.

58. Cooper GL: The safety of fluoxetine—an update. *Br J Psychiatry* 1988, 53(suppl 3):77–86.

59. Cooper BR, Hester TJ, Maxwell RA: Behavioral and biochemical effects of the antidepressant bupropion (Wellbutrin): evidence for selective blockade of dopamine uptake in vivo. *J Pharmacol Exp Ther* 1980, 215:127–134.

60. Hall RCW, Popkin MK, Devaul RA, *et al.*: Physical illness presenting as psychiatric disease. *Arch Gen Psychiatry* 1978, 35:1315–1320.

61. Schroeder DH: Metabolism and kinetics of bupropion. *J Clin Psychiatry* 1983, 44(5, sec 2):79–81.

62. Laizure SC, Devane CL, Stewart JT, *et al.*: Pharmacokinetics of bupropion and its major basic metabolites in normal subjects after a single dose. *Clin Pharmacol Ther* 1985, 38:586–589.

63. Van Wyck Fleet J, Manberg PJ, Miller LL, *et al.*: Overview of clinically significant adverse reactions to bupropion. *J Clin Psychiatry* 1983, 44(5, sec 2):191–196.

64. Horne RL, Ferguson JM, Pope HG, *et al.*: Treatment of bulimia with bupropion: a multicenter controlled trial. *J Clin Psychiatry* 1988, 49:262–266.

65. Weisler RH: A profile of bupropion: a nonserotonergic alternative. *J Clin Psychiatry Monogr* 1991, 9:29–35.

66. de Boer T: The effects of mirtazapine on central noradrenergic and serotonergic neurotransmission. *Int Clin Psychopharmacol* 1995, 4(suppl 10):19–23.

67. Sitsen JMA, Zivkov M: Mirtazapine: clinical profile. *CNS Drugs* 1995, 4(suppl 1):39–48.

68. Montgomery SA: Safety of mirtazapine: a review. *Int Clin Psychopharmacology* 1995, 4(suppl 10):37–45.

69. Cusack B, Nelson A, Richelson E: Binding of antidepressants to human brain receptors: focus on newer generation compounds. *Psychopharmacology* 1994, 114:559–565.

70. Feighner JP, Herbstein J, Damlouji N: Combined MAOI, TCA, and direct stimulant therapy of treatment-resistant depression. *J Clin Psychiatry* 1985, 46:206–209.

71. Gamble DE, Peterson LG: Trazodone overdose: four years of experience from voluntary reports. *J Clin Psychiatry* 1986, 47:544–546.

72. Fontaine R: Novel serotonergic mechanisms and clinical experience with nefazodone. *Clin Neuropharmacol* 1993, 16(suppl):S45–S50.

73. Rosenbaum JF, Fava M, Nierenberg AA: The pharmacologic treatment of mood disorders. *Psychiatric Clin North Am* 1994, 1:17–49.

74. Satel SL, Nelson JC: Stimulants in the treatment of depression: a critical overview. *J Clin Psychiatry* 1989, 50:241–249.

75. Beck AT, Rush AJ, Shaw BF, Emery G: *Cognitive Therapy of Depression.* New York: Guileford Press, 1979.

76. Bandura A: *Social Learning Theory.* Englewood Cliffs NJ: Prentice-Hall; 1977.

77. Ferster CB: A functional analysis of depression. *Am Psychol* 1973, 28:857–870.

78. Luborsky L: *Principles of Psychoanalytical Psychotherapy.* New York: Basic Books; 1984.

79. Strupp HH, Binder JL: *Psychotherapy in a New Key.* New York: Basic Books; 1984.

80. Depression Guidelines Panel: Depression in primary care: detection, diagnosis, and treatment. [Technical support. Number 5.] Rockville, MD: US Department of Health and Human Services, Public Health Service; 1993.

81. Welch CA: Electroconvulsive therapy. In *Treatment of Psychiatric Disorders. A Task Force Report of the American Psychiatric Association*, Vol 3. Washington, DC: American Psychiatric Association Press; 1989:1803–1813.

82. Rosenthal NE, Sack DA, Gillin JC, *et al.*: Seasonal affective disorder: a description of the syndrome and preliminary findings with light therapy. *Arch Gen Psychiatry* 1984, 41:72–80.

83. Kripke DF: Therapeutic effects of bright light in depression. In *The Medical and Biological Effects of Light.* Edited by Wurtman RJ, Baum MJ, Potts JT. *Ann NY Acad Sci* 1985, 453:270–281.

84. Yerevanian BJ, Anderson JL, Grota LJ, Bray M: Effects of bright incandescent light on seasonal and nonseasonal major depressive disorder. *Psychiatry Res* 1986, 18:355–364.

85. Rosenthal NE: Light therapy. In *Treatment of Psychiatric Disorders. A Task Force Report of the American Psychiatric Association*, Vol 3. Washington, DC: American Psychiatric Association Press; 1989:1890–1896.

86. Lewy AJ, Sack RL, Miller LS, Hoban TM: Antidepressant and circadian phase-shifting effects of light. *Science* 1987, 235:352–354.

87. Nierenberg AA, Amsterdam JD: Treatment-resistant depression: definition and treatment approaches. *J Clin Psychiatry* 1990, 51(suppl):39–47.

88. Popkin MK, Callies AL, Mackenzie TB: The outcome of antidepressant use in the medically ill. *Arch Gen Psychiatry* 1985, 42:1160–1163.

89. Fawcett J, Kravitz HM: Anxiety syndromes and their relationship to depressive illness. *J Clin Psychiatry* 1983, 44(suppl):8–11.

90. Clayton PJ, Grove WM, Coryell W, *et al.*: Follow-up and family study of anxious depression. *Am J Psychiatry* 1991, 148:1512–1517.

91. Joffe RT, Bagby M, Levitt A: Anxious and nonanxious depression. *Am J Psychiatry* 1993, 150:1257–1258.

92. Fava M, Rosenbaum JF, McGrath PJ, *et al.*: Lithium and tricyclic augmentation of fluoxetine treatment for resistant major depression: a double-blind, controlled study. *Am J Psychiatry* 1994, 151:1372–1374.

93. Rosenbaum JR, Fava M, Nierenberg AA, Sachs G: Treatment resistant mood disorders. In *Treatments of Psychiatric Disorders: The DSM-IV Edition.* Edited by Gabbard G. Topeka, KS: Meninger Clinic; 1995.

94. MacEwan WG, Remick RA: Treatment resistant depression: a clinical perspective. *Can J Psychiatry* 1988, 33:788–792.

95. Johnson FN: Lithium augmentation therapy. *Rev Contemp Pharmacother* 1991, 2:1–52.

96. Austin M-P, Souza FGM, Goodwin GM: Lithium augmentation in antidepressant resistant patients: a quantitative analysis. *Br J Psychiatry* 1991, 159:510–514.

97. Ontiveros A, Fontaine R, Elie R: Refractory depression: the addition of lithium to fluoxetine or desipramine. *Acta Psychiatr Scand* 1991, 83:188–192.

98. Thase ME, Kupfer DJ, Frank E, Jarrett DB: Treatment of imipramine-resistant recurrent depression: II. An open clinical trial of lithium augmentation. *J Clin Psychiatry* 1989, 50:413–417.

99. Prange AJ, Wilson IC, Robon AM: Enhancement of imipramine antidepressant activity by thyroid hormone. *Am J Psychiatry* 1969, 126:457–469.

100. Wilson IC, Prange AJ, McClaine TK: Thyroid hormone enhancement of imipramine in nonrelated depressions. *N Engl J Med* 1970, 282:1063–1067.

101. Earle BV: Thyroid hormone and tricyclic antidepressants in resistant depressions. *Am J Psychiatry* 1970, 126:1667–1669.

102. Ogura C, Okuma T, Uchida Y, *et al.*: Combined thyroid (triiodothyronine)–tricyclic antidepressant treatment in depressive states. *Folia Psychiatr Neurol Jpn* 1974, 28:179–186.

103. Banki CM: Triiodothyronine in the treatment of depression. *Orv Hetil* 1975, 116:2543–2547.

104. Tsutsui S, Yamazaki Y, Namba T, Tsushima M: Combined therapy of T_3 and antidepressants in depression. *J Int Med Res* 1979, 7:138–146.

105. Joffe RT, Singer W, Levitt AJ, MacDonald C: A placebo-controlled comparison of lithium and triiodothyronine augmentation of tricyclic antidepressants in unipolar refractory depression. *Arch Gen Psychiatry* 1993, 50:387–393.

106. Agnoli A, Ruggieri S, Casacchia M: Restatement and perspectives of ergot alkaloids in clinical neurology and psychiatry. *Pharmacology* 1978, 16(suppl 1):174–188.

107. Colonna L, Petit M, Lepine JP: Bromocriptine in affective disorders. *J Affect Disord* 1979, 1:173–177.

108. Nordin C, Siwers B, Bertilsson L: Bromocriptine in depressive disorders: clinical and biochemical effects. *Acta Psychiatr Scand* 1981, 64:25–33.

109. Silverstone T: Response to bromocriptine distinguishes bipolar from unipolar depressions. *Lancet* 1984, 1:903–904.

110. Bouras N, Bridges PK: Bromocriptine and depression. *Curr Med Res Opin* 1982, 8:150–153.

111. Theohar C, Fischer-Cornelssen K, Brosch H, *et al.*: A comparative, multicenter trial between bromocriptine and amitriptyline in the treatment of endogenous depression. *Arzneimittelforschung* 1982, 32:783–787.

112. Waehrens J, Gerlach J: Bromocriptine and imipramine in endogenous depression: a double-blind controlled trial in out-patients. *J Affect Disord* 1981, 3:193–202.

113. Bouckoms A, Mangini L: *Pergolide: An Antidepressant Adjuvant for Mood Disorders?* Boca Raton FL: New Clinical Drug Evaluation Unit; 1992.

114. Chiarello RJ, Cole JO: The use of psychostimulants in psychiatry. *Arch Gen Psychiatry* 1987, 44:286–295.

115. Linet LS: Treatment of a refractory depression with a combination of fluoxetine and *d*-amphetamine [Letter]. *Am J Psychiatry* 1989, 146:803–804.

116. Metz A, Shader RI: Combination of fluoxetine with pemoline in the treatment of major depressive disorder. *Int Clin Psychopharmacol* 1991, 6:93–96.

117. Fawcett JJ, Kravitz HM, Zajecka JM, Schaff MR: CNS stimulant potentiation of monoamine oxidase inhibitors in treatment-refractory depression. *J Clin Psychopharmacol* 1991, 11:127–132.

118. Amsterdam JD, Berwish NJ: High dose tranylcypromine therapy for refractory depression. *Pharmacopsychiatry* 1989, 22:21–25.

119. Schuckit MA, Feighner JP: Safety of high-dose tricyclic antidepressant therapy. *Am J Psychiatry* 1972, 128:140–143.

120. Cole JP, Schatzberg AF, Sniffin C, *et al.*: Trazodone in treatment-resistant depression: an open study. *J Clin Psychopharmacol* 1981, 1(6; suppl):49S–54S.

121. Fava M, Rosenbaum JF, Cohen L, *et al.*: High-dose fluoxetine in the treatment of depressed patients not responsive to a standard dose of fluoxetine. *J Affect Disord* 1992, 25:229–234.

122. Tyrer P, Murphy S: Efficacy of combined antidepressant therapy in resistant neurotic disorder. *Br J Psychiatry* 1990, 156:115–118.

123. Sheperd M, Lader M, Rodnight R: *Clinical Psychopharmacology*. London: English Universities Press; 1968:140.

124. Spiker DG, Pugh DD: Combining tricyclic and monoamine oxidase inhibitor antidepressants. *Arch Gen Psychiatry* 1976, 33:828–830.

125. White K, Simpson G: Combined MAOI–tricyclic antidepressant treatment: a re-evaluation. *J Clin Psychopharmacol* 1981, 1:264–282.

126. Lader M: Combined use of tricyclic antidepressants and monoamine oxidase inhibitors. *J Clin Psychiatry* 1983, 44:20–24.

127. Eisen A: Fluoxetine and desipramine: a strategy for augmenting anti-depressant response. *Pharmacopsychiatry* 1989, 22:272–273.

128. Seth R, Jennings AL, Bindman J, *et al.*: Combination treatment with noradrenaline and serotonin reuptake inhibitors in resistant depression. *Br J Psychiatry* 1992, 161:562–565.

129. Baettig D, Bondolfi G, Montaldi S, Amey M: Tricyclic antidepressant plasma levels after augmentation with citalopram: a case study. *Eur J Clin Pharmacol* 1993, 44:403–405.

130. Weilburg JB, Rosenbaum JF, Biederman J, *et al.*: Fluoxetine added to non-MAOI antidepressants converts nonresponders to responders: a preliminary report. *J Clin Psychiatry* 1989, 50:447–449.

131. Weilburg JB, Rosenbaum JF, Meltzer-Brody S, Shustari J: Tricyclic augmentation of fluoxetine. *Ann Clin Psychiatry* 1991, 3:209–213.

132. Bakish D: Fluoxetine potentiation by buspirone: three case histories. *Can J Psychiatry* 1991, 36:749–750.

133. Jacobsen FM: Possible augmentation of antidepressant response to buspirone. *J Clin Psychiatry* 1991, 52:217–220.

134. Joffe RT, Schuller DR: An open study of buspirone augmentation of serotonin reuptake inhibitors in refractory depression. *J Clin Psychiatry* 1993, 54:269–271.

135. McGrath PJ, Stewart JW, Harrison W, Quitkin FM: Treatment of tricyclic refractory depression with a monoamine oxidase inhibitor antidepressant. *Psychopharmacol Bull* 1987, 23:169–172.

136. Nolen WA, Van de Putte JJ, Dijken WA, *et al.*: Treatment strategy in depression. II. MAO inhibitors in depression resistant to cyclic antidepressants: Two controlled crossover studies with tranylcypromine versus L-5-hydroxytryptophan and nomifensine. *Acta Psychiatr Scand* 1988, 78:676–683.

137. Stern WC, Harto-Truax N, Bauer N: Efficacy of bupropion in tricyclic-resistant or intolerant patients. *J Clin Psychiatry* 1983, 44:148–152.

138. Delgado PL, Price LH, Charney DS, Heninger GR: Efficacy of fluvoxamine in treatment-refractory depression. *J Affect Disord* 1988, 15:55–60.

139. Nolen WA, Van de Putte JJ, Dijken WA, *et al.*: Treatment strategy in depression. I. Non-tricyclic and selective reuptake inhibitors in resistant depression: a double-blind partial crossover study on the effects of oxaprotiline and fluvoxamine. *Acta Psychiatr Scand* 1988, 78:668–675.

140. White K, Wykoff W, Tynes LL, *et al.*: Fluvoxamine in the treatment of tricyclic-resistant depression. *Psychiatr J Univ Ottawa* 1990, 15:156–158.

141. Prudic J, Sackeim HA, Devanand DP: Medication resistance and clinical response to electroconvulsive therapy. *Psychiatry Res* 1990, 31:287–296.

142. Pava JA, Fava M, Levenson JA: Integrating cognitive therapy and pharmacotherapy in the treatment and prophylaxis of depression: a novel approach. *Psychother Psychosom* 1994, 61:211–129.

143. Fava M, Kaji J: Continuation and maintenance treatments of major depressive disorder. *Psychiatr Ann* 1994, 24:281–290.

144. Prien RF, Kupfer DJ, Mansky PA, *et al.*: Drug therapy in the prevention of recurrences in unipolar and bipolar affective disorders: a report of the NIHM Collaborative Study Group comparing lithium carbonate, imipramine, and a lithium carbonate–imipramine combination. *Arch Gen Psychiatry* 1984, 41:1096–1104.

145. Loonen AJ, Peer PG, Zwanikken GJ: Continuation and maintenance therapy with antidepressive agents: meta-analysis of research. *Pharm Weekbl [Sci]* 1991, 13:167–175.

146. Kleinman I, Schachter D: Tricyclic maintenance therapy in unipolar depression. *Can J Psychiatry* 1988, 33:7–10.

CHAPTER 5

Treatment of Bipolar Disorder

Charles L. Bowden

The treatment of bipolar disorders is complex owing to the multiple types of episodes and the rapid onset of symptoms. In this chapter, we discuss the treatment of patients with acute manic and acute depressive phases of bipolar disorder, and patients with mixed mania, rapid and non-rapid cycling, mania secondary to general medical disorders, and mania concurrent with substance abuse. Drug therapies for bipolar disorders are multifaceted, and different adjunctive therapies are needed as a consequence of the stage of illness. However, the fundamental mood-stabilizing regimen is continued. Mood-stabilizing drugs such as lithium, valproate, divalproex (a derivative of valproate), and carbamazepine and their dosage and side effects are considered. We outline the use of these drugs in patients with the different phases of bipolar disorders. Even after diagnosis and successful treatment, many environmental factors can destabilize otherwise well-functioning patients. The key task for patients and their psychiatrists is to recognize early signs of relapse, which tend to be consistent across episodes for individuals regarding symptomatology and type of episode. Effective treatment is then possible.

Treatments for the acute manic episode are among the most effective for any psychiatric condition and, based on recent studies, often can be tailored to the particular characteristics of the patient's course of illness, symptomatology, and several associated illness features. The aims of treatment are clear: get the patient out of the episode without causing adverse effects that interfere with function, and establish the context for maintenance phase treatment. In today's managed care environment, when a patient with mania requires hospitalization the imperative for rapid symptom control is even greater as a result of efforts to reduce the duration of hospital stays.

Definition of and Rationale for the Term *Mood Stabilizer*

The term *mood stabilizer* has only entered psychiatric parlance in the past decade. It derives from the goal of mood stabilization, long discussed in literature and in practice. The need for the term stems from two distinct developments. Unlike in the early years of the use of lithium, other medications now warrant use for mood stabilization. For example, today services would not be organized around a so-called lithium clinic. The second source of need is the gradual recognition that some medications that benefit certain aspects of bipolar episodes have the potential to worsen other equally important aspects of the disease. This is most clearly established regarding the potential for all currently available antidepressants to precipitate manic, hypomanic, and mixed episodes, and to increase cycling frequency. The concept of mood stabilization helps to order the priorities for treatment of this disease and the classes of drugs used. Another term, *thymoleptic*, is also used. It derives from the Latin *thymos*, which means spirit. This seems to me deficient both in derivation and in practical utility, because its lack of self-evidence requires an explanation if used with a patient.

Herewith is a suggested definition for the term *mood stabilizer*: A drug that alleviates the frequency, intensity, or both, of manic, hypomanic, depressive, or mixed episodes in patients with bipolar disorder, and that does not increase the frequency or severity of any of the subtypes of bipolar disorder. Presently, this definition would apply to lithium, valproate, and carbamazepine. If a drug were developed that would alleviate depressive episodes without increasing the severity of manic or mixed episodes, it would qualify as a mood stabilizer within this definition. Perhaps the part of this definition most open to question is allowing a drug to qualify that only reduces episode frequency. I do so principally because it seems logically cleaner, in that the goal of mood stabilization is furthered by either reduced amplitude or frequency of episodes. Finally, it would seem awkward to require separate classes for drugs that reduce manic or depressive symptoms from those that reduce episode frequency. The term also facilitates the convenient grouping of other medications useful in various phases of bipolar disorder, but that are not mood stabilizers, to be classified under the general heading of adjunctive medications. The definition is offered here not as a final statement, but as an organizing concept to guide both research efforts and clinical practice.

Mood stabilization

Treatment with a mood stabilizer is the central, essential feature of care for the patient with acute mania. Lithium has the advantages of duration of experience, established efficacy, and low cost. It has the disadvantages of relatively slow onset of action, unsuitability for loading dose strategies, somewhat poorer early tolerability compared with divalproex [1], and relative ineffectiveness in many identifiable forms of mania. The divalproex form of valproate has the advantages of better quality of studies than those of either lithium or carbamazepine, a broader symptomatic spectrum of response, fewer adverse effects in most patients, a somewhat more rapid response than does lithium, and, unlike lithium or carbamazepine, tolerability with a loading dose strategy, which may further speed up the initial response [1,2]. The disadvantages of valproate are the lesser experience that many psychiatrists have had with it compared with their experience with lithium, and the small number of controlled studies of its long-term effectiveness.

The advantages of carbamazepine are somewhat better tolerability than lithium [3] and (probably) efficacy in lithium refractory patients. Its disadvantages are poor quality of studies, possibly somewhat lower efficacy than has lithium [4], pharmacokinetic complexities, high frequency of neuromuscular adverse effects, and severe dermatologic reactions.

Little support exists for other treatments as specifically antimanic. Neuroleptic drugs consistently were shown to be inferior to lithium (although equivalent to carbamazepine) in prospective clinical trials, and they have disadvantageous acute and long-term adverse effects that, in turn, contribute to poor compliance [5]. Case reports suggest no greater safety or efficacy for risperidone than for standard neuroleptic drugs [6,7]. Clozapine may be useful in a small group of patients with schizoaffective mania; however, the studies are open and uncontrolled, and clozapine's disadvantageous acute adverse effects, risk of agranulocytosis, and the nuisance of frequent leukocyte count monitoring are sufficient to dissuade its use in other than unusual cases [8].

Although there have been reports that verapamil has benefits, the studies are inadequate in patient number, design, and execution; are not placebo-controlled in randomized parallel group studies; and suggest that the symptoms of some patients with bipolar disorders worsen with verapamil treatment [9]. The best-designed and best-executed study reported no difference between verapamil and placebo [10]. The main positive report comes from a crossover study of just six patients, five of whom showed substantial improvement [11]. A study of 12 patients did not even clarify whether the patients were experiencing an acute manic episode [12], and a third study reported much greater use of neuroleptic drugs needed in verapamil than in patients treated with lithium [13].

Electroconvulsive therapy (ECT) can be effective in both the manic and depressive phases of bipolar disorder, although the small number of studies lack adequate controls. In arguably the best study, a randomized trial, for example, most patients treated with ECT also were receiving lithium [14]. There is suggestive evidence that only bilateral ECT, not unilateral ECT, is effective in the treatment of acute mania [15]. The main indications for ECT include psychotic episodes, nonresponsiveness to adequate medication trials, and patients' inability to safely take medications, such as women in the first trimester of pregnancy.

Clinical Factors Associated with Response to Specific Therapies
Mixed mania

Data are now strong that lithium is only infrequently of benefit in mixed mania. Rates of response are a little higher than are those seen with placebo [16,17•]. The relatively poor response to lithium is not only during acute mania, but at least through the first year of treatment of a mixed manic episode. In two studies, carbamazepine appeared to be less effective in patients with mixed mania than in those with classic mania [18].

Divalproex was equally effective in patients with mixed mania or pure mania in a well-designed prospective blinded study [1]. A blinded comparison of divalproex and lithium found mixed manic symptomatology associated with a relatively favorable response to divalproex [19]. A large open study of divalproex in patients with mixed mania reported a response rate of over 90% for the full year. This study is limited in that about half of patients received divalproex alone and about half received divalproex plus lithium [20]. Based on these data, divalproex generally should be the first drug tried for a patient with mixed mania.

The criteria for diagnosis of mixed mania remain unsatisfactorily established [21]. According to the Diagnostic and Statistical Manual (DSM)-IV, the patient must meet the symptomatic criteria for a major depressive episode for a minimum duration of 1 week. Many mixed episodes are much briefer than 1 week, especially in adolescents. Our recent study found that the presence of even mild degrees of purely depressive symptoms strongly differentiated patients with poor response to lithium from those with good response (Swann *et al.*, Unpublished data). Based on the previous considerations, psychiatrists should consider a different therapeutic approach in patients with pure depressive symptoms of shorter duration than those that currently exist in DSM-IV criteria. Attention to the number of previous depressive episodes also may be a useful guide. In the same study, we also found that patients with a larger number of previous episodes of depression did significantly better with divalproex treatment than they did with lithium treatment.

Rapid cycling

Lithium is relatively ineffective in patients with rapid cycling, both in acute and prophylactic treatments [22,23]. Divalproex was equally effective in alleviating acute mania in rapid cycling and nonrapid cycling patients in a blinded, randomized prospective trial [1]. Its effectiveness was equally good when even more stringent criteria of rapid cycling were applied, such as requiring four or more manic episodes in each of the 2 years preceding study entry. In an open trial, Calabrese and Delucchi [20] reported high rates of acute and maintained response in rapid cycling bipolar patients treated with divalproex, about half of whom also were receiving lithium [20]. Carbamazepine is less effective in rapid cycling patients than in nonrapid cycling patients [18,24]. Thyroid supplementation of lithium has been reported to be beneficial in a small series of patients [25].

A tentative recommended approach to rapid cycling patients is shown in Table 1. The medication recommendations are based on sparse data, especially for the more important longer term efficacy of the treatments. A large naturalistic long-term study recently reported that rapid cycling seems to be a temporary phase of illness [15]. By contrast, some patients may develop more frequent rapid cycling as they age, and some patients maintain high, regular rates of cycling for many years. It is plausible that different etiopathologic factors may be operational in these variants, which, in turn, would suggest different prognoses and treatment strategies.

Secondary mania

Mania that occurs consequent to other medical conditions that alter central nervous system function is referred to as mania secondary to a general medical disorder, or simply secondary mania. Patients with secondary mania respond relatively poorly to lithium. Carroll *et al.* [26] found that for patients with secondary mania, hospitalization was significantly longer among patients treated with lithium than it was for those treated with either carbamazepine or valproate. One randomized comparison of lithium and carbamazepine found carbamazepine to be more effective than lithium [27]. A retrospective medical record review found that patients with bipolar and schizoaffective disorders who also have neurologic abnormalities responded better to valproate than did patients without such abnormalities [28]. Case reports also indicate favorable response to divalproex in patients with secondary bipolar disorders, most of whom had previously been nonresponsive or intolerant to lithium [29].

A reasonable treatment strategy therefore is to treat optimally the primary general medical disorder, then consider carbamazepine or valproate as the mood-stabilizing agent. My experience is that valproate is better-tolerated than is lithium or carbamazepine in many patients with secondary mania, largely because of a lower frequency of cognitive and neuromuscular adverse effects (*eg*, ataxia, poor coordination, and diplopia) than occur with either lithium or carbamazepine.

Table I. Approach to Treatment of Rapid Cycling Bipolar Disorder

Assess for and eliminate destabilizing drugs
Initial treatment: valproate, carbamazepine, or lithium
No or partial response: add second mood stabilizer
No or partial response: evaluate thyroid, add T4
No or partial response: clozapine or electroconvulsive therapy

Bipolar disorder and substance abuse

Lithium is relatively ineffective in the large group of patients with concurrent substance abuse. This may be linked partly to the increased likelihood of mixed mania in patients who are substance abusers [30]. It also suggests that attention be given to the need for concurrent specific treatment for substance abuse in these patients. Other factors may be that patients who are substance abusers are particularly unlikely to adhere to a treatment with as high a frequency of subjectively distressing adverse effects as has lithium. An open case series suggests good tolerability and efficacy of divalproex in patients with bipolar disorder and concurrent substance abuse [31]. Days of drug use diminished, as did symptoms of mania and depression.

Previous lithium response

One of the strongest predictors of lithium responsiveness in acute manic episodes is prior response to lithium in an acute manic episode. Although the data are from one study, they are of practical importance for several reasons. The practicing psychiatrist can obtain as reliable information about the most recent lithium response as can an investigator. Several studies indicate that about half of patients do well with lithium treatment [32]. Once a patient's previous good response to lithium is established, that patient should be treated with lithium unless the drug is poorly tolerated. By contrast, patients who indicated that they had not done well with lithium previously had little short-term likelihood of response; therefore, these patients should generally be treated with divalproex, which was similarly effective in previous responders and nonresponders to lithium [1]. Because most patients with bipolar disorder have received lithium and because the illness commonly has recurrent episodes, this information will be available for most patients. Whereas other predictive variables may be relatively difficult to ascertain with confidence, this often will be quite clear. Only in instances in which poor compliance unrelated to poor tolerability is at issue is this information not likely to be useful.

Avoidance of destabilizing medications and activities

A wide range of potentially avoidable events may precipitate mania or hypomania, even in the face of adequate mood-stabilizing treatment. The evidence is most conclusive for currently available antidepressants, therefore shorter periods of use of the antidepressant are indicated, unless the patient relapses on discontinuation of the antidepressant. The importance of avoiding destabilizing substances that can be abused is widely understood. More difficult for the patient to avoid are the extensive array of medications that may precipitate mania or hypomania. Table 2 makes clear that it would be difficult for a patient to avoid all exposure to such a broad spectrum of commonly used drugs. Patients vary greatly in their sensitivity to such effects; therefore, over time, a useful sense of the needed degree of vigilance can be developed.

Drug Administration
Lithium

Lithium poses difficulties tied to its narrow therapeutic index, with concentrations about twice the average clinical level posing serious risks. Although a loading dose strategy is not feasible, dosage should be increased as rapidly as tolerated until the patient responds

Table 2. Medications That May Cause Manic or Hypomanic Episodes	
Corticosteroids	Isoniazid
Anabolic steroids	Procarbazine
Stimulants	Levodopa
Decongestants	Bromide
Beta blockers	Bronchodilators
Tricyclic antidepressants	Procyclidine
Selective serotonin reuptake inhibitors	Phencyclidine
Bupropion	Metaclopramide
Monoamine oxidase inhibitors	Hallucinogens
Alcohol	Sympathomimetic amines
Disulfiram	Barbiturates
Anticholinergics	Anticonvulsants

or until a plasma level of 1.2 to 1.4 mEq/L is achieved. Lithium is generally well tolerated in the acute treatment of mania. The most common acute phase adverse effects are gastrointestinal irritation, tremor, and cognitive dulling. Renal, thyroid, and cardiovascular adverse effects are largely limited to chronic therapy. Lithium excretion rates diminish after control of an acute manic episode [33]; therefore, some compensatory reduction in dosage during maintenance phase therapy is indicated. Although studies indicate an overall better response at levels of 0.8 mEq/L or greater, individual patients may do well at lower levels. Among the many body systems affected by lithium, thyroid function warrants the closest clinical monitoring for most patients, because at least one third of patients in therapy for as few as 6 months are likely to have clinical or subclinical evidence of suboptimal thyroid function. This can diminish responsiveness to lithium or other mood-stabilizing and antidepressant drugs. The most sensitive laboratory index of hypothyroidism is thyroid-stimulating hormone (TSH). Psychiatrists recommend that TSH levels of 5 µIU or greater be viewed as warranting treatment with replacement thyroid hormone.

Elderly patients

Elderly patients with bipolar disorder present a difficult subset of patients. Shulman *et al.* [34] found that 36% of patients over the age of 65 with late onset mania had a neurologic disorder, compared with only 8% of persons of similar age with late-onset depression. All bipolar disorders that occur in the elderly are not secondary. In general, treatments that worked earlier in life should be continued. Some patients who tolerated lithium well in their 50s begin to experience short-term memory difficulty in their 60s with the needed lithium serum concentration. For such patients a change to divalproex or carbamazepine may be salutary [35]. Elderly patients with other central nervous system diseases (*eg*, stroke and mild dementia) are particularly sensitive to the cognitive impairing effects of lithium. Severe and protracted neurotoxicity may occur at relatively low serum levels, at times below 0.6 mEq/L. Sinus bradycardia is also a greater risk in the elderly. In general, divalproex and carbamazepine are better-tolerated choices in the elderly; however, each also poses special difficulties in this age group. Valproate is highly protein bound, and in elderly patients lower plasma proteins may result in a higher free valproate level, which represents the active moiety. Therefore, a total plasma level as reported by a laboratory may misleadingly suggest a smaller drug effect than the patient is actually receiving. Cautious reduction of dosage to better-tolerated levels may yield a level that is both tolerable and effective. With carbamazepine, hyponatremia is more likely to be clinically significant than it is in younger patients. Ataxia and torpor also are more common. Exploration of lower plasma levels therefore is indicated.

Adjunctive Treatments for the Acute Phase Treatment of Mania

Use of an antimanic mood stabilizer is the central treatment for the acute phase treatment of mania. Many patients respond adequately to a single mood stabilizer with no adjunctive medication. However, more than half of patients require adjunctive medication at some point. Approximately one third of manic episodes include psychotic features at some point in the episode [36]. Although certain features suggest differences from schizophrenic disorders, none occur reliably. The presence of psychotic symptoms in a patient with a major depressive mood disorder is highly suggestive of a bipolar disorder. Such symptoms may resolve with achievement of mood stabilization. Accompanying problems with diminished insight, hostility, and other inappropriate behavior often necessitate symptomatic treatment in addition to the mood stabilizer. One study suggests that benzodiazepines may accomplish much that neuroleptic drugs do [37]. Therefore, a case can be made for first trying a benzodiazepine, or a benzodiazepine along with a relatively low dose of a neuroleptic drug, rather than a neuroleptic drug alone.

Inadequate sleep is both a symptom of mania and perhaps a contributor to manic episodes. Benzodiazepines may improve this problem. Choice among benzodiazepines should largely be tied to the goal of treatment. Difficulty getting to sleep calls for treatment with a drug with rapid onset of action (*eg*, alprazolam, triazolam, or diazepam). Restless sleep and early morning waking suggest the need for a medication with a longer half-life (*eg*, temazepam, estazolam, or clonazepam). In principle, it may be advisable to avoid a drug with an ultrashort half-life, such as triazolam, because the sharp decay in drug level might cause a rebound wakening or impaired sleep in the second half of the night. I know of no tests of this notion, however. Because of the high frequency of substance abuse in patients with bipolar disorder, psychiatrists are sometimes reluctant to use benzodiazepines out of concern for precipitating substance use, or abusive use of the benzodiazepine. Given the evidence that substance abuse is often a consequence or manifestation of bipolar disorder, and given the lack of reports of such destabilization, benzodiazepines should be used as clinically indicated in these patients, because of the importance of adequate sleep. Nondrug approaches to sleep hygiene also are important.

Acute Phase Treatment for Depression

Strategies for the acute phase treatment of the depressed phase of bipolar disorder suffer from a dearth of experimental data. Anecdotal evidence suggests that all approved antidepressant drugs, plus ECT, may benefit depressive episodes in bipolar disorder. Additionally, lithium may alleviate depression, based on early studies [38]. However, optimal treatment strategies are unclear, based on evidence that all antidepressants increase the short-term likelihood of manic or hypomanic episodes and that more frequent episodes may also be induced. Selective serotonin reuptake inhibitors (SSRIs) may pose lower risks than do tricyclic antidepressants (TCAs). Although bupropion has been suggested to be relatively safer regarding cycle induction, the supporting evidence is limited and inconclusive [39]. Both valproate and carbamazepine alleviate some depressive episodes; however, their efficacy in depression seems much lower than is that in mania [5]. Calcium channel blockers may alleviate some depressive episodes, but are actually causative of depression in some patients [40]. The one placebo-controlled comparison of lithium and a TCA found that imipramine was significantly more effective than was lithium [41]. Furthermore, the neuromuscular and cognitive adverse effects of lithium may worsen the subjective sense of depression. The recently introduced antidepressants venlafaxine and nefazadone have not been studied systematically in bipolar depression.

One is left with relatively too much expert opinion and too little solid data to guide treatment choices and practices. The present consensus, which this author supports, is roughly as depicted in Figure 1. The ease of use of SSRIs, their generally good tolerability, the negligible risk of lethality with overdose, and the two studies that suggest lower

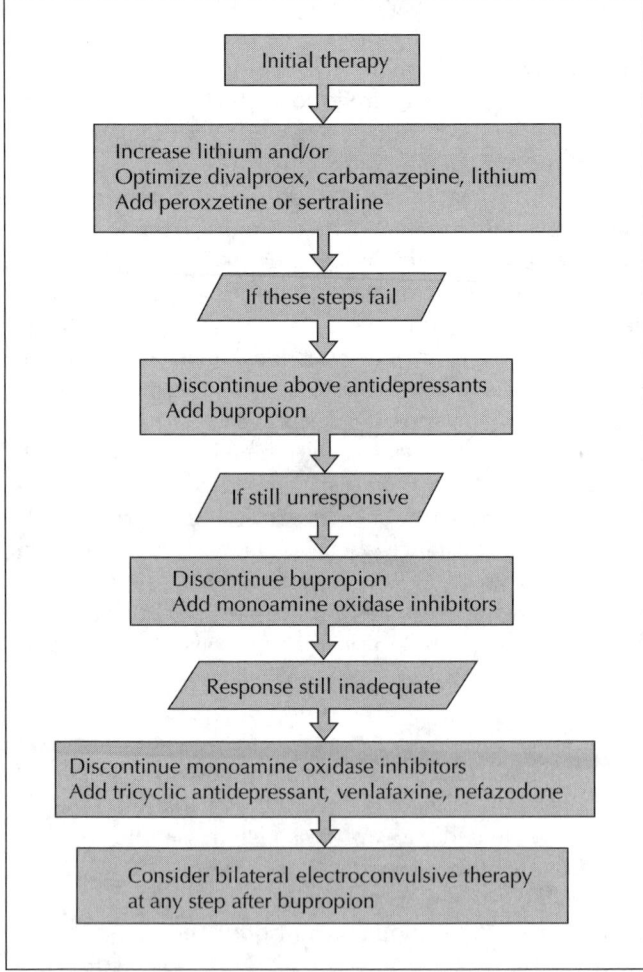

Figure 1. Algorithm for treatment of bipolar depression.

rates of mania in short-term treatment than those seen with tricyclic antidepressants make these the treatments of first choice for most patients with depressive episodes. Bupropion also may cause lower rates of manic episodes; however, data are very limited. Although monoamine oxidase inhibitors are effective, their adverse effect profile is not as favorable. The importance of dietary adherence is perhaps an even greater concern in bipolar disorder, given the impulsivity and impaired judgment that may accompany manic and mixed episodes.

Increase of lithium dosage

A trial increase of lithium may be warranted. However, higher lithium concentrations may contribute to worsened depression-like symptoms due to neuromuscular and cognitive side effects. Some depressed patients may benefit from valproate [42]. It is especially noteworthy that divalproex is the only mood stabilizer that appears to be as efficacious in mixed states as it is in classic mania. Mixed states may appear as predominantly depressive episodes. Indeed, some patients with mixed states spontaneously complain only of the depressive symptoms, viewing the manic features as not of clinical consequence. The importance of careful diagnostic assessment in such cases is clear.

Duration of antidepressant treatment

Because of the risks of precipitation of mania (hypomania, increasing cycle frequency or, perhaps even more commonly, short time-frame mood instability) the present view has shifted to a shorter, more episode-limited use of antidepressants. Although there are no good studies on the point, if a patient recovers from depression with treatment, the antidepressant should probably be tapered within 4 to 12 weeks of recovery. A gradual discontinuation over 4 to 8 weeks is plausibly desirable to reduce risk of relapse [43]; it also serves to allow identification of early signs of relapse, thereby allowing reinstitution for longer term use for the small percentage of patients who have such need.

Maintenance Phase Treatment

If treatment proceeds as we and our patients expect, most elapsed time, but not most contact time, will be spent in this essentially lifelong phase. Much of what has been presented earlier in this article also applies to maintenance phase treatment. We now focus on the differences.

A key task is for patients and psychiatrists to recognize early signs of relapse. These tend to be consistent across episodes for an individual, both as to symptomatology (eg, increased time talking about a political scheme) and type of episode (patients with more depressive than manic episodes historically are likely to continue that pattern). Subthreshold symptomatology has different implications if it is hypomanic rather than depressive. Most hypomanic periods lead to full manic ones, whereas mild depressive periods usually are self-limited (Table 3) [44]. Durational requirements of DSM-IV that an episode last a minimum of 7 days to be counted as manic, or 4 days as hypomanic, and that depressive symptoms be present at least 1 week during a manic episode are unsatisfactory criteria for use by the clinician with a patient diagnosed with a bipolar disorder.

The justification for the DSM perspective is that these limitations reduce the likelihood of a false-positive diagnosis. For the patient who already has been diagnosed with

Table 3. Relationship of First Subsyndrome to Major Relapse in Bipolar Disorder

	Patients, *n*	No relapse, %	Mania, %	Depression, %
Minor depression	33	61	27	12
Depression				
Hypomania	17	24	65	12

a bipolar disorder, a new episode can be devastating to daily functioning. Therefore, the psychiatrist must be able to recognize the early warning signs so that quick intervention can ward off a full-blown episode. Figure 2 addresses these issues in more detail.

Adjustment of dosage

Lithium

For lithium, dosage often may be reduced somewhat from that needed for control of mania, with correspondingly less adverse effects. This is an important tactic in that the most troublesome adverse effects of lithium do not occur during treatment for an acute episode, but only develop with longer term treatment. It is likely that this accounts for the consistent evidence of poor long-term tolerability of lithium in recent studies, compared with the more benign adverse effects acutely.

Although several studies indicate that both prevention of relapse and severity of adverse effects to lithium increase at levels of 0.8 mEq/L or greater, recent review of the data in the study by Gelenberg *et al.* [45] suggests a modified interpretation. Although patients maintained at 0.4 to 0.6 mEq/L did have more manic relapses, the increased rate was almost completely accounted for by patients who, clinically, had needed higher levels for good illness control and, for study purposes, were randomly assigned to the lower serum level range. Patients maintained at lower levels before the study did not have higher relapse rates if they were randomly assigned to the group with low serum levels [46].

Divalproex and valproate

It appears that patients treated with divalproex will need similar dosages for maintenance as for acute treatment, although the question has not been studied systematically. As with lithium, the adverse effects of concern acutely are somewhat different from those at issue in maintenance. Infrequent bleeding secondary to reduced platelet count, weight gain, and hair loss all may occur with long-term treatment. Valproate has minor interactions with drugs metabolized oxidatively by the P450 family of enzymes. Metabolism of lometraline is strongly inhibited, as both are metabolized by glucuronide conjugation. Empirically, psychiatrists now treat many patients with single daily doses of divalproex at bedtime, with the advantages this provides for better compliance (Maci *et al.*, Unpublished data).

Carbamazepine

Carbamazepine needs to be continued on a schedule of two to three times daily, because patients tend to have more neuromuscular adverse effects with higher peak plasma levels.

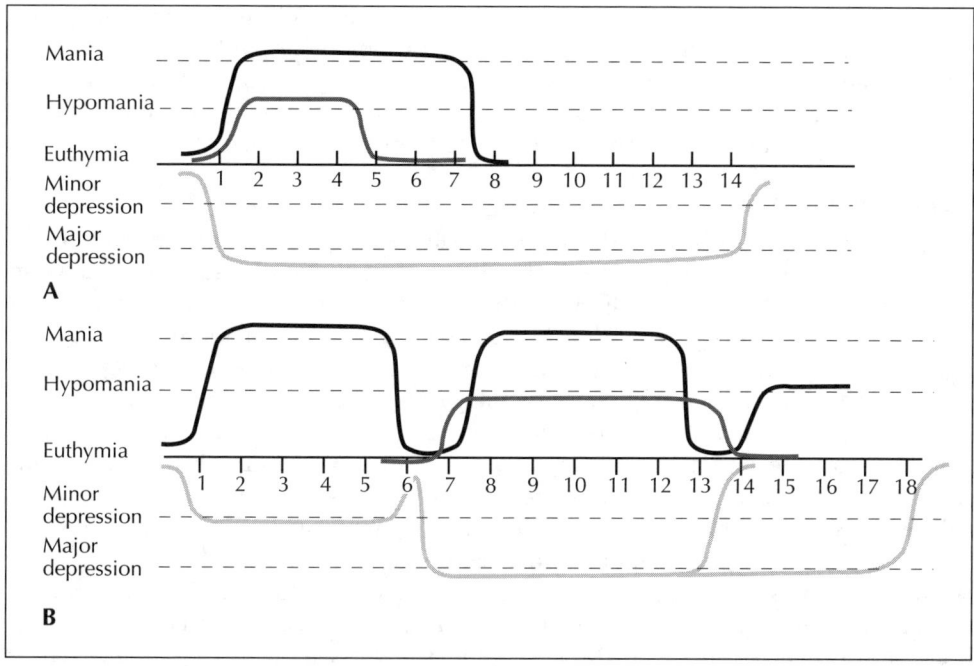

Figure 2. **A**, Acute episodes in bipolar disorder. **B**, Illness patterns not meeting the *Diagnostic and Statistical Manual of Mental Disorders-IV* criteria.

The enzyme induction effects of carbamazepine are now understood to be limited to drugs metabolized all or partly by the 3A4 isozyme of the CYP450 oxidative enzyme family. These include bupropion, nefazadone, alprazolam, triazolam, oral contraceptives, and warfarin, among a relatively large group of psychotropic and nonpsychotropic drugs. The magnitude of these effects is often large. When possible, drug levels of other medicines should be monitored closely during concomitant administration with carbamazepine.

For some but not all patients, the neuromuscular adverse effects of carbamazepine diminish with stable treatment, either as a function of lower plasma levels with autoinduction or organ system adaptation. Rash secondary to carbamazepine is one of the most frequent reasons for discontinuation of medication. In a recent study, 20% of patients terminated treatment with carbamazepine owing to these often hemorrhagic-type rashes [47]. Few systematic long-term data with carbamazepine in bipolar disorder have been published. Two groups have reported that patients initially responding to carbamazepine may lose their response over time [48,49].

Pregnancy

Because the onset of bipolar disorder most often occurs in adolescence or early adulthood, most women will face issues of adapting treatment needs to the wish to have a child. All three mood stabilizers pose some teratogenic risks, although the low base rate for Ebstein's atresia has made it difficult to ascertain the risk with lithium. Neural tube defects may occur in 2% to 4% of patients taking divalproex or carbamazepine, the risk of which is reduced with lower dosage and supplemental folic acid. However, for most patients, a preferred strategy is to discuss these issues well in advance of pregnancy, and develop a plan to discontinue the mood stabilizer promptly on evidence of pregnancy. Small studies indicate a reduced risk of developing an illness episode during pregnancy, although the risk increases dramatically in the postpartum period. It therefore is essential to return the patient to mood stabilization treatment after delivery [50].

Combined drug therapy

Many patients with bipolar disorder are best treated with more than one mood stabilizer, or long-term use of an adjunctive medication. Unlike schizophrenia, wherein adverse effects often drive the need for adjunctive medication, in bipolar disorder the reasons to use more than one drug stem from the inherent complexity of the illness, perhaps greater than any other in psychiatry. A patient may have manic symptomatology with or without irritability, depressive symptomatology, psychotic symptoms, hostility, sleep impairment, and anxiety, all of which may be a focus for treatment, in some instances over the same time period. Furthermore, bipolar disorder is comorbidly associated with panic disorder, migraine headaches, attention deficit hyperactivity disorder, and alcoholism and substance abuse, each of which may require treatment. Here I review some of the more common combinations with an emphasis on when to use, duration of combined use, and possible complications more likely to occur with combined therapy.

Lithium combined with divalproex have been reported effective in an open trial [20]. Their study is particularly instructive in that in a study design focusing on the effectiveness of divalproex in rapid cycling patients, a clinical decision to add lithium or other medications could be made. Under these conditions an approximately equal number of patients were treated with divalproex alone and with divalproex plus lithium. The patients were relatively severely ill—all had current rapid cycling—therefore it is possible that a smaller percentage of patients might need combined drug regimens when a full spectrum of patients, including those with milder symptoms and infrequent episodes, are included.

The regimen has some features to recommend it. There is no pharmacokinetic interaction between the two drugs. Divalproex has no effects on thyroid or renal function and relatively little on cognitive function. Both drugs may cause gastrointestinal adverse effects and weight gain. Based on my experience, it is possible that some patients who benefited but poorly tolerated a standard dose of lithium may be able to obtain adjunctive benefit from lower serum levels of lithium in conduction with divalproex. The report by Citrome [3] suggests that the percentage of patients having adverse effects is higher with combined drug therapy of lithium plus divalproex, as well as the combinations of lithium plus carbamazepine and carbamazepine plus divalproex; however, the sample is an unusual one, consisting of patients with diverse diagnoses treated at a state hospital [51]. Because the study was retrospective, it is possible that patients with more severe forms of the illness received combined treatment, and thus may have received higher doses of at least one drug.

Valproate plus carbamazepine has improved response in some patients [52]. The combination, however, does have the potential for pharmacokinetic interactions through the oxidative enzyme-inducing effects of carbamazepine, which may reduce the serum level of valproate. Lithium and carbamazepine also have been reported to be effective in patients who respond poorly to lithium alone [52].

Dosing Guidelines

Divalproex

Divalproex is comparatively well tolerated, allowing rapid dose escalation to achieve serum levels of at least 45 µg/mL. Acutely manic patients who were hospitalized tolerated well loading doses of 20 to 30 mg per kilogram of body weight, and showed improvement in manic symptoms within 2 days with such a regimen. Characteristic adverse effects of valproate are more likely at serum levels above 125 µg/mL. This provides a relatively broad therapeutic range. Although the half-life of valproate is less than 24 hours, many patients tolerate single bedtime dosing well and appear to retain a benefit similar to that present with divided dosing.

Divalproex may increase hepatic enzymes and elevate ammonia levels. Most authorities do not view modest increases (*eg,* hepatic enzymes that are as high as three times the upper limits of normal) as clinically significant *per se* with most psychotropic drugs, including divalproex and carbamazepine. Patients with current or previous hepatic disease may be at higher risk for valproate-related problems and require closer monitoring. Reduction in platelet count commonly occurs secondary to divalproex use. Only rarely do bleeding complications develop. Platelet counts below 150,000/mm^3 warrant closer assessments. Hair loss may occur secondary to divalproex. Use of the trace metals zinc and selenium in concentrations present in multiple vitamins often rectifies the problem. Elderly patients may have increased sensitivity to the obtunding cognitive impairing effects of divalproex. A trial using a reduced dose is indicated.

Carbamazepine

Carbamazepine requires a relatively slow dosage escalation to reduce the severity of the neuromuscular adverse effects such as ataxia, asthenia, diplopia, and slurred speech. Dosage is begun with 200 mg/d and increased in 200-mg increments every 3 to 5 days until improvement occurs or adverse effects develop. No clear serum level guides to efficacy have been established. Nonetheless, serum level monitoring is important to ensure that levels do not exceed 12 to 14 µg/mL.

Psychotherapy

There is a prima facia case for psychotherapeutic management of bipolar disorder; however, there has been little systematic study and much less experimental study of the issue. It is useful to group psychotherapy services by goals. Almost all patients will need an educational experience about the disease and its treatment. This can be accomplished in three stages. The focus during an acute manic episode is to help a person recognize his behavior as symptoms and signs of illness. This is sometimes difficult, because the inherent impaired judgment and impaired insight of the illness work against this effort. Once patients come to some degree of recognition, they can more usefully and collaboratively comment on the effects of medication. This knowledge also is an essential platform for the next stage of treatment.

The second stage of treatment is to recognize the impact that the behavior during the illness episode has on others, especially close family and coworkers. For this reason, it is useful to involve family members in treatment visits because understanding of the impact on the family is essential if the patient is to commit to long-term treatment. This second stage also can be aided by groups, Depressive and Manic Depressive Association programs, the several books about bipolar disorder for lay persons, and most of all time. For most persons it is difficult to accept the implications of an illness that is likely to be present for life. Procreativity, career options, and family relationships may all be effected, and the person must deal with medication regimens, side effects, and the cost and intrusiveness of treatments. If the disorder first occurs when the person is still a teenager, issues of maturity and development can make this even more emotionally difficult to negotiate.

A third stage of more traditional psychotherapy is not needed by most patients, but may be particularly important on an individual basis. This may need to address reconciliation of effects of the illness on life goals, or developmentally affected coping and character issues. A unique dimension is that many patients with bipolar disorder were reared by parents whose parenting behavior toward the patient and other children was influenced by the impulsive and erratic behavior and by the impaired judgment associated with expression of bipolar disorder in their own lives. Thus, the patient may have troubling memories and consequences of such unstable parental efforts.

Conclusions

Treatment of bipolar disorder is complex but gratifying. The complexity is a function of the multiple types of episodes that may occur, the rapidity of onset of symptoms in some individuals, and the many environmental factors that can destabilize otherwise well-functioning patients. Furthermore, treatments are multifaceted, with differing adjunctive treatments needed as a consequence of the stage of illness, but with the fundamental mood-stabilizing regimen continued throughout. The gratifying aspect is that most patients have responses that yield not only symptomatic recovery but, often, full functional capability.

References and Recommended Reading

Papers of particular interest, published recently, have been highlighted as:
* Of special interest
•• Of outstanding interest

1. Bowden CL, Brugger AM, Swann AC, et al.: Efficacy of divalproex vs lithium and placebo in the treatment of mania. *JAMA* 1994, 271:918–924.
2. Lambert PA, Venaud G: Comparative study of valpromide versus lithium as prophylactic treatment in affective disorders. *Nervure Journal de Psychiatrie* 1995, 7:1–9.
3. Citrome L: The use of lithium, carbamazepine, and valproic acid in a state operated psychiatric hospital. *J Pharm Technol* 1995, 11:55–59.
4. Lerer B, Moore N, Meyendorff, et al.: Carbamazepine versus lithium in mania: a double-blind study. *J Clin Psychiatry* 1987, 48:89–93.
5. Janicak PG, Davis JM, Preskorn SH, et al.: *Principles and Practice of Psychopharmacotherapy.* Baltimore: Williams & Wilkins; 1993.
6. Dwight MM, Keck PE, Stanton SP, et al.: Antidepressant activity and mania associated with risperidone treatment of schizoaffective disorder. *Lancet* 1994, 344:555–556.
7. Tohen M, Zarate CA, Jr, Centorrino F, et al.: Risperidone in the treatment of mania. *J Clin Psychiatry* 1996, 57:249–253.
8. Suppes T, McElroy SL, Gilbert J, et al.: Clozapine in the treatment of dysphoric mania. *Biol Psychiatry* 1992, 32:270–280.

9. Barton BM, Gitlin MJ: Verapamil in treatment-resistant mania: an open trial. *J Clin Psychopharmacol* 1987, 7:101–103.

10. Janicak PG, Sharma R, Peterson J, *et al.*: A double-blind, placebo-controlled trial of verapamil for acute mania: Preliminary results. *ACNP Abstracts of Panels and Posters* 1993:245.

11. Dubovsky SI, Franks RD, Allen S, *et al.*: Calcium antagonists in mania: a double blind study of verapamil. *Psychiatry Res* 18:1986, 309–320.

12. Giannini AJ, House WL, Loiselle RH: Antimanic effects of verapamil. *Am J Psychiatry* 1984, 141:1602–1603.

13. Garza-Trevino ES, Overall JE, Hollister LE: Verapamil versus lithium in acute mania. *Am J Psychiatry* 1992, 149:121–122.

14. Small JG, Klapper MH, Kellams JJ, *et al.*: Electroconvulsive treatment compared with lithium in the management of manic states. *Arch Gen Psychiatry* 1988, 45:727–732.

15. Black DW, Winokur G, Nasrallah H: Treatment of mania: a naturalistic study of electroconvulsive therapy versus lithium in 438 patients. *J Clin Psychiatry* 1987, 48:132–139.

16. Secunda SK, Katz MM, Swann A, *et al.*: Mania: diagnosis, state measurement and prediction of treatment response. *J Affect Disord* 1985, 8:113–121.

17.• Swann AC, Bowden CL, Morris D, *et al.*: Depression during mania: treatment response to lithium or divalproex. *Arch Gen Psychiatry* 1997, 54:37–42.

Most systematic data on responsive numbers of mixed mania to treatments.

18. Okuma T: Effects of carbamazepine and lithium on affective disorders. *Neuropsychobiology* 1993, 27:138–145.

19. Freeman TW, Clothier JL, Pazzaglia P, *et al.*: A double-blind comparison of valproate and lithium in the treatment of acute mania. *Am J Psychiatry* 1992, 149:108–111.

20. Calabrese JR, Delucchi GA: Spectrum of efficacy of valproate in 55 patients with rapid-cycling bipolar disorder. *Am J Psychiatry* 1990, 147:431–434.

21. McElroy SL, Keck PE Jr, Pope HG, *et al.*: Clinical and research implications of the diagnosis of dysphoric or mixed mania or hypomania. *Am J Psychiatry* 1992, 149: 1633–1644.

22. Dunner DL, Fieve RR: Clinical factors in lithium carbonate prophylaxis failure. *Arch Gen Psychiatry* 1974, 30:229–233.

23. Dunner DL, Fleiss JL, Fieve RR: The course of development of mania in patients with recurrent depression. *Am J Psychiatry* 1976, 133:905–908.

24. Denicoff KD, Smith-Jackson E, Disney E, et al.: Carbamazepine, lithium and the combination: a bipolar maintenance trial. *Proceedings of the American Psychiatric Association* 1995: 178.

25. Bauer MS, Whybrow PC: Rapid cycling bipolar affective disorder: II. Treatment of refractory rapid cycling with high-dose levothyroxine: a preliminary study. *Arch Gen Psychiatry* 1990, 47:435–440.

26. Carroll BT, Goforth HW, Dueno OR, *et al.*: Mood disorder due to general medical conditions: frequency, treatment, and response. *Psychosomatics* 1995, 36:167–168.

27. Himmelhoch JM, Garfinkel ME: Sources of lithium resistance in mixed mania. *Psychopharmacol Bull* 1986, 22:613–620.

28. Tohen M, Shulman KI, Satlin A: First-episode mania in late life. *Am J Psychiatry* 1994, 151:130–132.

29. Kahn D, Stevenson E, Douglas CJ: Effect of sodium valproate in three patients with organic brain syndromes. *Am J Psychiatry* 1988, 145:1010–1011.

30. O'Connell RA, Mayo JA, Flatow L, *et al.*: Outcome of bipolar disorder on long-term treatment with lithium. *Br J Psychiatry* 1991, 159:123–129.

31. Brady KT, Sonne SC: The relationship between substance abuse and bipolar disorder. *J Clin Psychiatry* 1995, 56:19–24.

32. Bowden CL, Calabrese JR, Wallin BA, *et al.*: Who enters therapeutic trials? Illness characteristics of patients in clinical drug studies of mania. *Psychopharmacol Bull* 1995, 31:103–109.

33. Vahip S, Ozkan B, Ayan A, *et al.*: Elevation of plasma lithium at the end of mania and some biochemical correlates [abstract]. *Second International Conference on New Directions in Affective Disorders, Jerusalem.* Jerusalem: Israel Psychiatric Association; 1995:31.

34. Shulman KI, Tohen M, Satlin A, *et al.*: Mania compared with unipolar depression in old age. *Am J Psychiatry* 1992, 149:341–345.

35. Stoll AL, Banov M, Kolbrener M, *et al.*: Neurologic factors predict a favorable valproate response in bipolar and schizoaffective disorders. *J Clin Psychopharmacol* 1994, 14:311–313.

36. Goodwin FK, Jamison KR: *Manic-Depressive Illness.* New York: Oxford University Press; 1990.

37. Lenox RH, Newhouse PA, Creelman WL, *et al.*: Adjunctive treatment of manic agitation with lorazepam versus haloperidol: a double-blind study. *J Clin Psychiatry* 1992, 53:47–52.

38. Dunner DL, Fieve RR: Clinical factors in lithium carbonate prophylaxis: tranylcypromine versus imipramine in anergic bipolar depression. *Am J Psychiatry* 1991, 148:910–916.

39. Sachs GS, Lafer B, Stoll AL, *et al.*: A double-blind trial of bupropion versus desipramine for bipolar depression. *J Clin Psychiatry* 1994, 55:391–393.

40. Barton BM, Gitlin MJ. Verapamil in treatment-resistant mania: an open trial. *J Clin Psychopharmacol* 1987, 7:101–103.

41. Fieve RR, Platman SR, Plutchik RR: The use of lithium in affective disorders: I. Acute endogenous depression. *Am J Psychiatry* 1968, 125:487–491.

42. Mitchell P: Valproate for rapid-cycling unipolar affective disorder. *J Nerv Ment Dis* 1991, 179:503–504.

43. Faedda GL, Tondo L, Baldessarini RJ, *et al.*: Outcome after rapid vs. gradual discontinuation of lithium treatment in bipolar disorders. *Arch Gen Psychiatry* 1991, 50:448–456.

44. Keller MB, Lavori PW, Coryell W, *et al.*: Differential outcome of pure manic, mixed/cycling, and pure depressive episodes in patients with bipolar illness. *JAMA* 1986, 255:3138–3142.

45. Gelenberg AJ, Kane JM, Keller MB, *et al.*: Comparison of standard and low serum levels of lithium for maintenance treatment of bipolar disorder. *N Engl J Med* 1989, 321:1489–1493.

46. Sachs GS, Lafer B, Truman CJ, *et al.*: Lithium monotherapy: miracle, myth and misunderstanding. *Psychiatr Ann* 1994, 24:299–305.

47. Denicoff KD, Smith-Jackson E, Disney E, *et al.*: Carbamazepine, lithium and the combination: a bipolar maintenance trial. *Proceedings of the American Psychiatric Association* 1995:178.

48. Frankenburg FR, Tohen M, Cohen BM, *et al.*: Long-term response to carbamazepine: a retrospective study. *J Clin Psychopharmacol* 1988, 8:130–132.

49. Post RM, Leverich GS, Rosoff AS, *et al.*: Carbamazepine prophylaxis in refractory affective disorders: a focus on long-term follow-up. *J Clin Psychopharmacol* 1990, 10:318–327.

50. Lier L, Kastrup M, Rafaelsen OJ: Psychiatric illness in relation to childbirth and pregnancy: II. Diagnostic profiles, psychosocial and perinatal aspects. *Nord Psychitr Tidsskrift* 1989, 43:535–542.

51. Ketter TA, Pazzaglia PJ, Post RM: Synergy of carbamazepine and valproic acid in affective illness: case report and review of the literature. *J Clin Psychopharm* 1992, 12:276–281.

52. Kramlinger KG, Post RM: Adding lithium carbonate to carbamazepine: anti-manic efficacy in treatment resistant mania. *Acta Psychiatr Scand* 1989, 79:378–385.

CHAPTER 6

Electroconvulsive Therapy for Mood Disorders

Joan Prudic and Harold A. Sackeim

This chapter reviews the recent literature on the role of electroconvulsive therapy in treating mood disorders. Topics covered include indications and evidence for efficacy, and technical aspects (eg, stimulus characteristics, electrode placement, treatment duration and frequency, use of drugs during treatment). Side effects and relapse rates are also discussed.

Convulsive therapy was introduced by Meduna in 1934, using intramuscular injection of camphor in oil for seizure induction. This method of seizure elicitation was soon replaced by use of pentylenetetrazol and, later, electrical stimulation. Electrical induction of seizures became the preferred method and the major form of biologic treatment in psychiatry until the emergence of psychotropic medications in the 1950s. In the following two decades, the use of electroconvulsive therapy (ECT) decreased, owing largely to the efficacy of pharmacologic strategies, the ease of their use, and the lack of the cognitive side effects that were seen with ECT. In the 1970s, greater awareness of the limitations of psychotropic medications, including concerns about medication resistance, safety, and persistent side effects, led to a renewed interest in ECT and more systematic inquiry about its use. The role of ECT in therapeutics was the subject of a National Institutes of Health (NIH) Consensus Conference in 1985 [1]. In 1990, the American Psychiatric Association Task Force on ECT issued a comprehensive statement of standards of care, training, and privileging [2].

Since the 1980s, rates of ECT use in the United States have stabilized and perhaps have increased [3]. In the current era, there is greater use of ECT in private hospitals and academic centers than in public facilities, contradicting the claims of ECT opponents that the treatment is a method of behavior control inflicted on the poor and disadvantaged. Within the United States, about 80% of those who receive ECT have major depression [3]. Hence, women are more likely to receive ECT than men. For the remaining 20%, schizophrenia and mania are the most common indications. Presumably, because of medication resistance and intolerance and the superior medical safety profile of ECT, the elderly are more likely to receive ECT than are younger patients [4].

Indications and Evidence for Efficacy

Major depression

The short-term efficacy of ECT for major depression, both unipolar and bipolar, is established. ECT may be used as a treatment of first choice when there is a need for rapid, definitive response on medical or psychiatric grounds; when the risks of other treatments outweigh the risks of ECT; or when there is a prior history of good ECT response in previous episodes. However, ECT is more frequently used as a second-line treatment, particularly when medication resistance or intolerance has occurred [5]. There continues to be concern about using ECT, the most effective antidepressant treatment, only as a last-resort treatment, particularly in inpatient settings. Not surprisingly, there also continues to be considerable variability in practice concerning when in the course of treatment ECT is employed.

Before the introduction of psychotropic medications, numerous uncontrolled studies of depressed patients reported response rates varying between 80% and 100% [1]. Many of these studies compared outcomes for patients who received inadequate or no somatic treatment with those of patients who received ECT, and none used prospective, randomized design. Nonetheless, results were largely uniform: ECT resulted in decreased chronicity, morbidity, and possibly mortality, particularly among the elderly [6].

Following the introduction of monoamine oxidase inhibitors (MAOIs) and tricyclic antidepressants (TCAs), the efficacy of these psychotropics was studied, using comparison with ECT as the gold standard. In a meta-analysis, Janicak et al. [7] reported that the average response rate for ECT was 20% higher relative to TCAs and 45% higher relative to MAOIs. Although the extent of residual symptomatology following pharmacologic treatment and ECT has not been extensively investigated, Hamilton [8] found that a higher percentage of depressed patients became asymptomatic after ECT compared with TCA therapy. Unfortunately, two methodologic limitations characterize this body of work relative to modern standards: the dosage and duration of medication was often suboptimal, and comparisons were not double-blind.

During the 1970s and 1980s, a group of double-blind, random assignment trials were conducted comparing ECT with "sham ECT," a condition in which anesthesia alone was administered. ECT was consistently found more effective than sham ECT, except in one study, now known to have employed a form of ECT that has limited efficacy (see Sackeim [6] for a review). This work demonstrated that the passage of an electrical stimulus or the elicitation of a generalized seizure are necessary for antidepressant effects.

Although ECT is an effective antidepressant treatment for all subtypes of depression, early work from the 1950s and 1960s indicated that melancholic or endogenous subtypes predicted positive clinical outcome (see Nobler and Sackeim [9] for a review). It appears that this association was largely due to the inclusion of patients with "neurotic" depression or dysthymia in samples. Later studies that required a diagnosis of major depression suggested no predictive value for melancholic or endogenous symptom presentation [10,11].

More recent studies have identified other clinical features as predictive of outcome. In several studies, age was positively associated with ECT response [6]. Another group of studies showed that a shorter duration of the current episode was also positively correlated with response [9]. Finally, some studies found better outcome among patients with psychotic depression than among those with the nonpsychotic form [12,13]. Unfortunately, the predictive relationships found in these studies are of insufficient strength to guide treatment recommendations.

Unlike the prepharmacologic era when ECT was used as treatment of first choice, the samples of patients with depression now referred for ECT have a high representation of those who have failed adequate trials of antidepressant medications. In spite of this altered profile, little research has examined whether expectations about response rates should be changed relative to the prepharmacologic era. Prudic *et al.* [5] reported that patients who failed one or more adequate TCA trials had a 50% response rate to subsequent bilateral ECT, compared with an 86% response rate for patients not determined to be medication-resistant. Although ECT was of considerable benefit to many patients who were treatment-resistant, TCA resistance was predictive of relative nonresponse.

A variety of biologic measures have been examined as potential predictors of ECT outcome, including neurotransmitter levels, neuroendocrine measures, and electroencephalographic (EEG) and other brain-imaging methods. None of these investigations has resulted in consistent findings [9,10]. There has been increasing emphasis on studies of treatment adequacy as an approach to ensuring optimal outcome. Although, in the past, it was believed that generalized seizures of sufficient duration were enough to ensure maximal therapeutic effect, it is now recognized that seizures of "adequate" duration can be reliably produced that lack efficacy, and that seizure duration bears little relation to efficacy [14]. Preliminary research suggests that specific features of the ictal EEG, such as the presence of postictal suppression, may be associated with superior clinical response [15].

Mania

A recent review of five decades of experience with ECT in the treatment of mania concluded that approximately 80% of 589 patients with this disorder responded [16]. Retrospective controlled comparisons found ECT to be equivalent to lithium and chlorpromazine [17] and superior to chlorpromazine alone [16]. A prospective study compared sham with real ECT in patients who were manic, and who had been maintained on chlorpromazine, and found a 75% response rate in the ECT group compared with a 6% response in the sham and neuroleptic group [18]. A prospective controlled study comparing ECT and lithium found equal response rates, with quicker onset of response with ECT [19]. A prospective study of patients who were manic and who failed potent trials of lithium or neuroleptics compared ECT with combination treatment with Li and haloperidol. There was a robust response to ECT, but no response to combination pharmacology [20]. Thus, it is evident that ECT is effective in the treatment of acute mania, and it may be especially helpful in patients who are medication-resistant. There is limited information of the efficacy of ECT among rapid-cycling patients, and no comparisons of ECT with anticonvulsant medications.

Schizophrenia

The use of ECT in schizophrenia is more uncertain than in mood disorders. Early reports of uncontrolled case series estimated response rates on the order of 75%. However, this information is qualified by limitations concerning the validity of diagnosis and questionable outcome criteria. In addition, there have been several prospective, controlled trials (*see* Krueger and Sackeim [21] for a review). The findings from real versus sham ECT studies were contradictory: four early studies with chronic samples failed to show an advantage for ECT; three later studies in which patients with less chronic disease were maintained on neuroleptics during the study showed superior short-term outcome with ECT versus sham treatment. The discrepancy between these two groups of studies may be due to the preponderance of acute versus chronic disease subtypes and the suspected advantage of combination ECT–neuroleptic treatment relative to ECT alone. A series of prospective, controlled studies comparing monotherapy with ECT to monotherapy with a neuroleptic generally found ECT to be equal or somewhat inferior in short-term outcome. These data were limited because they preceded the use of current diagnostic criteria and the development of study methods using random assignment and standardized, blind evaluation of outcome. However, these studies were among the first to suggest that, in the long-term, the use of ECT in the treatment of schizophrenia might result in superior outcome. Of particular note, all three comparisons of combination ECT and neuroleptic with ECT alone found the combination to be superior. Similarly, six of seven comparisons of combination ECT and neuroleptic with neuroleptic alone found that the combination treatment was superior in short-term outcome. This pattern held even though in several studies the neuroleptic dose in the combination treatment group was lower compared with that in the neuroleptic alone group. This body of research also suggested that there were lower relapse or recurrence rates among patients originally treated with combination ECT and a neuroleptic, although subsequent maintenance treatment was uncontrolled. Overall, it is not difficult to understand why there are differences in the recommendation of expert bodies on the role of ECT in the treatment of schizophrenia [1,2,22].

Currently, ECT is usually reserved for patients who are neuroleptic-resistant. There has not been a controlled, random assignment study of the usefulness of ECT in this subgroup. Eight reports, beginning in the 1960s, have indicated positive response, even in patients with a chronic form. Given the uncontrolled nature of these observations, there is reason to be circumspect. Combination ECT–clozapine treatments have been the subject of only a small case series [21].

Because ECT has both antipsychotic and antiparkinsonian effects, it may also have a role in the amelioration of movement disorders resulting from neuroleptics. Recently, evidence suggests that ECT may improve or forestall the development of neuroleptic-induced parkinsonism [16,23,24]. It is also possible that ECT may decrease the incidence of tardive dyskinesia, either by direct effects or by minimizing the need for neuroleptics [25–27].

Less common indications

Electroconvulsive therapy is occasionally used for other psychiatric and medical syndromes. There are anecdotal reports describing a favorable short-term outcome for obsessive–compulsive disorder (OCD) when treated with ECT [2]. Khanna et al. [28] reported a small, prospective sample of medication- and behavior-therapy resistant non-depressed patients with OCD who showed marked acute response to ECT. ECT may be efficacious for patients who are catatonic and who fail benzodiazepine treatment [29].

In addition to psychiatric syndromes, there are medical and neurologic entities that may respond to ECT. Delirium resulting from various causes, including alcohol withdrawal, phencyclidine, organic mental states associated with enteric fever, and systemic lupus erythematosus have been successfully treated with ECT [2], although it is now rarely used for these purposes. ECT ameliorates symptoms of idiopathic Parkinson disease and briefly reduces requirements for levodopa in both open and sham-controlled trials [2,10]. Neuroleptic malignant syndrome (NMS), a variety of iatrogenic lethal catatonia, appears to respond well to ECT compared with medical treatments, such as bromocriptine, dantrolene, levodopa, or amantadine [30], and may be useful when there is a need for antipsychotic treatment as well as treatment of NMS, after a patient has been autonomically stabilized. The case literature suggests that the anticonvulsant properties of ECT may be useful for medication-resistant epilepsy or prolonged status epilepticus [2].

Evaluation for Electroconvulsive Therapy
Standard evaluation
There are several components to preparation for ECT [2]. These include psychiatric, medical, and anesthesiologic evaluations. The psychiatric history and examination should include a determination of indications. A referral for ECT is often made in situations for which rapid, definitive response is necessitated on psychiatric or medical grounds (Table 1). Examples include imminent suicidal threat, inanition, or manic delirium. Under these circumstances, ECT may be a primary treatment. Other circumstances for which ECT may be used as a first-line treatment include patient preference and a history of poor response to psychotropic agents or a beneficial response to ECT. However, ECT is more often used when there has been failure to respond to psychotropic agents or intolerance of such agents. The history of prior ECT treatment courses should be specified. Pre-ECT cognitive evaluation should be made to establish a baseline and assist in identifying the need for further neurologic evaluation. At the least, this should include assessment of orientation, concentration, and remote and short-term memory. Evaluations of visuospatial performance and language function are recommended, particularly if patients are not confined to an inpatient unit during their treatment course. Both objective measures and subjective reports should be elicited.

There should be an evaluation by an individual privileged to administer ECT. Such an evaluation includes consideration of indications and risks of treatment, and may include recommendations for additional evaluations, alterations in ongoing medication regimens, and modification of ECT technique. It may be recommended that medical agents, which may be protective against adverse medical effects, be given during the period a patient is ordinarily fasted pretreatment. Such medications include antihypertensives, antiarrhythmics, antianginal agents, and steroids. Both psychotropic and medical agents should be reviewed for their effect on risks associated with ECT and on the efficacy of treatment. Benzodiazepines, sedative-hypnotics [31,32], anticonvulsants, and

---

Table 1. Indications for Use of Electroconvulsive Therapy

Primary use	Secondary use
Rapid definitive response on medical or psychiatric grounds is required	Failure to respond to pharmacotherapy
	Pharmacotherapy intolerance
Risks of alternative treatments outweigh benefits	Deterioration of patient's condition during pharmacotherapy such that need for rapid definitive response is necessary
History of poor response to psychotropics or good response to ECT in previous episode of illness	
Patient preference	

ECT—electroconvulsive therapy.

lidocaine [33] and its analogues may increase seizure threshold or decrease seizure duration, with possible consequences for the efficacy of ECT. Lithium increases the risk of delirium during treatment [34]. Reserpine has been associated with death at treatment, and theophylline is associated with increased risk of prolonged seizures, even if theophylline levels are within the therapeutic range [35,36]. Although it is often advisable to discontinue psychotropics, because presumably, there has been no response to them and there is no evidence of synergism with ECT for most agents, withdrawal effects are a consideration. Low- to moderate-dose neuroleptics can be useful for psychotic patients, and the combination of ECT with neuroleptics may be superior in some situations. It does not appear that an appreciable drug-free period is necessary for MAOIs as had been recommended in the past [37].

To identify risks, especially in the neurologic and cardiopulmonary systems, the medical evaluation should minimally include a history and physical examination, vital signs, electrolytes and hematocrit–hemoglobin values, and an electrocardiogram (ECG). Anesthesia evaluation should focus on the ability to tolerate anesthesia and the need to alter the usual medications and techniques used.

Situations of higher risk

Because ECT has been in use since the 1930s, the assessment of risk has changed over time. Initially, ECT was given without anesthetic modification, and the associated risks were fracture, prolonged or spontaneous seizures, and cardiac or cerebral decompensation, sometimes leading to death. With the introduction of the use of brief anesthetics and muscle relaxants, the risk of fracture has been practically eliminated. Seizure complications are managed with medications, and the probability of risk can often be estimated before pretreatment. Cerebral and cardiac problems are frequently recognized in the pre-ECT evaluation. With advances in techniques for the characterization and management of patients with brain lesions, even the presence of brain tumor is not an absolute contraindication to ECT. Patients with small, slow-growing lesions, without associated increased intracranial pressure, have received ECT safely [38]. Progress in cardiology has been applied to ECT procedure to minimize risks of cardiac decompensation as well.

As ECT is now practiced, each treatment situation should be evaluated for risk–benefit considerations. Such a rubric takes into account the severity of psychiatric illness and its threat to life, the likelihood of therapeutic success with ECT, the medical risk attendant to ECT, and the risks and benefits of alternative treatment or even no treatment. Medical conditions that substantially increase risk are described in Table 2. Retinal detachment is also accompanied by increased risk to sight.

Special populations

Advancing age does not correlate with any change in the efficacy of ECT. However, the elderly generally have increased medical burden, which is reflected in increased risk for all somatic treatments, including ECT. Other issues impinge on the use of ECT in the elderly. These include changes in pharmacokinetics, which may necessitate alterations in anesthetic medication doses. Another area requiring attention is the age-associated increase in seizure threshold, which affects the electrical dosage at treatment. Cognitive deficits are increasingly common with age, and preexisting cognitive deficits may increase

Table 2. Medical Conditions Associated with Increased Risk for Electroconvulsive Therapy

Medical condition	Intervention to decrease risk
Space-occupying brain lesions	Neurologic or neurosurgical consultation; ECT may be possible if mass is small and is not associated with increased intracranial pressure or edema
Increased intracranial pressure	Neurologic or neurosurgical consultation to determine risk of adverse events such as herniation
Recent intracranial bleeding	Consultation to assess degree of healing and risk of rebleeding; need to use antihypertensives at ECT
Recent myocardial infarct	Cardiologic consultation to determine stability of current cardiac status and to determine risk of ischemia, arrhythmia
Aneurysm	Consultation to determine instability of aneurysm and whether abolishing changes in blood pressure or heart rate associated with ECT will allow treatment
Retinal detachment	Ophthalmologic consultation to assess risk associated with increased intraocular pressure at ECT
Pheochromocytoma	Medical consultation to determine whether adequate blockade of blood pressure changes will permit ECT

ECT—electroconvulsive therapy.

vulnerability to the cognitive side effects of ECT [39•]. Patients should be frequently assessed, and modifications of electrode placement, stimulus intensity, and frequency of treatment should be considered, as determined by such assessments.

Electroconvulsive therapy may be used in all trimesters of pregnancy. Risks of teratogenesis from barbiturate anesthesia in the first trimester are not well understood, and they should be considered in the recommendation and consent processes. Brief exposure during ECT is probably less hazardous than constant exposure to psychotropic medications, such as lithium and benzodiazepines. Obstetric consultation and modifications of the treatment setting and technique may be necessary, including fetal monitoring, intubation, and equipment and personnel to manage obstetric emergencies.

Data on the use of ECT in children are sparse, partly because affective syndromes in children are less commonly identified and also because of theoretic concerns that induced seizures may be more toxic in children. No controlled studies have been conducted with ECT in children, and generally, other treatments must be considered first. However, youth is not an absolute contraindication. Case reports suggest that well-defined affective syndromes in children respond to ECT. Because of its rare use, special consultation is generally obtained and treatment is undertaken with anesthetists experienced with children. There is more experience in the use of ECT with adolescents, ages 13 to 17, but similar cautions are taken with this age group.

Technical Issues
Stimulus characteristics
The physical properties of the ECT electrical stimulus affect both efficacy and cognitive side effects. Over the several decades of ECT practice, a variety of devices that produced differing waveforms were used. Presently, the two basic waveforms are sine wave and

brief pulse. Sine-wave stimulation is characterized by a gradual increase in current intensity to maximum and a gradual offset, resulting in a long phase duration. Brief-pulse stimulation is characterized by near instantaneous peak current intensity, with quick return to baseline. Because the rising edge of current flow is largely responsible for neuronal depolarization, sine-wave stimulation is less efficient and is associated with greater cognitive side effects and greater disruption of EEG than brief-pulse stimulation [40,41].

Electrode placement and stimulus intensity

An earlier set of studies drew attention to the importance of seizure elicitation as fundamental to efficacy. Ulett *et al.* [42] found inferior clinical outcome with subconvulsive electrical stimuli. Comparisons of chemical induction of seizures with ECT suggested that chemical induction has at least equivalent therapeutic efficacy, but resulted in possibly less cognitive impairment. Ottosson [33] compared a standard suprathreshold stimulus, a standard stimulus attenuated by the anticonvulsant properties of lidocaine, and a stimulus substantially higher than the standard and unmodified by lidocaine. The lidocaine group had diminished therapeutic response, and the higher electrical intensity group had intensified cognitive side effects. These studies led to the view that the seizure was necessary and sufficient for antidepressant efficacy, and that the intensity of the electrical stimulus determined the magnitude of cognitive side effects, but had no role in efficacy.

More recent studies have modified these principles. Generalized seizures can be reliably produced and yet have very limited antidepressant effects [14]. Right unilateral ECT with stimulus dosage near threshold is ineffective, whereas bilateral ECT with stimulus near threshold is a powerful antidepressant. Robin and de Tissera [43] compared three electrical waveforms that differed in stimulus intensity and reported that less intense stimulation resulted in a slower rate of clinical response. Taken together, these studies suggested that electrical dosage influences the efficacy of right unilateral ECT and the speed of both right unilateral and bilateral ECT. These hypotheses were confirmed more recently [44]. This work also suggested that dosage above threshold, rather than absolute dosage, is the critical determinant of the effects on clinical response, rate of response, and cognitive side effects (Fig. 1).

Thus, the seizure may be necessary, but not sufficient, for ECT to be effective, and technical aspects of treatment delivery have a profound effect on clinical response. From a mechanistic perspective, the interaction of electrode placement and dosage in determining efficacy suggests that specific current pathways may be critical for antidepressant effects, and that there may be anatomic specificity in functional systems therapeutically altered by ECT.

Adequacy and number of treatments

Typically, a minimum seizure duration of 20 to 30 seconds by motor or EEG criteria has been recommended. However, little data support this recommendation. Were seizure duration contributory to efficacy, one would expect that patients with longer seizure duration require fewer treatments. This effect has never been observed. Indeed, elderly patients with high seizure thresholds have seizure durations that are short initially and can shorten below the 20-second limit early in the treatment course. These patients have not been shown to require more treatments than other patients. Furthermore, right unilateral treatment near

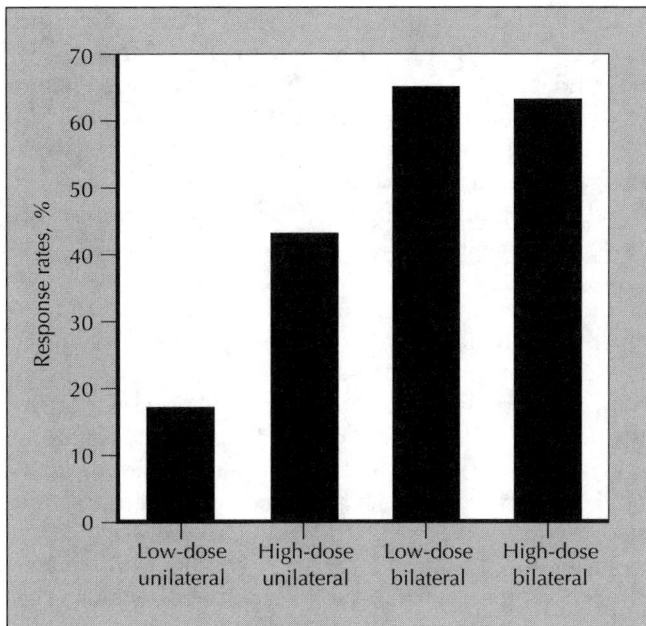

Figure 1. Response rates as a function of stimulus intensity and electrode placement during electroconvulsive therapy.

threshold, meeting duration requirements as just cited, can be remarkably ineffective [14,44]. Indeed, it is now accepted that high-intensity electrical stimulation results in a more robust EEG seizure expression, but a shorter seizure duration relative to treatments at lower electrical intensity [45]. There are, however, circumstances for which seizure duration may be of value in determining treatment adequacy: durations of less than 15 seconds are often indicators of inadequate stimulus intensity or the confounding effects of concurrent medication. Short durations in patients with high initial seizure thresholds, who typically experience substantial increases in threshold during the treatment course, may suggest the need for technical modifications that maintain electrical dosage above seizure threshold.

There is no substitute for close clinical evaluation in determining the adequacy of a treatment course and, in particular, the number of treatments needed. Complete absence of response after six to ten treatments indicates the need to reassess the original treatment indications or consider changes in treatment technique; for example, switching from unilateral to bilateral electrode placement or increasing stimulus dosage. The number of treatments administered is a function of achieving maximal therapeutic gain, either by the attainment of complete remission or a plateau in symptom change over two or three consecutive treatments. Finally, there is no benefit for additional treatments once this end point has been achieved [46].

Frequency of treatment

Practitioners in the United States generally give ECT three times weekly, whereas treatment courses in Britain and other settings are often on a twice-weekly schedule. Strömgren *et al.* [47,48] retrospectively compared patients who were depressed and who received unilateral treatment two or four times weekly and found a trend toward better response during the first six treatments with four-times weekly ECT, with no difference in cognitive side effects. McAllister *et al.* [49] randomly assigned patients with depression to two- or three-times weekly unilateral ECT in a single-blind fashion and found no difference in response at 2 and 4 weeks, but greater impairment of visual memory in the three-times weekly group. Kellner *et al.* [50] compared once weekly to three-times weekly ECT in a single-blind, randomized fashion, and found an advantage for three-times weekly ECT in the rate and speed of response, without differences in cognitive side effects. These studies, unfortunately, were single-blind or open in design and had limited cognitive-testing batteries.

Sham-controlled studies have also been conducted. Gangadhar *et al.* [51] randomly assigned patients with depression, many of whom were also receiving TCAs during the ECT course, to twice-weekly ECT with one sham session per week or to three-times weekly ECT. There was no difference in response at any time point; cognitive side effects were not assessed. More recently, Lerer *et al.* [52] conducted a double-blind, randomized trial, comparing twice-weekly ECT, with one sham session per week, with three-times weekly ECT, using bilateral, brief-pulse stimulation. Final response rates were similar, but the speed of response was more rapid with three-times weekly ECT. Cognitive side effects were less pronounced with twice-weekly treatment. In general, twice weekly ECT is effective, with the potential advantage of less severe cognitive side effects, whereas a three-times weekly schedule may be indicated when rapid onset of response is critical.

Pharmacologic agents during treatment

Agents that increase the risk of adverse effects are problematic. Adenosine antagonists, particularly theophylline, can lengthen seizure duration and have been implicated in status epilepticus following ECT, even when maintained at therapeutic levels [36]. Lidocaine and its analogues alter the seizure characteristics and attenuate efficacy [53,54]. Echothiopate, used for glaucoma, has anticholinesterase activity and may interact adversely with anesthetic agents. Early reports of deaths at ECT in the presence of reserpine [55,56] dictate that it be discontinued before ECT [2].

Psychotropic agents may also affect the safety and efficacy of ECT. Anticonvulsants may be required in epileptic patients receiving ECT, but their capacity to increase seizure threshold or interfere with seizure propagation suggests discontinuation in patients for whom the use of these medications is psychiatric. Pettinati *et al.* [57] reported that the use of benzodiazepines concurrently with unilateral ECT was associated with decreased antidepressant efficacy, and it has generally been recommended that sedative agents with shorter half-lives be used only when necessary. High-dose neuroleptics are considered a risk factor for prolonged seizures. Lithium can also lead to prolonged seizures and is associated with noticeable increases in confusional states when used with ECT in some patients [34].

In addition to adverse affects, there is evidence for potentiating or augmenting therapeutic effects with the use of pharmacologic agents. Low to moderate doses of neuroleptics may be superior to either neuroleptic or ECT alone when used for schizophrenia spectrum disorders [21]. There has been increasing interest in the thyroid axis as an area for intervention. Stern *et al.* [58] compared liothyronine with placebo in a double-blind study and found that patients receiving it required fewer ECT and exhibited fewer cognitive side effects. Khan *et al.* [59] reported a study of eight patients in whom 0.5 mg of thyrotropin-releasing hormone (TRH) was administered 5 minutes post-ECT in a randomized, double-blind, crossover design. Relative to placebo, TRH improved attention and verbal fluency, but did not impinge on tests of memory.

Side Effects

Mortality rates with ECT are comparable with those associated with general anesthesia for minor surgical procedures, approximately one death per 10,000 patients [10]. When adverse medical events occur, they typically take place during the ictal or immediately postictal period. ECT is believed to be safer than classic antidepressant medications, especially in patients with medical illness and in the elderly [60,61]. Naturalistic data for this claim are complicated by the high-risk nature of populations referred for ECT, and by the fact that few controlled studies have been conducted.

Cardiovascular

The electrical stimulus results in immediate vagal outflow, which decreases firing of the sinoatrial node, slowing heart rate and sometimes resulting in asystole under unmodified conditions, but rarely in modified treatments. Risk factors for asystole include subconvulsive stimulus, absence of anticholinergic premedication, use of a β-adrenergic blocker, and preexisting intracardiac conduction deficits [62]. A generalized seizure is accompanied by significant catecholamine release, principally from the adrenal glands, but also from direct sympathetic discharge. Significant elevations of heart rate and blood pressure result, although they return to baseline values within minutes of seizure termination. Benign arrhythmias are common [63].

Cardiovascular complications are the leading cause of morbidity and mortality with ECT [10]. Patients at greatest risk are those with preexisting cardiac illness, and the nature of adverse cardiovascular events is strongly predicted by the nature of cardiac condition [64]. Rice *et al.* [65], who used a case-control method, assessed the risk associated with ECT for patients with preexisting cardiovascular disease by examining the medical complications in patients older than 50 years of age undergoing ECT during a 1-year period. Although the at-risk group had more minor complications during ECT, the two groups did not differ in the rate of major complications. The routine practice of specific medical clearance for high-risk patients, cardiac monitoring during treatment, and the availability of medications to treat sympathetically induced arrhythmias were most likely responsible for the low rate of major complications.

Central nervous system

Cerebrovascular complications of ECT are rare, despite the increased cerebral blood flow and intracranial pressure during the seizure. Other possible complications include prolonged seizures (*ie*, those lasting more than 3 minutes) and tardive seizures. There is increased risk of prolonged seizures with the concomitant use of adenosine antagonists [36], high-dose neuroleptics, and lithium [66]. Preexisting electrolyte imbalance and possibly repeated induction of seizures also constitute risk factors. Failure to terminate prolonged seizures within 3 to 5 minutes may increase postictal confusion and amnesia. Tardive seizure (*ie*, seizures that develop following termination of the ECT-induced seizure) are not infrequently characterized by absence of motor manifestations and may be detected only by EEG. The development of spontaneous seizures following an ECT course is rare and probably does not differ from baseline rates in the general population. [67,68].

The evidence from neuropathologic investigations for the alteration of brain structure by ECT was recently reviewed [69•]. Prospective computed tomography and magnetic resonance imaging studies show no evidence of ECT-induced structural changes. Human postmortem studies have not linked neuronal cell loss to current ECT practice. In animal studies that used conditions comparable with human ECT and appropriate controls, blind ratings, and fixation techniques, no neuronal loss was observed. Several well-controlled studies have shown that neuronal loss occurs only after continuous seizure activity of at least 25 to 30 minutes, a condition not approached during ECT. Other studies found that the passage of electricity, thermal effects, and the transient disruption of the blood–brain barrier during ECT do not result in structural brain damage.

Cognition

During the immediate postictal period, patients may experience disorientation [70], attention deficits, disturbance of higher cognitive functions such as learning and memory [71], and transient sensorimotor and other neurologic abnormalities [72]. The magnitude and duration of the acute deficits can be affected by electrode placement, stimulus waveform, dosage higher than seizure threshold, cumulative number of treatments, and the frequency of treatment sessions (Table 3). For example, acute and short-term deficits are often substantially greater with bilateral than with right unilateral ECT [44] and with sine-wave relative to brief-pulse stimulation [40]. The acute and short-term cognitive side effects appear to be influenced more by electrical dosage higher than threshold than by absolute electrical dosage [44]. Because seizure threshold varies 40-fold among patients [73], determining seizure threshold and adjusting dosage accordingly is critical to minimizing cognitive side effects (Fig. 2). Recovery from a single ECT treatment is rapid, but, depending on technical factors, the recovery may be incomplete before the next treatment, leading to progressive deficits over the course of treatment

---

Table 3. Technical Factors Influencing the Degree of Cognitive Effects from Electroconvulsive Therapy

Technical factor	Approach associated with reduction of cognitive effects
Electrode placement	Right unilateral
Stimulus waveform	Brief pulse
Stimulus intensity	Threshold determination; dosage closer to threshold
Number of treatments	Fewest necessary to achieve remission or plateau of target symptoms
Frequency of treatment sessions	Less frequent: twice weekly for acute treatment
Number of seizures per session	One
Simultaneous use of psychotropic medications	Discontinue lithium, sedatives, antidepressants; reduce dose of neuroleptics
Dosage of anesthetic medications	Adjust dosage to produce light anesthesia

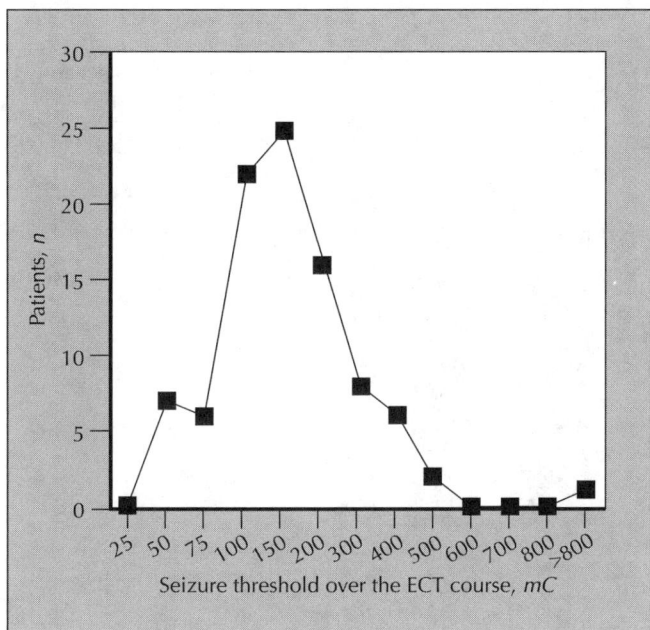

Figure 2. Variability in seizure threshold among 100 patients treated with titrated low-dose electroconvulsive therapy (ECT).

[74]. Thus, a larger cumulative number of treatments can have a negative effect on acute and short-term cognitive function. Increasing the spacing of treatments may be useful to decrease cognitive side effects.

Examination of the effect of ECT on learning and memory has focused mainly on anterograde and retrograde memory, the areas thought to be most affected [74] (Figs. 3 through 6). For anterograde verbal tasks, most studies have found a greater negative effect of bilateral ECT during and immediately following ECT. Nonverbal tasks are more challenging to evaluate because many of these tasks can involve verbal encoding. For anterograde nonverbal tasks, such as memory for faces or nonsense shapes, right unilateral and bilateral electrode placement may not be distinguishable. For retrograde memory tasks involving verbal memory, there is better performance with right unilateral than with bilateral ECT. For nonverbal retrograde memory tasks, there have been variable results, depending on the task, even when using face and nonsense shape recognition. Retrograde memory for both public and personal material appears to be more affected by bilateral than by right unilateral ECT, and material within the previous 3 years may be more vulnerable than more remote material. The magnitude of anterograde and retrograde amnesia is also sensitive to electrical dosage and waveform characteristics.

The associations between the cognitive side effects and technical aspects of ECT diminish over time, and 1 to 2 weeks following ECT, electrode placement effects are difficult to detect [40,44]. At this time, many domains of cognitive performance are improved relative to pretreatment baseline, including measures of attention, immediate learning, and intelligence. For anterograde tasks, performance is typically comparable with or superior to baseline [75], and patients who received sham and real ECT perform in a similar fashion [76]. For retrograde memory tasks, patients with right unilateral ECT may be comparable with patients without ECT.

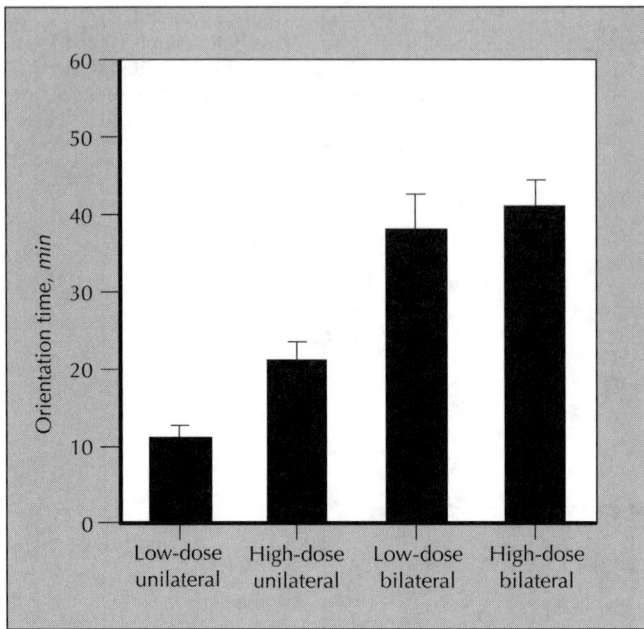

Figure 3. Recovery of orientation as a function of dosage and electrode placement in 96 patients who were tested immediately after electroconvulsive therapy. *T bars* indicate ±SEM.

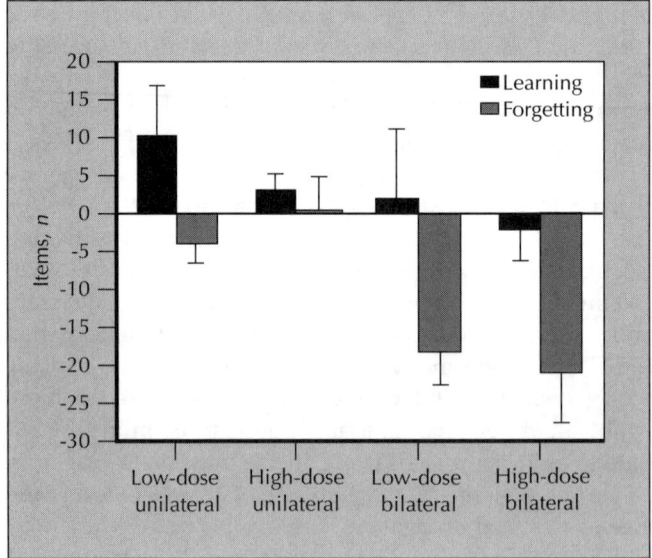

Figure 4. Anterograde memory measured by selective reminding as a function of dosage and electrode placement after completion of a course of electroconvulsive therapy in 96 patients. *T bars* indicate ±SEM.

Beyond the 1- to 2-week period, it is difficult to detect anterograde memory deficits. Weeks *et al.* [77] found it difficult to distinguish patients who had undergone ECT from those who had not at 3 and 6 months after ECT. Gangadhar *et al.* [78] reported similar findings. For retrograde memory, it appears that after 6 months to 1 year, the recall of remote events is no different in patients who have had ECT than in controls who had not [40,79]. Persistent deficits in the recall of recent events appears to be particularly vul-

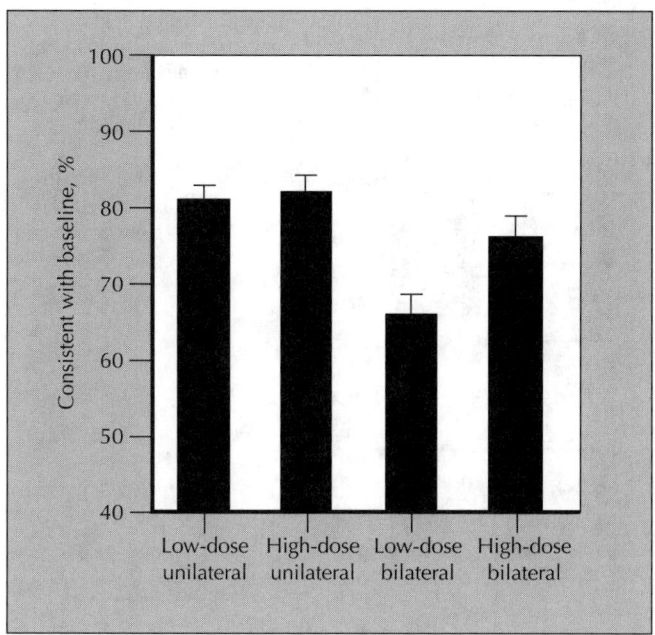

Figure 5. Retrograde memory as measured by autobiographic memory interview as a function of dosage and electrode placement in 96 patients after completion of a course of electroconvulsive therapy. *T bars* indicate ±SEM.

nerable, and the magnitude of this deficit is greater with bilateral and sine-wave stimulation [40,79,80]. Regardless of technical factors, patients who present with preexisting cognitive impairments or who show unusually prolonged acute disorientation may be at higher risk for deficits in the recall of recent, personal events [39•].

Relapse and Continuation Treatment

Relapse rates within the first 6 months following the remission of a depressive episode treated with medication are 50% or higher if no continuation treatment is given [81–83]. ECT is generally used to treat an acute episode of psychiatric illness and then discontinued when that episode remits. At minimum, similar rates of relapse can be expected when an ECT-induced remission is not followed by continuation treatment [84–86].

Continuation pharmacology

Standard treatment after remission with ECT usually consists of pharmacologic continuation therapies. This represents a departure from standard psychopharmacologic practice in which the treatment that induced remission is carried forward into the continuation phase. The belief that relapse rates following ECT can be markedly reduced by the use of a TCA or MAOI is based on three randomized, double-blind, placebo-controlled studies, conducted in England in the 1960s, that showed that relapse rates could be reduced from 50% to approximately 20% with these approaches [85,87,88]. Methodologic problems pose limitations to the findings. In particular, during the era of the studies, ECT was often a first-line treatment, but modern patient groups treated with ECT often comprise many who have failed adequate psychotropic trials [62,89].

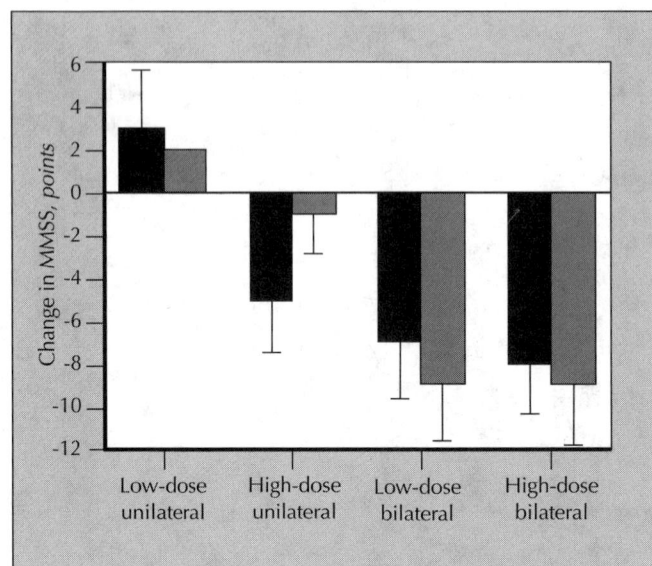

Figure 6. Change in global mental status as a function of dosage and electrode placement as measured by change in total score on the Mini-Mental State Score (MMSS) in 96 patients following electroconvulsive therapy (ECT). *Light shading* is score after six ECT treatments; *dark shading* is after completion of ECT. *T bars* indicate ±SEM.

In more recent studies, there is increasing evidence that relapse rates are high following ECT [90–92]. The preliminary evidence is that this may be particularly true of patients with established resistance to adequate trials of antidepressant medication during the index episode, and that adequate continuation therapy with a TCA may benefit only those who did not have established antidepressant resistance [91]. When pharmacotherapy is used as continuation treatment following ECT, it may be wise to select a class or combination of medications for which resistance was not manifest during the index episode.

Continuation electroconvulsive therapy

An alternative strategy is use of continuation ECT, which has been widely practiced for decades. Unfortunately, this practice has been little studied. Reports from the 1950s and 1960s indicated that the rate of rehospitalization was lower among patients who received continuation ECT compared with those who did not. From 1965 to 1986, no reports were published. Renewed interest is reflected in the 17 case reports from 1987 onward, which again found a reduction in rehospitalization rates and longer interepisode length in patients receiving continuation ECT. The case reports and a survey by Kramer [93] also emphasized that continuation ECT is practiced with widely different schedules, duration, and frequency of use among clinicians.

Conclusions

For major depression and mania, ECT is an effective treatment. Its role in the treatment of schizophrenia and other neuropsychiatric syndromes needs reevaluation. It is no longer thought that the generalized seizure alone is sufficient for efficacy with ECT. Technical factors, such as the extent to which electrical dosage exceeds seizure threshold and the interrelations of dosage with electrode placement, have considerable influence on the efficacy, efficiency, and the development of cognitive side effects. Substantial progress has been made in optimizing ECT technique. Progress in the management of adverse effects has added to the safety of ECT and made it more available. There is no credible evidence that ECT has adverse effects on brain structure. Relapse after brief treatment with ECT remains a critical clinical issue, and further research into the usefulness of various continuation treatment strategies, including continuation ECT, is important.

Acknowledgment

Supported in part by the National Institute of Mental Health grants MH-35636 and MH-47739.

References and Recommended Reading

Papers of particular interest, published recently, have been highlighted as:
* Of special interest
•• Of outstanding interest

1. NIH Consensus Conference: Electroconvulsive therapy. *JAMA* 1985, 254:2103–2108.
2. American Psychiatric Association. In *The Practice of ECT: Recommendations for Treatment, Training and Privileging*. Edited by Weiner RD, Fink M, Hammersley D, *et al.* Washington, DC: American Psychiatric Press; 1990.
3. Thompson JW, Weiner RD, Myers CP: Use of ECT in the United States in 1975, 1980, and 1986. *Am J Psychiatry* 1994, 151:1657–1661.
4. Sackeim HA: Use of electroconvulsive therapy in late life depression. In *Diagnosis and Treatment of Depression in Late Life*. Edited by Schneider LS, Reynolds CF III, Liebowitz BD, Friedhoff AJ. Washington, DC: American Psychiatric Press; 1993:259–277.
5. Prudic J, Sackeim HA, Devanand DP: Medication resistance and clinical response to electroconvulsive therapy. *Psychiatry Res* 1990, 31:287–296.
6. Sackeim HA: The efficacy of electroconvulsive therapy in treatment of major depressive disorder. In *The Limits of Biological Treatments for Psychological Distress: Comparisons with Psychotherapy and Placebo*. Edited by Fisher S, Greenberg RP. Hillsdale, NJ: Erlbaum; 1989:275–307.
7. Janicak PG, Davis JM, Gibbons RD, *et al.*: Efficacy of ECT: a meta-analysis. *Am J Psychiatry* 1985, 142:197–302.
8. Hamilton M: The effect of treatment on the melancholias (depressions). *Br J Psychiatry* 1982, 140:223–230.
9. Nobler MN, Sackeim HA: Electroconvulsive therapy: clinical and biological aspects. In *Prediction of Response to Antidepressant Treatments*. Edited by Goodnick P. Washington, DC: American Psychiatric Press; 1996: 1535–1556.
10. Abrams R: *Electroconvulsive Therapy*. New York: Oxford University Press; 1992.
11. Zimmerman M, Coryell W, Pfohl B: The treatment validity of DSM-III melancholic subtyping. *Psychiatry Res* 1985, 16:37–43.
12. Clinical Research Center, Division of Psychiatry: The Northwick Park ECT trial: predictors of response to real and simulated ECT. *Br J Psychiatry* 1984, 144:227–237.
13. Janicak PG, Easton MS, Comaty JE, *et al*: Efficacy of ECT in psychotic and nonpsychotic depression. *Convulsive Ther* 1989, 5:314–320.
14. Sackeim HA, Decina P, Kanzler M, *et al*: Effects of electrode placement on the efficacy of titrated, low-dose ECT. *Am J Psychiatry* 1987, 144:1449–1455.
15. Nobler MS, Sackeim HA, Solomou M, *et al.*: EEG manifestations during ECT: effects of electrode placement and stimulus intensity. *Biol Psychiatry* 1993, 34:321–330.
16. Mukherjee S, Sackeim HA, Schnur DB: Electroconvulsive therapy of acute manic episodes: a review of 50 years of experience. *Am J Psychiatry* 1994, 151:169–176.

17. Thomas J, Reddy B: The treatment of mania: a retrospective evaluation of the effects of ECT, chlorpromazine, and lithium. *J Affect Disord* 1982, 4:85–92.

18. Sikdar S, Kulhara P, Avasthi A, *et al.*: Combined chlorpromazine and ECT in mania. *Br J Psychiatry* 1994, 164:806–810.

19. Small JG, Klapper MH, Kellams JJ, *et al.*: Electroconvulsive treatment compared with lithium in the management of manic states. *Arch Gen Psychiatry* 1984, 45:727–732.

20. Mukherjee S, Sackeim HA, Lee C, *et al.*: ECT in treatment resistant mania. In *Biological Psychiatry 1985*. Edited by Shagass C, Josiassen RC, Bridger WH, *et al.* New York: Elsevier; 1986:732–34.

21. Krueger RB, Sackeim HA: Electroconvulsive therapy and schizophrenia. In *Schizophrenia*. Edited by Hirsch SR, Weinberger DR. Oxford: Blackwell; 1995:503–545.

22. Freeman CP, Crammer JL, Deakin JFW, *et al.*: *The Practical Administration of Electroconvulsive Therapy (ECT)*. London: Gaskell; 1989.

23. Goswami R, Dutta S, Kuruvilla K, *et al.*: Electroconvulsive therapy in neuroleptic-induced parkinsonism. *Biol Psychiatry* 1989, 26:234–238.

24. Mukherjee S, Debsikdar V: Absence of neuroleptic-induced parkinsonism in psychotic patients receiving adjunctive electroconvulsive therapy. *Convulsive Ther* 1994, 151:169–176.

25. Gardos G, Samu I, Kallos M, *et al.*: Absence of severe tardive dyskinesia in Hungarian schizophrenic out-patients. *Psychopharmacology (Berl)* 1980, 71:29–34.

26. Schwartz M, Silver H, Tal I, *et al.*: Tardive dyskinesia in northern Israel: preliminary study. *Eur Neurol* 1993, 33:264–266.

27. Cole JO, Gardos G, Boling LA, *et al.*: Early dyskinesia: vulnerability. *Psychopharmacology (Berl)* 1992, 107:503–510.

28. Khanna S, Gangadhar BN, Sinha V, *et al.*: Electroconvulsive therapy in obsessive-compulsive disorder. *Convulsive Ther* 1988, 4:314–320.

29. Pataki J, Zervas IM, Jandorf L: Catatonia in a university inpatient service (1985–1990). *Convulsive Ther* 1992, 8:163–173.

30. Davis JM, Janicak PG, Sakkas P, *et al.*: Electroconvulsive therapy in the treatment of the neuroleptic malignant syndrome. *Convulsive Ther* 1991, 7:111–120.

31. Strömgren LS, Dahl J, Fjeldborg N, *et al.*: Factors influencing seizure duration and number of seizures applied in unilateral electroconvulsive therapy: anaesthetics and benzodiazepines. *Acta Psychiatr Scand* 1980, 62:158–165.

32. Pettinati HM, Stephens SM, Willis KM, *et al.*: Evidence for less improvement in depression in patients taking benzodiazepines during unilateral ECT. *Am J Psychiatry* 1990, 147:1029–1035.

33. Ottosson J: Experimental studies of the mode of action of electroconvulsive therapy. *Acta Psychiatr Scand* 1960, 145(suppl):1–141.

34. el-Mallakh RS: Complications of concurrent lithium and electroconvulsive therapy: a review of clinical material and theoretical considerations. *Biol Psychiatry* 1988, 23:595–601.

35. Peters SG, Wochos DN, Peterson GC: Status epilepticus as a complication of concurrent electroconvulsive and theophylline therapy. *Mayo Clin Proc* 1984, 59:568–570.

36. Devanand DP, Decina P, Sackeim HA, *et al.*: Status epilepticus during ECT in a patient receiving theophylline. *J Clin Psychopharmacol* 1988, 8:153.

37. Freese KJ: Can patients safely undergo electroconvulsive therapy while receiving monoamine oxidase inhibitors? *Convulsive Ther* 1985, 1:190–194.

38. Maltbie AA, Wingfield MS, Volow MR, *et al.*: Electroconvulsive therapy in the presence of brain tumor: case reports and an evaluation of risk. *J Nerv Ment Dis* 1980, 168:400–405.

39.• Sobin C, Sackeim HA, Prudic J, *et al.*: Predictors of retrograde amnesia following ECT. *Am J Psychiatry* 1995, 152:995–1001.
Seventy-one depressed patients who had been randomly assigned to four ECT conditions underwent measures of cognitive side effects. The study found that pre-ECT global cognitive status, as measured by the modified mini-mental state examination, and the duration of postictal disorientation were strong predictors of the magnitude of retrograde amnesia for autobiographical memory immediately and 12 months following ECT. These relationships were maintained regardless of the technical parameters used in administration of ECT.

40. Weiner RD, Rogers HJ, Davidson JR, *et al.*: Effects of stimulus parameters on cognitive side effects. *Ann N Y Acad Sci* 1986, 462:315–325.

41. Weiner RD, Rogers HJ, Davidson JR, *et al.*: Effects of electroconvulsive therapy upon brain electrical activity. *Ann N Y Acad Sci* 1986, 462:270–281.

42. Ulett G, Smith K, Gleser G: Evaluation of convulsive and subconvulsive shock therapies utilizing a control group. *Am J Psychiatry* 1956, 112:795–802.

43. Robin A, De Tissera S: A double-blind controlled comparison of the therapeutic effects of low and high energy electroconvulsive therapies. *Br J Psychiatry* 1982, 141:357–366.

44. Sackeim HA, Prudic J, Devanand DP, *et al.*: Effects of stimulus intensity and electrode placement on the efficacy and cognitive effects of electroconvulsive therapy. *N Engl J Med* 1993, 328:839–846.

45. Sackeim HA, Devanand DP, Prudic J: Stimulus intensity, seizure threshold, and seizure duration: impact on the efficacy and safety of electroconvulsive therapy. *Psychiatry Clin North Am* 1991, 14:803–843.

46. Barton JL, Mehta S, Snaith RP: The prophylactic value of extra ECT in depressive illness. *Acta Psychiatr Scand* 1973, 49:386–392.

47. Strömgren LS: Therapeutic results in brief-interval unilateral ECT. *Acta Psychiatr Scand* 1975, 52:246–255.

48. Strömgren LS, Christiansen AL, Fromholt P: The effects of unilateral brief interval ECT on memory. *Acta Psychiatr Scand* 1976, 54:336–346.

49. McAllister DA, Perri MG, Jordan RC, *et al.*: Effects of ECT given two versus three times weekly. *Psychiatry Res* 1987, 21:63–69.

50. Kellner CH, Monroe RR Jr, Pritchett J, *et al.*: Weekly ECT in geriatric depression. *Convulsive Ther* 1992, 8:245–252.

51. Gangadhar BN, Janakiramaiah N, Subbakrishna DK, *et al.*: Twice versus thrice weekly ECT in melancholia: a double-blind prospective comparison. *J Affect Disord* 1993, 4:273–278.

52. Lerer B, Sapira B, Calev A, *et al.*: Antidepressant and cognitive effects of twice- versus three-times-weekly ECT. *Am J Psychiatry* 1995, 152:564–570.

53. Ottosson JO: Effect of lidocaine on the seizure discharge in electroconvulsive therapy. *Acta Psychiatr Scand Suppl* 1960, 145:7–32.

54. Hood DD, Mecca RS: Failure to initiate electroconvulsive seizures in a patient pretreated with lidocaine. *Anesthesiology* 1983, 58:379–381.

55. Gaitz CM, Pokornoy AD, Mills MJ: Death following electroconvulsive therapy. *Arch Neurol Psychiatry* 1956, 75:493–499.

56. Bross R: Near fatality with combined ECT and reserpine. *Am J Psychiatry* 1957, 113:933.

57. Pettinati HM, Stephens SM, Willis KM, *et al.*: Evidence for less improvement in depression in patients taking benzodiazepines during unilateral ECT. *Am J Psychiatry* 1990, 147:1029–1035.

58. Stern RA, Nevels CT, Shelhorse ME, *et al.*: Antidepressant and memory effects of combined thyroid hormone treatment and electroconvulsive therapy: preliminary findings. *Biol Psychiatry* 1991, 6:623–627.

59. Khan A, Mirolo MH, Claypoole K, *et al.*: Effects of low-dose TRH on cognitive deficits in the ECT postictal state. *Am J Psychiatry* 1994, 151:1694–1696.

60. Weiner RD, Coffey CE: Indications for use of electroconvulsive therapy. In *Review of Psychiatry*, vol 7. Edited by Frances AJ, Hales RE. Washington, DC: American Psychiatric Press; 1988:458–481.

61. Weiner, RD, Coffey CE: The use of ECT in patients with severe medical illness. In *Treatment of Psychiatric Disorders in Medical–Surgical Patients*. Edited by Stoudmire A, Fogel B. New York: Grune & Stratton; 1987:113–134.

62. McCall WV: Management of cardiovascular risk during ECT. *Abstracts from the 2nd international conference on new directions in affective disorders;* 1995.

63. Pitts FN: Medical physiology of ECT. In *Electroconvulsive Therapy: Biological Foundations and Clinical Applications*. Edited by Abrams R, Essman WB. New York: Spectrum; 1982:57–90.

64. Zielinski RJ, Roose SP, Devanand DP, *et al.*: Cardiovascular complications of ECT in depressed patients with cardiac disease. *Am J Psychiatry* 1992, 150:904–909.

65. Rice EH, Sombrotto LB, Markowitz JC, *et al.*: Cardiovascular morbidity in high-risk patients during ECT. *Am J Psychiatry* 1994, 151:1637–1641.

66. Weiner RD, Whanger AD, Erwin CW, *et al.*: Prolonged confusional state and EEG seizure activity following concurrent ECT and lithium use. *Am J Psychiatry* 1980, 137:1452–1453.

67. Blackwood DH, Cull RE, Freeman CP, *et al.*: A study of the incidence of epilepsy following ECT. *J Neurol Neurosurg Psychiatry* 1980, 43:1098–1102.

68. Small JG, Milstein V, Small IF, *et al.*: Does ECT produce kindling? *Biol Psychiatry* 1992, 16:773–778.

69.• Devanand DP, Dwork AJ, Hutchinson ER, *et al.*: Does ECT alter brain structure? *Am J Psychiatry* 1994, 151:957–970.
The evidence from neuropathologic investigations regarding the possibility of alteration of brain structure by ECT was reviewed. Prospective CT, MRI, human postmortem studies, animal electroshock studies (ECS) (using conditions comparable with ECT in patients and appropriate controls), blind ratings, and fixation techniques show no evidence to date of any ECT- or ECS-induced structural changes or neuronal cell loss. Other studies found that the passage of electricity, thermal effects, and the transient disruption of blood–brain barrier during ECS do not result in structural brain damage.

70. Daniel WF, Crovitz HF: Disorientation during electroconvulsive therapy: technical, theoretical, and neuropsychological issues. *Ann N Y Acad Sci* 1986, 462:293–306.

71. Squire LR, Slater P: Bilateral and unilateral ECT: effects on verbal and nonverbal memory. *Am J Psychiatry* 1978, 135:1316–1320.

72. Kriss A, Blumhardt LD, Halliday AM, *et al.*: Neurological asymmetries immediately after unilateral ECT. *J Neurol Neurosurg Psychiatry* 1978, 41:1135–1144.

73. Sackeim HA, Decina P, Prohovnik I, *et al.*: Seizure threshold in electroconvulsive therapy: effects of sex, age, electrode placement, and number of treatments. *Arch Gen Psychiatry* 1987, 4:355–360.

74. Sackeim HA: The cognitive effects of electroconvulsive therapy. In *Cognitive Disorders: Pathophysiology and Treatment.* Edited by Moos WH, Gamzu ER, Thal LJ. New York: Marcel Dekker; 1992:183–228.

75. Jackson B: The effects of unilateral and bilateral ECT on verbal and visual spatial memory. *J Clin Psychol* 1978, 34:4–13.

76. Frith CD, Stevens M, Johnstone EC, *et al.*: Effects of ECT and depression on various aspects of memory. *Br J Psychiatry* 1983, 142:610–617.

77. Weeks D, Freeman CP, Kendell RE: ECT: III. Enduring cognitive deficits? *Br J Psychiatry* 1980, 137:26–37.

78. Gangadhar BN, Kapur RL, Kalyanasundaram S: Comparison of electroconvulsive therapy with imipramine in endogenous depression: a double blind study. *Br J Psychiatry* 1982, 141:367–371.

79. Squire LR, Slater PC, Miller PL: Retrograde amnesia and bilateral electroconvulsive therapy: long-term follow-up. *Arch Gen Psychiatry* 1981, 38:89–95.

80. McElhinney MC, Moody BJ, Steif BL, *et al.*: Autobiographical memory and mood: effects of electroconvulsive therapy. *Neuropsychology* 1995, 9:501–517.

81. Mindham RHS, Howland C, Shepherd M: An evaluation of continuation therapy with tricyclic antidepressants in depressive illness. *Psychol Med* 1973, 3:5–17.

82. Paykel ES, Dimascio A, Haskell D, *et al.*: Effects of maintenance amitriptyline and psychotherapy on symptoms of depression. *Psychol Med* 1975, 3:5–17.

83. Prien RF, Kupfer DJ: Continuation drug therapy for major depressive episodes: how long should it be maintained? *Am J Psychiatry* 1986, 143:18–23.

84. Jarvie HF: Prognosis of depression treated by electric convulsive therapy. *Br Med J* 1954, 1:132–134.

85. Seager CP, Bird RL: Imipramine with electrical treatment in depression: a controlled trial. *J Ment Sci* 1962, 108:704–707.

86. Snaith RP: How much ECT does the depressed patient need? In *Electroconvulsive Therapy: An Appraisal.* Edited by Palmer RL. New York: Oxford University Press; 1981:61–64.

87. Imlah NW, Ryan E, Harrington JA: The influence of antidepressant drugs on the response to electroconvulsive therapy and on subsequent relapse rates. *Neuropsychopharmacology* 1965, 4:438–442.

88. Kay DW, Fahy T, Garside RF: A 7-month double-blind trial of amitriptyline and diazepam in ECT-treated depressed patients. *Br J Psychiatry* 1970, 117:667–671.

89. Prudic J, Sackeim HA, Devanand DP: Medication resistance and clinical response to electroconvulsive therapy. *Psychiatry Res* 1990, 31:287–296.

90. Aronson TA, Shukla S, Hoff A: Continuation therapy after ECT for delusional depression: a naturalistic study of prophylactic treatments and relapse. *Convulsive Ther* 1987, 3:251–259.

91. Sackeim HA, Prudic J, Devanand DP, *et al.*: The impact of medication resistance and continuation pharmacotherapy on relapse following response to electroconvulsive therapy in major depression. *J Clin Psychopharmacol* 1990, 10:96–104.

92. Spiker DG, Stein J, Rich CL: Delusional depression and electroconvulsive therapy: one year later. *Convulsive Ther* 1985, 1:167–172.

93. Kramer BA: Maintenance ECT: a survey of practice (1986). *Convulsive Ther* 1987, 3:260–268.

CHAPTER 7

Treatment of Geriatric Mood Disorders

Charles F. Reynolds III, George Alexopoulos, Ira Katz, and Benoit H. Mulsant

Geriatric mood disorders are both chronic and recurring; therefore the goals of treatment must always be complete remission of symptoms and prevention of relapse. In addition, although treating these common disorders must take into account concomitant general medical illness, the treatment benefits far outweigh the risks of not treating or undertreating elderly patients with mood disorders. This chapter describes the diagnosis and prognosis of geriatric mood disorders, treatment phases, treatment of specific syndromes, and the future directions for treatment research. The psychosocial and neuromedical pathways to mood disorders in later life are described. We also present the current status of diagnosis and treatment along with the current psychopharmacologic considerations of major depression, delusional depression, bipolar disorders, major and minor depressions in frail patients, depression in patients with dementing disorders, and bereavement-related depression. We describe the advantages, disadvantages, precautions, and side effects of the following: selective serotonin-reuptake inhibitors (SSRIs), nortriptyline, bupropion, venlafaxine, nefazodone, lithium, and anticonvulsants. Of particular interest, we discuss the new SSRIs—as of 1996—paroxetine and sertraline.

Geriatric mood disorders are common but treatable sources of disability, both in ambulatory patients and those who reside in long-term care facilities. It is important to take a long-term view of the treatment of mood disorders in later life, because they tend to be chronic and recurring. Treatment benefits clearly outweigh the risks, and the risks of not treating these mood disorders are considerable, especially when they co-occur with general medical and neurologic illnesses. Hence, the key concepts of treating depression and other geriatric mood disorders follow:

- Depression is a common but treatable source of disability in later life.
- A long-term view of treatment is necessary.
- Treatment benefits outweigh the risks.
- Risks of *not* treating are great.

It is appropriate to place a review of treatment of geriatric mood disorders within the broader context of research dealing with the pathways to mood disorders in later life. There are important psychosocial and neuromedical antecedents to major depression in later life (Table 1) [1]. Moreover, the relation between depression and general medical illness in later life is multifaceted. Although major or minor depression and physical illness may exist coincidentally, depression may also be 1) symptomatic of an underlying general medical illness, 2) a psychologic reaction to general medical illnesses and their sequelae, 3) an effect of neuromedical illness on brain neurotransmitter systems, 4) a side effect of treatment for a concurrent medical condition, or 5) some combination of

Table I. Pathways to Major Depression in Later Life*

Psychosocial antecedents	Neuromedical antecedents
Demographic variables (female gender)	Possible physical causes of depression in later life
Early events and achievements (childhood trauma)	Dementia (multi-infarct and Alzheimer's)
Later events and achievements (occupation, income, widowhood)	Stroke
	Parkinson's disease
Social integration (lack of religious affiliation, participation in volunteer organizations, neighborhood stability)	Cardiovascular disease
	Chronic pain
	Hypothyroidism
Vulnerability and protective factors (chronic stressors, social support versus isolation)	Cancer
	Possible drug-related causes of depression in later life
Provoking agents and coping efforts (life events, such as bereavement, major role transitions, or interpersonal conflicts; coping styles and strategies)	Alcohol use
	Antihypertensives
	Anticancer drugs
	Benzodiazepines
	Narcotics
	Histamine-receptor antagonists
	Glucocorticoids

*Adapted from George [2].

these. The importance of recognizing and treating depression in physically ill elderly patients is at least threefold. First, untreated or inadequately treated depression can influence the outcome of treatment or rehabilitation of physical illness, as well as both quality of life and survival in physically ill elderly patients. Second, major depression is an independent risk factor for mortality in patients who are hospitalized after myocardial infarction [2], or who have been admitted to a nursing home. Third, depressive disorders may cause or contribute to physical illness by such physiologic routes as neuroendocrine or immunologic alterations, or by behavioral routes, such as excess alcohol or tobacco use, or poor compliance with medical treatment.

Estimates of the point prevalence of major depressive episodes among community-dwelling elderly patients are about 2% to 3% [3]. Among nursing home residents, prevalence estimates have ranged from 15% to 25%, with approximately a 13% annual incidence of new episodes in major depression among residents of long-term care facilities. However, the burden of depressive illness in later life is not limited to major depression. Studies estimate an 8% to 15% prevalence of subsyndromal depressions (whether minor depression or depression not otherwise specified [NOS]) in community-residing elders. Such symptoms also represent an important source of disability, suffering, caregivers' burden, and diminished quality of life [4].

The National Institutes of Health (NIH) Consensus Development Conference on the Diagnosis and Treatment of Depression in Late Life [4] conceptualized several goals for treatment, including the reduction and resolution of depressive symptoms, and improvement in quality of life and enhancement in functional ability. The panel report emphasized that adequate treatment of mood disorders in later life would also likely result in an improvement in physical health status and a reduction of healthcare cost. The panel report further emphasized the importance of preventing relapse, recurrence, and suicide.

This chapter discusses the diagnosis and prognosis of geriatric mood disorders, phases of treatment, treatment of specific geriatric mood syndromes, and future directions for treatment research. Specific geriatric mood syndromes to be considered include major depression, delusional major depression, bipolar disorders, major and minor depressions in nursing-home and other very elderly and frail patients, depression in patients with dementing disorders, and bereavement-related depression and "complicated" bereavement (discussed later). Considerations pertaining to psychosocial, psychopharmacologic, and electroconvulsive (ECT) therapy interventions are considered with each disorder, when data exist.

Diagnosis of Geriatric Mood Disorders

Although there are many psychosocial (Table 1) and neuromedical (Table 2) pathways to mood disorders in later life, this heterogeneity need not complicate the clinician's diagnostic task relative to major depression. We advocate taking an *inclusive* view of symptoms, rather than an effort to assign specific symptoms to either depression or another general medical disorder [5,6]. An inclusive approach facilitates case finding and treatment initiation. There is a real danger that when depression strikes medically ill elderly patients, it often goes unrecognized and untreated [4]. Thus, we believe it appropriate to diagnose depression in the elderly medically ill patient if such a patient shows a depressed mood or loss of interest or pleasure with four or more other *Diagnostic and Statistical Manual of Mental Disorders* (DSM) symptoms of major depression for 2 or more weeks. In other words, in our view it is appropriate to consider symptoms in their entirety, without making causal attributions.

Phases of Treatment

The benefits of treating depression in elderly patients clearly outweigh the risk of not treating or of inadequate treatment. The risks of no treatment or inadequate treatment include chronic depression and its attendant psychosocial invalidism, ongoing or worsening cognitive impairment, poor compliance with medical treatment and worsening of general medical conditions, social impairments, reduction in quality of life (satisfaction and coping skills), and suicide [7]. Thus, patients should be vigorously treated and complete remission of symptoms should be one therapeutic goal. However, because depression in

---

Table 2. Phase-Specific Goals of Treatment for Recurrent Major Depression in Later Life

Acute phase
To achieve remission of symptoms

Continuation phase
To prevent relapse back into the index depressive episode

Maintenance phase
To preserve recovery
To prevent recurrence

the elderly is often a chronic illness, with a tendency to recur, many if not most elderly patients will benefit from treatment beyond acute-phase treatment of the index episode and a resolution of symptoms associated with treatment of the acute episode [8]. Although the purpose of initial treatment is to bring about remission of symptoms, the goal of continuation treatment is to prevent relapse into the current episode of major depression. The goal of maintenance treatment is to preserve recovery and to prevent recurrence (*ie*, the onset of a new episode) (Table 2).

The expected duration of treatment phases in major depression in later life can now be estimated from recent empirical research. The median time to full recovery in the short-term treatment of the index episode of major depression in ambulatory elderly outpatients is approximately 12 weeks [9]. We recommend continuing stabilization therapy for 16 to 20 weeks beyond the immediate therapy period. Maintenance therapy may well be indicated for the duration of the patient's life, particularly if the patient has had two or more major depressive episodes or if the index episode was severe, delusional, and protracted, or superimposed on chronic intermittent depression [10].

Treatment of Specific Geriatric Mood Disorders
Major depression
Adequate pharmacotherapy in major depression of late life depends not only on adequate dosing and steady-state blood levels, but also on duration of treatment. For example, when using a combination of nortriptyline and interpersonal psychotherapy, researchers have reported that the median time to remission in the initial treatment of the index episode is about 12 weeks [9,10]. Reliable discrimination of remitting from nonremitting patients is not possible until about week 4 or 5 [11•]. In the same study, relapse rates following discontinuation of nortriptyline after 16 to 20 weeks of continuation therapy was 24% among patients randomly assigned to placebo, but zero among patients randomly assigned to continue on active medication [9].

Elderly patients should probably be treated with the same dose of medication during continuation and maintenance therapy that attained a response during initial therapy [8]. Relapse rates of 17% for nortriptyline and 20% for phenelzine were reported in one series of elderly depressed patients during 4 to 8 months of continuation therapy [12]. Similarly, from open trial data in 27 elderly depressed patients, a recurrence rate of 15% was observed during 18 months of nortriptyline maintenance therapy at steady-state levels of 50 to 150 ng/mL [13]. In a subsequent controlled study, approximately 90% of elderly patients who suffered a recurrence of major depression after random assignment to a maintenance placebo condition could be successfully treated to remission using combined therapy with interpersonal psychotherapy and nortriptyline prescribed in the same dose used to treat the index episode of major depression [14].

Selecting an antidepressant for elderly patients involves a careful consideration of risk versus benefits. With the tricyclic antidepressants (TCAs) (Table 3), secondary amines (*eg*, nortriptyline or desipramine) are effective in elderly depressed patients and have a generally benign side-effect profile when selected with due cognizance of their medical contraindications (electrocardiographic [ECG] conduction disturbances, acute narrow angle glaucoma, and prostatic hypertrophy with urinary retention) [15,16]. Importantly, however, the adverse effects of the TCAs, particularly amitriptyline,

Table 3. Selecting an Antidepressant for Elderly Patients: Risk Versus Benefit

Tricyclic antidepressants	Selective serotonin-reuptake inhibitors (SSRIs)
Nortriptyline (NT) and desipramine (DMI) are safer and better tolerated than amitriptyline (AT) or imipramine (IMI).	Tolerable side-effect profile of newer SSRIs (eg, paroxetine and sertraline) supports their use in elderly depressed patients.
Target therapeutic blood level of 80–120 ng/mL (NT) and >115 ng/mL (DMI).	Most common side effects: nausea, diarrhea, somnolence, insomnia, headache.
An 80% efficacy of NT in combination with interpersonal psychotherapy.	Efficacy of SSRIs equals that of doxepin and amitriptyline (60–80% response rates; >50% reduction in Hamilton depression ratings).
Three atropinic side effects of NT persist but are generally mild: dry mouth, constipation, and modest increase in heart rate of seven to eight beats per minute.	Tolerability is superior to that of doxepin and amitriptyline (lower rates of anticholinergic effects with SSRIs).
Wide dose range of NT (20–200 mg/d) associated with steady-state therapeutic level.	

imipramine, and doxepin, may be worse in the elderly. These adverse effects are principally orthostatic hypotension (which is associated with falls and fractures), excessive sedation, anticholinergic symptoms (including delirium), and cardiac toxicity [17,18].

Therapeutic blood levels of 80 to 120 ng/mL of nortriptyline and higher than 125 ng/mL of desipramine are to be targeted. At these levels, an overall 80% efficacy rate of nortriptyline in combination with interpersonal psychotherapy has been reported for elderly patients with recurrent major depression [9]. Three side effects of nortriptyline are commonly noted in the elderly and are persistent, but generally mild: dry mouth, constipation, and a modest increase in heart rate of seven to eight beats per minute [16].

Recommendations for long-term treatment with tricyclic antidepressants in the elderly also require consideration of risk-benefit ratio. For example, it has recently been reported that nortriptyline is not a strong promoter of either weight gain or orthostasis in a placebo-controlled maintenance therapy trial [16]. In addition, the use of secondary agents, such as nortriptyline or desipramine, allows compliance to be verified by monitoring the blood levels of these agents. At the same time, however, their use is less straightforward than with newer selective serotonin-reuptake inhibitors (SSRIs). For example, a wide dose range of nortriptyline (20 to 200 mg/d) can be associated with steady-state therapeutic levels of 80 to 120 ng/mL.

Selective serotonin-reuptake inhibitors

Because of their favorable side-effect profiles and safety in overdose, as of 1995 newer SSRIs, such as paroxetine and sertraline, have arguably become first-line antidepressants in ambulatory or frail elderly patients with major depression, particularly those patients seen in primary care practice settings [19] (Table 3) (Fig. 1). These agents appear to be as effective overall as secondary tricyclic antidepressants, although direct, prospective head-to-head comparisons have not yet been published.

We tend to avoid prescribing fluoxetine to older patients because it has an efficacy similar to paroxetine or sertraline, but (with its active metabolite norfluoxetine) has the

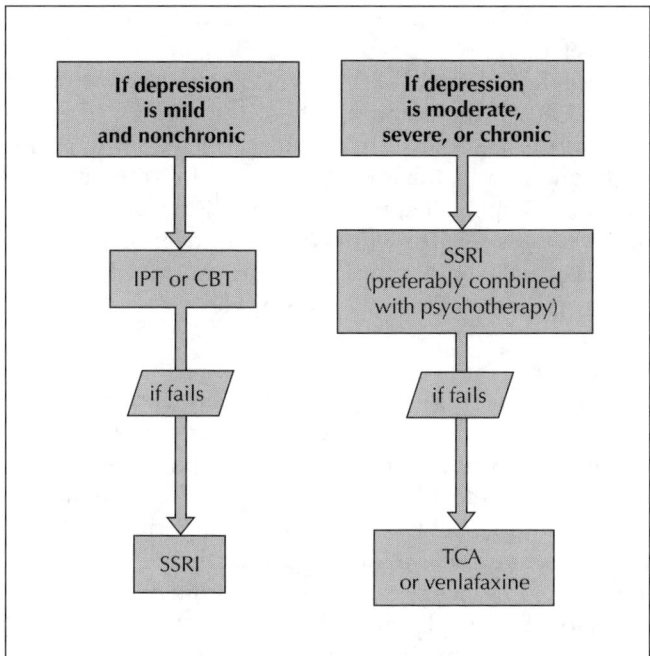

Figure 1. Preferred treatment algorithm for nonpsychotic major depressive disorders in the elderly. CBT—cognitive–behavioral therapy; IPT—interpersonal psychotherapy; SSRI—selective serotonin-reuptake inhibitor; TCA—tricyclic antidepressants.

longest half-life of the SSRIs (*ie,* 5 to 7 days) and the most potent inhibition of the cytochrome P-450 2d6 hepatic isoenzyme [20]. In addition, fluoxetine seems more likely to cause side effects, such as insomnia, agitation, weight loss, Parkinsonism, and the syndrome of inappropriate secretion of antidiuretic hormone (SIADH) [21]. If fluoxetine is prescribed to an elderly person, 10 mg/d, given in the morning, should be used.

Newer SSRIs have been reported to be equal in efficacy to doxepin and amitriptyline in older patients, as measured by response rates [22–24]. They clearly have superior tolerability to doxepin and amitriptyline relative to anticholinergic side effects. The most common side effects of the newer SSRIs are nausea, diarrhea, somnolence, insomnia, and headache. They are generally safer than tricyclic antidepressants in elderly depressed patients with coexisting medical conditions and treatments. However, very old, frail, or medically ill patients may be less tolerant of SSRIs and may experience apathy, anorexia, and SIADH [19]. A lower starting dose of paroxetine (10 mg) or sertraline (25 mg) should be considered, together with more gradual dosage increases in elderly patients (particularly those older than 75 years of age). The dose of the SSRI should be increased until optimal therapeutic response is obtained, with an upper dose limit of 40 mg for paroxetine and 200 mg for sertraline.

A recent placebo-controlled, multisite study of an SSRI in geriatric depression demonstrated rather low efficacy for fluoxetine [25]. Moreover, the work of Roose *et al.* [26] showed that those older patients with cardiac problems who have severe melancholic depression have a poor response to fluoxetine compared with nortriptyline. Although SSRIs may have fewer cardiac side effects and may be easier to use, they may be effective only in some types of geriatric depression. The issue requires further investigation.

Overall, the advantages of SSRI agents for use in elderly depressed patients include the absence of orthostasis, greater safety in overdose than with TCAs, smaller effect on the ECG, better tolerability and once-daily dosing (both of which may promote better compliance), and the moderate half-life of the newer agents or the absence of active metabolites (Table 4). Precautions for the use of SSRIs in the elderly include SIADH, the possibility of extrapyramidal symptoms, bradycardia, weight loss, apathy, drug interactions, and sexual dysfunction. As of this writing, it appears that the advantages of newer SSRIs greatly outweigh their disadvantages for treating medically ill depressed elderly patients. However, the newer SSRIs should be further studied in controlled trials of depressed elderly patients, especially those older than 75 years of age.

Bupropion, venlafaxine, and nefazodone

These other agents also represent important additions to the pharmacotherapeutic armamentarium for treating late-life depression [27]. Advantages of bupropion include efficacy equal to tricyclics and SSRIs in the treatment of major depression, fewer adverse side effects than tricyclic antidepressants, the lack of an association with cognitive impairment or sedation, a minimal cardiotoxicity profile, and relative safety in overdose (Table 4). Precautions in the use of bupropion include the necessity to use divided dosing to minimize the propensity to induce seizures, as well as the desirability of administering the last daily dose before bedtime because of a tendency to cause insomnia. In geriatric patients, bupropion may be initially prescribed at 50 to 75 mg twice daily, and the dose gradually increased to approximately 300 mg daily in two or three divided doses. Drug interactions are generally not a significant problem with bupropion, but it should not be administered concomitantly with a monoamine oxidase inhibitor (MAOI) antidepressant. Bupropion may be helpful in depressed elderly patients with Parkinson's disease.

Venlafaxine is a novel antidepressant that selectively inhibits both norepinephrine and serotonin uptake (Table 4). Venlafaxine has been reported to have efficacy in treatment-refractory patients with major depression, as well as in depressed patients with chronic pain [27,28]. Patients respond to a relatively wide range of daily doses, and no dosage adjustment is necessary based on age. The use of venlafaxine entails several precautions. For example, nausea may be minimized by beginning treatment with lower doses of 25 mg daily and gradually titrating up to a therapeutic dose. Blood pressure needs to be monitored because higher doses, in general more than 225 mg daily, can be associated with sustained increases in blood pressure. The drug must be administered in two to three divided doses a day, which may hinder compliance. As of this writing, venlafaxine appears to be an important addition to the pharmacotherapeutic armamentarium in the treatment of late-life major depression, particularly for treatment-refractory patients [28]. By starting at a low dose and escalating dosage slowly, the burden of nausea associated with early venlafaxine therapy may be diminished.

The recently approved agent nefazodone has several promising advantages for the treatment of late-life depression: its sleep-promoting and early anxiolytic effects, its high level of tolerability, safety in overdosage, and absence of sexual dysfunction or sleep architecture–disrupting effects (Table 4). As of now, nefazodone appears to be an interesting agent, although further research is needed, particularly in the elderly. That higher doses (300 to 500 mg/d) and twice-daily dosing are required for clinical efficacy may

Table 4. Advantages and Precautions with SSRIs, Bupropion, Venlafaxine, and Nefazodone

Selective serotonin-reuptake inhibitors (SSRIs)

Advantages	Precautions
No orthostasis	Drug interactions
Safer in overdose	Extrapyramidal symptoms
Less impact on electrocardiogram	Syndrome of inappropriate antidiuretic hormone
Well tolerated (may promote better compliance)	secretion
Once-daily dosing (may promote better compliance)	Weight loss
Moderate half-life of newer agents or absence of	Sexual dysfunction
active metabolites	Bradycardia

Bupropion

Advantages	Precautions
As effective as tricyclic antidepressants and SSRIs in treating major depression	Divided dosing necessary to minimize propensity to induce seizures
Few adverse side effects of tricyclic antidepressants	Administer last dose well before bedtime because of tendency to cause insomnia
Not associated with cognitive impairment or sedation	
Minimal cardiotoxicity profile and relative safety in overdose	

Venlafaxine

Advantages	Precautions
A novel antidepressant that selectively inhibits both norepinephrine and serotonin uptake	Nausea (may be minimized by starting treatment with lower doses of 25 mg/d and gradually titrating up to therapeutic level)
Has efficacy in treatment-refractory patients	Insomnia and anorexia
Has efficacy in depressed patients with chronic pain	Need to monitor blood pressure because higher doses can be associated with sustained increases in blood pressure
Patients respond to a relatively wide range of daily doses	
No dosage adjustment is necessary based on age	Must be administered in two or three divided doses a day (may hinder compliance)

Nefazodone

Advantages	Precautions
Sleep-promoting and early anxiolytic effects in depressed patients	Need more clinical trials in the elderly
Relatively well tolerated	High doses (300–500 mg) are required for clinical efficacy
Safe in overdose	Twice-daily dosing required (may limit compliance)
Does not cause sexual dysfunction or disruption in sleep architecture	

limit compliance. Its sedating property may make it beneficial or less acceptable, depending on the particular elderly patient.

Monoamine oxidase inhibitors

We are aware of at least one controlled study [29] showing comparable efficacy of the MAOI antidepressant phenelzine with that of nortriptyline (both 60% vs 13% efficacy for placebo) in the acute-phase treatment of elderly patients with major depression. In general, the use of MAOIs in elderly depressed patients needs to be based on a careful assessment of potential benefit, need, and risk. Because of the necessity for dietary restrictions and precautions over drug–drug interactions, these agents should probably be considered as third-line or fourth-line treatment for most patients, after the new-generation SSRIs, secondary TCAs, and venlafaxine, buproprion, or nefazodone. A recent study by Sunderland *et al.* [30] supported claims for the efficacy of high-dose selegiline in treatment-refractory elderly depressed patients.

Estrogen therapy

Sex hormones have known psychotropic properties. One recent study has shown mood-enhancing effects of exogenously administered estrogen, as shown by lower depression scores in psychologically healthy postmenopausal women [31]. This effect can be attenuated by progesterone treatment, which can cause symptoms of depression [32]. Estrogen replacement therapy (ERT) may also hasten the resolution of depressive symptoms [33]. However, most studies have selected subjects who were not clinically depressed. Studies in more severely depressed subjects showed no change, or worsening, of clinical condition [34,35]. There is one report, however, that showed improvement in severe refractory depression, but only with extremely high doses of ERT [36]. None of these studies controlled for serum levels of estradiol, which can vary widely with fixed-dosing strategies [37] and can cause supraphysiologic levels. More data are required to determine the antidepressant effect of physiologic levels of ERT on mildly to moderately depressed postmenopausal women who are frequently treated in primary care settings.

Psychosocial factors in the treatment of late-life depression

Stressful life events and ongoing difficulties contribute significantly to delayed treatment response and stabilization during acute therapy of major depressive episodes in later life [38]. Other factors may also contribute to delayed treatment response, including perceived lack of social support and eccentric personality features of a schizoid type. Psychotherapy, therefore, is an important and perhaps critical adjuvant to pharmacotherapy in the treatment of geriatric major depression. Interpersonal psychotherapy (IPT) is particularly useful in depression associated with bereavement, major role transitions, interpersonal conflicts, and social isolation. An elderly patient's course of recovery with IPT or with cognitive–behavioral psychotherapy (CBT) is probably greater than the open-ended (insight-oriented) psychotherapy that clinicians are more familiar with. Psychotherapy is also helpful for addressing hopelessness that may characterize elderly depressed patients, particularly those with a history of suicidal attempts and those who are likely to drop out of treatment [39].

Disability often accompanies geriatric depression and worsens its outcome. Disability contributes to the high rate of hospital admissions, nursing home placement, mortality [40], and even morbidity for specific medical conditions [41]. Disability, and especially impairment in activities of daily living, appears to be related to depressive symptomatology and particularly to anxiety, depressive ideation, retardation, and weight loss [42]. Although most of these symptoms respond to antidepressants, depressive ideation, and particularly hopelessness, may be an appropriate focus of psychotherapeutic intervention.

Obstacles in treating late-life depression to full recovery

Obstacles to adequate treatment include poor compliance with treatment by patients and their families, adverse effects associated with treatment (side-effect burden), inadequate family support for proper compliance with treatment, occult self-medication (particularly with alcohol), adverse psychosocial factors (such as bereavement or social isolation), and comorbid physical illness (complicating pharmacotherapy). Despite these obstacles, compliance can be enhanced by attention to side effects and by the use of appropriate countermeasures to decrease such side effects and improve the quality of life. Equally important, if not more so, the creation and maintenance of an alliance with the patient's family members permits education about depression in later life and the need for its treatment. Educational workshops, monthly telephone calls to family members, and family support groups, all are useful here. In addition, collaboration with the patient's primary care physician may enhance awareness about the challenge and treatment of depression in later life and may elicit support for participation and treatment. An attitude of caring and enthusiasm among clinicians is also very important in eliciting adequate compliance that will ultimately ensure a high-response rate.

Treatment of psychotic depression in later life

Psychotic depression, Kraepelin's melancholia gravis, occurs in 3.6% of elderly depressed patients living in the community [43] and in 20% to 45% of hospitalized elderly depressed patients [44]. Psychotic depression is a severe illness with profound depressive symptomatology accompanied by delusions and, less frequently, by hallucinations. Psychomotor retardation or agitation are more pronounced and frequent in psychotic than in nonpsychotic elderly depressive patients [45]. Delusions occur in successive episodes of geriatric depression if the severity of episodes is high [45,46]. However, in geriatric patients, psychotic depression is not merely a consequence of high severity of depression because high percentages of severely depressed elderly patients do not develop delusions [45,46]. Psychotic depression poses a risk for suicide [47], usually by violent means [48]. For this reason, recognition and treatment of psychotic depression can be lifesaving.

There is agreement that both young [49,50] and elderly patients with psychotic depression [45] (Alexpoulis *et al.*, Paper presented at the Annual Meeting of the American Psychiatric Association, New Orleans, 1991) respond poorly to initial treatment with tricyclic antidepressants and to placebo therapy [51]. Poor response to tricyclic antidepressants is not explained by the high severity of depression alone [49]. Combinations of tricyclic antidepressants and neuroleptics appear to be effective in psychotic depression both in controlled studies of younger patients [52] and in naturalistic treatment studies of elderly patients [45] (Alexpoulis *et al.*, Paper presented at the Annual Meeting of the American Psychiatric Association, New Orleans, 1991). The most frequently prescribed antidepressants are nortriptyline or desipramine at plasma levels comparable with those of younger adults (60 to 150 ng/mL for nortriptyline or higher than 115 ng/mL for desipramine). Perphenazine is the neuroleptic that has been used in most studies of psychotic depression [53] and appears to be effective at daily dosages of approximately 32 mg. It is unclear if elderly patients can respond to lower doses of neuroleptics or whether risperidone can be effective and better-tolerated than perphenazine.

Although there is agreement that psychotic depression requires combination drug therapy, these drugs may not be tolerated by elderly patients. Consequently, ECT is frequently the treatment of choice in geriatric psychotic depression. Studies comparing ECT with simulated ECT have demonstrated benefit in psychotic depression [54]. There is some evidence that bilateral ECT is more effective than unilateral ECT in psychotic depression. However, controlled studies are needed.

The requirement for special treatment makes it important to identify psychotic depression. Sometimes it is difficult to distinguish depressive delusions from overvalued ideas of worthlessness and hopelessness. Nondelusional depressed patients, as a rule, are able to recognize the exaggerated nature of their overvalued ideas, although they are unable to stop being preoccupied with them. Depressive delusions can be distinguished from delusions of demented patients in that the latter are less systematized and less congruent to the affective disturbance [55]. In contrast, depressive delusions usually are well-organized ideas of guilt, hypochondriasis, nihilism, persecution, or jealousy. However, geriatric depression with reversible dementia often is a psychotic depression with a poor long-term outcome [56]. Although the dementia syndrome initially subsides after effective antidepressant treatment, in the long run, a high percentage of these patients develop irreversible dementia. In this context, it is also important clinically to consider the possibility of a superimposed delirium.

Younger patients with psychotic depression have a poor outcome, at least during the first 2 years from recovery [57], but their outcome over 8 to 40 years is similar to the outcome of nonpsychotic depressive patients [58,59]. The long-term outcome of geriatric psychotic depression is, to some extent, comparable with that of younger adults. A geriatric study showed that approximately 80% of geriatric patients with psychotic depression recovered, and only 50% had a relapse within 3.5 to 8.5 years [45]. The recurrence rate of psychotic depression was similar to that of nonpsychotic depression, although psychotic depression often required hospitalization during recurrences. Relapses and recurrences are particularly frequent in elderly patients who achieve only partial recovery after short-term treatment of psychotic depression [60]. Therefore, it is important to treat the initial episode aggressively and provide continuation and maintenance therapy. Studies are underway to examine whether combinations of tricyclic antidepressants and neuroleptics are necessary, or whether neuroleptics alone are sufficient for this purpose. However, patients who recover after ECT should not receive continuation treatment with drugs that failed before ECT because, as a rule, these drugs are unable to prevent relapse.

Treatment of bipolar disorders in later life

Although the risk of mania declines with aging, mania and hypomania constitute 5% to 10% of the diagnoses of elderly psychiatric patients [61]. Mania first occurring in late life includes a substantial number of patients with unipolar depression who changed polarity. Mania associated with general medical illnesses or drugs as a rule has its onset at an age older than 40 years [62]. Cerebrovascular disease, and especially right-sided lesions, have been implicated in late-onset mania [63].

In principle, the management of mania in the elderly is similar to that of younger patients [64]. However, an effort should be made to identify patients with mania induced by drugs or medical or neurologic disorders and to treat the underlying condition. Weighing of the risks and benefits of treatment is particularly important in elderly patients.

Lithium remains the first-line initial treatment for geriatric mania [61]. Elderly patients require 30% to 60% lower lithium doses than do younger adults to develop equivalent plasma levels (Table 5), because age-induced decreases in glomerular filtration rate and in renal blood flow reduce lithium excretion. If one starts at 75 to 150 mg of lithium per day or uses a single nightly dose that is 150% of the daily dose every other night, side effects may be reduced and compliance improved, without decreasing efficacy [65]. The half-life of lithium is about 24 to 30 hours in the seventh decade of life. Therefore, steady-state pharmacokinetics are anticipated 5 or more days after the stabilization of the daily dosage. Lithium plasma levels of 0.8 to 1.2 mEq/L often are not tolerated by elderly manic patients. Some older manic patients may respond to low lithium plasma levels (0.4–0.6 mEq/L), although higher plasma levels appear to be more effective [66]. The onset of lithium action is slow and may require several days or weeks. Lorazepam or low doses of high-potency neuroleptics may be used in the early treatment of acutely agitated manic patients.

Elderly patients may be particularly vulnerable to the side effects of lithium. Delirium can develop at lithium levels at or even below the therapeutic lithium plasma level range, especially in patients with Parkinson's disease or in patients taking neuroleptics [67]. Delirium and cerebellar dysfunction may last for weeks after lithium discontinuation. Lithium-induced tremor is more frequent in the elderly than in younger patients. Lithium can worsen Parkinson's disease or produce parkinsonism in neurologically intact patients. It may worsen cognitive function, especially in demented patients. Sinoatrial block can be caused by lithium. Digitalis and β-adrenergic blockers increase the risk for sinoatrial block. Elderly patients often receive drugs that increase lithium plasma levels. These include thiazide diuretics, nonsteroidal anti-inflammatory drugs, and angiotensin-converting enzyme (ACE) inhibitors.

The anticonvulsants carbamazepine and valproate (divalproex sodium) are effective antimanic agents in younger adults [68] (Table 6) (Fig. 2). Although controlled studies are still lacking, case reports suggest that both carbamazepine [69] and valproate are effective

Table 5. Lithium in the Treatment of Geriatric Mania

Lithium doses 30%–60% lower than those of younger adults produce equivalent plasma levels in the elderly
The half-life ($t_{1/2}$ = 24–30 h) is prolonged in the elderly
Delirium may develop at lithium plasma levels below the therapeutic range
Lithium can cause sinoatrial block, especially in patients receiving digitalis or β-adrenergic receptor blockers

Table 6. Anticonvulsants in the Treatment of Geriatric Mania

Anticonvulsants are as effective as lithium
Anticonvulsants may be effective in those who respond to lithium as in those who do not
Anticonvulsants may be more effective than lithium in rapidly cycling and in dysphoric manic patients
Valproate may be more effective in patients with neurologic brain diseases than in neurologically intact patients
Leukopenia develops in 2% of carbamazepine-treated patients and 0.4% of valproate-treated patients

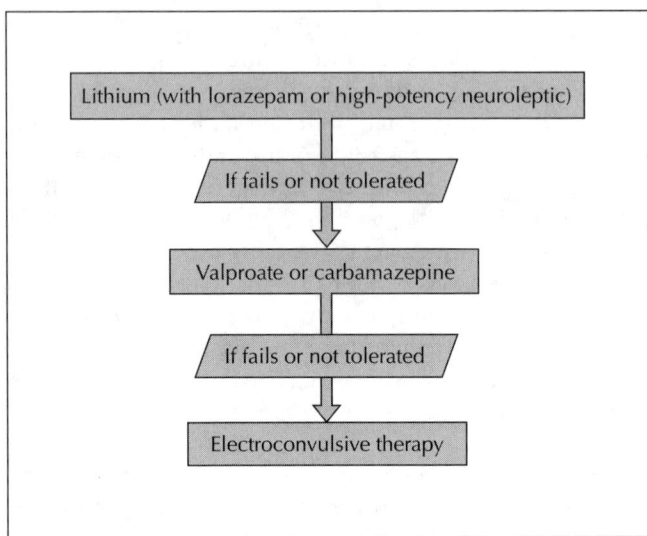

Figure 2. Preferred treatment algorithm for geriatric mania.

in geriatric mania [70–72]. Anticonvulsants appear to be effective in both lithium responders and nonresponders [68]. There is some evidence that anticonvulsants are more effective than is lithium in rapidly cycling patients and in patients with dysphoric mania [73]. Patients with neurologic brain diseases may be more responsive to valproate than are neurologically intact patients with mania [74]. Hematologic and liver function tests should be obtained before treatment with carbamazepine and valproate. A higher free fraction of valproate is found in the elderly than in younger patients; however, its clinical role is unclear [75]. Carbamazepine can cause sedation, confusion, and ataxia in a dose-dependent fashion [76]. Complete blood counts should be obtained frequently because carbamazepine can cause leukopenia (leukocyte count lower than $4000/mm^3$) in approximately 2% of cases [77]. Half of the patients who develop carbamazepine-induced leukopenia have a decrease in leukocyte count within the first 16 days of treatment. Valproate causes leukopenia in 0.4% of patients, a percentage comparable with that of tricyclic antidepressants.

Electroconvulsive therapy is an effective treatment of mania, leading to remission or marked clinical improvement in 80% of patients [78]. ECT is effective even in patients with mania who fail to respond to drug therapy. Remission following ECT is a primary therapeutic effect, rather than a secondary consequence of an ECT-induced organic brain syndrome. Geriatric patients with mania do not require a high frequency or prolonged course of ECT to respond, and they appear to have a lower seizure threshold than do depressed patients [78]. ECT is safe and well tolerated by most geriatric patients. Consequently, ECT is the treatment of choice for elderly patients with mania who are unable to tolerate drug therapy, or who have a severe behavioral disturbance that necessitates rapid response.

Continuation and maintenance treatment is necessary in elderly bipolar patients who achieve remission of a manic or a depressive episode. Although studies of geriatric populations are not available, studies of younger adults suggest that lithium, carbamazepine, and valproate are effective in prevention of both depressive and manic episodes. Therefore, continuation and maintenance treatment with these drugs should be considered in the elderly.

Treatment of depression in the frail elderly

The National Institutes of Health Consensus Conference [4] stated that "the hallmark of depression in older people is its comorbidity with medical illness." Although some authors in the lay press have claimed that depression in the elderly may be a natural and even an inevitable reaction to loss, illness, and disability, there is compelling evidence from placebo-controlled clinical trials that antidepressant medications are efficacious in patients with common comorbid medical disorders as diverse as stroke, parkinsonism, cancer, ischemic heart disease, chronic obstructive pulmonary disease, and arthritis [79]. Moreover, one seminal study [79] found that treatment of depression in patients with chronic lung disease led to improvements in day-to-day functioning as well as the alleviation of mood symptoms. Another study [81] suggested that treatment of depression in cancer patients could facilitate the administration of chemotherapy by helping patients tolerate its adverse effects.

Each of these studies was conducted in patient populations with a single, well-characterized comorbid condition. Analogous results were obtained in placebo-controlled studies of tricyclic antidepressants in an inpatient rehabilitation unit [82], where treatment of depression could facilitate recovery from acute illness or injury, and in a residential care setting, where patients were characterized by extreme old age and the interacting effects of many of the common disabling medical disorders of late life [83]. Although there have been recurring concerns that it may be difficult to distinguish between the somatic or vegetative symptoms of depression and those of medical illness, current evidence demonstrates that depression can be reliably diagnosed, even in the old and frail. The basic conclusion from this literature, therefore, must be that persistent symptoms of major depression in patients with adequately treated medical disorders should also be treated. There are, however, various special considerations that are relevant to treatment of depression in the frail elderly.

There has as yet been little research on the efficacy of either psychotherapy or newer antidepressants such as the SSRIs, venlafaxine, or nefazodone in older patients with significant general medical illnesses. Although they may still be appropriate first-line treatments for frail older patients with mild to moderate depressive symptoms, it is important to monitor affective symptoms closely during treatment and to switch to more established approaches, such as tricyclic antidepressants, if patients do not respond.

There is growing anecdotal literature on the use of stimulant medications, such as methylphenidate, for the short-term treatment of depressive symptoms in elderly patients with significant medical illness. This is supported by suggestive results from a recent small-scale, placebo-controlled crossover study [84].

Depression can be a key component of the often terminal physiologic decline that is frequently seen in the frail elderly. Thus, Morley and Kraenzle [85] found that depression was the most common cause of weight loss in a community nursing home, and Katz *et al.* [86] found that it was a critical part of the syndrome of "failure to thrive." It has been suggested by Katz *et al.* [83] that there may be a vicious cycle involving depression and malnutrition in the frail elderly; depression may cause protein–calorie undernutrition, and subnutrition may decrease antidepressant responses. Depressed older patients with weight loss and subnutrition must be viewed as highly vulnerable.

Drug–drug and drug–disease interactions can make older patients highly vulnerable to the adverse effects of tricyclic antidepressants; approximately 30% of a residential care population, average age 85, could not tolerate treatment with nortriptyline at therapeutic plasma levels [83]. Careful monitoring of both potential adverse effects and plasma levels is necessary to optimize the safety of these agents in the frail elderly.

Treatment of depression in patients with dementing disorders

Patients with major depression and cognitive impairment may have either a single illness, in which reversible cognitive impairment occurs as a component of depression (dementia syndrome of depression or depressive pseudodementia), or two separate disorders, in which major depression coexists with irreversible dementia and causes increased cognitive impairment, functional disability, behavioral disturbances, care needs, and caregiver burden. The latter condition, in which depression coexists with irreversible dementia, appears to be more common [87]. Recent clinical research focuses on both problems. Whereas earlier studies had suggested that patients for whom treatment of depression led to improvements in cognitive status were no more likely than control individuals to develop irreversible dementia, more recent findings [56] suggest that they are, in fact, at increased risk; thus, depressive pseudodementia may, in some cases, be a prodrome of Alzheimer's disease or related disorders. Although there is still controversy about the extent to which mild or minor depression early in the course of dementing illness represents a psychologic reaction to increasing disability, there is growing evidence that major depression occurring in association with Alzheimer's disease and related disorders can have biologic components. Pearlson *et al.* [88] noted that it tends to occur in individuals with family histories of affective disorder. Zweig *et al.* [89] and Zubenko and Moossy [90] reported that postmortem studies on patients with dementia demonstrate that a history of coexisting depression is associated with pathologic lesions of brain stem aminergic nuclei. Although there has been considerable ongoing research on methods for distinguishing between the two contexts in which depression and cognitive impairment exist, the issue facing clinicians is straightforward: depression that is significant and persistent should be treated whenever it occurs.

Although randomized clinical trials on homogeneous groups of patients with coexisting Alzheimer's disease and major depression remain an important area for research, clinicians caring for these patients should approach them with the working hypothesis that treatment should follow the same basic principles that apply with other older patients [91] (Table 7). The modifications in practice that may be necessary follow from the clinical features of the comorbid dementias: it is important to ensure that medication-taking is supervised, to involve caregivers both in assessing affective outcomes and in monitoring for adverse drug effects, and to recognize that patients with Alzheimer's disease exhibit increased vulnerability to cognitive impairment from anticholinergic medications. In patients with dementia, as in those who are cognitively intact, clinicians should consider psychosocial as well as biologic approaches for treating depression. Teri [92] developed a model for a brief, focused treatment that involves altering the aversive events that maintain depression, increasing pleasant events, maximizing cognitive abilities, and teaching caregivers strategies for problem solving and behavioral management.

Electroconvulsive therapy

Older patients with severe depression are more likely to present with psychosis, suicidality, or food refusal requiring a rapid response, and less likely to respond to SSRIs [25] or to tolerate the anticholinergic and cardiac side effects of TCAs. Thus, whereas age per se does not constitute an indication for, or a predictor of favorable response to ECT, older patients are particularly likely to meet the current indications for ECT [93,94] (Table 8). As a result, 16% of inpatients 65 years of age and older with a mood disorder are treated with ECT, and the elderly constitute more than one third of ECT recipients, even though they represent less than 10% of hospitalized psychiatric patients [95].

Modern ECT techniques, including careful medical assessment of risks, use of non-dominant unilateral ECT with stimulus energy well above seizure threshold, and intensive monitoring and management of physiologic side effects, have made ECT a safe and efficacious treatment in older depressed patients, even in the presence of general medical illnesses or dementia [96–100]. ECT may be most useful as a first-line treatment in older, severely depressed patients for whom a rapid response is needed [101]. Indeed, patients who have failed to respond to antidepressant medications have a relatively low probability of responding quickly to ECT [102], and the responders tend to relapse after only a few weeks, irrespective of the continuation pharmacotherapy they may receive [60]. Little empirical data are available to guide the selection of continuation and maintenance

---

Table 7. Treatment of Depression Associated with Cognitive Impairment

Cognitive impairment can result from depression or from a separate dementing disorder. In either one, the depression should be treated.

Follow the same basic principles that apply with older patients.

Special considerations:

Ensure that medication use is supervised.

Involve caregivers to assess the benefits and monitor for adverse effects of treatment.

Patients with Alzheimer's disease are highly sensitive to increasing cognitive impairment from anticholinergic medications.

Antidepressants with lowest anticholinergic effects are preferred:

SSRIs

Nortriptyline

Bupropion

Nefazodone

Venlafaxine

SSRI—selective serotonin-reuptake inhibitor.

Table 8. Electroconvulsive Therapy: Advantages and Disadvantages

Advantages	Disadvantages
Most rapid response	Requires comprehensive work-up and close monitoring (specialized team)
Efficacy similar or better than any available antidepressant medication	Diminished acute efficacy and high relapse rates in medication-refractory patients
Physiologic alterations are transient and typically occur while patient is intensely monitored	No validated/accepted strategy for continuation after therapy and maintenance pharmacotherapy
Low rate of complications	Stigma

pharmacotherapy following successful treatment of depression with ECT. There may be a role for continuation and maintenance ECT given on an outpatient basis, particularly for patients refractory to medications. Although this strategy has been supported by a growing clinical experience and some published case series, it has not yet been validated by any controlled study.

Bereavement-related depression and complicated bereavement

Syndromal major depression occurs in 10% to 20% of the estimated 800,000 older Americans who lose a spouse through death each year [103]. Syndromal depression tends to persist throughout at least the first year or two of bereavement, unless treated. Preliminary data, based on open clinical trials, suggest that early intervention (as early as 2 months after bereavement) with antidepressant medication (nortriptyline) may well reduce the burden of depressive symptoms and, thereby, allow bereaved patients to do the work of bereavement [104]. Further controlled evaluation of antidepressant medication and psychotherapy in bereavement-related major depression and minor depression is necessary, however. Even when antidepressant medication appears to reduce symptoms of major depression in bereaved elders, it may not affect the symptoms of grief or of complicated grief per se. Symptoms of complicated grief are associated with poorer psychiatric and functional outcomes generally at 18 months than occur in the absence of such symptoms, after controlling for concurrent levels of depression. The symptoms of complicated grief can be reliably measured and include inability to accept the loss, anger over the loss, preoccupation with the deceased, survival guilt, intrusive thoughts, avoidant behaviors, hallucinations about the deceased, and sleep disturbance. In many ways, complicated grief resembles the symptoms of posttraumatic stress disorder and may possibly be a variant of it [105•]. As such, these symptoms may be responsive to SSRI therapy in combination with psychotherapy appropriate for complicated grief.

Conclusions

When major depression strikes elderly patients, particularly those with concomitant general medical illness, it often goes unrecognized and untreated. Yet, treatment can be as effective and life-enhancing in the elderly as in younger medically healthy patients. Thus, an attitude of therapeutic optimism is supported. These conclusions are strongly buttressed by a recent comparison of initial treatment response in elderly and midlife patients with recurrent major depression. When using open, combined therapy with a tricyclic antidepressant (nortriptyline in the elderly [n = 150], imipramine in midlife patients [n = 225]), and interpersonal psychotherapy, researchers found similar rates of treatment response (about 65% in intent-to-treat samples) though somewhat more rapid remission of symptoms in midlife than in geriatric patients (on average about 12 weeks in geriatric depressed patients). Thus, medically burdened elderly patients with recurrent major depression appear to be as treatable as are patients in midlife with combined pharmacotherapy (under plasma level–controlled conditions) and IPT [106•]. These data also pose a challenge to the widely received strategy of "starting low, going slow" in the "young" elderly. Such a conservative approach may be more appropriate in the "old old" (patients 75 years of age and older).

Referral guidelines: the importance of being alert to suicide

Referral to a geriatrics specialist is appropriate if the patient is diagnostically complex or is severely ill, psychotic, suicidal, nonresponsive to an adequate trial of a first-line treatment, or judged to be in need of ECT. Referral back to the primary care clinician may occur after development of a treatment plan for a first-line treatment or after stabilization.

As recently emphasized by Conwell *et al.* [107], however, suicide in older patients frequently occurs in the context of first-episode major depression of moderate severity, without coexisting substance abuse or personality disorder. Yet, depression was not recognized by primary healthcare providers during office visits that occurred within the final month of the patient's life. Thus, for proper referral to take place, depression in the elderly must first be recognized at the initial point of clinical contact. The data from Conwell *et al.* [108] underscore that such recognition can be, literally, a matter of life and death. In this context, somatization appears to be a risk factor in elderly persons presenting to hospital [109]. Conwell *et al.* [108] described from their psychologic autopsy studies many elderly suicide cases preoccupied with health concerns, who did not seek mental health attention [108].

Directions for future research

Given current practice patterns, the field would benefit from additional data bearing on the comparative short- and long-term efficacy, tolerability, and safety of secondary TCAs, such as nortriptyline, versus the newer generation SSRIs, such as sertraline or paroxetine. There is good reason to think that the SSRIs may be safer and better tolerated, particularly in the "old old" or frail elderly, with more benign effects on measures of neuropsychologic function, but whether they are as effective in severely ill patients, or various subtypes of geriatric depression, on a short- or long-term basis is unknown.

Clinical practice also needs to be informed by data from clinical trials enrolling difficult patients at very high risk for severe chronic illness and suicide, such as those with delusional or bipolar forms of illness, as well as mood disorders associated with neurodegenerative illnesses. The role of psychosocial interventions with such disorders, particularly in ensuring compliance with treatment and easing the burden of caregiving, deserves special attention. Researchers need to develop and test treatment approaches to such patients that are transferable from university-based laboratory settings to other community-based settings dealing with more diverse heterogeneous populations than those that may be enrolled in controlled clinical trials. This is also true with the so-called minor depressions that are typically seen in primary care settings.

Finally, interventions with more rapid onset of clinical activity are highly desirable, given the sluggish course of antidepressant response in the elderly. For example, the controlled evaluation of total or partial short-term sleep deprivation, or the use of combined pharmacotherapy, as a means of accelerating clinical response should be tested.

Acknowledgments

Supported in part by National Institute of Mental Health (NIMH) Clinical Research Center grants MH52247 (CFR), MH49762 (GA), and MH52129 (IK). The authors thank Barry D. Lebowitz, PhD, Chief of the NIMH Aging Branch, for his review of this chapter; Jane Pearson, PhD; and Rick Martinez, MD, also of the NIMH Aging Branch.

References and Recommended Reading

Papers of particular interest, published recently, have been highlighted as:
*   Of special interest
•• Of outstanding interest

1. Kennedy GJ, Kelman HR, Thomas C: Persistence and remission of depressive symptoms in late life. *Am J Psychiatry* 1991, 148:174–178.

2. George LK: Social factors and depression in late life. In *Diagnosis and Treatment of Depression in Late Life: Results of the NIH Consensus Development Conference.* Edited by Schneider LS, Reynolds CF, Lebowitz BD, Friedhoff AJ. Washington, DC: American Psychiatric Press; 1994:131–153.

3. Blazer DG: Is depression more frequent in late life? An honest look at the evidence. *Am J Geriatr Psychiatry* 1994, 2:193–199.

4. National Institutes of Health Consensus Development Panel: diagnosis and treatment of depression in late life. *JAMA* 1992, 268:1018–1024.

5. Mulsant BU, Sweet RA, Rifai AH, *et al.*: The use of the Hamilton Rating Scale for depression in elderly patients with cognitive impairment and physical illness. *Am J Geriatr Psychiatry* 1994, 2:220–229.

6. Hendrie HC, Callahan CM, Levitt EE, *et al.*: Prevalence rates of major depressive disorders: the effects of varying the diagnostic criteria in an older primary care population. *Am J Geriatr Psychiatry* 1995, 2:119–131.

7. Schneider LS, Reynolds CF, Lebowitz DB, Friedhoff AJ, eds.: *Diagnosis and Treatment of Depression in Late Life: Proceedings of the NIH Consensus Development Conference.* Washington, DC: American Psychiatric Press; 1994.

8. Frank E: Long-term prevention of recurrences in elderly patients. In *Diagnosis and Treatment of Depression in Late Life: Proceedings of the NIH Consensus Development Conference.* Edited by Schneider LS, Reynolds CF, Lebowitz BD, Friedhoff AJ. Washington, DC: American Psychiatric Press; 1994:317–329.

9. Reynolds CF, Frank E, Perel JM, *et al.*: Combined pharmacotherapy and psychotherapy in the acute and continuation treatment of elderly patients with recurrent major depression: a preliminary report. *Am J Psychiatry* 1992, 149:1687–1692.

10. Reynolds CF: Treatment of depression in late life. *Am J Med* 1994, 97(suppl 6A):39–46.

11.• Reynolds CF, Frank E, Dew MA, *et al.*: Discrimination of recovery in the treatment of elderly patients with recurrent major depression: limits of prediction. *Depression* 1995, 2:218–222.
Reliable discrimination of recovery versus nonrecovery in the elderly generally takes about 4 weeks. Thus, persistence with a particular treatment approach is important.

12. Georgotas A, McCue RE, Cooper TB, *et al.*: How effective and safe is continuation therapy in elderly depressed patients? Factors affecting relapse rate. *Arch Gen Psychiatry* 1988, 435:929–932.

13. Reynolds CF, Perel JM, Frank E, *et al.*: Open-trial maintenance of pharmacotherapy in late-life depression: survival analysis. *Psychiatry Res* 1989, 27:225–231.

14. Reynolds CF, Frank E, Perel JM, *et al.*: Treatment of consecutive episodes of major depression in the elderly. *Am J Psychiatry* 1994, 151:1740–1743.

15. Miller MD, Pollock BG, Rifai AH, *et al.*: Longitudinal analysis of nortriptyline side effects in elderly depressed patients. *J Geriatr Psychiatry Neurol* 1991, 4:226–230.

16. Reynolds CF, Frank E Perel JM, *et al.*: Nortriptyline side effects during double-blind, randomized, placebo-controlled maintenance therapy in older depressed patients. *Am J Geriatr Psychiatry* 1995, 3:170–175.

17. Monane M, Avorn J, Beers MH, *et al.*: Anticholinergic drug use and bowel function in nursing home patients. *Arch Intern Med* 1993, 153:633–638.

18. Willcox SM, Himmelstein DU, Woodhandler S: Inappropriate drug prescribing for the community-dwelling elderly. *JAMA* 1994, 272:292–296.

19. Reynolds CF, Zubenko GS, Pollock BG, *et al.*: Depression in late life. *Curr Opin Psychiatry* 1994, 7:18–21.

20. Preskorn SH: Recent pharmacologic advances in antidepressant therapy for the elderly. *Am J Med* 1993, 94(suppl 5A):2–12.

21. Druckenbrod R, Mulsant BH: Fluoxetine-induced syndrome of inappropriate antidiuretic hormone secretion. *J Geriatr Psychiatry Neurol* 1994, 7:255–258.

22. Cohn CK, Shrivastava R, Mendels J, *et al.*: Double blind, multicenter comparison of sertraline and amitriptyline in elderly depressed patients. *J Clin Psychiatry* 1990, 51(suppl B):28–33.

23. Dunner DL, Cohn JB, Walsh T III, *et al.*: Two combined, multicenter double blind studies of paroxetine and doxepin in geriatric patients with major depression. *J Clin Psychiatry* 1992, 53(suppl):57–60.

24. Hutchinson DR, Tong S, Moon CAL, *et al.*: A double blind study in general practice to compare the efficacy and tolerability of paroxetine and amitriptyline in depressed elderly patients. *J Clin Res* 1991, 2:43–57.

25. Toleffson GD, Holman SL: Analysis of the Hamilton Depression Rating Scale factors from a double-blind, placebo controlled trial of fluoxetine in geriatric major depression. *Int Clin Psychopharmacol* 1993, 8:253–259.

26. Roose SP, Glassman AH, Attia E, *et al.*: Comparative efficacy of selective serotonin reuptake inhibitors and tricyclics in the treatment of melancholia. *Am J Psychiatry* 1994, 151:1735–1739.

27. Andrews JM, Nemeroff CB: Contemporary management of depression. *Am J Med* 1994, 17(suppl 6A):24–32.

28. Nierenberg AA, Feighner JP, Rudolph R, *et al.*: Venlafaxine for treatment-resistant unipolar depression. *J Clin Psychopharmacol* 1994, 14:419–423.

29. Georgotas A, McCue RE, Hapworth W, *et al.*: Comparative efficacy and safety of MAOIs versus TCAs in treating depression in the elderly. *Biol Psychiatry* 1986, 21:1155–166.

30. Sunderland T, Cohen RM, Molchan S, *et al.*: High-dose selegiline in treatment-resistant older depressive patients. *Arch Gen Psychiatry* 1994, 51:607–615.

31. Ditkoff EC Crary WG, Cristo M, *et al.*: Estrogen improves psychological function in asymptomatic postmenopausal women. *Obstet Gynecol* 1991, 78:991–995.

32. Sherwin BB: The impact of different doses of estrogen and progestin on mood and sexual behavior in postmenopausal women. *J Clin Endocrinol Metab* 1991, 72:336.

33. Montgomery JC, Brincat M, Tapp A, *et al.*: Effect of oestrogen and testosterone implants on psychological disorders in the climacteric. *Lancet* 1987, 1:297–299.

34. Schneider MA, Brotherton PL, Hailes G: The effect of exogenous estrogens on depression in menopausal women. *Med J Aust* 1977, 2:162–163.

35. Thomson J, Oswald I: Effect of estrogen on the sleep, mood, and anxiety of menopausal women. *Br Med J* 1977, 2:1317–1319.

36. Klaiber EL, Broverman DM, Vogel W, *et al.*: Estrogen therapy for severe persistent depressions in women. *Arch Gen Psychiatry* 1979, 36:550–554.

37. Tepper R, Goldberger S, Cohen I, *et al.*: Estrogen replacement in postmenopausal women: are we currently overdosing our patients? *Gynecol Obstet Invest* 1994, 38:113.

38. Karp JF, Frank E, Anderson B, *et al.*: Time to recovery in late-life depression: analysis of effects of demographic, treatment, and life-events measures. *Depression* 1993, 1:250–256.

39. Rifai AH, George CJ, Stack JA, *et al.*: Hopelessness continues to distinguish suicide attempters after acute treatment of major depression in later life. *Am J Psychiatry* 1994, 151:1687–1690.

40. Gurianik JM, LaCroix AZ, Branch LG, *et al.*: Morbidity and disability in older persons in the years prior to death. *Am J Public Health* 1991, 82:443–447.

41. Pahor M, Gurianik JM, Salive ME, *et al.*: Disability and severe gastrointestinal hemorrhage. A prospective study of community-dwelling older persons. *J Am Geriatr Soc* 1994, 42:816–825.

42. Alexopoulos GS, Vrontou C, Meyers BS, *et al.*: Disability in geriatric depression. *New Research Abstracts.* Miami: American Psychiatric Association; 1995:205.

43. Kivela SL, Pahkala K: Delusional depression in the elderly: a community study. *Gerontology* 1989, 22:236–241.

44. Meyers BS: Geriatric delusional depression. *Clin Geriatr Med* 1992, 8:299–308.

45. Baldwin RC: Delusional and non-delusional depression in later life: evidence for distinct subtypes. *Br J Psychiatry* 1988, 152:39–44.

46. Sands JR, Harrow M: Psychotic unipolar depression at followup: factors related to psychosis in the affective disorders. *Am J Psychiatry* 1994, 151:995–1000.

47. Roose SP, Glassman AH, Walsh T, *et al.*: Depression, delusions, and suicide. *Am J Psychiatry* 1983, 140:1150–1162.

48. Isometsa E, Henriksson M, Aro H, *et al.*: Suicide in psychotic major depression. *J Affect Disord* 1994, 31:187–191.

49. Glassman AH, Kantor SJ, Shostak M: Depression, delusion, and drug response. *Am J Psychiatry* 1975, 132:716–719.

50. Chan CH, Janicak PG, Davis JM, *et al.*: Response of psychotic and non-psychotic depressed patients to tricyclic antidepressants. *J Clin Psychiatry* 1987, 48:197–200.

51. Glassman AH, Roose SP: Delusional depression: a distinct entity? *Arch Gen Psychiatry* 1981, 38:424–427.

52. Prien RF: Somatic treatment of unipolar depressive disorder. In *Review of Psychiatry, Vol 7*. Edited by Frances AJ, Hales RE. Washington, DC: American Psychiatric Press; 1988.

53. Spiker DG, Weiss JC, Dealy RS, *et al.*: The pharmacological treatment of delusional depression. *Am J Psychiatry* 1985, 142:430–436.

54. Clinical Research Center: The Norwick Park ECT Trial: predictors of response to real and simulated ECT. *Br J Psychiatry* 1984, 114:227–237.

55. Greenwald BS, Kramer-Ginsber E, Marin DB, *et al.*: Dementia with coexistent major depression. *Am J Psychiatry* 1989, 146:1472–1478.

56. Alexopoulos GS, Meyers BS, Young RC, *et al.*: The course of geriatric depression with "reversible dementia:" a controlled study. *Am J Psychiatry* 1993, 150:1693–1699.

57. Robinson DG, Spiker DG: Delusional depression: a one-year follow-up. *J Affect Disord* 1985, 9:79–83.

58. Coryell M, Tsuang MT: Primary unipolar depression and the prognostic importance of delusions. *Arch Gen Psychiatry* 1982, 39:1181–1194.

59. Tsuang D Coryell W: An 8-year follow-up of patients with DSR-III-R psychotic depression, schizoaffective disorder, and schizophrenia. *Am J Psychiatry* 1993, 150:1182–1188.

60. Sackeim HA, Prudic J, Devanand DP: The impact of medication resistance and continuation pharmacotherapy on relapse following response to electroconvulsive therapy in major depression. *J Clin Psychopharmacol* 1990, 10:96–104.

61. Young RC, Klerman GL: Mania in late life: focus on age at onset. *Am J Psychiatry* 1992, 4:73–78.

62. Krauthammer C, Klerman G: Secondary mania. *Arch Gen Psychiatry* 1978, 35:1333–1339.

63. Starkstein SE, Robinson RG, Price TR: Comparison of patients with and without post-stroke major depression matched for size and location of lesion. *Arch Gen Psychiatry* 1988, 45:247–252.

64. Mirchandani IC, Young RC: Management of mania in the elderly: an update. *Ann Clin Psychiatry* 1993, 5:67–77.

65. Jensen HV, Olaffson K, Billie A, *et al.*: Lithium every second day: a new treatment regimen? *Lithium* 1990, 1:55–58.

66. Young RC, Mattis S, Kalayam B, *et al.*: Cognitive dysfunction in geriatric mania. *Abstracts of the Annual Meeting of the American Association for Geriatric Psychiatry*; 1992:14.

67. Lipsin B: Treatment of mania. In *Clinical Geriatric Psychopharmacology*. Edited by Salzman C. Baltimore: Williams & Wilkins; 1992:116–131.

68. Bowden CL, Brugger AM, Swann AC, *et al.*: Efficacy of divalproex vs. lithium and placebo in the treatment of mania. The Depakote Mania Study Group. *JAMA* 1994, 271:918–924.

69. Kellner MB, Neher F: A first episode of mania after age 80: a case report. *Can J Psychiatry* 1991, 36:607–608.

70. McFarland BH, Miller MR, Straumfjord AA: Valproate use in the older manic patient. *J Clin Psychiatry* 1990, 51:479–481.

71. Gnam W, Glint AJ: New onset rapid cycling bipolar disorder in an 87-year-old woman. *Can J Psychiatry* 1993, 38:324–326.

72. Yassa R, Cvejic J: Valproate in the treatment of posttraumatic bipolar disorder in a psychogeriatric patient. *J Geriatr Psychiatry Neurol* 1994, 7:55–57.

73. Dilsaver SC, Swann AC, Shoaib AM, *et al.*: The manic syndrome: factors which may predict a patient's response to lithium, carbamazepine and valproate. *J Psychiatry Neurosci* 1993, 18:61–66.

74. Stoll AL, Banov M, Kolbrener M, *et al.*: Neurologic factors predict a favorable valproate response in bipolar and schizoaffective disorders. *J Clin Psychopharmacol* 1994, 14:311–313.

75. Rimmer EM, Richens A: An update on sodium valproate. *Pharmacotherapy* 1985, 5:171–184.

76. Schneier HA, Khan D: Selective response to carbamazepine in a case of organic mood disorder [letter]. *J Clin Psychiatry* 1990, 52:485.

77. Tohen M, Castillo J, Baldessarini RJ, *et al.*: Blood dyscrasias with carbamazepine and valproate: a pharmacoepidemiological study of 2228 patients at risk. *Am J Psychiatry* 1995, 152:413–418.

78. Mukhergee S, Sackheim HA, Schnur DB:Electroconvulsive therapy of acute manic episodes; a review of 50 years' experience. *Am J Psychiatry* 1994, 151:169–176.

79. Katz IR: Drug treatment of depression in the frail elderly: discussion of the NIH Consensus Development Conference on the Diagnosis and Treatment of Depression in Late Life. *Psychopharm Bull* 1993, 29:101–108.

80. Borson S, McDonald GJ, Gayle T, *et al.*: Improvement in mood, physical symptoms, and function with nortriptyline for depression in patients with chronic obstructive pulmonary disease. *Psychosomatics* 1992, 33:190–201.

81. Costa D, Mogos I, Tuma T: Efficacy, and safety of mianserin in the treatment of depression of women with cancer. *Acta Psychiatr Scand Suppl* 1985, 72(suppl 320):85–92.

82. Lakshmanan M, Mion LC, Frengley JD: Effective low dose antidepressant treatment for depressed geriatric rehabilitation patients: a double-blind study. *J Am Geriatr Soc* 1986, 34:421–426.

83. Katz IR, Simpson GM, Curlik SM, *et al.*: Pharmacologic treatment of major depression for elderly patients in residential care settings. *J Clin Psychiatry* 1990, 51(suppl 7):41–47.

84. Wallace AE, Kofoed LL, West AN: Double-blind, placebo-controlled trial of methylphenidate in older, depressed, medically ill patients. *Am J Psychiatry* 1995, 152:929–931.

85. Morley JE, Kraenzle D: Causes of weight loss in a community nursing home. *J Am Geriatr Soc* 1994, 42:583–585.

86. Katz IR, Beaston-Wimmer P, Parmelee PA, *et al.*: Failure to thrive in the elderly: exploration of the concept and delineation of psychiatric components. *J Geriatr Psychiatry Neurol* 1993, 6:161–169.

87. Jones BN, Reifler BV: Depression coexisting with dementia: evaluation and treatment. *Med Clin North Am* 1994, 78:823–840.

88. Pearlson GD, Ross CA, Lohr WD, *et al.*: Association between family history of affective disorder and the depressive syndrome of Alzheimer's disease. *Am J Psychiatry* 1990, 147:452–456.

89. Zweig RM, Ross CA, Hedreen JC, *et al.*: The neuropathology of aminergic nuclei in Alzheimer's disease. *Ann Neurol* 1988, 24:233–242.

90. Zugenkok GS, Moossy J: Major depression in primary dementia. *Arch Neurol* 1988, 45:1182–1186.

91. Mulsant BH, Pollock BG, Nebes RD, *et al.*: Depression in Alzheimer's dementia. In *Progress in Alzheimer's Disease and Similar Conditions, Vol. 52*. Edited by Heston LL. [American Psychopathological Association Annual series.] Washington DC: American Psychiatric Press; 1997:161–179.

92. Teri L: Behavioral treatment of depression in patients with dementia. *Alzheimer Dis Assoc Disord* 1994, 8(suppl 3):66–74.

93. American Psychiatric Association Task Force on Electroconvulsive Therapy: *The Practice of Electroconvulsive Therapy: Recommendations for Treatment, Training and Privileging*. Washington, DC: American Psychiatric Association; 1990.

94. Sackeim HA: Use of electroconvulsive therapy in late-life depression. In *Diagnosis and Treatment of Depression in Late Life, Results of the NIH Consensus Development Conference*. Edited by Schneider LS, Reynolds CF, Lebowitz BD, Friedhoff AJ. Washington, DC: American Psychiatric Press; 1994:259–277.

95. Thompson JW, Weiner RD, Myers CP: Use of ECT in the United States in 1975, 1980, and 1986. *Am J Psychiatry* 1994, 151:1657–1661.

96. Knox GB, Sung YF: ECT anesthesia strategies in the high risk medical patient. In *Psychiatric Care of the Medical Patient*. Edited by Stoudemire A, Fogel BS. New York: Oxford University Press; 1993:225–240.

97. Mulsant BH, Rosen J, Thornton JE, *et al.*: A prospective naturalistic study of electroconvulsive therapy in late-life depression. *J Geriatr Psychiatry Neurol* 1991, 4:3–13.

98. Price TR, McAllister TW: Safety and efficacy of ECT in depressed patients with dementia: a review of clinical experience. *Convulsive Ther* 1989, 5:61–74.

99. Stoudemire A, Hill CD, Morris R, *et al.*: Long-term affective and cognitive outcome in depressed older adults. *Am J Psychiatry* 1993, 150:896–900.

100. Zielinski RJ, Roose SP, Devanand DP, *et al.*: Cardiovascular complications of ECT in depressed elderly patients with cardiac disease. *Am J Psychiatry* 1993, 150:904–909.

101. Mulsant BH, Singhal S, Kunik ME: New developments in the treatment of late-life depression. In *Practical Clinical Strategies in Treating Depression and Anxiety in a Managed Care Environment*. Edited by Holer RE, Yudolfsky SC. Washington, DC: American Psychiatric Press; 1996:55–61.

102. Prudic J, Sackeim HA, Devanand DP: Medication resistance and clinical response to electrocon-
      vulsive therapy. *Psychiatry Res* 1990, 31:287–296.

103. Zisook S, Shuchter SR, Sledge PA, *et al.*: The spectrum of depressive phenomena after spousal
      bereavement. *J Clin Psychiatry* 1994, 55(suppl 4):29–36.

104. Pasternak R, Reynolds CF, Frank E, *et al.*: Temporal course of depressive symptoms and grief
      intensity in late-life spousal bereavement. *Depression* 1993, 1:45–49.

105.● Prigerson HG, Frank E, Kasl SV, *et al.*: Complicated grief and bereavement-related depression: a
      literature review and a preliminary empirical validation among spousally bereaved elders. *Am J
      Psychiatry* 1995, 152:22–30.
This article reviews the psychiatric complications of bereavement and makes a case for traumatic grief
symptoms as being separate and distinct from those of bereavement-related depression and anxiety.

106.● Reynolds CF, Frank E, Kupfer DJ, *et al.*: Treatment outcome in recurrent major depression: a post-
      hoc comparison of elderly and midlife patients. *Am J Psychiatry* 1996, 153:1288–1292.
This study demonstrates that elderly depressed patients benefit as much as mid-life patients from treatment of major depression.

107. Conwell Y, Caine ED, Olson K: Suicide and cancer in late life. *Hosp Community Psychiatry* 1990,
      41:1334–1339.

108. Conwell Y, Rotenberg M, Caine ED: Completed suicide at age 50 and older. *J Am Geriatr Soc*
      1990, 38:640–644.

109. Horton-Deutsch SL, Clark DC, Farran CJ: Chronic dyspnea and suicide in elderly men. *Hosp
      Community Psychiatry* 1992, 43:1198–1203.

CHAPTER 8

Drug Interactions and Their Role in Patient Care

Sheldon H. Preskorn, Anne T. Harvey, and Christina Stanga

Polypharmacy is a clinical fact of life. For example, 30% to 80% of patients taking an antidepressant are also taking two or more other drugs, depending on the age and medical status of the population being surveyed. Although drug–drug interactions can be therapeutic, they also can have harmful and even fatal consequences. By being knowledgeable about the basis for such interactions, physicians can avoid adverse outcomes for their patients. Drug interactions can be broadly considered as pharmacodynamically and/or pharmacokinetically mediated. Pharmacodynamic interactions occur when the effect of the mechanism of action (MOA) of one drug amplifies or diminishes the response produced by the second drug through its MOA. Pharmacokinetic interactions occur when one drug affects the absorption, distribution, metabolism, or elimination of another drug. In addition, underlying biologic variance among patients can affect the pharmacodynamic response or alter the pharmacokinetics of one or more of the drugs. In this chapter, we examine these interactions and explain how physicians can organize their knowledge in terms of the effects of the drugs at specific sites of action. Using these principles, physicians can make appropriate treatment decisions to optimize patient outcome.

A significant percentage of patients being treated with an antidepressant may experience a drug–drug interaction. In four recent studies, 30% to 80% of outpatients in primary care or psychiatric settings being treated with an antidepressant were taking at least two other drugs [1,2] (Preskorn SH, Unpublished data; Wolf *et al.*, Abstract presented at the 148th Annual Meeting of the American Psychiatric Association, Miami, 1995). Given such prevalent use of polypharmacy, physicians have a duty to understand what potential interactions may occur and how to adjust therapy to optimize the patient's outcome.

Physicians use polypharmacy for many reasons [3]. When drugs are being used together to treat the same condition in a patient, the goal—wittingly or not—is to produce a drug–drug interaction that will either increase the therapeutic response or minimize an adverse effect (Table 1). Even when a patient is being administered more than one drug to treat different and pathophysiologically distinct illnesses, the potential exists for a drug–drug interaction. Because these cases involve a patient with more than one disease, the potential for unplanned drug–disease interaction also exists.

In the past, knowledge of drug–drug interactions was dependent primarily, if not solely, on memorization. New biochemical technology has allowed such interactions to be classified according to specific underlying mechanisms. This system can aid the physician in both remembering the potential interactions and anticipating whatever adjustments are needed to ensure an optimum outcome. This chapter presents such a system, rather than providing a catalog of drug–drug interactions.

Table 1. Parkinson's Disease as a Model of Rational Copharmacy*

Treatment	Effect†
L-Dopa	Increase synthesis of central dopamine (type: Pk)
L-Dopa plus carbidopa	Inhibit peripheral decarboxylase to reduce the dose of L-dopa needed to increase synthesis of central dopamine (type: Pk)
L-Dopa/carbidopa plus dopamine-reuptake inhibitor (eg, bupropion, amantadine)	Potentiate the effect of released central dopamine (type: Pk)
L-Dopa/carbidopa plus L-deprenyl (selegiline)	Increase synthesis of central dopamine and block its degradation (type: Pk)
L-Dopa/carbidopa plus bromocriptine	Potentiate central dopamine agonism by addition of direct dopamine agonist (type: Pd)

*Data from Preskorn and Lacey [3].
†"Type" refers to type of interaction.
Pd—pharmacodynamic; Pk—pharmacokinetic.

Types of Interactions

The patient's response to drug treatment is determined by three major variables: the mechanism of action of the drug, the concentration of the drug achieved at the site of action, and any underlying biologic variance in the patient that shifts the dose–response curve [4]. The following equations outline this relationship between pharmacodynamics, pharmacokinetics, and biologic variance in determining the overall result of drug treatment [4]:

1. Magnitude of effect = Pd × Pk × individual biologic variance (where Pd is pharmacodynamic and Pk is pharmacokinetic)
2. Clinical or clinical response = potency for MOA × drug concentration of site of action × underlying biology of patient

Drug–drug interactions can be understood in the same way. They are either pharmacodynamically or pharmacokinetically mediated. The magnitude of the interaction may be influenced by underlying biologic variance among patients. Individual differences can affect the pharmacodynamic response to one or more of the drugs or can alter the pharmacokinetics of one or more of the drugs.

The remainder of this article discusses drug–drug interactions as if they are either pharmacodynamically or pharmacokinetically mediated. This approach is being taken for the sake of simplicity. However, two drugs may interact pharmacodynamically and pharmacokinetically at the same time.

Pharmacodynamic interactions

Pharmacodynamic interactions occur when the effect of the MOA of one drug amplifies or diminishes the response produced by a second drug through its MOA. The sites of action may be in the same target cell, in different cell types in the same organ, or in different organs or body compartments. Drugs achieve a given response by engaging a mechanism at a site of action. However, the magnitude of that response is a function of the concentration of the drug at the site of action and the amount of time the drug remains there. This is discussed further in the last section, which deals with pharmaco-kinetically mediated drug interactions.

The potency of a drug that is required to affect a specific MOA can be determined using *in vitro* techniques [5,6]. In these studies, a concentration–response curve is constructed by incubating the isolated site of action with different concentrations of the drug to determine the drug's ability to affect the MOA. These studies may involve simply determining the binding affinity of the drug for the site, or determining the ability of the drug to engage the MOA. Examples of the latter would be 1) to measure the second-messenger response to stimulation by a drug with agonist properties, or 2) to study the ability of an antagonist to block response to an agonist. The second instance is important because a drug may act as an agonist, inverse agonist, or antagonist at a site of action. Simple binding studies determine the affinity of the drug for the site but not its effect.

From the results of such *in vitro* studies, the relative potency of the drug for multiple different MOAs can be determined. Given this information and a knowledge of the concentration of the drug that will occur under clinical conditions, one can determine which MOAs the drug is likely to affect under clinically relevant conditions. What these MOAs mediate in terms of physiologic responses and how they are interrelated both in normal physiology and under pathophysiologic conditions will allow the physician to determine whether a pharmacodynamically mediated drug–drug interaction is likely to occur and what the outcome is likely to be when two drugs are used together. The physician can estimate the magnitude of the interaction by 1) knowing the potency of each drug for its MOA; 2) either directly measuring the concentration of the drug achieved by the dose prescribed, or estimating the concentration that should be reasonably expected based on the dose prescribed; and 3) knowing how much agonism or antagonism is produced by affecting these different MOAs. With this information, the physician can make a reasonable initial dose adjustment and then further refine the dosing based on the patient's response.

Over its clinically relevant concentration range, a given drug may affect multiple MOAs or it may show selectivity such that it affects only one MOA [7]. The former is more characteristic of older drugs that were discovered by chance, whereas the latter is more typical of newer drugs, which were often designed rationally to affect only a specific MOA over the clinically relevant concentration range.

Obviously, the more MOAs a drug has the more likely it is to interact with other concomitantly prescribed drugs, depending on the concentration of each that is achieved by the dose prescribed. Table 2 provides a way of classifying drugs based on the MOAs that they affect over their clinically relevant dosing range. With this approach, the clinician can anticipate pharmacodynamically mediated drug–drug interactions and use them either therapeutically or to minimize adverse outcomes.

Pharmacodynamic interactions and neural wiring

Figure 1 illustrates potential components of the simplest type of interaction in which two pharmaceuticals act on the same neurotransmitter at the same synaptic site. Figure 1 also shows the various mechanisms known to be affected by specific types of psychopharmaceuticals and the physiologic and clinical consequences of affecting each MOA individually. With this type of conceptualization, the physician can determine the likely outcome of using two drugs together that can affect these different MOAs.

Table 2. Examples of Drugs Classified by Mechanism of Action

Serotonin (5-HT) uptake pump inhibition
  Paroxetine
  Sertraline
  Fluvoxamine
  Clomipramine
  Fluoxetine
  Amitriptyline
  Imipramine
  Venlafaxine
  Nefazodone
Norepinephrine uptake pump inhibition
  Maprotiline
  Desipramine
  Nortriptyline
  Venlafaxine
  Bupropion
Dopamine uptake pump inhibition
  Amphetamine
  Methylphenidate
  Pemoline
  Bupropion
Dopamine D_2-receptor antagonism
  Fluphenazine
  Haloperidol
  Perphenazine
  Risperidone
5-HT_{2A} antagonism
  Nefazodone
  Risperidone
  Trazodone
Muscarinic–cholinergic receptor blockade
  Benztropine
  Trihexyphenidyl
  Amitriptyline
  Chlorpromazine
  Thioridazine
  Doxepin
  Imipramine

Histamine H_1-receptor blockade
  Diphenhydramine
  Doxepin
  Amitriptyline
  Thioridazine
  Chlorpromazine
  Imipramine
Histamine H_2-receptor blockade
  Cimetidine
  Ranitidine
  Doxepin
  Amitriptyline
  Thioridazine
  Chlorpromazine
  Imipramine
α_1-Adrenergic receptor antagonism
  Prazosin
  Amitriptyline
  Thioridazine
  Chlorpromazine
  Doxepin
  Imipramine
α_2-Adrenergic receptor antagonism
  Yohimbine
  Amitriptyline
  Thioridazine
  Chlorpromazine
  Doxepin
  Imipramine
Sodium fast channel blockade
  Quinidine
  Amitriptyline
  Thioridazine
  Chlorpromazine
  Doxepin
  Imipramine

An example of a clinically relevant pharmacodynamic interaction involving a single neuron would be the proposed augmentation strategy of using pindolol in combination with a selective serotonin-reuptake inhibitor (SSRI) to shorten the time until onset of antidepressant efficacy [8]. This combination strategy also illustrates the emerging trend of using basic science to first model a potentially useful interaction and then test it in patients. A generally accepted and poorly understood limitation of most, if not all, antidepressants is a delayed onset of antidepressant efficacy. The delay is typically about 2 to 4 weeks. SSRIs are believed to act through the potentiation of central serotonin (5-hydroxytryptamine [5-HT]) neurotransmission. However, the immediate response to blockade of 5-HT uptake is to diminish the firing rate of the 5-HT neuron. This decrease appears to be the result of feedback inhibition mediated by the somatodendritic 5-HT_{1A} autoreceptor. After several weeks of continuous treatment with an SSRI, the 5-HT neuronal-firing rate returns to normal. Normalization is believed to be a result of the subsensitivity that develops in the 5-HT$_{1A}$ receptor. If the antidepressant efficacy of SSRIs is due to their promotion of central 5-HT transmission, an acute decrease in firing rate would temporarily counteract reuptake inhibition and efficacy would not become apparent until the firing rate returned to normal. If this line of reasoning is correct, one might be able to reduce the lag to onset of antidepressant efficacy by blocking the 5-HT$_{1A}$ receptor mediating the initial decrease in central 5-HT firing. Pindolol blocks the 5-HT$_{1A}$ receptor, and consistent with the basic science, iontophoretic application of pindolol onto central 5-HT neurons prevents a decrease in firing in response to the acute administration of an SSRI.

The next step will be to test the theory that preventing the decrease in 5-HT neuronal firing will prevent the delay in onset of efficacy. This could be accomplished by comparing the time to onset of antidepressant efficacy in patients treated with pindolol in combination with an SSRI with that of patients treated with an SSRI alone. As yet, there are only encouraging case reports; however, double-blind controlled studies are underway to test the theory formally. This work shows how drug interactions might be used to promote a desired clinical outcome in a relatively simple manner.

Figure 2 illustrates the complexity that can develop when drugs affect MOAs on different neurons and use different neurotransmitters. In this instance, the outcome is dependent on the way neurons interact in addition to the effect of the drugs on the different MOAs. The neurons may act in parallel to affect the same common pathway or they may interact in series. In the latter circumstance, one neuron may influence the other neuron through an effect on its dendritic input or by affecting its presynaptic terminal fields. In point of fact, all of these types of interaction may occur when two psychopharmaceuticals are used together, particularly when they affect fundamentally different MOAs.

Because the brain is a highly integrated organ, even simple drug combinations can have relatively far-reaching effects on brain function that may cause serious and possibly life-threatening adverse consequences. One example is the combination of an SSRI and a monoamine oxidase inhibitor (MAOI) in treating depression. SSRIs block the neuronal uptake pump for 5-HT, resulting in increased amounts of serotonin at the synapse. The MAOIs inhibit the major intracellular enzyme responsible for the degradation of

---

Following pages

Figure 1. (pages 150 and 151) **A,** Sites of action relevant to pharmacodynamically mediated drug–drug interactions affecting the central serotonin (5-HT) neurons. The illustration shows an idealized synapse between a presynaptic serotonin neuron and a postsynaptic cell. Not all postsynaptic cells will necessarily contain all of these receptors. They are presented here for purposes of illustration to show how drugs that affect the detailed sites of action could interact when administered together. **B,** A summary outlining the sites of interaction (cellular or receptor) and consequences of such interactions for representative neurotropic drugs. SSRIs—selective serotonin-reuptake inhibitors.

Figure 2. (pages 152 and 153) **A,** Potential components of complex pharmacodynamic interactions involving multiple neuronal connections or multiple neurotransmitters. How more than one neurotransmitter system may interact in parallel, or in series, is illustrated. For simplicity, all postsynaptic receptors are shown on one idealized postsynaptic neuron. Although such a situation does not exist in the brain, the goal is to illustrate how the effects of drugs that affect different sites of action can summate to produce the clinical effect observed in the patient. **B,** An outline of the sites of action and representative neurotropic drugs that act at these sites.

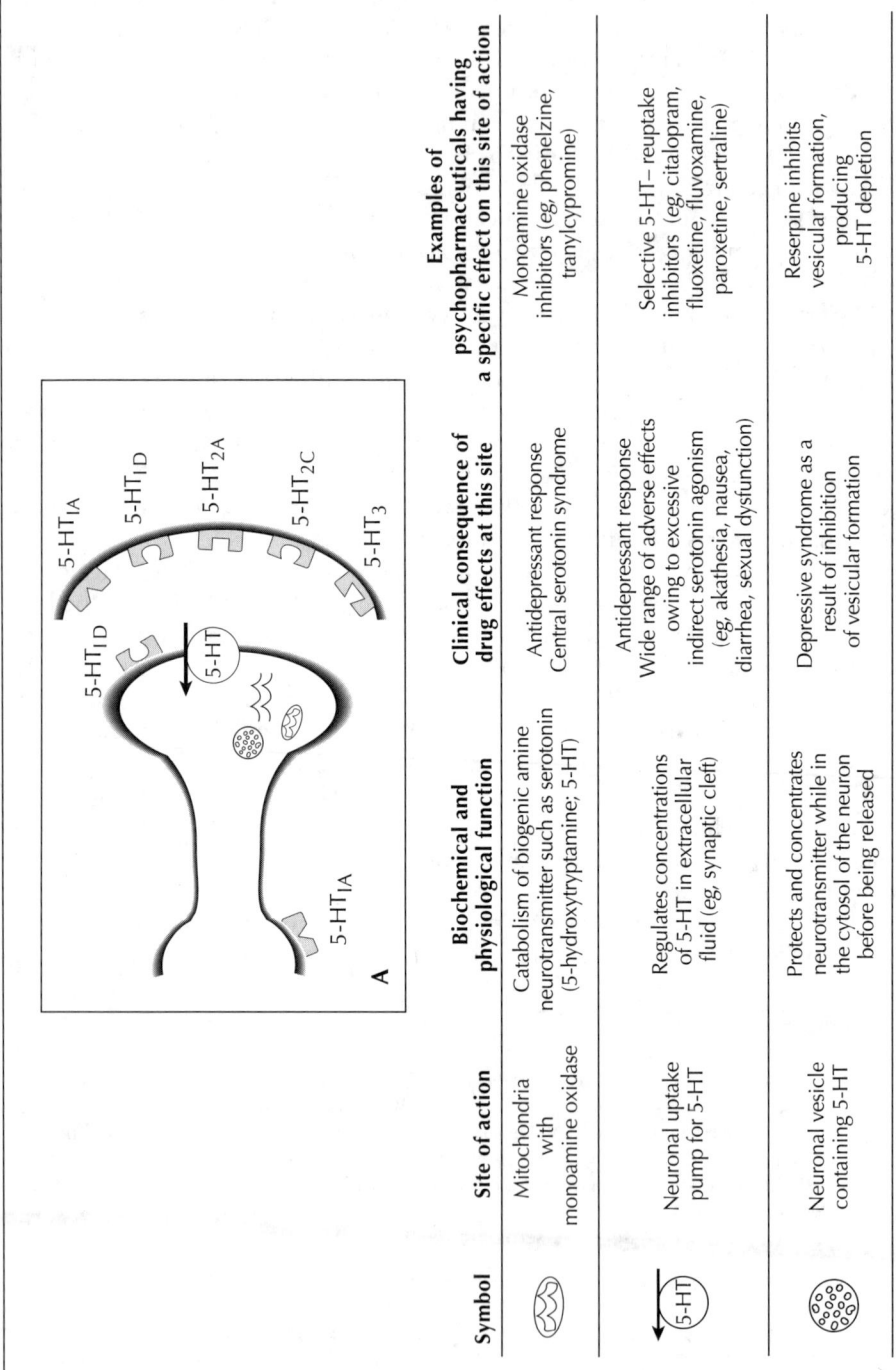

Symbol	Site of action	Biochemical and physiological function	Clinical consequence of drug effects at this site	Examples of psychopharmaceuticals having a specific effect on this site of action
	Mitochondria with monoamine oxidase	Catabolism of biogenic amine neurotransmitter such as serotonin (5-hydroxytryptamine; 5-HT)	Antidepressant response Central serotonin syndrome	Monoamine oxidase inhibitors (eg, phenelzine, tranylcypromine)
5-HT	Neuronal uptake pump for 5-HT	Regulates concentrations of 5-HT in extracellular fluid (eg, synaptic cleft)	Antidepressant response Wide range of adverse effects owing to excessive indirect serotonin agonism (eg, akathesia, nausea, diarrhea, sexual dysfunction)	Selective 5-HT–reuptake inhibitors (eg, citalopram, fluoxetine, fluvoxamine, paroxetine, sertraline)
	Neuronal vesicle containing 5-HT	Protects and concentrates neurotransmitter while in the cytosol of the neuron before being released	Depressive syndrome as a result of inhibition of vesicular formation	Reserpine inhibits vesicular formation, producing 5-HT depletion

B

Symbol	Site of action	Biochemical and physiological function	Clinical consequence of drug effects at this site	Examples of psychopharmaceuticals having a specific effect on this site of action
⌇	Mechanism for fusion of vesicle to plasmalemma of neuron	Facilitates migration of vesicle to and fusion with neuronal plasmalemma so neurotransmitter can be released into synaptic cleft in response to neuronal stimulation	Anorexia (?) Wide range of 5-HT–mediated adverse effects (see reuptake pump above)	Fenfluramine
	5-HT$_{1A}$ receptor	Presynaptic somatodendritic autoreceptor, the activation of which decreases 5-HT firing; also postsynaptic receptors; both inhibit adenylate cyclase	May medicate the delayed onset of antidepressant action produced by SSRIs; reduction in aggression	Busiprone: partial agonist presynaptically, closer to full agonist postsynaptically Pindolol: antagonist
	5-HT$_{1D}$ receptor	Presynaptic terminal auto- and heteroreceptor that inhibits vesicular release when neuron fires; inhibits adenylate cyclase	Antimigraine by blocking 5-HT–mediated vasoconstriction that produces migraine headache	Sumatriptan: agonist
	5-HT$_{2A}$ receptor	Linked to phosphatidylinositol turnover	Antidepressant Deficit symptoms reduction in schizophrenia	Nefazodone: antagonist Risperidone: antagonist
	5-HT$_{2C}$ receptor	Linked to phosphatidylinositol turnover	Anxiogenesis	Methylchlorpiperazine: agonist
	5-HT$_3$ receptor	Ion channel	Reduction of 5-HT–mediated nausea	Ondansetron: antagonist Cisapride: antagonist

B

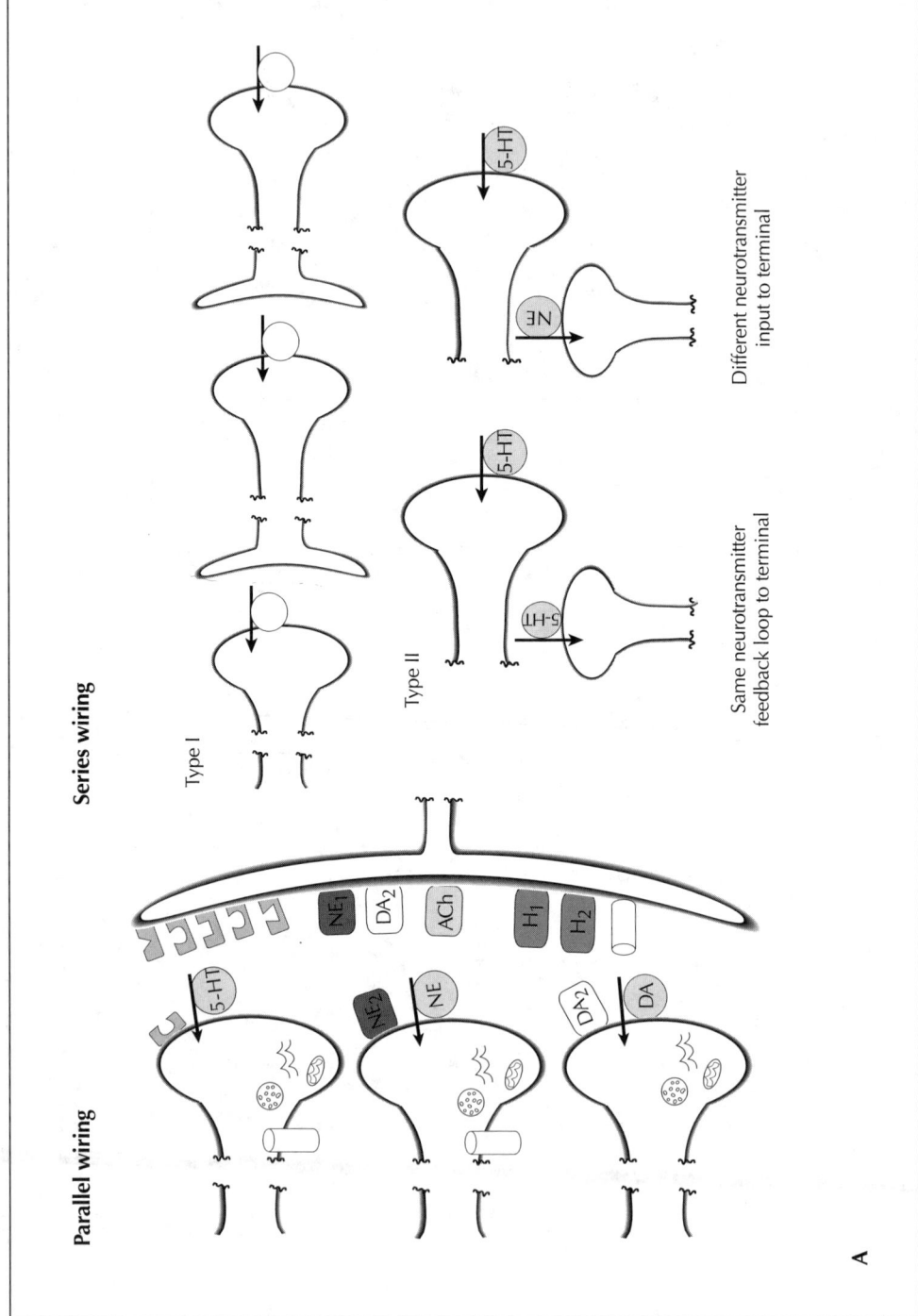

Class*	Symbol	Site of Action	Drug
2	5-HT	Uptake pump for serotonin (5-hydroxytryptamine; 5-HT)	Selective serotonin-reuptake inhibitor (SSRI; *eg,* sertraline) [†]
3	NE	Uptake pump for norepinephrine (NE)	Tricyclic antidepressant (TCA; *eg,* desipramine) [†]
4	DA	Uptake pump for dopamine (DA)	Dopamine uptake inhibitor (*eg,* bupropion)
5	ACh	Acetylcholinergic receptor (ACh)	Benztropine [†‡]
6	H_1	Histamine-1 receptor (H_1)	Diphenhydramine [†‡]
6	H_2	Histamine-2 receptor (H_2)	Ranitidine [†‡]
3	NE_1	α_1-Adrenergic receptor (NE_1)	Prasozin [†‡]
3	NE_2	α_2-Adrenergic receptor (NE_2)	Yohimbine [†‡]
4	DA_2	Dopamine-2 receptor (DA_2)	Haloperidol [‡]
1		Sodium fast channels	Quinidine [†‡]

*1—cellular; 2—serotonergic; 3—noradrenergic; 4—dopaminergic; 5—cholinergic; 6—histaminergic.
[†]Tertiary amine tricyclic antidepressants, such as amitriptyline, affect all of these sites.
[‡]Low-potency neuroleptics, such as thioridazine, affect all of these sites.

B

5-HT, thereby increasing its intracellular availability. However, MAOIs also affect norepinephrine, epinephrine, and dopamine. The monoamine neurotransmitter systems (involving serotonin, norepinephrine, epinephrine, and dopamine) are phylogenetically old and are key to basic brain function, projecting diffusely into many other neural structures. The combination of an SSRI and an MAOI for the treatment of depression may seem ideal, because these drug classes appear to have different and additive mechanisms, leading to enhancement of serotonergic transmission. However, the interconnectedness of the system affected, as illustrated in Figure 3, suggests that the combination of an SSRI and an MAOI could result in adverse and unexpected consequences. One known consequence is the potentially lethal serotonin syndrome [9]. The most frequent clinical features of this syndrome and plausible anatomic correlates are outlined in Table 3. These signs are most likely due to alterations in the function of the four monoamines within the central nervous system. This interaction underscores the problems posed by the interconnection of brain mechanisms and demonstrates the hazards of thinking in terms of a drug acting on one neurotransmitter system in isolation.

Pharmacodynamic interactions involving multiple organ systems

Two drugs may interact, even though each drug has a different site of action in different organ systems. Figure 4 illustrates such a scenario for blood pressure response to the combined use of a diuretic, a β-adrenergic receptor blocker, and an $α_1$-adrenergic receptor blocker. The diuretic can decrease vascular volume by its effects on renal clearance, the β-adrenergic blocker can decrease cardiac output by its effects on both stroke volume and heart rate, and an $α_1$-adrenergic blocker can decrease total peripheral resistance. The resulting change in blood pressure can be profound, because the various compensatory fail-safe mechanisms that the body uses to maintain blood pressure are simultaneously thwarted. Drugs normally thought of as psychotropic medications, such as tricyclic antidepressants (TCA) or low-potency phenothiazines, can have $α_1$-adrenergic–blocking activity (Table 3).

Pharmacokinetic interactions

Pharmacokinetic interactions occur when one drug affects the pharmacokinetics of another drug (*ie*, its absorption, distribution, metabolism, or elimination). Figure 5 illustrates the steps that occur during treatment with an orally administered medication in the outpatient setting. Two individuals determine the dosing rate: the physician who prescribes a given dose, and the patient who decides how much he or she will take, which may be more or less than the physician prescribed, or may be a variable rate over time. The dosing rate then is the amount of medication delivered to the body per interval of time, usually considered in terms of the daily dose. Once ingested, the drug passes down the alimentary canal until it is absorbed into the body, usually in the duodenum. As it crosses the bowel wall, the drug may undergo biotransformation before it ever reaches the systemic circulation. Such biotransformation is particularly true for drugs metabolized by the cytochrome P-450 enzyme, CYP3A3/4 [10]. Such biotransformation may convert the drug into an active or inactive metabolite that may be either absorbed or eliminated from the body at that point. In the latter instance, this process is termed *presystemic clearance* of the drug, because it occurs before the drug reaches the systemic circulation. Drugs that pass to the liver may be taken up by hepatocytes and there biotransformed by P-450 enzymes in the same way. Thus, presystemic clearance may occur either in the bowel wall

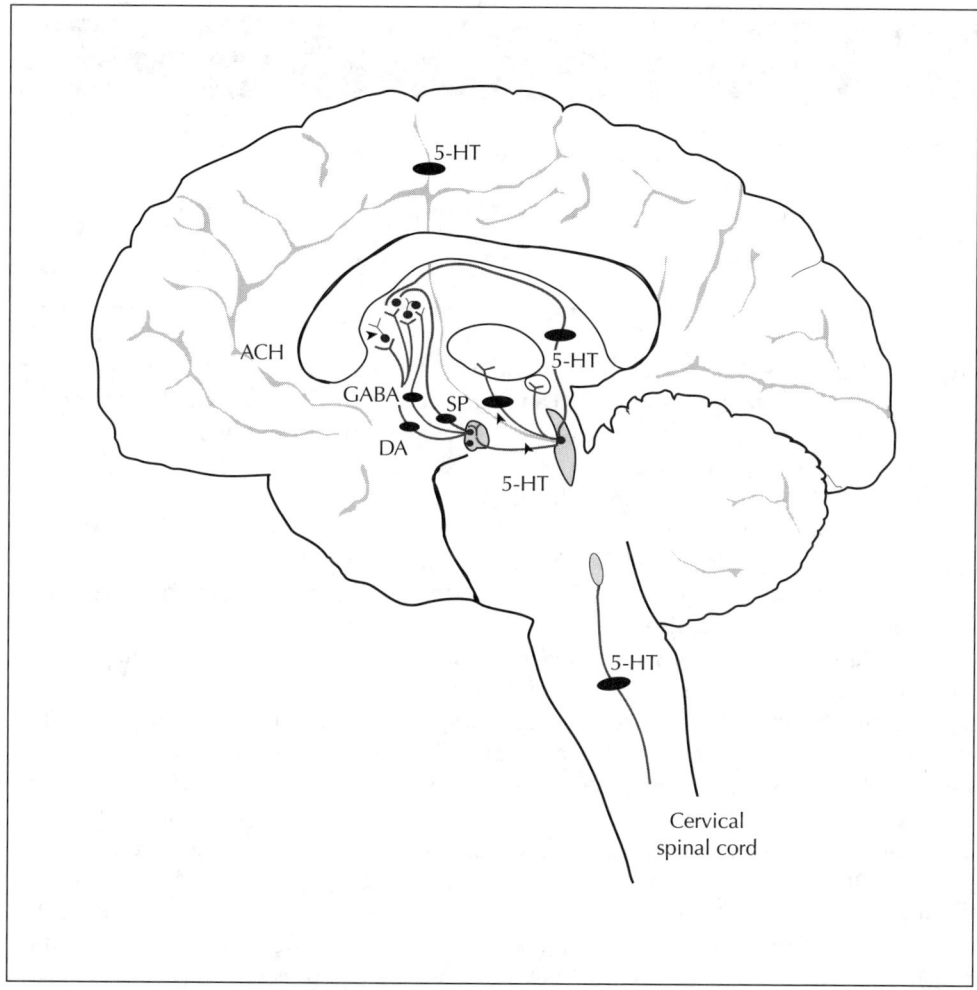

Figure 3. Some neuronal systems that can be affected by the combination of a selective serotonin-reuptake inhibitor and a monoamine oxidase inhibitor. Together these drug classes directly affect neurons containing serotonin (5-HT), norepinephrine, epinephrine, and dopamine (DA). Indirectly, the combination of serotonin-reuptake inhibitor and a monoamine oxidase inhibitor also affects neurons containing substance P (SP) and γ-aminobutyric acid (GABA). Changes in neuronal function occur in serotonergic projection areas of the cervical spinal cord, serotonin cell bodies in the raphe nuclei, motor centers of the substantia nigra and basal ganglia, autonomic centers of the hypothalamus, and higher cortical areas. ACH–acetylcholine.

or in the liver, but the net effect is the same. The drug and any metabolites that survive these two processes then enter the systemic circulation. From there, they are distributed to different body compartments, principally based on their lipophilicity, protein-binding characteristics, and blood flow to those compartments. The drug may act in one or more of those compartments, may be simply stored in other compartments (*eg*, adipose tissue) for later redistribution, or may be biotransformed or cleared in still other compartments (*eg*, liver or kidney). The clearance rate is the sum of these biotransformation and elimination

Table 3. Clinical Correlates of Serotonin Syndrome and Potential Anatomic Correlates

Sign	Anatomic correlate
Changes in mental status	Cerebral cortex
Fever, shivering, diaphoresis	Hypothalamus
Restlessness, tremor	Basal ganglia
Hyperreflexia, myoclonus	Spinal cord

processes. When the drug is administered on a prolonged basis, a steady-state concentration of the drug is achieved over time. That concentration is directly related to the dosing rate and is inversely related to the clearance rate. Hence, the concentration of the drug can be increased either by increasing the dosing rate or reducing the clearance rate. The concentration can be decreased by doing the opposite.

In a pharmacokinetic interaction, a second drug can alter the rate and extent of the absorption of the first drug, thereby altering its peak concentration (C_{max}) or its steady-state concentration (C_{ss}); or it can alter the relative distribution of the drug, the rate or the nature of its biotransformation, or its rate of elimination. This section focuses on pharmacokinetic interactions mediated by effects on the enzymes responsible for the biotransformation of drugs as a prerequisite for their elimination from the body. These types of interactions are the most common ones that are clinically important, and information now exists to permit classification of pharmaceuticals based on which enzymes are responsible for their biotransformation and which drugs affect which enzymes. Relative to drug–drug interactions, knowing whether a drug affects a xenobiotic-metabolizing enzyme is the same as knowing whether a drug affects any other specific site of action; it allows the physician to predict whether a drug is likely to produce a clinically meaningful pharmacokinetic interaction by affecting the site (*ie*, enzyme) responsible for the biotransformation of a concomitantly prescribed drug. It is useful to know which drugs affect which enzymes, the way in which the drug exerts its effects (*ie*, induction or inhibition) and whether these enzymes mediate the biotransformation of any concomitantly prescribed drugs.

Cytochrome P-450 enzymes

For some readers, this information will be relatively new because molecular biology has recently provided a substantial increase in knowledge about the cytochrome P-450 (CYP) enzymes that are responsible for the bulk of oxidative drug metabolism. Our knowledge about this process has increased over the past 100 years, but particularly so in the past 10 years.

By using molecular biology, the genes that code for specific P-450 enzymes have been identified, and the enzymes have been expressed in pure form. From amino acid sequences deduced primarily from cDNAs, a classification system that is based on their sequence homology has been developed for these enzymes [11••].

In vitro techniques have made it possible to determine which drugs are metabolized by which enzymes, to what extent, and to which active or inactive metabolites. There are

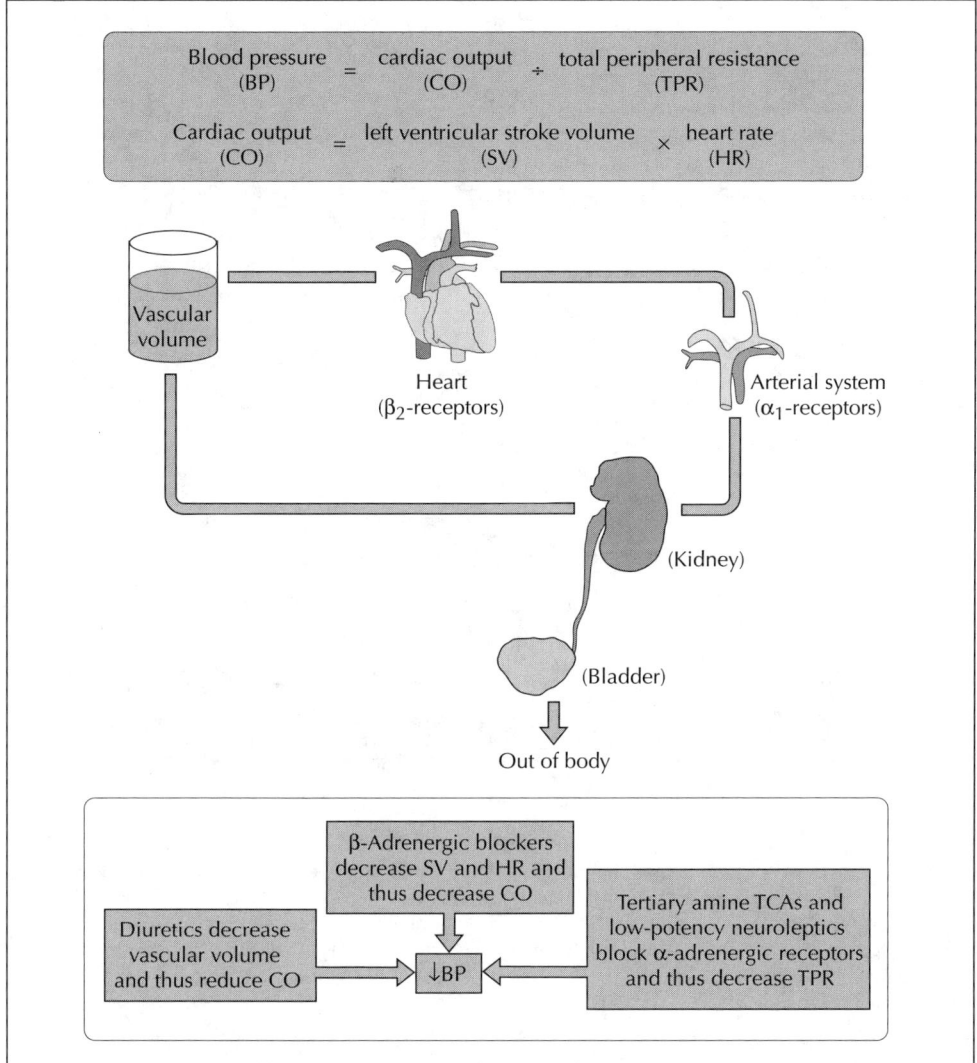

Figure 4. Consequences of combination therapy can be mediated by effects on different but interrelated organs. How blood pressure (BP) responds to the combined use of a diuretic, a β-adrenergic receptor blocker, and an α_1-adrenergic receptor blocker (tricyclic antidepressant [TCA] or neuroleptic) is illustrated. BP is determined by left ventricular stroke volume (SV), heart rate (HR), and total peripheral resistance (TPR). Diuretics decrease vascular volume at the level of the kidney; β-adrenergic receptor blockers act in cardiac tissue to change both SV and HR; and α_1-adrenergic receptor blockers act on the peripheral vasculature to decrease resistance. In consequence, the various compensatory fail-safe mechanisms that the body uses to maintain BP are simultaneously thwarted.

multiple such *in vitro* techniques, including those that use hepatic microsome preparations, liver slices, and purified enzyme [12]. They can be used in a way analogous to the *in vitro* studies, discussed in the pharmacodynamic section, to determine whether a given drug is capable of affecting the activity of a specific P-450 enzyme relative to the biotransformation

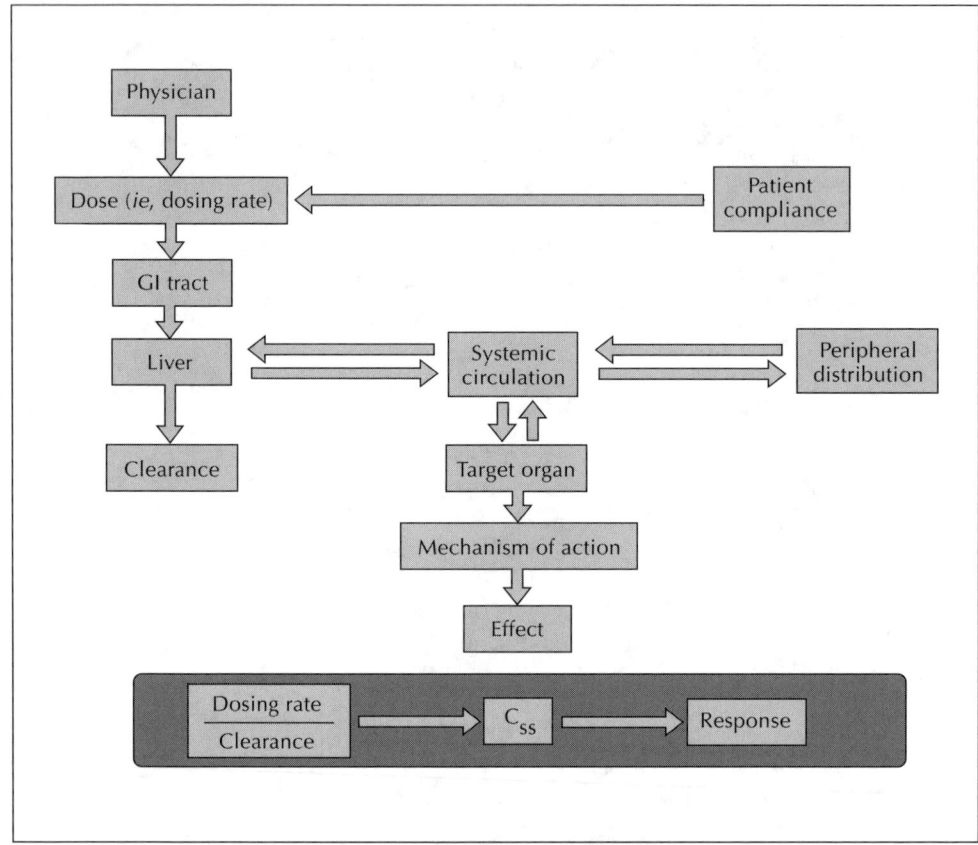

Figure 5. The steps at which pharmacokinetics can influence drug effects. Presystemic bioavailability depends on the dose taken, absorption, and first-pass metabolism in the gut and liver. Once a drug enters the systemic circulation, distribution and metabolism determine drug concentration at the site of action which, in turn, is a determinant of the drug's effect. The clearance rate is the sum of biotransformation and elimination processes. C_{ss}—steady-state concentration; GI—gastrointestinal. (*From* Greenblatt [35]; with permission.)

of another drug. Discussion of the nature and relative advantages and disadvantages of these techniques is beyond the scope of this article; suffice it to say that having multiple techniques permits cross-validation of results.

Figure 6 illustrates three of the major drug-metabolizing P-450 enzymes [13] (*ie*, CYP1A2, CYP2D6, and CYP3A3/4) in the endoplasmic reticulum of the cell. Drugs differ in their affinities for these enzymes, just as they do for sites of pharmacodynamic action. In addition, these enzymes differ in their rates and capacities for metabolism of drugs based on the structure of the drug. Finally, patients differ in that mutations in the genes encoding these enzymes can produce defective enzymes or, in rarer instances, mutations that are more efficient than the common wild-type. That mutations are genetic traits is one of the principal reasons for the substantial variability in the clearance rates of some drugs that can occur in specific populations, particularly along ethnic lines (*eg*, CYP2D6 deficiency in whites [14] and CYP2C19 deficiency in Asians

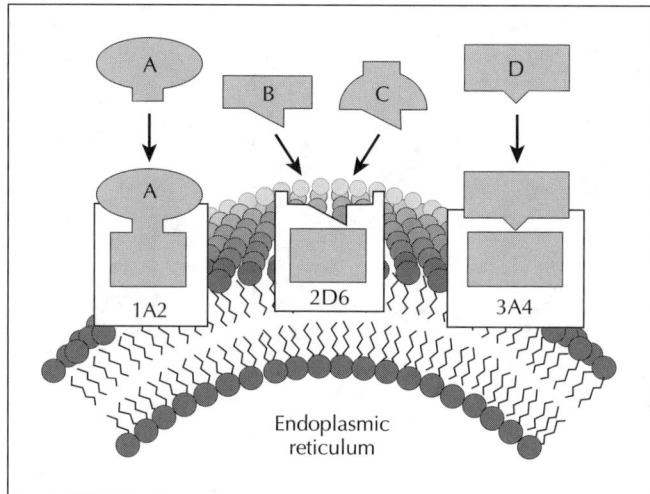

Figure 6. During metabolism by the cytochrome P-450 enzymes, the structures of drugs A, B, C, and D determine their relative affinities for the drug-metabolizing enzymes CYP1A2, CYP2D6, and CYP3A4. Drug A binds only to CYP1A2, and can be metabolized only by that enzyme. Drug C is an example of a drug that can be metabolized by more than one CYP enzymes, although one of these two may still be the preferred pathway. (*Adapted from* Watkins [36].)

[15]). This last point can be an important variable in determining the response to a specific drug in a specific patient.

Drugs can induce [16] or inhibit [17] specific P-450 enzymes. In induction, the drug increases production of the enzyme. Consequently, the clearance rate of drugs that are dependent on this enzyme for biotransformation is increased, and plasma drug levels fall unless there is a compensatory increase in the dosing rate. Inhibition is usually a competitive process; hence, the magnitude of the inhibition is a direct and immediate function of the concentration of drug and its potency for inhibiting the enzyme. In a fashion opposite that of induction, the levels of concomitantly prescribed drugs that depend on the affected enzyme for their biotransformation increase in proportion to the magnitude of the enzyme's inhibition.

There are several common misconceptions that may be useful to address at this point. One is that if a drug is metabolized by an enzyme, then it will inhibit that enzyme to a clinically relevant degree. There is no such axiomatic relationship. A drug may be metabolized by an enzyme, but not affect it. Alternatively, a drug may inhibit an enzyme, but not be metabolized by it.

The knowledge of specific P-450 enzymes and their role in oxidative drug metabolism is relatively recent. Thus, most drugs used in clinical practice were developed before this information and these techniques became available. Hence, it should not be surprising that a clear definition of which P-450 enzymes are responsible for the metabolism of which drugs is limited to only about 20% of marketed drugs. However, ascertainment of these relationships is now part of the drug development process and is part of the registration requirements. Thus, this information is available for the most recently developed medications, and the process of backfilling the missing information of other commonly used medications is in process. Physicians can expect to have an increasing amount of this type of information available to assist them when using multiple drugs in combination.

Table 4 lists common examples of clinically relevant pharmacokinetic interactions of this type. These are divided into the four main groups based on outcome: 1) buildup of

Table 4. Examples of Metabolically Mediated Pharmacokinetic Drug–Drug Interactions and Their Clinical Presentations

Type	Presentation	Affected drug	Causative drug	P-450 enzyme	Study
Buildup of drug levels owing to inhibition of clearance	Increase in incidence or severity of expected dose-dependent adverse effects	Carbamazepine	Erythromycin	3A3/4	Periti et al. [22]
		Dextromethorphan	Paroxetine	2D6	Harvey and Burke [23]
		Phenytoin	Fluoxetine	2C9/10	Woods et al. [24]
		Propranolol	Cimetidine	3A3/4?	Smith and Kendall [25]
		Theophylline	Fluvoxamine	1A2	Brosen et al. [26]
		Tricyclic antidepressants	Fluoxetine	2D6	Preskorn et al. [27]
		Tricyclic antidepressants	Fluvoxamine	1A2?, 3A3/4?	Harvey and Preskorn [28]
		Warfarin	Fluvoxamine	1A2?	Harvey and Preskorn [28]
Reduction of drug levels owing to induction of clearance	Loss of efficacy	Disopyramide	Phenytoin	3A3/4?	Nation et al. [29]
		Oral contraceptives	Phenytoin	3A3/4	Beck et al. [30]
		Propranolol	Rifampin	?	Herraiz et al. [31]
		Quinidine	Phenobarbital	3A3/4	Guengerich et al. [32]
		Theophylline	Phenytoin	1A2?	Nation et al. [33]
		Warfarin	Secobarbital	?	O'Reilly et al. [34]
Blockade of the production of an active metabolite	Loss of efficacy	Codeine	Neuroleptics / Tricyclic antidepressants	2D6	Dayer et al. [18]
Increased accumulation of an unusual toxic parent drug or metabolite	Unexpected toxicity given the usual pharmacology of the drug	Terfenadine	Ketoconazole	3A3/4	Honig et al. [19]

drug levels owing to inhibition of clearance; 2) reduction in levels owing to induction of clearance; 3) blockade of the production of an important active metabolite owing to enzyme inhibition; and 4) increased accumulation of a toxic parent drug or metabolite owing to a reduction in their clearance.

How Do Drug–Drug Interactions Present?

When two drugs interact pharmacodynamically or pharmacokinetically, the interaction may present as either a quantitative or qualitative change in the nature of the response. A *quantitative change* simply means that the magnitude of the response is either greater or less than would normally be expected. A *qualitative change* means that the fundamental nature of the response is different. An example of the latter would be the occurrence of the serotonin syndrome when a MAOI is used in combination with a SSRI, as opposed to the increase in antidepressant efficacy that might have been the original goal of using the two drugs together.

Either type of presentation can occur with either a pharmacodynamically or a pharmacokinetically mediated drug–drug interaction. As a general rule of thumb, qualitative changes are more likely due to a pharmacodynamically mediated drug–drug interaction, whereas pharmacokinetically mediated drug–drug interactions are more likely to produce a quantitative change (*see* equations 1 and 2). The most common outcome from a pharmacokinetic interaction is that the effective concentration of the concomitantly prescribed drug at its site of action changes; hence, the magnitude of the effect changes. In a pharmacodynamically mediated interaction, the effect on the second MOA may profoundly change the consequences of affecting the first MOA. This is because these two MOAs may mediate natural compensatory responses. When one MOA is affected, the other can offset the consequence unless it is also being affected by a concomitantly prescribed medication. Figure 4 provides an example in which cardiovascular collapse can occur as a result of the additive effect of volume depletion induced by a diuretic coupled with the decrease in peripheral arterial resistance produced by an α_1-adrenergic receptor blocker and the decrease in stroke volume and heart rate produced by a β-adrenergic receptor blocker.

Drug interactions that produce quantitative changes (*eg*, a pharmacokinetic interaction) in response may frequently be misattributed to a problem with the patient. Because these quantitative changes may mean either that there is diminished efficacy at usually therapeutic doses or that there are adverse effects at usually well-tolerated doses, the ready explanations are that the patient either is *resistant* to the beneficial effect of the medication or is *sensitive* to its adverse effects. What the physician may not realize is that the patient is essentially receiving a dose different from the prescribed dose because of a change in the clearance rate of the drug.

It may be difficult to formally substantiate the consequences of the interaction based on routine observation in clinical practice. The dose-dependent nature of seizures is seen when a patient receives two commonly used psychotropic medications: clozapine and bupropion. A concomitantly prescribed drug that slowed the clearance of one of these two drugs by twofold would have an effect equivalent to doubling the dosing rate. The result would be a greater than threefold increase in the patient's relative risk of having a seizure. However, it would be virtually impossible to detect this risk in routine clinical practice, because physicians treat one patient at a time. The clinician would simply observe the patient having a seizure at the prescribed dose. That most likely would not raise a special concern, because seizures are known to occur with these drugs in "sensitive" patients, even at relatively low doses. To detect a change in the relative risk, there would have to be an appropriate control group of an adequate size. To illustrate the difficulty in detecting this risk, over 700 patients randomly assigned to one of two treatment groups would have to be studied to detect a threefold increase in the relative risk of seizure produced by such a pharmacokinetically mediated drug–drug interaction involving a reduction in the clearance of buproprion or clozapine. Nonetheless, an interaction that leads to such an increased risk of seizures is clinically important. Thus, the prudent clinician will want to make appropriate dose adjustments when clozapine is coprescribed with drugs such as fluvoxamine and fluoxetine, because both have been reported to produce over 70% increases in the plasma concentrations of clozapine [20,21].

Although pharmacokinetically mediated drug interactions generally produce quantitative, rather than qualitative, changes in response, there are exceptions to this rule. One example occurs when the interaction leads to the unusual accumulation of a moiety that has a substantially different pharmacologic profile from the usual active substance. A case in point is a blockade of biotransformation of terfenadine to its active metabolite. Clinically meaningful levels of terfenadine do not usually occur when this drug is administered alone because it is converted to its acid metabolite by CYP3A3/4 during absorption (ie, presystemic clearance of terfenadine with production of the active metabolite). Although the active metabolite does not adversely affect intracardiac conduction, terfenadine can do so. When the presystemic clearance of terfenadine is blocked by the coadministration of a CYP3A3/4 inhibitor, such as the antifungal agent ketoconazole, high levels of terfenadine can develop. This results in unexpected and potentially life-threatening cardiac arrhythmias, which represent a qualitative change in the response to terfenadine.

Qualitative changes in drug response can also occur when the affected drug has more than one MOA over its clinically relevant dosing range. Here, reducing the clearance is equivalent to increasing the dose, and other MOAs become relevant to clinical outcome. For example, tertiary amine TCAs have action on sodium fast channels at higher concentrations and thus can slow intracardiac conduction which, in turn, can lead to serious and even life-threatening cardiac conduction disturbances.

Conclusions

Polypharmacy is common in clinical practice. With such practice comes the potential for clinically important drug–drug interactions that may be either helpful or harmful to the patient (see Ciraulo et al. [37••] and Janicak et al. [38••] for recent publications in this area). Such interactions can be broadly divided into two categories: pharmacodynamic and pharmacokinetic. The physician can organize his or her knowledge of the drugs in terms of their effects at specific sites of action, including specific cytochrome P-450 enzymes. In this way, the physician can anticipate drug interactions before they occur and make appropriate adjustments in the treatment plan to optimize the likelihood of the best possible outcome for the patient.

References and Recommended Reading

Papers of particular interest, published recently, have been highlighted as:
• Of special interest
•• Of outstanding interest

1. Coulehan JL, Schulberg HC, Block MR, *et al.*: Depressive symptomology and medical co-morbidity in a primary care clinic. *Int J Psychiatry Medicine* 1990, 20:335–347.

2. Rosholm J-U, Hallas J, Gram LF: Concurrent use of more than one major psychotropic drug (polypsychopharmacy) in out-patients: a prescription database study. *Br J Clin Pharmacol* 1994, 37:533–538.

3. Preskorn S, Lacey R: Polypharmacy: when is it rational? *J Practical Psychiatry Behav Health* 1995, 1:92–98.

4. Preskorn SH: Pharmacokinetics of psychotropic agents: why and how they are relevant to treatment. *J Clin Psychiatry* 1993, 54:(suppl 9):3–7.

5. Cusack B, Nelson A, Richelson E: Binding of antidepressants to human brain receptors: focus on newer generation compounds. *Psychopharmacology* 1994, 114:559–565.

6. Bolden-Watson C, Richelson E: Blockade by newly-developed antidepressants of biogenic amine uptake into rat brain synaptosomes. *Life Sci* 1993, 52:1023–1029.

7. Preskorn SH: Should rational drug development in psychiatry target more than one mechanism of action in a single molecule? *Int Rev Psychiatry* 1995, 7:17–28.

8. Artigas F, Perez V, Alvarez E: Pindolol induces a rapid improvement of depressed patients treated with serotonin reuptake inhibitors. *Arch Gen Psychiatry* 1994, 51:248–251.

9. Sternbach H: The serotonin syndrome. *Am J Psychiatry* 1991, 148:705–713.

10. Kolars JC, Schmiedlin-Ren P, Schuetz JD, *et al.*: Identification of rifampin-inducible P450IIIA4 (CYP3A4) in human small bowel enterocytes. *J Clin Invest* 1992, 90:1871–1878.

11.•• Nelson DR, Koymans L, Kamataki T, *et al.*: P450 superfamily: update on new sequences, gene mapping, accession numbers, and nomenclature. *Pharmacogenetics* 1996, 1:1–42.
The standard source of information on P-450 classification.

12. Guengerich FP, Shimada T: Oxidation of toxic and carcinogenic chemicals by human cytochrome P-450 enzymes. *Chem Res Toxicol* 1991, 4:391–407.

13. Wrighton S, Stevens J: The human hepatic cytochromes P450 involved in drug metabolism. *Crit Rev Toxicol* 1992, 22:1–21.

14. Steiner E, Bertilsson L, Sawe J, *et al.*: Polymorphic debrisoquin hydroxylation in 757 Swedish subjects. *Clin Pharmacol Ther* 1988, 44:431–435.

15. Caraco Y, Tateishi T, Wood AJJ: Ethnic effects on inhibition of drug metabolism [abstract]. *Clin Pharmacol Ther* 1994, 55:169.

16. Okey AB: Enzyme induction in the cytochrome P-450 system. *Pharmacol Ther* 1990, 45:241–298.

17. Murray M, Reidy GF: Selectivity in the inhibition of mammalian cytochromes P-450 by chemical agents. *Pharmacol Rev* 1990, 42:85–101.

18. Dayer P, Desmeules J, Striberni R: In vitro forecasting of drugs that may interfere with codeine bioactivation. *Eur J Drug Metab Pharmacokinet* 1992, 17:115–120.

19. Honig PK, Wortham DC, Zamani K, *et al.*: Terfenadine–ketoconazole interaction: pharmacokinetic and electrocardiographic consequences. *JAMA* 1993, 269:1513–1518.

20. Jerling M, Lindstrom L, Bondesson U, *et al.*: Fluvoxamine inhibition and carbamazepine induction of the metabolism of clozapine: evidence from a therapeutic drug monitoring service. *Ther Drug Monit* 1994, 16:368–374.

21. Centorrino F, Baldessarini RJ, Kando J, *et al.*: Serum concentrations of clozapine and its major metabolites: effects of cotreatment with fluoxetine or valproate. *Am J Psychiatry* 1994, 151:123–125.

22. Periti P, Mazzei T, Mini E, *et al.*: Pharmacokinetic drug interactions of macrolides. *Clin Pharmacol Ther* 1992, 23:106–131.

23. Harvey AT, Burke M: The serotonin syndrome associated with paroxetine, an over-the-counter cold remedy, and vascular disease [comment]. *Am J Emerg Med* 1995, 13:605–606.

24.   Woods DJ, Coulter DM, Pillans P: Interaction of phenytonin and fluoxetine. *N Z Med J* 1994, 107:19.

25.   Smith S, Kendall M: Ranitidine versus cimetidine: a comparison of their potential to cause clinically important drug interactions. *Clin Pharmacokinet* 1988, 15:44–56.

26.   Brosen K, Skjelbo E, Rasmussen BB, *et al.*: Fluvoxamine is a potent inhibitor of cytochrome P4501A2. *Biochem Pharmacol* 1993, 45:1211–1214.

27.   Preskorn SH, Alderman J, Chung M, *et al.*: Pharmacokinetics of desipramine coadministered with sertraline or fluoxetine. *J Clin Psychopharmacol* 1994, 14:90–98.

28.   Harvey AT, Preskorn SH. Cytochrome P450 enzymes: interpretation of their interactions with SSRIs (part II). *J Clin Psychopharmacol* 1996, 16:345–355.

29.   Nation RL, Evans AM, Milne RW: Pharmacokinetic drug interactions with phenytoin (part II). *Clin Pharmacokinet* 1990, 18:131–150.

30.   Beck DJ, Breckenridge AM, Crawford FE, *et al.*: Interindividual variation and drug interactions with hormonal steroid contraceptives. *Drugs* 1981, 21:46–61.

31.   Herraiz AG, Nakamura K, Wilkinson GR, *et al.*: Induction of propranolol metabolism by rifampicin. *Br J Clin Pharmacol* 1983, 16:565–569.

32.   Guengerich FP, Muller-Enoch D, Blair IA: Oxidation of quinidine by human liver cytochrome P-450. *Mol Pharmacol* 1986, 30:287–295.

33.   Nation RL, Evans AM, Milne RW: Pharmacokinetic drug interactions with phenytonin (part I). *Clin Pharmacokinet* 1990, 18:37–60.

34.   O'Reilly RA, Trager WF, Motley CH, *et al.*: Interaction of secobarbital with warfarin pseudoracemates. *Clin Pharmacol Ther* 1980, 28:187–195.

35.   Greenblatt DJ: *J Clin Psychiatry* 1993, 54(suppl 9):8–13.

36.   Watkins PB: *Gastroenterol Clin North Am* 1992, 21:511–526.

37.•• Ciraulo DA, Shader RI, Greenblatt DJ, Creelman WL, eds.: *Drug Interactions in Psychiatry*, edn 2. Baltimore: Williams & Wilkins; 1995.
Provides data on specific drug interactions, their clinical significance, and guidelines on identification and avoidance of potentially dangerous problems.

38.•• Janicak PG, Davis JM, Preskorn SH, Ayd FJ, eds: *Principles and Practice of Psychopharmacotherapy*. Baltimore: Williams & Wilkins; 1993.
A practical guide to the use of psychotropic medications in clinical practice.

CHAPTER 9

Treatment of Premenstrual Dysphoric Disorder

Kimberly A. Yonkers

This chapter reviews recent studies on premenstrual dysphoric disorder, a more severe form of premenstrual syndrome. Topics covered include epidemiology, diagnosis, and the psychobiology of the disorder. Regarding treatment, the author reviews recent studies on hormonal therapy, diuretics, gonadotropin-releasing hormone, bromocriptine, nonsteroidal anti-inflammatory drugs, and psychotropics. Finally, the author discusses long-term treatment.

Obstetricians, gynecologists, internists, family practitioners, and psychiatrists commonly see women with premenstrual complaints. In response to this, a number of aspects of premenstrual syndrome (PMS) have been investigated, including its prevalence, biology, and etiology. This review focuses on a form of PMS that is severe and characterized primarily by mood symptoms. Although an attempt has been made to be comprehensive, the reader is referred to other work in which information on milder forms of PMS is reviewed [1,2]. This work was presented partially in other publications [3,4].

Premenstrual syndrome is a disorder characterized by several days to 2 weeks of symptoms that commence during the luteal phase of the cycle and cease with menstruation or shortly thereafter. The most common symptoms include low mood, tension, anger, irritability, mood swings, headache, bloating, and changes in appetite and sleep. In the *Diagnostic and Statistical Manual of Mental Disorders* (DSM)-III-R [5], criteria were introduced for a proposed category termed *late luteal phase dysphoric disorder* (LLPDD). This entity was designed to identify a subset of women with PMS who have severe symptoms. The criteria stipulate a minimum of five symptoms, including at least one mood symptom and functional impairment in either the work or interpersonal domain. In addition, symptoms must be prospectively confirmed by keeping a daily diary of mood and behavior to illustrate an association between symptom expression and the luteal, but not follicular, phase of the cycle.

With publication of the DSM-IV [6], the category has been renamed *premenstrual dysphoric disorder* (PMDD) and is included in DSM-IV under the category "mood disorders not otherwise specified." The clinical criteria (Table 1) for this disorder changes in DSM-IV, with addition of the symptom "a subjective sense of being overwhelmed or out of control." Several researchers affirmed that these DSM-IV symptoms are those that are most frequently identified by patients with severe premenstrual complaints [7,8]. A DSM-IV workgroup reanalysis of data collected from over 600 patients from four large research centers further confirms this assessment [9,10]. The strength of this database is that all patients provided prospective ratings [9,10].

It is important to bear in mind that women who suffer from PMDD constitute a subset of women with PMS. Women who experience somatic symptoms in the absence of mood symptoms have PMS but would not meet the criteria.

Table 1. Research Criteria for Premenstrual Dysphoric Disorder*

A. For most cycles during the past year, at least five symptoms including one mood symptom (below) were present during the last week of the luteal phase. Symptoms remitted within a few days of menses and were absent during the postmenstrual week.

Depressed mood, hopelessness, or self-deprecating thoughts
Anxiety, tension or feeling "keyed up"
Affective lability
Persistent marked anger or irritability or increased interpersonal conflicts
Decreased interest in usual activities
Difficulty concentrating
Lethargy or fatigability
Change in appetite or food craving
Hypersomnia or hyposomnia
A subjective sense of being overwhelmed or out of control
Physical symptoms of breast tenderness or swelling, bloating, headache, joint, or muscle pain

B. Symptoms interfere with work, school, or usual social activities and relationships.
C. The disturbance is not merely the exacerbation of another disorder.
D. Symptoms are prospectively confirmed with daily ratings.

Adapted from American Psychiatric Association [6]; with permission.

Epidemiology

Previous research on PMS in community settings for which retrospective reports of symptomatology were used finds rates as high as 30% to 87% for mild symptoms and 2% to 9% for severe or disabling symptoms [7,11–14]. The difficulty of obtaining daily ratings from a community population is obvious. However, in two studies, prevalence was evaluated using prospective ratings. A population of nontreatment-seeking university women had a rate of 4.6% [13] whereas a second prospective study found a rate of 3.4% [15]. In addition, both figures are within the range of the previous estimates taken from retrospective community assessments.

Premenstrual symptoms have been investigated in nonwhite subgroups and other cultures. A reanalysis of data from the Epidemiological Catchment Area study, which used retrospective reports, found a rate in African American women equivalent to white women [16]. A community study of 120 Nigerian women has found at least one premenstrual complaint in 68% of women and work impairment in 7.5%. A study of Chinese women in Hong Kong found a PMS rate of 64%. The most common symptoms were fatigue, pain, bloating, and behavioral change. The rate of women with PMDD is likely to be lower because somatic symptoms such as pain were more problematic than was negative affect [17]. High prevalence rates (26%) of premenstrual symptoms also were found in an Italian community study. Women with severe mood symptoms were not independently identified in this study.

Course

The average age of onset of severe symptoms appears to be about age 26 [10,19,20], and several researchers [21,22], but not all [23,24], have found that symptoms associated with the premenstrual phase gradually worsen in both duration and severity. The latter may explain why the age of presentation is somewhat older, and averages between 33 and 36 [25,26]. One theory holds that the multiple increases and decreases in ovarian hormones are responsible for this worsening [27]. In support of this theory are data showing that in other cultures in which menstruation is infrequent, premenstrual complaints are rare [27]. This theory also is bolstered by data associating low parity with increased risk for PMDD [20,21,28,29]. Low parity yields a greater number of hormonal cycles, thus a woman has more exposure to and withdrawal from massive amounts of progesterone. Furthermore, the rate of premenstrual symptoms is lower among past users of oral contraceptives [20,21,30], again suggesting that less frequent exposure to peaks and troughs of endogenous hormones is protective against PMDD.

Age of onset, course, and duration of illness illustrate the accumulated morbidity from the disorder. If a woman has an age of onset of PMDD of 26 years [10,19,20], and if she has symptoms during the majority of the cycles until menopause, she will have had over 200 symptomatic cycles, or 1400 to 2800 symptomatic days (3 to 8 years). During that time, her life may be affected by her illness in a number of ways. One longitudinal study found that patients with PMDD experience luteal phase functional impairment most profoundly in relation to their interactions with their spouses and children, although impairment in social activities and work also occurs (Yonkers et al., Paper presented at the Annual Meeting of the American Psychiatric Association, Miami, 1995).

Detection and Diagnosis

As previously discussed, a stipulation for the diagnosis of PMDD is that retrospective reports of symptomatology are prospectively confirmed. This requirement grew from earlier research findings showing that only 20% to 50% of women retrospectively reporting severe PMS prospectively confirm severe symptoms isolated to the luteal phase [31–33]. Prospective charting reveals that women who present with retrospective reports of premenstrual difficulties will show symptom patterns 1) limited to the luteal phase; 2) intermittently during the cycle but not related to the luteal phase; or 3) throughout the cycle, possibly with worsening during the luteal phase [30,33]. Luteal phase worsening of mood or anxiety commonly occurs in women with dysthmic disorder or generalized anxiety disorder.

Current and past comorbid psychiatric illnesses are common in women with premenstrual complaints and in women with PMDD [16,34–37]. Concurrent DSM-III diagnoses in women presenting for evaluation of PMS were compared with the diagnoses found in a community epidemiologic study in one study [16]. Women with a retrospective report of PMS had much higher lifetime rates of dysthymia, phobia, mania, obsessive–compulsive disorder, alcohol abuse, and substance abuse. Others find that the lifetime rate for major depressive disorder in women with prospectively confirmed PMDD ranges between 30 and 70 [3]. Sixty percent of menstruating women with major depressive disorder (MDD) may experience premenstrual worsening [38,39], although the only report of women with MDD that used prospective ratings to confirm premenstrual worsening found that it occurred in about 30% of patients (Kornstein et al., Paper presented at the Annual Meeting of the New Clinical Drug Evaluation Program, Orlando, 1995). The role of premenstrual worsening is important because emergency room visits and hospitalizations increase during the premenstrual and menstrual phases of the cycle [40,41].

For women who fail to show premenstrual entrainment of symptoms, it is unclear why they misattribute symptoms to the premenstrual phase of the cycle. Hypotheses include the perception that it is more socially acceptable to have premenstrual symptoms versus another (psychiatric) illness, or that menses is a notable event that marks a time that is easier to remember.

Psychobiology

Proposed theories explaining the causes of premenstrual symptoms have been reviewed in greater detail by various authors [42–44]. The most common theories include 1) a relative deficit of progesterone, 2) an excess of estrogen, 3) a decrease in the progesterone-estrogen ratio, 4) alterations in progesterone metabolism and production of bioactive progesterone metabolism, 5) an excess of available androgens, 6) a relative deficiency of vitamin B, 7) a deficiency of the prostaglandin PGE_2, 8) an excess of prolactin, 9) a deficiency of β-endorphin, and 10) abnormal neurotransmitters, particularly serotonergic functioning.

Although these theories have been proposed for PMS, it is unclear whether they are relevant to the pathogenesis of PMDD, which is more severe than is PMS and which emphasizes mood symptoms. Differences between levels of progesterone, estrogen, or the ratio of the two have not yet been definitively shown in patients with premenstrual symptoms compared with control groups [22,42,44]. An association with neurotransmitter systems, particularly the serotonergic system, is more promising.

Serotonergic System

Sex steroids and serotonin interact in a number of ways [45]. *In vitro*, estradiol and testosterone inhibit serotonin uptake into platelets [46]. That this finding is physiologically relevant, and that it may be associated with the pathology of PMDD, is suggested by subsequent research. The first study to investigate platelet serotonin uptake in patients with premenstrual symptoms found that uptake is decreased more in the luteal than in the follicular phase of the cycle [47]. Three additional reports have evaluated platelet uptake of serotonin (5-hydroxytryptamine [5-HT]) during two times of the cycle in patients compared with control individuals. One study found no differences between groups at either time of the cycle [48], but two other studies found decreased platelet uptake of serotonin in symptomatic patients when compared with control groups during the luteal phase [49,50]. Similar findings are reported by a group using tritiated imipramine as a ligand, rather than serotonin [51]. A difference in V_{max} between groups was shown during both phases of the cycle, but was significant only during the midluteal phase. With the same ligand, a second group also found differences, but significance was achieved only during the follicular phase of the cycle [52]. Patients in these last two studies met the rigorous criteria for PMDD.

Other paradigms for investigating serotonergic functioning in women with severe premenstrual dysphoria suggest abnormalities. Subsensitivity of the 5-HT_{1A} receptor is postulated to underlie the blunted follicular phase prolactin response to buspirone challenge in PMDD patients compared with control groups [53]. Bancroft *et al.* [54] found that the prolactin response to L-tryptophan is blunted during the luteal phase in women with PMDD compared with control groups. They also found that the growth hormone and cortisol response is blunted more in patients than in control groups, but during both phases of the cycle. Finally, by using a paradigm of peripheral depletion of the serotonin precursor tryptophan to deplete stores of central serotonin, Menkes *et al.* [55] successfully provoked premenstrual symptoms during the follicular phase and exacerbated symptoms during the luteal phase. In sum, the evidence reviewed previously is suggestive of changes in serotonergic functioning or response in women who suffer from PMDD.

Adrenergic system

An increase in α_2-adrenergic receptor binding has been associated with depressive disorders [56]. Similarly, one study has found that α_2-adrenergic receptor binding is significantly higher during the mid-luteal phase of the cycle in women with PMDD than in control groups [57]. Our group has failed to replicate this finding in 18 symptomatic women and controls (Yonkers, Unpublished data). Binding at the imidizoline receptor shows even larger binding differences between PMDD patients and control groups [57].

γ-Aminobutyric acid system

Low γ-aminobutyric acid (GABA) levels are found in some patients with major depressive disorder [58]. A recent report also found that plasma GABA levels were lower in patients with PMDD compared with control groups. Women with PMDD and no lifetime history of major depressive disorder had lower levels during the luteal phase, whereas women with current PMDD and at least one previous episode of major depressive disorder had low plasma GABA levels at both times of the cycle [58].

Treatment

Several decades of treatment research have been conducted and, to date, over 30 compounds have been investigated. The treatment of PMS has been the subject of numerous detailed books and reviews [42–44,59]. In this article, the focus is on the treatment of the more severe syndrome, PMDD. Thus, the methodologic features used in older studies on the more heterogeneous group, PMS, are reviewed in this paper, with the intent of identifying treatment information that can be extrapolated to more severely afflicted populations.

To organize the large amount of work done, we summarize studies by class in a format similar to the DSM-IV work group [59], but with the inclusion of studies not available at that earlier date. In each group, we identify the number of trials that used solid, prospective criteria to define patients with luteal phase symptomatology who would be eligible for inclusion in a PMDD treatment trial. Many treatment trials describe response in terms of *continuous variables* (ie, the average amount of change in an active group compared with a control group). Although this offers a sense of how an active treatment compares with placebo, it does not illustrate how symptomatic an individual remains after treatment, and it does not describe the likelihood that women given adequate treatment will be rendered completely or nearly asymptomatic. Categorical measures can provide these data, for example, by identifying the number of patients who have total or near-total improvement or the number of patients who fall below a given threshold of a particular psychiatric instrument. In this review, we also identify trials according to whether they offer this type of information.

As noted in the DSM-IV work group summary for PMDD [59], treatments can be subsumed under six general categories: 1) hormones (estrogen, natural and synthetic progestins), 2) ovulation suppressors (gonadotropin-releasing hormone [GnRH] agonists and danazol), 3) vitamins and dietary supplements, 4) diuretics, 5) psychotropics (lithium, serotonin reuptake inhibitors, alprazolam, tryptophan, and nortriptyline), and 6) other miscellaneous treatments (naltrexone, nonsteroidal anti-inflammatory drugs).

Hormonal treatments, agonists, and antagonists

Hormonal treatments include natural and synthetic progestins, estrogen, and the combination of the two. Most studies test the use of progesterone, historically the most widely used agent for treatment of PMS. To date, 11 randomized, double-blind, placebo-controlled trials (RCTs) [19,60–69] have assessed the efficacy of progesterone. Three double-blind, randomized, placebo-controlled studies have evaluated the synthetic optical isomer, dydrogesterone [70–73] and two studies evaluated medroxyprogesterone [74,75] (Table 2). Only one study persisted as long as six cycles [71].

Table 2. Progesterone: Results of Randomized Placebo-Controlled Trials*

Study	Drug	Daily ratings as entrance criteria	Cycles, n	Outcome measures
Andersch et al. [60] (n = 15)	Prog 100 mg BID or placebo	No	2	CPRS Scale
Dennerstein et al. [61] (n = 23)	Prog or placebo 300 mg	Yes	2	MDQ, BDI, STAI, MACL, DRS
Freeman et al. [62••] (n = 121)	Prog 400 mg or placebo 300 mg	Yes	2	DRS, global improvement
Jordheim [63] (n = 21)	Prog + diuretic vs placebo	Yes	4	DRS
Maddocks et al. [64] (n = 20)	Prog 400 mg vs placebo	Yes	3	BDI, BUSS-DURKEE, STAI, Moos MDQ, PMTS
Richter et al. [65] (n = 22)	Prog 800 mg vs placebo	Yes	4	DRS
Sampson et al. [66] (n = 80)	Prog 400 mg prog vs placebo then 800 mg vs placebo	No	2	Moos MDQ
van der Meer et al. [67] (n = 13)	Prog 400 mg vs placebo	Yes	2	Authors' daily ratings
Magill [68] (n = 93)	Progesterone	Yes	4	Symptom score
Baker et al. [69] (n = 17)	Progesterone	Yes	7	Authors daily ratings, SADS, HRSD, BDI, STAI
West and Hillier [116] (n = 27)	Goserelin	Yes	3	VAS, HAD

*Change in worst symptom measured, but symptom differed between women.
†Except one subscale in SADS.
BDI—Beck Depression Inventory; BID—twice daily; CPRS—Comprehensive Psychiatric Rating Scale; DRS—daily rating scale; HAD—Hospital Anxiety and Depression scales; HRSD—Hamilton Rating Scale for Depression; MACL—Mood Adjective Check List; MDQ—Menstrual Distress Questionnaire; PMTS—premenstrual tension scale; Prog—progesterone; SADS—Schedule for Affective Disorders and Schizophrenia; STAI—State-Trait Anxiety Inventory.

In all progesterone trials, treatment was administered only during the luteal phase in daily doses between 200 and 400 mg/d, but entrance criteria was variable. Nine required daily ratings before randomization, but only three studies [19,61,62••] stipulated selection criteria rigorous enough to recruit women who met criteria for PMDD. Two of these investigations from the same group [19,62] also employed large sample sizes, more than 100 women, whereas others generally included fewer than 30 patients. Results from the first trial found that progesterone is no more effective than placebo for the treatment of severe premenstrual dysphoria [19]. The second study expanded this finding by showing that the benzodiazepine alprazolam is more effective for severe PMDD than either progesterone or placebo [62••].

Negative results are associated with most trials evaluating the optical isomer of progesterone, dydrogesterone or medroxyprogesterone (Table 3). Of the four studies that used this compound, two used daily ratings to confirm premenstrual symptoms; both studies

Results	Determination of efficacy	Comments	Definition of recovery
Prog = placebo	Statistical comparison of symptoms for each treatment group	Crossover; luteal phase treatment	None
Prog > placebo	Statistical comparison of daily ratings; other continuous variables	Crossover; luteal phase treatment	None
Prog = placebo	Statistical comparison of daily ratings	Luteal phase treatment	50% drop in DRS
Prog + diuretic = placebo	Statistical comparison of daily ratings; other continuous variables in each group	Luteal phase treatment	None
Prog = placebo	Statistical comparison of daily ratings; patient report of improvement	Luteal phase treatment	None
Prog = placebo	Statistical comparison of patients rating	Luteal phase treatment	"Degree of relief" although numbers for each degree not reported
Prog = placebo	Statistical comparison of daily ratings	Luteal phase treatment; crossover	None
Prog = placebo	Statistical	Luteal phase treatment	None
Prog > placebo	Change in score of worst symptom*	Only I treatment required for entry*	None
Prog = placebo	Statistical comparison of continuous measures	No difference in any measure†	None
Goserelins, placebo for somatic symptoms	Continuous	Mild benefit for anxiety, high placebo response	None

Table 3. Other Progestins: Results of Randomized Controlled Trials

Study	Drug	Daily ratings as entrance criteria	Cycles, n	Outcome measures
Dennerstein et al. [70] (n = 24)	Dydrogesterone 200 mg vs placebo	Yes	2	MDQ, STAI, MACL, daily ratings
Kerr et al. [71] (n = 67)	Dydrogesterone vs placebo	No	6	Symptom diaries
Hellberg et al. [74] (n = 38)	MPA vs spironolactone vs placebo	Yes (half cycle)	I	VAS
Sampson et al. [72] (n = 69)	Dydrogesterone 10 mg/BID vs placebo	Yes	2	MDQ
West [75] (n = 35)	MPA vs placebo; NET vs placebo	Yes	3	VAS
Williams et al. [73] (n = 300)	Dydrogesterone 10 mg/BID vs placebo	No	3	Patient diary

*Single-blind placebo-controlled initial placebo response in 43%.
†Luteal-phase treatment randomly with either MPA, spironolactone, or placebo.
‡Double-blind crossover; prospective criteria not described.
§Hormone treatment caused anovulatory placebo cycles; some carry-over effect; patients with premenstrual magnification included and had poorer response to MPA.
BID—twice daily; MACL—Mood Adjective Check List; MDQ—Menstrual Distress Questionnaire; MPA—medroxyprogesterone; NET—norethisterone; Rx–treatment; STAI—State-Trait Anxiety Inventory; VAS—visual analogue scale; TID—thrice daily.

are negative [70,72]. One study [71] has several problems, including the lack of daily prospective ratings, single-blinded conditions, and a lack of standard measures. This study found that dydrogesterone is superior to placebo for three of 13 symptoms [71].

At this point, research evidence does not show a role for either progesterone or dydrogesterone in the treatment of PMDD. Some clinicians continue to use these compounds, and many patients say that they are effective. It is likely that the positive response claimed by patients is a nonspecific response and is not due to therapeutic properties of the compounds.

The efficacy of estrogen or conjugated equine estrogens was assessed in three randomized, double-blind, placebo-controlled trials [76–78], two of which included a synthetic progestin with the estrogen [77,78] (Table 4). The duration of treatment was up to 10 cycles in one study and, perhaps, because less stringent entrance criteria were used, the rate of response to placebo was 94% during the first two cycles [77]. After 10 cycles, the response to estrogen was superior to placebo. In a subsequent study from the same group, estrogen was more effective than placebo [78]. A third study does not confirm this result [76].

It is not yet clear whether estrogen has a role in the treatment of PMDD. Given the high placebo response rate, the studies just cited pertain to less symptomatic patients. Studies on PMDD patients would be useful in clarifying this issue.

Results	Determination of efficacy	Comments	Definition of response
Dydrogesterone = placebo	Statistical comparison of Rx using continuous variables	Luteal phase Rx crossover	None
Dydrogesterone > placebo for 3/13 symptoms	Statistical comparison of treatments using continuous variables (percent of responders)	Luteal phase Rx	None
Bloatedness improved on spironolactone; depression somewhat improved on MPA	Statistical comparison of VAS scores for each Rx; patient self assessment	Not double-blind†	None
Dydrogesterone = placebo	Statistical comparison of treatments using continuous variables	Luteal phase Rx‡	Improvement/no improvement
NET = placebo except for breast tenderness; MPA > placebo for mood symptoms and breast tenderness	Statistical comparison of treatments using continuous variables	5 mg TID for 21 d§	None
Dydrogesterone = placebo; trends for improvement in dydrogesterone group	Statistical comparison of treatments using continuous variables	Multicenter trial	None

The best-designed oral contraceptive (OC) study shows that a triphasic type of OC is equivalent to placebo for mood, but better for breast tenderness and bloating [79]. A comparison trial of two different OCs found triphasic OCs more effective than monophasic OCs for all symptoms, but this study does not include a placebo comparison group [80]. These trials are three and four cycles, respectively; outcome is determined with continuous variables. Other reports comparing one OC with another, or to no OC therapy, used retrospective reports of symptoms or employed survey techniques [81], making results less reliable.

Given how frequently OCs are used as a treatment for premenstrual mood symptoms, the paucity of solid research is surprising (Table 5). The one well-designed study did not find benefit for mood symptoms. Further evaluations of OCs are needed.

Danazol has been used in five randomized, double-blind, placebo-controlled trials [82–86] and two open trials [87,88] (Table 6). The data from one open trial are compromised by the lack of daily ratings [82]. No trial lasted longer than three cycles. Watts *et al.* [86] used a 50% decrease in daily ratings and Hahn *et al.* [84] used a threshold criteria on the Premenstrual Tension Self-Rating Scale to define response. The study results are also notable in that investigators found treatment efficacious for some items (breast tenderness) but not as effective for others, such as mood [84].

Table 4. Estrogen and Conjugated Equine Estrogens: Results of Randomized Placebo-Controlled Trials

Study	Drug	Daily ratings as entrance criteria	Cycles, n	Outcome measures
Dhar and Murphy [76] (n = 11)	Premarin vs placebo	Yes	2	Authors daily rating
Magos et al. [77] (n = 68)	Estradiol 100 mg; NET 5 mg vs placebo	Yes	Up to 10	Retrospective VAS; concurrent modified MDQ (PDQ)
Watson et al. [78] (n = 40)	Estradiol 200 mg; NET 5 mg vs placebo	Yes	3	MDQ, PDQ

*Placebo response 94% in first two cycles, then waned after six cycles.
MDQ—Menstrual Distress Questionnaire; PDD—premenstrual dysphoric disorder; PDQ—Premenstrual Distress Questionnaire; NET—norethisterone; VAS—visual analogue scale.

Table 5. Oral Contraceptives: Results of Comparison, Randomized Placebo-Controlled and Open Trials

Study	Drug	Daily ratings as entrance criteria	Cycles, n	Outcome measures
Backstrom et al. [80]; n = 32	Triphasic vs monophasic	Yes	4	VAS
Bancroft and Rennie [81]; n = 552 (retrospective survey)	272 OC users vs 272 non-OC users	No	1	Self-ratings of well being
Graham and Sherwin [79]; n = 45	Triphasic vs placebo	Yes	3	VAS, DRF

*Breast pain less in OC users.
DRF—daily rating form; OC—oral contraceptive; VAS—visual analogue scale.

All studies found that danazol is more effective than placebo, but it is primarily beneficial for breast tenderness. Unfortunately, the treatment is poorly tolerated in most trials and dropouts in active treatment groups are high. Given these findings, danazol should be used only as a first-line treatment in women whose primary premenstrual complaint is severe breast tenderness and pain. Current evidence does not support a major role in the treatment of PMDD.

Diuretics

The diuretic spironolactone has been evaluated in four double-blind, placebo-controlled studies [89–92], and metazolone has been used in one trial [93] (Table 7). Treatment was given for a maximum of three cycles. Spironolactone was superior to placebo in two [90,92] of these four studies. The accuracy of one study [91] is compromised by the way in which the

Results	Determination of efficacy	Comments	Definition of response
Premarin < placebo	Statistic difference on daily ratings	Double-blind crossover	None
Estradiol and NET > placebo	Statistic difference on daily ratings	Prospective confirmation of only 1 symptom cluster after 1 cycle (not PDD criteria)*	None
Estradiol and NET > placebo	Statistic difference in MDQ	Double-blind crossover	None

Results	Determination of efficacy	Comments	Definition of recovery
Triphasic > monophasic	Statistic comparison of continuous variables	Included women with premenstrual aggravation; no psychologic assessment; no placebo group	None
OC = non-OC for depression and irritability*	Statistic comparison of continuous variables	Retrospective self reports; severity PDD: narrative survey; Rx not controlled by investigators	None
Triphasil = placebo for mood; Triphasil > placebo (breast tenderness/bloating)	Statistic comparison of continuous variables	1st Placebo-controlled study for OCs using prospectively confirmed PMS; no psychologic assessment	None

study was designed. Daily ratings were used in all four studies, but only one required confirmation of menstrual cycle changes as a diagnostic criterion [92]. This latter study included women who met criteria for PMDD. Notably, somatic symptoms were treated more effectively than were mood symptoms by spironolactone. Our group finds spironolactone helpful in alleviating bloating, headache, and breast pain. Because of this, it is useful as augmentation therapy to other treatments that more effectively treat mood symptoms.

Vitamins and dietary supplements

Vitamin B_6, evening of primrose oil, and the nutritional supplement, optivite, all have been evaluated as treatments for PMS (Tables 8 and 9) [94–107]. In the seven double-blind, placebo-controlled trials using vitamin B_6 [94–100], only one [94] used daily ratings to prospectively define participants suffering from luteal phase symptoms. No study

Table 6. Danazol: Results of Double-Blind Placebo-Controlled and Open Trials

Study	Drug	Daily ratings as entrance criteria	Cycles, n	Outcome measures
Day [88]; n = 25 (open)	Danazol 200–800 mg	No	2	Improvement vs no improvement
Deeny et al. [82]; n = 33	Danazol 100 mg BID vs placebo	No	3	VAS
Gilmore et al. [83]; n = 36	Danazol 400 mg BID vs placebo	Yes	3	Moos MDQ
Hahn et al. [84]; n = 28	Danazol 200 mg BID vs placebo	Yes	3	PMQ, VAS, BDI
Halbreich et al. [87]; n = 24 (open)	Danazol 200 mg/d	Yes	3	DRF
Sarno et al. [85]; n = 87	Danazol 200 mg vs placebo	Yes	2	MSQ
Watts et al. [86]; n = 88	Danazol (100, 200, 400 mg) or placebo	Yes	3	Weekly score of each symptom change in scales

*Placebo better than danazol for premenstrual depression.
BDI—Beck Depression Inventory; BID—twice daily; DRF—daily rating form; MDQ—Menstrual Distress Questionnaire; MSQ—Menstrual Symptom Questionnaire; PMQ—Premenstrual Questionnaire; PMTS—premenstrual tension scale; VAS—visual analogue scale.

Table 7. Diuretics: Results of Placebo-Controlled Trials

Study	Drug	Daily ratings as entrance criteria	Cycles, n	Outcome measures
Burnet et al. [89]; n = 41	Spironolactone vs placebo	No	3	Daily ratings
O'Brien et al. [90]; n = 28	Spironolactone vs placebo	No	2	VAS
Vellacott et al. [91]; n = 63	Spironolactone vs placebo	No	2	Daily ratings
Werch and Kane [93]; n = 33	Metazolone vs placebo	No	2	Weight and self-ratings
Wang et al. [92]; n = 35	Spironolactone vs placebo	Yes	3	Daily ratings

Rx—treatment; VAS—visual analogue scale.

Results	Determination of efficacy	Comments	Definition of response
Danazol helpful for severe symptoms of breast tenderness	Assessment of improvement	Open	None
Danazol > placebo	Statistical comparison of continuous variables	Double-blind crossover	None
Danazol > placebo	Statistical comparison of continuous variables	—	None
Danazol > placebo for all symptoms*	Statistical comparison of continuous variables	Side effects worsened scores on nonpremenstrual days	Threshold criteria on PMTS
Anovulatory cycles were less symptomatic	Statistical comparison of continuous variables	Efficacy depends on anovulation state	None
Danazol > placebo	Statistical comparison of MSQ for both groups	Luteal phase administration	None
Danazol 200–400 mg > placebo for breast pain, lethargy, anxiety, appetite, irritability	Statistical comparison of daily ratings	Baseline group differences confound results; small cell size; high drop-out rate in danazol group	50% drop in daily ratings

Results	Determination of efficacy	Comments	Definition of response
Spironolactone = placebo for most symptoms	Statistical comparison of 2 Rxs using continuous variables	Did not use daily ratings to select subjects	None
Spironolactone > placebo	Statistical comparison of VAS in luteal vs follicular phase	Did not use daily ratings to select subjects	None
Spironolactone = placebo except bloatedness	Comparison of success/failure in each condition	Did not use daily ratings to select subjects	At least 1 subject "better" and none "worse"
Metazolone > placebo	Statistical comparison of continuous variables	Luteal phase Rx; helpful for psychiatric and physical symptoms	None
Spironolactone > placebo	Statistical comparison of each symptom on a continuous scale	Crossover medication was more effective for somatic symptoms	None

Table 8. Vitamin B₆: Results of Randomized, Placebo-Controlled Trials

Study	Drug	Daily ratings as entrance criteria	Cycles, n	Outcome measures
Abraham and Hargrove [94]; n = 25	B₆ vs placebo	Yes (1 cycle)	2	Daily MSQ Scores
Hagen et al. [95]; n = 34	B₆ vs placebo	No	1	Monthly VAS and self-ratings
Barr et al. [99]	B₆ vs placebo	No	—	Luteal phase daily ratings
Kendall and Schnurr [96]; n = 55	B₆ vs placebo	No	2	MDQ
Stokes and Mendel [97]; n = 13	B₆ vs placebo	No	4–6	MDQ
Williams et al. [98]; n = 434	B₆ vs placebo	No	3	Self-report of symptoms

MDQ—Menstrual Distress Questionnaire; MSQ—Menstrual Symptom Questionnaire; Rx—treatment;
VAS—visual analogue scale.

Table 9. Nutritional Supplements: Results of Randomized, Placebo-Controlled Trials

Study	Drug	Daily ratings as entrance criteria	Cycles, n	Outcome measures
Callender et al. [102]; n = 10	Evening primrose oil and vitamins vs placebo	Yes	2	BDI; daily ratings; subjective improvement
Chakmakjian et al. [103]; n = 31	Optivite* vs placebo	Yes	3	MSD
Khoo et al. [104]; n = ?	Primrose oil vs placebo	No	3	Self-ratings
London et al. [100]; n = 29	Opitvite for 6 days vs Optivite for 12 days or placebo	No	3	MSQ
Stephenson et al. [105]; n = 70	Evening primrose oil vs placebo	No	3	MDQ
Stewart [101]; n = 118 and 104	High-dose Optivite vs placebo; low-dose Optivite vs placebo	No	3	Self-ratings in five patient scale
Thys-Jacob et al. [106]; n = 33	Calcium vs placebo	Yes	3	MDQ
Sayegh et al. [107]; n = 24	Carbohydrate-rich beverage	Yes	1	POMS

*Optimov Co., Torrance, CA.
BDI—Beck Depression Inventory; MDQ—Menstrual Depression Questionnaire; MSD—menstrual symptom diary;
MSQ—Menstrual Symptom Questionnaire; POMS—Profile of Mood States.

Results	Determination of efficacy	Comments	Definition of response
B_6 > placebo	Statistical comparison of continuous variables	Criteria for confirmation not stringent	None
B_6 = placebo	Statistical comparison of continuous variables	Crossover; poor methodology; results difficult to evaluate	None
B_6 > placebo	Comparison of patients self-rated as responders in each condition	Luteal phase Rx	Patient report of improvement
B_6 = placebo for affective and some physical symptom	Statistical comparison of continuous variables	Evaluation of prospective ratings were not used for entry criteria	None
B_6 = placebo	Statistical comparison of continuous variables	Crossover	None
B_6 = placebo	Statistical comparison of continuous variables	Did not use established instruments to evaluate outcome	None

Results	Determination of efficacy	Comments	Definition of response
Primrose oil > placebo only in subjective improvement	Statistical comparison of Patient Rating of Improvement	—	None
Optivite > placebo	Statistical comparison of Patient Rating of Improvement	Crossover; poor methodology; results difficult to evaluate	None
Primrose oil = placebo	Statistical comparison of continuous variables	Crossover	None
Optivite > placebo	Statistical comparison of continuous variables	Inappropriate statistical methods preclude meaningful results	None
Primrose oil = placebo	Statistical comparison of continuous variables	Ratings for 3 d/wk	None
High-dose Optivite > placebo	Comparison of percent improved under each condition	Luteal phase treatment	Patient reports of improvement
Calcium > placebo	Statistical comparison of continuous variables		Patient reports of improvement
Carbohydrate-rich beverage > control beverages	Statistical comparison of continuous variables	Luteal phase treatment	None

Table 10. Gonadotropin-Releasing Hormone Agonists: Results of Open and Placebo-Controlled Trials

Study	Drug	Daily ratings	Cycles, n	Outcome measures
Brown et al. [115]; n = 25	Leuprolide vs placebo	Yes	3	Premenstrual Tension Syndrome Scale
Hammarback and Backstrom [112]; n = 116	Buserelin (nasal) 400 µg vs placebo	Yes	Up to 6	VAS
Helvacioglu et al. [113]; n = 12	Leuprolide vs placebo	Yes	4	MSD
Mortola [114]; n = 8	Histrelin 100 µg and hormone replacement or placebo	Yes	2	COPE
Muse et al. [109]; n = 8	GnRH agonist vs placebo	Yes	3	Investigator scale
Bancroft [108]; n = 20	Buserelin 800 µg (open)	Yes	5–15	VAS
Freeman et al. [110]; n = 9	Leuprolide (open)	Yes	3	DSR
Mezrow et al. [111]; n = 10	Leuprolide (open)	Yes	12	Investigator scale

*Differential response for women with moderate to severe premenstrual depression.
†Subjects did not meet PDD criteria because follicular symptoms were high.
CGI—clinical global improvement; COPE—calendar of premenstrual experience; D/C—discontinue; DSR—daily symptom rating; GnRH—gonadotropin-releasing hormone; MDD—major depressive disorder; MSD—menstrual symptom diary; PMS—premenstrual syndrome; Rx—treatment; VAS—visual analogue scale.

employed entrance criteria as rigorous as those required for PMDD. The longest treatment study, six cycles, compares vitamin B_6 and placebo [97]. Only two [94,99] of the seven studies found B_6 more beneficial than placebo. The nutritional supplement optivite was superior to placebo in three [103, 104] but the lack of rigor in selecting study subjects limits the strength of these findings. Finally, a carbohydrate-rich drink was found to be superior to two isocaloric control beverages in a well-designed study of women with PMS [107]. Until well-designed studies are conducted on PMDD patients, the usefulness of these agents for treatment of this disorder has not been established.

Gonadotropin-releasing hormone

Gonadotropin-releasing hormone (GnRH) agonists putatively treat PMDD by inducing a cessation of menses. This method of "medical ovariectomy" was first used in a study by Muse et al. [109]. To date, three open trials [108–110] and six double-blind trials [111–116] have used GnRH agonists (Table 10). Because cessation of menses is associated with bone

Results	Determination of efficacy	Comments	Definition of response
Leuprolide > placebo in nonpremenstrually depressed group	Statistical comparison of pre and post Rx daily ratings for treatment groups	Double-blind crossover*	CGI assigned but the number of individuals with 1 or 2 was not reported
Modest benefit for buserelin	Statistical differences in daily ratings across cycle and between treatments	Included "pure" PMS and subjects with premenstrual aggravation; crossover	None
Leuprolide = placebo	Statistical comparison of daily ratings for treatment vs subjects baseline	Double-blind crossover	None
Histrelin > placebo or hormone replacement	Statistical differences in daily ratings across cycles	Sample size small; open	None
Agonist > placebo	Statistical differences in daily ratings across cycles and treatments	Single-blind placebo crossover†	None
10 patients felt worse and D/C prescribed	Statistical differences in daily ratings across treatment cycles	Drug administered nasally	None
Significant decrease in DSR scores in 6/9	Statistical comparison of daily ratings for treatment vs subjects baseline	Incudes 2 subjects with MDD; open trial	50% drop in symptoms
Leuprolide Rx decreased PMS symptoms	Statistical comparison of daily before and after Rx ratings	Open trial with hormone add-back therapy	None

loss, increased lipids, and a consequent risk of coronary artery disease, estrogen and progestin are commonly "added back" to approximate a menstrual cycle. This method was used in several investigations [111,112,114]. Although the first report showed success using GnRH agonists [109,114], only modest benefit was found for two subsequent trials [112,115], and no benefit was found in a third study [113]. Three studies found treatment ineffective for premenstrual depression. Given the risk associated with this treatment and the inconsistent findings, this type of treatment should be considered second-line therapy for women in whom other treatments have failed. Even then, patients undergoing this treatment may require ongoing treatment with agents effective in stabilizing mood, such as serotonin-reuptake inhibitors.

Bromocriptine

Bromocriptine has been the focus of eight double-blind, placebo-controlled, or comparison trials [117–124] (Table 11). Unfortunately, only two studies [122,123] used daily prospective ratings at baseline to confirm luteal phase symptomatology and continued treatment beyond one cycle. The positive study [123] is single-blind, whereas the double-blind study found bromocriptine equivalent to placebo [122]. In sum, three of eight studies found bromocriptine beneficial for mood and weight symptoms [119,120,123], but all three had flawed designs and none specifically found benefit for patients with PMDD.

Nonsteroidal anti-inflammatory drugs and other agents

The nonsteroidal anti-inflammatory drug (NSAID) mefenamic acid has been evaluated in three double-blind, placebo-controlled studies over a maximum of four cycles [125–127] Jakubowitz et al. [126] (Table 12). Only one study [127] used prospective ratings to diagnose participants. Some benefit for the agent is found in all three studies. A tightly designed study of naltrexone [128] used prospective ratings to define participants and response. This three-cycle study found benefit for naltrexone. To date, this positive result has not been replicated. Two studies of atenolol [129,130] failed to find substantial benefit for this agent compared with placebo. Other agents evaluated include naproxin [131], clonidine [132], and doxycycline [133]. Of these various agents, the most promising results are shown for naltrexone, although these results need to be replicated.

Psychotropic drug treatment

Aside from two early, negative lithium studies [135,136], psychotropic agents were not used for treatment of PMDD until 1987 [62,136–138] (Tables 13 and 14). Recent

Table 11. Dopamine Agonists: Single and Double-Blind Placebo-Controlled and Parallel Design Trials

Study	Drug	Daily ratings as entrance criteria	Cycles, n	Outcome measures
Andersch et al. [117]; n = 19	Bromocriptine vs bumetanid	No	1	CPRS; 3 point ratings
Andersen et al. [118]; n = 26	Bromocriptine vs placebo	No	1	4 point self-ratings
Benedek-Jaszmann and Hearn-Strutevant [119]; n = 10	Bromocriptine vs placebo	No	1	4 point scale
Graham et al. [120]; n = 8	Bromocriptine vs placebo	No	2	Daily symptoms rating
Ghose and Coppen [121]; n = 13	Bromocriptine vs placebo	No	1	4 point scale
Kullander and Svanber [124]; n = 10	Bromocriptine vs placebo	No	1	4 point scale
Steiner et al. [122]; n = 125	Bromocriptine (3 doses) vs placebo	Yes	3	VAS; MDQ; STAI; HRSD
Ylostalo et al. [123]; n = 18	Bromocriptine vs NET vs placebo	Yes	2	Daily symptom ratings

*Bromocriptine effective for psychologic symptoms and bloating.
†Three-point scale: good, insignificant, deterioration.
CPRS—Comprehensive Psychiatry Rating Scale; HRSD—Hamilton Rating Scale for Depression; MDQ—Menstrual Depression Questionnaire; NET—norethisterone; Rx—treatment; STAI—State-Trait Anxiety Inventory; VAS—visual analogue scale.

psychotropic drug trials are of interest because these studies generally use superior screening methods and study design, and psychotropic agents appear to be the most effective for all symptoms. There are 14 randomized, placebo-controlled trials and seven open trials, including studies on alprazolam and serotonin-reuptake inhibitors (SRIs). Studies using alprazolam ranged from two to four cycles [62,137–139]. Alprazolam is superior in four studies [62,143–145,146••] and equivalent to placebo in one study [140].

The most recent and promising acute-phase trials focus on psychopharmacologic agents that act at serotonin receptors (Tables 12 and 13). These include the 5-HT$_{1A}$ agonist buspirone [141]; 5-HT reuptake inhibitors clomipramine [142,143], fluoxetine [144–148], paroxetine [149,150], and sertraline [25]; the reuptake and 5-HT$_2$ antagonist nefazadone [151]; the 5-HT precursor tryptophan [152], and the 5-HT agonist, fenfluramine [153].

Four randomized placebo-controlled trials used fluoxetine [145,146••,147,148]. The longest acute-phase trial included six cycles [146••]. In three studies [145,146••,147], the outcome was determined by tests of statistical significance comparing placebo with active treatment. One also defined complete and partial response according to the number of standard deviations in treatment scores compared with baseline VAS scores [146••]. The only study to define response clinically is that of Stone *et al.* [148], who required an absolute score of 1 on clinical global improvement, a 50% reduction in premenstrual symptoms, or loss of entry criteria. All four studies show fluoxetine superior to placebo. The efficacy of fluoxetine is also supported by three open trials [144,154,155], two of which continued [154,155] beyond the acute phase.

Results	Determination of efficacy	Comments	Definition of response
Bromocriptine > bumetanid for tension and breast pain	Categorical	Overall bromocriptine superior to bumetanid; no placebo control	Clinician and self ratings†
Bromocriptine significantly improved breast pain	Statistical comparison of continuous variables	Crossover	None
Bromocriptine > placebo for mood and weight gain	Statistical comparison of continuous variables	Luteal phase Rx; crossover	None
Bromocriptine > placebo	Statistical comparison of continuous variables	Luteal phase Rx	None
Bromocriptine = placebo	Statistical comparison of continuous variables	Crossover	None
Bromocriptine = placebo	Statistical comparison of continuous variables	Luteal phase Rx; crossover	None
Bromocriptine = placebo	Statistical comparison of continuous variables	—	None
Bromocriptine > placebo	Statistical comparison of continuous variables	Single-blind administration vs placebo	None

Table 12. Nonsteroidal Anti-inflammatory Drugs and Other Nonpsychiatric Agents

Study	Drug	Daily ratings as entrance criteria	Cycles, n	Outcome measures
Choung et al. [128]; n = 16	Naltrexone vs placebo	Yes (3 cycles)	3	MDQ
Facchinetti et al. [131]; n = 34	Naproxen vs placebo	No	3	MDQ
Giannini et al. [132]; n = 24	Clonidine vs placebo	No	2	BPRS
Gunston [125]; n = 30	Mefanimic acid vs placebo	Yes (1 cycle)	4	Daily ratings
Jakubowitz et al. [126]; n = 19	Mefanimic acid vs placebo	Yes (1 cycle)	1	Daily ratings
Mira et al. [127]; n = 15	Mefanimic acid vs placebo	Yes	3	—
Parry et al. [130]; n = 13	Atenolol vs placebo	Yes (2 cycles)	2	VAS, HRSD
Rausch et al. [129]; n = 16	Atenolol vs placebo	Yes (3 cycles)	2	BDI, HRSD, MDQ, SRS, POMS, HAS
Toth et al. [133]; n = 30	Doxycycline vs placebo	Yes	2	VAS

*Pooled data showed naltrexane was better than placebo.
†Subjects with PDD of longer-standing duration improved more.
BDI—Beck Depression Inventory; BPRS—Brief Psychiatric Rating Scale; HAS—Hamilton Anxiety Scale; HRSD—Hamilton Rating Scale for Depression; MDQ—Menstrual Distress Questionnaire; PDD—premenstrual dysphoric disorder; PMS—premenstrual syndrome; POMS—Profile of Mood States; SRS—symptom rating scales; VAS—visual analogue scale.

Acute-phase efficacy for paroxetine is shown by one randomized, double-blind, placebo-controlled trial [150] and one open trial [151]. These studies used prospective ratings to define study-eligible patients and, in both instances, the participants met rigorous criteria for PMDD. In both studies, outcome was assessed by continuous and categorical variables. Both studies found paroxetine effective in the treatment of PMDD.

Other serotonergic compounds have yielded promising results. The tricyclic, clomipramine, was effective in an open five-cycle treatment study in which outcome was determined by categorical criteria using patient and spouse global assessment [142]. A subsequent double-blind study also measured outcome according to statistical comparison of the two treatment groups [143]. Symptom severity cutoffs (50% decrease in the Hamilton Rating Scale for Depression and daily ratings) and tests of statistical significance were used to define

Results	Determination of efficacy	Comments	Definition of response
5/7 on naltrexane and 6/9 on placebo showed response*	Statistical comparison of treatment groups on daily ratings	Double-blind crossover; treatment between day 9 and 18	Change of 10 patients on MDQ
Naproxen > placebo for pain	Statistical comparison of treatment groups on daily ratings	—	None
Clonidine > placebo	Statistical comparison of treatment groups on daily ratings	Crossover; PMS criteria not established	None
Mefanimic acid significantly better, only for questionable symptoms	Improvement or lack of improvement according to daily ratings	Luteal phase treatment; double-blind placebo-controlled crossover; participants not selected by daily-ratings criteria	Improvement/no improvement (no criteria given)
13/19 preferred mefanimic acid	Statistical comparison of treatment groups on daily ratings	PMS criteria not explained; luteal phase treatment	None
Mefanimic acid > placebo	Statistical comparison of treatment groups on daily ratings	Luteal phase treatment	None
Atenolol = placebo	Statistical comparison of treatment groups on daily ratings	Double-blind placebo-controlled crossover	None
Atenolol decreased premenstrual irritability	Statistical comparison of treatment groups on daily ratings	Double-blind crossover; luteal phase treatment†	None
Doxycycline > placebo	Statistical comparison of treatment groups on daily ratings	Double-blind placebo-controlled.	None

response for an open trial of the 5-HT$_2$ antagonist and reuptake inhibitor, nefazadone [150]. Buspirone significantly improved daily symptoms over placebo, but other measures, such as observer ratings, were not reported [141]. The 5-HT indirect agonist, D-fenfluramine, was more helpful than placebo for symptoms of depression and appetite in a trial of 17 patients [152]. Again, outcome was measured by continuous, rather than categorical variables.

There are only two negative trials of SRIs or serotonin agonists. Placebo was as effective as fluvoxamine in one study [156], but daily ratings were not used to screen patients. Although an open study of tryptophan revealed that some patients derive benefit, only 28% met outcome criteria of a 50% reduction in the Steiner Observer Rating Scale [152], suggesting less than optimal efficacy. This study is notable for its use of symptom criteria to categorically define response.

Table 13. Psychotropics: Results of Randomized, Controlled Trials

Study	Drug	Daily ratings as entrance criteria	Cycles, *n*	Outcome measures
Berger et al. [139]; *n* = 17	Alprazolam vs placebo	Yes	3 each treatment	VAS, BDI
Brzezinski et al. [153]; *n* = 17	d-Fenfluramine 30 mg vs placebo	Yes	3	HRSD
Eriksson et al. [149]; *n* = 65	Paroxetine vs maprotiline vs placebo	Yes	3	VAS, self-ratings
Freeman et al. [62••]	Alprazolam 0.25 mg/QID vs progesterone 300 mg QID vs placebo	Yes	3	DSR
Harrison et al. [136,137]; *n* = 152	Alprazolam 0.25–4 mg vs placebo	Yes	3	CGI, DRF, PAF, GAS
Menkes et al. [147]; *n* = 16	Fluoxetine vs placebo	Yes	3	PAF
Rickels et al. [141]; *n* = 34	Buspirone 25 mg vs placebo	Yes	3	DSR
Schmidt et al. [140]; *n* = 20	Alprazolam 0.75–2.25 mg vs placebo	Yes	4	DRF, SORS
Singer et al. [134]; *n* = 19	Lithium vs placebo	No	Up to 7 cycles	CGI; self-ratings
Steiner et al. [135]; *n* = 313	Fluoxetine 20 mg vs fluoxetine 60 mg and placebo	Yes	6	VAS
Smith [138]; *n* = 14	Alprazolam vs placebo	Yes	2	MSD
Stone et al. [148]; *n* = 20	Fluoxetine vs placebo	Yes	2	GAF
Sunblad et al. [143]; *n* = 29	Clomipramine 25–75 mg vs placebo	Yes	3	Spouse-rated VAS, subjects assessment
Veeninga et al. [156]; *n* = 9	Fluvoxamine 150 mg	No (weekly)	2	MDQ, SCL-90
Wood et al. [145]; *n* = 8	Fluoxetine vs placebo	Yes	3 each treatment	COPE, STAI, BDI, POMS

BDI—Beck Depression Inventory; CGI—clinical global improvement; COPE—Calendar of Premenstrual Experience; DRF—daily rating form; DSR—daily symptom rating; GAF—Global Assessment Form; GAS—Global Assessment Scale; HRSD—Hamilton Rating Scale for Depression; MDQ—Menstrual Distress Questionnaire; MSD—menstrual symptom diary; PAF—Premenstrual Assessment Form; POMS—Profile of Mood States; QID—four times per day; SCL—symptom checklist; STAI—State-Trait Anxiety Scale; VAS—visual analogue scale.

Long-term treatment of premenstrual dysphoric disorder

Steiner et al.'s [146••] study is a six-cycle fluoxetine study, and the estrogen study by Magos et al. [77] lasted up to 10 cycles. Only three other studies have investigated long-term treatment efficacy for agents that are beneficial in acute-phase treatment. Pearlstein et al. [155] followed 60 fluoxetine acute-phase responders for up to 2 years on an open basis and found continued well-being in at least 21 patients, all of whom continued

Results	Determination of efficacy	Comments	Definition of response
Alprazolam > placebo	Statistical comparison of continuous variables	Crossover; luteal phase treatment	None
d-Fenfluramine > placebo	Statistical comparison of continuous variables	Luteal phase treatment only	None
Paroxetine and maprotiline > placebo; paroxetine > maprotiline	Statistical comparison of continuous variables	Double-blind, placebo-controlled	Self-ratings of improvement
Alprazolam > progesterone; progesterone = placebo	Statistical comparison of continuous and categorical variables	Luteal phase treatment only	DRS, global improvement
Alprazolam > placebo	Statistical comparison of CGI, GAS, and continuous variables	Luteal phase treatment only	CGI, GAS
Fluoxetine > placebo	Statistical comparison of continuous variables	Crossover	None
Buspirone > placebo	Statistical comparison of continuous variables	Luteal phase treatment only	None
Alprazolam = placebo	Statistical comparison of continuous variables	Luteal phase treatment only	None
Lithium = placebo	Statistical comparison of continuous variables	Concurrent (anti-depressants allowed)	None
Fluoxetine 20 mg > fluoxetine 60 mg and placebo	Statistical comparison of continuous variables (VAS)	Luteal phase treatment	I SD from follicular phase score and percent decrease in VAS
Alprazolam > placebo	Statistical comparison of continuous variables	Double-blind placebo	None
Fluoxetine > placebo	Statistical comparison of continuous and categorical variables	Luteal phase treatment only	Failure to meet 30% ↑ 50% ↓ in patients
Clomipramine > placebo	Statistical comparison of continuous variables	Weekly prospective ratings only	None
Fluvoxamine = placebo	Statistical comparison of continuous variables	Crossover	None
Fluoxetine > placebo	Statistical comparison of continuous variables		None

pharmacotherapy. Six of the larger group developed an episode of major depression, and one developed recurrent hypomanic episodes. Elks [154] treated 11 women with fluoxetine and found continued moderate to marked relief during 3 to 20 months of treatment. Similarly, Freeman *et al.* [151] followed a subgroup of nefazadone acute-phase responders for a variable length of time, up to 1 year. In eight of 33 women who completed an additional 6 to 12 months, improvement has been maintained.

Table 14. Psychotropics: Results of Open Trials

Study	Drug	Daily ratings as entrance criteria	Cycles, n	Outcome measures
Brandenberg et al. [144]; n = 9	Fluoxetine	Yes	3	VAS
Elks [154]; n = 11	Fluoxetine	Yes	3–20	VAS
Eriksson et al. [142]; n = 5	Clomipramine	Yes	5	VAS
Freeman et al. [151]; n = 54	Nefazadone 100–600 mg	Yes	2	DRS, HRSD
Harrison et al. [157]; n = 11	Nortriptyline	Yes	3	CGI, DRF, PAF
Pearlstein [155]; n = 60	Fluoxetine	Yes	1–47	CGI
Steinberg et al. [152]; n = 13	Tryptophan 6 g; 2 wk of cycle	Yes	3	BDI, SORS
Steiner et al. [135]; n = 15	Lithium	Yes (1 cycle)	3	VAS, MDQ, MAACL, STAI, HDS, CDS
Rickels et al. [158]; n = 10	Fluoxetine	Yes	2	DRF

BDI—Beck Depression Inventory; CDS—Children's Depression Scale; CGI—clinical global improvement; DRF—daily rating form; DRS—Daily Rating Scale; HDS—Hamilton Depression Scale; MAACL—Multiple Affect Adjective Checklist; MDD—major depressive disorder; MDQ—Menstrual Distress Questionnaire; SORS—Stemer Observer Rating Scale; STAI—State-Trait Anxiety Scale; VAS—visual analogue scale.

Summary of Treatment Studies

As previously discussed, the strongest support for acute-phase treatment lies with alprazolam and SRIs (fluoxetine, clomipramine, paroxetine, and sertraline). Modest support is shown for the efficacy of danazol and GnRH agonists. Danazol is more effective for symptoms of breast tenderness than for other symptoms. The GnRH agonists appear to be less effective for mood symptoms associated with PMDD, but are very effective for other premenstrual symptoms [115]. They also confer the most morbidity because of the decreased estrogen production and the consequent risk of osteoporosis and atherosclerosis. Eventually, all women placed on a GnRH agonist regimen will require hormone replacement, and a risk of symptom recurrence is associated with this. As such, they should be considered a second-line treatment.

Results	Determination of efficacy	Comments	Definition of response
Efficacy preserved in assessment 3 mo after study	Statistical comparison of treatment with baseline	Open	None
10/11 had moderate to marked improvement	Clinical judgment	Open	None
Clomipramine helpful in 5 patients	Statistical comparison of treatment with baseline	—	None
45% of patients experienced 50% decrease	Statistical comparison of continuous and categorical variables with baseline	Most improved; some subjects still met entrance criteria at study end; included those with premenstrual worsening of MDD	Reduction in symptoms by at least 50%
—	Statistical comparison of continuous and categorical variables with baseline	—	—
100% had CGI of 1 or 2	Improvement on CGI (categorical)	95% of 21 patients relapsed after ↓ of fluoxetine	CGI
23% had 50% reduction in symptoms	Statistical comparison of continuous and categorical variables with baseline and significant percent reduction of symptoms (categorical)	3/13 had at least 50% reduction of symptoms	Reduction in symptoms by at least 50%
Lithium not beneficial	Statistical comparison of continuous and categorical variables with baseline	Some symptoms showed statistical improvement that was not deemed clinically meaningful	None
Fluoxetine effective	Statistical comparison of continuous and categorical variables with baseline	Fluoxetine primarily beneficial for mood, not somatic symptoms	None

Treatment Algorithm

The results of the studies reviewed and clinical practice has led to the following PMDD treatment algorithm (Fig. 1). The intent is to minimize drug exposure for more mild syndromes and to appropriately and aggressively treat the more severe form of the disorder.

Charting one's mood and behavior in and of itself is also palliative [150], probably because it functions as a mood monitor. Women with mild premenstrual syndromes that are not as severe as PMDD and do not cause functional impairment should have treatment tailored to the type of symptoms they experience and for the duration of symptom expression. Maintaining a daily diary can identify symptoms. For example, if bloating, weight gain, and headache during the late luteal phase are the predominant symptoms, a diuretic, such as spironolactone, taken during the symptomatic period is

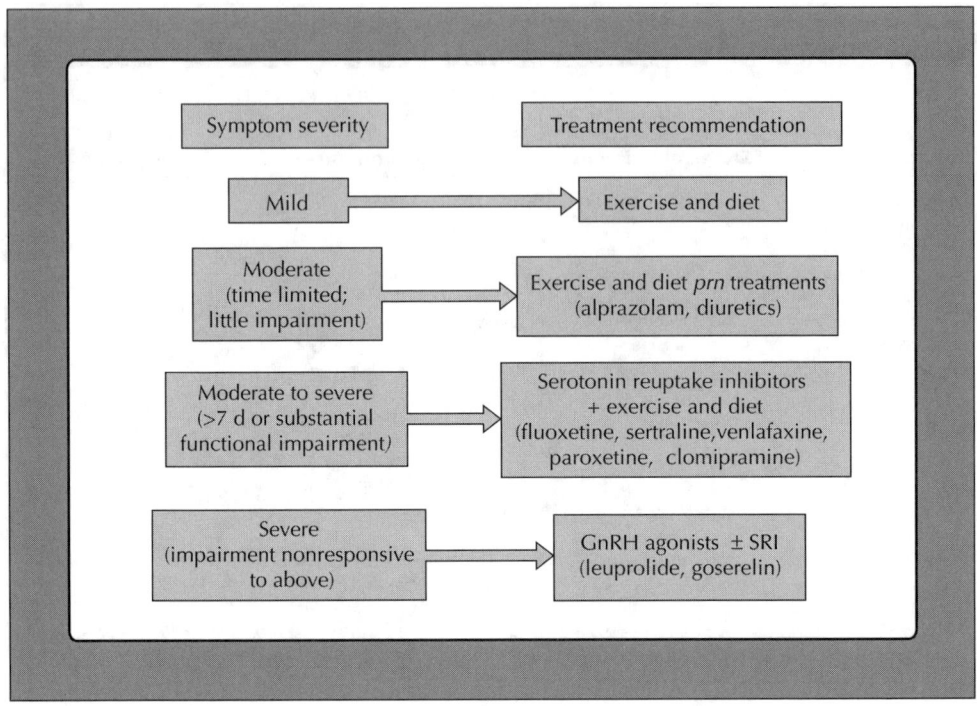

Figure 1. Premenstrual dysphoric disorder treatment algorithm. The symptom severity on the left is associated with a treatment recommendation on the right. GnRH—gonadotropin-releasing hormone; prn—as needed; SRI—serotonin-reuptake inhibitor.

helpful. Similarly, premenstrual symptoms of mastalgia can be treated by diuretics or a low dose of danazol. Mild, time-limited symptoms of irritability and mood swings can be treated by alprazolam. Alprazolam can also be used for more severe syndromes such as PMDD. However, if extended treatment (*eg*, 2 weeks) is required, another agent should be considered to avoid withdrawal or dependence.

Patients who have severe symptoms, such as those associated with PMDD, whether symptom expression is 1 week or 2 weeks, should be considered a candidate for SRI treatment. Ideally, treatment should commence after baseline ratings are obtained and after the most bothersome symptoms have been identified. Although not all patients are willing to maintain daily ratings, they should be encouraged to do so. After medication treatment is instituted, ongoing success can be determined from daily ratings. The SRI treatment may be most successful if it is commenced during the follicular phase so that the activating effects of most of these compounds do not exacerbate the tension and inner restlessness that is sometimes experienced by patients.

Preliminary evidence suggests that fluoxetine [146••] and clomipramine [144] can be effective if given only during the luteal phase. This may also be true of sertraline (Halbrach, Personal communication) and paroxetine [144]. However, patients who have no or a less than optimal response to luteal phase treatment should be prescribed medication taken on a daily basis. Finally, patients with severe debilitating illnesses who either relapse while taking medication or do not respond to other medications should be treated with a combination of SRIs and GnRH agonist. If this is successful, cyclic progestin and estrogen will need to be added by 6 months to preserve bone mass and protect the woman from atherosclerosis. After a period of stability, discontinuation from the SRI can be attempted.

Conclusions

Formalizing criteria for women who suffer from severe, mood-related premenstrual symptoms enhances well-designed research. Using rigorous criteria, researchers are able to clearly differentiate active treatments from placebo (SRIs, alprazolam, GnRH agonists) and are able to reevaluate the usefulness of progesterone. Many questions remain, such as whether there is a need for daily SRI treatment during both follicular and luteal phases; how long treatment should be continued; whether treatment efficacy is maintained during long-term treatment, and if ongoing treatment for PMDD decreases the likelihood that these patients will develop other mood disorders. It is hoped that future research will answer these questions.

References and Recommended Reading

Papers of particular interest, published recently, have been highlighted as:
* Of special interest
•• Of outstanding interest

1. Bancroft J: The premenstrual syndrome: a reappraisal of the concept and the evidence. *Psychol Med* 1993, 24(suppl):1–46.

2. Severino SK, Moline ML: *Premenstrual Syndrome: A Clinician's Guide*, edn 1. New York: The Guilford Press; 1989.

3. Yonkers KA: The association between premenstrual dysphoric disorder and other mood disorders. *J Clin Psychiatry* 1997, in press.

4. Yonkers KA, Brown WA: Pharmacologic treatments for premenstrual dysphoric disorder. *Psychiatric Ann* 1996, 26:1–4.

5. American Psychiatric Association: *Diagnostic and Statistical Manual of Mental Disorders*, edn 3. Washington, DC: American Psychiatric Association; 1987.

6. American Psychiatric Association: *Diagnostic and Statistical Manual of Mental Disorders*, edn 4. Washington, DC: American Psychiatric Association; 1994.

7. Logue CM, Moos RH: Perimenstrual symptoms: prevalence and risk factors. *Psychosom Med* 1986, 48:388–414.

8. Endicott J, Nee J, Cohen J, *et al.*: Premenstrual changes: patterns and correlates of daily ratings. *J Affect Disord* 1986, 10:127–135.

9. Frank E, Severino SK: Premenstrual dysphoric disorder: facts and meanings. *J Prac Psychol Behav Health* 1995,IX:20–28.

10. Hurt SW, Schnurr PP, Severino SK, *et al.*: Late luteal phase dysphoric disorder in 670 women evaluated for premenstrual complaints. *Am J Psychiatry* 1992, 149:525–530.

11. Ramcharan S, Love EJ, Fick GH, *et al.*: The epidemiology of premenstrual symptoms in a population-based sample of 2650 urban women: attributable risk and risk factors. *J Clin Epidemiol* 1992, 45:377–392.

12. Johnson SR: The epidemiology and social impact of premenstrual symptoms. *Clin Obstet* 1987, 30:369–384.

13. Rivera-Tovar AD, Frank E: Late luteal phase dysphoric disorder in young women. *Am J Psychiatry* 1990, 147:1634–1636.

14. Woods NF, Most A, Dery GK: Prevalence of premenstrual symptoms. *Am J Public Health* 1982, 72:1257–1264.

15. Haskett RF, Abplanalp JM: Premenstrual tension syndrome: diagnostic criteria and selection of research subjects. *Psychiatry Res* 1983, 9:125–138.

16. Stout AL, Grady TA, Steege JF, *et al.*: Premenstrual symptoms in black and white community samples. *Am J Psychiatry* 1986, 143:1436–1439.

17. Chang AM, Hoyd E, Chau SP: Premenstrual syndrome in employed Chinese women in Hong Kong. *Health Care for Women International* 1995, 16:551–561.

18. Monagle L, Dan V, Krogh V, *et al.*: Perimenstrual symptom prevalence rates: an Italian-American comparison. *Am J Epidemiol* 1993, 138:1070–1081.

19. Freeman E, Sondheimer S, Rickels K, *et al.*: Ineffectiveness of progesterone suppository treatment for premenstrual syndrome. *JAMA* 1990, 264:349–353.

20. Woods NF, Larson L, Williams R: Social and psychological factors in relation to premenstrual tension and menstrual pain. *Aust N Z J Obstet Gynaecol* 1979, 19:111–115.

21. Merikangas KR, Foeldenyl M, Angst J: The Zurich Study:XIX. Patterns of menstrual disturbances in the community: results of the Zurich Cohort Study. *Eur Arch Psychiatry Clin Neurosci* 1993, 243:23–32.

22. Reid RL: Premenstrual syndrome. *N Engl J Med* 1991, 324:1208–1210.

23. Freeman EW, Rickels K, Sondheimer SJ: Course of premenstrual syndrome symptom severity after treatment. *Am J Psychiatry* 1992, 149:531–533.

24. Metcalf MG, Braiden V, Livesey JH: Symptoms cyclicity in women with the premenstrual syndrome: an 8-year follow-up study. *J Psychosom Res* 1992:36:237–241.

25. Yonkers KA, Halbreich U, Freeman EW, *et al.*: Sertraline in the treatment of premenstrual dysphoric disorder. *Psychopharm Bull* 1996, 32:41–46.

26. Freeman EW, Rickels K, Schweiker E, Ting T: Relationships between age and symptom severity among women seeking medical treatment for premenstrual symptoms. *Psychol Med* 1995, 25:309–315.

27. MacDonald PC, Dombroski RA, Casey ML: Recurrent secretion of progesterone in large amounts: an endocrine/metabolic disorder unique to young women? *Endocr Rev* 1991, 12:372–401.

28. Hallman J: The premenstrual syndrome: an equivalent of depression? *Acta Psychiatr Scand* 1986, 73:403–411.

29. van Keep PA, Lehert P: The premenstrual syndrome: an epidemiological and statistical exercise. In *The Premenstrual Syndrome* vol 1, edn 1. Edited by van Keep PA, Utian WH. Lancaster, UK: MTP Press; 1981.

30. Warner P, Bancroft J: Factors related to self-reporting of the pre-menstrual syndrome. *Br J Psychiatry* 1990, 157:249–260.

31. Gise LH, Lebovits AH, Paddison PL, *et al.*: Issues in the identification of premenstrual syndromes. *J Nerv Ment Dis* 1990, 178:228–234.

32. Hamilton JA, Gallant S: Premenstrual syndromes: a health psychology critique of biomedically-oriented research. In *Psychophysiological Disorders*, edn 1. Edited by Gatchel RJ, Blanchard EB. Washington, DC: American Psychological Association; 1993.

33. Rubinow DR, Roy-Byrne P: Premenstrual syndromes: overview from a methodologic perspective. *Am J Psychiatry* 1984, 141:163–172.

34. Endicott J, Halbreich U, Schact S, *et al.*: Premenstrual changes and affective disorders. *Psychosom Med* 1981, 43:519–529.

35. Mackenzie TB, Wilcox K, Baron H: Lifetime prevalence of psychiatric disorders in women with perimenstrual difficulties. *J Affect Disord* 1986, 10:15–19.

36. Pearlstein TB, Frank E, Rivera-Tovar A, *et al.*: Prevalence of Axis I and Axis II disorders in women with late luteal phase dysphoric disorder. *J Affect Disord* 1990, 20:129–134.

37. DeJong R, Rubinow DR, Roy-Byrne P, *et al.*: Premenstrual mood disorder and psychiatric illness. *Am J Psychiatry* 1992, 53:289–292.

38. Wetzel RD, Reich T, McClure JN, *et al.*: Premenstrual affective syndrome and affective disorder. *Br J Psychiatry* 1975, 127:219–221.

39. Yonkers KA, White K: Premenstrual exacerbation of depression: one process or two? *J Clin Psychiatry* 1992, 53:289–292.

40. Tonks CM, Rack PH, Rose MJ: Attempted suicide and the menstrual cycle. *J Psychosom Res* 1968, 11:319–323.

41. Wetzel RD, McClure JN: Suicide and the menstrual cycle: a review. *Compr Psychiatry* 1972, 13:369–374.

42. Bancroft J: The premenstrual syndrome: a reappraisal of the concept and the evidence. *Psychol Med* 1993, 24(suppl):1–46.

43. Reid RL, Yen SSC: Premenstrual syndrome. *Am J Obstet Gynecol* 1981, 139:85–104.

44. Severino SK, Moline ML: *Premenstrual Syndrome: A Clinician's Guide*, edn 1. New York: Guilford Press; 1989.

45. Halbreich U, Tworek H: Altered serotonergic activity in women with dysphoric premenstrual syndromes. *Int J Psychiatry Med* 1993, 23:1–27.

46. Ehrenkranz JRL: Effects of sex steroids on serotonin uptake in blood platelets. *Acta Endocrinol* 1976, 83:420–428.

47. Taylor DL, Mathew RJ, Weinman ML: Serotonin levels and platelet uptake during premenstrual tension. *Neuropsychobiology* 1984, 12:16–18.

48. Malmgren R, Collins A, Nilsson CG: Platelet serotonin uptake and effects of vitamin B_6-treatment tension. *Neuropsychobiology* 1987, 18:83–88.

49. Ashby CRJ, Carr LA, Cook CL, *et al.*: Alteration of platelet serotonergic mechanisms and monoamine oxidase activity in premenstrual syndrome. *Biol Psychiatry* 1988, 24:225–233.

50. Ashby CRJ, Carr LA, Cook CL, *et al.*: Alteration of 5-HT uptake by plasma fractions in premenstrual syndrome. *J Neural Trans* 1990, 79:41–50.

51. Rojansky N, Halbreich U, Zander K, *et al.*: Imipramine receptor binding and serotonin uptake in platelets of women with premenstrual changes. *Gynecol Obstet Invest* 1991, 31:146–152.

52. Steege JF, Stout AL, Knight BS, *et al.*: Reduced platelet tritium-labeled imipramine binding sites in women with premenstrual syndrome. *Am J Obstet Gynecol* 1992, 167:168–172.

53. Yatham LN: Is 5HT-$_{1A}$ receptor subsensitivity a trait marker for late luteal phase dysphoric disorder? A pilot study. *Can J Psychiatry* 1993, 38:662–664.

54. Bancroft J, Cook A, Davidson D, *et al.*: Blunting of neuroendocrine responses to infusion of L-tryptophan in women with perimenstrual mood change. *Psychol Med* 1991, 21:305–312.

55. Menkes DB, Coates DC, Fawcett JP: Acute tryptophan depletion aggravates premenstrual syndrome. *J Affect Disord* 1994, 32:37–44.

56. Garcia-Sevilla JA, Guirron J, Garcia Vallejo P, Foster MJ: Platelet α-2 adrenergic receptors in major depressive disorder. *Arch Gen Psychiatry* 1981, 38:1327–1333.

57. Halbreich U, Piletz JE, Carson S, *et al.*: Increased imidazoline and α-2 adrenergic binding in platelets of women with dysphoric premenstrual syndromes. *Biol Psychiatry* 1993, 34: 676–686.

58. Halbreich U, Petty F, Yonkers K, *et al.*: Low plasma γ-aminobutyric acid levels during the late luteal phase of women with premenstrual dysphoric disorder. *Am J Psychiatry* 1996, 153:718–720.

59. Gold JH, Severino SK, eds. *Premenstrual Dysphorias: Myths and Realities*. Washington, DC: American Psychiatric Press; 1994.

60. Andersch B, Hahn L: Progesterone treatment of premenstrual tension: a double blind study. *J Psychosom Res* 1985, 29:489–493.

61. Dennerstein L, Spencer-Gardner C, Gotts G, *et al.*: Progesterone and the premenstrual syndrome: a double-blind crossover trial. *Br Med J* 1985, 290:1617–1621.

62.•• Freeman EW, Rickels K, Sondheimer SJ, *et al.*: A double-blind trial of oral progesterone, alprazolam, and placebo in treatment of severe premenstrual syndrome. *JAMA* 1995, 274:51–57.
Landmark article evaluating relative efficacy of alprazolam and progesterone.

63. Jordheim O: The premenstrual syndrome. *Acta Obstet Gynecol Scand* 1972, 51:77–80.

64. Maddocks S, Hahn P, Moller F, *et al.*: A double-blind placebo-controlled trial of progesterone vaginal suppositories in the treatment of premenstrual syndrome. *Am J Obstet Gynecol* 1986, 154:573–581.

65. Richter MA, Haltvick R, Shapiro SS: Progesterone treatment of premenstrual syndrome. *Curr Ther Res* 1984, 135:840–850.

66. Sampson G: Premenstrual syndrome: a double-blind controlled trial of progesterone and placebo. *Br J Psychiatry* 1979, 135:209–215.

67. Van der Meer YG, Benedek-Jaszmann LJ, Van-Loenen AC: Effect of high-dose progesterone on the premenstrual syndrome. *J Psychosom Obstet Gynecol* 1983, 2:220–222.

68. Magill PJ: Investigation of the efficacy of progesterone pessaries in the relief of symptoms of premenstrual syndrome. *Br J Gen Practice* 1995, 45:589–593.

69. Baker ER, Best RG, Manfredi RL, *et al.*: Reproductive endocrinology: efficacy of progesterone vaginal suppositories in alleviation of nervous symptoms in patients with premenstrual syndrome. *J Assisted Reproductive Genetics* 1995, 12:205–209.

70. Dennerstein L, Morse C, Gotts G, *et al.*: Treatment of premenstrual syndrome: a double-blind trial of dydrogesterone. *J Affect Disord* 1986, 11:199–205.

71. Kerr GD, Day JB, Munday MR, *et al.*: Dydrogesterone in the treatment of the premenstrual syndrome. *Practitioner* 1980, 224:852–855.

72. Sampson G, Heathcote P, Wordsworth J, *et al.*: Premenstrual syndrome: a double-blind cross-over study of treatment with dydrogesterone and placebo. *Br J Psychiatry* 1988, 153:232–235.

73. Williams JGC, Martin AJ, Hulkenberg-Tromp TEML: PMS in four European countries: Part 2. A double-blind placebo controlled study of dydrogesterone. *Br J Sex Med* 1983, 10:8–18.

74. Hellberg D, Claesson B, Nilsson S: Premenstrual tension: a placebo-controlled efficacy study with spironolactone and medroxyprogesterone acetate. *Int J Gynaecol Obstet* 1991, 34:243–248.

75. West CP: Inhibition of ovulation with oral progestins: effectiveness in premenstrual syndrome. *Eur J Obstet Gynecol Reprod Biol* 1990, 34:119–128.

76. Dhar V, Murphy BEP: Double-blind randomized crossover trial of luteal phase estrogens (premarin) in the premenstrual syndrome (PMS). *Psychoneuroendocrinology* 1991, 15:489–493.

77. Magos AL, Brincat M, Studd JWW: Treatment of the premenstrual syndrome by subcutaneous oestradiol implants and cyclical oral norethisterone: placebo controlled study. *Br Med J* 1986, 292:1629–1633.

78. Watson NR, Studd JWW, Savvas M, *et al.*: Treatment of severe premenstrual syndrome with oestradiol patches and cyclical oral norethisterone. *Lancet* 1989, 2:730–732.

79. Graham CA, Sherwin BB: A prospective treatment study of premenstrual symptoms using a triphasic oral contraceptive. *J Psychosom Res* 1992, 36:257–266.

80. Backstrom T, Hansson-Malmstrom Y, Lindhe B-A, *et al.*: Oral contraceptives in premenstrual syndrome: a randomized comparison of triphasic and monophasic preparations. *Contraception* 1992, 46:253–268.

81. Bancroft J, Rennie D: The impact of oral contraceptives on the experience of perimenstrual mood, clumsiness, food craving and other symptoms. *J Psychosom Res* 1993, 37:195–202.

82. Deeny M, Hawthorn R, McKay-Hart D: Low dose danazol in the treatment of the premenstrual syndrome. *Postgrad Med* 1991, 67:450–454.

83. Gilmore DH, Hawthorn RJ, Hart DM: Danazol for premenstrual syndrome: a preliminary report of a placebo-controlled double-blind study. *J Int Med Res* 1985, 13:129–130.

84. Hahn PM, Van Vugt DA, Reid RL: A randomized, placebo-controlled, crossover trial of danazol for the treatment of premenstrual syndrome. *Psychoneuroendocrinology* 1995, 20:193–199.

85. Sarno AP, Miller EJ, Lundblad EG: Premenstrual syndrome: beneficial effects of periodic, low-dose danazol. *Obstet Gynecol* 1987, 70:33–36.

86. Watts JF, Butts WR, Edwards RL: A clinical trial using danazol for the treatment of premenstrual tension. *Br J Obstet Gynaecol* 1987, 94:30–34.

87. Halbreich U, Rojansky N, Palter S: Elimination of ovulation and menstrual cyclicity (with danazol) improves dysphoric premenstrual syndromes. *Fertil Steril* 1991, 56:1066–1069.

88. Day J: Danazol and premenstrual syndrome. *Postgrad Med J* 1979, 55:87–89.

89. Burnet RB, Radden HS, Easterbrook EG, *et al.*: Premenstrual syndrome and spironolactone. *Aust N Z J Obstet Gynaecol* 1991, 31:366–368.

90. O'Brien PMS, Craven D, Selby C, *et al.*: Treatment of premenstrual syndrome by spironolactone. *Br J Obstet Gynaecol* 1979, 86:142–147.

91. Vellacott ID, Shroff NE, Pearce MY, *et al.*: A double-blind, placebo-controlled evaluation of spironolactone in the premenstrual syndrome. *Curr Med Res Opin* 1987, 10:450–456.

92. Wang M, Hammarback S, Lindhe B-A, Backstrom T: Treatment of premenstrual syndrome by spironolactone: a double-blind, placebo-controlled study. *Acta Obstet Gynecol Scand* 1995, 74(suppl):803–808.

93. Werch A, Kane RE: Treatment of premenstrual tension with metolazone: a double-blind evaluation of a new diuretic. *Curr Ther Res* 1976, 19:565–572.

94. Abraham GE, Hargrove JT: Effect of vitamin B-6 on premenstrual symptomatology in women with premenstrual tension syndromes: a double blind crossover study. *Infertility* 1980, 3:155–165.

95. Hagen I, Nesheim B, Tuntland T: No effect of vitamin B-6 against premenstrual tension. *Acta Obstet Gynecol Scand* 1985, 64:667–670.

96. Kendall KE, Schnurr PP: The effects of vitamin B-6 supplementation on premenstrual symptoms. *Obstet Gynecol* 1987, 70:145–149.

97. Stokes J, Mendels J: Pyridoxine and premenstrual tension. *Lancet* 1972, 1:1177–1178.

98. Williams MJ, Harris RI, Dean BC: Controlled trials of pyridoxine in the premenstrual syndrome. *J Int Med Res* 1985, 13:174–179.

99. Barr W: Pyridoxine supplements in the premenstrual syndrome. *Practitioner* 1984, 228:425–427.

100. London RS, Bradley L, Chiamori NY: Effect of a nutritional supplement on premenstrual symptomatology in women with premenstrual syndrome: a double-blind longitudinal study. *J Am Coll Nutr* 1991, 10:494–499.

101. Stewart A: Clinical and biochemical effects of nutritional supplementation on the premenstrual syndrome. *J Reprod Med* 1987, 32:435–441.

102. Callender K, McGregor M, Kirk P, Thomas CS: A double-blind trial of evening primrose oil in the premenstrual syndrome: nervous symptom subgroup. *Hum Psychopharmacol* 1988, 3:57–61.

103. Chakmakjian ZH, Higgins CE, Abraham GE: The effect of a nutritional supplement, Optivite for Women, on premenstrual tension syndromes, II: effect on symptomatology, using a double blind cross-over design. *J Appl Nutr* 1985, 37:12–17.

104. Khoo SK, Munro C, Battistutta D: Evening primrose oil and treatment of premenstrual syndrome. *Med J Aust* 1990, 153:189–192.

105. Stephenson MJ, Milner R, Lamont J: Treatment of premenstrual syndrome with oil of evening primrose: a randomized controlled trial. Proceedings of the 16th Annual Meeting of the North American Primary Care Research Group. Ottawa, Ontario, Canada; 1988.

106. Thys-Jacob S, Alvir MJ: Calcium-regulating hormones across the menstrual cycle: evidence of a secondary hyperparathyroidism in women with PMS. *J Clin Endocrinol Metab* 1995, 80:2227–2232.

107. Sayegh R, Schiff I, Wurtman J, *et al.*: The effect of a carbohydrate-rich beverage on mood, appetite, and cognitive function in women with premenstrual syndrome. *Obstet Gynecol* 1995, 86(4), Part 1:520–528.

108. Bancroft J, Boyle H, Warner P, *et al.*: The use of an LHRH agonist, buserelin, in the long-term management of premenstrual syndromes. *Clin Endocrinol* 1987, 27:171–182.

109. Muse KN, Cetel NS, Futterman LA, *et al.*: The premenstrual syndrome: effects of "medical ovariectomy". *N Engl J Med* 1984, 311:1345–1349.

110. Freeman EW, Sondheimer SJ, Rickels K, *et al.*: Gonadotropin-releasing hormone agonist in treatment of premenstrual symptoms with and without comorbidity of depression: a pilot study. *J Clin Psychiatry* 1993, 54:192–195.

111. Mezrow G, Soupe D, Spicer D, *et al.*: Depot leuprolide acetate with estrogen and progestin add-back for long-term treatment of premenstrual syndrome. *Fertil Steril* 1994, 62:932–937.

112. Hammarback S, Backstrom T: Induced anovulation as treatment of premenstrual tension syndrome: a double-blind cross-over study with GnRH-agonist versus placebo. *Acta Obstet Gynecol Scand* 1988, 67:159–166.

113. Helvacioglu A, Yeoman RR, Hazelton JM, *et al.*: Premenstrual syndrome and related hormone agonist treatment. *J Reprod Med* 1993, 38:864–870.

114. Mortola JF, Girton L, Fischer U: Successful treatment of severe premenstrual syndrome by combined use of gonadotropin-releasing hormone agonist and estrogen/progestin. *J Clin Endocrinol Metab* 1991, 72:252A–252F.

115. Brown CS, Ling FW, Andersen RN, *et al.*: Efficacy of depot leuprolide in premenstrual syndrome: effect of symptom severity and type in a controlled trial. *Obstet Gynecol* 1994, 84:779–786.

116. West CP, Hillier H: Ovarian suppression with the gonadotrophin-releasing hormone agonist goserelin (Zoladex) in management of premenstrual tension syndrome. *Hum Reprod* 1994, 9:1058–1063.

117. Andersch B, Hahn L, Wendestam C, *et al.*: Treatment of premenstrual tension syndrome with bromocriptine. *Acta Endocrinol* 1978, (suppl 88)216:165–174.

118. Anderson AN, Larsen JF, Steenstrup OR, et al.: Effect of bromocriptine on the premenstrual syndrome: a double-blind clinical trial. Br J Obstet Gynaecol 1977, 84:370–374.

119. Benedek-Jaszmann LJ, Hearn-Sturtevant MD: Premenstrual tension and functional infertility: aetiology and treatment. Lancet 1976, 1:1095–1098.

120. Graham JJ, Harding PE, Wise PH: Prolactin suppression in the treatment of premenstrual syndrome. Med J Aust 1978, 2:18–20.

121. Ghose K, Coppen A: Bromocriptine and premenstrual syndrome: controlled study. BMJ 1977, 1:147–148.

122. Steiner M, Haskett RF, Osmun JN: The treatment of severe premenstrual dysphoria with bromocriptine. J Psychosom Obstet Gynecol 1983, 2:223–227.

123. Ylostalo P, Kauppila A, Puolakka J, et al.: Bromocriptine and norethisterone in the treatment of premenstrual syndrome. Obstet Gynecol 1981, 58:292–298.

124. Kullander S, Svanberg: Bromocriptine treatment of the premenstrual syndrome. Acta Obstet Gynecol Scand 1979, 58:375–378.

125. Gunston KD: Premenstrual syndrome in Cape Town: Part II. A double-blind placebo-controlled study of the efficacy of mefenamic acid. S Afr Med J 1986, 70:159–160.

126. Jakubowicz DL, Godard E, Dewhurst SJ: The treatment of premenstrual tension with mefenamic acid: analysis of prostaglandin concentrations. Br J Obstet Gynaecol 1984, 91:78–84.

127. Mira M, McNeil D, Fraser IS, et al.: Mefenamic acid in the treatment of premenstrual syndrome. Obstet Gynecol 1986, 68:395–398.

128. Choung CJ, Coulan CB, Kao PC, et al.: Neuropeptide levels in premenstrual syndromes. Fertil Steril 1985, 44:760–765.

129. Rausch JL, Janowsky DS, Golshan S, et al.: Atenolol treatment of late luteal phase dysphoric disorder. J Affect Disord 1988, 15:141–147.

130. Parry BL, Rosenthal NE, James SP, et al.: Atenolol treatment of late luteal phase dysphoric disorder. J Affect Disord 1991, 37:131–138.

131. Facchinetti F, Fioroni L, Sances G, et al.: Naproxen sodium in the treatment of premenstrual symptoms: a placebo-controlled study. Gynecol Obstet Invest 1989, 28:205–208.

132. Giannini AJ, Sullivan B, Sarachene J, Loiselle RH: Clonidine in the treatment of premenstrual syndrome: a subgroup study. J Clin Psychiatry 1988, 49:62–63.

133. Toth A, Lesser ML, Naus G, et al.: Effect of doxycycline on pre-menstrual syndrome: a double-blind randomized clinical trial. J Int Med Res 1988, 16:270–279.

134. Singer K, Cheng R, Schou M: A controlled evaluation of lithium in the premenstrual tension syndrome. Br J Psychiatry 1974, 124:50–51.

135. Steiner M, Haskett RF, Osmun JN, Carroll BJ: Treatment of premenstrual tension with lithium carbonate. Acta Psychiatr Scand 1980, 61:92–102.

136. Harrison WM, Endicott J, Rabkin JG, et al.: Treatment of premenstrual dysphoria with alprazolam and placebo. Psychopharmacol Bull 1987, 23:150–153.

137. Harrison WM, Endicott J, Nee J: Treatment of premenstrual dysphoria with alprazolam. Arch Gen Psychiatry 1990, 47:270–275.

138. Smith S, Rinehart JS, Ruddock VE, et al.: Treatment of premenstrual syndrome with alprazolam: results of a double-blind, placebo-controlled, randomized crossover clinical trial. Obstet Gynecol 1987, 70:37–43.

139. Berger CP, Presser B: Alprazolam in the treatment of two subsamples of patients with late luteal phase dysphoric disorder: a double-blind, placebo-controlled crossover study. Obstet Gynecol 1994, 84:379–385.

140. Schmidt PJ, Grover GN, Rubinow DR: Alprazolam in the treatment of premenstrual syndrome. Arch Gen Psychiatry 1993, 50:467–473.

141. Rickels K, Freeman E, Sondheimer S: Buspirone in treatment of premenstrual syndrome. Lancet 1989, 4:777.

142. Eriksson E, Lisjo P, Sundblad C, et al.: Effect of clomipramine on premenstrual syndrome. Acta Psychiatr Scand 1989, 81:87–88.

143. Sundblad C, Hedberg MA, Eriksson E: Clomipramine administered during the luteal phase reduces the symptoms of premenstrual syndrome: a placebo-controlled trial. Neuropsychopharmacology 1993, 9:133–145.

144. Brandenberg S, Tuynman-Qua H, Verheij R, *et al.*: Treatment of premenstrual syndrome with fluoxetine: an open study. *Int Clin Psychopharmacol* 1993, 8:315–317.

145. Wood S, Mortola J, Chan Y-F, *et al.*: Treatment of premenstrual syndrome with fluoxetine: a double-blind, placebo-controlled crossover study. *Obstet Gynecol* 1992, 339–334.

146.•• Steiner M, Steinberg S, Stewart D, *et al.*: Fluoxetine in the treatment of premenstrual dysphoria. *N Engl J Med* 1995, 332:1529–1534.
Large multicenter trial evaluating the efficacy of two fixed doses of fluoxetine for premenstrual dysphoric disorder.

147. Menkes DB, Taghavi E, Mason PA, *et al.*: Fluoxetine treatment of severe premenstrual syndrome. *Br Med J* 1992, 305:346–347.

148. Stone AB, Pearlstein TB, Brown WA: Fluoxetine in the treatment of late luteal phase dysphoric disorder. *J Clin Psychiatry* 1991, 52:290–293.

149. Eriksson E, Hedberg MA, Andersch B, Sundblad C: The serotonin reuptake inhibitor paroxetine is superior to the noradrenaline reuptake inhibitor maprotiline in the treatment of premenstrual syndrome. *Neuropsychopharmacology* 1995, 12:169–176.

150. Yonkers KA, Gullion C, Williams A, *et al.*: Paroxetine as a treatment for premenstrual dysphoric disorder. *J Clin Psychopharm* 1995, Submitted.

151. Freeman EW, Rickels K, Sondheimer SJ, *et al.*: Nefazodone in the treatment of premenstrual syndrome: a preliminary study. *J Clin Psychopharm* 1994, 14:180–186.

152. Steinberg S, Annable L, Young YN, *et al.*: Tryptophan in the treatment of late luteal phase dysphoric disorder: a pilot study. *J Psychiatr Neurosci* 1994, 19:114–119.

153. Brzezinski AA, Wurtman JJ, Wurtman RJ, *et al.*: d-Fenfluramine suppresses the increased calorie and carbohydrate intakes and improves the mood of women with premenstrual depression. *Obstet Gynecol* 1990, 76:296–300.

154. Elks ML: Open trial of fluoxetine therapy for premenstrual syndrome. *South Med J* 1993, 86:503–507.

155. Pearlstein TB, Stone AB: Long-term fluoxetine treatment of late luteal phase dysphoric disorder. *J Clin Psychiatry* 1994, 55:332–335.

156. Veeninga AT, Westenberg HGM, Weusten JTN: Fluvoxamine in the treatment of menstrually related mood disorders. *Psychopharmacology (Berlin)* 1990, 102:414–416.

157. Harrison WM, Endicott J, Nee JC: Treatment of premenstrual depression with nortriptyline: a pilot study. *J Clin Psychiatry* 1989, 50:136–139.

158. Rickels K, Freeman EW, Sondheimer S, Albert J: Fluoxetine in the treatment of premenstrual syndrome. *Curr Ther Res* 1990, 48:161–166.

CHAPTER 10

Management of Mood and Anxiety Disorders in Primary Care

Herbert C. Schulberg, Wayne Katon,
and M. Katherine Shear

The primary care physician's extensive role in diagnosing and treating mood and anxiety disorders creates both opportunities and challenges as we strive to enhance the quality of care for these psychiatric conditions. We review the epidemiology of mood and anxiety disorders in the ambulatory medical sector, present *Diagnostic and Statistical Manual of Mental Disorders*, edition 4 criteria for diagnosing these disorders in patients whose comorbid organic and medically unexplained symptoms possibly confound the assessment process, and describe state-of-the-art psychosocial and pharmacologic treatments that can be applied in routine primary care practice.

It has been consistently shown that persons experiencing mental disorders seek help as often from primary care physicians as from psychiatric specialists [1,2]. This pattern will continue, if not grow, during the coming years as third-party payors shift mental health services to the generalist medical sector where direct costs are only 33% to 50% of those incurred in the specialist sector [3]. Primary care physicians, thus, will need to become more skilled and efficient in diagnosing and treating mental disorders if the quality of their care and its clinical outcomes are to meet contemporary standards. With these developments in mind, this chapter focuses on mood and anxiety disorders, which are two of the most prevalent psychiatric disorders presenting in primary care practice [4,5]. The American Psychiatric Association's (APA) *Diagnostic and Statistical Manual of Mental Disorders*, edition 4 (DSM-IV) classification system [6] describes a large range of depressive and anxiety disorders. We limit ourselves here, however, to those conditions most likely to be identified and directly managed by the primary care physician. They include major and minor depression and dysthymic mood disorders; panic and generalized anxiety disorders among the anxiety disorders; and mixed anxiety-depression. We will review the epidemiology of these conditions in the ambulatory medical sector, present criteria for diagnosing them in patients whose comorbid organic and medically unexplained symptoms possibly confound the assessment process, and describe psychosocial and pharmacologic treatments that can be applied in routine clinical practice.

Epidemiology of Mood and Anxiety Disorders

Knowledge of the prevalence of mood and anxiety disorders in primary care practice serves many scientific and clinical purposes. In the assessment of patients presenting with complex histories, symptoms, and complaints, higher base rates for particular conditions lead the physician to focus on them in the diagnostic decision-making process. The present scientific standard for establishing valid prevalence rates requires the administration of structured interviews yielding diagnoses within the DSM-IV system. Rates generated through physician estimates of psychiatric morbidity in their practices or patient responses to a screening instrument are no longer considered valid or reliable for epidemiologic purposes [4].

Mood disorders

Of the several epidemiologic indices that can be calculated, point prevalence rates are most commonly reported in the primary care literature. Few studies have investigated period prevalence or incidence rates. With regard to major depression's point prevalence, Katon and Schulberg's review [4] of 11 studies administering structured interview schedules to primary care patients found this disorder's rate to range from 4.8% to 8.6% across diagnostic instruments and primary care settings. More recently, a point prevalence of 11.5% was obtained for major depression in the Primary Care Evaluation of Mental Disorders (PRIME-MD 1000) study [7] and a rate of 13.5% was obtained in a study using an instrument that did not require the symptoms to meet impairment criteria [8]. Given that investigators from the Epidemiologic Catchment Area Program [9] and the National Comorbidity Survey [10] obtained point prevalence rates of 1.6% to 2.9% and 4.9%, respectively, among community samples, major depression is at least twice as prevalent among ambulatory medical patients as in the general population.

Fewer reports are available about the point prevalence of less severe forms of depression among primary care patients. The studies of this population reviewed by Katon and Schulberg [4] yielded rates of between 2.1% and 3.8% for dysthymia and 3.4% and 4.7% for minor depression. An almost similar rate of 8.8% for current subthreshold depression was reported by Simon and Von Korff [11], but Williams *et al.* [12] diagnosed 16% of their primary care sample as experiencing minor depression. As for mixed anxiety-depression, which DSM-IV defines as presenting with a nonspecific symptom pattern below threshold criteria for either depression or anxiety [6], its point prevalence was found to be 8% when studied in several primary care centers [13].

Anxiety disorders

A major change in studying the epidemiology of anxiety disorders occurred in 1980 with publication of DSM-III, which no longer considered anxiety a unidimensional condition. Instead, it proposed specific diagnostic categories marked by carefully delineated symptom clusters, each of which has unique etiologic, treatment, and prognostic implications. This nosologic change led investigators [14–18] administering structured clinical interviews to estimate that the point prevalence of generalized anxiety disorder (GAD) among primary care patients ranges from 1.6% to 9.1% and that for panic disorder ranges from 1.4% to 6.7%. GAD rates among men typically resemble those among women, but the diagnosis of panic disorder has been assigned to 2.5 to 3.0 times as many women as men seeking health care [19]. As with depressive disorders, GAD and panic disorder appear more prevalent in medical than community populations. Primary care physicians, indeed, rated anxiety disorders as the most common psychiatric problem in their practices [20]. Panic disorder and GAD are particularly prevalent among psychologically distressed high-volume users of primary medical care [21]; approximately 20% were assigned the diagnosis of panic disorder and 40% the diagnosis of GAD. These disorders are also highly comorbid with depressive morbidity, with 25% to 54% of primary care patients exhibiting the mood disorder and current GAD [22].

Diagnosing Mood and Anxiety Disorders in the Medical Setting

Leaders in psychiatry and primary care medicine have long recognized that individuals with psychiatric disorders often are seen only in primary care settings and that these disorders often remained unrecognized. Consequently, the APA and nine medical groups initiated deliberations in 1990 in order to develop a DSM for primary care physicians (DSM-IV-PC) that would be user friendly, have clinical and educational utility, and be compatible with DSM-IV and International Classification of Diseases, 9th Revision, Clinical Modification (ICD-9-CM). These deliberations resulted in DSM-IV-PC [23,24], a manual that was reviewed and revised after field tests in various primary care settings. A major strength of the manual are the algorithms to be used by the physician in assessing a patient's presenting complaints and in selecting a proper diagnosis. The DSM-IV-PC framework is highly compatible with that proposed for mood disorders by the Depression Guideline Panel of the Agency for Health Care Policy and Research (AHCPR) [25]. The DSM-IV-PC diagnostic algorithms are more fully illustrated in the succeeding discussion of criteria for diagnosing mood and anxiety disorders in the ambulatory medical setting.

Before doing so, we note the growing availability of psychiatric screening instruments explicitly designed for use by primary care physicians wishing to determine whether a fuller diagnostic interview is indicated. When suspicious that a patient is experiencing a mood or anxiety disorder, the physician can administer the screening component of the PRIME-MD [7] or the Symptom Driven Diagnostic System-Primary Care (SDDS-PC) [26]. When the patient acknowledges a sufficient number of symptoms pertinent to a particular disorder, a more extended assessment is conducted to ascertain whether DSM-IV-PC criteria are met.

Mood disorders

In comparison with depressed persons seeking help from mental health specialists, depressed persons presenting to primary care physicians describe more physical-psychophysiologic symptoms, perceive their health as worse, experience more pain, and exhibit poorer physical functioning [27,28]. The chronic disorders and physical symptoms that often trouble primary care patients and the medications that they may be taking at any given time further contribute to the complex differential diagnosis facing the internist or family physician. When affective symptoms such as "feeling blue" or having lost interest in daily activities accompany physical complaints, the physician is challenged to determine whether the patient is experiencing a general medical illness producing depression-like symptoms, a depression producing organic-like symptoms, a depression that is comorbid with a general medical illness, or whether substances or medications are producing depression-like symptoms [29]. General medical illnesses [30] and substances or medications [25] that may induce depression-like symptoms are listed in Tables 1 and 2, respectively.

Table 1. General Medical Conditions Inducing Mood Symptoms*

Endocrine disorders	Tumors	Others
Addison's disease	Central nervous system	Anemia
Cushing's disease	Lung	Electrolyte abnormalities
Diabetes mellitus	Pancreas	Heavy metal poisoning
Hyperparathyroidism	Neurologic disorders	Hypertension
Hypopituitarism	Cerebrovascular disease	Systemic lupus erythematosus
Hypothyroidism	Dementia	
Infections	Epilepsy, particularly with a	
Epstein-Barr virus	temporal lobe focus	
Encephalitis	Huntington's disease	
HIV	Parkinson's disease	
Postinfluenza	Postconcussion	
Pneumonia	Progressive supranuclear palsy	
Syphilis	Multiple sclerosis	
Hepatitis	Stroke	

*Adapted from Hall et al. [30].

Table 2. Substances and Medications Associated with Mood Symptoms*

Analgesics and anti-inflammatory	Antimicrobials	Immunosuppressive agents
agents	Ampicillin	Tranquilizers
Ibuprofen	Cycloserine	Barbiturates
Indomethacin	Dapsone	Major tranquilizers
Baclofen	Griseofulvin	Minor tranquilizers
Opiates	Isoniazid	Miscellaneous
Pentazocine	Metronidazole	Alcohol
Phenacetin	Nalidixic acid	Amphetamine or cocaine
Phenylbutazone	Nitrofurantoin	withdrawal
Anticonvulsants	Procaine penicillin	Caffeine
Antihistamines	Streptomycin	Cimetidine
Antihypertensive agents	Sulfonamides	Digitalis
Clonidine	Tetracycline	Disulfiram
Guanethidine	Trimethoprim sulfamethoxazole	Fenfluramine
Hydralazine	Antiparkinsonian agents	Halothane
Methyldopa	Cytotoxic agents	Lysergic acid diethylamide (LSD)
Propranolol	Hormones	Methysergide
Reserpine	Adrenocorticotropic hormone	Metrizamide
	Corticosteroids	Phenylephrine
	Estrogen	
	Oral contraceptives	

*Adapted from Depression Guideline Panel [25].

Before describing an algorithm with which the physician can test these diagnostic possibilities, we consider the DSM-IV criteria for a mood disorder that involves symptoms of both affective and somatic types. Major depressive disorder is diagnosed when at least five of nine symptoms (including either depressed mood or markedly diminished interest in most activities) are present almost daily for at least 2 weeks. Dysthymia is diagnosed when depressed mood is present more often than not over a

2-year period but wherein fewer than four concurrent symptoms are present, which are not so disabling as in major depression. Minor depression is marked by depressed mood or lost interest over a 2-week period, although an insufficient number of additional symptoms needed to meet criteria for a major depression are present. The diagnosis of mixed anxiety-depression is contained in the appendix rather than the text of DSM-IV but it is, nevertheless, of interest to primary care physicians given the condition's high prevalence in their practices [13]. As noted previously, this condition is marked by persistent or recurrent dysphoric mood as well other symptoms of depression and anxiety but in insufficient numbers to meet threshold criteria for either of these disorders (Table 3).

Given these criteria for the various mood disorders likely to challenge the primary care physician, several algorithms developed by the Depression Guideline Panel [25] can assist in diagnostic decision making. Figure 1 presents a conceptual sequence for organizing symptom levels and clinical histories into a specific diagnosis. Its several steps include determining the following: 1) whether the patient's presenting symptomatology is sufficiently extensive to warrant the diagnosis of major depression; and 2) whether the diagnosis of bipolar rather then unipolar disorder is more appropriate in light of past episodes of the former mood disorder.

Patients in the primary medical care sector often experience general medical conditions and may be taking medications of some type [31]. Thus, it is necessary for physicians to ascertain that the depressive symptoms reflect a true mood disorder rather than a general medical illness and separate or concurrent side effects from a drug. The algorithm in Figure 2 indicates that this can be accomplished by initially optimizing treatment of the general medical disorder with or without modifying the medication regimen.

Table 3. Research Criteria for Mixed Anxiety–Depressive Disorder*

Persistent or recurrent dysphoric mood lasting at least 1 month
The dysphoric mood is accompanied for at least 1 month by four (or more) of the following symptoms:
  Difficulty concentrating or mind going blank
  Sleep disturbance (difficulty falling or staying asleep, or restless unsatisfying sleep)
  Fatigue or low energy
  Irritability
  Worry
  Being easily moved to tears
  Hypervigilance
  Anticipating the worst
  Hopelessness (pervasive pessimism about the future)
  Low self-esteem or feelings of worthlessness
The symptoms cause clinically significant distress or impairment in social, occupational, or other important
  areas of functioning
The symptoms are not due to the direct physiologic effects of a substance (eg, drug abuse, medication) or a
  general medical condition
All of the following:
  Criteria have never been met for major depressive disorder
  Criteria are not currently met for any other anxiety or mood disorder (including an anxiety or mood
    disorder in partial remission)
  The symptoms are not better accounted for by any other mental disorder

*Adapted from Diagnostic and Statistical Manual of Mental Disorders, edn 4 [6]; with permission.

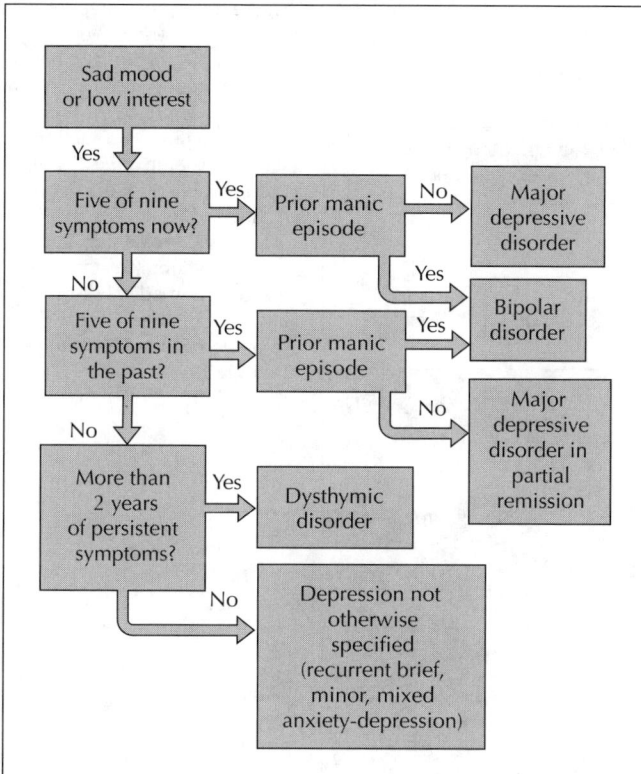

Figure 1. Decision tree for the differential diagnosis of several primary mood disorders when sad mood or low interest is a prominent clinical symptom. (*Adapted from* Depression Guideline Panel [25].)

This strategy is particularly appropriate when the clinical history indicates onset of the mood symptoms after the patient started taking a medication or developed the general medical disorder. If the depression persists despite these interventions, the morbidity may be considered psychiatric and treatment for a mood disorder may be initiated.

A further differential diagnosis that the physician should consider before concluding that the patient is experiencing, and should be treated for, a primary mood disorder is presented in Figure 3. Because the majority of depressed ambulatory medical patients experience comorbid psychiatric (Axis I) and personality (Axis II) disorders [32], the relationship between depression and other psychopathology must be weighed. For example, the physician should suspect alcohol or drug abuse rather than depression as the primary diagnosis when the patient presents with labile hypertension, multiple accidents, absenteeism, abnormal liver function tests, needle marks, skin abscesses, or HIV positivity. The algorithm in Figure 3 indicates that substance abuse, eating disorders, and obsessive compulsive disorder warrant treatment before the depressive disorder. Conversely, depression is to be treated before GAD and personality disorders.

Personality disorders are often comorbid with depressive disorders and have been associated with a poorer short-term treatment response of the depression's symptoms and functional limitations [33]. However, an 18-month follow-up of primary care patients meeting these Axis I and II diagnoses found no differences in ratings of depression and social functioning between these patients and mood-disordered patients lacking an Axis

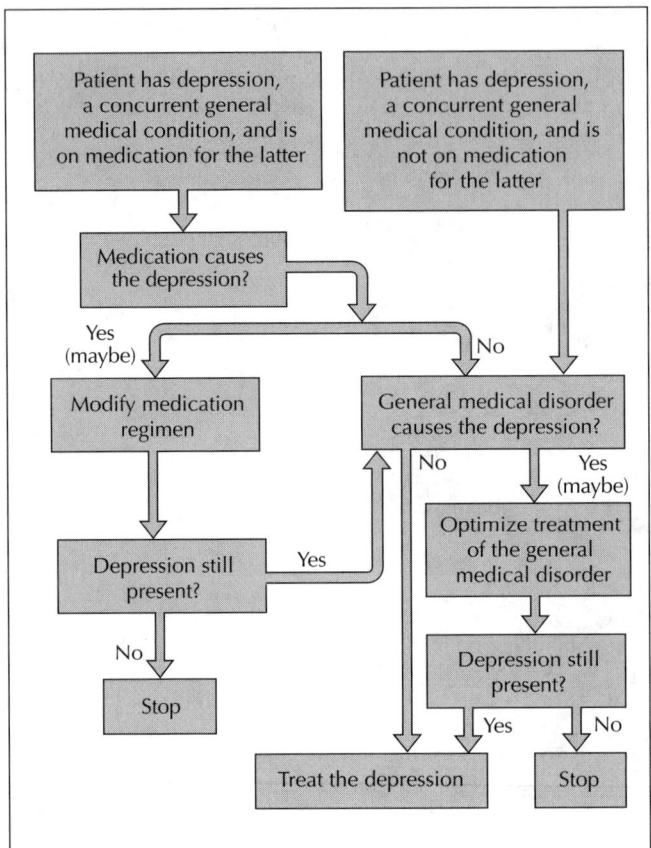

Figure 2. Decision tree for determining whether or not a medication or general medical disorder causes the depression. Strategies are presented for intervening in either circumstance. In some clinical situations, treatment of the depression (*eg*, if severe, incapacitating, or life-threatening) cannot be delayed until treatment for the general medical disorder has been optimized. (*Adapted from* Depression Guideline Panel [25].)

II diagnosis [34]. Aggressive and extended treatment of the depression is indicated, therefore, with reevaluation of the symptoms and functioning at a later time.

Anxiety disorders

Anxiety disorders are more difficult to diagnose in primary care than psychiatric settings because a medical patient's chief complaint when experiencing anxiety often is that of physical symptoms rather than psychic distress. Approximately 80% of clinically anxious primary care patients present with a somatic symptom or complaints about a chronic medical illness [35]. Not surprisingly, therefore, physicians were found to diagnose clinically significant anxiety or depression improperly in 52% of their patients presenting with physical symptoms. On the other hand, only 4% of such episodes were missed among patients expressing psychologic difficulties [35].

Panic disorder

The majority of patients with panic disorder initially present in a general medical setting [36] with their most frightening autonomic symptom such as chest pain, palpitations, or shortness of breath. Primary care patients experiencing panic disorder, therefore, most commonly present with the following three physical symptom clusters: 1) cardiologic

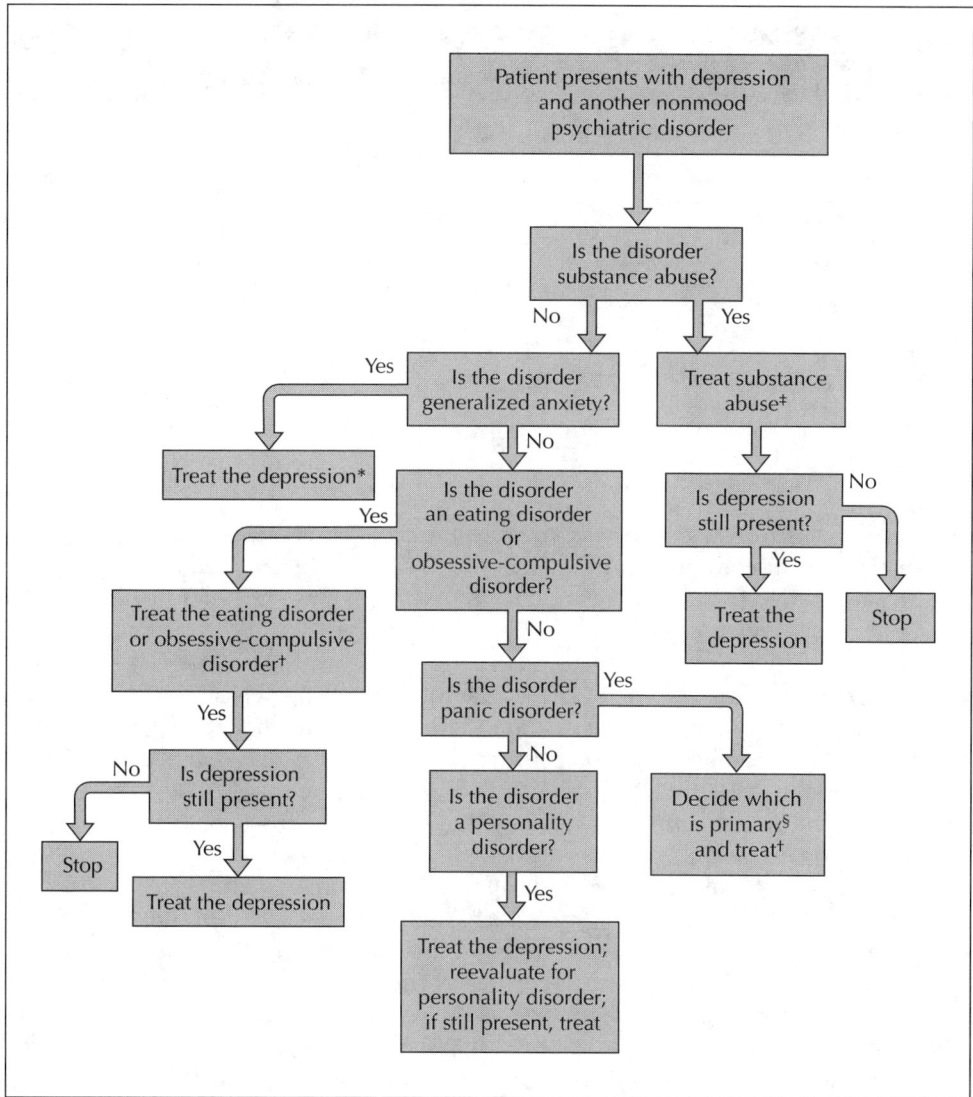

Figure 3. Decision tree for determining whether depression or a coexisting psychiatric disorder should be the initial treatment target. *When the depression is treated, the anxiety disorder should resolve as well. †Choose medications known to be effective for both the depression and the other psychiatric disorder. ‡In certain cases (based on history), both major depression and substance abuse may require simultaneous treatment. §Primary is the most severe, the longest standing by history, or the one that runs in the patient's family. (*Adapted from* Depression Guideline Panel [25].)

complaints, *eg*, chest pain or rapid heart beat; 2) gastrointestinal complaints, *eg*, epigastric pain or symptoms of irritable bowel syndrome; and 3) neurologic complaints, *eg*, headache or dizziness. Less common somatic presentations of panic disorder include near-syncopal episodes, breathlessness, and choking sensation [37]. Medical disorders and substances that can mimic panic symptoms are listed in Table 4.

Table 4. Medical Disorders and Substances that can Mimic Panic Symptoms*

Alcohol withdrawal	Hyperparathyroidism
Amphetamines	Hyperthyroidism
Asthma	Hypoglycemia
Caffeine consumption	Hypothyroidism
Cardiac arrhythmias	Marijuana
Cardiomyopathies	Menopausal symptoms
Cocaine	Mitral valve prolapse
Coronary artery disease	Pheochromocytoma
Cushing's syndrome	Pulmonary embolus
Drug withdrawal	Temporal lobe epilepsy
Electrolyte abnormalities	True vertigo

*Adapted from Katon [47].

Because marked overlap exists in the phenomenology of anxiety and organic disorders, which key and unique features of this psychiatric disorder should the primary care physician consider in the differential diagnosis? DSM-IV criteria for panic disorder require that the patient experience recurrent panic attacks of unexpected sudden onset that are marked by intense apprehension, fear, or terror, and at least four somatic symptoms. Furthermore, at least one of the attacks is followed by persistent concern about future attacks, worry about the attack's implications, or altered behavior. Application of these criteria to the physician's diagnostic decision-making is illustrated in Table 5, which follows the DSM-IV-PC [23] anxiety algorithm. Each of its seven steps specifies the information needed to refine the clinical formulation and the diagnostic alternatives available to the physician.

In addition to familiarity with the diagnostic algorithm for anxiety disorders (Fig. 4), the primary care physician's assessment of panic disorder should consider its chronologic development [38]. A patient's initial attacks are often associated with stressful life events that the patient perceives as threatening and unavoidable (Fig. 4). Some patients recover uneventfully from their first or initial attacks with reassurance and education. Others progress to a second stage where the panic attacks increase in frequency and anticipatory anxiety develops, ie, constant fear of a recurrent attack. During this second stage, patients may associate specific environmental events or circumstances with an attack, especially when they feel trapped for social or physical reasons. In this second stage, patients often visit physicians focusing on an autonomic symptom of panic (ie, rapid heart beat or chest tightness) or a physical sequela of the attack, such as headaches or diarrhea. Some patients develop a third stage of the illness in which they are agoraphobic. This stage may result in job loss and marital problems and can be marked by "doctor shopping" for help with unexplained physical symptoms and hypochondriacal fears.

As noted with regard to mood disorders, the physician diagnosing anxiety disorders must consider the possible role of medical illnesses and medications (at therapeutic or toxic levels) in precipitating psychiatric morbidity. For example, an asthmatic patient with a toxic theophylline level or a patient with diabetes whose dosage of insulin was

Table 5. Steps for Distinguishing Between Several Anxiety Disorders based on the Patient's Presenting Symptoms*†

Step 1
Consider the etiologic role of generalized medical conditions or substance use, and whether the anxiety is
    better accounted for by another mental disorder:
Anxiety disorder due to a general medical condition
Substance-induced (including medication) anxiety disorder
Other mental disorders

Step 2
If the presenting symptom is one or more panic attacks, consider:
Panic disorder with agoraphobia
Panic disorder without agoraphobia
Other anxiety disorders (eg, social phobia, specific phobia, posttraumatic stress disorder, obsessive-
    compulsive disorder)

Step 3
If the presenting symptom is fear, avoidance, or anxious anticipation about one or more specific situations,
    consider:
Social phobia (avoidance of a social situation in which the person may be exposed to scrutiny)
Specific phobia
Agoraphobia without history of panic disorder (avoidance of a situation in which escape may be difficult or
    interrelated, overlapping phobias involving specific situations)

Step 4
If presenting symtpoms include fear of separation, consider:
Separation anxiety disorder (anxiety concerning separation from major attachment figure)

Step 5
If the presenting worry or anxiety is related to recurrent and persistent thoughts (obsessions) or ritualistic
    behaviors or recurrent mental acts (compulsions), consider:
Obsessive-compulsive disorder

Step 6
If the presenting symptoms are related to reexperiencing highly traumatic events, consider:
Posttraumatic stress disorder (if symptoms persist at least 4 weeks)
Acute stress disorder (if symptoms persist for 2 to 4 weeks)

Step 7
If pervasive symptoms are associated with a variety of events or situations and have persisted for at least
    6 months, consider:
Generalized anxiety disorder

Step 8
If symptoms are in response to a specific, psychosocial stressor, consider:
Adjustment disorder with anxiety

Step 9
If the criteria are not met for any of the previously described specific disorders, consider:
Anxiety disorder not otherwise specified

Step 10
If the clinician has determined that a disorder is not present, but wishes to note the presence of
    symptoms, consider:
Anxiety

*Adapted from Diagnostic and Statistical Manual of Mental Disorders, edn 4, Primary Care Version [23];
with permission.
†Presenting symptoms might also include fear; worry; repetitive, intrusive, inappropriate thoughts or actions;
and unexplained general medical complaint.

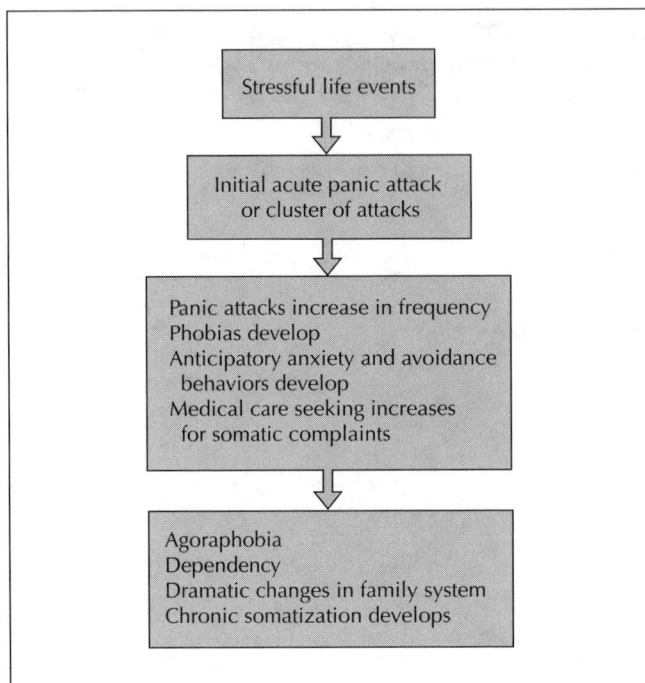

Figure 4. Sequence of chronologic stages leading from stressful life events to development of panic attacks, panic disorder, and agoraphobia. (*Adapted from* Katon [47].)

recently increased could present with heightened anxiety. Although medical illnesses can cause symptoms resembling panic (*eg*, cardiac arrhythmias, temporal lobe epilepsy, pheochromocytoma), drug toxicity and withdrawal are the far more common precipitants of this anxiety disorder.

Physicians must determine whether medical conditions and medications play an etiologic role in the onset of a panic attack (*see* Table 5, Step 1), but they should also recognize that panic disorder and medical illness may coexist. For example, patients with medical illness had a 41% higher rate of anxiety disorders than those with no medical illness in the Epidemiologic Catchment Area study [39]. Primary care patients with a chronic medical illness who develop panic disorder frequently experience intensified medical distress, possibly due to sympathetic nervous system arousal from the anxiety disorder, which can lead to physiologic worsening of illnesses like angina pectoris, peptic ulcer, or hypertension.

A particularly well-studied association between anxiety and medical disorders is that between panic disorder and mitral valve prolapse (MVP). Although the prevalence of panic disorder is no higher among MVP patients than patients with other cardiac conditions [40], patients with panic disorder have a higher prevalence of MVP than controls. Nevertheless, MVP associated with panic disorder is of questionable medical significance because it is mild and not associated with thickened mitral valve leaflets or small ventricular size [41]. Indeed, MVP may originate in autonomic arousal, which is thought to play a role in the genesis of panic attacks. The MVP neither alters the response to lactate nor the response of panic patients to imipramine; in fact, it disappears in some patients after adequate treatment of panic disorder.

Panic disorder is occasionally associated with labile hypertension and leads to medical work-ups for pheochromocytoma, a rare catecholamine-secreting tumor. One study found that 40% of patients with negative results of laboratory tests for pheochromocytoma met panic disorder criteria on a structured psychiatric interview versus only 5% in a hypertensive control group receiving cholesterol work-ups. Only one of 300 laboratory work-ups for pheochromocytoma was positive in two large hospitals during this same time period [42].

Generalized anxiety disorder

The key clinical feature of GAD as defined by DSM-IV is excessive or uncontrollable worry occurring over a 6-month period accompanied by at least three of the following symptoms: restlessness, fatigue, difficulty concentrating, irritability, muscle tension, or sleep disturbance. These symptoms must be associated with clinically significant impairment in social, vocational, or other important areas of the patient's life [43,44]. As when assessing symptoms of depression and panic disorder, the primary care physician should ascertain that the presenting symptoms are not precipitated by the physiologic effects of a medication or medical illness before diagnosing the patient's morbidity as generalized anxiety. The differential diagnosis should also consider that many patients meeting criteria for GAD also experience more severe psychopathology, *eg*, major depression or another form of anxiety, *eg*, panic disorder or posttraumatic stress disorder. When such additional psychopathology is present, DSM-IV requires that the anxiety and worry not be confined to the other Axis I disorder if the patient is to meet diagnostic criteria for GAD.

Treating Mood and Anxiety Disorders in the Medical Setting

The initial step in the primary care physician's decision on how to treat a depressed or anxious patient is determining whether an active intervention is indicated. Although a sizable literature laments improper management of these disorders in ambulatory medical practice, it should not be assumed that all diagnosed cases necessarily need immediate treatment. As Schulberg and Pajer [45] have indicated, the treatment decision should consider the disorder's clinical severity, the extent of social and vocational dysfunction associated with it, the presence of medical and psychiatric comorbidity, and the patient's probability of complying with a prescribed treatment.

When the physician concludes that immediate treatment is indicated, it must next be determined whether to provide the intervention personally or whether to refer the patient to a mental health specialist. Most episodes of depression and anxiety can be managed by primary care physicians; indeed, they typically are in prepaid health care plans [46]. Katon [47] and the Depression Guideline Panel of the AHCPR [48] suggest, however, that mental health specialists be involved under the following clinical circumstances: 1) complexities in the management of antidepressant or anxiolytic medications such as when the patient is hypersensitive to a drug's side effects or when the patient has a serious medical illness; 2) the patient exhibits behavioral problems associated with a personality disorder or with current substance abuse; 3) the patient requires psychotherapy as well as pharmacotherapy; 4) the patient expresses suicidal ideation; and 5) the patient displays only a partial response to the initial treatment or has a symptom breakthrough after a positive acute phase response.

Having concluded an active intervention will produce a better clinical outcome than "watchful waiting" and that the patient often can be treated by a generalist in the ambulatory medical care setting, the primary care physician has various treatment options for mood and anxiety disorders, which are reviewed in the following sections.

Mood disorders

The effectiveness of particular treatments for depression is less well studied with primary care patients than it is with psychiatric patients. Nevertheless, the Depression Guideline Panel of the AHCPR concluded from a meta-analysis of evidence tables that the available body of findings from studies of psychiatric patients is scientifically valid enough to formulate caregiving principles to be followed in primary care practice [48]. This conclusion was confirmed in recent primary care randomized controlled trials that found psychosocial and pharmacologic interventions equally effective with a general medical population experiencing major depression and more effective than the primary care physician's "usual care" [49•,50•]. However, virtually no randomized controlled trials have been conducted with either psychiatric or primary care populations to test the efficacy of interventions for the subclinical condition of mixed anxiety-depression. The study by Katon et al. [49•] suggests that most patients experiencing this condition have a good prognosis when treated with low doses of antidepressants and supportive psychotherapy.

Treatment aims to eliminate the dysphoric mood and somatic symptoms characterizing the depression and at minimizing the social and vocational dysfunctioning resulting from this disorder. Various psychosocial and pharmacologic interventions effectively achieve these objectives although their relative costs remain unstudied. Without cost-effectiveness analyses, primary care physicians should select among scientifically validated treatments on the basis of clinical considerations and patient preference. The latter criterion warrants particular attention given its profound implications for the patient's regular and full adherence to the prescribed treatment regimen.

Psychosocial treatments

More than 250 psychosocial treatments have been described in the literature but relatively few aim to achieve the depression-specific therapeutic objectives already described. Moreover, psychotherapies directed at depression have been largely developed and validated with psychiatric patients. Brown and Schulberg [51] identified only seven studies in which primary care patients were diagnosed as depressed with a structured interview schedule and the efficacy of a psychosocial intervention, before being studied within a research design using randomized treatment assignments.

Despite this limited but growing primary care database, the AHCPR Depression Guideline Panel [48] extrapolated findings from studies with psychiatric patients and concluded that cognitive, behavioral, and interpersonal psychotherapies are efficacious in treating medical patients experiencing major depression. These time-limited interventions generally are as efficacious as antidepressant medication when delivered within "treatment manual" standards. More than 50% of treated patients will recover with either psychologic or pharmacologic intervention. The restrictions imposed by behavioral managed care administrators, therefore, are unnecessary and possibly even deleterious to a patient's clinical outcome [52]. Whether psychotherapy alone and medication alone have similar efficacy when the depression is severe remains unclear. Elkin et al. [53] found imipramine superior to cognitive-behavioral therapy or interpersonal psychotherapy in treating psychiatric patients whose baseline Hamilton Rating Scale-Depression score exceeded 19. The paper by Schulberg *et al.* [50•], however, found no 4- or 8-month outcome differences between such severely depressed primary care patients treated with nortriptyline alone or with interpersonal psychotherapy alone. In a more complex analysis of treatment efficacy, Thase *et al.* [54] concluded that a neurobiologic boundary rather than severity alone limits response to interpersonal psychotherapy, since patients with abnormal sleep profiles fared poorly when provided this treatment but improved with pharmacotherapy.

The research-validated depression-specific psychotherapies generally are more similar than different in overall efficacy as well as in impact on targeted symptoms despite their varied theoretic principles and therapeutic foci [55]. When selecting formal psychotherapy as the sole treatment, the Depression Guideline Panel [48] suggests that the physician apply the following principles: 1) the time-limited psychotherapy should focus on current problems and aim at symptom reduction rather than personality reconstruction; 2) the therapist should be trained in the psychotherapy's use with patients who have a major depression; and 3) clinical course should be monitored and medication considered for patients failing to show any improvement by 6 weeks or nearly full remission by 12 weeks.

Pharmacologic treatments

Tricyclic and heterocyclic agents and monoamine oxidase inhibitors (MAOIs) formed the mainstay of pharmacologic treatment of depression until the late 1980s when selective serotonin reuptake inhibitors (SSRIs) were introduced. The efficacy of these several classes of medications has been demonstrated in almost 200 studies with psychiatric outpatients and approximately 10 studies with primary care patients. Meta-analyses of this literature by the Depression Guideline Panel [48] led it to conclude that all antidepressant medications are equally efficacious; 50% to 60% of patients prescribed any such drug will recover. No single drug results in remission for all patients.

The primary care physician's selection of a particular antidepressant for a specific patient should be guided by the following considerations: the medication's short- and long-term side effects, the patient's previous positive or negative response to the medication, the history of first-degree relatives responding to an antidepressant, comorbid medical illnesses affecting the drug's safety and toxicity, concomitant use of other medications that can alter the drug's metabolism or increase its side effects, cost of the medication, and the physician's experience with the medication. When the patient's medical state is fragile or unstable, SSRIs are preferable to a tricyclic or heterocyclic antidepressant because they have a less adverse effect on the heart's electrical conduction system. Since patient acceptance or rejection of the antidepressant drug is strongly influenced by awareness of the psychiatric disorder and its consequences [56], physicians must properly educate their patients about the benefits of pharmacotherapy and the adverse consequences of refusing it.

The most problematic aspect of using antidepressants is their side effects, which can be particularly troublesome for medical patients already experiencing various physical symptoms. SSRIs produce fewer side effects than tricyclic and heterocyclic antidepressants and, therefore, are thought to increase patient adherence to the prescribed regimen [57–59]. Nevertheless, the primary care physician should recognize that even SSRIs are not fully devoid of side effects. The frequency of specific central nervous system and cardiovascular side effects of a given antidepressant, as rated by the Depression Guideline Panel [48], are presented in Table 6 as a guide to physicians considering the choice of a particular medication. Although medication costs measured in cost per pill are higher for SSRIs than for generic antidepressants, primary care ambulatory costs and inpatient costs are higher for patients treated with tricyclics [60,61].

Having selected the antidepressant most suited to the patient, the primary care physician must decide on the dosage at which it is to be prescribed. These clinicians typically err on the side of underdosing, with the rationale that medical patients respond to lower doses of the drug and that they are less tolerant of its side effects. However, clinical trials support neither assumption [45]. Primary care physicians, thus, should prescribe the antidepressant at full dosages needed to achieve therapeutic efficacy. Dosages recommended by the Depression Guideline Panel [48] for each such medication are presented in Table 7. With medically fragile patients, however, the initial dosage should be only half that used with younger adults and it should be increased more slowly than in routine practice. Therapeutic drug monitoring is of great value when implemented properly, *eg*, ascertaining that nortriptyline's plasma concentration ranges within the empirically-validated therapeutic window of 50 to 150 ng/mL. The lack of a validated relationship, however, among dosage, plasma concentrations, and clinical effect for most other antidepressants at present precludes routine therapeutic drug monitoring in primary care practice.

Treatment phases

The treatment of depression is now recognized as proceeding through successive phases that clinicians classify as being of the acute, continuation, and maintenance types. The objective of acute treatment is to relieve the intense mood and neurovegetative symptoms characterizing the disorder. As indicated previously, both psychosocial and pharmacologic treatments are efficacious for this purpose. When accomplished successfully, the depression is deemed in remission. Acute phase treatment should be carefully and regularly monitored by the physician through clinical judgment and the administration to patients of standardized instruments such as the 13-item Beck Depression Inventory [62]. Physical and mental disabilities associated with depression are increasingly recognized as additional problems to be monitored [63], and brief instruments such as the 12-item Short Form Health Survey [64] are now available for this purpose. The algorithm that the Depression Guideline Panel [48] constructed to specify the clinical decisions required of physicians during the approximately 12-week time frame of acute phase treatment is presented in Figure 5.

Patients whose symptoms have remitted require an additional 4 to 6 months of treatment to prevent relapse. Although the efficacy of psychotherapy as a continuation phase treatment remains unclear, pharmacotherapy has been found efficacious in preventing relapse when the patient is prescribed the medication for this more extended period at the dosage level that resolved the acute episode [65]. Finally, because many patients experience repeated episodes of depression, interest has turned most recently to preventing such recurrences and minimizing the disorder's chronic and debilitating consequences. The findings of Frank *et al.* [66] about the benefits of extending treatment for 3 to 5 years for patients who have experienced at least three depressive episodes, or two episodes and who have first-degree relatives with bipolar or recurrent major depression, have led to a growing appreciation of maintenance therapy's value for patients meeting these criteria. Although primary care physicians are familiar with the recommendations

Table 6. Side-effect Profiles of Antidepressant Medications*

| Drug | Anticholinergic‡ | Central nervous system | | Cardiovascular | | Gastrointestinal distress | Other |
		Drowsiness	Insomnia-agitation	Orthostatic-hypotension	Cardiac arrhythmia		Weight gain (over 6 kg)
Amitriptyline	4+	4+	0	4+	3+	0	4+
Desipramine	1+	1+	1+	2+	2+	0	1+
Doxepin	3+	4+	0	2+	2+	0	3+
Imipramine	3+	3+	1+	4+	3+	1+	3+
Nortriptyline	1+	1+	0	2+	2+	0	1+
Protriptyline	2+	1+	1+	2+	2+	0	0
Trimipramine	1+	4+	0	2+	2+	0	3+
Amoxapine	2+	2+	2+	2+	3+	0	1+
Maprotiline	2+	4+	0	0	1+	0	2+
Trazodone	0	4+	0	1+	1+	1+	1+
Nefazadone	1+	2+	0	1+	0	2+	0
Bupropion	0	0	2+	0	1+	1+	0
Fluoxetine	0	0	2+	0	0	3+	0
Paroxetine	0	0	2+	0	0	3+	0
Sertraline	0	0	2+	0	0	3+	0
Fluvoxamine	0	0	2+	0	0	3+	0
Venlafaxine	0	0	2+	0	0	3+	0
Monoamine oxidase inhibitors	1−	1+	2+	2+	0	1+	2+

Side effect†

*Adapted from Depression Guideline Panel [48].
† 0—absent or rare; 1+, 2+—in between; 3+, 4+—relatively common.
‡Dry mouth, blurred vision, urinary hesitancy, constipation.

Table 7. Pharmacology of Antidepressant Medications*

Drug	Therapeutic dosage range, mg/d	Average and range of elimination half-lives, h†	Potentially fatal drug interactions
Tricyclics			
Amitriptyline	75–300	24 (16–46)	Antiarrhythmics, MAOIs
Clomipramine	75–300	24 (20–40)	Antiarrhythmics, MAOIs
Desipramine	75–300	18 (12–50)	Antiarrhythmics, MAOIs
Doxepin	75–300	17 (10–47)	Antiarrhythmics, MAOIs
Imipramine	75–300	22 (12–34)	Antiarrhythmics, MAOIs
Nortriptyline	40–200	26 (18–88)	Antiarrhythmics, MAOIs
Protriptyline	20–60	76 (54–124)	Antiarrhythmics, MAOIs
Trimipramine	75–300	12 (8–30)	Antiarrhythmics, MAOIs
Heterocyclics			
Amoxapine	100–600	10 (8–14)	MAOIs
Bupropion	225–450	14 (8–24)	MAOIs (possibly)
Maprotiline	100–225	43 (27–58)	MAOIs
Trazodone	150–600	8 (4–14)	—
Nefazadone	200–500	6 (5–8)	MAOIs
Selective serotonin reuptake inhibitors			
Fluoxetine	10–40	168 (72–360)‡	MAOIs
Paroxetine	20–50	24 (3–65)	MAOIs§
Sertraline	50–150	24 (10–30)	MAOIs§
Fluvoxamine	100–300	15 (10–20)	MAOIs
Venlafaxine	37.5–225	8 (5–11)	MAOIs
Monoamine oxidase inhibitors¶			
Isocarboxazid	30–50	Unknown	For all three MAOIs: vasocon-
Phenelzine	45–90	2 (1.5–4.0)	strictors,** decongestants,**
Tranylcypromine	20–60	2 (1.5–3.0)	meperidine, and possibly other narcotics

*Adapted from Depression Guideline Panel [48].
†Half-lives are affected by age, sex, race, concurrent medications, and length of drug exposure.
‡Includes both fluoxetine and norfluoxetine.
§By extrapolation from fluoxetine data.
¶MAO inhibition lasts longer (7 days) than drug half-life.
**Including pseudoephedrine, phenylephrine, phenylpropanolamine, epinephrine, norpinephrine, and other.
MAOI—monoamine oxidase inhibitors.

for acute and even continuation phase treatments, many remain unfamiliar with guidelines regarding when and how to extend treatment into a maintenance phase for selected patients whose depressions are chronic and recurring.

Anxiety disorders

Anxiety disorders are among the most difficult psychiatric disorders to diagnose and treat among primary care patients because, as indicated previously, they often present with complex autonomic or neurovegetative symptoms with or without comorbid physical illness. Thus, it is not surprising that many patients remain untreated for their anxiety symptoms [67]. The consequences are remarkable from both public health and economic perspectives. In addition to the needless distress experienced by people who

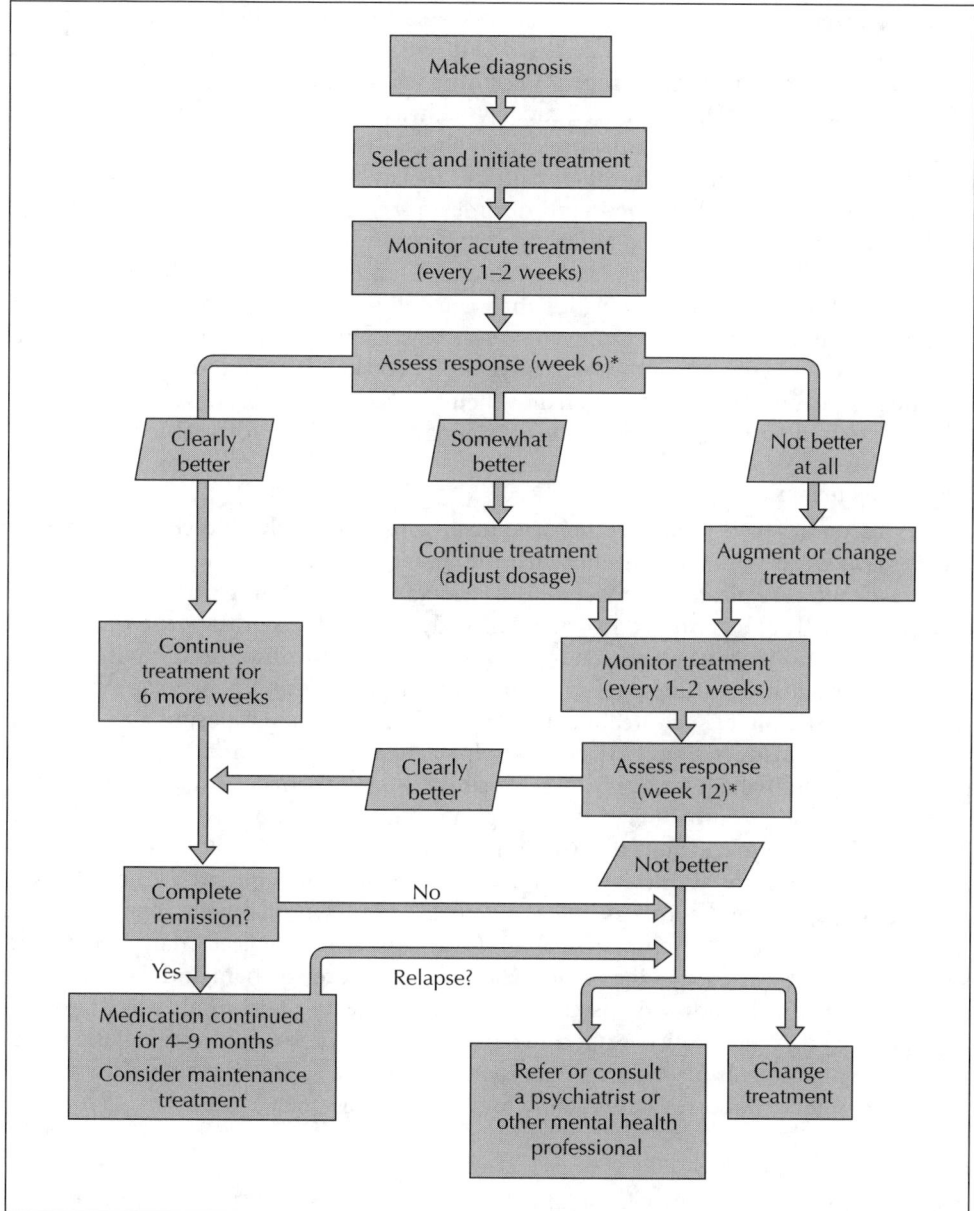

Figure 5. Algorithm specifying time points during acute treatment phase at which clinician should monitor patient's depressive status to determine whether the treatment plan requires modification or augmentation. *Times of assessment (weeks 6 and 12) rest on very modest data. It may be necessary to revise the treatment plan earlier for patients who fail to respond. (*Adapted from* Depression Guideline Panel [48].)

remain untreated for anxiety, lost productivity associated with these disorders totalled $35.4 billion in the United States in 1990 (Dupont *et al.* Paper presented at the Annual Meeting of Anxiety Disorders Association of America, Charleston, SC, 1993).

Panic disorder, GAD, and mixed anxiety-depression are prevalent in primary care practice and produce significant physical and social dysfunction when left untreated [68]. Nevertheless, anxiety disorders continue to lack definitive treatment guidelines such as those formulated for the mood disorders [48], and even basic research conventions for clinical trials [69]. Available efficacy data were generated largely in studies conducted with psychiatric patients, and experienced clinicians have considered findings from these clinical trials equally valid when generalized to medical populations. Thus, available treatments have been delivered with reasonable confidence in their efficacy [70]. However, practice guidelines reflecting expert consensus about how anxiety disorders are best diagnosed and treated are now being developed by the APA and, when published, likely will constitute state of the art standards during the forseeable future.

Psychosocial treatments

Numerous studies have found psychosocial treatments sufficiently efficacious in reducing the impairment and dysfunction associated with panic disorder and GAD that their role in national health care plans requires serious consideration [71]. With regard to panic disorder, Clum *et al.* [72] determined from a meta-analysis of earlier studies that psychological coping strategies involving relaxation training, cognitive restructuring, and exposure yielded beneficial outcomes comparable with both antidepressant and benzodiazepine medications. An example of such treatment is the combined somatic exposure and cognitive therapy used by Barlow *et al.* [73], which helps patients confront and alter maladaptive cognitions, *eg*, thoughts of a heart attack or stroke when experiencing rapid heartbeat. A related meta-analysis of the literature dealing with the treatment of GAD by Durham and Allan [74] led them to conclude that psychologic therapies of the cognitive-behavioral type are more efficacious than control conditions and at least equal in efficacy to anxiolytics in treating this psychiatric disorder as well. Given these findings, primary care physicians need not rely as predominantly on pharmacologic treatments as they typically have [75,76] and should consider psychosocial interventions if the patient prefers them and they are available. No controlled studies of psychosocial treatments for subclinical mixed anxiety-depression could be identified. Supportive psychotherapy or watchful waiting, thus, may be the initial treatments of choice for a period of up to 4 weeks at which time clinical nonresponse should be followed with a more formal and active intervention.

Pharmacologic treatments

Patients with panic disorder can be difficult to treat with medications because they are hypervigilant to minor side effects, often interpreting them as symptomatic indicators of a catastrophic event that could lead to death. The physician, therefore, should advise patients of the likely side effects to be produced by the medication, indicate that these side effects will gradually fade, and note that therapeutic effects will become evident within 2 to 4 weeks. The physician should also emphasize that the medication is not to be discontinued because of side effects without consulting the physician.

Medication dosages should be increased to the point of completely alleviating the anxiety, not simply ameliorating it. The patient should be informed by the physician of the approximate dosage at which the medication is therapeutic and permitted to control its incremental increases. Very low starting dosages which are increased quite gradually can minimize the potential for jitteriness and other troublesome side effects.

A review of developments in the psychopharmacology of anxiety disorders [77] found that the following four types of medication have demonstrated efficacy in treating panic disorder or GAD.

1. Tricyclic antidepressants (TCAs). The TCAs are as effective as benzodiazepines and significantly more effective than placebos for both of these anxiety disorders [78–81]. It is useful to start the TCA at 10 mg per day and gradually increase it by 10 mg every 2 to 3 days until the anxiety attacks are completely ameliorated. Despite low starting dosages, most patients with GAD or panic disorder will require 100 to 300 mg daily of a TCA to achieve this clinical outcome. Dose ranges and plasma level–response relationships are available for imipramine to guide the physician's selection of a therapeutic dosage [82]. Perhaps 20% of patients experience heightened jitteriness when prescribed a TCA. When this or other side effects are experienced, the medication's upward titration should be slowed or even halted until the side effects become tolerable. Approximately 20% of patients prescribed TCAs are unable to continue taking them because they find the side effects intolerable. Occasionally, however, addition of a low dosage benzodiazepine can decrease the initial jitteriness produced by tricyclics and help the patient adhere to necessary increments in this antidepressant medication.

2. Serotonin reuptake inhibitors. Controlled studies have demonstrated the efficacy of fluvoxamine, clomipramine, and paroxetine in treating panic disorder [83–85]. Unpublished data from pharmaceutical companies and clinical experience also suggest that fluoxetine and sertraline have equal efficacy for this anxiety disorder. Although controlled studies are lacking on the efficacy of serotonin reuptake inhibitors (SRIs) in treating GAD, clinical experience suggests they are useful for treating it as well. As with TCAs, SRIs should initially be prescribed at lower dosages and titrated upwards until the panic attacks have ceased or the symptoms of generalized anxiety have been ameliorated. Most patients require antidepressant-type daily dosages of an SRI, *eg*, 20 mg of fluoxetine, to achieve this clinical outcome; however, an adequate therapeutic level can only be reached with careful titration.

3. Monoamine oxidase inhibitors. The MAOIs, particularly phenelzine, have been proven effective for treating panic disorder in double-blind, placebo-controlled trials [86, Sheehan *et al.*, paper presented at the Annual Meeting of American Psychiatric Association, Los Angeles, 1984]. Clinical experience suggests that patients with GAD or anxious depression also respond well to this class of drugs. Nevertheless, the MAOIs frequently are regarded as second- or third-order medications for panic disorder or GAD because of the dietary restrictions which they impose on patients (the need to adhere to a low-tyramine diet), their adverse interaction with such other medications as vasoconstrictors and decongestants, and their potential for creating a hypertensive crisis. When prescribed, phenelzine can be started at a dose of 15 mg orally, twice a day, without concern for the overstimulation or jitteriness possibly occurring with TCAs or SRIs. To effectively ameliorate GAD and eliminate panic attacks, phenelzine often must be prescribed in the dosage range of 45 to 90 mg.

4. Benzodiazepines (BZDs). Primary care physicians often treat anxiety disorders with BZDs [87,88] because they decrease both psychic and somatic symptoms, have a quick onset of action, and are relatively safe in overdoses. Three high potency BZDs (alprazolam, clonazepam, lorazepam) have demonstrated efficacy in controlling panic disorder [89,90]; at least one study [91] has similarly found high-dose diazepam efficacious for this purpose. Despite the faster rate at which high-potency BZDs ameliorate anxiety compared with TCAs, SRIs, or MAOIs, many physicians are reluctant to prescribe BZDs given concerns about their potential to create physical-psychologic dependence, and difficulty tapering them after usage at therapeutic dosage levels for extended periods of time [70,92]. Despite the controversies associated with physical dependence, Davidson [93] concluded that BZDs can be considered a primary treatment for panic disorder with or without agoraphobia. This is particularly true if the primary care physician does not prescribe BZDs to patients at high risk for abuse potential, ie, those with prior histories of alcohol or substance abuse, chronic pain, personality disorders, and perhaps even family histories of substance abuse.

Given such safeguards and the fact that some patients cannot tolerate antidepressant medications, primary care physicians will continue to prescribe BZDs selectively. When doing so, initial dosages again should be low and increased appropriately until anxiety is ameliorated or panic attacks cease. If a patient experiences break-through anxiety within 3 to 5 hours of alaprozalam's last dose given its short half-life, a medication with a longer half-life such as clonazepam should be considered by the physician. For clinically anxious patients who are also experiencing a serious medical illness, a benzodiazepine or buspirone prescribed at half the usual young adult dosage constitutes safe and effective treatment.

Treatment phases

As with mood disorders, the treatment of anxiety disorders can be divided into acute, continuation, and maintenance phases. The acute phase aims to block spontaneous panic attacks or persistent symptoms of anxiety and generally extends for a duration of 4 months. During this treatment phase, clinicians should encourage patients to reenter physical environments and to participate in social situations that were avoided so as to decrease the onset of agoraphobic behaviors.

It is crucial that the physician quickly develop an understanding of the patient's health concerns and beliefs and provide reassurance and education about their treatability. Patients with panic disorder or GAD are often convinced that they have a cardiac or neurologic disorder, and that their anxiety or nervousness is secondary to their physical symptoms. When informed by the physician that the primary disorder is anxiety, the patient may feel that the physician does not believe the physical symptoms are real. Thus, it is helpful to educate the patient about biologic research findings on panic disorder and GAD, eg, that panic disorder likely results from dysfunction of the sympathetic nervous system in which bursts of catecholamine are released into the peripheral circulation, causing symptoms such as tachycardia, chest pain, and dyspnea. Describing panic attacks as analogous to the "fight-or-flight" response may also be helpful. Educational materials regarding anxiety disorders can be provided distressed patients who typically are hypervigilant about bodily symptoms and interpret them in a catastrophic manner.

Such materials can help patients appreciate that somatic manifestations of anxiety are uncomfortable, even distressing, but not dangerous.

During the acute treatment phase, the clinical course of the patient's anxiety disorder should be monitored within a time frame similar to that applicable to a mood disorder (Fig. 5). In addition to the physician's using clinical judgement about the patient's state, the physician can also have the patient complete a standardized instrument to determine whether the symptoms have remitted. Instruments available for this purpose are the Anxiety scale of the Hopkins Symptom Check List [94] and the Zung Self-Rating Anxiety Scale [95]. There is limited evidence that patients completing the acute treatment phase maintain short-term gains in the absence of further therapy. Therefore, they should be entered into a continuation treatment phase of approximately 4 to 6 months that aims to stabilize and extend the therapeutic gains achieved earlier. Patients who have experienced lifelong recurring episodes of GAD or panic disorder should be provided prolonged maintenance treatment in a manner similar to that provided patients whose depression is chronic or recurring. Nevertheless, since it is difficult to predict the optimal duration of therapy for an individual patient, future research should focus on developing optimal treatment algorithms incorporating pharmacologic and psychotherapeutic options [97].

Conclusions

Mood and anxiety disorders are prevalent among patients presenting in the primary medical care sector and physicians are increasingly cognizant of the need to diagnose and treat such psychopathology. The assessment process is particularly complex with medical patients because their complaints and symptoms are more often somatic rather than psychic, and potentially mimic organic disorders or substance withdrawal. Nevertheless, careful review of the symptom picture and ruling out of alternative syndromes will lead to an accurate diagnosis of these psychiatric disorders. After the psychopathology has been identified, clinicians can often choose among various pharmacologic or psychotherapeutic interventions of relatively equal efficacy. Consequently, patient preference should serve as a major criterion in selecting a particular treatment. The need to carefully and regularly monitor the course of treatment cannot be overemphasized. Changes in the intensity or type of treatment should be initiated if symptom reduction is not evident within 6 to 8 weeks. The value of continuing pharmacotherapy for periods up to 9 months has been clearly demonstrated, as has the value of maintenance medication for periods up to 5 years for patients whose disorder is chronic or recurrent.

References and Recommended Readings

Papers of particular interest, published recently, have been highlighted as
•   Of special interest
••   Of outstanding interest

1.   Regier D, Goldberg I, Taube C, *et al.*: The de facto US mental health services system: a public health perspective. *Arch Gen Psychiatry* 1982, 35:685–693.

2.   Narrow W, Regier D, Rae D, *et al.*: Use of services by persons with mental and addictive disorders. *Arch Gen Psychiatry* 1993, 50:95–107.

3. Sturm R, Wells K: How can care for depression become more cost-effective? *JAMA* 1995, 273:51–58.

4. Katon W, Schulberg H: Epidemiology of depression in primary care. *Gen Hosp Psychiatry* 1992, 14:237–247.

5. Shear M, Schulberg H: Anxiety disorders in primary care. *Bull Menniger Clin* 1995, 59:A73–A85.

6. American Psychiatric Association: *Diagnostic and Statistical Manual of Mental Disorders*, edn 4. Washington, DC: American Psychiatric Association; 1994.

7. Spitzer R, Williams J, Kroenke K, *et al.*: Utility of a new procedure for diagnosing mental disorders in primary care. The PRIME-MD 1000 study. *JAMA* 1994, 272:1749–1756.

8. Coyne J, Fechner-Bates S, Schwenk T: Prevalence, nature and comorbidity of depressive disorders in primary care. *Gen Hosp Psychiatry* 1994, 16:267–276.

9. Weissman M, Bruce M, Leaf P, *et al.*: Affective disorders. In *Psychiatric Disorders in America*. Edited by Robins L, Regnier D. New York: The Free Press; 1991:53–80.

10. Blazer D, Kessler R, McGonagle K, *et al.*: The prevalence and distribution of major depression in a national community sample: The National Comorbidity Survey. *Am J Psychiatry* 1994, 151:979–986.

11. Simon G, Von Korff M: Recognition, management, and outcomes of depression in primary care. *Arch Fam Med* 1995, 4:99–105.

12. Wiliams J, Kerber C, Mulrow C, *et al.*: Depressive disorders in primary care. Prevalence, functional disability, and identification. *J Gen Int Med* 1995, 10:7–12.

13. Zinbarg R, Barlow D, Liebowitz M, *et al.*: The DSM-IV field trial for mixed anxiety-depression. *Am J Psychiatry* 1994, 151:1153–1162.

14. Barrett J, Barrett J, Oxman T, *et al.*: The prevalence of psychiatric disorders in a primary care practice. *Arch Gen Psychiatry* 1988, 45:1100–1106.

15. Katon W, Vitaliano P, Russo J, *et al.*: Panic disorder: epidemiology in primary care. *J Fam Pract* 1986, 23:233–239.

16. Kessler L, Cleary P, Burke J: Psychiatric disorders in primary care: results of a followup study. *Arch Gen Psychiatry* 1985, 42:583–587.

17. Von Korff M, Shapiro S, Burke J, *et al.*: Anxiety and depression in a primary care clinic. *Arch Gen Psychiatry* 1987, 44:152–156.

18. Fifer S, Mathias S, Patrick D, *et al.*: Untreated anxiety among adult primary care patients in a health maintenance organization. *Arch Gen Psychiatry* 1994, 51:740–750.

19. Sheehan D: *The Anxiety Disease*. New York: Scribner; 1987.

20. Orleans C, George L, Houpt J: How primary physicians treat psychiatric disorders: a national survey of family physicians. *Arch Gen Psychiatry* 1985, 42:52–57.

21. Katon W, Von Korff M, Lin E, *et al.*: Distressed high utilizers of medical care. *Gen Hosp Psychiatry* 1990, 12:355–362.

22. Sherbourne C, Jackson C, Meredith L, *et al.*: Prevalence of comorbid anxiety disorders in primary care outpatients. *Arch Fam Med* 1996, 5:27–34.

23. American Psychiatric Association: *Diagnostic and Statistical Manual of Mental Disorders*, edn 4: *Primary Care Version* (DSM-IV-PC). Washington, DC: American Psychiatric Association; 1995.

24. Pincus H, Vettorello N, McQueen L, *et al.*: Bridging the gap between psychiatry and primary care: the DSM-IV-PC. *Psychosomat* 1995, 36:328–335.

25. Depression Guideline Panel: *Depression In Primary Care*, vol 1. *Detection and Diagnosis. Clinical Practice Guideline*, No. 5. AHCPR Publication No. 93-0550. Rockville, MD: U.S. Department of Health and Human Services, Public Health Service, Agency For Health Care Policy and Research; 1993.

26. Broadhead W, Leon A, Weissman M, *et al.*: Development and validation of the SDDS-PC screen for multiple mental disorders in primary care. *Arch Fam Med* 1995, 4:211–219.

27. Wells K, Rogers W, Burnam A, *et al.*: How the medical comorbidity of depressed patients differs across health care settings: results from the Medical Outcomes Study. *Am J Psychiatry* 1991, 148:1688–1696.

28. Stewart A, Sherbourne C, Wells K, *et al.*: Do depressed patients in different treatment settings have different levels of well-being and functioning? *J Consult Clin Psychol* 1993, 61:849–857.

29. Rodin G, Craven J, Littlefield C: *Depression in the Medically Ill*. New York: Brunner/Mazel; 1991.

30. Hall R, Gardner E, Stickney S, *et al.*: Physical illness manifesting as psychiatric disease. II. Analyses of a state hospital inpatient population. *Arch Gen Psychiatry* 1980, 37:989–995.

31. Fann J, Tucker G: Mood disorders with general medical conditions. *Curr Opin Psychiatry* 1995, 8:13–18.

32. Schulberg H, Madonia M, Block M, *et al.*: Major depression in primary care practice. Clinical characteristics and treatment implications. *Psychosomat* 1995, 36:129–137.

33. Shea, M, Widiger T, Klein M: Comorbidity of personality disorders and depression: implications for treatment. *J Consult Clin Psychol* 1992, 60:857–868.

34. Patience D, McGuire R, Scott A, *et al.*: The Edinburgh Primary Care Depression Study: personality disorder and outcome. *Br J Psychiatry* 1995, 167:324–330.

35. Bridges K, Goldberg D: Somatic presentation of DSM-III psychiatric disorders in primary care. *J Psychosomat Res* 1985, 29:563–569.

36. Ballenger J: Panic disorder in the medical setting. *J Clin Psychiatry* 1997, 58 (suppl 2):13–17.

37. Katon W: Panic and somatization: a review of 55 cases. *Am J Med* 1984, 77:101–106.

38. Katon W: *Panic Disorder in the Medical Setting.* Washington, DC: American Psychiatric Press; 1991:29–40.

39. Wells K, Golding J, Burnam M: Psychiatric disorder in a sample of the general population with and without chronic medical conditions. *Am J Psychiatry* 1988, 145:176–181.

40. Margraf J, Ehlers A, Roth W: Mitral valve prolapse and panic disorder: a review of the relationship. *Psychosomat Med* 1988, 50:93–113.

41. Gorman J, Goetz R, Fyer M, *et al.*: The mitral valve prolapse-panic disorder connection. *Pychosomat Med* 1988, 50:114–122.

42. Fogarty J, Engel C, Russo J, *et al.*: Hypertension and pheochromocytoma testing: the association with anxiety disorders. *Arch Fam Med* 1994, 3:55–60.

43. Brawman-Mintzer O, Lydiard B: Generalized anxiety disorders: issues in epidemiology. *J Clin Psychiatry* 1996, 57(suppl 7):3–8.

44. Schweizer E, Rickels K: The long-term management of generalized anxiety disorder: issues and dilemmas. *J Clin Psychiatry* 1996, 57(suppl 7):9–12.

45. Schulberg H, Pajer K: Treatment of depression in primary care. In *Mental Disorders In Primary Care*. Edited by Miranda J, Hohmann A, Attkisson C, Larson D. San Francisco: Jossey-Bass; 1994:259–286.

46. Sturm R, Meredith L, Wells K: Provider choice and continuity for the treatment of depression. *Med Care* 1996, 34:723–734.

47. Katon W: *Panic Disorder In The Medical Setting.* DHHS Pub. No. (ADM) 89–1629. Washington, DC: Supt. of Docs., US Govt. Printing Office., 1989.

48. Depression Guideline Panel: *Depression in Primary Care*, vol 2. *Treatment of Major Depression. Clinical Practice Guideline*, No. 5. AHCPR Publication No. 93-0551. Rockville, MD: U.S. Department of Health and Human Services, Public Health Service, Agency For Health Care Policy and Research; 1993.

49.• Katon W, Von Korff M, Lin E, *et al.*: Collaborative management to achieve treatment guidelines. *JAMA* 1995, 273:1026–1031.

This paper describes the effect of a brief intervention that provided increased patient education and integrated a psychiatrist into the care of primary care patients with major depression. This intervention was found to improve patient adherence to antidepressant medication, increase satisfaction with care of depression, and improve depressive outcomes compared with that resulting from "usual care."

50.• Schulberg H, Block M, Madonia J, *et al.*: Treating major depression in primary care practice: eight-month clinical outcomes. *Arch Gen Psychiatry* 1996, 53:913–919.

This paper presents the findings from a randomized, controlled trial that demonstrated that significantly more primary care patients recover from a major depression when treated with medication or psychotherapy delivered in a standardized manner than when provided a physician's "usual care."

51. Brown C, Schulberg H: The efficacy of psychosocial treatments in primary care: a review of randomized clinical trials. *Gen Hosp Psychiatry* 1995, 17:414–424.

52. Elkin I, Gibbons R, Shea M, *et al.*: Initial severity and differential treatment outcome in the National Institute of Mental Health Treatment of Depression Collaborative Research Program. *J Consult Clin Psychol* 1995, 63:841–847.

53. Elkin I, Gibbons R, Shea M, *et al.*: Initial severity and differential treatment outcome in the National Institute of Mental Health Treatment of Depression Collaborative Research Program. *J Consult Clin Psychol* 1995, 63:841–847.

54. Thase M, Buysse D, Frank E, *et al.*: Which depressed patients will respond to interpersonal psychotherapy? The role of abnormal EEG sleep profiles. *Am J Psychiatry* 1997, 154:502–509.

55. Imber S, Pilkonis P, Sotsky S, *et al.*: Mode-specific effects among three treatments for depression. *J Consult Clin Psychol* 1990, 58:352–359.

56. Benkert E, Graf-Morgenstern M, Hillert A, *et al.*: Public opinion of psychotropic drugs: an analysis of the factors influencing acceptance or rejection. *J Nerv Ment Dis* 1997, 185:151–158.

57. Anderson I, Tomenson B: Treatment discontinuation with selective serotonin reuptake inhibitors compared with tricyclic antidepressants: a meta-analysis. *BMJ* 1995, 315:1433–1438.

58. Katon W, Von Korff M, Lin E, *et al.*: Adequacy and duration of antidepressant treatment in primary care. *Med Care* 1992, 30:67–76.

59. Simon G, Von Korff M, Wagner E, *et al.*: Patterns of antidepressant use in community practice. *Gen Hosp Psychiatry* 1993, 15:399–408.

60. Sclar D, Robison L, Skaer T, *et al.*: Antidepressant pharmacotherapy: economic outcomes in a health maintenance organization. *Clin Ther* 1994, 16:715–730.

61. Simon G, Von Korff M, Heiligenstein J, *et al.*: Initial antidepressant choice: effectiveness and cost of fluoxetine vs tricyclic antidepressants. *JAMA* 1995, 275:1897–1902.

62. Beck A, Beck R: Screening depressed patients in family practice: a rapid technique. *Postgrad Med* 1972, 52:81–85.

63. Hays R, Wells K, Sherbourne C, *et al.*: Functioning and well-being outcomes of patients with depression compared with general medical illnesses. *Arch Gen Psychiatry* 1995, 52:11–19.

64. Ware J, Kosinski M, Keller S: A 12-item Short Form Health Survey: construction of scales and preliminary tests of reliability and validity. *Med Care* 1996, 34:220–233.

65. Prien R, Kupfer D: Continuation drug therapy for major depressive episodes: how long should it be maintained? *Am J Psychiatry* 1986, 143:18–23.

66. Frank E, Kupfer D, Perel J, *et al.*: Three-year outcomes for maintenance therapies in recurrent depression. *Arch Gen Psychiatry* 1990, 47:1093–1099.

67. Fifer S, Mathias S, Mazonson P, *et al.*: Untreated anxiety among adult primary care patients in a Health Maintenance Organization. *Arch Gen Psychiatry* 1994, 51:740–750.

68. Roy-Bryne P: Generalized anxiety and mixed anxiety-depression: association with disability and health care utilization. *Clin Psychiatry* 1996, 57(suppl 7):86–91.

69. Shear M, Maser J: Standardized assessment for panic disorder research: a conference report. *Arch Gen Psychiatry* 1994, 51:346–354.

70. Katon W: Primary care-psychiatry panic disorder management module. In *Treatment of Panic Disorder*. Edited by Wolfe B, Maser J. Washington, DC: American Psychiatric Press; 1994:41–56.

71. Barlow D, Lehman C: Advances in the psychosocial treatment of anxiety disorders. Implications for national health care. *Arch Gen Psychiatry* 1996, 53:727–735.

72. Clum G, Clum G, Surls R: A meta-analysis of treatments for panic disorder. *J Consult Clin Psychol* 1993, 61:317–326.

73. Barlow D, Craske M, Cerny J, *et al.*: Behavioral treatment of panic disorder. *Behav Res Ther* 1989, 20:261–282.

74. Durham R, Allan T: Psychological treatment of generalized anxiety disorder. *Br J Psychiatry* 1993, 163:19–26.

75. Tyrer P, Casey P, Seiverwright H, *et al.*: A survey of the treatment of anxiety disorders in general practice. *Postgrad Med J* 1988, 64 (suppl 2):27–31.

76. Hecker J, Fink C, Fritzler B: Acceptability of panic disorder treatments: a survey of family practice physicians. *J Anx Dis* 1993, 7:373–384.

77. Lydiard R, Brawman-Mintzer O, Ballenger J: Recent developments in the psychopharmacology of anxiety disorders. *J Consult Clin Psychol* 1996, 64:660–668.

78. Rickels K, Downing R, Schweizer E, *et al.*: Antidepressants for the treatment of generalized anxiety disorder. *Arch Gen Psychiatry* 1993, 50:884–895.

79. Lydiard R, Roy-Byrne P, Ballenger J: Recent advances in the psychopharmacological treatment of anxiety disorders. *Hosp Comm Psychiatry* 1988, 39:1157–1165.

80. Noyes R, Perry P: Maintenance treatment with anti-depressants in panic disorder. *J Clin Psychiatry* 1990 (suppl A), 51:24–30.

81. Wilkinson G, Balestrieri M, Ruggeri M: Meta-analysis of double-blind placebo-controlled trials of antidepressants and benzodiazepines for patients with panic disorders. *Psychol Med* 1991, 21:991–998.

82. Mavissakalian M, Perel J: Imipramine treatment of panic disorder with agoraphobia: dose ranging and plasma level-response relationships. *Am J Psychiatry* 1995, 152:673–682.

83. McTavish D, Benfield P: Clomipramine: an overview of its pharmacologic properties in obsessive-compulsive disorder and panic disorder. *Drugs* 1990, 39:136–153.

84. Den Boer J, Westenberg H: Serotonin function in panic disorder: a double blind placebo controlled study with fluvoxamine and ritanserin. *Psychopharmacology* 1990, 102:85–94.

85. Christiansen P, Behnke K, Ocherberg S, *et al.*: Paxoretine in the treatment of panic disorder: a randomized double blind, placebo controlled trial. *Br J Psychiatry* 1995, 167:374–379.

86. Sheehan D, Ballenger J, Jacobsen G: Treatment of endogenous anxiety with phobic, hysterical, and hypochondriacal symptoms. *Arch Gen Psychiatry* 1980, 37:51–59.

87. Hollister L: A look at the issues: use of minor tranquilizers. *Psychosomat* 1980, 21:4–6.

88. Peden J: Benzodiazepine use at the medicine/psychiatry interface. *Psychiatry Ann* 1993, 23:301–308.

89. Ballenger J, Burrows G, DuPont R, *et al.*: Alprazolam in panic disorder and agoraphobia: results from a multicenter trial. *Arch Gen Psychiatry* 1988, 45:413–422.

90. Tesar G, Rosenbaum J: Successful use of clorazepam in patients with treatment resistant panic disorder. *J Nerv Ment Dis* 1986, 174:477–482.

91. Dunner D, Ishiki D, Avery P, *et al.*: Effect of alprazolam and diazepam in patients with panic disorder: a controlled study. *J Clin Psychiatry* 1986, 47:458–460.

92. Noyes R, Garvey M, Cook B: Benzodiazepine withdrawal: a review of the evidence. *J Clin Psychiatry* 1988, 49:382–389.

93. Davidson J: Use of benzodiazepines in panic disorder. *J Clin Psychiatry* 1997, 58(suppl 2):26–28.

94. Derogatis L, Lipman R, Rickels K, *et al.*: The Hopkins Symptom Checklist (HSCL): a self-report symptom inventory. *Behav Sci* 1975, 19:1–15.

95. Zung W: A rating instrument for anxiety disorders. *Psychosomat* 1971, 12:371–379.

96. Milrod B, Busch F: Long-term outcome of panic disorder treatment: a review of the literature. *J Nerv Ment Dis* 1996, 184:723–730.

97. Pollack M, Otto M: Long-term course and outcome of panic disorder. *J Clin Psychiatry* 1997, 58(suppl 2):57–60.

CHAPTER 11

Management of Personality Disorders in the Context of Mood and Anxiety Disorders

John F. Clarkin and Robert Abrams

Major advances in the treatment of affective and anxiety disorders involve the use of specific medications and psychotherapies, often alone and sometimes in combination. However, in the initial treatment trials, it has become clear that a substantial number of patients with anxiety and mood disorders suffer concomitantly from personality disorders. Furthermore, the presence of personality disorders has an influence on the patients' response to treatment, both the timing and degrees of response. There has been less development of the treatment of personality disorders in relation to the development of treatment for the symptom or Axis I disorders. Thus, in this chapter, we do not focus on the treatment of personality disorders either alone or in combination with anxiety and mood disorders, but rather, on the management of the personality disorders in the context of treatment of the symptomatic conditions. Even this latter topic is one that lacks much empirical investigation, and therefore this chapter will be of most use in defining the terrain and stimulating future investigation.

We first review the literature on the relation between personality disorders from both a theoretical and an empirical point of view; *ie*, both cross-sectional data showing the prevalence of personality disorders, given the presence of mood disorders or anxiety disorders, and longitudinal data on the trajectory of each in the presence of the other.

Relation Between Personality Disorders and Symptom Constellations

Theoretical considerations

The general issue of comorbidity is fraught with oversimplification and confusion [1,2]. Klein *et al.* [3] have delineated models of the relations between personality and depression (Fig. 1) that may help guide research and eventually lead to foci for treatment. Most relevant here are the models postulating that the interaction between affect and personality disorder will influence the treatment phase or the recurrence of the mood disorder. For example, a *pathoplasty* or *exacerbation* model makes the assumption that depression and personality disorder are etiologically distinct, but could each influence the clinical presentation or severity of the other when they occur together, depending on the clinical circumstances. For example, an increase in impulsive self-mutilation by a patient with borderline personality disorder could be understood as an exacerbation of the personality disorder

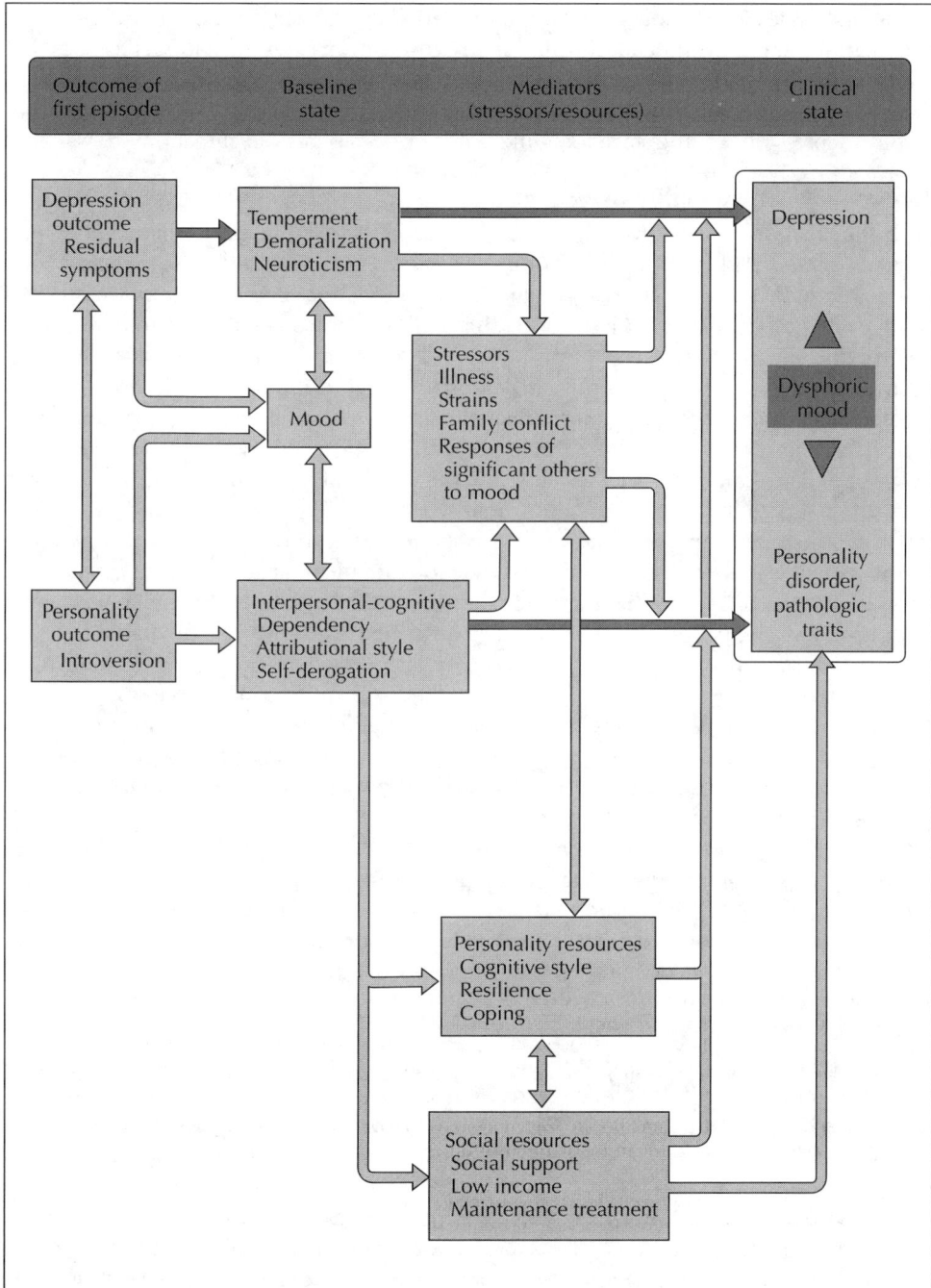

Figure 1. Integrated model of personality-depression relationships: subsequent episodes. (*Adapted from* Klein *et al.* [3]; with permission.)

symptom by the acute mood state, or as a primarily depressive symptom modified by the patient's long-standing difficulties with impulse control. A *predisposition* model implies that one condition, usually the personality disorder, encourages or in some way increases the likelihood of the other condition, usually depression. However, it is also possible that chronic depression sets the stage for some aspects of personality dysfunction.

Assessment of personality disorders

With the creation of the third edition of the *Diagnostic and Statistical Manual of Mental Disorders* (DSM-III) [4], the articulation of the criteria for personality disorders spawned a veritable industry for their assessment. Various semistructured interviews were developed, and these instruments have been the predominant research tool for the assessment of personality disorders. Some have used self-report instruments, but there has been concern that subjects overreport personality abnormalities on self-report instruments. There remains concern about the adequacy of assessing personality abnormality with data from the patient alone. For example, Riso *et al.* [5] found a low correlation between patients and their informants using the personality disorder examination. Data from the patients indicated more abnormality than data from the informants. On the other hand, many of the personality traits obtained from informants were not reported by the patients. These authors concluded that concordance was poor for personality disorder diagnoses, but somewhat better for dimensional scores. Interestingly, there was no indication that the patients were inclined to describe themselves in a favorable light.

Most relevant here is how current symptoms of depression or anxiety might influence the patients' report of personality disorders. It is quite conceivable, for example, that patients with current depression may overemphasize their report of personality disorders and difficulties on either a self-report or on a semistructured interview of personality disorders. The fact that acutely depressed patients temporarily overemphasize the extent of their maladaptive personality traits on self-report personality inventories or interviews has, for some time, been almost an axiom of research in this area [6]. More recent findings suggest that this "state confound" is especially applicable to cluster A and cluster C disorders [7]. However, Loranger *et al.* [8] have found that the semistructured interview that asks for examples of behavior may be less influenced by state depression.

Empirical findings on comorbidity of mood and personality disorders
Rate of concurrent comorbidity

A recent review [9] indicates that the rate of personality disorder among clinical samples of patients with affective disorder is high. Rates of personality disorder for depressive patients range from 23% to as high as 87%, with most reporting from 30% to 40%. Samples of inpatients have higher rates of cluster B personality disorders, and outpatient samples have more cluster C disorders. Rates of comorbid personality disorders among bipolar patients range from 23% to 62%. The rate of comorbidity may be influenced by other characteristics of the sample. For example, in a recent study of married outpatient bipolar patients, a rate of 22% was found for those who had at least one personality disorder [10].

Pepper *et al.* [11] compared the rate of comorbid Axis II disorders in patients with dysthymia and those with episodic major depression. There was a greater proportion of dysthymic patients (60%) than patients with episodic major depression (18%) manifesting

Axis II disorders. The most common personality disorders in the dysthymic population were borderline, histrionic, and avoidant personality disorder.

Although DSM-III [4] and subsequent revisions have suggested that personality disorders become attenuated by middle age, several recent studies have found substantial rates of comorbid personality disorder in older adults with major depression [12]. Kunik *et al.* [12], for example, reported a 24% rate of personality disorder among geriatric patients hospitalized for major depression. In addition to the relatively high rates of cluster C comorbidity, both the study of Kunik *et al.* [12] and another by Abrams *et al.* [13] found high rates of personality disorder not otherwise specified in their depressed elderly patient samples, suggesting a lack of specificity in the criteria as applied to the geriatric-aged group, but not a paucity of personality symptomatology in this population. Abrams *et al.* [13] also observed a higher level of lifetime personality dysfunction among depressed elderly patients who had their first mood episode in young adulthood than among those with late-onset depression, suggesting that first depressions in old age are less likely to be "characterological" in nature. However, dysthymia is quite common in the elderly, appearing in as many as 15% of the geriatric population [14]. Dysthymia, at least as manifest in elderly patients, could equally well be deemed an affective disorder with character pathology, or a personality disorder with secondary affective symptomatology. Double depression, or intermittent, acute depressive episodes superimposed on chronic subthreshold symptoms [15] and masked depressions [16], are other low-grade depression syndromes common in geriatric patients, in whom both affective and personality features may be present.

Criteria for depressive personality disorder were developed and field trials were done for inclusion in DSM-IV [17]. It is reported that the criteria identify a group of patients who are distinct from those with major depression and dysthymia, and who manifest significant social and occupational difficulty.

Causes of comorbidity

In a discussion of depressive phenomena in affective and personality disorders, Siever [18] argues that depressive symptoms found in individuals suffering from major depressive disorder can be distinguished from the dysphoria experienced by individuals with personality disorders. In major depression, the mood symptoms are relatively persistent, impervious to environmental influence, and associated with vegetative signs, whereas the affective features of personality disorder patients are more transient, often extremely reactive, and less likely to be associated with vegetative signs. Some patients may have both disorders, particularly those with the anxiety-related personality dysfunctions of cluster C, who seem particularly prone to develop a concurrent major depressive disorder.

There have been recent suggestions that depressive signs and symptoms in the personality disorders may have biologic substrates, in some ways unique from, and in other ways in common with, depressive disorder. For example, reduced serotonergic neurotransmitter activity can be generally present in depression, but also may underlie the specifically impulsive aspect of dysphoric mood instability [19].

Depression and borderline personality disorder

Discussion continues about the relation between depression and borderline personality disorder. In describing the depression of borderline personality disorder, psychoanalytically oriented theorists have emphasized aspects of the patient's internal experience rather than interpersonal behaviors. The psychoanalysts use constructs such as abandonment depression, characterized by hopeless longing for the lost object and subsequent alienation [20]; a sense of inner badness driving self-destructive sadomasochistic impulses [21]; and feelings of aloneness and transience owing to the lack of stable internal object representations [22,23].

Patients with concurrent borderline personality disorder and major depression may have a distinctive depression, characterized by deficient interpersonal functioning [24]. Bellodi *et al.*[25] found that patients with comorbid depression and borderline personality disorder had high scores in "anger-hostility" and in "interpersonal sensitivity" on the Hopkins Symptom Checklist. Rogers *et al.* [26], using both interview and self-report measures, found that the features of depression most strongly associated with borderline psychopathology were self-condemnation, emptiness, abandonment fears, self-destructiveness, and hopelessness; there was no particular association with boredom and somatic complaints. This raises the issue of which symptoms of depression respond to medication treatment in these patients, and which ones do not. The characteristics of borderline personality disorder were studied in an unselected sample of depressed individuals [27]. Those depressed individuals with borderline personality disorder had an earlier age of onset of depression and more dense Axis I and Axis II comorbidities than those depressed individuals without borderline personality disorder. In addition, those with borderline personality disorder had more elevated scores on psychoticism and anger-hositility.

Consistent with the overall pathoplastic model for the relation between depression and personality disorder referred to earlier, the depression seen in cluster B patients may also be distinctive in its course. For example, Shea *et al.* [28] reported from the collaborative study data that depressed patients with cluster B personality disorders were younger at the time of their first depressive episode and had a history of more suicide attempts than depressed patients without personality disorders. Personality disorder patients, in general, had more prior episodes of depression, as well as a longer duration of the index episode than other depressive patients.

Anxiety and personality disorders

Interest in the co-occurrence of anxiety and personality disorders has focused on both their intrinsic relations and the clinical implications of comorbidity. Personality disorders, in general, and cluster C disorders in particular (especially avoidant and obsessive-compulsive personality disorder), have been thought to be relatively frequent among patients with anxiety disorder, although perhaps less prevalent than in those who are depressed [29]. Thirty-five percent of these patients had at least one personality disorder, and the percentage was highest in those with social phobia (61%) and generalized anxiety disorder (4%). However, some of the overlap of disorders on Axis I and Axis II may be due to item overlap [30].

The prevalence of personality disorders was investigated in patients with social phobia and panic disorder [31]. Avoidant features, but not avoidant personality disorder, were found significantly more often in social phobia patients than in those with panic disorder. In general, the patients with social phobia were more disturbed on Axis II than the patients with panic disorder.

In a recent attempt to find meaningful subtypes of obsessive-compulsive disorder (OCD), Baer [32] used factor analysis to find three symptom factors: 1) symmetry and hoarding, 2) contamination and cleaning, and 3) pure obsessions. Only the first group was associated with concurrent obsessive-compulsive personality disorder. The author suggests that those patients with hoarding and symmetry behaviors, the group with the highest percentage of comorbid obsessive-compulsive personality disorder, are more difficult to treat with behavioral therapy because they do not habituate easily to exposure therapy.

In comorbid anxiety and personality disorders, the directionality of effects has been a matter of speculation. Does the personality disorder predispose to the development of the Axis I disorders, or is the reverse true? Presumably the same theoretical models discussed earlier for the comorbid relation between depression and personality disorder could also apply here. As with depression and personality disorders, the Axis I and Axis II syndromes may be virtually indistinguishable. However, in the anxiety disorder field, some specific relations have also been proposed. For example, dependent personality disorder may have a special relation to panic, at least partly accounting for the avoidance seen in panic patients [33,34]. Similarly, strong associations have been reported for avoidant personality disorder and social phobia [35]; and features of both avoidant and dependent personality disorders may be related to symptom severity in agoraphobia [36]. In contrast, patients with simple phobia appear to be diagnosed with personality disorders relatively infrequently [29]. As found in depression, state effects, or a subject's temporary exaggeration of maladaptive personality traits on self-report inventories have been reported for some acute anxiety conditions [33].

Management Issues

The prior review of comorbidity of disorders in patients with anxiety and affective disorders provides a beginning road map of what Axis II features must be managed while treating the symptoms. The complicated, and relatively unexplored nature of the relation between Axis I and Axis II disorders is intimately related to how one approaches the Axis I disorders in the presence of Axis II disorders. This issue was discussed earlier. When related to treatment, however, it implies that one might be able to treat the Axis I disorders while ignoring the Axis II disorders or, if the two are more causally linked, one might be able to treat the Axis I disorder and have some felicitous effect on the Axis II conditions [37]. Alternatively, although not a direct focus of intervention or outcome, the personality disorders may be patient variables that either foster or interfere with a treatment alliance [9].

There is some beginning definition and detailed description of the psychologic treatment of personality disorders, per se [38–40]. However, here we will not focus on the treatment of personality disorders, but on how the clinician might manage personality disorders during the process of treating the anxiety and mood disorders. As the forgoing review of the prevalence of mood and anxiety disorders occurring together with personality disorders indicates, the problem is of such a magnitude that it requires attention.

For the medication treatment of depression and anxiety, the patient must take the medication as prescribed. A primary question therefore is: do the behaviors of a patient with personality disorder interfere with medication compliance, and if so, which specific behaviors? For the psychotherapy of patients with depression and anxiety, we have the treatments, as presented in manuals, that have proved effective in clinical trials. Most of these treatments are directive (*ie*, the therapist indicates the focus of the discussion and gives homework assignments). It has been postulated that for a patient to respond to directive intervention, the patient must be low on reactance, *ie*, the patient must be willing to take direction from the authority figure in the form of the therapist [41]. Some patients with dependent disorders may actually be quite accepting of direction, whereas others (*eg*, narcissistic or antisocial patients) may resist compliance or feign such. Another helpful indication in this area is the speculation by Pilkonis [42] that the intensity and nature of depression may be related to the manner in which the patient has attached to key figures in their interpersonal history. It is possible that the patient's attachment style will influence that nature of attachment to the therapist, thereby either positively or negatively influencing the treatment of symptoms.

Management in the context of mood disorders

Depressed patients who were admitted to an acute disorder ward of a psychiatric hospital were assessed for symptom severity and personality disorder using Tyrer's Personality Assessment Schedule [43]. A large proportion (75.4%) of the sample met criteria for a personality disorder diagnosis. In terms of treatment response, those depressed patients with a concurrent personality disorder improved more slowly and had significantly higher symptom scores after 2 weeks of treatment (Table 1).

A large number of outpatients, with a diagnosis of major depression, were randomly assigned to one of four treatment modalities in the National Institute of Mental Health (NIMH) Treatment of Depression Collaborative Research Program [44]. The treatments included cognitive-behavioral therapy, interpersonal therapy, imipramine in the context of clinical management, and placebo in the context of clinical management. Treatment response was examined in relation to comorbid personality disorders [45]. Seventy-four percent of the patients had personality disorders. These patients had a significantly worse outcome in social functioning and were significantly more likely to have residual symptoms of depression when compared with those without personality disorders.

In one of the few studies to assess which particular personality disorders might impede treatment, Sato *et al.* [46] studied the treatment outcome of outpatient depressive patients treated with a course of antidepressant therapy for 4 months. A log-linear analysis showed that the presence of a personality disorder (DSM-III-R) [47] from cluster A was significantly correlated with poorer outcome of treatment. The authors speculated that patients with disorders in cluster A, such as schizoid and schizotypal personality disorder, might have diminished social support.

Peselow *et al.* [7] examined personality disorders using the SIDP before and after 4 to 5 weeks of treatment with desipramine. For those patients who recovered from depression (39 of the total of 68 patients), Axis II cluster A and C personality traits were significantly reduced. The authors concluded that the cluster A and C traits are interwoven with depressive features, and therefore are subject to change, whereas cluster B traits are more enduring and characteristic modes of thinking and behaving.

Reduced serotonergic activity may link impulsivity to affective instability, an observation that now has treatment implications with the wide use of selective serotonin reuptake inhibitors. One study [48] of responses to fluoxetine in depressed patients suggested that presence or absence of personality disorders (as measured by patient self-report) did

Table 1. Treatment of Mood and Anxiety Disorders in the Presence of Personality Disorders			
Study	**Depression or anxiety**	**Treatment**	**Results**
Brophy [43]	Depression	Two-week hospitalization	Patients with personality disorders improved more slowly
Peselow et al. [7]	Depression	Desipramine	For those who recovered from depression (39 of 68), Axis II clusters A and C symptoms were significantly reduced
Fava et al. [48]	Depression	Fluoxetine	Significant reductions in personality disorder diagnoses and dimensional score of personality disorder
Sato et al. [46]	Depression	Antidepressant drugs	Cluster A personality disorder was associated with poorer outcome
AuBuchon and Malatesta [50]	Anxiety	Behavioral therapy	Obsessive-compulsive disorder patients were more resistant to treatment
Shea et al. [45]	Depression	Pill placebo, imipramine, cognitive therapy, interpersonal therapy, psychotherapy	Patients with personality disorders showed significantly less improvement in all treatments except cognitive therapy

not predict the patient's symptom outcome. More narrowly, however, patients with a cluster B personality disorder before treatment showed a significantly greater drop in depression compared with those patients without a cluster B diagnosis. In fact, 44% of the patients with a cluster B diagnosis of borderline personality disorder before treatment lost the diagnosis following treatment.

Other neurotransmitter systems are also likely to be involved in typical characterological symptoms. For example, Siever [18] points out that although reduced noradrenergic activity is probably associated with a purely depressive diathesis, increased reactivity of the noradrenergic system caused by dysregulation might underlie impulse or aggressive behaviors. Tricyclic antidepressant prescriptions in such patients could well be addressing both conditions of neurotransmitter deficiency and neurotransmitter dysregulation.

One observation relevant to the maintenance phase of treatment is that suicide attempts in patients with borderline and other personality disorders often occur when the depressive state is relatively quiescent [49]. This is consistent with the frequent observation that suicide risk in depression increases when mood is beginning to improve, and also with the observation that suicide attempts in patients with personality disorder often arise in the context of impulsivity and anger. The impulsivity and anger are experienced more profoundly than depression, and indeed may represent a line of psychologic defense against depression [49].

Management in the context of anxiety disorders

Several suggestions have been made that a personality disorder's comorbidity renders the Axis I anxiety disorder less amenable to treatment. For example, AuBuchon and Malatesta [50] found that patients with OCD who also had personality disorders responded less satisfactorily to comprehensive behavior therapy than OCD patients without personality disorders. The OCD patients with personality disorders also had more hospitalizations and premature terminations of treatment. In addition, OCD patients with comorbid cluster A personality disorders have been reported to be less responsive to clomipramine treatment than OCD patients without personality disorder [32,51].

Unexplored treatment issues

Clinical awareness concerning the treatment of patients with both Axis I and Axis II disorders now exceeds our empirical information. Two such limitations in our knowledge are apparent. First, we have only speculation on which Axis II disorders one must treat clinically if one is to have success in treating the Axis I disorder. A likely candidate for this situation is one involving Axis I major depression and Axis II borderline personality disorder. The patient's need for relationships, despite the impulsive and angry qualities they possess that may drive others away may, in a reciprocal fashion, lead to further depression, especially depression with the particular qualities noted in one of the studies reviewed here previously [24–26].

Apart from treating the personality disorder per se when treating the Axis I disorder, one may need to manage the Axis II disorder to successfully treat the Axis I disorder. It is interesting to note the speculation on the relation between Axis II disorders and more general personality traits, as described by current theories of personality [52]. The conceptualization of the Axis II personality disorders in terms of more generalized personality traits, rather than in the mixture of behaviors, attitudes, and traits of Axis II, is helpful in planning treatment. For example, in treating an Axis I disorder in an individual with a paranoid personality disorder, hostility is the primary trait that the therapist will encounter and must manage to carry the treatment forward. Likewise, clinicians treating individuals with Axis I disorder and comorbid narcissistic personality disorder will be faced with the necessity of dealing with the traits of hostility, vulnerability, and extreme assertiveness.

Conclusions

Patients with personality disorders do not respond to treatment for mood or anxiety disorders—either pharmacotherapy or psychotherapy—as well as those symptomatic individuals without personality disorders. This issue has been explored mainly in patients suffering from depression, with fewer studies of patients who have anxiety disorders.

There is as yet no clear pattern in the empirical data relative to which personality disorders impede treatment response. In the absence of any clear pattern for which personality disorders impede treatment, it is difficult to alert the clinician to when and how to directly manage personality disorders while treating the symptom constellations.

It is possible that some specific personality disorders might actually foster a favorable treatment response. For example, dependent personality disorder might foster a treatment alliance.

The mechanism by which personality disorders influence treatment response has not been examined directly. Therefore, it is not totally clear what the clinician must manage while treating mood and anxiety disorders in the presence of a personality disorder. Shea *et al.* [9] have speculated on the multiple ways in which patients with personality disorders might interfere with treatment: 1) poorer compliance with treatment procedures;

2) reduced ability to form a therapeutic relationship with the treatment provider; and 3) provide a negative influence on the ability of the treatment provider to deliver good treatment.

A specific issue concerning drug or psychotherapeutic treatment of the symptom constellations during the continuation and maintenance phase of treatment is the prevalence of symptom breakthroughs that are related to the presence of comorbid personality disorders. The existing studies provide no information on this important clinical issue, and we can only look to future studies to eliminate this gap in our knowledge.

Several studies have suggested that drug therapy reduces disorders or personality disorder traits [7,48]. Studies such as these are hard to interpret, however. One issue is the test-retest reliability of the instruments that measure personality disorders, especially those instruments that depend solely on patient self-report. Another issue is the definition of personality disorder traits in terms of duration (*eg*, at least 5 years) and how the time frame is used in the Axis II assessment instrument. Another more basic issue is the variable nature of criteria on Axis II, which includes traits, attitudes, feelings, and behaviors. Despite these difficulties, some reports take theoretical stands. Akiskal *et al.* [53] suggest that remitted depressive states may lead to alterations in personality that are qualitatively different from the baseline condition. Bronisch and Klerman [37] make a distinction between personality and personality functioning, and they suggest that the latter category changes with treatment of anxiety and mood disorders.

References

1. Clarkin JF, Kendall PC: Comorbidity and treatment planning: summary and future directions. *J Consult Clin Psychol* 1992, 60:904–908.
2. Kendall PC, Clarkin JF: Special section: comorbidity and treatment implications. *J Consult Clin Psychol* 1992, 60:833–908.
3. Klein MH, Wonderlich S, Shea MT: Models of relationships between personality and depression: toward a framework for theory and research. In *Personality and Depression: A Current View*. Edited by Klein MH, Kupfer DJ, Shea MT. New York: Guilford Press; 1993.
4. American Psychiatric Association: *Diagnostic and Statistical Manual of Mental Disorders*, edn 3. Washington, DC: American Psychiatric Association; 1980.
5. Riso LP, Klein DN, Anderson RL, *et al.*: Concordance between patients and informants on the personality disorder examination. *Am J Psychiatry* 1994, 151:568–573.
6. Hirschfeld RM, Klerman GL, Clayton PJ: Assessing personality: effects of the depressive state on trait measurement. *Am J Psychiatry* 1983, 140:695–699.
7. Peselow ED, Sanfilipo MP, Fieve RR, Gulbenkian G: Personality traits during depression and after clinical recovery. *Br J Psychiatry* 1994, 164:349–354.
8. Loranger AW, Lenzenweger M, Gartner A, *et al.*: Trait-state artifacts and the diagnosis of personality disorders. *Arch Gen Psychiatry* 1991, 48:720–728.
9. Shea MT, Widiger TA, Klein MH: Comorbidity of personality disorders and depression: implications for treatment. *J Consult Clin Psychol* 1992, 60:857–868.
10. Carpenter D, Clarkin JF, Glick ID, Wilner PJ: Personality pathology among married adults with bipolar disorder. *J Affect Disord* 1995, 34:269–274.
11. Pepper CM, Klein DN, Anderson RL, *et al.*: DSM-III-R Axis II comorbidity in dysthymia and major depression. *Am J Psychiatry* 1995, 152:239–247.
12. Kunik ME, Mulsant BH, Rifai AH, *et al.*: Diagnostic rate of comorbid personality disorder in elderly psychiatric inpatients. *Am J Psychiatry* 1994, 151:603–605.
13. Abrams RC, Rosendahl E, Card C, Alexopoulos G: Personality disorder correlates of late and early onset depression. *J Am Geriatr Soc* 1994, 42:727–731.

14. Blazer D, Williams CD: Epidemiology of dysphoria and depression in an elderly population. *Br J Psychiatry* 1980, 137:439–444.

15. Post F: The management and nature of depressive illness in late life: a follow-through study. *Br J Psychiatry* 1972, 121:393–404.

16. Lesse S: The multivariant masks of depression. *Am J Psychiatry* 1968, 124:35–40.

17. Hirschfeld RM, Holzer CE: Depressive personality disorder: clinical implications. *J Clin Psychiatry* 1994, 55(suppl):10–17.

18. Siever LJ: Commentary. In *Personality and Depression: A Current View.* Edited by Klein MJ, Kupfer D, Shea MT. New York: Guilford Press; 1993.

19. Coccaro EF, Siever LJ, Klar HM, *et al.*: Serotonergic studies in patients with affective and personality disorders: correlates with suicidal and impulsive aggressive behavior. *Arch Gen Psychiatry* 1989, 46:587–599.

20. Masterson J: *Psychotherapy of the Borderline Adult: A Developmental Approach.* New York: Brunner/Mazel; 1976.

21. Kernberg OF: Borderline personality organization. *J Am Psychoanal Assoc* 1967, 15:641–685.

22. Kernberg OF: *Object Relations Theory and Clinical Psychoanalysis.* New York: Jason Aronson; 1976.

23. Buie DH, Adler G: Definitive treatment of the borderline personality. *Int J Psychoanal Psychother* 1982, 9:51–87.

24. Westen D, Moses MJ, Silk KR, *et al.*: Quality of depressive experience in borderline personality disorder and major depression: when depression is not just depression. *J Pers Disord* 1992, 6:382–393.

25. Bellodi L, Battaglia M, Gasperini M, *et al.*: The nature of depression in borderline depressed patients. *Compr Psychiatry* 1992, 33:128–133.

26. Rogers JH, Widiger TA, Krupp A: Aspects of depression associated with borderline personality disorder. *Am J Psychiatry* 1995, 152:268–270.

27. Sullivan PF, Joyce PR, Mulder RT: Borderline personality disorder in major depression. *J Nerv Ment Dis* 1994, 182:508–516.

28. Shea MT, Glass DR, Pilkonis PA, *et al.*: Frequency and implications of personality disorders in a sample of depressed outpatients. *J Pers Disord* 1987, 1:27–42.

29. Sanderson WC, Wetzler S, Beck AT, Betz F: Prevalence of personality disorders among patients with anxiety disorders. *Psychiatry Res* 1994, 51:167–174.

30. Brown TA, Barlow DH: Comorbidity among anxiety disorders: implications for treatment and DSM-IV. *J Consult Clin Psychol* 1992, 60:835–844.

31. Jansen MA, Arntz A, Merckelbach H, *et al.*: Personality disorders and features in social phobia and panic disorder. *J Abnorm Psychol* 1994, 103:391–395.

32. Baer L: Factor analysis of symptom subtypes of obsessive compulsive disorder and their relations to personality and tic disorders. *J Clin Psychiatry* 1994, 55(suppl):18–23.

33. Reich J, Noyes R, Troughton BA: Dependent personality disorder associated with phobic avoidance in patients with panic disorder. *Am J Psychiatry* 1987, 144:323–326.

34. Reich J, Perry JC, Shera D, *et al.*: Comparison of personality disorders in different anxiety disorder diagnoses: panic, agoraphobia, generalized anxiety, and social phobia. *Ann Clin Psychiatry* 1994, 6:125–134.

35. Liebowitz MR, Gorman JM, Fyer AJ, Klein DF: Social phobia: review of a neglected anxiety disorder. *Arch Gen Psychiatry* 1985, 42:729–736.

36. Hoffart A, Thornes K, Hedley LM, Strand J: DSM-III-R Axis I and II disorders in agoraphobic patients with and without panic disorder. *Acta Psychiatr Scand* 1994, 89:186–191.

37. Bronisch T, Klerman GL: Personality functioning: change and stability in relationship to symptoms and psychopathology. *J Pers Disord* 1991, 5:307–317.

38. Linehan MM: *Cognative-Behavioral Treatment of Borderline Personality Disorder.* New York: Guilford Press; 1993.

39. Beck AT, Freeman A, *et al.*: *Cogntive Therapy of Personality Disorders.* New York: Guilford Press; 1990.

40. Kernberg OF, Selzer MA, Koenigsberg HW, *et al.*: *Psychodynamic Psychotherapy of Borderline Patients.* New York: Basic Books; 1989.

41. Beutler L, Clarkin JF: *Systemic Treatment Selection.* New York: Brunner/Mazel; 1990.

42. Pilkonis PA: Personality prototypes among depressives: themes of dependency and autonomy. *J Pers Disord* 1988, 2:144–152.

43. Brophy JJ: Personality disorder, symptoms, and dexamethasone suppression in depression. *J Affect Disord* 1994, 31:19–27.

44. Elkin I, Shea MT, Watkins JT, *et al.*: The National Institute of Mental Health Treatment of Depression Collaborative Research Program: general effectiveness of treatments. *Arch Gen Psychiatry* 1989, 33:971–982.

45. Shea MT, Pilkonis PA, Beckham E, *et al.*: Personality disorders and treatment outcome in the NIMH treatment of depression collaborative research program. *Am J Psychiatry* 1990, 147:711–718.

46. Sato T, Sakado K, Sato S, *et al.*: Cluster A personality disorder: a marker of worse treatment outcome of major depression? *Psychiatry Res* 1994, 53:153–159.

47. American Psychiatric Association: *Diagnosis and Statistical Manual of Mental Disorders*, edn 3, Revised. Washington, DC: American Psychiatric Association; 1987.

48. Fava M, Bouffides E, Pava JA, *et al.*: Personality disorder comorbidity with major depression and response to fluoxetine treatment. *Psychother Psychosomat* 1994, 62:160–167.

49. Soloff PH, Lis JA, Kelly T, *et al.*: Risk factors for suicidal behavior in borderline personality disorder. *Am J Psychiatry* 1994, 151:1316–1323.

50. AuBuchon PG, Malatesta VJ: Obsessive compulsive patients with comorbid personality disorder: associated problems and response to a comprehensive behavior therapy. *J Clin Psychiatry* 1994, 55:448–453.

51. Baer L, Jenike MA, Black DW, *et al.*: Effect of Axis II diagnoses on treatment outcome with clomipramine in 55 patients with obsessive compulsive disorder. *Arch Gen Psychiatry* 1992, 49:862–866.

52. Widiger TA, Trull TJ, Clarkin JF, *et al.*: A description of the DSM-III-R and DSM-IV personality disorders with the five-factor model of personality. In *Personality Disorders and the Five-Factor Model of Personality*. Edited by Costa PT, Widiger TA. Washington DC: American Psychologcial Association; 1994:41–56.

53. Akiskal HS, Hirschfeld RM, Yerevanian BI: The relationship of personality to affective disorders: a critical review. *Arch Gen Psychiatry* 1983, 40:801–810.

CHAPTER 12

Treatment of Borderline Personality Disorder

Caron Zlotnick and M. Tracie Shea

In this chapter we review treatment approaches that are grounded in both theory and research for patients with borderline personality disorder (BPD). The overview evaluates the efficacy of treatment modalities broadly categorized as: 1) pharmacotherapeutic, 2) psychodynamic, 3) dialectic-behavioral, 4) dynamic-cognitive-behavioral, and 5) interpersonal. In addition, we propose a three-stage model of treatment for BPD patients with histories of childhood abuse. Directions for future research are also discussed.

Over the years the concept of *borderline* has stimulated much debate, although it is rooted in a strong theoretical framework. Some of the controversy has stemmed from divergent views on what constitutes the salient features of borderline personality disorder (BPD). Authors with a psychodynamic viewpoint have used the term *borderline* to connote a particular structure of personality characterized by primitive defenses, poor object relationships, and diffuse identity [1]. Others, such as the cognitive theorists, have emphasized as central aspects of their psychopathology specific maladaptive assumptions or schemas of BPD, such as dichotomous thinking or schemas of abandonment [2,3]. Theorists with an interpersonal orientation have focused on aspects of the patient's social learning experiences that create and maintain the disorder [4]. Although some experts have rejected the term *borderline* as misleading, they still acknowledge the clinical phenomenon of a certain personality structure. For instance, Millon [5] maintains that the term should be replaced by the term *cycloid*, since behavior and mood instability are the defining characteristics of the disorder [5]. Still others consider the term *borderline* as pejorative and biased toward women [6]. In clinical settings, the term *borderline* has, for the most part, been used to describe patients who were difficult to diagnose or difficult to treat.

The concept is further confounded by the heterogeneity of patients with BPD. They frequently present with other psychiatric disorders, especially thought disorders, depression, and posttraumatic stress disorder (PTSD). The high rates of comorbidity have led some authors to consider BPD a form of a mood disorder [7] or to believe that BPD is associated with schizophrenia [8]. There is also an overlap between BPD and other personality disorders [9]. These findings raise the question of whether BPD represents a unique entity or whether it is a variant of other mental disorders. Nonetheless, most authors agree that the *Diagnostic and Statistical Manual of Mental Disorders* (DSM) criteria for BPD provides a heuristically useful definition.

Diagnostic Criteria for Borderline Personality Disorder

The diagnostic criteria for BPD first appeared in the third edition of the DSM (DSM-III), which was published by the American Psychiatric Association in 1980. The most current definition of BPD, listed in DSM-IV [10], defines BPD as a pervasive pattern of instability of interpersonal relationships, self-image, and affects, and marked impulsivity beginning by early adulthood and present in a variety of contexts. Table 1 details the DSM-IV diagnostic criteria for BPD. In an attempt to increase the specificity and reliability of the DSM-IV diagnosis of BPD, the DSM-IV workgroup for BPD modified some of the DSM-III criteria [11]. Based on theoretical, clinical, and empirical considerations, changes in DSM-IV criteria for BPD include: 1) dysphoria has replaced depression in criterion 6 to point out that the affects are reactive; 2) criterion 3 was revised to emphasize a central feature of BPD, instability of self-image; 3) in criterion 7, chronic feelings of emptiness replaced chronic boredom, since the characteristics of emptiness appear to distinguish BPD from other personality disorders; and 4) a new criterion (criterion 9) was added based on empirical research that has consistently demonstrated that transient cognitive-perceptual dysfunctioning is a core and discriminating feature of BPD.

Borderline Personality Disorder as a Mental Health Challenge

Since BPD afflicts 11% to 23% of psychiatric patients [12], most mental health professionals will encounter patients with BPD in their clinical practice. Estimates of the community prevalence of BPD have ranged from 1.8% to 4% [13,14]. The diagnosis appears to be unrelated to socioeconomic status or education. However, BPD is a disorder that is predominantly found among women.

Borderline personality disorder is a serious mental health problem that can result in great personal, relational, and social morbidity. Suicide rates for patients with BPD have been estimated between 3% and 9% [15,16]. Parasuicidal behavior (*ie*, intentional self-injurious behavior) is common among BPD patients, with reported rates ranging from 69% to 80% [17–19]. Besides violence toward self, individuals diagnosed with BPD are at

---

Table I. DSM-IV Diagnostic Criteria for Borderline Personality Disorder

A pervasive pattern of instability of interpersonal relationships, self-image, and affects, and marked impulsivity beginning by early adulthood and present in a variety of contexts, as indicated by five (or more) of the following:

1. Frantic efforts to avoid real or imaged abandonment
   Note: Does not include suicidal or self-mutilating behavior covered in criterion 5
2. A pattern of unstable and intense interpersonal relationships characterized by alternating between extremes of idealization and devaluation
3. Identity disturbance: markedly and persistently unstable self-image or sense of self
4. Impulsivity in at least two areas that are potentially self-damaging (eg, spending, sex, substance abuse, reckless driving, binge eating)
   Note: Does not include suicidal or self-mutilating behavior covered in criterion 5
5. Recurrent suicidal behavior, gestures, threats, or self-mutilating behavior
6. Affective instability due to a marked reactivity of mood (eg, intense episodic dysphoria, irritability, or anxiety usually lasting a few hours and only rarely more than a few days)
7. Chronic feelings of emptiness
8. Inappropriate intense anger or difficulty controlling anger (eg, displays of temper, constant anger, recurrent physical fights)
9. Transient, stress-related paranoid ideation or severe dissociative symptoms

DSM-IV—Diagnostic and Statistical Manual of Mental Disorders, edn 4.

risk of being violent toward family members and engaging in criminal behaviors [15,18]. In addition, BPD patients are also more likely than those with any other psychiatric diagnoses, except those with antisocial personality, to abuse alcohol and drugs [15,20]. Finally, the financial burden of BPD is high. Treatment of BPD is demanding, and 30% of hospitalized BPD patients require further psychiatric hospitalizations, often two or more subsequent hospitalizations [21]. Furthermore, prospective long-term follow-up research on BPD patients shows that 46% are chronically incapable of working [22].

Treatment Approaches

Despite the vast amount of literature on the topic of BPD and its high social cost, there have been relatively few studies concerning effective treatment for BPD. Generally, research on treatment for BPD has targeted changes in specific features of patients with BPD or focused on subgroups of BPD patients, such as those who are parasuicidal.

This chapter includes only treatments of BPD that have been studied empirically, including naturalistic treatment studies, studies in which treatment is standardized but there is no control group, and studies with random assignment, standardized treatment, and control groups. To date, treatment modalities that have been studied empirically can be broadly categorized as: 1) pharmacotherapy, 2) psychodynamic, 3) dialectic-behavioral, 4) dynamic-cognitive-behavioral, and 5) interpersonal. Finally, as part of this review we have proposed a stage model of treatment for BPD patients with histories of childhood abuse.

Pharmacotherapy

The pharmacotherapy approach to BPD arises from biologic formulations of BPD. Serotonergic abnormalities, dopaminergic neurotransmitter pathology, and dyscontrol of limbic regions of the brain are among the biologic models of BPD.

Serotonergic abnormalities have been associated with irritable and impulsive aggressive behavior and suicide attempts in patients with BPD [23]. Research has found reductions in prolactin response to fenfluramine, a serotonin-releasing agent, in patients with BPD [24]. Recently, a 13-week, placebo-controlled, double-blind study found that treatment with selective serotonin reuptake inhibitors was effective in reducing anger in patients with BPD [25]. Although the number of subjects in this study was small, the findings supported previous clinical data and uncontrolled observations that fluoxetine appears to reduce anger in patients with BPD. Lithium is another pharmacologic agent that has been hypothesized to impact serotonergic functioning and thereby influence the mood of BPD patients. A preliminary report of a double-blind, randomized, placebo-controlled crossover trial of lithium carbonate and desipramine in 17 patients with BPD found no significant differences between lithium versus placebo and desipramine versus placebo in depressive symptoms, anger, or suicidality [26]. In contrast, therapists in this study reported a positive response to lithium compared with placebo for impulsive aspects of BPD.

Studies of other psychotropic agents that have direct or indirect effects on the serotonergic systems have shown some significant but modest efficacy in BPD patients. Monoamine oxidase inhibitors, such as phenelzine, have been found to decrease behavioral impulsivity and, to a lesser degree, depressive symptoms [27]. In a recent randomized, double-blind, placebo-controlled study comparing phenelzine with haloperidol in inpatients with a primary diagnosis of BPD, phenelzine was found to be more effective than haloperidol and placebo in reducing subjective hostility and anger [28]. However, the study was unable to replicate earlier findings that phenelzine was effective against atypical depression that includes symptoms of hypersomnia, leaden paralysis, rejection sensitivity, and excessive mood reactivity [27]. Soloff *et al.* [28] attributed this failure, in part, to their conservative daily dose of phenelzine sulfate (average 60.45 mg), and the modest length of treatment trial (5 weeks). Furthermore, unlike BPD patients with a primary diagnosis of atypical depression who respond to phenelzine, patients with the primary diagnosis of BPD may be too heterogeneous to demonstrate medication effects on any one type of depression.

Reduced dopaminergic activities have been hypothesized to be associated with the cognitive-perceptual symptoms of patients with BPD [29]. However, the use of neuroleptics with BPD patients has been found to have a nonspecific and mostly tranquilizing effect [30,31]. Furthermore, a controlled treatment trial found that a low-dose neuroleptic is no more effective than a placebo in acute treatment for the less severely impaired BPD patient [28]. In support of the dopaminergic hypothesis, research has shown that there is a more favorable response to neuroleptics in BPD patients who present with severe schizotypal symptoms, hostility, and suspiciousness, although the effects of the medication are not specific to cognitive and schizotypal symptoms [32].

Another biologic model of BPD, the dyscontrol of the primitive limbic regions of the brain, has been linked to the affective instability of BPD patients. Studies have reported electroencephalographic abnormalities, seizure activity, and increased neurologic soft signs in BPD patients [33]. Based on these findings, researchers have hypothesized that anticonvulsant medications alter limbic dysfunctioning by interrupting neuronal kindling [34]. An 8-week open trial of valproate in eight patients with BPD found that four of the patients showed improvement in mood, anxiety, irritability, and impulsivity, but specific therapeutic effects varied from patient to patient [35]. Other preliminary data on the use of anticonvulsant medication in BPD patients have shown that use of carbamazepine is related to reductions in behavior dyscontrol [34]. Table 2 summarizes findings from studies of the effects of various classes of drugs on patients with BPD.

Research on the pharmacotherapeutic treatment of BPD patients has methodologic problems that limit any conclusive evidence concerning the efficacy of medication for BPD. Few studies have involved large samples, used randomized control designs, controlled for psychosocial treatment, or replicated previous findings. Other major difficulties in pharmacotherapy studies have been the inability of some BPD patients to tolerate therapeutic dosages, noncompliance with prescribed medication, and high attrition rates. Finally, in almost all studies, patients were exposed to medication for a short duration, on average 5 to 12 weeks, which possibly limited the efficacy of the treatments and introduced a large amount of variance into long-term results.

Despite these methodologic constraints, there has been some consensus among researchers concerning the efficacy of psychotropic medications in BPD patients. Conclusions drawn from empirical findings are: 1) there is no drug of choice in the treatment of BPD patients [36]; 2) the short-term use of psychotropic medication produces modest changes in acute symptoms; 3) pharmacotherapy does not change the character

Table 2. Summary Findings From Selected Pharmacotherapy Studies of Patients with Borderline Personality Disorder

Study	Drug	Patients, n	Type of study	Results
Links and Steiner [26]	Lithium vs despiramine	17	Placebo-controlled, double-blind	Therapists rated lithium as signifcantly superior to placebo
Salzman et al. [25]	Fluoxetine (SSRI)*	21	Placebo-controlled, double-blind	Fluoxetine associated with significant decrease in anger
Soloff et al. [28]	Phenelzine (MAOI)* vs haloperidol (neuroleptic)	108	Placebo-controlled, double-blind	Superior efficacy for phenelzine in self-perceived anger and hostility
Soloff et al. [32]	Amitriptyline (tricyclic)* vs haloperidol (neuroleptic)	90	Placebo-controlled, double-blind	Amitriptyline was no more effective than placebo; haloperidol showed most improvement in depressive and schizotypal symptoms
Stein et al. [35]	Valproate (anticonvulsant)	8	Open trial	Overall improvement in 50% of sample

*Antidepressants.
MAOI—monoamine oxidase inhibitor; SSRI—selective serotonin reuptake inhibitor.

structure of the BPD patient; 4) there are difficulties with treatment compliance; 5) pharmacotherapy is, at best, a useful supplement to psychotherapy in the treatment of BPD patients; and 6) there are inadequate empirical guidelines concerning pharmacologic treatment for the continuation therapy of BPD.

Psychodynamic therapy

Psychodynamic treatment approaches to patients with BPD have been prominent in the clinical literature. Among the several psychodynamic approaches proposed in the literature, Kernberg's expressive psychotherapy [37,38] has been one of the most influential and well-articulated treatment models. Although to date there exists no empirical research on the efficacy of Kernberg's treatment model, Kernberg's work represents a substantial contribution to the field. Thus, we selected expressive psychotherapy as the psychodynamic modality to discuss in this article.

A central assumption of expressive psychotherapy is that the BPD patient's display of behavioral, emotional, and interpersonal disturbances are manifestations of an unconscious pathologic structure. This underlying ego structure of the patient with BPD is characterized by dissociated, "split off" aspects of the patient's internalized perceptions of self and others, the affect associated with these perceptions, and the use of defense mechanisms, such as splitting, to separate the positive and negative internal objects.

A primary aim of expressive psychotherapy is to facilitate the patient's experience of the self and others as integrated, coherent, and realistic. Other treatment goals include more effective affect modulation, impulse control, anxiety tolerance, and enhanced interpersonal relationships. In order to promote self-awareness or insight, the therapist repeatedly identifies, clarifies, and interprets the "split-off" aspects of the patient's internalized world as they are expressed in the therapeutic relationship. Transference analysis, interpretation, and uncovering techniques are also used to target defenses that maintain the dissociation and split-off ego states. Highest priority is given to suicidal behaviors and therapist-interfering behaviors.

Generally, the format of expressive therapy consists of two to three 45-minute individual psychotherapy sessions per week. Treatment is expected to last several years. Pharmacotherapy is managed by a psychiatrist other than the individual therapist. In the tradition of psychoanalysis, Kernberg emphasizes the neutrality of the therapist so intrapsychic conflicts of the patient can be revealed during therapy. Expressive psychotherapy has modified the psychoanalytic model so that therapists focus on here-and-now issues and assume an active role.

Results from a naturalistic study of expressive treatment with BPD, the Menninger study [38], suggest that expressive treatment combined with environmental structuring may be more beneficial than another form of psychodynamic therapy, supportive therapy. A concern about testing the efficacy of expressive therapy has been whether therapists can deliver expressive psychotherapy according to the dictates of a standardized manual, a requirement for empirical research on treatment. Currently, the gathering of pilot data concerning the feasibility of a manualized version of this treatment is in progress, and preliminary data suggest that therapists adhere to the psychodynamic aspects of treatment when working with BPD patients (Clarkin, Paper presented at the 5th European Conference on Psychotherapy Research, Cernobbio, Italy, 1996). Once the groundwork has been laid to test the efficacy of expressive psychotherapy, controlled outcome studies on this treatment modality should advance our knowledge concerning effective and cost-effective treatments for BPD.

Dialectic-behavioral therapy

Dialectic-behavioral therapy (DBT), developed by Linehan [39], considers emotional dysregulation a key characteristic of BPD. Based on a biosocial model, DBT proposes that the BPD patient's difficulties in regulating affect arise from biologic dysfunctioning that over time interacts with an "invalidating" environment (*ie*, an environment in which significant others negate the individual's affective responses). DBT views many of the BPD patient's behaviors, such as self-injurious behaviors, as manifestations of poor affect regulation. A primary goal of DBT is to facilitate the development of affect management skills in patients with BPD.

Dialectic-behavioral therapy is a cognitive-behavioral psychotherapy for the treatment of BPD with parasuicidal behaviors (*ie*, nonfatal, deliberate, acute self-injury or harm, including suicidal behaviors). DBT emphasizes a dialectic process that involves a balance between accepting patients (by both themselves and their therapists) and at the same time teaching them to change. The behavioral component of DBT includes skill training and problem-orientated techniques.

Dialectic-behavioral therapy, a manualized treatment [40], consists of weekly individual therapy (typically 1 hour per week), group skills training (1.5 to 2.5 hours per week), consultation and supervision meetings for therapists, and telephone consultation as needed between the patient and individual psychotherapist. The main focus of the group skills training is to teach skills that are postulated to be most often deficient in patients with BPD. In contrast to the group skills training, which is heavily didactic and follows a particular sequence, individual therapy is determined by the current maladaptive behavior of the patient. DBT is very clear in specifying a hierarchy of treatment targets for individual therapy. In order, these targets are: 1) suicide-related behaviors, 2) therapy-interfering behaviors, such as noncompliance, 3) quality-of-life–interfering behaviors, such as substance abuse and excessive hospitalizations, and 4) skills acquisition and practice.

Dialectic-behavioral therapy is beginning to be used by clinicians across the country in both inpatient and outpatient settings. Although limited, there is empirical support for the use of DBT in BPD patients [41,42]. Using randomized assignment, DBT was compared with treatment as usual (TAU) in a sample of 44 parasuicidal women meeting criteria for BPD. The duration of both treatments was 1 year, and the majority of patients in the TAU group received some form of individual or group psychotherapy. Results of this study suggest that DBT is more effective than TAU in reducing parasuicidal behavior, number of days of inpatient psychiatric hospitalization, and attrition rates. Although there were some differences between the two groups in various measures of adjustment at the end of treatment and at 1-year follow-up, at the end of treatment patients in both groups remained in the impaired range compared with normal samples. However, DBT did not affect level of depression, hopelessness, suicidal ideation, or reasons for living. The researchers concluded that one year of DBT appeared to have helped BPD patients in being more adept at tolerating their distressing situations and at functioning while emotionally distressed.

Further empirical support for DBT was found in a study of inpatients with BPD and parasuicidal behaviors [43]. In this study, monthly rates of parasuicidal behavior were found to decrease significantly after DBT was implemented on an inpatient unit. Moreover, in contrast with the unit that introduced the DBT program, the hospital's standard treatment did not show comparable changes in rates of parasuicidal behavior over the same time period.

Future research is needed to demonstrate that therapists can adhere to the DBT treatment manual, deliver the therapy competently, and obtain outcomes comparable to those at the University of Washington, where DBT originated. Another research direction is for DBT to be compared with other manualized psychosocial treatments or to a specific form of drug treatment.

In summary, DBT appears to be effective in its treatment targets of increasing distress tolerance and control of parasuicidal behavior. Also, DBT seems to be a cost-effective treatment compared with other types of intensive psychotherapy for BPD patients. Another positive finding is the low attrition rate in DBT, since attrition rates usually plague most studies and clinicians working with BPD patients. On a less encouraging note, DBT was not as successful in improving internal states and level of negative affect. Perhaps changes in "maladaptive schemas" and "phenomenologic relief" in BPD can only be expected in treatment that extends beyond a 1-year duration.

Dynamic-cognitive–behavioral therapy

Another cognitive-behavioral treatment model for BPD, dynamic-cognitive–behavioral therapy (DCBT) is based on principals of affective change processes, short-term psychodynamically oriented psychotherapy, and cognitive-behavioral therapy (Turner, Paper presented at the 27th Annual Meeting of the Association for the Advancement of Behavior Therapy, Atlanta, 1993). Psychodynamic techniques are used to conceptualize and interpret interpersonal conflicts. A broad range of cognitive-behavioral interventions are used that include skill training, implosive therapy, role playing, and the challenging of dysfunctional beliefs. The format for DCBT includes individual, dyadic, and group therapy sessions. Unlike DBT, group therapy in DBCT does not involve other patients. A unique component of DCBT is that groups are composed of significant persons in the patient's natural environment, such as partners, family members, friends, and other community support persons. In a preliminary investigation comparing the effectiveness of DCBT with a client-centered therapy control condition (CCTC), 24 BPD patients were randomly assigned to DCBT or CCTC. Patients received 49 to 84 sessions of treatment over a 12-month period (Turner, Paper presented at the Annual Meeting of the Association for the Advancement of Behavior Therapy, Philadelphia, 1984). Outcomes showed that the DCBT group improved more than the CCTC group on most measures of self-harm behaviors, affective states, and global psychologic functioning. However, therapists differed in their success with DCBT and CCTC. These findings raise the issue that therapists' attitudes and expectancies about treatment and about treating BPD patients may influence outcome, an area of research that warrants further investigation.

Interpersonal therapy

A major premise of interpersonal therapy is that the pathology of BPD should be understood in the context of learned patterns of interpersonal relating. Furthermore, the maladaptive interpersonal behavior of the patient with BPD stems from early experiences. Among interpersonal approaches to BPD is Benjamin's structural analysis of social behavior (SASB) [6]. The SASB interpersonal behavior nosologic system identifies specific interpersonal patterns of BPD that include a profound fear of abandonment; a desire for protective nurturance; friendly dependence on the nurturer, which becomes hostile if the nurturer fails to deliver enough; a belief that the provider likes dependency and neediness; and an internal response toward self-attack triggered by happiness or success.

In applying this theory of BPD, Benjamin views the role of therapist as helping the patient to learn about destructive patterns and their origin, make the decision to change, and replace current maladaptive patterns with more adaptive ones. In order to facilitate therapeutic change, Benjamin suggests that therapists use standard techniques such as dream analysis, free association, role-playing, interpretation of transference, and educational assignments. Benjamin states that "anything that helps the BPD learn about her patterns (without harming herself) is correct." Unfortunately, little is known about the efficacy of this form of interpersonal treatment for BPD.

Another approach that emphasizes the interpersonal dimension of BPD is interpersonal group psychotherapy (IGP), which was developed by Marziali and Munroe-Blum [44]. An aim of IGP is to provide a context in which patients are able to express and process internalized conflicts and expectations concerning the self in relation to others. In addition, the feedback of the group and the support of the therapist allow the patient to test and learn about modified self-attributes. Unlike other models of therapy for patients with BPD, IGP avoids genetic and transference interpretations, as well as education and advice giving. Instead, most interventions of IGP therapists are tentatively phrased and communicated with uncertainty, and the therapist maintains unwavering interest in the patient's dialogue. A randomized, controlled trial was conducted on 110 subjects with BPD to compare IGP with a control condition, individual dynamic psychotherapy (or TAU) [45]. IGP was manual-guided and consisted of 30 sessions of treatment for 1.5 hours, whereas the comparison group was open ended. Seventy-nine of the 110 subjects accepted their treatment assignment and entered treatment. Results showed that at 12- and 24-month follow-up, there were no significant differences between the two groups in behavioral indicators, social adjustment, psychologic distress, and depression [45]. The study found that both groups of subjects showed significant improvements on all outcome variables at follow-up. However, given the brevity of IGP therapy, it is possible that a longer period of IGP treatment may have resulted in the superiority of IGP compared with the control group. The researchers concluded that despite the comparability of the two treatments in outcome, IGP was more cost effective than open-ended psychodynamic psychotherapy. With the current increased fiscal constraints on mental health services, the cost benefits of interpersonal group therapy compared with open-ended psychodynamic psychotherapy is an important consideration. More controlled studies are needed to test the efficacy of interpersonal therapy for BPD. Table 3 summarizes research findings on the effects of various psychosocial treatments for BPD patients.

A three-stage treatment

Recently there has been a growing interest in the relationship between BPD and PTSD [46]. It has been estimated that approximately one third of the population with BPD meets criteria for PTSD [47]. Also, several studies have demonstrated that between 50% to 76% of patients with BPD have a history of childhood sexual abuse [48,49].

Table 3. Psychosocial Treatment Modalities for Borderline Personality Disorder

Study	Treatment modality	Approach	Key techniques	Empirical findings
Kernberg et al. [37,38]	Expressive psychotherapy	Psychodynamic-individual	Here-and-now interpretations, transference analysis, and limited setting	More beneficial than supportive psychodynamic therapy
Linehan [41,42]	Dialectic-behavioral therapy	Cognitive-behavioral, individual and group	Identification of deficits, teaching of skills, and daily life application of skills	More effective in reducing parasuicidal behavior and length of hospitalization than "treatment as usual" group
Turner*	Dynamic-cognitive–behavioral therapy	Integrated psychosocial, individual and group	Interpretation of conflicts, self-management skills, and other cognitive-behavioral strategies	More effective than a comparison treatment in negative behavior and mood
Marziali and Munroe-Blum [45]	Interpersonal group treatment	Group only	Observation and processing of the interactions between patients and co-therapists	No more effective than an open-ended comparison group

*Paper presented at the 27th Annual Meeting of the Association for the Advancement of Behavior Therapy, Atlanta, 1993.

These findings of an overlap between BPD and PTSD are so marked that questions have been raised concerning the distinctiveness of BPD, especially in survivors of early trauma. One view holds that when BPD arises out of a history of early trauma, other factors such as the premorbid character structure (immature defenses or coping mechanisms) and a "complex intermingling of familial emotional neglect and misunderstandings" interact with the abuse to shape the personality [46]. A contrasting view contends that early trauma can lead to enduring and pervasive changes in personality development that include disturbances in affect regulation, impulse control, dissociation, and reality testing, key features of BPD [50]. A third possibility is that BPD pathology is a secondary adaptation to the core features of chronic PTSD, rather than to the trauma per se.

Irrespective of which view one holds, it appears that individuals with BPD and histories of early trauma may represent a subgroup of BPD with their own set of clinical difficulties. In support of this view, research has found that patients with BPD and early trauma are more likely to engage in more serious forms of self-mutilation and have higher levels of dissociation than those with BPD and no histories of early trauma [51,52]. Treatment of BPD patients with histories of abuse that do not target the specific sequelae of trauma may be ineffectual. For instance, BPD patients who use dissociation to defend against any reminder of the trauma or any affectively laden material may be unable to use therapy unless their dissociative symptomatology is addressed at the onset of treatment. Furthermore, treatments that prematurely explore the origins of destructive behaviors may intensify symptoms of arousal, affect dysregulation, and dissociation in this subgroup of patients. Thus, it is plausible that patients with BPD and histories of childhood abuse may benefit from Herman's stage model of treatment [50]. Herman developed a three-stage treatment for survivors of trauma that progresses from symptomatic stabilization to integration of memories to restored social connection.

Stage one of treatment, a symptom-oriented intervention, emphasizes safety, trust, education, and stress management. For patients with BPD and histories of abuse, stage one consists of cognitive-behavioral strategies (such as DBT) that target current distress and dysfunctioning central to this subgroup of patients, strategies such as dissociation, self-mutilation, and affect dysregulation. As an adjunct, pharmacotherapy, such as fluoxetine or lithium, that is effective in reducing behavior dysregulation in both patients with BPD and patients with PTSD should reinforce stabilization of mood and adaptive behaviors. After patients have mastered emotional flooding and control of their dysfunctional behaviors , the next phase of treatment is the exploration and reconstruction of the trauma story. Stage two can involve traditional forms of therapy with trauma survivors, such as flooding or systematic desensitization, that expose the patient to a controlled reliving of the experience. Herman cautions that careful timing of "uncovering work" is critical for successful treatment. Finally, the task of stage three is for the survivor to "create a new self" in relation to himself or herself and others. Interpersonal group therapy that provides "the opportunity to test modified expectations of self and others" may achieve the goals of stage-three treatment for BPD patients with histories of abuse.

In our work with BPD patients with histories of childhood abuse and PTSD, we have found that they often decompensate in recovery groups that facilitate the disclosure of traumatic experiences. Based on these clinical observations, we have developed a group treatment model that targets affect dysregulation and presents skill-strengthening and behavioral strategies. Our experience using this structured treatment group as an adjunct to individual therapy with BPD patients with histories of childhood abuse and PTSD has been that both patients and treating individual therapists reported posttreatment improvement in self-destructive behaviors, tolerance of anxiety and anger, and enhanced mood. In addition, some BPD patients noted that the affect-regulation group was their first positive group experience, since their previous group experiences ended prematurely due to interpersonal conflict with other group members. However, we found that some BPD patients failed to complete the group treatment. Follow-up interviews with these patients revealed that reasons for early termination included the overwhelming prospect of ending the group, frustration with the group process for not promoting intimacy among group members, and limited contact with group therapists. Clearly, empirical data is needed to test the efficacy of an affect-management group and three-stage treatment for BPD patients with histories of abuse.

Conclusions

Efforts to treat patients with BPD have been extensive, as reflected by the broad range of available treatment modalities. Furthermore, for the most part, treatment approaches are characterized by comprehensive descriptions of strategies and interventions based on theoretical formulations of BPD. As this review shows, current knowledge concerning effective treatments for BPD is limited. However, general conclusions from the literature can be gleaned (Table 4).

Although research on treatment for BPD has become more advanced, there are still many unanswered questions. These include: 1) What are the critical "healing" elements in the treatment of BPD patients? The different psychosocial treatments each use a composite of interventions. In addition, treatment outcome studies have used concurrent modalities of treatment, psychotherapy, drug therapy, and sometimes individual and group therapy. Thus, it becomes difficult to know which specific factors account for improvement or absence of change. In addition, since the psychosocial treatments of patients with BPD all emphasize the importance of establishing a trusting and collaborative relationship with BPD patients and the need to set firm limits with patients, it is possible that the therapeutic relationship is the key to successful treatment of patients with BPD. 2) Given the heterogeneity of patients with BPD, should treatments be matched to areas of impairment? For instance, it is possible that patients with BPD without parasuicidal behavior respond

---

Table 4. General Conclusions regarding Treatment of Borderline Personality Disorder

Borderline patients benefit from treatment, especially in reducing their behavior dyscontrol.
Treatment of up to 1 year is unlikely to impact most character trait disturbances of BPD.
There is no evidence of the superiority of one treatment over another for BPD.
Pharmacotherapy is useful as an adjunct to psychotherapy for BPD.
There is no drug of choice in the treatment of borderline patients.
Borderline patients often fail to complete treatment.
There are inadequate empirical guidelines on maintenance treatment for BPD.

BPD—borderline personality disorder.

more favorably to interpersonal therapy rather than DBT. Currently, no systematic research exists that has investigated whether a particular treatment is more effective for specific clusters of BPD patients than another treatment. 3) How does the presence of a comorbid disorder impact treatment of patients with BPD? Clinicians have no guidelines in terms of whether treatment should also address the comorbid illness, and if so, what type of treatment should be implemented. 4) Would a combined treatment of psychotherapy and medication be more effective than one modality of treatment? To date, a treatment modality does not exist that integrates both approaches, although combined treatment is probably common clinical practice. 5) What are the possible and likely benefits of extended periods of treatment? Treatment studies have used time periods that range from 4 to 6 months to 1 year. Since patients with BPD have persistent and enduring patterns of dysfunction, long-term therapy may be indicated for this population. Other questions that have been raised are whether patients with BPD can be expected to eliminate serious depression or to achieve stable and satisfying interpersonal relationships [53]. Thus, given the serious nature of BPD and its impact on society, as well as our limited knowledge concerning effective treatment for this disorder, further research on treatments for BPD is needed to inform and guide clinical practice.

References

1. Kernberg O: Borderline personality organization. In *Essential Papers on Borderline Disorders. One Hundred Years At The Border.* Edited by Stone MH. New York: New York University Press; 1985:279–329.

2. Beck AT, Freeman A: *Cognitive Therapy of Personality Disorders.* New York: The Guilford Press; 1990.

3. Young J: *Cognitive Therapy for Personality Disorders: A Schema-focused Approach.* Sarasota, FL: Professional Resource Exchange; 1990.

4. Benjamin LS: *Interpersonal Diagnosis and Treatment of Personality Disorders.* New York: The Guilford Press; 1993.

5. Millon T: On the genesis and prevalence of the borderline personality disorder: a social learning thesis. *J Pers Disord* 1987, 1:354–372.

6. Becker D, Lamb S: Sex bias in the diagnosis of borderline personality disorder and posttraumatic stress disorder. *Prof Psych Res Pract* 1994, 25:55–61.

7. Akiskal HS, Chen SE, Davis GC, *et al.*: Borderline: an adjective in search of a noun. *J Clin Psychiatry* 1985, 46:41–48.

8. Blatt SJ, Auerbach JS: Differential cognitive disturbances in three types of borderline patients. *J Pers Disord* 1988, 2:198–211.

9. Nurnberg HG, Raskin M, Levine PE, *et al.*: The comorbidity of borderline personality disorder and other DSM-III-R axis II personality disorders. *Am J Psychiatry* 1991, 148:1371–1377.

10. American Psychiatric Association: *Diagnostic and Statistical Manual of Mental Disorders*, edn 4. Washington, DC: American Psychiatric Association; 1994.

11. Gunderson JG, Zanarini MC, Kisiel CL: Borderline personality disorder: a review of data on DSM-III-R descriptions. *J Pers Disord* 1991, 5:340–352.

12. Widiger TA, Frances AJ: Epidemiology, diagnosis, and comorbidity of borderline personality disorder. In *Review of Psychiatry*, vol 8. Edited by Tasman A, Hales RE, Frances AJ. Washington, DC: American Psychiatric Press; 1987:8–21.

13. Swartz M, Blazer D, George L, Winfield I: Estimating the prevalence of borderline personality disorder in the community. *Disorders* 1990, 4:257–272.

14. Gunderson JG, Zanarini M: Current overview of the borderline diagnosis. *J Clin Psychiatry* 1987, 48(suppl):5–11.

15. Stone MH: The course of borderline personality disorder. In *Review of Psychiatry*. Edited by Tasman A, Hales RE, Frances AJ. Washington, DC: American Psychiatric Press; 1987:103–122.

16. Kullgren G, Renberg E, Jacobsson L: An empirical study of borderline personality disorder and psychiatric suicides. *J Nerv Mental Dis* 1986, 174:328–331.

17. Gunderson JG: *Borderline Personality Disorder*. Washington, DC: American Psychiatric Press; 1984.

18. Stone MH: *The Fate Of Borderline Patients*. New York: The Guilford Press; 1990.

19. Shearer SL, Peter CP, Quaytman MS, Wadman BE: Intent and lethality of suicide attempters among female borderline inpatients. *Am J Psychiatry* 1988, 145:1424–1427.

20. Inman DJ, Bascue LO, Skoloda T: Identification of borderline personality disorders among substance abuse inpatients. *J Subst Abuse Treat* 1985, 2:229–232.

21. Gunderson JG: Borderline personality disorder. In *Comprehensive Textbook of Psychiatry*, vol 5. Edited by Kaplan HI, Sadock BJ. Baltimore: Williams & Wilkins; 1989:1387–1395.

22. Antikainen R, Hintikka J, Lehtonen J, et al.: A prospective three-year follow-up study of borderline personality disorder patients. *Acta Psychiatr Scand* 1995, 92:327–335.

23. Caccaro EF, Siever LJ, Klar H, et al.: Serotonergic studies in patients with affective and personality disorders: correlates with suicidal and impulsive aggressive behavior. *Arch Gen Psychiatry* 1989, 46:587–599.

24. Siever LJ, Trestman RL: The serotonin system and aggressive personality disorders. *Int Clin Psychopharmacol* 1993, 2(suppl):33–39.

25. Salzman C, Wolfson AN, Schatzberg A, et al.: Effect of fluoxetine on anger in symptomatic volunteers with borderline personality disorder. *J Clin Psychopharmacol* 1995, 15:23–29.

26. Links PS, Steiner M: Psychopharmacologic management of patients with borderline personality disorder. *Can J Psychiatry* 1988, 33:355–359.

27. Parsons B, Quitkin FM, McGrath PJ, et al.: Phenelzine, imipramine, and placebo in borderline patients meeting criteria for atypical depression. *Psychopharmacol Bull* 1989, 25:524–534.

28. Soloff PH, Cornelius J, George A, et al.: Efficacy of phenelzine and haloperidol in borderline personality disorder. *Arch Gen Psychiatry* 1993, 50:377–385.

29. Kalus O, Siever LJ, Coccaro EF, et al.: Dopaminergic dysfunction in schizotypal personality disorder [abstract]. *Biol Psychiatry* 1990, 27:166–167.

30. Brinkley JR, Beitman BD, Friedel RO: Low-dose neuroleptic regimens in the treatment of borderline patients. *Arch Gen Psychiatry* 1979, 36:319–326.

31. Teicher MH, Glod CA, Aaronson ST, et al.: Open assessment of the safety and efficacy of thioridazine in the treatment of patients with borderline personality disorder. *Psychopharmacol Bull* 1989, 25:535–549.

32. Soloff PH, George A, Nathan RS, et al: Amitriptyline vs haloperidol in borderlines: final outcomes and predictors of response. *J Clin Psychopharmacol* 1989, 9:238–246.

33. Cowdry RW, Pickar D, Davies R: Symptoms and EEG findings in the borderline syndrome. *Int J Psychiatry Med* 1985–1986, 15:201–211.

34. Cowdry RW, Gardner DL: Pharmacotherapy of borderline personality disorder: alprazolam, carbamezapine, trifluoperazine, and tranylcypromine. *Arch Gen Psychiatry* 1988, 45:111–119.

35. Stein DJ, Simeon D, Frenkel M, et al.: An open trial of valproate in borderline personality disorder. *J Clin Psychiatry* 1995, 56:506–510.

36. Soloff PH: Is there any drug treatment of choice for the borderline patient? *Acta Psychiatr Scand* 1994, 89(suppl):50–55.

37. Kernberg OF, Bernstein E, Coyne L, et al.: *Psychotherapy and Borderline Patients*. New York: Basic Books; 1989.

38. Kernberg OF, Bernstein E, Coyne L, et al.: Psychotherapy and psychoanalysis: final report of the Menninger Foundation's Psychotherapy Research Project. *Bull Med Menin Clin* 1973, 36:1–275.

39. Linehan MM: *Cognitive-Behavioral Treatment of Borderline Personality Disorder*. New York: The Guilford Press; 1993.

40. Linehan MM: *Skills Training Manual for Treating Borderline Personality Disorder*. New York: The Guilford Press; 1993

41. Linehan MM, Armstrong HE, Suarez A, et al.: Cognitive-behavioral treatment of chronically parasuicidal borderline patients. *Arch Gen Psychiatry* 1991, 48:1060–1064.

42. Linehan MM, Tutek DA, Heard HL, et al.: Interpersonal outcome of cognitive behavioral treatment for chronically suicidal borderline patients. *Am J Psychiatry* 1994, 151:1771–1776.

43. Barley WD, Buie SE, Peterson EW, *et al.*: Development of an inpatient cognitive-behavioral program for borderline personality disorder. *J Pers Disord* 1993, 7:232–240.

44. Munroe-Blum H, Marziali E: A controlled trial of short-term group treatment for borderline personality disorder. *J Pers Disord* 1995, 9:190–198.

45. Marziali E, Monroe-Blum H: An interpersonal approach to group psychotherapy with borderline personality disorder. *J Pers Disord* 1995, 9:179–189.

46. Gunderson JG, Sabo AN: The phenomenological and conceptual interface between borderline personality disorder and PTSD. *Am J Psychiatry* 1993, 150:19–27.

47. Swartz M, Blazer D, George L, Winfield, I: Estimating the prevalence of borderline personality disorder in the community. *Disorders* 1990, 4:257–272.

48. Herman JL, Perry JC, van der Kolk BA: Childhood trauma in borderline personality disorder. *Am J Psychiatry* 1989, 146:490–495.

49. Paris J, Zweig-Frank H: A critical review of the role of childhood sexual abuse in the etiology of borderline personality disorder. *Can J Psychiatry* 1992, 37:125–128.

50. Herman JL: *Trauma and Recovery*. New York: Basic Books; 1992.

51. Brodsky BS, Cloitre M, Dulit RA: Relationship of dissociation to self-mutilation and childhood abuse in borderline personality disorder. *Am J Psychiatry* 1995, 152:1788–1792.

52. Wagner AW, Linehan MM: Relationship between childhood sexual abuse and topography of parasuicide among women with borderline personality disorder. *J Pers Disord* 1994, 8:1–9.

53. Shea MT: Standardized approaches to indivdiual psychotherapy of patients with borderline personality disorder. *Hosp Community Psychiatry* 1991, 42:1034–1037.

Treatment of Obsessive-Compulsive Disorder in Adults

Roberto A. Dominguez

Obsessive-compulsive disorder (OCD) is typically a continuous and secretive disorder. Family, friends, and sometimes even the patient's spouse do not suspect the impairment and distress associated with these symptoms. Specific medications and psychosocial interventions are helpful for its treatment. The use of antidepressants and behavioral therapy are complementary. Serotonin reuptake inhibitors are preferentially effective in the treatment of OCD. Because the patient's response to pharmacologic treatment is independent of their baseline degree of depression, these medications can truly be considered "antiobsessive" drugs. Unfortunately, only 40% to 60% of patients will respond, at least partially, to pharmacologic treatment. If a favorable response to treatment is realized, long-term maintenance therapy is usually indicated.

Before 1985 there were few reports in the United States psychiatric literature regarding pharmacologic treatment of obsessive-compulsive disorder (OCD). The development and introduction of clomipramine (Anafranil; Ciba-Geigy Co., Summit, NJ) led to an increased interest in this disorder within the psychiatric community in the United States. There are now large controlled studies demonstrating unmistakable efficacy for some antidepressant agents in combating OCD. Recent epidemiologic studies show that this disorder, once considered rare, is much more prevalent (about 2% lifetime prevalence) [1,2]. Its lifetime prevalence (Table 1), coupled with its potentially serious effect on social, vocational, and even physical functioning, makes recognition of OCD by health care providers extremely important.

Diagnostic Features and Associated Disorders

Obsessive compulsive disorder is classified as an anxiety disorder [3]. This group of psychiatric conditions is characterized by symptoms of anxiety and avoidance. The pivotal symptoms required to make the diagnosis of OCD are obsessions, compulsions, or both (Table 2). Obsessions are defined as recurrent unwanted thoughts, ideas, or impulses. Compulsions are repetitive intentional rituals or behaviors. Unlike most Axis I disorders, the *Diagnostic and Statistical Manual of Mental Disorders*, edn 4 (DSM-IV) does not specify a minimum duration of symptoms for patients to meet the diagnostic criteria for OCD. This is unnecessary, because when most adult patients present for treatment, they have suffered from symptoms for several years. Some patients may suffer from covert compulsions, such as mental checking and counting. Most patients with OCD, perhaps well over 90%, are troubled by both obsessions and compulsions, and typically have multiple obsessions and compulsions.

Table 1. Five-site Lifetime Prevalence Rates from the Epidemiological Catchment Area Study*

Disorder	Lifetime prevalence, %
Anxiety disorders	14.6
Phobias	12.6
Panic	1.6
Obsessive-compulsive	2.5
Affective disorders	8.3
Major depression	4.9
Bipolar disorder	1.3
Other disorders	
Schizophrenia	1.4
Alcohol-related disorders	13.5

Adapted from Regier et al. [2].

Table 2. DSM-IV Criteria for Obsessive-Compulsive Disorder

Requires either obsessions or compulsions
Symptoms must be viewed as excessive and unreasonable
Symptoms must produce marked distress, must be time-consuming, and interfere with social or work functioning
Excludes obsessions and compulsions associated with eating disorders, body dysmorphic disorder, alcohol and substance abuse, trichotillomania, paraphilias, hypochondriasis, major depression, and others

DSM-IV—Diagnostic and Statistical Manual of Mental Disorders, edn 4.

Based on their presenting symptoms, three groups of patients with OCD can be recognized. There are those with a persistent fear of contamination (Table 3). They are usually excessively concerned about incompleteness, and their typical compulsions include washing or cleaning. For others, "doubt" is the primary concern, which gives rise to a large and heterogeneous group of patients referred to as *checkers*. It is common to evaluate patients who report both washing and checking compulsions. Finally, there are those who can be classified as having a *primary obsessive disorder*. These patients, also called *ruminators*, are seemingly free from compulsions. They may have multiple obsessions that usually comprise unwanted aggressive, sexual, somatic, or religious themes.

Of those patients who present for treatment, men are more typically checkers. Common repetitive behaviors in adults within and around the home involve checking electrical appliances, doors and windows, faucets and toilets, and mechanical tools and equipment, including the vehicles in the home. Related behaviors may involve counting (especially money), general ordering and arranging, and concerns with symmetry. An interesting group of checkers are those patients who fear they might have caused an accident while driving. These persons, typically overly concerned with the health and safety of others, will drive around in circles (circumnavigators) [4] and seldom arrive at their destination.

Women are often washers as well as checkers. Sometimes all compulsions revolve strictly around washing or cleaning. Typical areas that are washed repeatedly are the hands and the genitalia. Cleaning concerns may be highly "territorial;" for example, in the home, the kitchen and bathroom may be immaculate, whereas the garage and the yard (the "husband's domain") may be comparatively ignored. Generally, women who suffer from washing compulsions are much more symptomatic, distressed, impaired in their occupational functioning, and they are more likely to report severe depressive symptoms than pure checkers.

In addition, there are other psychiatric disorders, not classified within the realm of anxiety disorders, for which their symptoms include repetitive unwanted thoughts or behaviors. Some investigators consider these OCD variants. These conditions include trichotillomania (excessive hair pulling), body-dysmorphic disorder (excessive concern with an imagined defect in appearance), and scrupulosity (excessive unwanted religiosity). There are even variants of these disorders that can also resemble OCD. For example, quite similar to body-dysmorphic disorder is a condition referred to as *olfactory reference syndrome* [5,6]. A patient with such a disorder may be overly concerned about his or her excessive sweating offending others. There are also similarities between those patients troubled by OCD and others who suffer from disorders such as (compulsive) drinking, smoking, gambling, shopping, fire-setting, paraphilias, onychophagia, and eating disorders. These disorders may be collectively referred by some as *OCD-spectrum disorders* [7•].

There are a several psychiatric disorders that can coexist with OCD [8]. The most frequent of these in adults include major depression, specific and social phobias, and eating and panic disorders. In addition, in some patients it is difficult to separate OCD from a principal diagnosis of obsessive-compulsive personality disorder, a somatoform disorder, or a psychotic disorder including schizophrenia.

It is particularly challenging separating those patients who may suffer from a somatoform disorder, such as hypochondriasis, from those who could be classified as obsessive-compulsive. This is particularly true when one specific somatic symptom or concern dominates the clinical presentation. For example, some patients are overly concerned or believe that they suffer from a terminal illness, such as AIDS (AIDS phobia). Interestingly, these patients may benefit from the same antiobsessive medications now recommended for the more typical patient with OCD [9].

The Neurobiology of Obsessive-Compulsive Disorder

Obsessive-compulsive disorder has been associated with various biologic factors. From a genetic perspective, some studies have reported a much higher rate of OCD in monozygotic, in contrast to dizygotic, twins, or between siblings [10,11]. However, the principal lead linking biologic factors and OCD is provided by pharmacologic response studies.

Elegant work, based principally on neuroimaging and pharmacologic challenge studies, has been published to help explain the pathophysiology of OCD. A model that integrates some of these neuroanatomic and neurophysiologic observations has been proposed [12]. In this model, environmental, visual, and emotional stimuli are first processed by the orbitofrontal cortex. Thereafter, internal brain circuits (in the area of the basal ganglia), linked to these cortical areas by certain neurotransmitters, process and filter this information, allowing an adequate response. Obsessive-compulsive symptoms

Table 3. Common Compulsions
Checking appliances, plumbing, windows and doors, automobiles ("circumnavigators")
Washing and cleaning
Ordering, rearranging, symmetry
Grooming behavior, hoarding
Covert compulsions
Need to tell, repeat, ask, or confess
Counting

result from a dysfunction of this circuit that does not allow the appropriate filtering of irrelevant information. Neuroimaging studies have repeatedly demonstrated imbalances in function of specific cortical areas as well as internal structures in patients with OCD [13•,14]. Furthermore, adequate patient response to pharmacologic and behavioral treatments can reverse these imbalances.

These neuroanatomic and physiologic observations can be partially integrated into the serotonin (5-hydroxytrytamine [5-HT]) hypothesis of OCD [15]. Some cerebrospinal fluid studies indicating changes in 5-hydroxy indoleacetic acid (5-HIAA), a 5-HT metabolite [16], as well as 5-HT platelet activity in patients with OCD [17], support this hypothesis. In addition, pharmacologic challenge studies that assess behavioral and physiologic serotonin-mediated activity, such as response to m-chlorophenylpiperazine (m-CPP), a 5-HT agonist, strengthen the serotonin theory [18,19]. However, it is unlikely that the dysfunction of only one neurotransmitter fully explains the pathophysiology of such a heterogeneous disorder as OCD. The principal support for the serotonin hypothesis of OCD comes from the favorable treatment response to medications that putatively influence central nervous system (CNS) serotonin activity. Notably, less than half of OCD patients treated with medications attain full remission.

Therapeutic Strategies
Behavior therapy
Most mental health professionals view behavior therapy (BT) as the cornerstone in the treatment of OCD [20]. In most patients BT should be the first treatment alternative. The specific strategy employed most successfully in the behavioral treatment of OCD is exposure, coupled with ritual prevention (also known as response prevention). However, for some patients, BT should not be the first or only consideration. For those with concomitant depression (approximately 50% of patients with OCD in our experience), those with very severe symptoms, or those who cannot fully cooperate with BT, pharmacotherapy combined with psychotherapeutic support is a preferred initial strategy. Behavioral and pharmacologic treatments for OCD are both compatible and complementary [21•].

The efficacy of BT, which uses exposure and response prevention, has been reported in numerous case series [22–30]. These case reports 1) refined the techniques, 2) provided initial comparisons of efficacy with other psychosocial interventions, 3) reported on durability of effects, and 4) provided comparisons of the efficacy of BT (exposure and response prevention) with pharmacologic treatment. A report summarizing the worldwide experience with exposure and response prevention for OCD showed that 51% of patients treated showed a 70% improvement in symptoms [20]. In addition, another 39% of these patients had reductions of symptoms between 30% and 69%.

Since the introduction of the Yale-Brown Obsessive-Compulsive Scale (Y-BOCS) [31], controlled studies using BT have been published employing this instrument as an outcome measure. A recent report using both individual and group BT without concomitant medication showed a reduction of OCD symptoms that was greater than most published pharmacologic trials (Table 4) [32]. Another large National Institute of Mental Health (NIMH)-sponsored two-site, randomized, controlled trial now underway is comparing pharmacotherapy with BT and with a combination of the two. A preliminary report of partial results suggests that BT is superior to pharmacotherapy for OCD (Table 4) [Foa, Paper presented at the National Conference of the Anxiety Disorders of America, Santa Monica, CA, 1994].

The principle behind the use of exposure plus ritual prevention seems simple, and the apparent ability of the patient to tackle these tasks seems easy. However, BT for OCD is neither simple nor easy. The basic theory that drives this therapeutic model is that most patients' obsessions are "anxiogenic" (increase anxiety), whereas the subsequent rituals generally serve an "anxiolytic" (anxiety-reducing) effect. Unfortunately, the anxiolytic effect from these rituals or compulsions is typically short-lived and incomplete. Thus, the obsessions quickly return and the behaviors necessary to quench these must be repeated. An endless vicious cycle is created. The patient feels trapped and overwhelmed.

After the diagnosis is confirmed, one strategy in beginning BT for OCD is to first perform a thorough behavioral analysis [33]. The patient is asked to carefully record their obsessive thoughts and compulsive behaviors over a period of several days. The patient is also encouraged to rank these in the order of their severity. Once the precise obsessions and rituals identified, an effort is made between the patient and therapist to carefully confirm their degree of distress. Typically, both patient and therapist try to agree on a set of obsessions and compulsions that fit somewhere in the middle of this severity and

Table 4. Results from Controlled Studies of Behavior Therapy Showing Improvement using the Yale-Brown Obsessive-Compulsive Scale for Obsessive-Compulsive Disorder

Investigator	Group	Patients, n	Baseline, Y-BOCS	Endpoint, Y-BOCS
Fals-Stewart et al. [32]	Wait-list	32	20	21
	Individual behavior therapy	31	20	13
	Group behavior therapy	30	22	12
Foa*	Placebo	12	24	23
	Clomipramine	15	26	19
	Individual behavior therapy	10	25	11
	Clomipramine + individual behavior therapy	10	26	10

*Paper presented at the National Conference of the Anxiety Disorders of America, Santa Monica, CA, 1994.
Y-BOCS—Yale-Brown Obsessive-Compulsive Scale.

distress hierarchy. Thereafter, the focus is to design strategies wherein the patient consciously resists performing the compulsions when confronted with the obsessions.

After a basic understanding of the exposure and ritual-prevention strategy, and with much patience and time, the motivated patient will be able to slowly move toward those thoughts and behaviors that are most distressing. As therapy progresses, exposure and ritual prevention lead to habituation. The need to perform the compulsions subsides, and because the thoughts typically drive the rituals, these begin to decrease as well.

During the treatment period, many fears, distractions, and stressors can sabotage the success of BT. However, with the help of an experienced therapist, motivated patients should experience marked relief from their symptoms over a period of a few weeks. After the initial phase of treatment is completed, occasional "booster" sessions may be indicated. The principal value of BT, when successful, is its durability. Just as the use of relaxation techniques for the treatment of other anxiety disorders, the principles and strategies learned through BT serve to teach the patient to combat symptoms when they worsen because of stress.

Pharmacotherapy

Initial considerations

The Y-BOCS [31] has become the primary outcome measure for controlled pharmacotherapy trials. The Y-BOCS allows comparative efficacy trials to dissect effective treatments from placebo. The first section of the Y-BOCS provides a thorough inventory of current obsessions and compulsions. The scale is helpful in clinical practice as well since such a measure provides justification for initial and subsequent treatment decisions (Table 5).

Clomipramine is the most widely studied and clinically accepted pharmacologic treatment for OCD [34–38]. Clomipramine is a tertiary amine tricyclic agent, similar in structure to imipramine, and it is a more potent 5-HT-reuptake blocker than imipramine or any other tricyclic antidepressant [39]. However, clomipramine is not a selective serotonin reuptake inhibitor (SSRI) because its principal metabolite, desmethyl-clomipramine, potently inhibits the reuptake of norepinephrine.

Controlled trials with clomipramine reveal a decisive improvement in approximately 50% to 60% of patients. In sharp contrast, the placebo response rate in the large multicenter study that established the safety and efficacy of clomipramine in the United States was less than 10% [40]. However, few patients experience a complete

Table 5. Summary of Scoring of the Yale-Brown Obsessive-Compulsive Scale

Obsessions	Compulsions	Each item scored 0–4
Time occupied	Time occupied	0 = not present
Interference	Interference	1 = mild
Distress	Distress	2 = moderate
Resistance	Resistance	3 = severe
Degree of control	Degree of control	4 = extreme
		Maximum total score = 40

remission of symptoms with pharmacotherapy alone, making concomitant BT an important early consideration. Furthermore, clomipramine is often associated with anticholinergic, sedative, sexual dysfunction, and other side effects. A subsequent analysis of the 10-week clomipramine multicenter study reveals some interesting relationships between early typical side effects and ultimate response to clomipramine [41]. Although improvement may occur at smaller doses for some patients, our experience is that the optimal therapeutic dose of clomipramine in adult outpatients with OCD lies between 150 and 250 mg/day.

Of additional interest is that fluoxetine (Prozac; Eli Lilly Co., Indianapolis, IN), an SSRI, is also clearly effective for OCD [34,42••]. Our clinical experience suggests that approximately 25% of patients prescribed clomipramine discontinue treatment prematurely because of side effects. Fluoxetin, initially prescribed at 20 mg/day followed by gradual subsequent increases depending on response, results in fewer than 10% of patients discontinuing this drug because of its side effects. No definitive double-blind studies comparing the efficacy of fluoxetine with that of clomipramine in OCD are available, although some investigators suggest that clomipramine may be more effective than fluoxetine for OCD [35,43••]. Based on our clinical experience, we believe that fluoxetine and clomipramine are of comparable efficacy in the treatment of checkers; clomipramine may be preferred in the treatment of washers.

The design of the fluoxetine study established the model employed by subsequent fixed-dose pharmacologic trials in OCD [42••] (Fig. 1). This was a double-blind, randomized, 13-week acute phase trial, preceded by a 1-week placebo run-in period. There were four treatment cells, as noted in Figure 1. The Y-BOCS [31] was used as the principal outcome measure. Study completers who responded entered a 6-month extension phase at the acute phase dose, whereas nonresponders could be treated with open-label fluoxetine (20 to 80 mg/day).

A total of 355 patients who met DSM-IIIR criteria for OCD were randomized to the four-cell trial [42••]. There were approximately 90 subjects in each treatment group or cell (Table 6). Baseline Y-BOCS scores were generally lower than for the clomipramine trial; nevertheless, most patients were ranked as markedly ill by the Clinical Global Impressions (CGI) severity rating. Study subjects could have concomitant depressive symptoms as long as a mood disorder was not the primary diagnosis.

Endpoint analysis revealed that all three active treatment groups were superior to placebo for all endpoint outcome measures, including the HAM-D (Hamilton Depression Rating Scale) results (all comparisons $P<0.01$). For both the Y-BOCS and CGI there was an apparent dose-response relationship, but none of these comparisons reached statistical significance. From a most conservative definition of response (a 35% or greater decrease in total Y-BOCS score from baseline), 8.5% of evaluable subjects (those completing at least 7 weeks of treatment) responded to placebo, whereas between 32% and 35% of subjects assigned to active treatment were considered responders (Table 7). The retention rate for study subjects was excellent, since 79.2% of those randomized completed the trial. There was a clear relationship between assigned dose and the percentage of subjects who discontinued treatment prematurely because of side effects (Table 8). This finding highlights the need for the gradual escalation of the dose of fluoxetine in OCD. For this trial, as with studies of fluoxetine in depression, steady-state plasma levels of fluoxetine or its metabolite norfluoxetine were not related to efficacy [44].

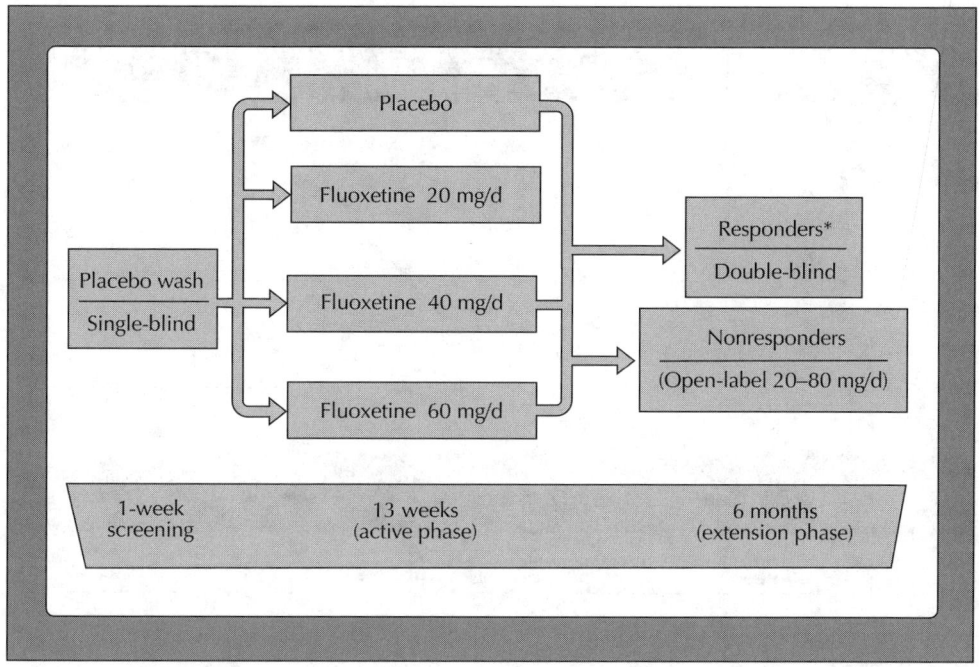

Figure 1. Study design for fixed-dose study of fluoxetine in obsessive-compulsive disorder. *≥25% Reduction in the Yale-Brown Obsessive-Compulsive Scale from baseline and at least "much improved" in the Clinical Global Impressions scale.

Depressive symptoms significantly improved for each group who received fluoxetine compared with the group who received placebo. Of note, the concomitant depressive symptoms accompanying OCD responded optimally to 20 and 40 mg/day of fluoxetine, but concomitant depressive symptoms of OCD patients did not improve with placebo.

Other SSRIs also appear effective for OCD. Fluvoxamine (Luvox; Solvay Pharmaceuticals, Marietta, GA), an effective antidepressant, has efficacy for OCD that may be comparable with that of clomipramine and fluoxetine [45,46,47•]. Fluvoxamine's side effect profile is similar to other SSRIs. Nausea, gastrointestinal distress, tremor, restlessness, and sexual dysfunction are possible. Our impression is that fluvoxamine is slightly more sedative than other SSRIs. Unlike fluoxetine, fluvoxamine is not a strong inhibitor, nor does it significantly depend on the cytochrome P-450-IID6 hepatic enzyme system for its metabolism. However, fluvoxamine inhibits the activity of the IA2, IIC9, and the IIIA4 isoenzymes, leading to other pharmacokinetic interactions [48]. Of importance to psychiatrists is that the coadministration of fluvoxamine and a triazolobenzodiazepine, such as alprazolam, for which metabolism depends on the IIIA4 isoenzyme, can significantly increase the benzodiazepine's serum levels. Fluvoxamine has a half-life of approximately 24 hours and has no major active metabolites. Elimination half-life, and the production of clinically significant active metabolites [49•], are two of the most salient pharmacokinetic differences among the SSRIs (Table 9).

Clomipramine, fluoxetine, and fluvoxamine should now be considered as first-line antiobsessive drugs [49•]. There are also controlled studies that have demonstrated

Table 6. Baseline Scores by Treatment Group in Fixed-dose Fluoxetine Obsessive-Compulsive Disorder Study*

Measure	Placebo (n = 89)	20 mg (n = 87)	40 mg (n = 89)	60 mg (n = 90)
Y-BOCS (total)	24.3	23.6	23.5	24.4
HAM-D (17-item)	9.0	9.2	9.6	9.4
CGI (severity)	5.0	5.0	5.1	5.1
CPRS	10.7	11.2	11.3	11.2

*Data from Tollefson et al. [42••].
CGI—Clinical Global Impressions; CPRS—Comprehensive Psychopathological Rating Scale;
HAM-D—Hamilton Depression Rating Scale; Y-BOCS—Yale-Brown Obsessive-Compulsive Scale.

Table 7. Summary of Response Rates (Endpoint Analysis) in Fixed-dose Fluoxetine Study*

Treatment group	n	Improved, %†	P value vs placebo
Placebo	82	8.5	
Fluoxetine 20 mg	78	32.1	< 0.001
Fluoxetine 40 mg	74	32.4	< 0.001
Fluoxetine 60 mg	77	35.1	< 0.001

*Data from Tollefson et al. [42••].
† > 35% Reduction from baseline on the Yale-Brown Obsessive-Compulsive Scale.

some efficacy for sertraline in OCD [50–53]. However, the sertraline studies suffered from an unexpectedly high placebo-response rate [51]. This seriously blunted the net effect of sertraline (as measured by either the Y-BOCS or CGI) in the treatment of OCD.

Comparisons between the fixed-dose study of sertraline [51] and fluoxetine [42••] are possible, although difficult. Study design was surprisingly similar. A total of 325 patients entered the double-blind acute phase of the 12-week sertraline trial. Study subjects were randomized to receive sertraline in doses of 50, 100, or 200 mg/day, or placebo. The sertraline trial failed to report endpoint analysis of the Y-BOCS for each treatment group versus placebo, making direct comparisons with the fluoxetine results impossible. Furthermore, the sertraline results also failed to report response rates for each treatment group based on a decrease in Y-BOCS scores. With the CGI as a response measure, the pooled sertraline group showed a 38.9% response rate, whereas the placebo response was 30%.

Preliminary results from a fixed-dose study of paroxetine also suggest efficacy [Smith-Kline Beecham, Unpublished data]. The design of this study was very similar to the design of the fluoxetine fixed-dose trial. A total of 348 patients with OCD were randomized into an active treatment period of 12 weeks. Patients received paroxetine in fixed doses of 20, 40, or 60 mg/day, or placebo. Results show that, in contrast with fluoxetine, paroxetine's efficacy in OCD is perhaps limited to higher doses (40 or 60 mg/day). It is notable that a 60 mg/day dose exceeds the maximum recommended

Table 8. Premature Discontinuations in the Fixed-dose Fluoxetine Study*†

Reason for discontinuation	Premature discontinuations, %			
	Placebo	Fluoxetine 20 mg	Fluoxetine 40 mg	Fluoxetine 60 mg
Adverse events	2	3	13	19
Lack of efficacy	8	0	0	0
Lost to follow-up	2	3	1	1
Protocol violation	0	2	3	1
Nontreatment-related reasons	2	7	8	6

*Data from Tollefson et al. [42••].
†A total of 355 patients were randomized to the "active" phase; 87.6% completed at least 7 weeks of treatment; and 79.2% completed all 13 weeks.

Table 9. Half-life and Metabolites of SSRIs Marketed in United States

SSRI	Half-life	Active metabolite	Clinical significance
Fluoxetine	3–8 d	Yes	yes
Fluvoxamine	15 h	No	—
Sertraline	26 h	Yes (weak)	±
Paroxetine	17 h	No	—

SSRI—selective serotonin reuptake inhibitor.

for the treatment of depression. Abrupt discontinuation of high doses of paroxetine could result in withdrawal symptoms [54]. Endpoint analysis of net (drug-placebo) results show that paroxetine's efficacy at any dose is numerically inferior to that of fluoxetine. Although endpoint results suggest a dose-response relationship for paroxetine with the Y-BOCS, no dose-response relationship emerged with the CGI. Paroxetine's Food and Drug Administration–approved labeling has now been expanded to include OCD.

Only one large, double-blind, placebo-controlled study comparing an SSRI with clomipramine for OCD has been published [55•]. At total of 406 patients were randomized to flexible doses of paroxetine, clomipramine, or placebo for a period of 12 weeks. Results revealed that both active drugs were statistically superior to placebo and similar in efficacy. The response rates, based on a 25% decrease of Y-BOS scores, were 55.1% and 55.3% for paroxetine and clomipramine, respectively. However, this trial also suffered from an unexpectedly high and confounding placebo response rate. The percentage of placebo patients considered "responders" by the Y-BOS scale was 35.4%, and the percentage of those considered "improved" by the CGI scale was 53.5%. Adverse experiences generally favored paroxetine over clomipramine.

It is possible to make some rough comparisons of treatment results between the fixed-dose studies of fluoxetine, sertraline, and paroxetine for OCD. A limiting factor is that there are no published endpoint results for each sertraline treatment group. When using the decrease in the Y-BOCS from baseline, it appears that fluoxetine is at least numerically superior to the other two drugs. Other comparisons are also possible. In contrast with most 6- to 8-week–controlled depression studies, a surprisingly high number of patients completed the trials (Table 10). In addition, the percentage of patients who discontinued treatment prematurely owing to adverse events is surprisingly similar for each trial. However, for the fluoxetine trial, there is a strong relationship between the dose and the percentage of patients who discontinued treatment because of adverse events. Perhaps because higher doses of SSRIs may be prescribed for OCD than for depression, clinicians should be aware that some rare events, such as spontaneous seizures, manic and hypomanic symptoms, and elevations in liver function test values, may be more frequent with higher doses of these drugs.

Dose-response relationships for the SSRIs in the treatment of OCD may be different from those for depression. When prescribed for depression, the SSRIs appear to have a flat dose-response curve [56]. For fluoxetine and paroxetine at 20 mg/day, and perhaps also for sertraline at 50 mg/day, fixed-dose studies reveal little additional benefit from increasing the initial dose. Thus, for the treatment of depression, the initial recommended dose of fluoxetine and paroxetine (20 mg/day) may be the optimal dose. With perhaps sertraline being the only exception, it appears that for OCD, an increase in the dose beyond the initial dose recommended for depression may be necessary for optimal response. For both fluoxetine and paroxetine, a gradual increase in the daily dose to 60 mg may prove more beneficial than staying at 20 mg/day. However, the controlled trials

Table 10. Comparison of Fixed-dose Obsessive-Compulsive Disorder Studies With Selective Serotonin Reuptake Inhibitors*

Drug	Discontinuations from adverse events, %	Discontinuations from lack of efficacy, %
Fluoxetine[†]		
Low dose (20 mg/d)	3	0
Medium dose (40 mg/d)	12	0
High dose (60 mg/d)	19	0
Total	11	0
Sertraline[‡]		
Low dose (50 mg/d)	8	6
Medium dose (100 mg/d)	14	9
High dose (200 mg/d)	8	9
Total	10	8
Paroxetine[§]		
Low dose (20 mg/d)	11	2
Medium dose (40 mg/d)	10	6
High dose (60 mg/d)	16	1
Total	13	2

*Data from Tollefson et al. [42••], Griest et al. [51], and Smith-Kline Beecham, Unpublished data.
[†]Percent completing study, 79.2.
[‡]Percent completing study, 76.2.
[§]Percent completing study, 77.6.

generally demonstrate only a numerical advantage, and not a statistical difference [42••, Smith-Kline Beecham, Unpublished data), favoring the higher doses. Interestingly, for fluoxetine, there may be little additional benefit from escalating the dose beyond 60 mg/day [57]. No large fixed-dose studies with fluvoxamine have been published, but our limited clinical experience suggests that it also appears to have an ascending dose-response curve.

Can presenting symptoms predict a favorable response to pharmacotherapy in OCD? Our group has learned that a greater percentage of checkers will respond compared with washers. It is also our experience that another surprising predictor of good response is the patient's ability to relate the onset of symptoms to a specific stressor. Finally, and not surprisingly, we have learned that longer duration of symptoms is a predictor of poor response to pharmacotherapy. A recently published report is in agreement with some of our unpublished impressions [58].

Early options for the treatment-resistant patient

For pharmacotherapy alone, there seems to be little difference between clomipramine and an SSRI as the initial treatment for OCD. For some patients, clomipramine may be more effective [35,43••,59,60], but it is not tolerated as well. Thus, the pivotal issue initially is whether the initial medication is prescribed at an appropriate dosage and for a sufficient duration. At least 10 weeks of treatment, at a therapeutic dose, is recommended before considering a medication trial a failure. For clomipramine, the minimum dosage that a patient should receive before moving to other alternatives is 150 mg/day. However, if tolerated, escalating the dosage to 250 mg/day before abandoning this medication is preferred. Similar dosing parameters apply to fluvoxamine. In patients in whom there is unsatisfactory response, fluoxetine should also be increased to 60 mg/day before moving on to other alternatives (Table 11). Concommitant behavior therapy must also be an early consideration.

What is the next step if the initial medication fails? Recommendations vary. Some endorse immediately combining clomipramine and an SSRI [61]. In our opinion, because of the potential metabolic drug interactions, we do not prefer this alternative [62]. Others recommend augmentation strategies if a partial response was achieved, or switching from an SSRI to clomipramine or vice versa if no response was apparent [35,63]. Our strategy has been to switch drug groups when an initial response is insufficient (Table 12). A detailed rational treatment algorithm for OCD has been published [64]. However, as its author observes, "treating OCD with medication requires a blend of science and art."

Table 11. Minimum Daily Dose Required to Consider a Patient with Obsessive-Compulsive Disorder a Treatment Failure

Clomipramine: 250 mg/d
Fluoxetine: 60 mg/d
Fluvoxamine: 300 mg/d
Paroxetine: 60 mg/d
Sertraline: 200 mg/d

There are differences in the pharmacologic approach to OCD and the pharmacologic approach to depression (Table 13). Only those antidepressants that are potent serotonin reuptake blockers seem helpful. The pharmacologic response is independent from the patient's baseline depressive symptoms. Thus, these medications can truly be considered antiobsessive drugs. Treatment should be continued for a minimum of 10 to 12 weeks before it is abandoned, and generally higher doses are required. Only 40% to 60% of patients respond to pharmacotherapy alone, and the magnitude of their response is only partial. Upon discontinuation of treatment, a larger number of patients will relapse, and long-term therapy is typically indicated.

Other monotherapies and early augmentation strategies

Lithium augmentation is often decisively helpful for treatment-resistent depression. Yet, perhaps with the exception of low-dose neuroleptic therapy, no specific pharmacotherapeutic combination has been found consistently effective in treatment-resistant OCD [49•]. Reports using lithium, buspirone, clonazepam, and others have been generally

---

Table 12. Strategies to use After an Initial Drug Treatment Failure in Obsessive-Compulsive Disorder

Sufficient dose and duration?
Consider behavior therapy
Switch to another antiobsessive drug
Add a neuroleptic?
   Tourette's spectrum OCD
   Schizotypal personality?
Possible augmentation strategies:
   Lithium   Clonazepam
   Buspirone   Tryptophan
   Fenfluramine Others
Consider an antiobsessive drug combination (clomipramine + SSRI), or an MAOI
Electroconvulsive therapy?
Psychosurgery

MAOI—monoamine oxidase inhibitor; OCD—obsessive-compulsive disorder; SSRI—selective serotonin reuptake inhibitor.

Table 13. Contrasting the Use of Antidepressants for Obsessive-Compulsive Disorder or Depression*

Serotonin reuptake inhibitors (clomipramine, fluoxetine, fluvoxamine) are preferentially effective for OCD
Initial duration of treatment longer with OCD (10–12 wks) than depression (4–6 wks)
Higher doses needed for OCD?
Percentage of responders lower with OCD (40%–60%) than with depression (70%–80%)
Magnitude of response lower with OCD, more complete with depression
Relapse rate higher with OCD after discontinuation of pharmacologic treatment

Adapted from Goodman WK, Personal communication.
OCD—obsessive-compulsive disorder.

disappointing [65–71] (Table 14). A complex double-blind crossover trial with clonazepam found this drug helpful for OCD using mean daily doses of 6.85 mg [70]. However, diphenhydramine, included to serve as the study's active placebo, was also effective. For enhancement, most reports have used an SSRI as the anchor antiobsessive drug. There is no reason to believe that the results would be different with clomipramine.

A group of investigators have advanced the concept of *Tourette's spectrum OCD* [72,73]. Often children troubled with OCD, and occasionally adults, suffer from or have a history of chronic multiple tics or clear Tourette's syndrome. In addition, close relatives may have a history of tics or Tourette's. In patients in whom the Tourette's spectrum coexists with a primary diagnosis of OCD, the combination of high-potency neuroleptics and a primary antiobsessive drug appears extremely effective [72]. Haloperidol and pimozide have been the most commonly used neuroleptics, usually prescribed at comparatively low doses. Earlier reports from the same group also suggested the same strategy for OCD patients with schizotypal features.

Other psychotropics that have been reported as effective in either monotherapy or as enhancement strategies for OCD include lithium, buspirone, and clonazepam. Our group has often tried lithium in combination with a primary antiobsessive drug for treatment-

Table 14. Summary of Controlled Studies of Lithium, Buspirone, and Neuroleptic Augmentation of Patients with Obsessive-Compulsive Disorder

Investigator	Drug	Patients, *n*	Duration of treatment, *wks*	Outcome
McDougle *et al.* [66]				
	FLV + lithium for 2 wks	11	2	18% response
	FLV + placebo for 2 wks	9	2	No response
	FLV + lithium for 4 wks	5	4	No response
	FLV + placebo for 4 wks	5	4	No response
Pigott *et al.* [65]				
	CIMI + T3 + lithium	16	4	No response
	CIMI + lithium			No response
Pigott *et al.* [67]				
	CIMI + buspirone	14	10	Four patients responded
McDougle *et al.* [68]				
	FLV + buspirone	19	6	No response
	FLV + placebo	14	6	No response
Grady *et al.* [69]				
	FLX + buspirone	13	4	One patient responded
	FLX + placebo			No response
McDougle *et al.* [72]				
	FLV + HDL	17 (8 tics)	4	65% response (all with tics responded)
	FLV + placebo	17 (7 tics)	4	No response

CIMI—clomipramine; FLV—fluvoxamine; FLX—fluoxetine; HDL—haloperidol; T3—triiodothyronine.

resistant patients. Although an occasional patient responds favorably to the combination, it is our experience that this strategy is not consistently helpful. However, we continue to believe that it is often worth a trial. Recent small controlled studies reveal a similar experience by other groups [65,66].

We have not found buspirone or clonazepam helpful for the core symptoms of OCD, either as monotherapies or in combination. A recent controlled trial with buspirone supports our impressions [68]. Buspirone may be helpful when residual anxiety symptoms remain after the core symptoms improve from a primary antiobsessive drug. We have often prescribed clonazepam, as well as other benzodiazepines, in combination with antiobsessive drugs. This is a reasonably safe augmentation strategy the value of which can be assessed within a few days after its initiation. We have repeatedly tried clonazepam for periods longer than 4 weeks in doses exceeding 4 mg/day. Although it can be very helpful in combating residual generalized anxiety symptoms, it does not appear useful for the core OCD symptoms.

Other pharmacologic alternatives

After some of these combinations have been explored, most other choices in the pharmacotherapy of OCD are based on case reports. Perhaps the only exception is the use of a monoamine oxidase inhibitor (MAOI). Case reports dating back as far as 1959 [74–76], as well as a more recent controlled study [77], suggest that the efficacy of an MAOI in OCD is comparable with that of clomipramine. However, this controlled European trial failed to use standard rating instruments. Thus, the efficacy of an MAOI for OCD after more common alternatives have been tried remains speculative.

Other options include trazodone and perhaps its cousin nefazodone. Given some neuropharmacologic observations, using a specific 5-HT-2 antagonist may be attractive. However, neither of these drugs has been effective for OCD [78, Bristol-Myers Squibb Co., Personal communication]. Exploring different mechanisms, fenfluramine, clonidine, and cyproterone acetate (not available in the United States) have also been reported effective in small case series [79–81]. In addition, a small controlled crossover study of inositol, a second messenger presursor, showed it was also helpful [82]. Other options, reported to be at least modestly effective, include tryptophan [83–85], which is no longer available in the United States, and stimulants such as methylphenidate [86]. If the serotonin theory is at least partially correct [15], stimulants should worsen OCD. Some clinicians, sensing common features between attention deficit disorder and OCD, have tried stimulants with occasional success. In the handful of patients for whom our group has tried methylphenidate for OCD, they have been generally intolerant to relatively small doses, and core obsessive-compulsive symptoms have worsened.

Other medications may be effective in treatment-refractory OCD. Several case reports [87–89] and a case series [90] with venlafaxine showed favorable effects for this drug. However, controlled studies are lacking. There is also a positive case report with carbamazepine [91]. Some investigators have recently begun to use atypical neuroleptics, such as clozapine and risperidone. Two separate reports of open trials with clozapine suggest little, if any, therapeutic benefit [92,93]. Others report worsening of OCD symptoms with clozapine. Reports with risperidone, as either monotherapy or as an adjunct, have not been consistently favorable [94–99], but a recent larger case series showed a > 50% response rate in treatment-resistant patients [100]. We have little experience with these strategies. Serial intravenous clomipramine infusions [101] appear safe and effective [102,103], and although the experience in the United States has been limited, the results have been promising [104,105]. However, some report a paradoxical worsening of symptoms for intravenous comipramine in contrast to oral therapy [106].

A final option is the combination of an SSRI, such as fluoxetine, with clomipramine [51,107,108]. This option must be approached with great caution because even low doses of fluoxetine will markedly inhibit the metabolism of tricyclic antidepressants, resulting in potentially toxic serum levels [62]. Our group has followed this approach with several patients. We have failed to detect any additional benefits from this disputable combination. If treatment with a combination of clomipramine and an SSRI seems indicated, fluvoxamine, which is neither a substrate nor an inhibitor of the enzyme system that metabolizes tricyclics, may be a better alternative [109].

Continuation and maintenance therapy

There is little guidance from the literature regarding continuation and maintenance phase therapy for OCD. Some controlled studies and a wealth of clinical experience show that the premature discontinuation of an effective medication will often result in a rapid relapse, usually within 6 to 8 weeks [57,110–112,113•,114,115]. How long should treatment continue after an initial response? At least 1 year, and preferably 2, seem reasonable targets. Thereafter, therapy could be gradually interrupted to assess its continued beneficial effects. If the patient has been managed with pharmacotherapy alone, considering BT during the continuation phase of treatment would be timely. This would capitalize on the enduring effects of this treatment (Table 15).

Interestingly, it has been our observation that when some patients relapse after the medication is interrupted, it may take them longer to respond favorably to the same medication when started. However, so far all patients for whom we have interrupted treatment have responded once more. For some patients facing maintenance therapy we have tried to reach the lowest therapeutic dose. For a few of these as little as 60 mg of fluoxetine a week seems clearly beneficial, whereas discontinuing the drug altogether often results in a relapse [34]. Other investigators have also reported that after an adequate response to clomipramine or fluvoxamine, a reduction in dosage is possible for maintenance purposes [116]. A double-blind continuation study monitored 30 OCD patients who had benefitted from at least 10 weeks of acute treatment over a period of 102 days [117]. Patients were randomly assigned to three different magnitudes of dose reduction, from no reduction to a decrease of 60% to 66% of the original dose. There were no significant differences in worsening of symptoms across the different dose reduction groups.

Table 15. Guidelines for Discontinuing Pharmacologic Treatment for Obsessive-Compulsive Disorder After an Initial Response

Consider continuation treatment for *at least* 1 year
Gradually taper dose of serotonin uptake blocker with a relatively short half-life
After totally discontinuing treatment, follow the patient closely for the first 8 to 10 weeks
Consider behavior therapy

Electroconvulsive therapy, neurosurgery, and hospitalization

For the treatment-refractory OCD patient, electroconvulsive therapy (ECT) does not seem predictably beneficial. It is the experience of many clinicians that ECT will improve the concomitant depressive symptoms [118]. However, ECT has not been reported consistently useful in combating the core obsessive-compulsive symptoms.

Another factor in choosing ECT is that these patients will often need hospitalization. It is our experience that OCD patients have extreme difficulty adjusting to the milieu of a heterogenous inpatient psychiatric unit. In some specialized inpatient settings, where intensive behavior therapy is provided, severely ill OCD patients can respond more favorably. In most other cases where hospitalization is considered, this decision is often driven by secondary symptoms or complications. OCD patients with concomitant depression or suicidal thoughts will need to enter a protected environment. In addition, occasionally patients have such a fear of contamination that they neglect their nutrition and need to be hospitalized. Otherwise, even the most severely ill OCD patients can be managed as outpatients.

Various surgical strategies have been employed for OCD in the United States and abroad [119]. Anterior capsulotomy, cingulotomy, and limbic leukotomy all aim in some way to interrupt the connections between the basal ganglia and related structures, and the cortex. Understandably, neurosurgery for OCD should be considered an option only after intense inpatient behavior therapy and aggressive pharmacologic strategies have clearly failed. There is some suggestion, primarily from the European literature, that the gamma knife may be an option to older neurosurgical procedures for severe intractable anxiety disorders, including OCD. The experience in the United States with this technique has been limited to a few patients.

Family therapy

The serious social and vocational disability that can affect those who suffer from OCD will also invariably affect their relatives. A health care provider does not ignore the effect on the family of serious psychiatric disorders, such as schizophrenia or chronic depression. It would also be unwise to ignore how family interactions may impinge on treatment outcome for those who suffer from OCD. The constant ruminations and rituals, plus the accompanying depressive symptoms, often lead to a decrease in productivity and independence. This causes much friction within the family, transferring the financial and physical burden of care to relatives, and leading to strained relationships, marital difficulties, and excessive arguing.

It is also common for family members to be drawn into the ritualizing by the obsessive-compulsive patient [120]. Although the relatives often recognize that assisting with the compulsions may not be therapeutic, they often feel helpless and overwhelmed by the constant requests for help from the patient. The family needs guidance on how to cope, as well as how to effectively and consistently respond to the patient's compulsive behaviors.

Family therapy for OCD is a relatively new field. It recognizes that families need much support to deal with those who suffer from this disorder. Communication skills often need to be improved. Referrals to family support groups in the area must be considered. Some investigators have documented the necessity of identifying important family factors and the influence that these factors may have on the patient [121,122]. In addition, recent findings report the favorable outcome that family intervention may have in OCD [123].

Support Groups and the Obsessive-Compulsive Foundation

In most large cities support groups for OCD sufferers began to emerge in the late 1980s. These groups have grown and thrived. They are often led by those recovering from the disorder, or sometimes they are professionally assisted. Family members are usually welcomed. Frequent topics include local treatment resources, improvement of communication skills, and discussion of relevant educational material [124]. Most importantly, these support groups allow members to vent their symptoms as well as their intense frustrations and overwhelming fears. Members begin to recognize OCD as a distinct disorder, with biologic, genetic, psychologic, and social contributions, and begin to deal with the guilt and the impairment caused by their symptoms.

The Obsessive-Compulsive Foundation (OCF) was also established during the late 1980s. Through its newsletter and its national educational programs, it provides a wide spectrum of information of vital interest to its membership. This includes reports discussing treatments and resources, as well as information on related symptoms and disorders. The foundation is very active in the area of consumer advocacy, media relations, national and regional educational programs, and supporting and publicizing research.

We routinely provide our patients with specific information about the OCF and its mission. Also, a recent copy of the OCF newsletter is usually well received by both patient and family. We further encourage our patients to become members of the foundation. We also recommend that our patients and their families read certain medical reports as well as descriptive and self-help books about OCD. Although many excellent self-help books have been published, two that have become popular include *When Once is not Enough* [33] and *Stop Obsessing* [125]. In addition, *The Boy Who Couldn't Stop Washing* [126] is on our "must read" list. These, and many other psychoeducational publications, are available through the OCF. Their address is Obsessive-Compulsive Foundation, Inc., PO Box 70, Milford, CT 06460; telephone, (203) 878-5669.

References and Recommended Reading

Papers of particular interest, published recently, have been highlighted as:
* Of special interest
•• Of outstanding interest

1. Robins LN, Helzer JE, Weissman MM, *et al*: Lifetime prevalence of specific psychiatric disorders in three sites. *Arch Gen Psychiatry* 1984, 41:958–967.

2. Regier DA, Farmer ME, Rae DS, *et al*.: Comorbidity of mental disorders with alcohol and other drug abuse. *JAMA* 1990, 264:2511–2518.

3. American Psychiatric Association: *Diagnostic and Statistical Manual of Mental Disorders*, edn 4. Washington, DC: American Psychiatric Association; 1994.

4. Dominguez RA, Goldstein BJ: Treatment of obsessive-compulsive disorder. *J Florida Med Assoc* 1988, 75:91–94.

5. Martin P, Scharfetter C: Olfactory hallucinations in depression. *Fortschr Neurol Psychiatr* 1993, 6:293–300.

6. Dominguez RA, Puig A: Olfactory reference syndrome responds to clomipramine but not fluoxetine: a case report. *J Clin Psychiatry,* in press.

7.• McElroy SL, Phillips KA, Keck PE: Obsessive compulsive spectrum disorder. *J Clin Psychiatry* 1994, 55:(suppl 10):33–51.
This paper discusses the OCD-spectrum disorders. There are similarities between those who suffer from disorders such as compulsive drinking, gambling, shopping, and others, and those with OCD.

8. Pigott TA, L'Heureux F, Dubbert B, *et al.*: Obsessive compulsive disorder: comorbid conditions. *J Clin Psychiatry* 1994, 55 (suppl 10):15–27.

9. Fallon BA, Liebowitz MR, Salzman E, *et al.*: Fluoxetine for hypochondriacal patients without major depression. *J Clin Psychopharmacol* 1993, 13:438–441.

10. Hoaken PCS, Schnurr R: Genetic factors in obsessive-compulsive neurosis: rare case of discordant monozygotic twins. *Can J Psychiatry* 1980, 25:167–172.

11. Woodruff R, Pitts FN: Monozygotic twins with obsessional neurosis. *Am J Psychiatry* 1964, 120:1075–1080.

12. Baxter LR, Schwartz JM, Bergman KS, *et al.*: Caudate glucose metabolic rate changes with both drug and behavior therapy for obsessive-compulsive disorder. *Arch Gen Psychiatry* 1992, 49:681–689.

13.• Baxter LR: Positron emission tomography studies of cerebral glucose metabolism in obsessive compulsive disorder. *J Clin Psychiatry* 1994, 55 (suppl 10):54–59.
Neuroimaging studies like this one demonstrate imbalances in function of specific cortical areas as well as internal structures in those suffering from OCD.

14. Anath J, Villanueva-Meyer J, Trajmar PG, *et al.*: Regional 133 xenon cerebral blood flow and cerebral 99mTc-HMPAO uptake in patients with obsessive-compulsive disorder before and during treatment. *Biol Psychiatry* 1995, 38:429–437.

15. Barr LC, Goodman WK, Price LH, *et al.*: The serotonin hypothesis of obsessive compulsive disorder: implications of pharmacologic challenge studies. *J Clin Psychiatry* 1992, 53(suppl 4):17–28.

16. Insel TR, Mueller EA, Alterman I, *et al.*: Obsessive-compulsive disorder and serotonin: is there a connection? *Biol Psychiatry* 1985, 20:1174–1188.

17. Bastani B, Arora RC, Meltzer HY: Serotonin uptake and imipramine binding in the blood platelets of obsessive-compulsive disorder patients. *Biol Psychiatry* 1991, 30:131–139.

18. Zohar J, Mueller EA, Insel TR, *et al.*: Serotonergic responsivity in obsessive-compulsive disorder: comparison of patients and healthy controls. *Arch Gen Psychiatry* 1987, 49:21–28.

19. Zohar J, Insel TR, Zohar-Kadouch RC, *et al.*: Serotonergic responsivity in obsessive-compulsive disorder: effect of chronic clomipramine treatment. *Arch Gen Psychiatry* 1988, 45:167–172.

20. Foa EB, Steketee GS, Ozarow BJ. Behavior therapy with obsessive-compulsives: from theory to treatment. In *Obsessive-Compulsive Disorder: Psychological and Pharmacological Treatment.* Edited by Mavissakalian M, Turner SM, Michelson L. New York, N.Y.: Plenum Press; 1985:49–129.

21.• Griest JH: Behavior therapy for obsessive compulsive disorder. *J Clin Psychiatry* 1994, 55(suppl 10):60–68.
This review of behavioral therapy for OCD shows that the pharmacotherapy and psychotherapy strategies are compatible and complementary.

22. Foa EB, Goldstein A: Continuous exposure and complete response prevention of obsessive-compulsive disorder. *Behav Ther* 1978, 9:821–829.

23. Foa EB, Grayson JB, Steketee GS, *et al.*: Success and failure in the behavioral treatment of obsessive-compulsives. *J Consult Clin Psychol* 1983, 51:287–297.

24. Emmelkamp PMG, Hoekstra RJ, Visser S: The behavioral treatment of OCD: prediction of outcome at 3.5 years follow-up. In *Psychiatry: the State of the Art.* Edited by Pichot P, Berner P, Wolf R, *et al.* New York: Plenum Press; 1985.

25. Foa EB, Staketee GS, Grayson JB, *et al.*: Deliberate exposure and blocking of obsessive rituals: immediate and long-term effects. *Behav Ther* 1984, 15:450–472.

26. Hoogduin CAL, Hoogduin WA: The outpatient treatment of patients with an obsessional-compulsive disorder. *Behav Res Ther* 1984, 22:455–459.

27. Emmelkamp PMG, Visser S, Hoekstra RJ: Cognitive therapy vs. exposure in vivo in the treatment of obsessive-compulsives. *Cogn Ther Res* 1988, 12:103–114.

28. Marks IM, Lelliot P, Basogly M, *et al.*: Clomipramine, self-exposure and therapist-aided exposure for obsessive compulsive rituals. *Br J Psychiatry* 1988, 152:522–534.

29. Emmelkamp PMG, van den Heuvell CVL, Ruphan L, *et al.*: Home-based treatment of obsessive-compulsive patients: intersession interval and therapist involvement. *Behav Res Ther* 1989, 27:89–93.

30. Foa EB, Kozak MJ, Steketee GS, *et al.*: Imipramine and behavior therapy in the treatment of depressive and obsessive-compulsive symptoms: immediate and long-term effects. *Br J Clin Psychiatry* 1992, 31:279–292.

31. Goodman WK, Price LH, Rasmussen SA, *et al.*: The Yale-Brown Obsessive-Compulsive Scale. *Arch Gen Psychiatry* 1989, 46:1001–1006.

32. Fals-Stewart W, Marks AP, Schafer J: A comparison of behavioral group therapy and individual behavior therapy in treating obsessive-compulsive disorder. *J Nerv Ment Dis* 1993, 181:189–193.

33. Steketee GS, White K: *When Once is Not Enough*. Oakland, CA: New Harbinger Press; 1990.

34. Dominguez RA: Serotonergic antidepressants and their efficacy in obsessive compulsive disorder. *J Clin Psychiatry* 1992, 53(suppl 10):56–59.

35. Pigott TA, Pato MT, Bernstein SE, *et al.*: Controlled comparisons of clomipramine and fluoxetine in the treatment of obsessive-compulsive disorder. *Arch Gen Psychiatry* 1990, 47:926–932.

36. Flament MF, Rapoport JL, Berg CJ, *et al.*: Clomipramine treatment of childhood obsessive compulsive disorder: a double-blind controlled study. *Arch Gen Psychiatry* 1985, 42:977–983.

37. Anath J, Pecknold JC, Van Den Steen N, *et al.*: Double-blind comparative study of clomipramine and amitriptyline in obsessive neurosis. *Prog Neuropsychopharmacol Biol Psychiatry* 1981, 5:257–262.

38. Insel TR, Murphy DL, Cohen RM, *et al.*: Obsessive-compulsive disorder: double-blind trial of clomipramine and clorgyline. *Arch Gen Psychiatry* 1983, 40:605–612.

39. Zohar J, Insel TR: Obsessive-compulsive disorder: psychobiological approaches to diagnosis, treatment, and pathophysiology. *Biol Psychiatry* 1987, 22:667–687.

40. The Clomipramine Collaborative Study Group: Clomipramine in the treatment of patients with obsessive-compulsive disorder. *Arch Gen Psychiatry* 1991, 48:730–738.

41. Ackerman DL, Greenland S, Bystritsky A, *et al.*: Relationship between early side effects and therapeutic effects of cloipramine therapy in obsessive-compulsive disorder. *J Clin Psychopharmacol* 1996, 16:324–328.

42.•• Tollefson GD, Rampey AH, Potvin JH, *et al.*: A multicenter investigation of fixed-dose fluoxetine in the treatment of obsessive-compulsive disorder. *Arch Gen Psychiatry* 1994, 51:559–567.
This important study found fluoxetine to be clearly effective for OCD.

43.•• Griest JH, Jefferson JW, Koback KA, *et al.*: Efficacy and tolerability of serotonin transport inhibitors in obsessive-compulsive disorder. *Arch Gen Psychiatry* 1995, 52:53–60.
These authors suggest that clomipramine may be more effective than the SSRIs for OCD, although no definitive double-blind studies are available.

44. Koran LM, Cain JW, Dominguez RA, *et al.*: Are fluoxetine plasma levels related to outcome in obsessive-compulsive disorder? *Am J Psychiatry* 1996, 153:1450–1454.

45. Freeman CP, Trimble MR, Deakin JF, *et al.*: Fluvoxamine versus clomipramine in the treatment of obsessive compulsive disorder: a multicenter, randomized, double-blind, parallel group comparison. *J Clin Psychiatry* 1994, 55:301–305.

46. Koran LM, McElroy SL, Davidson JR, *et al.*: Fluvoxamine versus clomipramine for obsessive-compulsive disorder: a double-blind comparison. *J Clin Psychopharmacol* 1996, 16:121–129.

47.• Goodman WK, Kozak MJ, Liebowitz M, *et al.*: Treatment of obsessive-compulsive disorder with fluvoxamine: a multicentre, double-blind, placebo-controlled trial. *Int Clin Psychopharmacol* 1996, 11:21–29.
This study found that fluvoxamine's efficacy for OCD may be comparable with that of clomipramine and fluoxetine.

48. DeVane CL: Pharmacokinetics of the newer antidepressants: clinical relevance. *Am J Med* 1994, 97(suppl 6A):13–23.

49.• Dominguez RA, Mestre SM: Management of treatment-refractory obsessive compulsive disorder patients. *J Clin Psychiatry* 1994, 55 (suppl 10):86–92.
This review suggests that clomipramine, fluoxetine, and fluvoxamine should be considered as first-line antiobsessive drugs.

50. Chouinard G. Sertraline in the treatment of obsessive compulsive disorder: two double-blind, placebo-controlled studies. *Int Clin Psychopharmacol* 1992, 2(suppl 7):37–41.

51. Griest J, Chouinard G, DuBoff E, *et al.*: Double-blind parallel comparison of three dosages of sertraline and placebo in outpatients with obsessive-compulsive disorder. *Arch Gen Psychiatry* 1995, 52:289–295.

52. Greist JH, Jefferson JW, Kobak KA, *et al.*: A 1 year double-blind placebo-controlled fixed dose study of sertraline in the treatment of obsessive-compulsive disorder. *Int Clin Psychopharmacol* 1995, 10:57–65.

53. Bisserbe JC, Wiseman RL, Goldberg MS, *et al.*: A double-blind comparison of sertraline and clomipramine in outpatients with OCD. In *New Research Abstracts APA Annual Meeting*; 1995:173.

54. Dominguez RA, goodnick PJ: Adverse events after the abrupt discontinuation of paroxetine. *Pharmacotherapy* 1995, 15:778–780.

55.• Zohar J, Judge R, *et al.*: Paroxetine versus clomipramine in the treatment of obsessive-compulsive disorder. *Br J Psychiatry* 1996, 169:468–474.
Results of this study revealed that flexible doses of paroxetine and clomipramine, given for a period of 12 weeks, were statistically superior to placebo and similar in efficacy.

56. Preskorn SH, Janicak PG, Davis JM, *et al.*: Advances in the pharmacotherapy of depressive disorders. In *Principles and Practice of Psychopharmacotherapy* Edited by Janicak PG. Baltimore: Williams & Wilkins; 1995:1–24.

57. Tollefson GD, Birkett M, Koran L, *et al.*: Continuation treatment of OCD: double-blind and open-label experience with fluoxetine. *J Clin Psychiatry* 1994, 55(suppl 10):69–76.

58. Ravizza L, Barzega G, Bellino S, *et al.* Predictors of drug treatment response in obsessive-compulsive disorder. *J Clin Psychiatry* 1995, 56:368–373.

59. Stein DJ, Spadaccini E, Hollander E: Meta-analysis of pharmacotherapy trials for obsessive-compulsive disorder. *Int Clin Psychopharmacol* 1995, 10:11–18.

60. Piccinelli M, Pini S, Bellantuono C, *et al.*: Efficacy of drug treatment in obsessive-compulsive disorder: a meta-analytic review. *Br J Psychiatry* 1995, 166:424–443.

61. Feigner JP, Boyer WF, *et al.*: Selective serotonin re-uptake inhibitors. In *Perspectives in Psychiatry*, vol 1: Chichester, UK: John Wiley & Sons; 1991.

62. Preskorn SH, Alderman J, Chung M, *et al.*: Pharmacokinetics of desipramine co-administered with sertraline or fluoxetine. *J Clin Psychopharmacol* 1994, 14:90–98.

63. Goodman WK, McDougle CJ, Barr LC, *et al.*: Biological approaches to treatment-resistant obsessive-compulsive disorder. *J Clin Psychiatry* 1993, 54(suppl 6):16–26.

64. Jefferson JW, Greist JH: The pharmacotherapy of obsessive-compulsive disorder. *Psychiatric Ann* 1996, 26:202–209.

65. Pigott TA, Pato MT, L'Heureux F, *et al.*: A controlled comparison of adjuvant lithium carbonate or thyroid hormone in clomipramine-treated patients with obsessive-compulsive disorder. *J Clin Psychopharmacol* 1991, 11:242–248.

66. McDougle CJ, Price LH, Goodman WK, *et al.*: A controlled trial of lithium augmentation in fluvoxamine-refractory obsessive-compulsive disorder. *J Clin Psychopharmacol* 1991, 11:175–184.

67. Pigott TA, L'Heureux F, Hill JL, *et al.*: A double-blind study of adjuvant buspirone hydrochloride in clomipramine-treated patients with obsessive-compulsive disorder. *J Clin Psychopharmacol* 1992, 12:11–18.

68. McDougle CJ, Goodman WK, Leckman JF, *et al.*: Limited therapeutic effect of addition of buspirone in fluvoxamine-refractory obsessive-compulsive disorder. *Am J Psychiatry* 1993, 150:647–649.

69. Grady TA, Pigott TA, L'Heureux F, *et al.*: Double-blind study of adjuvant buspirone for fluoxetine-treated patients with obsessive-compulsive disorder. *Am J Psychiatry* 1993, 50:819–821.

70. Hewlett WA, Vinogradov S, Agras WS: Clomipramine, clonazepam and clonidine treatment of obsessive-compulsive disorder. *J Clin Psychopharmacol* 1992, 12:420–430.

71. Pigott TA, L'Heureux F, Rubenstein CS, *et al.*: A controlled trial of clonazepam augmentation in OCD patients treated with clomipramine or fluoxetine. In *New Research Program and Abstracts of the 145th Annual Meeting of the American Psychiatric Association*. Washington, DC, 1992:Abstract NR144:82.

72. McDougle CJ, Goodman WK, Price LH, *et al.*: Neuroleptic addition in fluvoxamine-refractory obsessive-compulsive disorder. *Am J Psychiatry* 1990, 147:652–654.

73. McDougle CJ, Goodman Wk, Leckman JF, *et al*.: The efficacy of fluvoxamine in obsessive-compulsive disorder: effects of comorbid chronic tic disorder. *J Clin Psychopharmacol* 1993, 13:354–358.

74. Jenike M: Rapid response of severe obsessive-compulsive disorder to tranylcypromine. *Am J Psychiatry* 1981, 138:1249–1250.

75. Joel SW: Twenty month study of iproniazid therapy. *Dis Nerv Syst* 1959, 20:14.

76. Joffee RT, Swinson RP: Tranylcypromine in primary obsessive-compulsive disorder. *J Anx Disord* 1990, 4:365–367.

77. Vallejo J, Olivares J, Marcos T, *et al*.: Clomipramine vs phenelzine in obsessive-compulsive disorder: a controlled clinical trial. *Br J Psychiatry* 1992, 161:665–670.

78. Pigott TA, L'Heureux F, Rubenstein CS, *et al*.: A double-blind, placebo-controlled study of trazodone in patients with obsessive-compulsive disorder. *J Clin Psychopharmacol* 1992, 12:156–162.

79. Hollander E, DeCaria CM, Schneier F, *et al*.: Fenfluramine augmentation of serotonin uptake blockade antiobsessional treatment. *J Clin Psychiatry* 1990, 51:119–123.

80. Lipsedge MS, Prothero W: Clonidine and clomipramine in obsessive-compulsive disorder. *Am J Psychiatry* 1987, 144:965–966.

81: Casas M, Alvarez E, Duro P, *et al*.: Antiandrogenic treatment of obsessive-compulsive neurosis. *Acta Psychiatr Scand* 1986, 73:221–222.

82. Fux M, Levine J, Aviv A, *et al*.: Inositol treatment of obsessive-compulsive disorder. *Am J Psychiatry* 1996, 153:1219–1221.

83. Yaryura-Tobias JA, Bhagavan HN: Tryptophan in obsessive-compulsive disorders. *Am J Psychiatry* 1977, 134:1298–1299.

84. Blier P, Bergeron R: Sequential administration of augmentation strategies in treatment -resistant obsessive-compulsive disorder: preliminary findings. *Int Clin Psychopharmacol* 1996, 11:37–44.

85. Montgomery SA, Fineberg N, Montgomery D, *et al*.: L-tryptophan in obsessive-compulsives. *Eur Neuropsychopharmacol* 1992, 2:384–385.

86. Joffe RT, Swinson RP: Methylphenidate in primary obsessive-compulsive disorder. *J Clin Psychopharmacol* 1987, 7:420–422.

87. Zajecka JM, Fawcett J, Guy C: Coexisting major depression and obsessive-compulsive disorder treated with venlafaxine. *J Clin Psychopharmacol* 1990, 10:152–153.

88. Grossman R, Hollander E: Treatment of obsessive-compulsive disorder with venlafaxine. *Am J Psychiatry* 1996, 153:576–577.

89. Ananth J, Burgoyne K, Smith M, *et al*.: Venlaxafine for treatment of obsessive-compulsive disorder. *Am J Psychiatry* 1995, 152:1832.

90. Rauch SL, O'Sullivan RL, Jenike MA: Open treatment of obsessive-compulsive disorder with venlaxafine: a series of ten cases. *J Clin Psychoparmacol* 1996, 16:81–84.

91. Khanna S: Carbamazepine in obsessive-compulsive disorder. *Clin Neuropharmacol* 1988, 11:478–481.

92. Barr LC, Aronson SC, Anand A, *et al*.: Clozapine in treatment-resistant obsessive-compulsive disorder. *Soc Neurosci Abstr* 1993, 19:383.

93. McDougle CJ, Barr LC, Goodman WK, *et al*.: Lack of efficacy of clozapine monotherapy in refractory obsessive-compulsive disorder. *Am J Psychiatry* 1995, 152:1812–1814.

94. Jacobsen FM: Risperidone in the treatment of affective illness and obsessive-compulsive disorder. *J Clin Psychiatry* 1995, 56:423–429.

95. Berigan TR, Harazin JS: Response to risperidone addition in fluvoxamine-refractory obsessive-compulsive disorder: three cases. *J Clin Psychiatry* 1996, 57:594–595.

96. McDougle CJ, Fleishman RL, Epperson CN, *et al*.: Risperidone addition in fluvoxamine-refractory obsessive-compulsive disorder: three cases. *J Clin Psychiatry* 1995, 56:526–528.

97. Remington G, Adams M: Risperidone and obsessive-compulsive symptoms. *J Clin Psychopharmacol* 1994, 14:358–359.

98. Kopala L, Honer WG: Risperidone, serotonergic mechanisms, and obsessive-compulsive symptoms in schizophrenia. *Am J Psychiatry* 1994, 151:1714–1715.

99. Saxena S, Wang D, Bystinsky A, *et al*.: Risperidone augmentation of SRI treatment for refractory obsessive-compulsive disorder. *J Clin Psychiatry* 1996, 57:303–306.

100. Ravizza L, Barzega G, Bellino S, *et al*.: Therapeutic effect and safety of adjunctive risperidone in refractory obsessive-compulsive disorder (OCD). *Psychopharmacol Bull* 1996, 32:677–682.

101. Hollander E: Developments in obsessive-compulsive disorder, II: obsessive-compulsive "spectrum disorders." *Curr Affect Illness* 1994, 13:5–13.

102. Warneke L: Intravenous chlorimipramine therapy in obsessive-compulsive disorder. *Can J Psychiatry* 1989, 34:853–858.

103. Thakur AK, Remillard AJ, Meldrum LH, *et al.*: Intravenous clomipramine and obsessive-compulsive disorder. *Can J Psychiatry* 1991, 36:521–524.

104. Fallon BA, Campeas R, Schneier FR, *et al.*: Open trial of intravenous clomipramine in five treatment-refractory patients with obsessive-compulsive disorder. *J Neuropsychiatry Clin Neurosci* 1992, 4:70–75.

105. Koran LM, Sallee FR, Pallanti S: Rapid benefit of intravenous pulse loading of clomipramine in obsessive-compulsive disorder. *Am J Psychiatry* 1997, 154:396–401.

106. Mundo M, Bellodi L, Smeraldi E: Effects of acute intravenous clomipramine on obsessive-compulsive symptoms and response to chronic treatment. *Biol Psychiatry* 1995, 38:525–531.

107. Simeon JG, Thatte S, Wiggins D: Treatment of adolescent obsessive-compulsive disorder with a clomipramine-fluoxetine combination. *Psychopharmacol Bull* 1990, 26:285–290.

108. Browne M, Horn E, Jones TT: The benefits of clomipramine-fluoxetine combination in obsessive compulsive disorder. *Can J Psychiatry* 1993, 38:242–243.

109. Szegedi A, Wetzel H, Leal M, *et al.*: Combination treatment with clomipramine and fluvoxamine: drug monitoring, safety, and tolerability data. *J Clin Psychiatry* 1996, 57:257–264.

110. Fontaine R, Chouinard G: Fluoxetine in the long-term treatment of obsessive-compulsive disorder. *Psychiatry Ann* 1989, 19:88–91.

111. Levine R, Hoffman JS, Knepple ED, *et al.*: Long-term fluoxetine treatment of a large number of obsessive-compulsive patients. *J Clin Psychopharmacol* 1989, 9:281–283.

112. Fraenkel A, Rosenthal J, Nezu A, *et al.*: Efficacy of long-term fluoxetine treatment of obsessive-compulsive disorder. *Mt Sinai J Med* 1990, 57:348–352.

113.• Orloff LM, Battle MA, Baer L, *et al.*: Long-term follow-up of 85 patients with obsessive-compulsive disorder. *Am J Psychiatry* 1994, 151:441–442.
This study showed that premature discontinuation of an effective medication will result in rapid relapse.

114. Pato MT, Zohar-Kadouch R, Zohar J, *et al.*: Return of symptoms after discontinuation of clomipramine in patients with obsessive-compulsive disorder. *Am J Psychiatry* 1988, 145:1521–1525.

115. Ravizza L, Barzega G, Bellino S, *et al.*: Drug treatment of obsessive-compulsive disorder (OCD): long-term trial with clomipramine and selective serotonin reuptake inhibitors (SSRIs). *Psychopharmacol Bull* 1996, 32:167–173.

116. Mundo E, Bareggi SR, Pirola R, *et al.*: Long-term pharmacotherapy of obsessive-compulsive disorder: a double-blind controlled study. *J Clin Psychopharmacol* 1997, 17:4–10.

117. Maletzky BM, McFarland B, Burt A: Refractory obsessive-compulsive disorder and ECT. *Convuls Ther* 1994, 10:34–42.

118. Baer L, Rauch SL, Ballantine HT Jr, *et al.*: Cingulotomy for intractable obsessive-compulsive disorder: prospective long-term follow-up of 18 patients. *Arch Gen Psychiatry* 1995, 52:384–392.

119. Mindus P. Neurosurgical treatment of malignant obsessive compulsive disorder. *Psychiatr Clin North Am* 1992, 15:921–928.

120. Calvocoressie L, Lewis B, Harris M, *et al.*: Family accommodation in obsessive compulsive disorder. *Am J Psychiatry* 1995, 152:441–443.

121. Emmelkamp PMG, Kloek J, Blaauw E: Obsessive-compulsive disorders. In *Principles and Practice of Relapse Prevention*. Edited by Wilson PH. New York: Guilford Press; 1992:213–234.

122. Steketee G: Social support and treatment outcome of obsessive-compulsive disorder, a nine-month follow-up. *Behav Psychother* 1993, 21:81–95.

123. Mehta M: A comparative study of family-based and patient-based behavioral management in obsessive-compulsive disorder. *Br J Psychiatry* 1990, 157:133–135.

124. Black DW, Blum NS: Obsessive-compulsive disorder support groups: the Iowa model. *Compr Psychiatry* 1992, 33:65–71.

125. Foa EB, Wilson R: *Stop Obsessing!* New York: Bantam; 1991.

126. Rapoport JL: *The Boy Who Couldn't Stop Washing.* New York: EP Dutton; 1989.

CHAPTER 14

Eating Disorders
and Mood Disorders

Joel Yager and Brenda Erickson

The comorbidity between eating disorders and mood disorders is so high that in many case series eating disorder patients who lack mood disorders are the exception rather than the rule. This chapter reviews these issues and delineates current treatment considerations. Clinically, eating disorders may contribute to the vulnerability for mood disorders, and mood disorders may contribute to the vulnerability for eating disorders. Comprehensive assessment and treatment of these patients demands close attention to both disorders, as well as to other common concurrent disorders such as anxiety disorders; obsessive-compulsive disorders, especially in anorexia nervosa patients; substance abuse, especially in bulimia nervosa patients; and personality disorders. Mood disorders often improve with adequate treatment of eating disorders, but specific attention to both the eating and mood disorder is required. Current empirically based treatment strategies for managing these patients include the judicious admixture of nutritional rehabilitation, cognitive-behavioral and interpersonal therapies, as well as antidepressant medications, particularly tricyclics and selective serotonin reuptake inhibitors.

E ating disorders include anorexia nervosa (AN), bulimia nervosa (BN), atypical eating disorders and, in the *Diagnostic and Statistical Manual of Mental Disorders*, edn 4 (DSM-IV), a proposed new entity, binge eating disorder (BED). AN and BN may occur individually or concurrently. AN is characterized by refusal to maintain body weight at or above a minimum for height and age, with maintenance weight less than 85% of expected; an intense fear of gaining weight or becoming fat, even though underweight; a disturbance in body image, so that the patient perceives himself or herself to be fat even when malnourished; and, in postmenarcheal women, the absence of at least three consecutive menstrual periods. AN is subcategorized into restricting types and binge eating or purging types.

Bulimia nervosa is characterized by recurrent episodes of binge eating; a sense of lack of control over the eating binges; recurrent inappropriate compensatory behavior to prevent weight gain (*eg*, self-induced vomiting, use or abuse of laxatives, diuretics, enemas, diet pills, fasting, excessive exercise); the occurrence of binge eating and compensatory symptoms at least twice a week for a period of at least 3 months; and self-evaluation excessively influenced by weight and body shape. The disturbance does not occur exclusively during episodes of AN. BN is subcategorized into purging and nonpurging types, the former more prominent than the latter.

Binge eating disorder, in many ways akin to what is commonly called *compulsive overeating*, is episodic in nature like BN, but lacks the compensatory behaviors. In addition, the binge eating episodes are typically the same as those associated with BN: eating until uncomfortably full, eating large quantities when not hungry, eating alone because of embarrassment about how much one eats, and feeling disgusted, depressed, or guilty when overeating. Marked distress about binge eating is present, and the eating episodes must occur for a minimum of twice a week for 6 months to meet criteria. Symptoms in these patients frequently tend to wax and wane, and individuals may evolve from AN to BN or vice versa, with varying degrees of subclinical or atypical disorders at other points.

Patients with eating disorders frequently have disturbances in mood and often merit concurrent diagnoses of mood disorders. Clinicians working with these patients face complex assessments; they must evaluate the significance of these symptoms, consider possible explanations for their co-occurrence, and contend with frequently difficult treatment problems. In some groups of eating disorders, patients' lifetime and concurrent mood disorder diagnoses are the rule rather than the exception.

Several formulations have been suggested for this connection between eating disorders and mood disorders. The most prominent are 1) eating disorders are manifestations and equivalents of mood disorders; 2) eating disorders increase vulnerability to disturbances in mood through malnutrition; 3) mood disorders increase vulnerability for eating disorders; and 4) eating disorders and mood disorders are both related to common antecedents, and both reflect maladaptive attempts to cope with difficult biologic, developmental, or environmental circumstances. Evidence can be found in existing literature to partially support each of these views, reflecting in part the diverse nature of both eating disorders and mood disorders, as well as their complex interrelationships; no single explanation fits all cases.

Assessment and Diagnosis of Depression in the Context of Eating Disorders

Symptoms of depressed mood, low self-esteem, worthlessness, hopelessness, anergy, irritability, and sleep disturbances are extremely common in patients with AN, BN, combined syndromes (AN-BN) and, to a somewhat lesser extent, in patients with BED and atypical eating disorders. Tables 1 and 2 present data from several representative reports of formal diagnostic studies of comorbidity in AN and BN [1,2••,3•,4,5]. In addition to the high prevalence of mood disorders, these tables also illustrate considerable comorbidity with other major types of psychiatric disorders.

Whether specific mood disorder manifestations differ in patients with eating disorders remains unclear. Available evidence suggests that, for the most part, depression in patients with BN is predominantly cognitive and emotional, whereas patients with AN have a higher rate of somatic symptoms. In a study of 83 patients with AN and 115 patients with BN that used a structured clinical interview based on DSM-III-R (revised) [6], 43% of patients met criteria for major depression. As a group they averaged 30.9 on the Beck Depression Inventory, indicating severe depression. Among those with BN, cognitive symptoms had the greatest discriminating power (discouragement, expectation of punishment, and difficulty with decision making), whereas among those with AN a wider group of somatic and affective symptoms predominated, particularly loss of satisfaction, feelings of failure, suicidal ideation, and worry about physical problems in the AN-BN group.

Some research suggests that the highest rates of major depression are found among those patients with eating disorders who suffer from both AN and BN [7].

Bipolar II affective disorder may be particularly common among inpatients with eating disorders. Of 22 carefully diagnosed inpatients with persistent eating disorders, 59% were thought to have had a lifetime diagnosis of bipolar II disorder, a finding requiring additional investigation [8]. Additionally, seasonal changes in mood, weight, and energy,

Table 1. DSM-III-R Lifetime Comorbidity in Anorexia Nervosa

	Halmi et al. [1]* Patients/controls, %	Walters and Kendler [2••]† Odds ratios
Bulimia nervosa		11.8
Any affective disorder	72.5/22.5	
Major depression	67.7/20.9	4.0
Mania	3.2/1.6	
Dysthymia	32.2/3.2	
Bipolar	3.2/0	
Atypical bipolar	9.7/0	
Any anxiety disorder	62.9/20.9	
Obsessive compulsive	25.8/6.5	
Agoraphobia	14.5/3.2	2.9 (all phobias)
Simple phobia	12.9/14.5	
Social phobia	33.9/3.2	
Panic	8.1/8.1	2.7
Schizophrenia	6.5/0	
Any substance abuse	17.8/25.8	
Alcohol abuse	8.1/14.5	1.9
Cannabis abuse	12.9/24.2	
Amphetamine abuse	1.6/8.1	

*Hospitalized population.
†Community population—odds of comorbidity among those meeting criteria for anorexia nervosa compared with others in the population.
DSM-III-R—Diagnostic and Statistical Manual of Mental Disorders, edn 3, revised.

corresponding to patterns seen in seasonal affective disorder (SAD), are more common in patients with BN and combined AN-BN than in those with AN alone or in population-based comparison samples. SAD or subsyndromal SAD was found to occur in 47% to 48% of BN and AN-BN patients, respectively, but only in 28% of AN patients [9].

Other complexities relevant to comprehensive diagnosis of patients manifesting both eating disorders and mood disorders abound. Patients with eating disorders score significantly higher in dissociative psychopathology than comparison subjects, and these experiences have been linked to a propensity for self-mutilation and suicidal ideation in these groups [10]. The extent to which these phenomena may be linked to increased rates of assorted combinations of childhood physical, psychologic, and sexual abuse remains unclear [11•,12]. These factors may all contribute to developmental difficulties with affective self-regulation and vulnerabilities to mood disorders.

Disturbances in personality, described later in this article, are also extremely common. Many appear to predate the occurrence of mood and eating disorders and may also contribute to the appearance of both disorders. Personality disturbances are also important in treatment and prognostic considerations for patients with comorbid eating disorders and mood disorders.

Studies on the coincidence of BED and mood disorders have shown the incidence of depression to be higher among obese patients with BED than nonobese patients with BED in some studies [13, 14], but not in others [15,16].

Table 2. DSM-III-R Lifetime Comorbidity in Bulimia Nervosa

	Garfinkel et al. [3•]* Subjects/controls, %	Hudson et al. [4]† Subjects/controls, %	Kendler et al. [5]‡ Odds ratios
Anorexia nervosa			8.23
Any affective disorder		67/29	
Major depression	38.2/10.1	55/29	2.20
Dysthymia		3/3	
Bipolar		11/0	
Atypical bipolar			
Any anxiety disorder	58.2/25.8	43/21	
Generalized anxiety disorder	10.9/2.5		2.61
Obsessive-compulsive disorder		33/7	
Agoraphobia	34.5/7.5		2.37 (any phobia)
Panic	20.0/2.6		3.00
Agoraphobia with or without panic		17/14	
Simple phobia	40.0/11.4		
Social phobia	45.5/15.2		
Schizophrenia		0/0	
Any substance abuse		49/11	
Alcohol abuse	30.9/5.0	36/11	3.23

*Community population.
†Clinical population derived from clinic and advertisments.
‡Community population—odds of comorbidity among those meeting criteria for anorexia nervosa compared with others in the population.

Personality and developmental issues

Certain personality disorders are seen much more frequently in patients with mood disorders than in the population at large. Although the percentage of patients with eating disorders reported to have one or more personality disorders ranges from 27% to 93% in various studies, and although rates vary with different methods of ascertainment and diagnosis, patients with AN are more generally likely to have avoidant personality disorders, and patients with BN are more likely to have borderline personality disorders [17]. Higher depression-symptom ratings are reported in BN patients with borderline personality disorder than other BN patients [18]. Among AN patients, the presence of obsessive-compulsive characteristics may contribute to the occurrence of depressive illness [19]. Strober [20] suggested that an essential core of AN lies in its genotypic personality structure and temperament, and that this personality may predispose individuals to a lower than optimal threshold for experiencing inner tensions, leading to a greater need to maintain unwavering control over threatening affective states and, ultimately, to difficulties with affective self-regulation. Conceivably, all personality disturbances already described tend to alienate individuals with eating disorders from potential sources of social and emotional support, and may thereby increase vulnerability to depression.

To sum up, the complex clinical problems presented by patients with eating disorders frequently include comorbid mood disorders, other Axis I disorders, frequent Axis II disorders, and other significant developmental issues. These combinations test the diagnostic and therapeutic skills of the best clinicians and often show the severe limitations of simplistic assessment and treatment algorithms.

Relationships of Mood and Weight

Disturbances in mood are closely connected to disturbances in appetite and weight. Classically, major depression is associated with "true" anorexia: a lack of appetite and even revulsion toward food, and often concurrent weight loss, sometimes in the range of 10 to 20 pounds or more. These conditions constitute well-known vegetative signs of depression. Similarly, "atypical" depressions are associated with increases in appetite, increases in eating (*eg*, "stress eating"), and weight gain. Many of the neurotransmitter and neuromodulating systems affected in primary depressions are also involved in regulating the basic biologic programs mediating appetite, weight regulation, gastrointestinal function, and sleep, among others.

Conversely, substantial literature confirms that decreases in weight significantly alter mood. In a classic study, Keys *et al.* [21] showed that profound alterations in behavior and personality were evident in states of prolonged starvation. Reducing the weight of previously healthy young men by 25% to 30% through controlled food restriction resulted most consistently in depressive symptoms of irritability, generalized apathy, fragmented sleep, decreased libido and concentration, anhedonia, social withdrawal, and dysphoria. Impaired cognitive performance occurs in dieters consuming 70% of their maintenance caloric intake [22]. These studies have been taken to show that in AN, starvation may lead to symptoms of depression. Some degree of starvation often occurs in normal weight BN as well, as evidenced by metabolic and endocrine adaptation to starvation in these patients [23]. This finding has been invoked to account for vulnerability to depressive disorders in BN patients.

Therefore, although the patterns of true anorexia and weight loss initially seen in primary major depressive disorders are not typical of those seen in AN or BN, it is possible that in patients whose profound depressions lead to severe weight loss and malnutrition, psychologic sequelae and cognitive impairment may partly be due to starvation. Weight loss in the starvation experiments did not, however, typically result in low self-esteem, guilt, or hopelessness, cardinal cognitive characteristics of clinical depressions.

Normalization of eating with or without weight restoration typically results in remission of these starvation-induced psychologic and biologic effects. With refeeding, metabolic indicators of starvation (*eg*, levels of free fatty acids, ketones, glucose tolerance) disappear first, whereas endocrine findings related to triiodothyronine, luteinizing hormone, follicle-stimulating hormone, cortisol, among others, normalize at a much slower pace [24,25]. Mood and other psychologic changes appear to normalize slowly as well; some of the starvation-induced psychopathologic signs and symptoms seen in malnourished normal subjects may last for up to 1 year following weight restoration [21].

Many theories have been postulated to link externally imposed starvation with the appearance of depressive symptoms. In animal models, starvation reduces hypothalamic norepinephrine and dopamine turnover [26]; serotonin systems are also affected [27]. Individually, or in combination, these disturbances in neurotransmission could lead to both neuroendocrine and mood disturbances. Kaye *et al.* [28] postulate that alterations in the serotonergic system can account for symptoms consistent with both AN and BN;

they have also found that alterations in serotonin systems persist even after weight restoration in both AN and BN. These systems have, of course, been linked to the pathogenesis of mood disorders as well as eating disorders.

At the same time, patterns of increased appetite, coinciding with "stress eating" seen in patients with atypical depression, may bear some clinical relationship to binge eating that occurs in BN and in BED. The extent to which such patterns of overeating may represent failures in preexisting patterns of restrained eating, which may at times induce mild chronic, subclinical starvation states, is unclear.

Primary and Secondary Depression in Eating Disorders

Distinguishing primary from secondary depressions in the presence of concurrent eating disorders is often problematic. The diagnosis of a primary mood disturbance is easy to make when a definitive episode of depression or mania clearly precedes the onset of eating disorder symptomatology. The presence of a strong family history of mood disorder may also contribute, presumptively, to the diagnosis of a primary mood disorder. Finding a clear sequence of depression followed by eating disorder, however, or visa versa, is frequently difficult to do in practice; the disorders often seem to begin virtually concurrently. Few studies have systematically examined this relationship. In a retrospective study of 24 AN patients among whom 83% had a lifetime diagnosis of major depressive disorder, almost half of those with depression developed the mood disorder roughly 1 year prior to the AN, the others coincident to or following the onset of AN [29•]. In a similar study of patients with BN who had lifetime major depression, approximately one third reported their first episode of depression to have occurred at least 1 year prior to the onset of BN, one third within the same year, and the remainder at least 1 year following the onset of the eating disorder [4]. These findings parallel unpublished data collected in the University of California Los Angeles (UCLA) Eating Disorders Clinic, where among 50 BN patients with major depression, the finding of mood disorder appeared to be evenly divided between those mood disorders that preceded the appearance of BN and those that followed. However, when early and subtle symptoms of the two disorders were carefully elicited, the timing of their onsets often seemed indistinguishable.

We have discussed how eating disorders might contribute to the appearance of mood disturbance. Clinical impressions suggest that when AN begins prior to significant mood disturbance, the appearance of depression follows significant weight loss with or without increasing chronicity, ie, when the patient realizes that he or she is helpless against the overwhelming nature of their symptoms. In patients in whom mood disorder follows the onset of BN, a similar sequence appears to operate, ie, the mood disturbance follows periods in which eating becomes chaotic, subtle malnutrition may exist, and the patient feels increasingly impaired by his or her symptoms and powerless to control them. The frequent observation that depressive symptoms improve in the wake of successful treatment for eating disorders also suggests that symptoms of depression, if not major mood disorders, may respond to the presence of eating disorder psychopathology [30].

To what extent might preexisting depression increase vulnerability to developing an eating disorder? In theory, this is relationship should be likely, because depression probably increases vulnerability to many psychiatric disturbances. Although many clinical anecdotes and some cross-sectional correlational studies are consistent with this association, substantiating prospective data clearly demonstrating that depression increases vulnerability for AN, BN, or even BED are not available. Furthermore, because not all patients with AN or BN develop major depressions, identifying what distinguishes BED patients who develop significant mood disturbance from those who do not is an important matter for research.

Familial Factors Linking Mood Disorders and Eating Disorders

A sizeable amount of literature points to an increased risk of depression not only in patients with AN, but in their first-degree relatives as well [31–34]. The familial association of eating disorders with mood disorders has led investigators to raise the possibility that these disorders share a common diathesis, and possibly a genetic basis. Strober [20] reviewed nine family studies to conclude that rates of major depression are higher among first- and second-degree relatives of BN and AN probands than in normal controls or in other psychiatric comparison groups. The range of familial risk for major depression was estimated between 7% and 22%, two to three times that of control families.

Strong familial associations exist between BN and major depression. Rates of familial major depression are highest when probands have both BN and depression compared with BN alone [35,36]. Probands with BN without depression, however, still demonstrated higher familial rates of major depression than controls [33,35]. Examining this question from another perspective, when BN patients who had family histories of affective disorder in at least one first-degree relative were compared with patients without such a family history, those with a positive family history were more likely to have been treated for depression themselves, to report problems in social and vocational functioning, and to attribute binge eating to depressive symptoms [37]. Parental psychopathology among those with BN includes significantly more depression, suicide attempts, drinking problems, and histories of psychiatric treatment than among comparison groups. For example, in a community sample, 49.1% of subjects with BN reported histories of parental depression and 18.2% reported parental suicide attempts [3•].

In a genetic analysis of the co-occurrence of BN and major depression in 1033 women twin pairs in a population-based register using personal interviews and DSM-III-R criteria, additive genes, but not family environment, were found to be etiologically important for both BN and major depression. The genetic liabilities of the two disorders correlated at about 0.456. These analyses suggest that some genetic correlation exists between the disorders, in addition to which each disorder has some unique genetic and environmental risk factor [38].

Controversy exists regarding whether increased rates of depression occur in relatives of depressed versus nondepressed AN patients [31,34,39]. Halmi *et al.* [1] found no significant differences in the lifetime diagnoses of affective disorders between mothers of patients with AN and mothers of controls, 12% in this sample. Other studies, however, some using different diagnostic methods and methods of obtaining patient samples, have found higher rates of mood disorders among mothers and other first-degree relatives of patients with AN than in comparison samples [31,39]. For example, Winokur *et al.* [39] found unipolar depression in 36% of mothers of patients with AN.

Controversy also exists as to whether the presence of mood disorder in patients with AN predicts mood disorder in their relatives. Some studies find more incidence of mood disorder in the relatives of AN patients who have mood disorders [34], whereas others do not [1]. Careful examination of these studies suggests that discrepancies may be resolved by considering that patients with AN who have family histories of mood disorders may be susceptible to developing mood disorders at an earlier age.

Further strengthening the view that AN and mood disorders do have familial linkages, a population-based study of identical twins found the relative risk for major depression in co-twins of subjects with AN to be 2.3 times higher than that among co-twins of unaffected twins. Even when comorbidity of major depression in the twin with AN was controlled for, the relative risk for depression among the co-twins of twins with AN was still 2.0 compared with those of unaffected twins [2••]. This same study showed that co-twins of those with narrowly defined AN were 2.6 times more likely to have BN as the co-twin of an unaffected twin, suggesting that a common set of familial factors appear to influence risk for both eating disorders.

On the other hand, the fact that first-degree relatives of patients with mood disorders do not show an increase in rates of eating disorders, a finding replicated in several studies, has been taken as evidence that eating disorders are not merely forme frustes of mood disorders [20,35,40].

Treatment Strategies

Because few controlled studies have explicitly addressed the treatment of patients with comorbid eating disorders and mood disorders, suggestions for treatment are based on the few reports that consider this comorbidity, other treatment studies that at least mention comorbid issues, and the consensus of clincial experience. Because patients with both eating disorders and mood disorders may in some instances respond differently to various treatments than patients with eating disorder without such comorbidities, future studies need to examine this particular issue.

Anorexia nervosa

For the patient presenting with AN and significant symptoms of depression, the clinician should first attempt to ascertain whether the presenting mood disorder meets criteria for major depression or seems primarily to reflect symptoms of apathy, lethargy, sleep disturbance, and irritability resulting fundamentally from malnutrition. Although these conditions are not always easy to distinguish from one another, the presence of cognitive signs and symptoms of depression, such as morbid guilt, low self-esteem, self-blame, and hopelessness point toward a true mood disorder. Family history of depression and appearance of the mood disorder before the onset of significant eating disorder symptoms also strengthens the diagnosis of major depression. Symptoms that are predominantly vegetative and unaccompanied by corresponding cognitive symptoms may more directly result from malnutrition.

Most authorities agree that the primary intervention for AN is nutritional rehabilitation [41]. With weight gain and good nutrition, many of the symptoms of depression appear to resolve, particularly those related to energy, affect, and sleep. Several months may be necessary before the full benefits of good nutrition can be realized. The extent to which intensive psychotherapy with or without antidepressant medication adds benefit to nutritional rehabilitation and empathic, supportive, reality-based nursing programs at the early stages of treating the severely malnourished patient remains unclear. Some believe that severely malnourished patients with AN are not able to take advantage of traditional psychotherapies during this phase of treatment, whereas others believe that individual and family psychotherapy may help. Certainly, after the initial period of weight gain, individual and family psychotherapy appears to benefit patients with AN to maintain recovery [42,43]. The impact of concurrent mood disorder on treatment outcome is unclear, and some modification of individual psychotherapy to address the mood disorder, using cognitive and interpersonal techniques, seems appropriate. Given the demonstrated salutary impact of couples' therapy on the treatment of depression in married women experiencing marital discord [44], by extension family therapy should also be practical and useful for many depressed patients with eating disorder.

With regard to antidepressant medication, the few available controlled trials showed little value for amitriptyline at doses of 40 to 160 mg/day [45], or for low dose, 50 mg/day, clomipramine [46]. Furthermore, most clinicians have been reluctant to use tricyclic antidepressants in severely malnourished patients with AN, concerned that because of these drugs' anticholinergic and cardiotoxic side effects, these medications might cause more harm than good, exacerbating hypotension in patients already prone to hypotensive episodes, and risking potentially fatal arrhythmias in patients whose cardiac conduction systems are compromised by malnutrition.

Clinicians have, however, been less reluctant to use selective serotonin reuptake inhibitors (SSRIs) in the treatment of AN. In an open series of six patients with previously unresponsive long-term AN, clinical improvement in eating behaviors, weight, obsessionality, compulsive behaviors (including some reduction in compulsive exercise), and mood was reported following treatment with up to 60 mg/day of fluoxetine [47]. When patients with AN who recovered weight were treated for 1 year following hospitalization in a controlled trial, patients treated with fluoxetine had less loss of weight and, furthermore, reported less exacerbation of depressive symptoms than the placebo group during the posthospital year. Doses were 10 to 80 mg/day, with most patients receiving 20 to 60 mg/day of fluoxetine. None of these patients reported weight loss as a side effect of fluoxetine at these dosages [28].

However, many patients with AN with and without concurrent mood disorder do not respond to fluoxetine, and, at least anecdotally, not uncommonly experience troubling side effects including headaches, anorgasmia, and akathisia. In the absence of controlled trials, the decision to use SSRIs as part of initial treatment in low-weight patients with AN must be made after considering all aspects of the case, and after careful discussion with patients and families. When mood disorders and obsessive-compulsive disorders are also clearly present, many clinicians opt to use SSRIs in earlier phases of treatment, and in the event of unresponsiveness to treatment, to proceed with algorithms designed for patients resistant to treatment.

In cases in which patients with AN suffer from persistent, treatment-resistant depressions, treatment with monoamine oxidase inhibitors (MAOIs) has sometimes been helpful [48]. Electroconvulsive therapy (ECT) has also been reported to be of value for some patients [49].

Bulimia nervosa

A large number of controlled treatment trials for BN have been published [50]. Although relatively few of these studies explicitly focus on the impact of treatment on those with comorbid diagnoses [51], many have used a variety of self-report rating scales for depressive symptoms. In virtually all studies, improvement in BN symptoms is accompanied by corresponding improvements in depressive symptoms. Some medication studies report improvement in depressive symptoms even in the absence of significant improvement in BN symptoms [52].

Psychotherapy

Although several types of psychotherapy are effective for the treatment of BN, the influence of coexisting depression on treatment outcome has not been evaluated systematically. Certain studies using psychotherapy alone are reviewed by Mitchell *et al* [50]. Psychotherapies that are effective for BN also tend to reduce symptoms of depression [53,54]. Results of these studies can be summarized as follows. Cognitive-behavioral therapy has been shown both in individual and group treatment settings to result in significant improvement in symptoms of BN, with short-term rates of reduction in symptoms of binge eating and purging in the range of 77%, and abstinence rates averaging around 38% according to an analysis by Abbott and Mitchell [55]. Elements of cognitive-behavioral therapy include psychoeducation; monitoring of eating using logs that also record cognitive, emotional, and behavioral antecedents and consequences of binge eating and purging; goal setting with contingencies; elucidating and challenging maladaptive attitudes related to eating, body image, and related issues; and enhancing alternative styles of coping. Long-term maintenance of symptomatic gains are common, and improvement seems to be enhanced by participation in ongoing maintenance–relapse prevention treatment (individually or in groups) and by initial insistence on abstinence from binge eating and purging [55]. Although cognitive-behavioral therapy may be more effective initially than interpersonal psychotherapy (specifically modified to remove discussion of eating disorder issues) or behavior therapy alone in the treatment of BN, after a period of several years, those treated with interpersonal psychotherapy have as much sustained improvement as those treated with cognitive-behavioral therapy, and both do significantly better than patients treated with behavioral therapy alone [56]. Approaches that use high intensity outpatient treatments and that favor an emphasis on abstinence may be more effective than others, at least initially [57]. Table 3 [56–61] provides summaries of some illustrative, larger, controlled psychotherapy studies for BN.

Because approaches using cognitive-behavioral therapy and interpersonal therapy have both been successful in the treatment of mood disorders, particularly nonpsychotic major depressions as well as eating disorders, approaches that combine features targeted at symptoms of both eating and mood disorders should be designed and implemented.

Medication

A substantial literature of controlled trials for BN exists, illustrated by the representative studies delineated in Tables 3 and 4 [62–75,76••], with other new medications being regularly tested as well [72]. To summarize, double-blind, placebo-controlled studies have shown significantly reduced binge eating and purging to be associated with administration of the tricyclic antidepressants imipramine and desipramine, tradazodone, the SSRI fluoxetine, and the MAOIs phenelzine and isocarboxazid. In the most extensive short-term studies available, with hundreds of subjects enrolled in 8-week [74] and 16-week trials [76••], fluoxetine was superior to placebo in reducing symptoms of binge eating and purging. The 60 mg/day dosing schedule was found to be more effective than 20 mg/day. Other SSRIs also appear to have promise. For example, specific 5-HT 1A agonists and partial agonists such as ipsapirone reduce both BN behaviors and depressive symptoms [77], further supporting the notion that serotonin systems may be involved in both conditions. However, none of these studies has shown depressed patients with BN to be better responders to antidepresant treatment than nondepressed patients [52].

Pharmacotherpeutic agents that have been ineffective compared with placebo in controlled trials are listed in Table 5 [78–82]. One agent, perhaps as yet inadequately evaluated on its own, is d-fenfluramine. In an 8-week controlled trial in which 43 patients received 45 mg/day of d-fenfluramine or placebo together with cognitive-behavioral therapy, patients in both the drug and placebo groups showed significant improvement; those receiving active drug received no added benefit [83].

In an analysis specifically aimed at patients suffering from both atypical depression and BN, Rothschild *et al.* [51] found phenelzine to be somewhat better than imipramine, and both to be significantly better than placebo. In spite of the demonstrated efficacy of MAOIs, however, many clinicians prefer starting with an SSRI or a tricyclic because of a lower incidence of untoward effects and concerns about eating binges that might include foods containing tyramine. As with psychotherapy, medication responders whose symptoms of BN improve often show parallel improvement in their depressive symptoms as well. This holds true for those improving on placebo as well as those taking active medication [52,80].

Combined psychotherapy and medication

Several studies have examined the combined use of psychotherapy and medication. Many differences in the design of these studies concerning medications used, doses, types of psychotherapy, lengths of treatment, and timing of follow-ups, make direct comparisons difficult and leave several issues unresolved [55]. To date, studies have shown that 1) combinations of cognitive-behavioral therapy and tricyclics used for 24 weeks are somewhat more effective in reducing binge eating and purging than individual treatment with either modality alone [53,84, and Walsh, Unpublished paper presented at New Directions in Diagnosis and Treatment of Eating Disorders, American Psychiatric Association Annual Meeting, Miami, 1995], and that adding medication may help prevent relapse after cognitive-behavioral therapy has ended [55]; 2) depending on the study design and other variables, medication sometimes adds little discernable advantage in reducing eating disorder symptoms when patients are treated with outpatient cognitive-behavioral therapy [83,Walsh,85]; and 3) intensive outpatient [64] or inpatient [75] therapy programs produce considerable benefit, and that adding medication in these situations yields small, if any, additional advantages with respect to eating disorder symptoms. Combined medication plus outpatient psychotherapy treatment, however, produces greater improvement in depression and anxiety measures [64].

One suggestion for resolving the dispute as to whether prescribing medication in addition to intensive psychotherapies really adds anything of discernable value pertains to potential "ceiling effects" of psychotherapies. When very intensive psychotherapy regimens are used, (eg, Mitchell *et al.* [50] used an average of 45 hours over 10 weeks, front loaded to be more intensive during the first 3 to 4 weeks), medications may add little; but, when an outpatient psychotherapy program is less intensive (eg, Agras *et al.* [84]

Table 3. Illustrative Recent Controlled Psychotherapy Trials for Bulimia Nervosa

Study	Design	Patients, n

Fairburn et al. [56]	Prospective follow-up of two randomized controlled trials:
	    Individual CBT vs FIT
	    Individual CBT vs FIT vs BT
		24
		75

Mitchell et al. [57]	Controlled four-cell group CBT trial: varied by intensity
	    (Hi I/Lo I) and emphasis on early abstinence (Hi A/Lo A)
		143 (each cell had
		    33–41 patients)

Garner et al. [58]	Individual psychodynamic vs CBT	60 (30 patients in each)
Fairburn et al. [59]	Individual CBT vs IPT vs BT	75
Agras et al. [60]	Three group treatment: Self-monitoring CBT CBT plus ERP	58
Freeman et al. [61]	Individual CBT vs individual BT vs group	92

BT—behavioral therapy; CBT—cognitive-behavioral therapy; ERP—exposure response prevention; FIT—focal interpersonal psychotherapy; IPT—interpersonal psychotherapy.

used 50 minutes per week of psychotherapy for a total of about 18 hours), medications may offer additional benefit [50].

Other approaches

Following the observation that some BN patients have seasonal disorders, in a controlled trial with 17 patients Lam et al. [86] found that 2 weeks of bright light therapy resulted in significantly greater improvement in eating and mood symptoms in seven patients with seasonal bulimia than in 10 without a seasonal component.

Treatment implications

What do these studies imply, and what is the current level of clinical practice? Most clinicians would agree that some sort of focused, active psychotherapy, preferably one with strong cognitive-behavioral and psychoeducational aspects dealing with eating disorders, and with

Duration of treatment	Time of follow-up	Results
18 wk 18 wk	5.8 years	Abstinence rates, % FIT=52 CBT=50 BT=18
1. Hi I/Hi A 45 hr/12 wk 2. Hi I/Lo A 45 hr/12 wk 3. Lo I/Hi A 22.5 hr/12 wk 4. Lo I/Lo A 22.5 hr/12 wk	Endpoint analysis: treatment or dropping out	Abstinence rates by group, % 1. 64 2. 68 3. 68 4. 21
18 wk	Endpoint	Abstinence from purging, % Psychodynamic, 12 CBT, 36
18 wk	Endpoint	Reductions in binge frequency, % CBT, 97 IPT, 89 BT, 91 Abstinence from binges, % CBT, 71 IPT, 62 BT, 62
14 wk	Endpoint	Reductions in binge frequency, % Self-monitoring, 63 CBT, 75 CBT plus ERP, 52 Abstinence, % Self-monitoring, 24 CBT, 56 CBT plus ERP, 31 Only significant finding CBT > wait-list control
15 wk	Endpoint	Reduction in binge frequency, % Individual CBT, 79 Individual BT, 87 Group, 87

attention to interpersonal issues as well, is indicated in the initial treatment of virtually all patients with BN. For patients without concurrent major depression, this treatment often suffices and is successful, but if little improvement has occurred after 2 months, treatment with medication should be instituted. However, because the onset of clinical improvement may be faster among patients taking antidepressants whether or not clinical depression is present, the option of starting medication immediately should be discussed with every patient.

For the many patients with BN who present with concurrent major depression (a group not yet specifically studied in this respect given what we know), a medication trial should be advised along with psychotherapy from the beginning of treatment. For patients with atypical depression, an MAOI trial may be considered. Because in clinical practice several trials of different types of antidepressant medication may be necessary before an effective one is found, this potential course should be discussed with patients at the start of medication treatment to prepare them for this possibility.

Table 4. Effective Medication Treatments for Bulimia Nervosa (Double-blind, Placebo-controlled Trials)

Medication	Patients, n	Maximum dose, mg	Duration, wk	Drug/placebo reduction, % Binge eating	Drug/placebo reduction, % Purging	Abstinent at end of treatment, %
Tricyclics						
Imipramine						
Pope et al. [62]	22	200	6	70/0		0
Agras et al. [63]	22	300	16	72/43	72/35	30
Desipramine						
Barlow et al. [65]	47	150	6			4
Hughes et al. [66]	22	200	6	91/-19	68/0	
McCann et al. [67]	23	300	12	63/-16	*	
Walsh et al. [68]	78	300	6	47/-7		
Blouin et al. [69]	36	150	6		45	12.5/7.9
Trazadone						
Pope et al. [70]	46	625	6	31/-21		10/0
MAOIs						
Phenelzine						
Walsh et al. [71]	50	60–90	6	64/5		35/4
Isocarboxide						
Kennedy et al. [72]	18	90	12	35/-7.0		
SSRIs						
Fluoxetine						
Freeman et al. [73]	40	60	6	51/17		
FBNC study group [74]	382	20/60	8	67/45/33†		
Goldstein et al. [76••]	398	60	16	51/36‡	53/35†	19/12

*Nonpurging bulimics.
†60 mg/20 mg/placebo.
‡Percentage improving≥ 50%.
FBNC—Fluoxetine Bulimia Nervosa Collaborative; MAOI—monoamine oxidase inhibitor; SSRIs—selective serotonin reuptake inhibitors.

With regard to effectiveness, early treatment with medication for BN may be associated with better sustained recovery. As part of a prospective, naturalistic study of patients with BN who sought treatment, Herzog and Sacks [87] found that patients with BN who had received medication treatment within the first 13 weeks were more likely to demonstrate sustained recovery over the course of the first year than those who were not receiving medications. In this survey, the modal form of medication treatment was fluoxetine in doses of 20 to 60 mg/day taken for at least 6 months.

Similarly, although several medications have been demonstrated to be effective for BN, we are unaware of studies that have prospectively compared their efficacy in depressed and nondepressed patients with BN.

Binge eating disorder

Few published treatment studies have targeted BED and none has looked specifically at the treatment of depressed binge eaters. Two double-blind, placebo-controlled medication trials have been reported. Marcus et al. [88] treated obese binge eaters and obese nonbinge

Table 5. Ineffective Treatments for Bulimia Nervosa (Double-blind, Placebo-controlled Trials)

Medication	Patients, n	Maximum dose, mg	Duration, wk	Drug/placebo reduction, % Binge eating	Purging	Abstinent at end of treatment, %
Tricyclics						
Amitriptyline						
Mitchell et al. [78]	38	150	8	72/52	78/5	19/19
Imipramine						
Alger et al. [79]	22	200	8			
MAOIs						
Brofaromine						
Kennedy et al. [52]	36	200	8	62/50	75/24*	19/13
Mianserine						
Sabine et al. [82]	50	60	8			
Lithium carbonate						
Hsu et al. [80]	91	600–1200	8	40/63	50/58	
		(blood levels 0.62 mEq/L ± .12)				
Naltrexone						
Alger et al. [79]	22	150	8	22/40/30/†		
Mitchell et al. [81]‡	18	50	6	14	8	

*Not significant for binge eating; significant for purging.
†200 mg/150 mg/placebo.
‡Crossover trial.
MAOI—monoamine oxidase inhibitor.

eaters for 52 weeks with 60 mg/day fluoxetine plus basic behavior modification techniques (in a total of 13 visits) and found that those treated with medication lost significantly more weight; however, there was no differential beneficial effect for binge eaters versus nonbinge eaters. McCann *et al.* [67] showed that desipramine in doses of up to 300 mg/day resulted in decreased binge eating, greater dietary restraint, and less hunger in a group of overweight nonpurging bulimic women (essentially BED patients). Based on Beck Depression Inventory scores at the start of the study, these patients were not suffering from depression.

With regard to psychotherapy, cognitive-behavioral and group support treatments specifically designed to address binge eating may yield better short-term symptomatic improvement and weight loss among severe binge eaters than moderate binge eaters or nonbinge-eating obese patients [89]. Several additional controlled trials using psychotherapies with or without medications for treating BED are currently under way.

Prognostic Implications of Comorbid Eating Disorders and Mood Disorders

Given the frequency with which they coexist, surprisingly little has been examined with respect to the extent to which comorbid mood disorder affects treatment outcome and prognosis for eating disorders [90]. In reviewing 33 long-term follow-up studies of AN, Herzog *et al.* [91] mention only one study that explicitly considered depressive symptoms and another that considered the presence of previous secondary psychiatric diagnoses in relation to outcome (in both cases they were predictors of negative outcome); in none of the other studies reviewed were mood disturbances even listed, neither as predictors of negative or positive outcome nor as nonpredictors. In a study of 30 hospitalized patients with BN followed 2 to 5 years later, patients who were moderately or severely depressed on admission, as assessed by the Beck Depression Inventory and Hamilton Rating Scale for Depression, tended to fall into the intermediate or poor outcome category at follow-up, whereas those with milder depression on admission were more likely to fall into the good outcome groups; depression on admission was not related to depression at follow-up [92].

Conclusions

Mood disorders are frequently concomitant with eating disorders. Their co-occurrence suggests some combination of common antecedents, which may partly be related to as yet obscure genetic factors, partly due to preexisting vulnerabilities related to personality, trauma, and other developmental issues, and partly related to the profound psychobiologic effects of malnutrition. Comprehensive assessment of these patients must be sensitive to these multiple biologic, psychologic, and social contributing factors. Current treatment strategies are based on those available for eating disorders and mood disorders, and include judicious combinations of nutritional rehabilitation, psychoeducation, cognitive-behavioral therapies, interpersonal psychotherapies, family therapies, and medications. Further research is necessary to delineate more carefully the full implications of these associations for treatment and prognosis.

References and Recommended Reading

Papers of particular interest, published recently, have been highlighted as:
- Of special interest
- • Of outstanding interest

1.   Halmi KA, Eckert K, Marchi P, et al.: Comorbidity of psychiatric diagnoses in anorexia nervosa. Arch Gen Psychiatry 1991, 48:712–718.
2.•• Walters EE, Kendler KS: Anorexia nervosa and anorexic-like syndromes in a population based female twin sample. Am J Psychiatry 1995, 152:64–71.
This excellent epidemiologic study examined risk factors for AN and examined the relationship between narrowly defined AN and anorexia-like syndromes in a population-based sample of 2163 female twins. Co-twins of twins with AN were a significantly higher risk for lifetime AN, bulimia, BN, major depression, and current low body mass index. The results support the hypothesis of a spectrum of anorexic-like syndromes in women and found that these syndromes share familial etiologic factors with major depression and BN.
3.• Garfinkel PE, Lin E, Goering P, et al.: Bulimia nervosa in a Canadian community sample; prevalence and comparison of subgroups. Am J Psychiatry 1995, 152:1052–1058.
The authors sought to define the prevalence of BN and its comorbidity in a nonclinical community sample of 8116 Canadian subjects. Subjects with full- and partial-syndrome BN showed significant vulnerability for mood and anxiety disorders, and lifetime rates of alcohol dependence were high in the full-syndrome group. Both bulimic groups were significantly more likely to experience childhood sexual abuse than a healthy female comparison.
4.   Hudson JI, Pope Jr HG, Yurgelun-Todd D, et al.: A controlled study of lifetime prevalence of affective and other psychiatric disorders in bulimic outpatients. Am J Psychiatry 1987, 144:1283–1287.

5. Kendler KS, Maclean C, Neale M, *et al.*: The genetic epidemiology of bulimia nervosa. *Am J Psychiatry* 1991, 148:1627–1637.

6. Kennedy SH, Kaplan AS, Garfinkel PE, *et al.*: Depression in anorexia nervosa and bulimia nervosa: discriminating depressive symptoms and episodes. *J Psychosom Res* 1994, 38:773–782.

7. Fornari V, Kaplan M, Sandberg DE, *et al.*: Depressive and anxiety disorders in anorexia nervosa and bulimia nervosa. *Int J Eating Disord* 1992, 12:21–29.

8. Simpson SG, Al-Mufti R, Andersen AE, *et al.*: Bipolar II affective disorder in eating disorder inpatients. *J Nerv Ment Dis* 1992, 180:719–722.

9. Fornari VM, Braun DL, Sunday SR, *et al.*: Seasonal patterns in eating disorder subgroups. *Comp Psychiatry* 1994, 35:450–456.

10. Demitrack MA, Putnam FW, Brewerton TD, *et al.*: Relation of clinical variables to dissociative phenomena in eating disorders. *Am J Psychiatry* 1990, 147:1184–1188.

11.• Andrews B, Valentine ER, Valentine JD: Depression and eating disorders following abuse in childhood in two generations of women. *Br J Clin Psychol* 1995, 34:37–52.
The relation of sexual and physical abuse in childhood to subsequent depression and eating disorders was explored in a community sample of mothers and their teenage and young adult daughters, respectively. Both physical and sexual abuse were related to bulimia in the daughters, but not in the mothers, as only one mother had such a disorder. This suggests a cohort effect for bulimia, perhaps related to cultural pressures that differed for daughters compared with mothers.

12. Rorty M, Yager J, Rossotto E: Childhood sexual, physical and psychological abuse and their relationship to comorbid psychopathology in bulimia nervosa. *Int J Eating Disord* 1994, 16:317–334.

13. Marcus MD, Wing RR, Hopkins J: Obese binge eaters: affect, cognitions, and response to behavioral weight control. *J Consult Clin Psychol* 1988, 56:433–439.

14. Fichter MM, Quadflieg N, Bradl B: Recurrent overeating: an empirical comparison of binge eating disorder, bulimia nervosa and obesity. *Int J Eating Disord* 1993, 14:1–16.

15. Katzman MA, Wolchik SA: Bulimia and binge eating in college women: a comparison of personality and behavioral characteristics. *J Consult Clin Psychol* 1984, 52:423–428.

16. de Zwaan M, Bach M, Mitchell JE, *et al.*: Alexithymia, obesity, and binge eating disorder. *Int J Eating Disord* 1995, 17:135–140.

17. Skodol AE, Oldham JM, Hyler SE, *et al.*: Comorbidity of DSM-III-R eating disorders and personality disorders. *Int J Eating Disord* 1993, 14:403–416.

18. Steiger H, Leung F, Thibaudeau J, *et al.*: Comorbid features in bulimics before and after therapy: are they explained by axis II diagnoses, secondary effects of bulimia, or both? *Comp Psychiatry* 1993, 34:45–53.

19. Rothenberg A: Differential diagnosis of anorexia nervosa and depressive illness: a review of 11 studies. *Comp Psychiatry* 1988, 29:427–432.

20. Strober M: Family-genetic studies of eating disorders. *J Clin Psychiatry* 1991, 52:(suppl), 9–12.

21. Keys A, Brozek J, Henschel A, *et al.*: *The Biology of Human Starvation.* Minneapolis: University of Minnesota Press; 1950.

22. Green MW, Rogers PJ, Elliman NA, *et al.*: Impairment of cognitive performance associated with dieting and high levels of dietary restraint. *Physiol Behav* 1992, 55:447–452.

23. Pirke KM, Palh J, Schweiger U, *et al.*: Metabolic and endocrine indices of starvation in bulimia: a comparison with anorexia nervosa. *Psychiatry Res* 1985, 15:33–40.

24. Pahl J, Pirke KM, Schweiger U, *et al.*: Anorectic behavior, mood, and metabolic and endocrine adaptation to starvation in anorexia nervosa during inpatient treatment. *Biol Psychiatry* 1985, 20:874–887.

25. Kennedy SH, Brown GM, Ford CG, *et al.*: The acute effects of starvation on 6-sulphatoxy-melatonin output in subgroups of patients with anorexia nervosa. *Psychoneuroendocrinology* 1993, 18:131–139.

26. Pirke KM, Spyra B: Catecholamine turnover in the brain and the regulation of luteinizing hormone and corticosterone in starved male rats. *Acta Endocrinol* 1982, 100:168–176.

27. Broochs A, Liu J, Pirke KM: Influence of hyperactivity on the metabolism of central monoaminergic neurotransmitters and reproductive function in the semi-starved rat. In *The Menstrual Cycle and Its Disorders.* Edited by Prick KM, Wuttke W, Schweiger UH. New York: Springer Verlag; 1989:88–96.

28. Kaye WH, Weltzin TE, Hsu LKG, *et al.*: An open trial of fluoxetine in patients with anorexia nervosa. *J Clin Psychiatry* 1991, 52:464–471.

29.• Deep AL, Nagy LM, Weltzin TE, *et al.*: Premorbid onset of psychopathology in long-term recovered anorexia nervosa. *Int J Eating Disord* 1995, 17:291–297.

In a retrospective study of 24 subjects who were recovered from AN for more than 1 year, the authors examined the extent to which these subjects experienced other psychiatric illnesses before the onset of anorexia. In this sample, 58% reported the onset of one or more childhood anxiety disorder diagnoses at the age of 10 +/- 5 years, 5 years before the mean age of onset of AN. The onset of depression was about 1 year before the onset of AN in about half of the subjects, and alcohol and substance abuse or dependency tended to occur after the onset of AN and only occurred in anorexic subjects who binged or purged. The early and common onset of anxiety disorders raises the possibility that childhood anxiety disorders herald the first behavioral expression of a biologic vulnerability in some subjects who develop AN.

30. Cooper PJ, Fairburn CG: Confusion over the core psycopathology of bulimia nervosa. *Int J Eating Disord* 1993, 13:385–389.

31. Gershon E, Schrieber J, Hamovit J, *et al.*: Clinical findings in patients with anorexia nervosa and affective illness in their relatives. *Am J Psychiatry* 1984, 149:1419–1422.

32. Hudson JI, Pope HG, Jonas JM, *et al.*: A family history study of anorexia nervosa and bulimia nervosa. *Br J Psychiatry* 1983, 142:133–138.

33. Kassett JA, Gershon ES, Maxwell ME, *et al.*: Psychiatric disorders in the first-degree relatives of probands with bulimia nervosa. *Am J Psychiatry* 1989, 146:1468–1471.

34. Strober M, Lampert C, Morrell W, *et al.*: A controlled family study of anorexia nervosa: evidence of familial aggregation and lack of shared transmission with affective disorders. *Int J Eating Disord* 1990, 9:239–253.

35. Hudson JI, Pope HG Jr, Jonas JM, *et al.*: A controlled family history study of bulimia. *Psychol Med* 1987, 17:883–890.

36. Wilson GT, Lindholm L: Bulimia nervosa and depression. *Int J Eating Disord* 1987, 6:725–732.

37. Mitchell JE, Hatsukami D, Pyle RO, *et al.*: Bulimia with and without a family history of depressive illness. *Comp Psychiatry* 1986, 27:215–219.

38. Walters EE, Neale MC, Eaves LJ, *et al.*: Bulimia nervosa and major depression: a study of common genetic and environmental factors. *Psychol Med* 1992, 22:617–622.

39. Winokur A, March V, Mendels J: Primary affective disorder in relatives of patients with anorexia nervosa. *Am J Psychiatry* 1980, 137:695–698.

40. Logue CM, Crowe RR, Bean JA: A family study of anorexia nervosa and bulimia. *Comp Psychiatry* 1989, 30:179–188.

41. American Psychiatric Association: Practice guideline for eating disorders. *Am J Psychiatry* 1993, 150:212–228.

42. Russell GF, Szmukler GI, Dare C, *et al.*: An evaluation of family therapy in anorexia nervosa and bulimia. *Arch Gen Psychiatry* 1987, 44:1047–1056.

43. Gowers S, Norton K, Halek C, *et al.*: Outcome of outpatient psychotherapy in a random treatment allocation study of anorexia nervosa. *Int J Eating Disord* 1994, 15:165–177.

44. Beach SRH, Sandeen EE, O'Leary KD: *Depression in Marriage*. New York: Guilford; 1990.

45. Halmi KA, Eckert E, LaDu TJ, *et al.*: Anorexia nervosa: treatment efficacy of cyroheptadine and amitriptyline. *Arch Gen Psychiatry* 1986, 43:177–181.

46. Lacey JH, Crisp AH: Hunger, food intake and weight: the impact of clomipramine on a refeeding anorexia nervosa population. *Postgrad Med J* 1980, 56:79–85.

47. Gwirtsman HE, Guze BH, Yager J, *et al.*: Fluoxetine treatment of anorexia nervosa: an open clincial trial. *J Clin Psychiatry* 1990, 51:378–382.

48. Hudson JI, Pope HG Jr, Jonas JM, *et al.*: Treatment of anorexia nervosa with antidepressants. *J Clin Psychopharmacol* 1985, 5:17–23.

49. Ferguson JM: The use of electroconvulsive therapy in patients with intractable anorexia nervosa. *Int J Eating Disord* 1993, 13:195–201.

50. Mitchell JE, Raymond N, Specker S: A review of the controlled trials of pharmacotherapy and psychotherapy in the treatment of bulimia nervosa. *Int J Eating Disord* 1993, 14:229–248.

51. Rothschild R, Quitkin HM, Quitkin FM, *et al.*: A double-blind placebo controlled comparison of phenelzine and imipramine in the treatment of bulimia in atypical depressives. *Int J Eating Disord* 1994, 15:1–9.

52. Kennedy SH, Goldbloom DS, Ralevski E, *et al.*: Is there a role for selective monoamine oxidase inhibitor therapy in bulimia nervosa: a placebo-controlled trial of brofaromine. *J Clin Psychopharmacol* 1993, 13:415–422.

53. Agras WS, Rossiter EM, Arnow B, *et al.*: One-year follow-up of psychosocial and pharmacologic treatments for bulimia nervosa. *J Clin Psychiatry* 1994, 55:179–183.

54. Fairburn CG, Jones R, Peveler C, *et al.*: Psychotherapy and bulimia nervosa: longer term effects of interpersonal psychotherapy, behavior therapy and cognitive behavior therapy. *Arch Gen Psychiatry* 1993, 50:419–428.

55. Abbott DW, Mitchell JE: Antidepressants versus psychotherapy in the treatment of bulimia nervosa. *Psychopharm Bull* 1993, 29:115–199.

56. Fairburn CG, Norman PA, Welsch SL, *et al.*: A prospective study of outcome in bulimia nervosa and the long-term effects of three psychological treatments. *Arch Gen Psychiatry* 1995, 52:304–312.

57. Mitchell JE, Pyle RL, Pomeroy C, *et al.*: Cognitive-behavioral group psychotherapy of bulimia nervosa: importance of logistical variables. *Int J Eating Disord* 1993, 14:277–289.

58. Garner DM, Rockert W, Davis R, *et al.*: Comparison of cognitive-behavioral and supportive-expressive psychotherapy for bulimia nervosa. *Am J Psychiatry* 1993, 150:37–46.

59. Fairburn CG, Jones R, Peveler RC, *et al.*: Three psychological treatments for bulimia nervosa. *Arch Gen Psychiatry* 1991, 48:463–469.

60. Agras WS, Schneider JA, Arnow B, *et al.*: Cognitive-behavioral and response-prevention treatment for bulimia nervosa. *J Consult Clin Psychol* 1989, 57:215–221.

61. Freeman CPL, Barry F, Bunkeld-Turnbull J, *et al.*: Controlled trial of psychotherapy for bulimia nervosa. *BMJ* 1988, 296:521–525.

62. Pope HG Jr, Hudson JI, Jonas JM, *et al.*: Bulimia treated with imipramine: a placebo-controlled, double-blind study. *Am J Psychiatry* 1983, 140:554–558.

63. Agras WS, Dorian B, Kirkley BG, *et al.*: Imipramine in the treatment of bulimia: a double blind controlled study. *Int J Eating Disord* 1987, 6:29–38.

64. Mitchell JE, Pyle RO, Eckert ED, *et al.*: A comparison study of antidepressants and structured intensive group psychotherapy in the treatment of bulimia nervosa. *Arch Gen Psychiatry* 1990, 47:149–157.

65. Barlow J, Blouin A, Perez E: Treatment of bulimia with desipramine: a double-blind cross over study. *Can J Psychiatry* 1988, 33:129–133.

66. Hughes PL, Wells LA, Cunningham CJ, *et al.*: Treating bulimia with desipramine: a double-blind placebo controlled study. *Arch Gen Psychiatry* 1986, 43:182–186.

67. McCann UD, Agras WS: Successful treatment of nonpurging bulimia nervosa with desipramine: a double-blind, placebo-controlled study. *Am J Psychiatry* 1990, 147:1509–1513.

68. Walsh BT, Hadigan CM, Devlin MJ, *et al.*: Long-term outcome of antidepressant treatment for bulimia nervosa. *Am J Psychiatry* 1991, 148:1206–1212.

69. Blouin AG, Blouin JH, Perez E, *et al.*: Treatment of bulimia with fenfluramine and desipramine. *J Clin Psychopharmacol* 1988, 8:261–269.

70. Pope HG Jr, Keck PE Jr, McElroy SL, *et al.*: A placebo-controlled study of trazodone in bulimia nervosa. *J Clin Psychopharmacol* 1989, 9:254–259.

71. Walsh BT, Gladis M, Roose SP, *et al.*: Phenelzine versus placebo in 50 patients with bulimia. *Arch Gen Psychiatry* 1988, 45:471–475.

72. Kennedy SH, Prian N, Warsh JJ, *et al.*: A trial of isocarboxazid in the treatment of bulimia nervosa. *J Clin Psychopharmacol* 1988, 8:391–396.

73. Freeman CPL, Mundro JKM: Drug and group treatments for bulimia/bulimia nervosa. *Psychosom Res* 1988, 32:647–660.

74. Fluoxetine Bulimia Nervosa Collaborative Study Group: Fluoxetine in the treatment of bulimia nervosa: a multicenter placebo controlled, double blind trial. *Arch Gen Psychiatry* 1992, 49:139–147.

75. Fichter MM, Leibl K, Rief W, *et al.*: Fluoxetine versus placebo: a double-blind study with bulimic inpatients undergoing intensive psychotherapy. *Pharmacopsychiatry* 1991, 24:1–7.

76.•• Goldstein DJ, Wilson MG, Thompson VL, et al.: Long term fluoxetine treatment of bulimia nervosa. Br J Psychiatry 1995, 166:660–666.
This paper presents the results of a well-conducted, large-scale, pharmaceutical company–sponsored, 16-week, placebo-controlled, double-blind study using fluoxetine in the treatment of BN. Fifteen outpatient clinics participated, 483 patients entered, 398 were randomized at a 3:1 ratio, fluoxetine 60 mg/day or placebo, and 225 completed the study. Compared with placebo, fluoxetine treatment resulted in significantly greater reductions in vomiting and binge eating episodes per week at endpoint and improvement in other outcome measures. Adverse event, vital sign, and laboratory analyses indicated fluoxetine was safe.

77.   Geretseeger C, Greimel KV, Roed IS, et al.: Ipsapirone in the treatment of bulimia nervosa: an open pilot study. Int J Eating Disord 1995, 17:359–363.

78.   Mitchell JE, Groat R: A placebo-controlled, double-blind trial of amitryiptyline in bulimia. J Clin Psychopharmacol 1984, 4:186–193.

79.   Alger SA, Schwalberg MD, Bigaoutte JM, et al.: Effect of a tricycle antidepressant and opiate antagonist on binge-eating behavior in normal weight bulimic and obese binge eating subjects. Am J Clin Nutr 1991, 53:545–555.

80.   Hsu LKG, Clement L, Santhouse R, et al.: Treatment of bulimia nervosa with lithium carbonate: a controlled study. J Nerv Ment Dis 1991, 179:351–355.

81.   Mitchell JE, Christenson G, Jennings J, et al.: A placebo-controlled, double-blind cross over study of naltrexone hydrochloride in outpatients with normal weight bulimia. J Clin Psychopharmacol 1989, 9:94–97.

82.   Sabine EJ, Yonance A, Farrington AJ, et al.: Bulimia nervosa: a placebo controlled, double-blind study of mianserin. Br J Clin Pharmacol 1983, 15:1958–2028.

83.   Fahy TA, Eisler I, Russell GFM: A placebo-controlled trial of d-fenfluramine in bulimia nervosa. Br J Psychiatry 1993, 162:597–603.

84.   Agas WS, Rossiter EM, Arnow B, et al.: Pharmacologic and cognitive-behavioral treatment for bulimia nervosa: a controlled comparison. Am J Psychiatry 1992, 149:82–87.

85.   Leitenberg H, Rosen JC, Wolf J, et al.: Comparison of cognitive-behavior therapy and desipramine in the treatment of bulimia nervosa. Behav Res Ther 1994, 32:37–45.

86.   Lam RW, Goldner EM, Solyom L, et al.: A controlled study of light therapy for bulimia nervosa. Am J Psychiatry 1994, 151:744–750.

87.   Herzog DB, Sacks NR: Bulimia nervosa: comparison of treatment responders vs non-responders. Psychopharmacol Bull 1993, 29:121–125.

88.   Marcus MD, Wing RR, Ewing L, et al.: A double-blind placebo controlled trial of fluoxetine plus behavior modification in the treatment of obese binge eaters. Am J Psychiatry 1990, 147:876–881.

89.   Porzelius LK, Houston C, Smith M, et al.: Comparison of a standard behavioral weight loss treatment and a binge eating weight loss treatment. Behav Ther 1995, 26:119–134.

90.   Hsu LFG: Outcome studies in patients with eating disorders. In Psychiatry Treatment: Advances in Outcome Research. Edited by Mirin SM, Gossett JT, Grob MC. Washington, DC: American Psychiatric Press; 1991:159–180.

91.   Herzog DB, Keller MB, Lavori PW: Outcome in anorexia nervosa and bulimia nervosa: a review of the literature. J Nerv Ment Dis 1988, 176:131–143.

92.   Swift WJ, Kalin NH, Wamboldt FS, et al.: Depression in bulimia at 2–5 year follow-up. Psychiatr Res 1985, 16:111–122.

CHAPTER 15

Treatment of Anxiety Disorders in Children and Adolescents

Carroll W. Hughes and Graham J. Emslie

This chapter on the treatment of anxiety disorders in children and adolescents is a treatise on limitations in research and precautions in psychopharmacotherapy. Such a chapter should characterize the disorder, establish what is known about the disorder, and determine what research supports the recommendations for pharmacotherapy or other therapeutic interventions. This chapter attempts to put the current treatment of childhood anxiety disorders in perspective.

At issue first are the short-lived and evolving concepts and definitions of anxiety disorders in childhood. The most recent *Diagnostic and Statistical Manual of Mental Disorders*, edn 4 (DSM-IV) definitions were last revised in 1994. Second, childhood disorders, more so than adult disorders, are typically comorbid with other childhood disorders, sharing many overlapping symptoms and developmental considerations. Biologic foundations for the disorders remain speculative, based primarily on a limited number of adult studies. Hence, diagnosis is frequently uncertain. Finally, research and case studies on child and adolescent anxiety disorders to date are scarce in comparison with the number of studies on adults and the amount of research on other disorders (*eg*, depression). Diagnosis is also limited by methodologic flaws. Nonetheless, on the horizon there are patterns of pharmacotherapy and behavior therapy treatments evolving along with the definitions of the disorders, ongoing research studies, and promise for new receptor-specific medications [1•].

Brief History

As shown in Table 1 [2–6], the evolution of anxiety disorders in children and adolescents has had an interesting history over the past 40 years. In the original DSM [2], anxiety disorders in children and adolescents were not considered, and only a few references were made to other childhood disorders. By the time of the second edition (DSM-II) [3], child and adolescent anxiety disorders were considered a subsection of behavior disorders and were restricted to "overanxious" and "withdrawing" reactions. It wasn't until the changes associated with DSM-III [4] that three distinct types of anxiety disorders in children and adolescents were spelled out: overanxious, avoidant, and separation anxiety disorder. Additionally, DSM-III recognized that children and adolescents could meet the criteria for the adult anxiety disorders: panic attacks, phobia, posttraumatic stress disorder (PTSD), and obsessive-compulsive disorder (OCD). Other than modification of some criteria, DSM-III-R [5] added no new anxiety disorders but did indicate that a child or

---

Table 1. Evolving Definition of Childhood Anxiety Disorders

DSM (1952): Anxiety disorders in children and adolescents are not considered [2].

DSM-II (1968): "Overanxious" and "withdrawing reaction"
These two disorders of adolescents and children were conceptualized as subcategories of behavior disorders [3].

DSM-III (1980): "Overanxious," "avoidant," and "separation anxiety"
Three unique anxiety disorders of adolescents and children are defined. Additionally, children and adolescents could be considered for the adult disorders of panic attacks, posttraumatic stress disorder, obsessive-compulsive disorder, and phobias [4].

DSM-III-R (1987): "Overanxious," "avoidant," and "separation anxiety"
Minor changes were made in criteria and with the explanation that children and adolescents could have any of these disorders in combination with the adult anxiety disorders [5].

DSM-IV (1994): "Generalized anxiety disorder"–childhood overanxious disorder is changed to adult generalized anxiety disorder.
"Social phobia" or "social anxiety disorder" are substituted for the deleted avoidant disorder.
"Separation anxiety disorder" is retained as a unique disorder of children and adolescents based on developmental considerations.
If criteria for the adult anxiety disorders are met, they are defined as "childhood onset" [6].

DSM—Diagnostic and Statistical Manual of Mental Disorders.

---

adolescent could have any of the adult anxiety disorders, as well as the three childhood anxiety disorders. Nosology of these disorders continued to evolve, and in DSM-IV [6], childhood overanxious disorder was eliminated. Instead, those children who met this criteria were now classified as having generalized anxiety disorder (GAD) with childhood onset. In addition to GAD, children could now have childhood-onset OCD, phobias, PTSD, and panic attacks, all defined as similar to the adult disorders. By contrast, separation anxiety disorder is seen as a unique developmental anxiety disorder of childhood. School refusal or phobia is often associated with separation anxiety [7]. The DSM-III childhood avoidant disorder was dropped in DSM-IV in favor of childhood-onset social phobia or social anxiety disorder. Selective mutism (elective mutism as defined in DSM-III-R) is thought to be a variant of social phobia [8,9]. Clearly, the ever-evolving definition of anxiety disorders in children and adolescents significantly affects pharmacotherapy research on the topic and our understanding of the disorders. Consequently, studies over time have thus far been limited in comparability due to changing diagnostic criteria. But as the conceptualization of childhood anxiety disorders becomes more similar to those of adults,' research efforts will also become more uniform, comparable, and generalized.

What, then, are the rates of these disorders in children and adolescents? Berenson [10] reports an incidence rate of anxiety disorders in children between 8% and 9% in community samples. Use of a semistructured interview with a normal sample found that from 9.8% to 30.6% of the children had overanxious symptoms below the criteria necessary to diagnose an actual disorder; the numbers were 10.7% to 22.6% for phobias [11]. Even though below diagnostic threshold, these anxiety symptoms can cause difficulty with functioning [12]. A survey conducted in the early 1980s by the National Institute of Mental Health suggested that OCD, in particular, affected more than 2% of the population, a number that exceeds the incidence of bipolar disorder, schizophrenia, and panic disorder. Economic and social costs of OCD alone have been estimated to be as high as \$8.4 billion in 1990 [13]. OCD in children and adolescents is frequently underdiagnosed, and only recently has it been studied systematically (a multisite study is currently being conducted). Readers can refer to Bernstein *et al.* [14••] for a more thorough discussion of anxiety disorder frequency in children and adolescents.

Conceptualization of Disorder

As shown in Table 2, significant overlap exists in the symptom profile of some of the childhood disorders, often making diagnosis more difficult and tentative. Obviously, had the other anxiety disorders been included, there would have been a lot of overlap between them as well. As indicated in Table 2, generalized anxiety disorder, depression, and bipolar disorders all cause disturbances in sleep, symptoms of irritability, difficulty concentrating (*eg,* flight of ideas), fatigue (bipolar children frequently become fatigued as well from heightened activity), changes in appetite (weight gains or losses or failure to gain weight), restlessness to excessive motor activity or agitation, and so forth. Manifesting three or four of these symptoms would make the patient potentially eligible for meeting criteria for each disorder. Distinct differences exist among the disorders based on nonoverlapping symptoms and criteria. Nonetheless, the high frequency of overlapping symptoms complicates diagnosis, particularly in settings in which a premium is set on the amount of time available for assessment and diagnostic evaluation. Careful assessment of the full symptom profile is necessary along with onset, course, and family history. Single to multiple diagnoses will affect the treatment recommended, as described below.

As noted, children and adolescents seen in the clinic are frequently characterized as having multiple disorders. The individual with a single disorder is the exception rather than the rule. The question remains whether these are all separate disorders, a result of the confusing overlap of symptoms, or part of the same disorder expressed differently in children and adolescents than in adults. Nevertheless, estimates of comorbidity of anxiety and depression range from 12% to 69%, to cite but a few of the studies indicating

Table 2. Comparison of Overlap between Anxiety Disorder Symptoms with other Childhood Disorders

Generalized anxiety disorder	Depression	Childhood manic disorder
Irritability	Depressed mood/irritability in childhood	Elevated, expansive, irritable mood
Fatigue		Sleep disturbance
Sleep disturbance	Fatigue, loss of energy	Flight of ideas
Difficulty concentrating	Sleep disturbance	Excessive speech
Restlessness	Difficulty concentrating	Distractibility
Muscle tension	Psychomotor agitation/retardation	Increased goal activity
Anxiety and worry	Anhedonia	Excessive pleasure activities
	Feelings of worthlessness	Grandiosity
	Weight/appetite change	
	Suicidal ideation	

comorbid depression and anxiety [15••,16–20]. There are similar findings for anxiety and attention deficit disorder [19,21–23]. Only recently has recognition grown that bipolar disorder in children and adolescents has been misdiagnosed as attention deficit disorder with or without an anxiety overlay. The overlap of anxiety disorders is a common finding as well, as noted in a study in which one third of the children with a primary diagnosis of separation anxiety disorder had a concurrent diagnosis of overanxious disorder [24]. One anxiety disorder study reported that 36% of the subjects met criteria for two or more anxiety disorders [25]. What accounts for this comorbidity? Some researchers have speculated that anxiety and depressive disorders are on a continuum and represent different manifestations of the same basic disorder [25, 26]. Continued genetic studies may answer the question someday [27]. Comorbidity must be assessed, a timeline of disorder onset established, and a hierarchy of relative dysfunction established.

Assessment of Anxiety Disorders

Psychopharmacologic intervention necessitates accurate diagnosis as part of a comprehensive treatment plan. As suggested above and elaborated below, comorbid disorders with an anxiety disorder often dictate a different treatment intervention [20,28,29••]. How can diagnosis for anxiety disorders in children and adolescents be improved [30••]? Diagnosis can be enhanced with the use of structured diagnostic instruments. As indicated in Table 3 [4], there are at least four structured interviews available, two of which are semistructured, one that is more structured, and one that is highly structured [31–44]. A lot of research has gone into the development of these instruments, and they are very helpful in identifying comorbidities that might otherwise be glossed over [30]. One has computer programs (eg, Diagnostic Interview for Children and Adolescents [35]) with child, adolescent, and parent versions that can be self-administered with higher functioning individuals. However, this highly structured interview, although computer-driven, requires a trained interviewer to conduct the interview and simultaneously enter the answers. Patients report that answering the structured diagnostic questions is helpful in gaining personal insight, and that parents better understand and empathize with their child's problems. Frequently, children and adolescents are more open to computer questioning than a face-to-face initial interview. The summary reports of either instrument assist the clinician in focusing on critical areas to explore further, resolve item discrepancies between the child and parents, confirm the accuracy of the diagnosis, and establish the course, family history, and any prior treatments.

The other childhood anxiety instruments listed in Table 3 include self-reports, parent reports, and clinician-administered rating scales. All of these instruments, in addition to helping the clinician, help educate parents and children about the disorders, assess severity levels, and aid in monitoring clinical response to treatment intervention. An additional aid is to teach the child and parent to keep diaries and to rate the level of severity on a one-to-10 scale, with one being normal with no anxiety and 10 being the most severe of anxiety states. For very young children who have difficulty with the one-to-10 scale, the clinician can create a picture scale with a calm normal face (no anxiety) at one extreme and a very anxious face (severe anxiety) at the other end and ask the patient to point where they are on the scale (see [29••] for an example). They can also use the revised Visual Analogue Scale for Anxiety [39]. Clearly, these instruments are not

Table 3. Instruments for Assessment of Anxiety in Children and Adolescents*

Measure	Type of measure	Informant
Schedule for Affective Disorders and Schizophrenia for School-Age Children [32]	Semistructured psychiatric interview; information from all available sources used to derive a summary score	Parent and child; epidemiologic version available (K-SADS-E)
Anxiety Disorders Interview Schedule for Children [33]	Semistructured psychiatric interview does include other disorders but focuses on anxiety disorders	Parent and child versions
Diagnostic Interview for Children and Adolescents-Revised [34]	Structured psychiatric interview	Parent, child, and adolescent versions
National Institute of Mental Health Diagnostic Interview Schedule for Children [35]	Highly structured psychiatric interview designed for lay interviewers	Parent and child versions
State-Trait Anxiety Inventory for Children [36]	Severity measure assesses state and trait anxiety	Self-report
Revised Children's Manifest Anxiety Scale [37]	Severity measure with three anxiety subscales and a lie subscale	Self-report
Revised Fear Survey Schedule for Children [38]	Severity measures examine fears	Self-report
Visual Analogue Scale for Anxiety-Revised [39]	Visual analogues to quantify anxiety-related to anxiety-producing situations	Self-report
Social Anxiety Scale for Children-Revised [40]	Severity measure of social anxiety	Self-report
Multidimensional Anxiety Scale for Children [41]	Severity measure with four main anxiety factors	Self-report
Hamilton Anxiety Rating Scale [42]	Clinician rating scale for adults that has been validated for adolescents	Clinician rating using adolescent report
Anxiety Rating for Children-Revised [31]	Clinician rating scale assesses severity; has anxiety subscale and physiologic subscale	Clinician rating using child or adolescent report
Personality Inventory for Children [43]	Multiple scales including anxiety scale	Parent report
Child Behavior Checklist [44]	Multiple scales including anxious-depressed scale	Parent report

*Adapted from Bernstein et al. [14••]; with permission.
K-SADS-E—Kiddie-Schizophrenia and Affective Disorders Scale-Epidemiology.

a substitute for good clinical assessment but do provide important measures for establishing baselines and providing comparison to established norms. Side-effect scales specific to the type of medications used are also an important adjunct to pharmacotherapy (*see* buspirone example in [29••]).

Finally, as a part of the assessment phase for anxiety disorders, it is particularly important to include a thorough medical history and physical examination, which should include panels for electrolytes, metabolic, thyroid, fasting blood glucose determinations, and electrocardiogram. If the anxiety disorder appears to be panic disorder, tests to rule out mitral valve prolapse should also be considered. The potential impact of caffeine, nicotine, or substance abuse needs to be considered, and in some settings a drug screen should be included.

Biologic Basis for Anxiety Disorders

The exact mechanism or biologic basis for anxiety disorders is not known, but recent work is promising [45•,46]. At least some of the disorders appear to have a familial component [27,47], suggesting a genetic base [48], although the strong role of the environment can not be ruled out as witnessed by the PTSD syndromes that occur in nonanxious families. There is every reason to believe that the limbic system in combination with the hypothalamic pituitary adrenal axis (the classic "fight or flight" mechanism) is involved in the disorder, since most of the physiologic symptoms of anxiety are driven by these systems. Assuming a normal distribution of the physiologic basis for these mechanisms, one may argue that anxiety is the extreme 5% to 10% of the "fight or flighters," resulting in a certain hypervigilance and anxious state, perhaps similar to that which results from too much caffeine. Similar to taking too much caffeine, anxiety is potentially dysfunctional. Cloniger [49] has argued for two other states as well, including a hypovigilance. At least for panic attacks in childhood, a study by Haywood et al. [50] demonstrated a developmental relationship with pubertal stage in a large study of sixth- and seventh-grade girls, suggesting a developmental neurobiologic base. Additional epidemiologic work suggests that peak onset of panic disorder occurs in late adolescence [51]. Panic disorder in adults has been linked to neurobiologic factors [52]. Neuroimaging is being used to investigate the mediating neuroanatomy of adult OCD symptoms [45•,46,53,54], and these studies suggest significant roles for paralimbic and limbic regions, including the caudate, thalamus, anterior cingulate, orbitofrontal cortex, and amygdala. Interested readers should see the chapter by Coplan et al. [55] on anxiety and the serotonin$_{1A}$ receptor, and Baxter's review [56] of neuroimaging studies of human anxiety disorders to further appreciate the current understanding of the biologic bases for anxiety disorders.

That the principal pharmacotherapies for anxiety disorders to date involve anxiolytics, antidepressants, and serotonin-specific reuptake inhibitors (SSRIs), including buspirone, a 5-HT specific drug, also suggests an identifiable neurobiologic basis for the disorder. For example, benzodiazepines (BZDs) produce their pharmacologic effects in conjunction with BZD receptor sites. The BZD receptors in turn are a part of the γ-aminobutyric acid (GABA) inhibitory neurotransmitter system of the central nervous system (CNS), which make up about 40% of the terminals in the cortex [57]. Recent work suggests that the 5-HT receptors are also involved in anxiety [55]. However, the 5-HT receptors are primarily responsive to non-BZD azapirone agents such as buspirone or the SSRIs described later in this chapter. Increased GABAergic transmission is believed to be a contributing factor in mediating anxiety disorders; hence, BZD binding with these receptor sites and blocking GABA reuptake help to modulate anxiety by increasing GABA bioavailability. In addition to BZD anxiolytic effects, they also have anticonvulsant, hypnotic, and muscle-relaxant properties because of their action. Two major classes of GABA receptors, GABA$_A$ and GABA$_B$, have been discovered , along with a third similar to GABA$_A$, called GABA$_C$, [58] but with a different pharmacologic profile (limited research on the latter is available at this time). GABA$_A$ functions as a ligand-activated ion channel receptor, whereas GABA$_B$ is a large G protein–coupled receptor (Fig. 1) [59]. Both types of GABA receptors are found on the terminals of GABAergic neurons and act as autoreceptors to modulate GABA release by the terminals. However, the distribution of GABA$_A$ and GABA$_B$ differs throughout the CNS. An excellent detailed description of the mechanism of action for these receptors is found in a chapter by Davies [59]. Finally, there is recent work suggesting a role for cholecystokinin as a centrally acting neuropeptide in anxiety disorders [60].

In contrast to the BZDs, buspirone, an azapirone, is an antianxiety agent that is neither chemically nor pharmacologically related to the BZDs, barbiturates, or to the sedative-anxiolytic drugs. The exact mechanism of action for buspirone is not known but appears to involve both pre- and postsynaptic receptor sites of action [55]. Unlike the benzodiazepines, buspirone does not have any muscle-relaxant or anticonvulsant effects, nor does it have any pronounced sedative effects. Studies indicate that buspirone has a high affinity for serotonin (5-HT$_{1A}$) receptors but no affinity for BZD receptors [61]. Furthermore, it does not appear to affect GABA binding in preclinical models. It does appear to have moderate affinity for D$_2$-dopaminergic [62] and noradrenergic [63] receptors. That the newer SSRIs (*eg*, fluoxetine, fluvoxamine) are also proving effective for the treatment of some of the anxiety disorders (*eg*, OCD and panic disorder) supports the role of serotonergic systems in anxiety. The SSRIs are also proving to be effective for comorbid anxiety and depressive disorders [15].

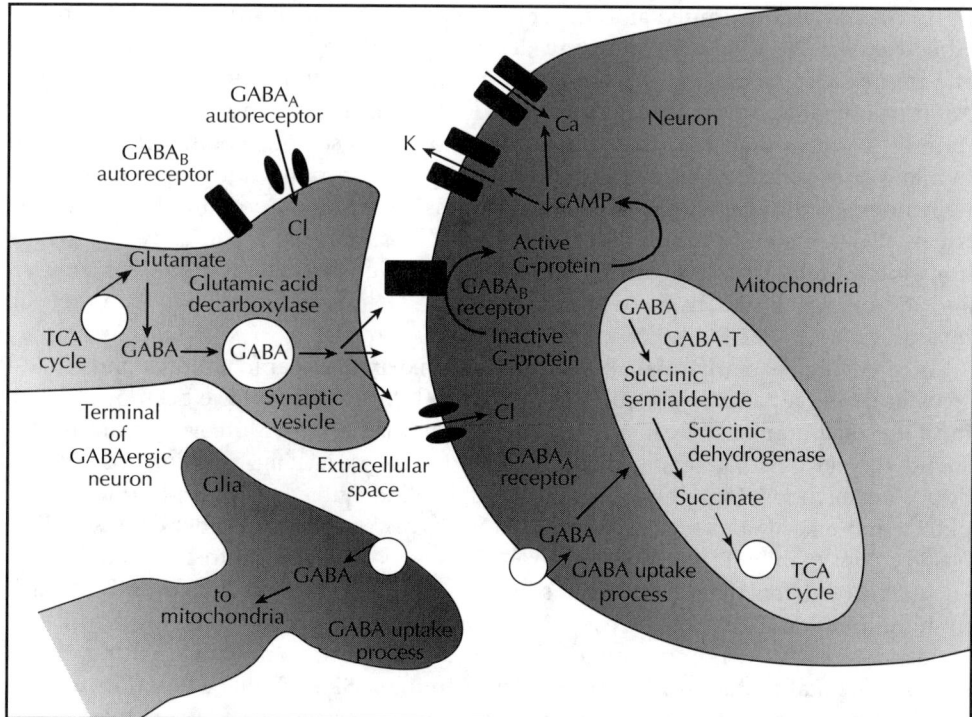

Figure 1. Schematic presentation of the synthetic pathways and receptor activator of the γ-aminobutyric acid (GABA)ergic system. TCA—tricyclic antidepressant. (*Adapted from* Davies [59]; with permission.)

Childhood Anxiety Disorders Research

Few systematic nonpharmacotherapy psychosocial treatment studies of childhood anxiety disorders have been conducted. Most studies to date have been of behavioral interventions to address specific fears or phobias [64]. Unfortunately, from a research and clinical application perspective, these anxiety disorders only represent about 3% to 4% of the population [65] and only infrequently present in the clinic compared with other childhood anxiety disorders more commonly seen [66]. One of the best childhood psychosocial studies to date is a recent randomized clinical trial that compared 16 weeks of cognitive-behavioral therapy with a wait-list control [67]. Kendall [67] found significantly reduced symptoms with the cognitive-behavioral therapy compared with the wait-list control. Cognitive therapy appeared to have a long-term effect as well, in that these subjects met fewer criteria for an anxiety disorder 1 year later. Cognitive-behavioral treatment has also been recommended as effective for OCD [68,69], and even potentially more cost-effective than pharmacotherapy [70,71••]. One earlier study indicated that participant modeling is superior to other behavior techniques for childhood fears [72], and another demonstrated a cognitive-behavior technique to be effective for childhood anxiety [73]. Clearly, this cursory review of the limited childhood psychosocial treatment studies suggests that cognitive-behavioral therapy offers a viable treatment alternative in some cases [70,74,75]. Family therapy is also an important adjunct to any treatment strategy for childhood anxiety disorders [12,76–78], particularly since there is a high frequency of familial anxiety disorder [79].

In contrast to the limited amount of psychosocial treatment studies in children and adolescents is the wealth of literature demonstrating overwhelming evidence for the effectiveness of psychosocial treatment for every type of adult anxiety disorder [80••]. Adult treatment approaches vary from disorder to disorder, but most incorporate some form of cognitive therapy in combination with problem solving, coping strategies, and in many cases, exposure-based procedures. As the authors point out [80••], despite the tremendous amount of successful research in this area, these procedures have not been widely disseminated to health care delivery systems or clinicians, and consequently are not widely available to patients. This situation is obviously even more true for children and adolescents, in whom these procedures are used even less frequently than they are in adults.

A recent review of pharmacologic studies of anxiety disorder in children and adolescents indicated a paucity of studies to date [29••]. Most studies have been open-label, involved small numbers of patients, or are based on case reports. Moreover, as already discussed, they are based on outdated diagnostic notions or are lacking in systematic structured diagnostic methods. There have been five double-blind studies for OCD, four for school phobia and refusal, and five for generalized anxiety-overanxious disorder or mixed diagnostic groups (Table 4) [81–94]. Uncontrolled case reports and open trials are not indicated or reviewed here [14••,29••,31]. As shown in Table 4, there is a trend for early research from the 1960s and 1970s to be based on BZDs, followed by work on the various tricyclic antidepressants (TCAs) (or combinations of TCAs and BZDs), to recently newly developed serotonin reuptake inhibitors (SRIs) (eg, clomipramine), SSRIs (eg, fluoxetine, fluvoxamine, paroxetine, and sertraline), and buspirone. Unfortunately, as discussed later in this chapter, with the exception of recent work on OCD, research is not conclusive to support rational psychopharmacologic treatment protocols for all childhood anxiety disorders.

The earliest double-blind crossover study involved children with depression or phobic symptoms in a comparison of chlordiazepoxide plus phenelzine versus phenobarbital [90]. Chlordiazepoxide plus phenelzine was found to be superior to phenobarbital in reducing symptoms. In contrast, other early anxiety studies found no difference between diazepam and placebo in 12 hospitalized children and adolescents [91] and no differences for diphenhydramine versus placebo [92]. More recently, neither alprazolam [93] nor clonazepam [94] were more effective than placebo in treating overanxious and avoidant disorders. In contrast to the one early study that found differences [90]—by today's standards a methodologically weak study restricted to depression and phobias—these studies provide no solid research basis for a rational pharmacologic intervention for these anxiety disorders.

The research on school phobia and school refusal provides mixed findings. Imipramine was demonstrated to be more effective than placebo [81], but another study failed to replicate these findings [82]. A study of clomipramine versus placebo showed no difference [83]. An open-label study that found imipramine or alprazolam superior to placebo did not replicate these findings when conducted in a double-blind setting [18]. That these particular drugs result in definitive improvement in addressing school phobias remains to be demonstrated. More research is needed and merits a randomized cognitive behavior trial as well [67].

Findings for treatment of childhood OCD appear more promising. Four separate studies have demonstrated that clomipramine is superior to placebo [85–87,89], one of which was a multicenter trial [89]. A couple of these studies [86,87], using a crossover design to desipramine, also showed a significant relapse of anxiety symptoms when switched to desipramine, indicating the importance of maintenance with clomipramine. Another recent study also found fluoxetine superior to placebo in reducing anxiety [88]. However, a recent review of the effectiveness of fluoxetine in treating juvenile OCD [95] indicated that concurrent medications (BZDs, TCAs, mood stabilizers, stimulants, and clonidine) were required with fluoxetine in 42% of the cases. These studies suggest that either fluoxetine or clomipramine is effective in treating childhood OCDs.

To summarize, research to date using double-blind, randomized trials finds little support for pharmacologic effectiveness for the treatment of school phobias (avoidance) or GAD. In contrast, the research on childhood-onset OCD has proven fruitful, demonstrating both clomipramine and fluoxetine as effective treatment options, although a recent study indicated that fluoxetine is frequently supplemented with other medications as well. In contrast to the childhood pharmacologic research, the psychosocial studies with a particular emphasis on behavior desensitization and cognitive therapies are proving to be very effective, although to date they too are limited in the actual number of well-designed and controlled studies conducted in children and adolescents.

Contemporary Treatment Approaches To Childhood Anxiety Disorders

Treatment guidelines for anxiety disorder have been recently reported [12] that support a multimodal approach, including pharmacologic and nonpharmacologic strategies (*eg,* psychosocial exposure-based behavior therapy as the treatment choice for simple phobias). The reader interested in the cognitive behavioral and family therapies for treating childhood anxiety disorders is referred to excellent current reviews for more extensive

Table 4. Double-Blind Pharmacotherapy Anxiety Disorder Studies in Children and Adolescents

Study	Pharmacotherapy	Results
School phobia/refusal		
Gittleman-Klein and Klein [81]	Imipramine vs placebo plus persuasion and desensitization	After 6 weeks, subjects receiving imipramine were more successful in returning to school than those on placebo.
Gittelman-Klein and Klein [82]	Imipramine vs placebo	Did not replicate; imipramine did not differ from placebo, with about half in each condition showing improvement.
Berney et al. [83]	Clomipramine vs placebo	No differences between groups in response. Depressive disorder was comorbid in 44% of the subjects.
Bernstein et al. [84]	Imipramine, alprazolam, and placebo	Open label showed improvement on imipramine or alprazolam (n = 17), but double blind (n = 24) did not demonstrate a drug effect.
Obsessive-compulsive		
Flament et al. [85]	Clomipramine vs placebo	Seventy-five percent had a moderate-to-marked response on clomipramine (approximately 3 mg/kg/d) vs placebo.
Leonard et al. [86]	Clomipramine crossed over to desipramine (after 5 weeks)	Replicated earlier study, but subjects switched to desipramine after 5 weeks on clomipramine had a 66% relapse rate, indicating the importance for maintenance on clomipramine.
Leonard et al. [87]	Clomipramine randomized to clomipramine vs desipramine (after 2 months)	Subjects blindly switched to desipramine after 2 months on clomipramine had a 90% relapse rate indicating the importance for maintenance on clomipramine.
Riddle et al. [88]	Fluoxetine vs placebo	Forty-four percent decrease in obsessive-compulsive disorder with fluoxetine (fixed dose of 20 mg/d) vs a 27% decrease with placebo.
DeVeaugh-Geiss et al. [89]	Clomipramine vs placebo	Clomipramine significantly more effective than placebo was demonstrated in multiple-site study.
Generalized anxiety–mixed diagnostic groups		
Frommer [90]	Chlordiazepoxide plus phenelzine vs phenobarbital	A double-blind, crossover trial found chlordiazepoxide plus phenelzine superior to phenobarbital for children with depression with or without phobic symptoms.
Lucas and Palsey [91]	Diazepam vs placebo	A double-blind, crossover trial found equivocal results for diazepam and placebo for anxiety symptoms in 12 hospitalized children and adolescents.
Korein et al. [92]	Diphenhydramine vs placebo	A double-blind, placebo-controlled study found no difference for childhood anxiety symptoms in a heterogenous group of pediatric patients.
Simeon et al. [93]	Alprazolam vs placebo	A double-blind, placebo controlled study found no difference between alprazolam (up to 0.04 mg/kg per day, mean daily dose of 1.57 mg) and placebo.
Graae et al. [94]	Clonazepam vs placebo	A double-blind, placebo-controlled crossover trial study found no difference between clonazepam (up to 2 mg/d) from placebo as measured by Brief Psychiatric Rating Scale or clinical global improvement.

details than have been covered in the review of literature earlier in this chapter [71••,77,80••] and to Table 5, which summarizes the treatment of childhood anxiety disorders. Emphasis here is on the pharmacotherapies.

Pharmacokinetic considerations

Ideally, drug doses in children and adolescents should be based on studies in children and adolescents, but as clearly evident from the review of research to date, adequate, well-designed, controlled trials in children and adolescents frequently do not exist. Because many of the doses are based initially on adult studies, several pharmacokinetic differences between children and adults should be taken into consideration [96]. For example, many of the psychotropic medications are highly lipophilic. The percentage of total body fat, which is a reservoir for lipid soluble compounds, increases during the first year of life and then decreases until the prepubertal increase [97]. Consequently, children at different developmental stages have different volumes of deep storage that affect the overall residual time that a drug remains in the body after discontinuation. Although hepatic enzyme activity is fully developed by 1 year of age, the rate of drug metabolism is also in part dependent on liver mass. Relative to body weight, the liver of a toddler is 40% to 50% greater than that of an adult, and the liver of a 6-year-old child is 30% greater [97]. The effect is often for children to clear drugs at a much more rapid rate than adults, and as a result they frequently need higher doses on a milligram per kilogram basis to achieve the same plasma drug levels and clinical effect. More frequent dosing may be required, which in turn leads to additional compliance issues. This is particularly noteworthy when one is attempting to titrate a dose for a chronic anxiety disorder in a child if the drug has a short half-life. What may appear as a worsening of symptoms in childhood disorders may reflect a withdrawal effect rather than an actual worsening of the disorder. The assessment of the timing of symptoms relative to dosing becomes critical. This is most likely to occur with drugs possessing anticholinergic properties, such as tertiary amine TCAs (*eg*, imipramine).

Puberty is another significant pharmacokinetic period in childhood, since in the few months prior to its onset there appears to be a transient decrease in drug metabolism. High levels of circulating sex hormones compete for hepatic enzyme sites [98], which can result in a rapid elevation in the plasma drug concentration without any change in body weight or dose [99]. Finally, interindividual variability in children's rates of biotransformation and elimination can be substantial [100], causing plasma levels of drug to be unusually low or high in some individuals taking average doses.

Approaches to pharmacotherapeutic intervention

With the significant lack of well-designed and controlled studies on childhood anxiety disorders, concerns for dependency and abuse of anxiolytics, and the fact that most childhood anxiety disorders are comorbid with other childhood disorders, the anxiolytics are being used less as a first line of treatment (particularly the large class of BZDs). This current trend contrasts with the approach in the 1980s, when BZDs were reported to be the most commonly prescribed psychotropic agents for children and adolescents [101]. Rather, the current tendency is to assess for and presume a more likely source of the anxiety symptoms based on a more treatable disorder. For example, major depressive disorders have many symptoms that overlap with anxiety, as noted in Table 2, and they

Table 5. Treatment of Childhood Anxiety Disorders

Anxiety disorder	Psychosocial-behavior therapies*

Generalized anxiety disorder	Relaxation/meditation plus
	    Cognitive therapy
	    Problem solving and coping
	    Psychodynamic therapy
	    Cognitive family therapy

Separation anxiety disorder	Systematic desensitization with *in vivo* practice, problem solving and coping that is
	    age appropriate
	    Cognitive therapy
	    Cognitive family therapy

Obsessive-compulsive disorder	Systematic desensitization by exposure and response prevention
	    Less effective
	        Cognitive therapy
	        Cognitive family therapy

Panic attack (with or without agoraphobia)	Systematic desensitization (*in vivo* exposure procedures vs imagination)
	    Cognitive therapy
	    Cognitive family therapy

Specific phobias Heights, animals, flying, injections	Systematic desensitization based on exposure combined with procedures specific to phobia (eg, muscle tension with blood/injury/injection phobia to maintain blood pressure)
Social (school) phobias	Systematic desensitization based on exposure combined with cognitive therapy
Selective mutism	Systematic desensitization based on exposure combined with cognitive therapy

Posttraumatic stress disorder	Direct exposure, combined cognitive restructuring, stress management, and relaxation with problem solving (similar to generalized anxiety disorder)
	    Anger management in some cases
	    Family therapy

Substance-induced anxiety disorder	Substance abuse therapy Cognitive family therapy

Anxiety (not otherwise specified)	Relaxation-meditation plus problem solving and coping
	    Cognitive therapy
	    Cognitive family therapy
	    Psychodynamic therapy

*See Barlow and Lehman [80] for complete review of psychosocial treatments.
†There is a growing reluctance to prescribe anxiolytics for these childhood disorders given 1) the lack of empiric research to support the effectiveness of anxiolytics; 2) the potential for abuse and dependence; and 3) that the disorders typically have a comorbid diagnosis. Rather, drug selection tends to be driven by predominant comorbidity such as mood or behavior disorder. Polypharmacy typically follows lack of adequate response to single drug selections.
ADHD—attention deficit–hyperactivity disorder; BZDs—benzodiazepines; MDD—major depressive disorder; SSRI—serotonin-specific reuptake inhibitor; TCA—tricyclic antidepressant.

are frequently a concomitant disorder. Experience finds that alleviation of the depression typically reduces the anxiety symptoms as well. In the case of the individual with attention deficit–hyperactivity disorder, treating the disorder often reduces the anxiety that is secondary to poor school performance, interference in social function, and frequent disciplinary consequences of unruly behavior and family discord. Likewise, use of mood stabilizers for bipolar disorders similarly reduces associated anxiety symptoms. This

Pharmacologic therapies[†]

Comorbid diagnoses:
  MDD—TCAs or SSRIs
  Bipolar—mood stabilizers
  ADHD—stimulants
  Anxiolytics reluctantly and only acutely; buspirone has been effective in open trials.

A good response to behavioral intervention often precludes need for pharmacotherapeutics, unless comorbid disorder exists; some recommend imipramine or BZDs.

Prolonged use of clomipramine may be more effective than behavior therapies alone, but best used in combination; fluoxetine may be effective in some cases.

Comorbidities drive selection of drug; high potency BDZs have been used short term in combination with exposure and cognitive restructuring based on a tapering off of anxiolytic.

A good response to behavioral intervention often precludes need for pharmacotherapeutics, unless a comorbid disorder exists.

Beta blockers are sometimes used in adult performance anxiety but are not recommended for school phobias; comorbidity drives drug selection.

Similar to social (school) phobias

A good response to behavioral intervention often precludes need for pharmacotherapeutics unless a comorbid disorder exists.

Other than treatment of acute withdrawal symptoms, pharmacotherapeutic intervention is not recommended unless significant comorbidity requires treatment.

Treatment is determined by presence of comorbidity or nature of anxiety producing situation based on alternatives above.

pharmacologic approach is then combined, when resources allow, with the various psychosocial, family, and behavior alternatives indicated in Table 5.

Treatment with benzodiazepines

Despite the increasing hesitancy to prescribe the BZDs, they can be used to manage anxiety disorders or for the short-term relief of the symptoms of anxiety in both children and adults. In general, the anxiety of tension associated with the stress of everyday life usually does not require treatment with an anxiolytic. Generalized anxiety, as characterized by DSM-IV, indicates the need for a persistent, generalized anxiety of at least 1 months' continual duration and manifested by a number of symptoms from three of the four categories of multiple symptoms: motor tension, autonomic hyperactivity, apprehensive expectation, and vigilance and scanning. These symptoms should not be due to other disorders. Assuming these symptoms plus dysfunction are present, the BZDs are best used in combination with one of the behavior therapies in which the drug can be tapered off after a short period.

The BZDs vary significantly in terms of milligram potency presumably due to differential affinity for receptor sites. Whereas many of the clinical doses are as low as 2 mg (eg, triazolam) others often exceed 20 mg (ie, halazepam, prazepam, clorazepate) (Table 6). The actual clinical action among the various BZDs is not very discernible. Basically, all of the BZDs share similar anxiolytic, anticonvulsant, and sedative-hypnotic features when dose, half-life, and blood levels are taken into account. There is very little data to support differences in anxiolytic, hypnotic, or anticonvulsant properties. The most pronounced difference is half-life, which can be used for short-acting clinical symptoms (difficulty falling asleep) versus more chronic generalized anxiety in which the lasting effects of a longer half-life are desirable.

In terms of chemical structure, BZD derivatives are weak organic bases that become very lipid soluble in vivo. The more lipid soluble the BZD, the more readily it passes from the plasma through the blood-brain barrier, and hence the more rapid the onset of pharmacologic action. The BZD chemical structure consists of a core benzene ring fused to a 7-member 1,4 diazepine ring and a 5-aryl substituent ring. The BZDs differ by different attachments to the diazepine ring, the benzene ring, or the 5-aryl ring. These different attachment possibilities result in five major pharmacologic subgroups, consisting of the triazolo BZD, the alpha-keto BZD, the 7-nitro BZD, the imidazo BZD, and the 3-OH BZD. These derivatives are all metabolized in a similar fashion by the liver and have half-lives in similar ranges [102]. Differing structures in BZDs vary quite a bit in terms of their rate of absorption, sedating properties, potency, type and frequency of adverse effects and withdrawal phenomena, as well as onset and duration of clinical activity.

Buspirone is a structurally unique (azapirone) anxiolytic that functions as an SRI. It has differential effects on noradrenergic and dopanergic systems as opposed to affecting the BZD-GABA ion–receptor system. It has been effective in treating adult anxiety disorders [103–105] and appears to also have antidepressant effects [104,106]. The side-effect profile is relatively benign and appears to have a low abuse potential. It has no significant muscle relaxant or sedative-hypnotic properties or annoying withdrawal symptoms. Although not studied well, it has potential for treatment of childhood anxiety disorders due to its safety, low potential for abuse and withdrawal reactions, and minimal side effects.

Treatment precautions for benzodiazepines

There is a strong tendency toward both physical and psychologic dependency on the BZDs. Withdrawal symptoms similar to those seen in alcohol dependence, and sedative-hypnotics effects have occurred following the discontinuation of BZDs. The symptoms tend to range from mild dysphoria and insomnia to a major syndrome that often includes abdominal and muscle cramps, vomiting, tremors, and convulsions. Individuals who have a tendency toward substance abuse are particularly vulnerable to the addictive properties of the BZDs. The symptoms of withdrawal and the original manifestation of a disorder can easily be confused, although the former typically include some new symptoms, occur near the end of tapering off the medication, and tend to diminish with time. To manage withdrawal symptoms, it may be necessary to reinstitute the BZD at a dose sufficient to manage the symptoms and then begin a more gradual withdrawal of the drug.

Treatment with antidepressants, serotonin-specific reuptake inhibitors, and mood stabilizers

Readers are referred to the other articles in this series for more specific details on treatment with the antidepressants and mood stabilizers [15••,102]. The choice of a TCA as the first-line pharmacotherapeutic intervention for a childhood anxiety disorder should be supported by diagnostic evidence of a depressive disorder, or at a minimum, significant functionally impairing depressive symptoms (Tables 7 and 8). Historically, imipramine, nortriptyline, and desipramine have been used in different studies [81,82,84,107,108]. As shown in Table 7, the TCAs have a number of significant side effects. Safety precautions require regular monitoring for cardiotoxicity, liver function, and so on, and determination of plasma levels to facilitate clinical effect [1]. Unlike the possibility for abuse and dependency with the BZDs, the major concern with TCAs is the potential for lethal overdose. Consequently, the SSRIs have become much more popular due to less susceptibility to overdose, less nuisance, and fewer potentially dangerous side effects (Table 9). The SSRIs have been demonstrated to be successful in treating OCD (Table 4), and a recent study has demonstrated fluoxetine superior to placebo for major depression in children and adolescents [15••]. Clomipramine, although one of the better-studied SRI options in children and adolescents, appears not to be that well tolerated, and due to its safety profile, is not a first-line choice as an anxiolytic. As indicated earlier, both the TCAs and SSRIs, through their direct effect on affective symptoms, frequently reduce anxiety symptoms either directly or indirectly. The mood stabilizers have been included in Table 10 due to the increased frequency with which they are being used to treat childhood disorders. Unfortunately, there have been no studies to date that systematically study the relationship between bipolar disorders and anxiety.

Other pharmacotherapeutic options

As briefly reviewed elsewhere [74], there is no supportive data for the use of barbiturates (since they are often toxic), neuroleptics (since there are too many potentially serious side effects associated with them), or antihistamines in the treatment of childhood anxiety disorders. Propranolol, as a highly lipophilic beta-blocker with both central and peripheral effects, does have antianxiety properties. One study reported it to be effective in treating childhood hyperventilation syndrome, which possibly corresponds to panic disorder [109]. It is sometimes prescribed for adult performance anxiety, although studies have not found it to be effective for anxiety disorders [110]. It might be considered for short-term use in combination with behavioral techniques for initial exposure to phobic or anxiety-producing stimuli.

Table 6. Pharmacotherapy of Anxiolytics*

Medication	Dosage schedule†	Serum level, ng/mL	Indications
Benzodiazepine Anxiolytics			
Lorazepam	0.05 mg/kg/dose (range: 0.02–0.09 mg/kg) every 4–8 h	20	Anxiety (long acting), irritability or agitation, insomnia, status epilepticus, preoperative sedation, amnesia
Chlordiazepoxide	5 mg, 2–4 times/d	N/A	Anxiety, alcohol withdrawal, preoperative anxiety
Oxazepam	Adults: 10–30 mg 3–4 times/d	N/A	Anxiety disorders, alcohol withdrawal, anticonvulsant in simple partial seizures
Diazepam	0.12–0.8 mg/kg/d every 6–8 h	196–341	Anxiety and panic disorders, status epilepticus, preoperative sedation, skeletal muscle relaxant, tetanus
Alprazolam	Adults: 0.25–0.5 mg 2–3 times/d	8–37	Anxiety disorders, panic disorders, adjunct to treatment of depression
Clonazepam	Children <10 years of age or 30 kg: 0.1–0.2 mg/kg/d in 3 divided doses not to exceed 0.2 mg/kg/d Adults: 0.05–0.2 mg/kg/d in 3 divided doses not to exceed 20 mg/d	N/A	Prophylaxis of absence seizure (petit mal), prophylaxis of Lennox-Gastaut (akinetic and myoclonic seizures)
Azaspirone serotonergic anxiolytic: buspirone	Adults: 5 mg bid or tid, range: 10–60 mg/d	1–6	Anxiety disorders

*From Weinberg et al. [102]; with permission.
†Approximate dosage ranges. Some children and adolescents will require higher dosages; some may respond to lower doses.
bid—twice daily; N/A—not applicable; tid—three times daily.

Treatment precautions

Given the high frequency of comorbid disorders in childhood and the likelihood that more than one medication may be prescribed to treat the disorders [95], it is important to consider the synergistic effects of polypharmacy. An obvious one that can be a frequent problem with teenagers is the combination of alcohol and many of the drugs of abuse. Such abuse is frequently glossed over in assessment when time is short. Alcohol is well documented to increase both peripheral and central levels of many medications to potentially cardiotoxic levels. Routine drug screens may be necessary to assure such abuse is not

Risk factors	Potential adverse effects	Drug interactions
Note: For all benzodiazepines below: Drug specific or benzodiazepine sensitivity in general, pregnancy, acute narrow angle glaucoma, tendency to chemical abuse	Note: For all benzodiazepines below: Physical and psychologic dependence with prolonged use	
See note above, severe hypotension, comatose states. Use caution in patients with: renal or hepatic impairment, myasthenia gravis, Parkinson's disease	Confusion, central nervous system depression, sedation, drowsiness, lethargy, hangover effect, dizziness, bradycardia, circulatory collapse, transitory hallucinations, diplopia, ataxia, nystagmus, constipation, dry mouth, nausea, vomiting, urinary incontinence or retention, respiratory depression, hypertension or hypotension	Alcohol, central nervous system depressants
See note above	Drowsiness, ataxia, confusion, syncope, electroencephalogram changes, blood dyscrasias	N/A
See note above, preexisting depression	Circulatory collapse, respiratory depression, tachycardia, blurred vision, orthostatic hypotension, dizziness, drowsiness	None
See note above, comatose patients, respiratory depression, patients with low albumin levels, hepatic dysfunction	Decrease in respiratory rate, apnea, cardiac arrest, drowsiness, confusion, dizziness, ataxia, blurred vision, diplopia, amnesia, slurred speech, impaired coordination, hypotension, bradycardia, cardiovascular collapse, laryngospasm, phlebitis, excitement or rage	Central nervous system depressants, enzyme inducers, cimitedine, valproic acid
See note above, respiratory depression	Constipation, diarrhea, nausea and vomiting, drowsiness, blurred vision, headache, dizziness, dry mouth, confusion, sedation, ataxia	Cimetidine, enzyme inducers, central nervous system depressants
See note above, severe liver disease, impaired renal function, chronic respiratory disease	Drowsiness, ataxia, changes in behavior or personality, hypotonia, choreiform movements, headache, hypersalivation and bronchial hypersecretion, nystagmus, tremor, vertigo, confusion, anemia, leukopenia, eosinophilia, thrombocytopenia, rash, respiratory depression	Central nervous system depressants, phenytoin
Buspirone sensitivity, not used with monoamine oxidase inhibitors	Dizziness, nausea, headache, nervousness, lightheadedness, excitement	Monoamine oxidase inhibitors

occurring prior to beginning treatment or contracted with the patient on an ongoing basis if potential abuse is a concern. It is not possible to review all of the possible drug combinations and possible interactions in a single review, but an example may suffice to alert the reader to possible effects with two frequently prescribed medications. In one of the early SSRI studies, a 33% increase in alprazolam plasma levels occurred after only 4 days of coadministration of a loading dose of 60 mg/day of fluoxetine [111]. In a second study, at a loading dose of 40 mg/day, a 25% decrease in the clearance of alprazolam occurred. Consequently, it has been predicted that a steady state of 20 mg/day would be expected

Table 7. Pharmacotherapy of Tricyclic Antidepressants*

Medication	Dosage schedule	Serum level, ng/mL	Indications
Imipramine	Children 1–3 mg/kg/d (if monitored) Adolescents 100–200 mg/d	150–250 (sum of imipramine plus desipramine)	Depression, migraine, tic syndrome, parasomnia
Amitriptyline	Children 1–3 mg/kg/d (if monitored) Adolescents 100–200 mg/d	100–250 (sum of amitriptyline plus nortriptyline)	Depression, migraine, painful neuropathy, parasomnia, cyclic vomiting, narcolepsy, tic syndrome, absence epilepsy
Nortriptyline	Children 1–3 mg/kg/d Adolescents 50–150 mg/d	50–150	Depression, migraine, parasomnia, panic, urticaria, premenstrual syndrome
Doxepin	Children 1–3 mg/kg/d Adolescents 100–200 mg/d	75–200	Depression, chronic urticaria, phobic states, overanxious states, parasomnia
Protriptyline	Children 5–10 mg bid or tid Adolescents 5–15 mg bid or tid	70–260	Depression, narcolepsy/cataplexy, hypovigilance, encopresis, obstructive sleep apnea
Desipramine	Children 1–3 mg/kg/d (if monitored) Adolescents 100–200 mg/d	50–300	Depression, anorexic/bulimic states, substance abuse
Clomipramine	Children 25 mg/d–3 mg/kg/d or 100 mg/d Adolescents 100–250 mg/d	70–200 Desclomipramine 150–300	Obsessive-compulsive disorder, tic syndrome, panic disorders, pain syndromes

*From Weinberg et al. [102]; with permission.
bid—twice daily; tid—three times daily.

Table 8. Tricyclic Antidepressant Drug Interaction*

Drugs that increase TCA concentration	Drugs that decrease TCA concentration	Others
Cimetidine Fluoxetine Disulfiram† Haloperidol Birth control pills Phenothiazines	Barbiturates Charcoal Smoking	Anticholinergics: potentiate anticholinergic side effects Clonidine†: marked increase in blood pressure Guanethidine†: Antihypertensive effect of guanethidine is masked Levodopa: Decreased intestinal levodopa absorption Monoamine oxidase inhibitor†: potentiates "tyramine" effect

*Adapted from Olin [114].
†Combinations are best avoided.
TCA—tricyclic antidepressant.

Risk factors	Potential adverse effects
Significantly underweight or with anorexia,' history of paroxysmal atrial tachycardia or other cardiac conduction disturbances, liver or renal disease (closely monitored)	Induction or promotion of mania, atrophic side effects, mild tremor, worsening of depressive symptoms, decreased appetite and excessive weight loss, excessive daytime sleepiness, rash, electrocardiogram evidence of cardiac conduction changes and hypertension
Obesity, excessive daytime sleepiness, history of paroxysmal atrial tachycardia or other cardiac conduction disturbances, liver or renal disease (closely monitored)	Same as imipramine but increased appetite and excessive weight gain
History of paroxysmal atrial tachycardia or other cardiac conduction disturbances, liver or renal disease (closely monitored)	Same as amitriptyline except with less effect on appetite and weight, "therapeutic window" in which subtherapeutic dosages worsen depression
Same as amitriptyline	Same as amitriptyline, except infrequently induces or promotes mania
Same as nortriptyline	Same as imipramine but rarely hypovigilance, insomnia
Same as nortriptyline	Same as imipramine, insomnia
Same as imipramine	Same as imipramine

to increase alprazolam plasma levels 30% to 40% [1•]. Clearly, these studies reinforce the importance of monitoring possible synergistic effects when more than one medication is prescribed. The effects of a third or fourth medication are not well studied; consequently, precaution must be taken with additional monitoring of levels where possible. The toxicity of many of these medications has been well studied [1•] and documented, as have the withdrawal and dependency of the BZDs.

Future Studies

There are a number of ongoing studies looking at other SSRIs (*eg*, paroxetine) and OCD. Of particular importance to childhood anxiety are well-designed, controlled studies that combine the various behavioral and cognitive therapies with pharmacotherapy. Exciting studies in adults involve neuroimaging, and some neuroimaging studies will be done in adolescents too as the techniques become more refined and safety issues are addressed. Much more precise genetic studies are clearly on the horizon. New medications are continually coming on the market that are more and more receptor specific or combine different receptor systems that may prove fruitful. One fairly recent drug on the market is mirtazapine, which has been studied primarily as an antidepressant [112,113]. Interestingly, because of its mechanism of action (it is a potent antagonist of 5-HT$_2$, 5-HT$_3$, and H$_1$, but

Table 9. Pharmacotherapy of Serotonin-specific Reuptake Inhibitors and Other Antidepressants*

Medication	Dosage schedule	Serum level, *ng/mL*	Indications
Fluoxetine	Children: 10–20 mg qam Adolescents: 20–40 mg qam	100–900 (fluoxetine and norfluoxetine combined)	Depression, OCD, migraine
Paroxetine	Children: 10–30 mg qam Adolescents: 10–40 mg qam	N/A	Depression, anxiety, OCD
Sertraline	Children: 25–50 mg qam Adolescents: 50–150 mg qam	30–200	Depression, OCD, migraine, primary disorder of vigilance
Venlafaxine	50–200 mg/d	N/A	Depression, ADHD
Trazodone	25–300 mg/d	800–1600	Depression, anxiety, insomnia
Nefazodone	50–300 mg/d	N/A	Depression, anxiety
Buproprion	Children: 37.5–75 mg bid or tid (preferably tid) Adolescents: 75–150 mg bid or tid (preferably tid)	10–30 or 50–100 depending on laboratory studies	Depression, ADHD

*From Weinberg et al. [102]; with permission.
ADHD—attention deficit–hyperactivity disorder; bid—twice daily; NA—not applicable; OCD—obsessive-compulsive disorder; qam—given in the morning; tid—three times daily.

Risk factors	Potential adverse effects	Drug interactions
Significantly underweight or with anorexia, history of paroxysmal atrial tachycardia or other cardiac conduction disturbances, liver or renal disease (closely monitored), prominent anger, excessive daytime sleepiness	Induction or promotion of mania, hypovigilance, decreased appetite and excessive weight loss, confusion, incoordination, insomnia, rash, akathisia, nervousness, gastrointestinal symptoms	Monoamine oxidase inhibitors (due to risk of severe toxic reaction); L-tryptophan; increased levels of phenytoin, tricyclic antidepressants, trazodone, ?diazepam; ?increase, decrease lithium levels; barbiturates, carbamazepine decrease levels; cimetidine, phenothiazine, methylphenidate may increase levels; ?buspirone; ?serotonin antagonists (eg, ondansetron)
Same as fluoxetine	Same as fluoxetine, fatigue/drowsiness, abnormal ejaculation/orgasm	Same as fluoxetine
Same as fluoxetine except for excessive daytime sleepiness	Same as fluoxetine but infrequent hypovigilance, drowsiness, ?weight gain, tremor, abnormal ejaculation/orgasm	Same as fluoxetine
Hypersensitivity to venlafaxine, hypertension, history of paroxysmal atrial tachycardia or other cardiac conduction disturbances	Blood pressure change, nausea, drowsiness, dizziness, nervousness, abnormal ejaculation/orgasm	Same as fluoxetine, ?potentiate sympathomimetic agonists
Obesity, excessive daytime sleepiness, history of paroxysmal atrial tachycardia or other cardiac conduction disturbances, liver or renal disease (closely monitored), primary disorder of vigilance	Induction or promotion of mania, atropinic side effects, mild tremor, worsening of depressive symptoms, increased appetite and excessive weight gain, excessive daytime sleepiness, rash, electrocardiogram evidence of cardiac conduction changes, hypertension, priapism	Barbiturates, carbamazepine decrease levels; cimetidine, phenothiazines, methylphenidate may increase levels; increased levels of digoxin, phenytoin
Same as trazodone	Dizziness, sedation	Increased levels of alprazolam; ?potentiate sedative-hypnotics (eg, ethanol)
Significantly underweight or with anorexia, history of paroxysmal atrial tachycardia or other cardiac conduction disturbances, liver or renal disease (closely monitored), active seizure disorder, abnormal electroencephalogram, liver disease, anorexia	Seizures, induction of liver enzymes, rash	Potentiates monoamine oxidase inhibitors; L-dopa; barbiturates, carbamazepine decrease levels; cimetidine, phenothiazines, methylphenidate may increase levels

Table 10. Pharmacotherapy of Mood Stabilizers*

Medication	Dosage schedule	Serum level	Indications
Lithium carbonate	Children: 20–40 mg/kg/d (600–1200 mg/d) (use tid dosage schedule for regular tablets and bid schedule for sustained-release tablets, take after eating) Adolescents: 600–1800 mg/d (dosage as above)	0.8–1.4 mEq/L	Conduct disorder, bipolar I disorder, encopresis, mental retardation with SIB, Prader Willi Syndrome, Klein-Levin Syndrome
Carbamazepine	Children: 10–20 mg/kg/d (use bid or tid dosage) Adolescents: 200–1200 mg/d (dosage as above)	4–12 µg/mL	Trigeminal neuralgia, temporal lobe epilepsy, diabetes insipidus, bipolar I disorder
Valproate	Children: 20–40 mg/kg/d (use bid or tid dosage) Adolescents: 375–1200 mg/d (dosage as above)	50–100 µg/mL	Bipolar I disorder, simple and complex absence seizures

*From Weinberg et al. [102]; with permission.
bid—twice daily; NSAIDS—nonsteroidal anti-inflammatory drugs; SGOT—serum glutamate oxaloacetate transaminase; SGPT—serum glutamate pyruvate transaminase; SIB—self-injurious behavior; tid—three times a day.

not 5-HT$_{1A}$ or 5-HT$_{1B}$ receptors, and a modest antagonist of alpha$_1$ and muscarinic receptors), mirtazapine has also been shown to reduce anxiety and sleep disturbance symptoms [113]. To date, however, no studies specifically addressing anxiety have occurred, nor have any studies been done of children or adolescents with this new drug. The refined DSM-IV definitions to make the childhood disorders more developmentally specific and in line with adult disorders should bring more uniformity to our conceptualization of the disorder and help us make better generalizations between childhood and adult studies.

Conclusions

With the exception of OCD, the pharmacotherapy studies of childhood anxiety disorders have been uniformly disappointing and do not serve as a sound basis for making treatment recommendations. BZDs are being used less and less often due to ineffectiveness and the potential for dependence and abuse. The SSRIs are proving to be much safer, with a better tolerated side-effect profile, and are effective in treating many of the disorders. The cognitive-behavioral studies, likewise, are proving to be effective for many of the anxiety disorders and are safe, cost-effective, and apparently long lasting. Studies are only recently beginning to be conducted that combine pharmacotherapy and behavioral approaches for the treatment of anxiety disorders. Contemporary treatment approaches consider childhood comorbidities and developmental aspects of the disorders unique to childhood. Comorbid disorders such as attention deficit–hyperactivity disorder, major depressive disorder, and bipolar illness often drive the pharmacologic treatment of choice since many of the anxiety symptoms will respond to their respective treatments. As neuroimaging studies continue to define

Risk factors	Potential adverse effects	Drug interactions
Pregnancy, significant renal or cardiovascular disease, severe dehydration, sodium depletion	Nausea, weight gain, excessive sedation, tremor, headache, thirst, acne, hypothyroidism, electrocardiogram changes, polyuria, polydipsia	Increase: indomethacin, piroxicam, NSAIDs, enlapril, captopril Decrease: acetalozamide
Clozapine treatment, history of bone marrow depression, monoamine oxidase inhibitor treatment within 21 days	Sedation, ataxia, dizziness, blurred vision, nausea, aplastic anemia/agranulocytosis, thrombocytopenia, elevated SGOT, SGPT, alkaline phosphatase	Increase: erythromycin, cimetidine, propoxyphene, fluoxetine, isoniazid, calcium channel blockers Decrease: phenobarbital, phenytoin, premidone
Significant hepatic disease, pregnancy	Nausea, sedation, tremor, weight gain, elevated SGOT, SGPT, alkaline phosphatase, hepatotoxicity	Increase: phenobarbital, phenytoin, primidone

the biologic bases for the anxiety disorders more precisely, and as additional receptor-specific drugs are developed, the treatment of anxiety will improve.

References and Recommended Reading

Papers of particular interest, published recently, have been highlighted as:
- • Of special interest
- •• Of outstanding interest

1.• Preskorn SH: *Clinical Pharmacology of Selective Serotonin Reuptake Inhibitors.* Caddo, OK: Professional Communications, Inc.; 1996.
An excellent recent book that serves as a guide to the clinical pharmacology of SSRIs. The basic neuropharmacology of the SSRIs is explained, comparisons are made to the TCAs, cytochrome P450 mechanisms are discussed, and the ways all these relate to clinical use of SSRIs are explained.

2. American Psychiatric Association: *Diagnostic and Statistical Manual of Mental Disorders.* Washington, DC: American Psychiatric Association; 1952.

3. American Psychiatric Association: *Diagnostic and Statistical Manual of Mental Disorders*, edn 2. Washington, DC: American Psychiatric Association; 1968.

4. American Psychiatric Association: *Diagnostic and Statistical Manual of Mental Disorders*, edn 3. Washington, DC: American Psychiatric Association; 1980.

5. American Psychiatric Association: *Diagnostic and Statistical Manual of Mental Disorders*, edn 3 (revised). Washington, DC: American Psychiatric Association; 1987.

6. American Psychiatric Association: *Diagnostic and Statistical Manual of Mental Disorders*, edn 4. Washington, DC: American Psychiatric Association; 1994.

7. Leonard HL, Rapoport JL: Separation anxiety, overanxious, and avoidant disorders. In *Textbook of Child and Adolescent Psychiatry.* Edited by Wiener JM. Washington, DC: American Psychiatric Press; 1991:311–322.

8.   Black B, Unde TW: Case study: elective mutism as a variant of social phobia. *J Am Acad Child Adolesc Psychiatry* 1992, 31:1090.

9.   Leonard HL, Topol D: Elective mutism. *Child Adolesc Psychiatry Clin North Am* 1993, 2:695–708.

10. Berenson CK: Evaluation and treatment of anxiety in the general pediatric population: a clinician's guide. *Child Adolesc Psychiatry Clin North Am* 1993, 2:763–747.

11. Bell-Dolan DJ, Last CG, Strauss CC: Symptoms of anxiety disorders in normal children. *J Am Acad Child Adolesc Psychiatry* 1990, 29:759–765.

12. American Academy of Child and Adolescent Psychiatry, AACAP official action: Practice parameters for the assessment and treatment of anxiety disorders. *J Am Acad Child Adolesc Psychiatry* 1993, 32:1089–1098.

13. National Institute of Mental Health: *Obsessive-Compulsive Disorder* NIH publication No. 94-3755; 1994.

14.•• Bernstein GA, Borchardt CM, Perwien AR: Anxiety disorders in children and adolescents: a review of the past 10 years. *J Am Acad Child Adolesc Psychiatry* 1996, 35:1110–1119.
A review article of childhood anxiety disorders based on the past 10 years of research from a developmental perspective. Authors conclude that more research is needed in the areas of neurobiologic bases for the disorders, longitudinal studies, and treatment.

15.•• Emslie GA, Rush AJ, Weinberg WA, *et al.*: A double-blind, randomized placebo-controlled trial of fluoxetine in depressed children and adolescents. *Arch Gen Psychiatry* 1997, in press.
The first research in children and adolescents to demonstrate fluoxetine superior to placebo in treating childhood depression. A significant number of the individuals had comorbid anxiety disorders.

16. McGee R, Feehan M, Williams S, *et al.*: DSM III disorders in a large sample of adolescents. *J Am Acad Child Adolesc Psychiatry* 1990, 29:611–619.

17. Kashani JH, Orvaschel H: Anxiety disorders in mid-adolescence: a community sample. *Am J Psychiatry* 1988, 145:960–964.

18. Bernstein GA: Comorbidity and severity of anxiety and depressive disorders in a clinic sample. *J Am Acad Child Adolesc Psychiatry* 1991, 30:43–50.

19. Anderson JC, Williams S, McGee R, *et al.*: DSM-III disorders in preadolescent children: prevalence in a large sample from the general population. *Arch Gen Psychiatry* 1987, 44:69–76.

20. Kendall PC, Kortlander E, Chansky TE, *et al.*: Comorbidity of anxiety and depression in youth: treatment implications. *J Cons Clin Psychology* 1992, 60:869–880.

21. Biederman J, Newcorn J, Sprich S: Comorbidity of attention deficit hyperactivity disorder with conduct, depressive, anxiety, and other disorders. *Am J Psychiatry* 1991, 145:564–577.

22. Last C, Hersen M, Kazdin A, *et al.*: Comparison of DSM III separation anxiety and overanxious disorders: demographic characteristics and patterns of comorbidity. *J Am Acad Child Adolesc Psychiatry* 1987, 26:527–531.

23. Strauss CC, Last CG, Hersen M, *et al.*: Association between anxiety and depression in children and adolescents with anxiety disorders. *J Abnorm Child Psychol* 1988, 16:57–68.

24. Last CG, Strauss CC, Francis G: Comorbidity among childhood anxiety disorders. *J Nerv Ment Dis* 175:726–730.

25. Kashani JH, Orvaschel H: A community study of anxiety in children and adolescents. *Am J Psychiatry* 1990, 147:313–318.

26. Kovacs M, Gastonsis C, Paulauskas SL, *et al.*: Depressive disorders in childhood: IV. A longitudinal study of comorbidity with and risk for anxiety disorders. *Arch Gen Psychiatry* 1989, 46:776–782.

27. Pauls DL, Alsobrook JP, Goodman W, *et al.*: A family study of obsessive-compulsive disorder. *Am J Psychiatry* 1995, 152:76–84.

28. Kutcher SP, Reiter S, Gardner DM, *et al.*: The pharmacotherapy of anxiety disorders in children and adolescents. *Pediatr Psychopharmacol* 1992, 15:41–67.

29.•• Allen AJ, Leonard H, Swedo, SE: Current knowledge of medications for the treatment of childhood anxiety disorders. *J Am Acad Child Adolesc Psychiatry* 1995, 34:976–986.
An excellent recent article that reviews the benefits and risks of medication for the treatment of childhood anxiety disorders. Most of the research supporting the use of medications came from the study of OCD. The other anxiety disorders have either no support or conflicting reports.

30.•• Carlson GA: Classification and assessment of mood and anxiety disorders in children and adolescents. *Curr Rev Mood Anx Disord* 1996, 1:12–25.

Excellent recent article that reviews the classification and assessment of mood and anxiety disorders in children and adolescent. The emphasis is both cross-sectional and longitudinal and takes developmental considerations into account.

31. Bernstein GA, Crosby RD, Perwien AR, *et al.*: Anxiety rating for children–revised: reliability and validity. *J Anx Disord* 1996, 10:97–114.

32. Chambers WJ, Puig-Antich J, Hirsch M, *et al.*: The assessment of affective disorders in children and adolescents by semistructured interview: test-retest reliability of the Schedule for Affective Disorders and Schizophrenia for School-Age Children, Present Episode. *Arch Gen Psychiatry* 1985, 42:696–702.

33. Silverman WK, Nelles WB: The Anxiety Disorders Interview Schedule for Children. *J Am Acad Child Adolesc Psychiatry* 1988, 27:772–778.

34. Welner Z, Reich W, Herjanic B, *et al.*: Reliability, validity and parent-child agreement studies of the Diagnostic Interview for Children and Adolescents (DICA). *J Am Acad Child Adolesc Psychiatry* 1987, 26:649–653.

35. Shaffer D, Fisher P, Dulcan MK, *et al.*: The NIMH Diagnostic Interview Schedule for Children Version 2.3 (DISC-2.3): description, acceptability, prevalence rates, and performance in the MECA study. *J Am Acad Child Adolesc Psychiatry* 1996, 35:865–877.

36. Spielberger C: *Manual for the State-Trait Anxiety Inventory for Children.* Palo Alto, CA: Consulting Psychologists Press; 1973.

37. Reynolds CR, Richmond BO: What I think and feel: a revised measure of children's manifest anxiety. *J Abnorm Child Psychol* 1978, 6:271–280.

38. Ollendick TH: Reliability and validity of the Revised Fear Survey Schedule for Children (FSSC-R). *Behav Res Ther* 1983, 21:685–692.

39. Bernstein GA, Garfinkel BD: The Visual Analogue Scale for Anxiety-Revised: psychometric properties. *J Anx Disord* 1992, 6:223–239.

40. LaGreca AM, Stone WL: Social Anxiety Scale for Children-Revised: factor structure and concurrent validity. *J Clin Child Psychol* 1993, 22:17–27.

41. March JS: *Manual for the Multidimensional Anxiety Scale for Children (MASC).* Toronto: Multi-Health Systems; 1996.

42. Hamilton M: The assessment of anxiety states by rating. *Br J Med Psychol* 1959, 32:50–55.

43. Wirt RD, Lachar D, Klinedinst JK, *et al.*: *Multidimensional Description of Child Personality: A Manual for the Personality Inventory for Children.* Los Angeles: Western Psychological Services; 1977.

44. Achenbach TM: *Manual for the Child Behavior Checklist/4-18 and 1991 Profile.* Burlington, VT: University of Vermont Department of Psychiatry; 1991.

45.• Breiter HC, Rauch SL, Kwong KK, *et al.*: Functional magnetic resonance imaging of symptom provocation in obsessive-compulsive disorder. *Arch Gen Psychiatry* 1996, 52:595–606.

Functional magnetic resonance imaging was used to study the mediating neuroanatomy of OCD symptoms in adults. Statistical maps showed activation for 70% or more of patients with OCD in medial orbitofrontal, lateral frontal, anterior temporal, anterior cingulate, and insular cortex areas, as well as in the caudate, lenticulate, and amygdala. No normal subjects exhibited activation in any brain region.

46. Aylward EH, Harris GJ, Hoehn-Saric R, *et al.*: Normal caudate nucleus in obsessive-compulsive disorder assessed by quantitatiive neuroimaging. *Arch Gen Psychiatry* 1996, 53:577–584.

47. Biederman J, Faraone SV, Keenan K, *et al.*: Familial association between attention deficit disorder and anxiety disorders. *Am J Psychiatry* 1991, 148:251–256.

48. Last CG: Conclusions and future directions. In *Anxiety across the Lifespan: A Developmental Perspective.* Edited by Last CG. New York: Springer-Verlag; 1993.

49. Cloninger CR: Recent advances in the genetics of anxiety and somatoform disorders. In *Psychopharmacology: The Third Generation of Progress.* Edited by Meltzer HY. New York: Raven Press; 1987:955–965.

50. Hayward C, Killen JD, Hammer LD, *et al.*: Pubertal stage and panic attack history in sixth- and seventh-grade girls. *Am J Psychiatry* 1992, 149:1239–1243.

51. Von Korff MR, Eaton WW, Keyl PM: The epidemiology of panic attacks and panic disorder: results of three community surveys. *Am J Epidemiol* 1985, 122:970–981.

52. Sallee R, Greenwald J: Neurobiology. In *Anxiety Disorders in Children and Adolescents*. Edited by March JS. New York: Guilford; 1995:3–34.

53. Insell TR: Toward a neuroanatomy of obsessive-compulsive disorder. *Arch Gen Psychiatry* 1992, 49:739–744.

54. Rauch SL, Jenike MA: Neurobiological models of obsessive-compulsive disorder. *Psychosomatics* 1993, 34:20–32.

55. Coplan JD, Wolk SI, Klein DF: Anxiety and the serotonin$_{1A}$ receptor. In *Psychopharmacology: The Fourth Generation of Progress*. Edited by Bloom FE, Kupfer DJ. New York: Raven Press; 1995:1301–1310.

56. Baxter LR: Neuroimagining studies of human anxiety disorders. In *Psychopharmacology: The Fourth Generation of Progress*. Edited by Bloom FE, Kupfer DJ. New York: Raven Press; 1995:1287–1299.

57. Bloom FE, Iversen LL: Localizing 3H-GABA in nerve terminals of rat cerebral cortex by electron microscopic autoradiography. *Nature* 1971, 229:628.

58. Shimada S, Cutting G, Uhl GR: Gamma-aminobutyric acid A or C receptor? Gamma-aminobutyric acid rho 1 receptor RNA induces bicuculline- barbiturate-, and benzodiazepine-insensitive gamma-aminobutyric acid responses in Xenopus oocytes. *Mol Pharmacol* 1992, 41:683.

59. Davies MF: The pharmacology of the gamma-aminobutyric acid system. In *Brain Mechanisms and Psychotropic Drugs*. Edited by Baskys A, Remington R. Boca Raton, FL: CRC Press; 1996:101–116.

60. Shader RI, Greenblatt DJ: The pharmacotherapy of acute anxiety. In *Psychopharmacology: The Fourth Generation of Progress*. Edited by Bloom FE, Kupfer DJ. New York: Raven Press; 1995:1341–1348.

61. Sprouse JS, Aghajanian GK: Electrophysiological responses of serotoninergic dorsal raphe neurons to 5-HT1A and 5-HT1B agonists. *Synapse* 1987, 1:3–9.

62. Riblet L, Taylor D, Eison M, *et al.*: Pharmacology and neurochemistry of buspirone. *J Clin Psychiatry* 1982, 43:11–16.

63. Sanghera MK, McMillen BA, German DC: Buspirone, a nonbenzodiazepine anxiolytic, increases locus coeruleus noradrenergic neuronal activity. *Eur J Pharmacol* 1982, 86:107–110.

64. Beutler L, Clarkin J: *Systematic Treatment Selection: Toward Targeted Therapeutic Perspective*. New York: Basic Books; 1990.

65. Ollendick T, Francis G: Behavioral assessment and treatment of childhood phobias. *Behav Modif* 1988, 12:165–204.

66. Last CG, Phillips JE, Statfeld A: Childhood anxiety disorders in mothers and their children. *Child Psychiatry Hum Dev* 1987, 18:103–117.

67. Kendall PC: Treating anxiety disorders in children: results of a randomized clinical trial. *J Consult Clin Psychol* 1994, 62:100–110.

68. March JS, Mulle K, Herbel B: Behavioral psychotherapy for children and adolescents with obsessive-compulsive disorder: an open trial of a new protocol-driven treatment package. *J Am Acad Child Adolesc Psychiatry* 1994, 33:333–341.

69. March JS: Cognitive-behavioral psychotherapy for children and adolescents with OCD: a review and recommendations for treatment. *J Am Acad Child Adolesc Psychiatry* 1995, 34:7–18.

70. March JS, Leonard HL: Obsessive-compulsive disorder in children and adolescents: a review of the past 10 years. *J Am Acad Child Adolesc Psychiatry* 1996, 35:1265–1273.

71.•• March JS: Cognitive-behavioral psychotherapy for children and adolescents with OCD: a review and recommendations for treatment. *J Am Acad Child Adolesc Psychiatry* 1996, 34:7–18.
A comprehensive, recent review of OCD in children and adolescents. This review of 32 separate studies found that all but one demonstrated some benefit in the treatment of childhood disorders with some version of cognitive therapy. Graded exposure and response prevention form the core of treatment; anxiety management training and OCD-specific family interventions may play an adjunctive role.

72. Graziano AM, DeGiorann I, Garcia K: Behavioral treatment of child's fear. *Psychol Bull* 1979, 56:804–830.

73. Kendall PC, Howard BL, Epps J: The anxious child: cognitive-behavioral treatment strategies. *Behav Modif* 1988, 12:281–310.

74. King N, Hamilton DH, Ollendick T: *Children's Phobias: A Behavioural Perspective*. Chichester, England: Wiley; 1988.

75. Kendall PC, Kirtlander E, Chansky TE, *et al.*: Comorbidity of anxiety and depression in youth: treatment implication. *J Consult Clin Psychol* 1992, 60:869–880.

76. McDermott JF, Werry J, Petti T, *et al.*: Anxiety disorders in childhood or adolescence. In *Treatment of Psychiatric Disorders*, vol 1. Washington, DC: American Psychiatric Association; 1989:401–446.

77. Howard BL, Kendall PC: Cognitive-behavioral family therapy for anxiety–disordered children: a multiple-baseline evaluation. *Cognitive Ther Res* 1996, 20:423–444.

78. Barrett PM, Dadds MR, Rupee RM: Family treatment of childhood anxiety: a controlled trial. *J Consult Clin Psychology* 1996, 64:333–342.

79. Last CG, Hersen M, Kazdin AE, *et al.*: Psychiatric illness in mothers of anxious children. *Am J Psychiatry* 1987, 144:1580–1583.

80.•• Barlow DH, Lehman CL: Advances in the psychosocial treatment of anxiety disorders. *Arch Gen Psychiatry* 1996, 53:727–735.
Reviews the current status of psychosocial interventions that complement psychopharmacologic treatment of anxiety disorders. Finds support for some form of psychosocial treatment (predominately behavioral and cognitive-behavioral) for every anxiety disorder. Suggests where research is going for each anxiety disorder.

81. Gittleman-Klein R, Klein D: Controlled imipramine treatment of school phobia. *Arch Gen Psychiatry* 1971, 25:204–207.

82. Gittleman-Klein R, Klein D: School phobia: diagnostic considerations in the light of imipramine effects. *J Nerv Ment Dis* 1973, 156:199–215.

83. Berney T, Kolvin I, Bhate SR, *et al.*: School phobia: a therapeutic trial with clomipramine and short-term outcome. *Br J Psychiatry* 1981, 138:110–118.

84. Bernstein G, Garfinkel B, Borchardt C: Comparative studies of pharmacotherapy for school refusal. *J Am Acad Child Adolesc Psychiatry* 1990, 29:773–781.

85. Flament MR, Rapoport JL, Berg CJ, *et al.*: Clomipramine treatment of childhood obsessive-compulsive disorder: a double-blind controlled study. *Arch Gen Psychiatry* 1985, 42:977–983.

86. Leonard HL, Swedo SE, Rapoport JL, *et al.*: Treatment of obsessive-compulsive disorder with clomipramine and desipramine in children and adolescents: a double-blind crossover comparison. *Arch Gen Psychiatry* 1989, 46:1088–1092.

87. Leonard HL, Swedo SE, Lenane MC, *et al.*: A double-blind desipramine substitution during long-term clomipramine treatment in children and adolescents with obsessive-compulsive disorder. *Arch Gen Psychiatry* 1991, 48:922–927.

88. Riddle MA, Scahill L, King RA, *et al.*: Double-blind, crossover trial of fluoxetine and placebo in children and adolescents with obsessive-compulsive disorder. *J Am Acad Child Adolesc Psychiatry* 1992, 31:1062–1069.

89. DeVeaugh-Geiss J, Moroz G, Biederman J, *et al.*: Clomipramine hydrochloride in childhood and adolescent obsessive-compulsive disorder: a multicenter trial. *J Am Acad Child Adolesc Psychiatry* 1992, 31:45–49.

90. Frommer EA: Treatment of childhood depression with antidepressants. *BMJ* 1967, 1:729–732.

91. Lucas AR, Palsey C: Psychoactive drugs in the treatment of emotionally disturbed children: haloperidol and diazepam. *Compr Psychiatry* 1969, 10:376–386.

92. Korein F, Fish B, Shapiro T, *et al.*: EEG and behavioral effects of drug therapy in children: chlorpromazine and diphenhydramine. *Arch Gen Psychiatry* 1971, 24:552–563.

93. Simeon JG, Ferguson HB, Knott V, *et al.*: Clinical, cognitive, and neurophysiological effects of alprazolam in children and adolescents with overanxious and avoidant disorders. *J Am Acad Child Adolesc Psychiatry* 1992, 31:29–33.

94. Graae F, Milner J, Rizzotto L, *et al.*: Clonazepam in childhood anxiety disorders. *J Am Acad Child Adolesc Psychiatry* 1994, 33:372–376.

95. Geller B, Biederman J, Reed ED, *et al.*: Similarities in response to fluoxetine in the treatment of children and adolescents with obsessive-compulsive disorder. *J Am Acad Child Adolesc Psychiatry* 1995, 34:36–44.

96. Hughes CW, Preskorn SH: Pharmacokinetics in child/adolescent psychiatric disorders. *Psych Ann* 1994, 24:76–82.

97. Briant RH: An introduction to clinical psychopharmacology. In *Pediatric Psychopharmacology: The Use of Behavior Modifying Drugs in Children*. Edited by Werry JS. New York: Brunner/Mazel; 1978.

98. Popper CW: Child and adolescent psychopharmacology. In *Psychiatry*. Edited by Cavenar JO, Michels R, Guze SB, Helzer JE. Philadelphia: JB Lippincott; 1985:1–23.

99. Pippinger CE: Rational and clinical application of therapeutic drug monitoring. *Pediatr Clin North Am* 1980, 27:891–925.

100. Preskorn SH, Bupp S, Weller E, *et al.*: Plasma levels of imipramine and metabolites in 68 hospitalized children. *J Am Acad Child Adolesc Psychiatry* 1989, 28:373–375.

101. Smart RG, Adlaf EM: Alcohol and other drug use among Ontario students in 1987 and trends since 1977. Toronto: Addiction Research Foundation; 1989.

102. Weinberg WA, Schraufnagel CD, Chudnow RS, *et al.*: Neuropsychopharmacology II. Antidepressants, mood stabilizers, neuroleptics (antipsychotics), and anxiolytics. In *Textbook of Pediatric Neuropsychiatry*. Edited by Coffey CE, Brumback RA. Washington, DC: American Psychiatric Press; 1997: in press.

103. Cohn J, Wilcox C: Low-sedation potential of buspirone compared with alprazolam and lorazepam in the treatment of anxious patients: a double-blind study. *J Clin Psychiatry* 1986, 47:409–412.

104. Goldberg H: Buspirone hydrochloride: a unique new anxiolytic agent. *Pharmacotherapy* 1984, 4:315–324.

105. Taylor D, Eison M, Riblet L, *et al.*: Pharmacological and clinical effects of buspirone. *Pharmacol Biochem Behav* 1985, 23:687–694.

106. Kastenholz K, Crimson M: Buspirone, a novel benzodiazepine anxiolytic. *Drug Rev* 1984, 3:600–607.

107. Gittleman R, Koplewicz H: Pharmacotherapy of childhood anxiety disorders. In *Anxiety Disorders of Childhood*. Edited by Gittleman R. New York: Guilford Press; 1986: 188–203.

108. Pliszka S: Effect of anxiety on cognition, behaviour, and stimulant response in ADHD. *J Am Acad Child Adolesc Psychiatry* 1989, 28:882–887.

109. Jorrabchi B: Expressions of the hyperventilation syndrome in childhood. *Clin Pediatr* 1977, 16:1110–1115.

110. Rickels K, Schweizer E: Current pharmacotherapy of anxiety and panic. In *Psychopharmacology, The Third Generation of Progress*. Edited by Meltzer H. New York: Raven Press; 1987:1193–1204.

111. Lasher TA, Fleishaker JC, Steenwyk RC, *et al.*: Pharmacokinetic-pharmacodynamic evaluation of the combined administration of alprazolam and fluoxetine. *Psychopharmacol* 1991, 104:323–327.

112. Bremner JD: A double-blind comparison Org 3770, amitriptyline, and placebo in major depression. *J Clin Psychiatry* 1995, 56:519–525.

113. Claghorn J, Lesem M: A double-blind placebo-controlled of Org 3770 in depressed outpatients. *J Affect Disord* 1996, 34:165–171.

114. Olin BR: *Drug Facts and Comparisons: Loose-leaf Drug Information Service*. St. Louis: Facts and Comparisons Inc.; 1996.

CHAPTER 16

The Effect of Personality Disorders on Outcome in the Treatment of Depression

Wilson McDermut and Mark Zimmerman

In this chapter we review the results of published empirical studies that examined the influence of personality disorder on outcome in the treatment of depression. Our search of the literature revealed 27 studies that have examined this topic. With few exceptions, these studies consistently show that compared with depressed individuals without a comorbid personality disorder, depressed persons with a personality disorder are less likely to recover and are more symptomatic after treatment. Methodologic issues and directions for future research are discussed.

D epression is a serious chronic medical problem with morbidity comparable to that of cardiovascular disease [1]. Estimated prevalence rates suggest that in any given year about 8% of men and 13% of women will experience an episode of major depression [2]. Several efficacious treatments for depression have been developed including both pharmacotherapies and psychotherapies. Despite the availability of effective treatments, many researchers now recognize that depression is often difficult to treat [3]. Even when effectively treated, depressed patients remain at substantial risk for relapse [4]. Consequently, increasing attention is being directed toward identifying predictors of treatment responsiveness and nonresponsiveness in the short and long term among individuals affected by depression.

An increasingly large body of research literature supports the suspicion held by many clinicians that compared with depressed patients without a comorbid personality disorder, depressed patients with a personality disorder respond less favorably to treatment. Our search of the psychiatry and psychology literature revealed 27 published reports based on 25 datasets that examined the effect of personality disorder on outcome in the treatment of depression. In this chapter we review and qualitatively evaluate the findings of these studies. In addition to reviewing the work in this area, we discuss pertinent methodologic considerations in conducting this type of research, and directions for future research.

Definitions of Depression and Personality Disorder

As used in this article, the terms *depression* and *personality disorder* refer to those disorders defined and described in established classification systems such as the *Diagnostic and Statistical Manual of Mental Disorders*, edition 3 (DSM-III) [5] and edition 3-revised

(DSM-III-R) [6], Research Diagnostic Criteria (RDC) [7], and International Classification of Diseases (ICD) [8]. At the writing of this paper, no published reports studying the effect of personality disorder on outcome of treatment for depression had employed the criteria in edition 4 of the DSM [9]. In the text that follows, the term *depression* refers to unipolar, nonpsychotic major depression as described in the aforementioned diagnostic schemes. *Personality disorder* refers to the Axis II disorders defined and described in the DSM-III and DSM-III-R, *ie*, enduring, inflexible, maladaptive patterns of perceiving and relating to oneself and the environment that result in either psychosocial functional impairment or subjective distress. The studies reviewed in this article assessed personality disorder in any number of ways (*eg*, paper-and-pencil self-report, informant interview, interview with the patient), but these studies subsequently categorized the personality disorder diagnoses according to the DSM-III or DSM-III-R. In addition to the DSM-III and DSM-III-R schemes for classifying personality disorder, several articles categorized personality diagnoses according to the Personality Assessment Schedule [10]. These articles are included in this review because the classification method is similar to the scheme elaborated in the DSM-III and DSM-III-R. What is not included in this review are studies that assessed personality traits such as neuroticism and then examined the effect of these traits on outcome in the treatment of depression (reviews of studies that measured personality as a continuous trait can be found in Reich and Green [11], and Reich and Vasile [12]).

Methodologic Considerations

Research involving the diagnosis of Axis II disorders presents several methodologic challenges. In the section that follows we discuss a number of important issues that should be addressed when conducting research that involves diagnosing Axis II pathology. For a more in-depth discussion of these issues, as well as an overview of the reliability of measures of personality disorder, the interested reader is referred to Zimmerman [13•]. Three questions that the researcher faces upon deciding to study personality disorders in patients with depression are: 1) who should be interviewed and provide the information for determining the presence or absence of a personality disorder—the patient or an informant; 2) what instrument should be used to make a diagnosis; and 3) when should one attempt to diagnose a personality disorder—on presentation for treatment when the patient is symptomatic, or after symptom improvement?

Who should be interviewed?

The evaluation of personality disorders presents special problems that may require the use of an informant. Unlike symptoms of Axis I pathology, the defining features of personality disorders are based on an extended longitudinal perspective of how individuals act in different situations, how they perceive and interact with a constantly changing environment, and the perceived reasonableness of their behaviors and cognitions. Only a minority of the personality disorder criteria are discrete, easily enumerated behaviors. For any individual to describe validly his or her normal personality, he or she must be somewhat introspective and aware of the effect his or her behavior has on himself or herself and others. The task is more formidable for acutely ill psychiatric patients because state effects might taint their perceptions of their usual personality.

To obtain putatively more accurate information, clinicians and researchers sometimes interview an informant of the patient such as a spouse or other family member.
Research on the concordance between information obtained from the patient and information obtained from an informant has generally failed to demonstrate adequate agreement (Kappas usually < .40) [14,15].

Given the failure to establish acceptable levels of agreement between patient and
informant, who should be interviewed? Which source of information is more valid?
Should both the patient and an informant be interviewed? Unfortunately, very little
research has addressed this question. What little evidence there is suggests that there is no
particular advantage to gathering information from two sources (patient plus informant)
rather than simply interviewing the patient. We are aware of only one study that examined the respective validities of different sources of information. Zimmerman *et al.* (Paper
presented at the 143rd Annual Meeting of the American Psychiatric Association, New
York, 1990) made personality disorder diagnoses in 66 depressed inpatients based on
independent interviews of the patient and a close informant. As noted above, they found
that the patients and informants differed markedly in their descriptions of the patients'
baseline personality. In order to examine validity, it was hypothesized that compared with
depressed patients without a personality disorder, those with a personality disorder
would be characterized by younger ages of onset, poorer social support, greater life stress,
more marital separations and divorces, a more unstable occupational history, a higher
morbid risk for alcoholism and drug abuse in their first-degree relatives, poorer overall
functioning during the 5 years prior to admission, and a poorer hospital course. Almost
all of the predictions were confirmed when diagnoses were based on the patient information and few were confirmed when diagnoses were based on the informant interview.
When the personality disorder diagnoses were derived from a combination of the patient
and informant information, the results were similar to the patient-only data. These data
therefore do not support the increased expenditure of time and resources needed to supplement the patient interview with information from an informant.

What instrument should be used?

What type of measure should be used—an interview or a questionnaire? After this is
decided, which of the several interviews and questionnaires should be chosen? Nine features distinguish the different personality measures.

Coverage

Some measures assess only one or two personality disorders [16,17], whereas others cover
all of the DSM disorders [18–24]. The International Personality Disorder Examination
covers DSM-III-R and the ICD, 10th Revision (Loranger, Paper presented at the 145th
Annual Meeting of the American Psychiatric Association, Washington, DC, 1992).

Correspondence to DSM-III-R and DSM-IV

Many instruments measure personality disorder constructs that are related, but not identical to those of the DSM criteria, such as the Personality Assessment Schedule [10] and
the Millon Clinical Multiaxial Inventory (MCMI) [24]. In contrast, other measures, such
as the Personality Disorder Examination (PDE) [19], the Structured Clinical Interview for
DSM-III-R Personality Disorders (SCID-II) [20], the Diagnostic Interview for Personality

Disorders (DIPD) [22], the Personality Diagnostic Questionnaire (PDQ) [23], and the Structured Interview for DSM-III-R Personality (SIDP) [18], were explicitly developed to assess DSM criteria.

Method of administration

Both self-administered questionnaires and semistructured interviews are commonly used. Unique to the SCID is the concurrent use of a screening questionnaire that is completed by the respondent and reviewed by the interviewer before the interview. The interviewer only inquires about the criteria that are endorsed on the questionnaire.

Interviewer requirements

The amount of clinical experience recommended for interviewer competence varies greatly. At one end of the continuum is the Personality Interview Questionnaire that was designed explicitly for use by lay interviewers. At the other end of the experience continuum is the PDE that was designed for use by experienced psychiatrists, clinical psychologists, or other professionals with comparable training. The authors of the SIDP recommend an intermediate level of experience (ie, an undergraduate degree in social sciences, at least 6 months experience in interviewing psychiatric patients, and about 1 month of specific training in using the SIDP).

Organization

Personality disorder assessment instruments vary in the way the questions are grouped. The questions on the SIDP and PDE are grouped into similar content areas, such as interpersonal relationships, emotions, and so forth. In contrast, the SCID-II, DIPD, and PDQ are organized by diagnosis. A topically oriented interview is smoother and less redundant, and should facilitate rapport between the subject and interviewer. This type of interview is also less prone to halo effects in which ratings of individual criteria are influenced by how close the individual is to meeting the criteria for the disorder. Because the bias of the halo effects is minimized, thematically organized instruments are more appropriate for studies of comorbidity.

Time frame

On the PDQ, the respondent is instructed to consider the past several years. The DIPD evaluates attitudes and behaviors for the 2 years prior to the interview, the SCID-II and the PDE evaluate attitudes and behaviors for the past 5 years, and the SIDP focuses on the individual's "usual self." If there is a dramatic recent change in the individual's personality, then the functioning that predominated for the greatest amount of time during the past 5 years is considered typical. On the PDE, the interviewer also inquires about age of onset of pathologic attitudes and behavior, and at least one criterion must be present before the age of 25 years to make a personality disorder diagnosis. Thus, the PDE emphasizes persistence and early onset more than the other measures, and it is more concordant with the DSM definition of a personality disorder.

Rating guidelines

The PDE is the only interview that is accompanied by a detailed item-by-item scoring manual. The items are scored from 0 through 2 with descriptors provided for each severity level.

The SIDP items are also scored from 0 through 2 with accompanying anchor point descriptions. In contrast, the SCID-II interviewer rates whether the item is absent, subthreshold, or is present at the threshold level, and there are general guidelines for distinguishing subthreshold and threshold severity levels. The DIPD ratings follow the same format as that of the SCID-II.

Scoring

On the SIDP several criteria are listed at the end of each section, and their ratings are based on the responses to all the questions in the section, though specific questions are identified as corresponding most closely to specific criteria. On the other interviews, the questions used to rate each criterion are listed immediately below or to the side of the item.

Content

Interestingly, the various assessment instruments use different questions to assess the same criteria. The questions are sufficiently different on the different instruments so that it cannot be assumed that individuals who are rated positive on one measure will be positive on the others.

Given the array of available choices, the first question one might want to address is whether to use a questionnaire or an interview. Research on the assessment of personality has a long history of using paper-and-pencil tests. These tests are convenient and have lower costs than conducting interviews. They are also free from biases of interviewers. Intuitively, one might expect interviews to be more valid because questions can be clarified, examples of pathology can be elicited, and positive responses can be followed up to confirm that apparent pathology was not situational or state-dependent, but rather represented aspects of the patient's long-term functioning. In addition, the rater can use the patient's interview behavior and demeanor as another source of data.

A number of studies comparing interview and self-report questionnaire assessments have consistently shown poor agreement between the measures. For example, Hunt and Andrews [25] compared agreement between the PDE and PDQ-R in a sample of 59 outpatients. They found that 7.5% of outpatients had a personality disorder according to the PDE, and 67.5% had a personality disorder according to the PDQ-R. Similar to Hunt and Andrews' results, most comparisons of self-report and interviews show that questionnaires tend to overdiagnose personality disorders in both patient and nonpatient samples [13•]. If studies rely solely on self-report measures, too many false-positives would be assigned to the personality disorder–positive group, thus increasing the similarity of the two groups and decreasing the likelihood of finding "true" differences in response to treatment.

The next question one might ask is: which of the interview-based measures should be employed? Research comparing different interview techniques would help answer this question. However, this kind of research is sparse because it is technically difficult. It requires independent administration of the measures so that the results of one do not influence the other. Thus, at least two raters who are trained to conduct both interviews are needed. These raters must demonstrate high levels of test-retest reliability with each measure, otherwise interinstrument diagnostic discordance might be due to rater variance. Additionally, interview measures have modest short-interval, test-retest reliability. Therefore, it is not surprising that the only studies comparing two different interviews [26–29] found generally poor to fair agreement.

When should the personality disorder assessment be conducted?

Given what is known about negative cognitive bias in depression and mood-state–dependent recall, wouldn't we expect to see greater levels of reported, Axis II pathology when someone is in the midst of an episode of major depression? Studies that have tested this hypothesis have typically administered personality assessment instruments to patients prior to the start of treatment and then again at the conclusion of treatment. The results fairly consistently show that compared with pretreatment levels of personality pathology, less personality pathology is reported following treatment. This result has been found in several different patient populations including patients with depression [30], eating disorders [31], and anxiety disorders [32]. In addition, the available data suggest that both personality disorder interviews and self-report inventories are susceptible to overreporting bias due to the acute psychiatric state. These results might suggest that symptom abatement be a prerequisite for personality disorder assessment, since personality pathology seems to be overreported during the acute stage of psychiatric illness.

However, despite the inflated rates of personality pathology seen during acute Axis I illness, we would argue that personality assessments should be conducted during the acute stage of an Axis I disorder, because this is usually the time when treatment decisions are made. If personality disorder assessments are to have treatment implications, they should be made at this early date. Moreover, as the literature review that follows will attest, assessments made during the acute stage of psychiatric illness do indeed have strong, consistent, prognostic value.

Review of the Literature

Our search of the literature identified 27 reports published between 1981 and 1996 based on 25 separate data sets. The preponderance of the available evidence shows that compared with depressed patients without a personality disorder, presence of a personality disorder is related to slower response to treatment, decreased likelihood of recovery from an episode of depression, and higher levels of depressive symptomatology and social impairment at treatment termination and up to a year after treatment termination. Of the 27 studies we reviewed, 23 (85%) found statistically significant evidence that the presence of a personality disorder is associated with worse outcome. Only two studies found statistically significant evidence that personality pathology was related to better outcome [33,34]. One study found no outcome differences between depressed patients with and without personality disorders [35]. Another study [36] obtained mixed results, with some evidence pointing toward worse outcome in depressed patients with a personality disorder and some evidence suggesting better outcome in depressed patients with a personality disorder.

The finding that personality disorder is associated with worse outcome has been replicated in several different patient populations including inpatients, outpatients, patients referred from primary care, and the elderly. The finding is consistent regardless of the type of treatment involved. Whether the treatment studied was naturalistic (Table 1) [33,37–44], medication only (Table 2) [34–36,45–50], psychotherapy with or without medication (Table 3) [51–57•], or electroconvulsive therapy (ECT) (Table 4) [58, 59•], the majority of studies demonstrated poorer outcome for depressed patients diagnosed with a comorbid personality disorder.

Though most published studies have been conducted in the United States and United Kingdom, one study [48] and a re-analysis [50] from Japan and another from Switzerland [41] are consistent with the majority of studies indicating that the presence of a personality disorder predicts poorer outcome. The poorer outcome in patients with a personality disorder has been noted in several studies at 6 months after treatment termination [39,47,58], and up to 1 year after treatment termination [56]. Andrews *et al.* [42] found evidence that the presence of personality pathology accounts for a significant amount of the variance in outcome up to 15 years after index treatment.

Is there any one personality disorder diagnosis or cluster of diagnoses that most strongly predicts treatment nonresponse?

There were two commonly used methodologies employed in studies to determine if type of personality disorder affects treatment response. One approach was to compare depressed patients with one or more personality disorder to depressed patients without any personality disorder diagnosis in terms of the likelihood of recovery or improvement. A second common approach was to identify treatment responders and nonresponders and compare those two groups in terms of whether or not they had significant characterologic pathology.

Four studies of the 27 we reviewed examined the degree to which each of the personality disorders affected outcome. The findings of these studies were often in conflict, and no systematic pattern emerged. Frank *et al.* [51] found that a higher percentage of slow responders were classified as avoidant or dependent. In contrast, Thompson *et al.* [53] found a trend toward more treatment successes among depressed patients diagnosed with dependent or avoidant personality disorders, and more treatment failures among those diagnosed as passive-aggressive or compulsive. Hoencamp *et al.* [36], found that subjects rated as passive-aggressive by their therapists or as dependent or self-defeating according to the SCID-II had worse outcome. Interestingly, this study also found that therapist ratings of obsessive-compulsive personality, and SCID-II-based diagnoses of obsessive-compulsive personality disorder were associated with better outcome. Joffe and Regan [34], on the other hand, found that treatment responders had higher scores on the Antisocial and Paranoid scales of the MCMI when they completed the measure while acutely depressed. In sum, though a few research groups have reported that certain personality disorders undermine recovery while others seem to enhance recovery, there is no convincing evidence that depressed individuals with any particular personality disorder have a poorer (or better) prognosis than depressed subjects with any other disorder.

The paucity of research comparing the relative impact of specific personality disorder is a consequence of the difficulty inherent in trying to recruit enough patients with each type of disorder to conduct meaningful analyses. As several researchers noted [38,45], their samples included sparse numbers of certain diagnoses. Pfohl *et al.* [38, 39] and Black *et al.* [40] had so few Cluster A diagnoses that they did not even have sufficient numbers to comprise a Cluster A group to be compared with Clusters B and C.

Ten studies [34,35,38–40,47,48,50,52,54] compared the effect of pathology in Clusters A, B, C on outcome in depression. The studies that compared the influence of different clusters found that slower improvement, or worse outcome, was accounted for primarily by Cluster A or C pathology [47,48,50,52] compared with subjects with no

Table 1. Studies Involving Uncontrolled Naturalistic Treatment

Study	Patients, n	Patient status	PD measure	Time of assessment
Charney et al. [37]	64	Inpatient	Chart review	N/A
Pfohl et al. [38]	78	Inpatient	SIDP	Within first week of admission
Pfohl et al. [39]	78	Inpatient	SIDP, PDQ	Within first week of admission
Black et al. [40]	228	Inpatient	Chart review	N/A
Andreoli et al. [41]	16	Inpatient	Clinical interview	At discharge (diagnosis subject to revision at 2-year follow-up)
Andrews et al. [42]	212	Inpatient	"Evidence for personality disorder (ICD-9)"	During hospitalization
Mazure et al. [33]	52	Inpatient	Not reported	Within 3 days of admission
Reich [43]	37	Outpatient	PDQ	Within 1 week of intake
Brophy [44]	57	Inpatient	PAS	Within 3 days of admission

BDI—Beck Depression Inventory [67]; BEC—a multidimensional psychiatric evaluation form developed in Europe [69]; ECT—electroconvulsive therapy; GAS—Global Assessment Scale [68]; HRSD—Hamilton Rating Scale for Depression [66]; ICD—International Classification of Diseases; N/A—not applicable; PAS—Personality Assessment Schedule; PD—personality disorder; PDQ—Personality Diagnostic Questionnaire; RDS—Raskin Depression Scale [70]; SIDP—Structured Interview for Diagnostic and Statistical Manual-III Personality [65].

personality disorder. One exception to this [36] found better outcome for patients rated as obsessive-compulsive either by themselves or their therapists. In contrast to the clinical lore that individuals with Cluster B personality disorders are more difficult to treat, no study found that Cluster B pathology accounted for the differences in outcome between personality disorder and non–personality disorder subjects. In fact, Fava et al. [35] found that patients with a Cluster B diagnosis exhibited a greater drop in depressive symptomatology compared with patients without a Cluster B diagnosis. Similarly, Joffe and Regan [34] found that subjects who had high levels of Cluster B pathology (specifically "antisocial") when depressed fared better in treatment than those with lower levels of Cluster B pathology. However, these authors argue that the antisocial dimension of the MCMI taps assertiveness, competitiveness, independence, and social aggressiveness rather than true sociopathy.

A number of investigators have noted significant overlap in personality disorder diagnoses, so that individuals with personality pathology in one cluster also demonstrate pathology in one or more of the other clusters. This finding suggested that measures of

Treatment	Outcome variables	Results and comment
Inpatient psychosocial treatment and/or anti-depressants	Improvement at discharge rated on scale of 1 to 5	Non-PD patients had better response to treatment than PD patients
"Doctor's choice"	HRSD, BDI, GAS, days hospitalized	Non-PD patients more likely to improve on outcome measures; PD patients less responsive to medication
"Doctor's choice"	HRSD, BDI, GAS, number of depressive symptoms, weeks on antidepressants	Patients with higher numbers of SIDP or PDQ criteria had poorer outcome at discharge and 6-month follow-up
ECT, antidepressants, or neither ECT nor anti-depressants	Ratings of degree of improvement were based on physician chart notes	PD patients less likely to recover at discharge and more likely to attempt suicide after discharge
Hospital treatment as usual (mean 3 weeks) or crisis intervention (6 weeks)	BEC, measures of global function-ing and social functioning	Presence of PD associated with worse outcome; however, analyses were not conducted on the depressed subsample
Inpatient hospitalization (median length of stay about 4 weeks)	Global outcome, time in hospital, time psychiatrically ill, work incapacity	Personality variables (eg, presence vs absence of PD) accounted for 20% of variance in 15-year outcome in nonendogenous depressives
One week inpatient hospitalization (no somatic treatment)	HRSD	Absence of PD was associated with lack of response to 1 week of hospitalization
Naturalistic (97% on antidepressants)	GAS, employment status, physician visits during follow-up, rehospi-talizations	Non-PD group had higher GAS scores and was more likely to achieve full employment at 6-month follow-up
Two weeks, routine inpa-tient hospitalization	HRSD, RDS	PD patients more depressed or anxious after 2 weeks

global personality pathology could be valid predictors of outcome [39]. Indeed, the research we reviewed consistently found that higher levels of overall personality pathology (as measured by diagnoses in more than one cluster or the sum total of personality criteria) was related to worse outcome. Of the seven studies that examined the relation between sheer number of personality disorder criteria and treatment outcome (assessed either via interview or self-report), four studies found that higher numbers of personality disorder criteria were associated with worse outcome [39,47,48,52]. This suggests that measures of overall personality pathology have some validity in predicting response to treatment.

Why does the presence of a personality disorder have an adverse effect on response to treatment of depression?

Several researchers have suggested that depression in isolation and depression in the presence of a personality disorder are biologically distinct phenomena. In support of this supposition is the fact that depression in the context of a personality disorder is not associated with the presence of conventional biologic markers of depression. For example,

Table 2. Treatment Studies Involving Medication Only

Study	Patients, n	Patient status	PD measure	Time of assessment
Tyrer et al. [45]	60	48 (outpatient) 12 (inpatient)	PAS	Pretreatment
Sauer et al. [46]	52	Inpatient	Clinical interview	"When the patients had improved"
Joffe and Regan [34]	42	Outpatient	MCMI	Responders completed MCMI after 4 weeks; nonreponders completed MCMI after 4-week point when HRSD < 5
Peselow et al. [47]	68	Outpatient	SIDP	Pretreatment
Sato et al. [48]	96	Outpatient	SCID-II	After at least 2 months of treatment and HRSD < 11
Fava et al. [35]	83	Outpatient	PDQ-R	Pretreatment
Hoencamp et al. [36]	119	Outpatient	SCID-II	Pretreatment
Nelson et al. [49]	68	Inpatient	Clinical interview of patient and informants	During first week of hospitalization
Sato et al. [50]	96	Outpatient	SCID-II	After at least 2 months of treatment and HRSD < 11

CGI—Clinical Global Impressions; HRSD—Hamilton Rating Scale for Depression; MCMI—Millon Clinical Multiaxial Inventory; PAS—Personality Assessment Schedule; PD—personality disorder; PDQ-R—Personality Diagnostic Questionnaire-Revised [71]; SCID-II—Structured Clinical Interview for Diagnostic and Statistical Manual-III-Revised personality disorders; TRIM—tricyclic response in major depression [72].

research shows that personality disorders are less frequent in patients with endogenous depression [60]. Depressed patients with personality disorders are also less likely to be dexamethasone suppression test nonsuppressors than depressed patients without personality disorders [38]. Personality pathology is also inversely correlated with an array of neuroendocrine and polysomnographic markers for depression [51].

Another reason that depressed patients with personality disorder may not be as responsive to treatment may be because of poor compliance or higher dropout rates. The reasons for dropout or noncompliance vary depending on the nature of the personality pathology. A person with schizoid features might be noncompliant for different reasons than a patient with borderline features, nevertheless the end result (ie, noncompliance or withdrawal from treatment) might be the same. The available evidence, however, does not support the prediction that patients with personality disorder are more likely to dropout or be noncompliant.

Shea et al. [54] found no difference in rates of attrition between depressed subjects with (31%) and without (36%) personality disorder. They found some differences

Treatment	Outcome variables	Results and comment
Four weeks, phenelzine	HRSD	Nonresponders were significantly more likely to have a PD compared with responders; 30 subjects had phobic or anxiety neuroses
Three weeks, amitriptyline	HRSD, days hospitalized	PD, sudden onset of depression, and depressive psychotic features were negatively correlated with 21-day outcome and explained 34% of outcome variance
Four weeks, desipramine or imipramine	HRSD	Responders had higher mean scores on antisocial and paranoid scales of MCMI
Four to 5 weeks, desipramine	HRSD, CGI	Treatment responders had lower level of overall personality pathology; patients with lower total personality pathology fared better at 6-month follow-up
Naturalistic treatment with antidepressants (mean 8.5 months)	HRSD, social functioning	PD patients had significantly worse 4-month outcome; Cluster A PD and number of schizoid features had strongest association with failure to remit
Eight weeks, fluoxetine	HRSD	Presence of PD was *not* associated with worse outcome
Eighteen weeks, antidepressants	HRSD	Dependent, self-defeating, passive-aggressive PD associated with worse outcome; obsessive PD associated with better outcome
Four weeks, desipramine	HRSD, CGI, TRIM	Presence of PD associated with worse 4-week outcome
Naturalistic treatment with antidepressants (mean 8.5 months)	HRSD, social functioning	Re-analysis and replication of Sato et al. [48], (ie, presence of Cluster A PD worsened outcome)

between clusters in attrition, noting that attrition rates were highest for Cluster B patients (40%) and lowest in the Cluster C patients (28%). Statistical significance of this difference was not reported. Sato *et al.* [48] found that depressed patients with personality disorders continued on medication treatment for just as long as depressed patients without personality disorders (8.6 months vs 8.4 months). In the studies we reviewed there is no systematic pattern of evidence suggesting that noncompliant patients or those who drop out are more likely to have personality disorders than compliant patients. However, most studies did not explicitly analyze the degree to which personality pathology was associated with noncompliance or early dropout.

Another plausible explanation for reduced treatment responsiveness in depressed patients with personality disorder may have to do with failure to establish a working alliance with the clinician [61]. Given that one of the hallmarks of personality pathology is impaired interpersonal functioning, one would anticipate (and clinical wisdom would suggest) that establishing a working alliance with patients with personality disorders is more difficult than establishing a working alliance with patients without

Table 3 Treatment Outcome Studies Involving Psychotherapy

Study	Patients, n	Patient status	PD measure	Time of assessment
Frank et al. [51]	68	Outpatient	PAF	During acute treatment at the point that HRSD ≤ 7 and RDS ≤ 5 for 3 consecutive weeks
Pilkonis and Frank [52]	119	Outpatient	PAF	Upon recovery during acute treatment
Thompson et al. [53]	79	Outpatient	SIDP	Within 12 to 24 months following completion of treatment
Shea et al. [54]	239	Outpatient	PAF	Pretreatment
Diguer et al. [55]	25	Outpatient	PAF	Within 1 week of intake
Hardy et al. [56]	114	Outpatient	PDE	Pretreatment
Patience et al. [57•]	113	Outpatient	PAS	At end of 16-week treatment phase or earlier if HRSD < 7

BDI—Beck Depression Inventory; CBT—cognitive-behavioral therapy; GAS—Global Assessment Scale; GLFS—General Life Functioning Scale [76]; HRSD—Hamilton Rating Scale for Depression; HSCL-90—Hopkins Symptom Checklist-90 [75]; HSRS—Health-Sickness Rating Scale [77]; IIP—Inventory of Interpersonal Problems [79]; MCMI—Millon Clinical Multiaxial Inventory; PAF—Personality Assessment Form [73]; PD—personality disorder; PDE—Personality Disorders Examination; P-IPT—psychodynamic-interpersonal psychotherapy; RDS—Raskin Depression Scale; SAS—Social Adjustment Scale [74]; SCL-90-R—Symptom Checklist-90-Revised [78]; SE—self-esteem measure [80]; SFS—Social Functioning Scale [81]; SIDP—Structured Interview for Diagnostic and Statistical Manual-III Personality.

Table 4. Electroconvulsive Therapy Studies

Study	Patients, n	Patient status	PD measure	Time of assessment
Zimmerman et al. [58]	25	Inpatient	SIDP	Within first week of admission
Casey et al. [59•]	40	Inpatient	PAS	After discharge from hospital

ECT—electroconvulsive therapy; HRSD—Hamilton Rating Scale for Depression; PAS—Personality Assessment Schedule; PD—personality disorder; SFS—Social Functioning Scale; SIDP—Structured Interview for Diagnostic and Statistical Manual-III Personality.

Treatment	Outcome variables	Results and comment
Twenty sessions of interpersonal psychotherapy plus imipramine	HRSD	Slow responders had more personality pathology
Twenty sessions of interpersonal psychotherapy plus imipramine	HRSD, RDS	Slow responders more likely had a PD and had higher levels of overall personality pathology
Twenty-four to 28 sessions of cognitive therapy, behavior therapy, or psychodynamic therapy	Presence or absence of major depression	Non-PD patients were more likely to not meet criteria for depression at posttreatment
At least 12 sessions of cognitive behavior therapy, interpersonal psychotherapy, clinical management plus imipramine, or clinical management plus placebo	HRSD, SAS, HSCL-90, GLFS	PD patients less likely to recover and had poorer social functioning
Sixteen sessions, psychodynamic psychotherapy	BDI, HSRS	PD patients were more depressed at intake, posttreatment, and 6-month follow-up
Eight or 16 sessions of cognitive-behavioral or psychodynamic psychotherapy	BDI, SCL-90-R, IIP, SE	Cluster C PD patients fared worse in P-IPT psychotherapy than those in CBT
Sixteen weeks of either routine care by general practitioner, pharmacotherapy by psychiatrist, cognitive-behavioral therapy by psychologist, or counseling by social worker	HRSD, SFS	Fewer patients with PD recovered by end of treatment; no differences in recovery rates at 12- and 18-month follow-ups

Treatment	Outcome variables	Results and comment
ECT (mean number treatments = 10.7)	HRSD, number of symptoms	PD patients less likely to recover; PD patients had more hospitalizations and more symptoms during 6-month follow-up
ECT	HRSD, SFS, rehospitalization	Patients with PD were more depressed and had more social dysfunction at discharge, but not at 6-month follow-up

personality disorders. To date, no studies that we are aware of have addressed the issue of whether the connection between personality pathology and outcome is mediated by the quality of the bond established between the clinician and the patient.

The psychosocial research on correlates of depression yields other clues as to why depressed patients with personality disorders may be less responsive to conventional treatments. A substantial body of literature has shown a connection between poor social support and depression [62]. One of the hallmarks of personality pathology is impaired interpersonal functioning. Thus, depressed persons with personality disorder may be less responsive to treatment because they lack the social resources that are conducive to recovery.

Personality pathology might interfere with the treatment responsiveness of depressed patients because the personality pathology is associated with "chaotic" lifestyles [38] that engender the types of stressful life events (eg, job loss, divorce) that are believed to be associated with depression [63]. Thus, the presence of personality pathology may complicate the process of recovering from a depressive episode by maintaining or creating circumstances that exacerbate depressive symptomatology and delay the recovery process.

Finally, depressed patients with personality disorders may have poorer coping skills. Some research has shown that depressed patients with a personality disorder show poorer coping abilities than depressed subjects without a personality disorder [64].

Conclusions and Future Directions

The extant empirical literature indicates that personality pathology predicts worse outcome in the treatment of depression. This finding is fairly robust, and has been found in several different patient populations and is generally true regardless of whether or not the treatment is medication, psychotherapy, or a combination of both. At this time, there is not enough evidence to suggest that any one particular personality disorder is most deleterious to the process of recovering from depression. There is evidence to suggest that character pathology in any of the three clusters is associated with worse outcome. If anything, available evidence supports the notion that Cluster A and C pathology are more deleterious to recovery than Cluster B pathology.

Several different hypotheses have been advanced to explain why personality pathology impedes the process of recovery from depression.

1. Depression in the context of a personality disorder may have a distinct biologic substrate that is not amenable to conventional somatic or psychotherapeutic treatments.
2. Personality disordered patients may be less compliant with treatment.
3. It may be more difficult for clinicians to establish a constructive working alliance with personality disordered patients.
4. Patients with personality disorders may have poorer social support.
5. Personality disordered patients may be more prone to chaotic lifestyles, and thus are prone to producing life events that are associated with depression.
6. Patients with personality disorders may have impaired coping abilities.

A major drawback of this research is that personality disordered patients are treated as a homogeneous population. Future research should attempt to discern to what degree each of the personality disorders is associated with nonresponsiveness to treatment of depression. Future research should also be directed at understanding why personality disorders impair recovery from depression. Once we have a better understanding of the reasons why depressed patients with comorbid personality disorders have poorer outcome, we may be in a better position to develop novel treatment approaches to improve recovery rates for this subpopulation of depressed patients.

Acknowledgment

We thank Dr. Mark Bauer for his helpful comments on this chapter.

References and Recommended Reading

Papers of particular interest, published recently, have been highlighted as:
- Of special interest
- • Of outstanding interest

1. Wells KB, Stewart A, Hays RD: The functioning and well-being of depressed patients: results from the Medical Outcomes Study. *JAMA* 1989, 262:914–919.
2. Kessler RK, McGonagle K, Zhao S: Lifetime and 12-month prevalence of DSM-III-R psychiatric disorders in the United States. *Arch Gen Psychiatry* 1994, 51:8–19.
3. Keller MB, Shapiro RW, Lavori PW, *et al*.: Recovery in major depressive disorder: analysis with the life table and regression models. *Arch Gen Psychiatry* 1982, 39:905–910.
4. Keller MB, Shapiro RW, Lavori PW, *et al*.: Relapse in major depressive disorder: analysis with the life table. *Arch Gen Psychiatry* 1982, 39:911–915.
5. American Psychiatric Association: *Diagnostic and Statistical Manual of Mental Disorders*, edn 3. Washington, DC: American Psychiatric Association; 1980.
6. American Psychiatric Association: *Diagnostic and Statistical Manual of Mental Disorders* edn 3, revised. Washington, DC: American Psychiatric Association; 1987.
7. Spitzer RL, Endicott J, Robins E: Research Diagnostic Criteria: rationale and reliability. *Arch Gen Psychiatry* 1978, 35:773–782.
8. World Health Organization: *Manual of the International Statistical Classification of Diseases, Injuries, and Causes of Death*, revised edn. Geneva, Switzerland; 1978.
9. American Psychiatric Association: *Diagnostic and Statistical Manual of Mental Disorders*, edn 4. Washington, DC: American Psychiatric Association; 1994.
10. Tyrer P, Alexander MS, Cicchetti D, *et al*.: Reliability of a schedule for rating personality disorder. *Br J Psychiatry* 1979, 135:163–167.
11. Reich JH, Green AI: Effect of personality disorders on outcome of treatment. *J Nerv Ment Dis* 1991, 179:74–82.
12. Reich JH, Vasile RG: Effect of personality disorders on the treatment outcome of Axis I conditions: an update. *J Nerv Ment Dis* 1993, 181:475–484.
13.• Zimmerman M: Diagnosing personality disorders: a review of issues and research methods. *Arch Gen Psychiatry* 1994, 51:225–245.
This paper contains a comprehensive review of the reliability and validity of measures of personality disorders and discusses the most important methodologic issues related to assessing personality disorders.
14. Dowson JH: Assessment of DSM-III-R personality disorders by self-report questionnaire: the role of informants and a screening test for co-morbid personality disorders (STCPD). *Br J Psychiatry* 1992, 161:344–352.
15. Zimmerman M, Pfohl B, Coryell WH, *et al*.: Diagnosing personality disorder in depressed patients: a comparison of patient and informant interviews. *Arch Gen Psychiatry* 1988, 45:733–737.

16. Gunderson JG, Kolb JE, Austin V: The diagnostic interview for borderlines. *Am J Psychiatry* 1981, 138:896–903.

17. Kendler KS, Lieberman JA, Walsh D: The structured interview for schizotypy (SIS): a preliminary report. *Schizophrenia Bull* 1989, 15:559–571.

18. Pfohl B, Blum N, Zimmerman M, *et al.*: *Structured Interview for DSM-III-R Personality SIDP-R.* Iowa City, IA: Department of Psychiatry, University of Iowa; 1989.

19. Loranger AW: *Personality Disorder Examination (PDE) Manual.* Yonkers, NY: DV Communications; 1988.

20. Spitzer RL, Williams JBW, Gibbon M, *et al.*: *Structured Clinical Interview for DSM-III-R Personality Disorders (SCID II).* Washington, DC: American Psychiatric Association Press; 1990.

21. Widiger TA, Trull TJ, Hurt SW, *et al.*: A multidimensional scaling of the DSM-III personality disorders. *Arch Gen Psychiatry* 1987, 44:557–563.

22. Zanarini MC, Frankenburg FR, Chauncey DL, *et al.*: The Diagnostic Interview for Personality Disorders: interrater and test-retest reliability. *Comp Psychiatry* 1987, 28:467–480.

23. Hyler SE, Rieder RD, Williams JBW, *et al.*: The Personality Diagnostic Questionnaire: development and preliminary results. *J Pers Disord* 1988, 2:229–237.

24. Millon T: The MCMI provides a good assessment of DSM-III disorders: the MCMI-II will prove even better. *J Pers Assess* 1985, 49:379–391.

25. Hunt C, Andrews G: Measuring personality disorder: the use of self-report questionnaires. *J Pers Disord* 1992, 6:125–133.

26. O'Boyle M, Self D: A comparison of two interviews for DSM-III-R personality disorders. *Psychiatry Res* 1990, 32:85–92.

27. Skodol AE, Oldham JM, Rosnick L, *et al.*: Diagnosis of DSM-III-R personality disorders: a comparison of two structured interviews. *Int J Meth Psych Res* 1991, 1:13–26.

28. Hyler SE, Skodol AE, Kellman D, *et al.*: Validity of the Personality Diagnostic Questionnaire—Revised: comparison with two structured interviews. *Am J Psychiatry* 1990, 147:1043–1048.

29. Oldham JM, Skodol AE, Kellman D, *et al.*: Diagnosis of DSM-III-R personality disorders by two structured interviews: patterns of comorbidity. *Am J Psychiatry* 1992, 149:213–220.

30. Stuart S, Simons AD, Thase ME, *et al.*: Are personality assessments valid in acute major depression? *J Affect Disord* 1992, 149:829–831.

31. Ames-Frankel J, Devlin MJ, Walsh BT, *et al.*: Personality disorder diagnoses in patients with bulimia nervosa: clinical correlates and changes with treatment. *J Clin Psychiatry* 1992, 53:90–96.

32. Ricciardi JN, Baer L, Jenike MA, *et al.*: Changes in DSM-III-R Axis II diagnoses following treatment of obsessive-compulsive disorder. *Am J Psychiatry* 1992, 149:829–831.

33. Mazure CM, Nelson JC, Jatlow PI: Predictors of hospital outcome without antidepressants in major depression. *Psychiatry Res* 1990, 33:51–58.

34. Joffe RT, Regan JJ: Personality and response to tricyclic antidepressants in depressed patients. *J Nerv Ment Dis* 1989, 177:745–749.

35. Fava M, Bouffides E, Pava JA: Personality disorder comorbidity with major depression and response to fluoxetine treatment. *Psychother Psychosomat* 1994, 62:160–167.

36. Hoencamp E, Haffmans PMJ, Duivenvoorden H, *et al.*: Predictors of (non)-response in depressed outpatients treated with a three-phase sequential medication strategy. *J Affect Disord* 1994, 31:235–246.

37. Charney DS, Nelson JC, Quinlan DM.: Personality traits and disorder in depression. *Am J Psychiatry* 1981, 138:1601–1604.

38. Pfohl B, Stangl D, Zimmerman M: The implications of DSM-III personality disorders for patients with major depression. *J Affect Disord* 1984, 7:309–318.

39. Pfohl B, Coryell W, Zimmerman M, *et al.*: Prognostic validity of self-report and interview measures of personality disorder in depressed inpatients. *J Clin Psychiatry* 1987, 48:468–472.

40. Black DW, Bell S, Hulbert J, *et al.*: The importance of Axis II in patients with major depression: a controlled study. *J Affect Disord* 1988, 14:115–122.

41. Andreoli A, Gressot G, Aapro N, *et al.*: Personality disorders as a predictor of outcome. *J Pers Disord* 1989, 3:307–320.

42. Andrews G, Neilson M, Hunt C, *et al.*: Diagnosis, personality and the long-term outcome of depression. *Br J Psychiatry* 1990, 157:13–18.

43. Reich JH: Effect of DSM-III personality disorders on outcome of tricyclic antidepressant-treated nonpsychotic outpatients with major or minor depressive disorder. *Psychiatry Res* 1990, 32:175–181.

44. Brophy JJ: Personality disorder, symptoms and dexamethasone suppression in depression. *J Affect Disord* 1994, 31:19–27.

45. Tyrer P, Casey P, Gall J: Relationship between neurosis and personality disorder. *Br J Psychiatry* 1983, 142:404–408.

46. Sauer H, Kick H, Minne HW, *et al.*: Prediction of amitriptyline response: psychopathology vs. neuroendocrinology. *Int Clin Psychopharmacol* 1986, 1:284–295.

47. Peselow ED, Fieve RR, DiFiglia C: Personality traits and response to desipramine. *J Affect Disord* 1992, 24:209–216.

48. Sato T, Sakado K, Sato S: Is there any specific personality disorder or personality disorder cluster that worsens the short-term treatment outcome of major depression? *Acta Psychiatr Scand* 1993, 88:342–349.

49. Nelson JC, Mazure CM, Jatlow PI: Characteristics of desipramine-refractory depression. *J Clin Psychiatry* 1994, 55:12–19.

50. Sato T, Sakado K, Sato S, *et al.*: Cluster A personality disorder: a marker of worse treatment outcome of major depression? *Psychiatry Res* 1994, 53:153–159.

51. Frank E, Kupfer DJ, Jacob M, *et al.*: Personality features and response to acute treatment in recurrent depression. *J Pers Disord* 1987, 1:14–26.

52. Pilkonis PA, Frank E: Personality pathology in recurrent depression: nature, prevalence, and relationship to treatment response. *Am J Psychiatry* 1988, 145:435–441.

53. Thompson LW, Gallagher D, Czirr R: Personality disorder and outcome in the treatment of late-life depression. *J Geriatr Psychiatry* 1988, 21:133–146.

54. Shea MT, Pilkonis PA, Beckham E, *et al.*: Personality disorders and treatment outcome in the NIMH treatment of depression collaborative research program. *Am J Psychiatry* 1990, 147:711–718.

55. Diguer L, Barber JP, Luborksy L: Three concomitants: personality disorders, psychiatric severity, and outcome of dynamic psychotherapy of major depression. *Am J Psychiatry* 1993, 150:1246–1248.

56. Hardy GE, Barkham M, Shapiro DA, *et al.*: Impact of Cluster C personality disorder on outcomes of contrasting brief psychotherapies for depression. *J Consult Clin Psychol* 1995, 63:997–1004.

57.• Patience DA, McGuire RJ, Scott AIF, *et al.*: The Edinburgh Primary Care Depression Study: personality disorder and outcome. *Br J Psychiatry* 1995, 167:324–330.
This study (n=113) examined the effect of personality on outcome in the treatment of depressed outpatients in primary care in Scotland. All patients were referred by general practitioners and treated in the primary care setting. Patients with any personality disorder had higher levels of depressive symptoms and more impaired social functioning prior to treatment and at treatment completion (16 weeks), but there were no differences at 18-month follow-up. The investigators concluded that "the presence of personality pathology delays, but does not prevent, improvement from major depressive illness." Interestingly, there were no differences in outcome between the four treatments to which patients were assigned (routine care by a general practitioner, pharmacotherapy by a psychiatrist, cognitive-behavioral therapy by a psychologist, or "counseling" by a social worker).

58. Zimmerman M, Coryell W, Pfohl B, *et al.*: ECT response in depressed patients with and without a DSM-III personality disorder. *Am J Psychiatry* 1986, 143:1030–1032.

59.• Casey P, Meagher D, Butler E: Personality, functioning, and recovery from major depression. *J Nerv Ment Dis* 1996, 184:240–245.
This study (n=40) examined the effect of personality pathology on the efficacy of electroconvulsive therapy in severely depressed inpatients in Ireland. Patients with and without presonality disorders did not differ in levels of depressive symptoms prior to treatment. Patients with personality pathology were more depressed and more socially impaired at discharge. There were no differences in levels of depressive symptoms or social functioning at 12-month follow-up. The authors conclude that in their sample of depressed patients, personality pathology delayed recovery of social functioning but did not influence the speed of symptomatic recovery or readmission rates.

60. Zimmerman M, Coryell W, Pfohl B, *et al.*: An American validation study of the Newcastle Diagnostic Scale: II. Relationship with clinical, demographic, familial and psychosocial features. *Br J Psychiatry* 1987, 150:526–532.

61. Shea MT, Widiger TA, Klein MH: Comorbidity of personality disorders and depression: implications for treatment. *J Consult Clin Psychol* 1992, 60:857–868.

62. Brown GW, Harris T, Copeland JR: Depression and loss. *Br J Psychiatry* 1977, 130:1–18.

63. Paykel ES, Cooper Z: Life events and social stress. In *Handbook of Affective Disorders*. Edited by Paykel ES. New York: Guilford Press; 1992:149–170.

64. Roy-Byrne PP, Vitaliano PP, Cowley DS, *et al*.: Coping in panic and major depressive disorder: relative effects of symptom severity and diagnostic comorbidity. *J Nerv Ment Dis* 1992, 180:179–183.

65. Pfohl B, Stangl D, Zimmerman M: *The Structured Interview for DSM-III Personality Disorders (SIDP)*. Iowa City, IA: Department of Psychiatry, University of Iowa; 1982.

66. Hamilton M: A rating scale for depression. *J Neurol Neurosurgery Psychiatry* 1960, 23:56–62.

67. Beck AT, Ward CH, Mendelson M, *et al*.: An inventory for measuring depression. *Arch Gen Psychiatry* 1961, 4:561–571.

68. Endicott J, Spitzer RL, Fleiss RL, *et al*.: The Global Assessment Scale: a procedure for measuring overall severity of psychiatric disturbance. *Arch Gen Psychiatry* 1976, 33:766–771.

69. Gerin P: *L'evaluation des psychotherapies*. Paris: Payot; 1984.

70. Raskin A, Schulterbrandt J, Reatig N, *et al*.: Replication of factors of psychopathology in interview, ward behavior and self-report ratings of hospitalized depressives. *J Nerv Ment Dis* 1969, 148:87–98.

71. Hyler SE, Rieder RO: *PDQ-R: Personality Diagnostic Questionnaire-Revised*. New York: New York State Psychiatric Institute; 1987.

72. Nelson JC, Mazure CM: A scale for rating tricyclic response in major depression: the TRIM. *J Clin Psychopharmacol* 1990, 10:252–260.

73. Shea MT, Glass DR, Pilkonis PA, *et al*.: Frequency and implications of personality disorders in a sample of depressed outpatients. *J Pers Disorder* 1987, 1:27–42.

74. Weissman MM, Paykel ES: *The Depressed Woman: A Study of Social Relationships*. Chicago: University of Chicago Press; 1974.

75. Lipman RS, Covi L, Shapiro AK: The Hopkins Symptom Checklist: factors derived from the HSCL-90. *J Affect Disord* 1979, 1:9–24.

76. Elkin I, Parloff M, Hadley S, *et al*.: The National Institute of Mental Health Treatment of Depression Collaborative Research Program: background and research plan. *Arch Gen Psychiatry* 1985, 42:305–316.

77. Luborsky L, Bachrach HM: Factors influencing clinician's judgments of mental health: experiences with the Health-Sickness Rating Scale. *Arch Gen Psychiatry* 1974, 31:292–299.

78. Derogatis LR: *SCL-90-R: Administration, Scoring and Procedures Manual II-Revised version*. Towson, MD: Clinical Psychometric Research; 1983.

79. Barkham M, Hardy GE, Startup M: The structure, validity and clinical relevance of the Inventory of Interpersonal Problems (IIP). *Br J Med Psychol* 1994, 67:171–185.

80. O'Malley PM, Bachman JG: Self-esteem and education: sex and cohort comparisons among high school seniors. *J Pers Soc Psychol* 1979, 37:1153–1159.

81. Remington M, Tyrer P: The social functioning schedule—a brief semi-structured interview. *Soc Psychiatry* 1979, 14:151–157.

Stroke and Depression

Laura H. Lacritz and C. Munro Cullum

The development of depression and other affective symptoms following stroke or other brain injury is not uncommon, and is impacted by a multidimensional host of factors. Studies suggest that poststroke depression does not simply reflect a reaction to acquired neurologic, cognitive, or physical deficit, but represents an intricate interaction between intraindividual cognitive and personality variables and neurobiologic effects of lesion parameters. In this chapter we present an overview of the more recent literature pertaining to the frequency of poststroke depression, its relation to primary or "psychiatrically based" depressive disorders, and implications of lesion parameters such as size, location, and duration. Methodologic challenges of conducting research in this area and hypothesized neuroanatomic underpinnings of poststroke depression are also discussed, along with implications for recovery of function and treatment response. Following a summary and integration of the relevant literature from the past few years, many of the complex issues involved in identification, assessment, and treatment of poststroke depression are highlighted and illustrated through case examples.

The phenomenon of mood disturbance associated with stroke and other neurologic disorders has gained more attention and acceptance over the past 10 to 15 years, although the association between emotional experiences and underlying anatomic structures was postulated more than 50 years ago [1]. As with many acute neuromedical conditions, the initial focus after stroke is on medical stabilization and physical functioning, rather than emotional or even cognitive status. While this is understandable early in recovery, the plethora of research documenting the prevalence of depression following stroke and the impact it can have on cognition, physical recovery, and mortality, not to mention quality of life, emphasize the importance of correct assessment and treatment of mood disturbance in this population. In the past, and to a lesser extent today, poststroke depression (PSD) has been viewed primarily as a natural psychosocial reaction to an acute catastrophic stressor. Such an explanation makes common sense, and while such factors may contribute to the syndrome, there is much research to indicate that robust neurostructural correlates of depression exist [2,3••4,5]. In the following sections an overview of the features of PSD are presented, with particular emphasis on methodologic issues involved in studying such complex phenomena. Implications of PSD in relation to treatment and outcome will also be discussed and illustrated by case examples.

Depression Following Stroke

The prevalence of depression after stroke has been reported to be between 30% and 60%, with many studies reporting an average prevalence of around 40% [6–8]. The incidence of PSD, however, may even be higher, as up to 30% of individuals who are not initially depressed after stroke may develop symptoms of depression over a 2-year period [4].

Andersen *et al.* [9] found prevalence of PSD to be highest in the first month after stroke, with a 41% incidence rate of depression within 1 year after initial stroke.

The diagnosis of depression is often made using American Psychiatric Association (APA) *Diagnostic and Statistical Manual of Mental Disorders*, edition 4 (DSM-IV) [10] criteria for major depressive disorder (MDD), although these criteria exclude such a diagnosis when an organic factor is found to have initiated and maintained the disturbance. While individuals who have recently suffered a stroke may be more likely to experience various neurovegetative symptoms often associated with depression (*eg*, sleep disturbance, fatigue, weight loss), DSM criteria for depression seem to have adequate sensitivity and specificity in identifying PSD. For example, Robinson *et al.* [11] found that when using DSM criteria, MDD was only overdiagnosed in 2% and underdiagnosed in 5% of a sample of 205 poststroke patients. There is a subset of poststroke patients who may experience depressive symptoms, but not severe enough to qualify for a diagnosis of MDD. Robinson *et al.* [8] and Morris *et al.* [12] have typically used DSM criteria for dysthymia (excluding the mandatory duration criterion of 2 years) to characterize such subclinical cases, and they refer to this condition as *minor depression*.

Other studies have relied on International Classification of Diseases (ICD-10) [13] criteria or level of depression as measured by various depression rating scales [14,15] in the identification of PSD. In a review of PSD, Hosking *et al.* [16] discuss the reliability and validity of various depression screening instruments in the identification of PSD. They reported that the Geriatric Depression Scale (GDS) [17] has been found to be one of the best self-rating scales of depression, followed by the Zung Depression Rating Scale [18], with one study claiming the latter to have a 93% positive predictive value.

Duration of poststroke depression

Not unexpectedly, reports regarding the duration of depressive symptoms in poststroke patients, as well as the impact of time since stroke on affective complaints, have shown variability in the literature. Among those who do become depressed following stroke, some clearly experience a remission of depression with time, as in primary depression. Others, however, may demonstrate the delayed onset of depressive symptoms. In fact, the general consensus in 1- and 2-year follow-up studies is that the development and degree of depression may increase over time in many patients. Cullum and Bigler [6] compared patients' profiles on a short form of the Minnesota Multiphasic Personality Inventory (MMPI) who were classified as either short duration (2 to 6 months) or long duration (7 to 24 months) since stroke. As illustrated in Figure 1, the long duration group demonstrated higher elevations on many of the clinical scales than the short duration group, with clinically significant elevations on MMPI scales 2, 7, and 8. While the only statistically significant difference between the groups was on scale 2 (D, depression), it is worth noting that the long duration group scored higher on six of the ten clinical scales.

While Cullum and Bigler [6] used a cross-sectional sample, several longitudinal studies support their findings. Over a 6-month period, Robinson *et al.* [8] found that the prevalence of depressive symptoms increased from 23% among inpatients immediately after stroke to 34% at 6-month follow-up. Of those who were depressed when first seen in the hospital, 95% were still depressed at 6 months, and 32% of those who were not depressed initially were found to be depressed at 6 months. Robinson *et al.* [19] found that the overall prevalence of depression increased over a 2-year period in their hospitalized stroke

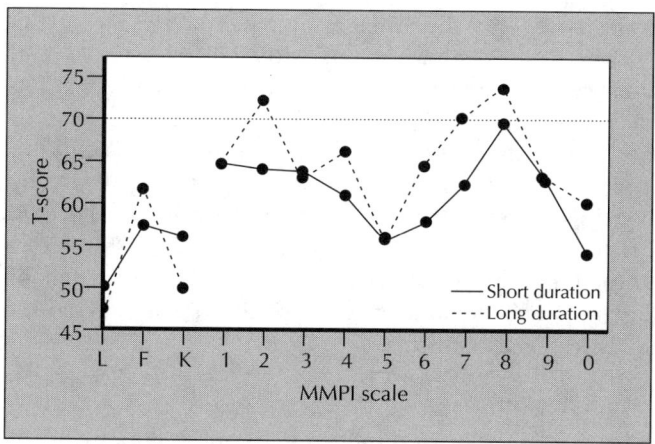

Figure 1. Mean Minnesota Multiphasic Personality Inventory (MMPI) profiles for short- and long-duration (time since stroke) groups. (*Adapted from* Cullum and Bigler [6].)

sample (33% to 42%), although the course of depression varied for different subgroups with depressive symptoms. They found that those who were initially diagnosed with major depression in the hospital shortly after their stroke improved overall by 2 years, while the majority of patients with minor depression got worse, and one third of patients who were not depressed initially developed depressive symptoms over the 2-year period. Thus, there was some degree of spontaneous recovery in those diagnosed with major depression, while prognosis was poorer for those identified with dysthymia or minor depression in this sample. The course of depression did not appear to be related to degree of cognitive or physical impairment, although an important finding was that there was a lack of improvement in daily living skills in those patients who remained depressed over 1 to 2 years.

The issue of major versus minor depression has not been extensively explored, and it should be noted that not all studies that have examined PSD have supported the poor prognosis of minor depression as described above. Morris *et al.* [12], for example, found a greater prevalence of minor versus major depression at 2 months in a sample of post-stroke rehabilitation patients, but only four of 19 (26%) of their minor depression group were still depressed at 15-month follow-up, compared with five of eight (62%) of their major depression group. Similarly, in a previous investigation, Morris *et al.* [7] found that mean duration of major depression following stroke was three times longer than in minor depression (mean=39 weeks, SD=31.8; mean=12.2 weeks, SD=18.2, respectively). However, the large standard deviations point to the wide variability in duration of depression that is seen in stroke patients. Even though many patients show improvement within 2 years after stroke, as many as 20% may continue to be depressed for up to 10 years after their stroke [20]. Clearly, many situational and interindividual differences contribute to the variability seen across studies. Since no two life situations are ever identical for patients, some variability in the emotional consequences of stroke must be expected.

The majority of research in this area has used hospital-based samples. This research may not be representative of the general stroke population in which up to 40% to 50% of patients may not be admitted to the hospital after stroke. Using a community-based sample, Wade *et al.* [14] found a 25% to 30% prevalence rate of depression 3 weeks following stroke, which remained stable over 6 months. However, there were some individual differences in course of depression, as 25% of the initial sample who were not initially depressed became so by 6 months, and 50% of patients with PSD at 3 weeks had improved by 12 months. Another community study found greater levels of depression (as measured by Beck Depression Inventory [BDI] [21] and Present State Examination [PSE] [22]) in patients 1 month after stroke compared with healthy controls [23]. However, by 12 months poststroke, there were no differences between the groups, aside from the poststroke group reporting lower energy and increased worry on the PSE. Furthermore, they found only two of 128 stroke patients consistently met DSM criteria for MDD during the duration of the study. Because this sample was composed of patients who were less physically impaired overall than some of the hospital-based samples [8,12,24], the findings may be more generalizable.

Risk factors for depression after stroke

There remains debate over risk factors for depression following stroke, and many of the studies investigating such factors are retrospective. Table 1 lists a number of variables that have been reported to be associated with increased risk for depression after stroke. By and large, the greatest risk factor reported has been location of lesion, with higher rates of depression reported in individuals with strokes in the left hemisphere, particularly more anterior lesions. Whereas less information regarding subcortical lesions and mood disturbance is available, left basal ganglia strokes have been noted to be associated with increased levels of depression compared with other left and right hemisphere lesion sites [25]. Despite such findings, a number of studies have found little or no relationship between side of lesion and level of depression. This controversy is discussed in more detail below.

Table 1. Potential Risk Factors for Developing Depression Following Stroke

Reported risk factors	Study
Location of lesion (left hemisphere > right hemisphere)	Herrmann et al. [26] Morris et al. [27] Cullum and Bigler [28] Starkstein et al. [25]
Preexisting subcortical atrophy	Starkstein et al. [29]
Time since stroke (increased risk of depression over time)	Cullum and Bigler [6] Robinson et al. [19]
Past psychiatric history	Morris et al. [7] Eastwood et al. [30]
Family psychiatric history (particularly for patients with right hemisphere lesions)	Morris et al. [7] Morris et al. [12]
Prior stroke	Thompson et al. [15]
Perceived lack of social support	Morris et al. [31]
Residence in an institution following stroke	Sharpe et al. [32]

While variables such as those listed in Table 1 have been identified as potential risk factors for depression [26–32], many studies investigating PSD have excluded individuals with one or more of these variables in addition to other potential risk factors (*eg*, prior head injury, substance abuse history) to reduce the possibility of confounding results. Consequently, there has been less opportunity to study the impact of these factors on the development and course of PSD. There has also been some debate regarding cause and effect for some variables in relation to PSD. For example, a positive, albeit modest, correlation between degree of physical impairment and depression rating scores has been reported, although level of physical malfunctioning accounted for only 10% of the variance on depression scores [33]. However, individuals with PSD have been found to require longer hospital stays and demonstrate greater functional disability compared with nondepressed stroke patients [30]. In addition, those who meet criteria for MDD after stroke have a higher mortality rate [7] and tend to make a slower physical recovery compared with nondepressed stroke patients [4].

Comparison of poststroke depression with major depressive disorder

Given the frequency of depression after stroke, it is of interest to better understand how "neurologically based" depression after stroke compares with primary major depressive disorder (*ie*, depression not associated with any known neurologic cause). Table 2 outlines some of the similarities and differences that have been found between these two forms of depression [34]. As can be seen in the table, there are many commonalities between the depressive symptomatology of PSD and so-called primary major depressive disorder.

Even though the symptom patterns are quite similar between the two types of depression, patients with PSD tend to experience more autonomic symptoms than those with primary major depressive disorder, and even nondepressed stroke patients reported an average of at least one neurovegetative symptom of depression (*eg*, increased fatigue, insomnia) [11]. Scores on depression rating scales tend to be similar between the two groups (*eg*, Hamilton Depression Rating Scale [35], BDI, PSE), although depressed stroke patients tend to endorse greater psychomotor slowness (69% versus 35%), while MDD patients report a greater lack of interest in activities and decreased concentration more frequently than PSD patients (98% versus 70%) on the PSE [34]. Not surprisingly,

Table 2. Similarities and Differences between Poststroke and Primary Major Depressive Disorder

Similarities	Differences
Similar duration of depression if untreated (6–12 mo)	Greater cognitive impairment in PSD
Both respond to treatment with antidepressant medication	Greater functional impairment in PSD
Both associated with abnormal dexamethasone suppression test results	PSD involves a response to a neurologic event (structurally or psychosocially), while primary depression entails no necessary precipitant
Similar performance on depression rating scales	Fewer PSD patients with past personal history of psychiatric disorder
Similar symptom patterns	

PSD—poststroke depression.

PSD patients tend to demonstrate greater cognitive impairment than MDD patients [34], and the degree of deficit has been shown to be correlated with severity of depression [24].

In comparing PSD patients with those with primary affective disorder in the absence of neurologic disease, Mayberg [3••] found similar patterns of abnormal brain metabolism involving areas with limbic connections. Both groups demonstrated similar levels of decreased metabolism bilaterally on positron emission tomography (PET) scans, particularly in the paralimbic frontal and temporal cortex. The similarities between these two types of depression, both in terms of clinical presentation and physiologic mechanisms, support the concept of PSD and highlight the importance of properly diagnosing and treating depression following stroke.

Hemispheric Lateralization and Depression

A considerable amount of research in the area of stroke and depression has focused on the prevalence of depression in relation to lesion location. In a review of PSD, Robinson and Starkstein [4] described 14 studies that found a greater frequency of depression following left versus right hemisphere stroke. Furthermore, this is one area that has seen a great deal of consensus in the literature, with numerous reports of an association between left hemisphere stroke and depression [eg, 26,36,37]. This finding has been supported even when factors such as lesion size and degree of physical dysfunction following stroke have been accounted for [27].

Location of lesion within the hemispheres has also been found to be important in the occurrence of PSD, with more anterior left hemisphere lesions showing a particularly strong association with depression. This relationship has generally been measured by calculating correlations between scores on various depression inventories and the distances of the lesions from the frontal poles. Correlations as high as −.92 between these variables among left hemisphere stroke patients have been reported [30,33,38]. In fact, Robinson et al. [33] found a double dissociation between level of depression in left versus right stroke patients and distance of the lesion from the frontal pole. This double dissociation is illustrated in Figure 2, which displays a negative correlation in left lesion patients (depression x distance from frontal pole) and a positive correlation in right lesion patients.

The frequency of depression after stroke appears to be similar for both cortical and subcortical (basal ganglia) lesions within the left hemisphere [39]. Similar to research that has examined lateralization with cortical lesions, a much higher percentage of depression has been reported in patients with left (88%) versus right (14%) basal ganglia lesions (Fig. 3), although studies of subcortical stroke and depression have been fewer [4]. An association between subcortical dysfunction and depression is also supported by the high prevalence of depression in other disorders that involve the basal ganglia or subcortical white matter, such as Parkinson's disease (40%) [40] and multiple sclerosis (27% to 54%) [41]. The contribution of basal ganglia dysfunction per se to depression is highlighted by a review of the literature in this area that found that depression in Parkinson's disease and multiple sclerosis tends to be more severe than for patients with other disorders that produce a similar level of physical disability, such as spinal cord injury, rheumatoid arthritis, and muscular dystrophy [42]. Furthermore, the review by Rao et al. [42] noted that a reduction in depression has not been found with improvement in physical functioning with the introduction of medications to treat Parkinson's disease. These researchers also reported that magnetic

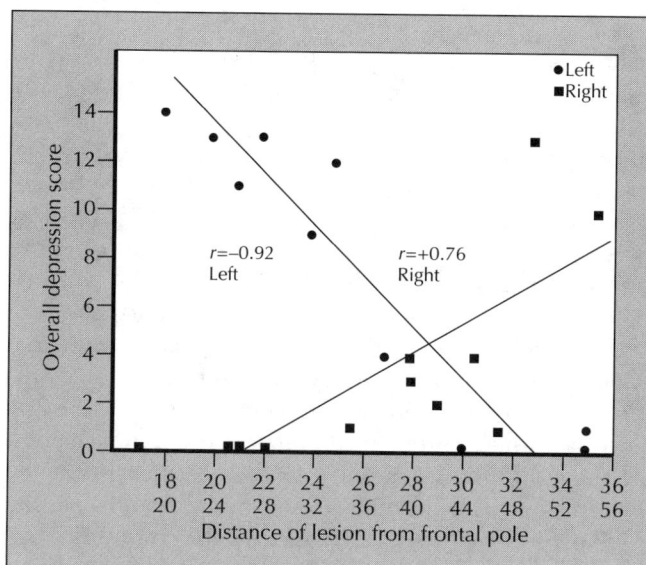

Figure 2. Relationship between level of depression and distance of lesion (expressed as a percentage of the total antero-posterior distance) from the frontal pole in left ($P < 0.001$) and right ($P < 0.01$) hemisphere lesion patients. (*Adapted from* Robinson *et al.* [33].)

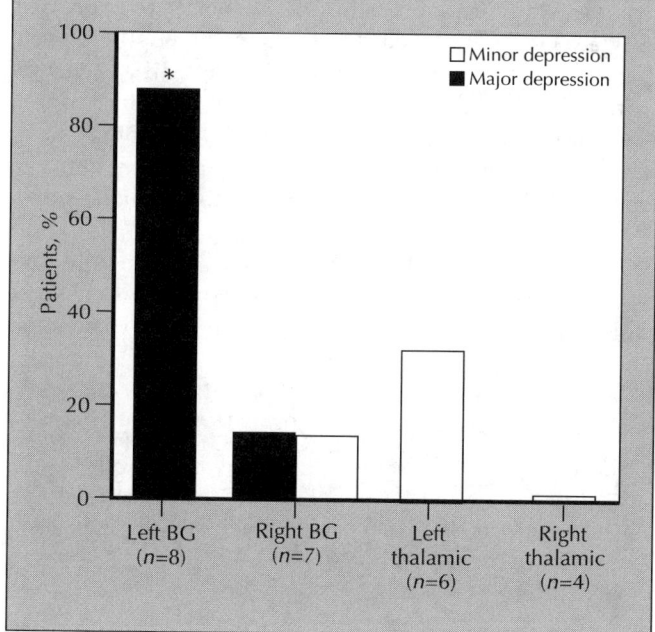

Figure 3. Percentage of major and minor depression in patients with left or right basal ganglia (BG) or thalamic lesions. *Significant difference. (*Adapted from* Robinson and Starkstein [4].)

resonance imaging (MRI) studies have not shown a systematic relationship between total lesion load and degree of affective disturbance in multiple sclerosis patients, thereby lending further support to the notion that location of lesion may be more important to the development of depression than size of lesion.

Lesion location may also influence the course of depression, both in terms of the development and remission of depressive symptoms. Consistent with previously reported research, Starkstein *et al.* [39] found lower levels of depression in patients who had experienced brainstem and cerebellar infarcts compared with those with middle cerebral artery (MCA) strokes (20% vs 82%, respectively) acutely after stroke. At 1- to 2-year follow-up, only 9% of patients with brainstem and cerebellar infarcts remained depressed, while 45% of patients with MCA strokes continued to meet criteria for depression (Fig. 4). Differential recovery rates of depression were also reported in relation to hemispheric side of lesion, with left hemisphere stroke patients showing a slower rate of recovery than right hemisphere patients at 2 months (compared with initial 2-week levels) [43]. However, at 6-month follow-up, right hemisphere subjects displayed a decline in their emotional functioning, while left hemisphere subjects remained relatively stable.

Ross *et al.* [44] examined hemispheric lateralization of emotions, advocating that the right and left hemispheres play different roles in the regulation of emotions. This notion was supported by examining the emotional content of life stories told by seizure patients while undergoing right hemisphere Wada procedures, in which sodium amobarbital is injected into the right internal carotid artery via a femoral catheter, thereby causing an acute, but reversible, anesthesia of the ipsilateral hemisphere. In the majority of both right and left seizure focus patients (eight of ten), the emotional content of life experiences was minimized or denied during right-sided Wada testing compared with both pre- and post-Wada test recollections of the same events. In addition, when emotional reactions to the Wada test procedure were elicited, depressive responses were most often associated with left-sided injections, while euphoric emotions were more likely to be reported following right-sided injections. In a review of the literature on asymmetric affective organization, Cullum [38] described a number of studies that support an association between depression and left hemisphere functioning. Furthermore, several studies were cited that report an association between right hemisphere dysfunction and emotional responses such as lability, denial, uncontrollable crying, and mania.

Despite the majority of studies reporting a relationship between left-sided lesions and depressive symptoms, a number of studies, even some involving many of the same researchers, have reported contradictory data. For example, several studies have failed to

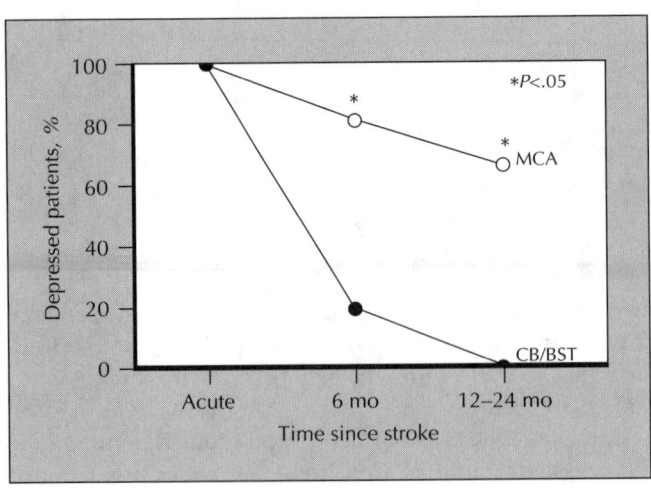

Figure 4. Course of depression over time in patients with either middle cerebral artery (MCA) or cerebellum or brainstem (CB/BST) lesions. (*Adapted from* Robinson and Starkstein [4].)

find any association between depression and location of lesion [12,45], and Wade *et al.* [14] found that the association between laterality of stroke and depression was no longer significant 6 months poststroke. It has been hypothesized that the failure to find a significant relationship between depression and side of lesion (*eg*, in left hemisphere lesions) may be related to the exclusion of aphasic patients in some studies, given the difficulty in assessing depression in these patients.

In analyzing level of depression and lesion size and location in groups of right and left hemisphere damaged patients (stroke and head injured), Cullum and Bigler [28] found that scores on scale 2 (D, depression) of the MMPI did not systematically relate to total lesion size in either of the lateralized groups. However, when the lateralized groups were further broken down by quadrants (left-right, anterior-posterior), estimated left frontal lesion size and scale 2 were significantly related, but in a negative direction ($r = -.56$, $P = .038$), while right posterior lesion size was positively correlated with scale 2 ($r = .38$, $p = .031$). These authors suggested that smaller lesion size in left hemisphere patients may result in a greater awareness of or sensitivity to their deficits, which may lead to higher depression scores in these patients. Furthermore, larger right hemisphere lesions may be required to elicit depressive symptomatology, although the frequency of anosognosia in right hemisphere damage [46] makes a clear interpretation of these findings difficult and suggests the existence of more complex brain structure–function relationships.

Time since stroke may also be an important variable in examining this issue, as Nelson *et al.* [43] found differential recovery curves for depression in left hemisphere and right hemisphere stroke patients over a 6-month period of time. Left hemisphere PSD patients showed a trend toward decreased depression over 6 months, while right hemisphere PSD patients displayed a reduction in depression at 2 months and then an increase in level of depression at 6 months. Therefore, the poststroke time at which patients are assessed may influence the presence and level of depression differentially for right and left hemisphere stroke patients.

While the association between lesion location and depression is not completely understood, lesion site has been found to account for the greatest amount of variance (50% to 70%) in depression rating scales when correlating distance of lesions from the frontal poles. In comparison, degree of physical impairment accounted for only 10% to 20% of the variance in depression scores [33]. Although these factors do not explain all of the variance, hence leaving room for other factors (*eg*, environmental, psychosocial, premorbid personality, and so forth) as potential contributors to the development of PSD, patients with left frontal and left basal ganglia strokes have been found to have a higher likelihood of developing PSD (75%) than patients with lesions elsewhere in the left hemisphere (8%) or those with right hemisphere lesions (29%), even when lesion size, stroke-related disability, and level of cognitive impairment have been controlled for [27].

Emotional dysfunction following right hemisphere stroke

Depression following right hemisphere stroke has also been reported, particularly with posterior lesions [47]. Finset [48] provided support for this notion by examining patients within 6 months after right hemisphere stroke, finding that depression was more likely to occur in patients with lesions involving parietal white matter than in any other area of the right hemisphere. While depression may be more common following left hemisphere lesions, there are a number of syndromes that occur with greater frequency after right hemisphere damage. For example, secondary mania is relatively rare following stroke, but has been reported in patients with right- sided lesions, particularly in the right basotemporal region and in other limbic-related structures [49,50]. Furthermore, patients with bipolar mood disorder have been found significantly more likely to have right subcortical lesions than patients with mania alone, who tended to have right orbitofrontal or basotemporal lesions [36]. In an elegant series of studies, Mayberg [3••] has provided additional support for these findings by showing that patients with mania tend to demonstrate right-sided temporal hypometabolism on PET images. A review by Dupont et al. [51] cited several studies showing that other psychiatric symptoms, including paranoia and delusional disorders, occur more frequently in right hemisphere stroke patients, although the prevalence of such disorders has not been well documented.

Indifference and anosognosia have also been associated with right hemisphere lesions. Starkstein et al. [46] determined that 34% of their sample of 80 acute stroke patients demonstrated anosognosia, with increased frequency among right hemisphere lesions (29% compared with 4% of left hemisphere lesion patients), particularly those involving the temporoparietal junction, thalamus, and basal ganglia. The presence of anosognosia in some individuals following right hemisphere stroke may help to explain why an increase in depression has been reported in some right hemisphere patients months after stroke, while left hemisphere patients improve or stabilize [43]. The recovery process for right hemisphere patients may result in increased awareness of their deficits over time, which may in turn exacerbate or initiate the presence of depression.

Anxiety following stroke

Interestingly, as the preceding review has suggested, while depression has been the most commonly examined psychologic disturbance following stroke, other syndromes have been reported, but have received less frequent investigation. The presence of depression following stroke with and without a comorbid anxiety disorder has been proposed as two distinct phenomena, possibly having different underlying anatomic or neurophysiologic explanations. Starkstein et al. [47] examined location of lesion and presence of depression and anxiety after stroke and found that patients who reported depression without anxiety were more likely to have lesions in the left basal ganglia, while comorbidity of depression and anxiety was associated with left cortical lesions (84% compared with 41% in the depressed-only group). Castillo et al. [52] also found an association between left cortical lesions and comorbid depression and anxiety, while anxiety alone was associated more with right hemisphere lesions.

Structural Basis for Depression

Mayberg [3••] examined the association between subcortical dysfunction and secondary depression across several neurologic disorders through a series of functional imaging studies. Her studies focused on depressed and nondepressed patients with basal ganglia disorders (Huntington's disease, Parkinson's disease, caudate stroke), given the high prevalence of depression in these disorders [40,53], as well as patients with primary depression. PET images from the basal ganglia level revealed bilateral frontal lobe hypometabolism in depressed Huntington's disease, Parkinson's disease, caudate stroke, and primary unipolar depressed patients, while metabolism in the frontal cortex appeared normal across all nondepressed neurologic patients, with the exception of those with strokes (Fig. 5). These findings raise the possibility that disruption of neural pathways mediated through the basal ganglia (*eg*, orbitofrontal-ganglia-thalamic pathway) may play an important role in the development of depression in certain neurologic patients. However, this relationship may not be so straightforward in stroke patients, as both depressed and nondepressed patients with left caudate strokes showed evidence of frontal hypometabolism.

The importance of subcortical structures in the development of depression following stroke has also been implicated when examining ventricular-brain ratios (VBR) using computed tomography (CT). Comparison of depressed and nondepressed stroke patients matched for lesion size and location (mostly left hemisphere lesions) found larger VBRs in depressed patients than in their nondepressed cohorts, while no differences were observed in background or demographic characteristics [29]. Since CT scans were obtained during the acute stage following stroke, these findings were thought to predate the occurrence of stroke. Therefore, it has been proposed that subcortical atrophy may actually represent a vulnerability to the development of depression following stroke.

Mayberg [3••] also examined temporal lobe metabolism through PET images from patients with single caudate lesions and different mood states (euthymic, depressed, and manic). Interestingly, she found that all subjects with either euthymic or depressed mood had left hemisphere lesions, while lesions in subjects with secondary mania were restricted to the right hemisphere. Both euthymic lesion subjects and controls demonstrated symmetric temporal lobe metabolism, while manic patients showed primary right-sided temporal hypometabolism and depressed patients had bilateral temporal hypometabolism (Fig. 6). It was suggested that the orbitofrontal cortex may in fact be disrupted in depressed stroke patients through involvement of basotemporal pathways that are connected to this region. Comparison of depressed and nondepressed Huntington's disease and Parkinson's disease patients as well as patients with primary depression revealed bilateral temporal hypometabolism in depressed patients, while

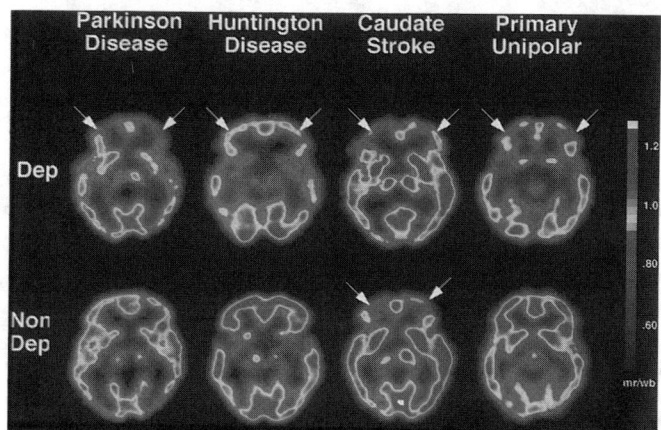

Figure 5. Position emission tomography images across diagnostic groups with and without depression (Dep) at basal ganglia level. Hypometabolism is indicated by *arrows*, showing bilateral frontal lobe hypometabolism in all depressed neurologic groups and in primary depression, as well as in nondepressed stroke patients. (*From* Mayberg [3••]; with permission.)

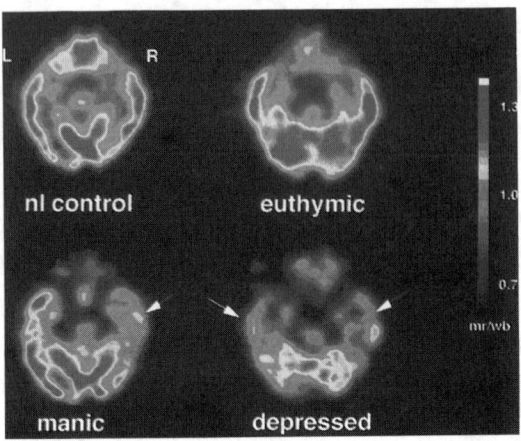

Figure 6. Position emission tomography images in controls and patients with caudate stroke and euthymic, manic, or depressed mood states. Temporal hypometabolism indicated by *arrows*. (*From* Mayberg [3••]; with permission.)

temporal metabolism was normal in nondepressed patients across diagnostic groups. Grasso *et al.* [54] also provide support for involvement of the temporal cortex in depression by examining single photon emission computed tomography (SPECT) and cerebral blood flow (CBF) in depressed and nondepressed subcortical stroke patients. While both depressed and nondepressed stroke patients demonstrated hypoperfusion in ipsilateral versus contralateral cortical regions on SPECT, lower CBF values in the mesial temporal cortex of the affected hemisphere were only found in depressed patients.

In an eloquent review of studies examining depression in various neurologic groups, Cummings [2] reported an association between depression and regional brain abnormalities as assessed by structural and functional imaging techniques. For example, involvement of the frontal lobes and caudate nuclei in the pathogenesis of depression in Parkinson's disease patients was supported through findings of decreased metabolic activity in the caudate and orbital regions of the frontal lobes in depressed Parkinson's disease patients compared with their nondepressed counterparts. Cummings' review also noted that depressed Huntington's disease patients showed hypometabolism in the orbitofrontal and inferior prefrontal cortices compared with nondepressed Huntington's disease patients, and it was reported that depressed temporal lobe epilepsy patients have been found to show reduced inferior frontal metabolism compared with nondepressed patients with epilepsy. In left hemisphere stroke patients, evidence was provided to suggest a relationship between depression and a lack of compensatory serotonergic receptors compared with right hemisphere stroke patients who actually demonstrate an increase in these receptors.

Mayberg *et al.* [55] described the possible relationship between serotonin and depression in more detail, reporting that left-sided stroke patients show greater failure to upregulate serotonin compared with right-sided stroke patients. In addition, they found a significant negative correlation in left hemisphere patients between the severity of depression and the ratio of serotonin receptor binding in the ipsilateral to contralateral area of the temporal cortex (ie, higher levels of depression were associated with lower serotonin receptor binding in the left temporal lobe). Disruption of the biogenic amine systems in the left hemisphere has been a widely proposed mechanism for PSD [4], although more research needs to be conducted in this area.

Complications of Poststroke Depression

Poststroke depression has been found to have a number of detrimental effects in relation to cognitive impairment, physical recovery, and mortality. Several studies have reported a negative relationship between PSD and intellectual/cognitive function. Robinson *et al.* [24] found that stroke patients with major depression had significantly lower scores on the Mini-Mental State Examination (MMSE) than those with minor depression and nondepressed stroke patients (MMSE = 13.0 [5.8], 25.0 [4.5], and 22.0 [6.0], respectively). While there was also a significant negative correlation between lesion size and MMSE scores across all subjects ($r = -.73$), patients with major depression had greater cognitive impairment for similar lesion sizes compared with nondepressed patients. Furthermore, when cognitive impairment was held constant, depressed patients were found to have significantly smaller lesion volumes than nondepressed patients. Therefore, presence of depression following stroke appears to negatively impact cognitive functioning independent of lesion size. Morris *et al.* [7] also found significantly lower MMSE scores in depressed compared with nondepressed stroke patients, but only for those with left hemisphere lesions (MMSE = 16.4 vs 23.0 for nondepressed left hemisphere stroke patients).

Detrimental effects of depression on cognition in stroke patients have also been found using more comprehensive batteries of neuropsychologic measures as opposed to the MMSE, which provides only a crude estimate of global cognitive functioning. Performances of depressed and nondepressed stroke patients with either left or right hemisphere lesions were compared across various cognitive domains in one investigation [56]. Results revealed greater cognitive dysfunction in depressed left hemisphere stroke patients compared with nondepressed left hemisphere and depressed and nondepressed right hemisphere patients. Left hemisphere lesion patients demonstrated lower scores in orientation, language, executive-motor, and frontal lobe domains, while there were no differences between the groups in terms of lesion size.

Poststroke depression has also been reported to have a negative effect on physical recovery following stroke. In one study, researchers who followed patients with PSD over a 6-month period found that those with major depression failed to show any improvement in physical functioning as measured by the Johns Hopkins Functioning Inventory [57], while nondepressed patients and those with minor depression demonstrated significant improvement over the same period. While none of the groups demonstrated an improvement in cognitive functioning over the 6-month period, the depressed group obtained lower MMSE scores than the minor depressed and nondepressed patients (MMSE scores = 19, 25, and 26, respectively) [8].

Support for the detrimental effects of PSD on activities of daily living was provided by results from a 2-year prospective study of 63 patients following stroke [58]. Depression was diagnosed using DSM-III criteria elicited through a structured clinical interview as part of the PSE. While depressed and nondepressed patients initially did not differ in terms of their level of physical functioning in the acute stage after stroke as measured by the Johns Hopkins Functioning Inventory, the depressed patients showed significantly less functional recovery over a 2-year period than nondepressed patients (Fig. 7). In addition, there was no significant difference in scores on depression rating scales at 2-year follow-up, indicating a general remission of PSD in the depressed group. This suggests that the initial presence of depression after stroke may have lingering effects on physical recovery, even after the remission of depressive symptoms.

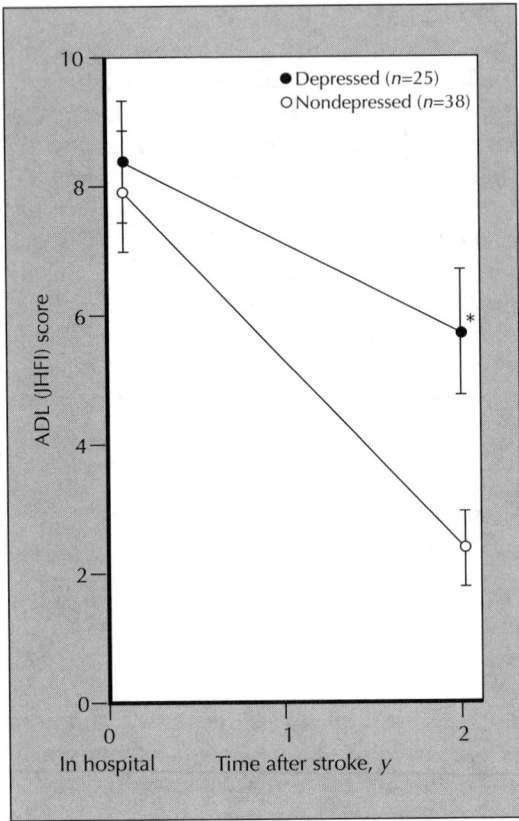

Figure 7. Activities of daily living (ADL), as measured by the Johns Hopkins Functioning Inventory (JHFI), in depressed and non-depressed stroke patients over 2 years. A group by time interaction can be observed, with the depressed patients scoring significantly higher (*ie*, greater impairment) than nondepressed patients at 2-year follow-up. *$P < 0.05$. (*Adapted from* Parikh *et al.* [58]; with permission.)

In addition to negative effects on cognitive and physical functioning, patients with depression several weeks after stroke have shown a trend toward increased mortality. For example, PSD patients were 3.4 times more likely to have died than nondepressed stroke patients at 10-year follow-up [59]. While lesion size was significantly associated with mortality (*ie*, patients who died had lesions twice as large as those who survived), a similar trend toward increased mortality in depressed patients was seen even when depressed and nondepressed patients were matched for lesion size. Social isolation and lack of support systems were also found to contribute to increased mortality among the depressed patients, further underscoring the complexities of relationships between depression and outcome following stroke.

Treatment

It has been noted that stroke patients often fail to receive treatment for their depression [11,60], and few attempts have been made to study different treatment modalities in this population. While many of their symptoms may remit over time (as do depressive symptoms in most cases of primary depression), the possible negative effects of depression on outcome emphasize the importance of treatment for these patients, who have been found to respond well to pharmacotherapy with different classes of antidepressants.

Early studies focused on medications such as nortriptyline and trazadone for treating this population. In a double-blind investigation assessing the benefit of nortriptyline in patients with PSD, the nortriptyline patients showed significantly greater improvement in their depression over a 6-week period compared with the placebo group (Fig. 8) [49,61]. A similar trend has also been reported in patients treated with trazadone [62].

Given the undesirable side effects of tricyclic antidepressants (*eg*, anticholinergic and cardiac effects), recent trends have focused on the use of selective serotonin reuptake inhibitors (SSRIs) in depression [63], which makes particular sense in light of the proposed role of serotonin disruption in PSD discussed above. Subjects treated with the SSRI citalopram in a double-blind, placebo-controlled study showed significant improvement in depressive symptoms compared with the control group [64•]. The usefulness of SSRIs in accelerating functional recovery after stroke has also been examined. Dam *et al.* [65] compared the effects of maprotiline (a norepinephrine reuptake blocker), fluoxetine (an SSRI), and a placebo on functional recovery after severely debilitating stroke in hemiplegic patients as assessed by activities of daily living, degree of neurologic impairment, and depression. After a 3-month period, patients who had been treated with fluoxetine showed the greatest improvement in activities of daily living and neurologic recovery, while no difference across treatment groups for depressive symptomatology was noted (BDI decreased equally with both fluoxetine and maprotiline). Despite the apparent effectiveness of psychopharmacologic treatment of PSD, there have been few systematic efficacy studies, and more research in this area is clearly needed.

Another treatment option for depression is electroconvulsive therapy (ECT), which has been found to be effective in treating patients whose depression was refractory to antidepressant medication. In a small study of poststroke ECT, 12 of 14 patients showed a significant improvement in their depression with ECT [66]. In a review of PSD treatment,

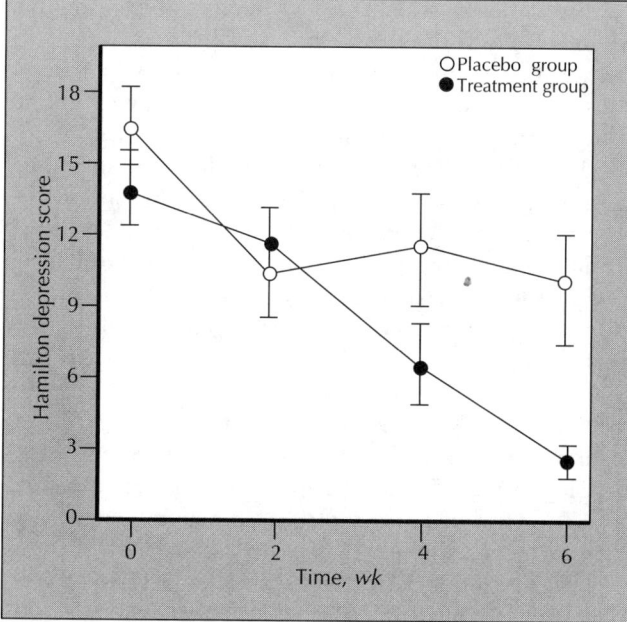

Figure 8. Mean depression rating scores on the Hamilton Depression Rating Scale in nortriptyline-treated depressed stroke patients (*closed circles*) and a depressed stroke placebo group (*open circles*), demonstrating significant ($P < 0.006$) improvement in the treatment group over a 6-week period. (*Adapted from* Robinson *et al.* [61]; with permission.)

Gustafson *et al.* [67] discuss several other small studies that found ECT a well tolerated and useful treatment option in this population. Thus, as with other depressed populations, ECT may be an effective treatment option for stroke patients who cannot tolerate or who do not benefit from pharmacotherapy for their depression. Psychotherapy, particularly cognitive-behavioral intervention, is another treatment modality that has been shown to be quite effective (equal to medication in some cases) in treating primary depression [68]. While the efficacy of this type of treatment in stroke patients has received little attention in the literature, patients in one study who received group therapy after stroke reported this intervention to be helpful with respect to their symptoms [69]. However, well-controlled systematic analysis of this topic is needed in order to further understand the effectiveness of such interventions after stroke.

Methodologic Issues

There are many variables that may potentially impact the presence and assessment of PSD that are often not taken into consideration when studying this population. It is important to be aware of these factors, as it can be difficult to compare groups of studies and generalize results if variables such as lesion size, lesion location, time since stroke, prior neurologic condition, psychiatric history, method of depression measurement, and other demographic variables are not taken into consideration. For example, location of lesion has been considered in a number of studies as illustrated above; however, inclusion of lesion location without controlling for lesion size may confound the conclusions made based on this variable. Morris *et al.* [59], for example, found that depression several weeks after stroke resulted in a threefold increase in mortality rates 10 years later. However, when size of lesion was controlled for, the association was no longer significant, although a trend was still present. Table 3 provides a list of several important factors that may play a role in the assessment or development of PSD and that deserve consideration in interpreting results of PSD research.

There may also be an interaction that occurs between certain variables, making it important to consider the above factors simultaneously. For example, depression and time since stroke may not have a linear relationship. While some researchers have reported an increase in depression over time [6], others have found a curvilinear relationship, with similar rates of depression immediately following stroke and at 3-year follow-up, and lower levels at 1 and 2 years after stroke [70]. Furthermore, variables such as lesion location and degree of dysphasia may be more important in the development of PSD in the acute stage following stroke, while psychosocial factors such as social support or premorbid personality may play a greater role in the perpetuation of depression over time. Furthermore, the method by which the level of depression is assessed may be very important. For instance, Grasso *et al.* [54] reported a significant correlation between depression scores on the BDI and cerebral blood flow values in affected hemispheres, while they found no such relationship when using other depression rating scales (Hamilton Rating Scale for Depression, Zung Self-Rating Depression Scale). Differential associations between various depression rating scales and selected neuroanatomic and other factors may be related to item content of these measures. In particular, depression measures that are composed of a greater number of cognitive versus neurovegetative symptom items may result in higher correlations with selected variables.

Table 3. Methodologic Considerations in Interpreting Poststroke Depression Research

Variable	Possible implication
Time since stroke	Level and presence of depression may vary depending on time since stroke
Lesion size	Inconsistent findings regarding size of lesion and impact on depression
Lesion location	Depression more common with left (anterior and subcortical) hemisphere stroke, although left hemisphere lesion case selection may be biased toward smaller lesions due to aphasia
Aphasia in left hemisphere stroke	Exclusion of patients with aphasia may bias sample
Inpatient-outpatient population	Inpatient sample more likely to have had a more severe stroke and greater functional impairment
Measurement of depression	Depression scales that emphasize neurovegetative, physical, or cognitive symptoms may over-identify the presence of depression in stroke patients
Sample size	Many studies use small sample sizes that reduce generalizability of results
Use of control groups	Many studies fail to include a control group in assessing PSD
Premorbid personality	No systematic assessments conducted to date, although this variable may influence the development or course of PSD
Cognitive dysfunction	Few studies have examined neuropsychologic patterns of stroke patients with and without PSD, though this may be a critical mediating variable
Physical impairment	Rate of physical recovering following stroke tends to be slower in depressed vs nondepressed stroke patients, although the direction of this relationship and bearing on the development of PSD has not been thoroughly studied

PSD—*poststroke depression.*

Case Studies

Two case studies are presented below in order to illustrate the types of affective changes seen following stroke. Family members and physicians are often more likely to focus on the physical manifestations of stroke and other brain injuries, particularly in the acute stages of illness, and may not be readily aware of affective and personality changes that can also occur. Furthermore, when they do notice something different in a patient's presentation, they may ascribe it to the traumatic nature of what the patient has undergone and assume that it will resolve with time. Understanding that there may be a neurologic basis underlying various affective conditions following stroke may help others to identify these conditions and facilitate proper treatment as needed.

The first case illustration involves a 45-year-old woman who was seen as an outpatient 6 months following a right frontal hemorrhagic stroke (Fig. 9), which initially resulted in left hemiparesis, severe memory deficits, and periods of confusion and disorientation. After several months of physical and cognitive rehabilitation, the patient was able to attend to most of her self- care skills with minimal prompting, and her hemiparesis had largely resolved. She had previously been a very active individual who was involved in competitive sports and many community and family activities, but now spent her time watching television and working on word puzzles. While her family described continued problems with short-term memory, judgement, impulsivity, spatial organization, and apathy, the patient reported few cognitive concerns and denied any emotional problems despite the radical change in her functional abilities. Her MMPI-2 profile (Fig. 10) was consistent with her verbal report regarding the lack of any emotional problems, but was completed in a highly defensive and overly optimistic manner, representing her lack of insight and awareness of her deficits.

The patient was seen again 5 months later (11 months poststroke), by which time she had become depressed and suicidal, requiring psychiatric hospitalization, after malfunction

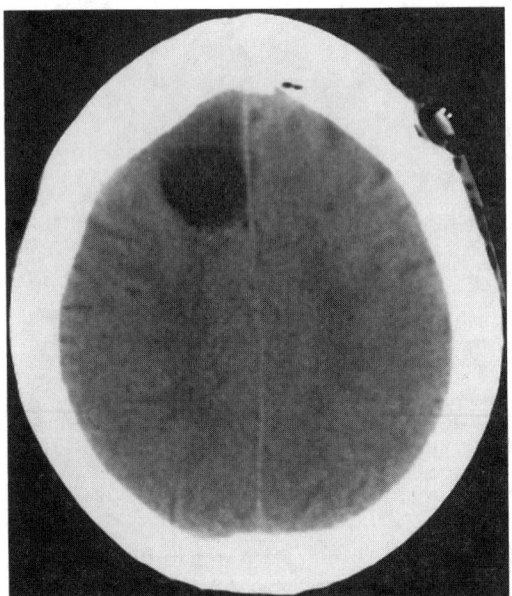

Figure 9. Computed tomography scan showing a large right frontal hemorrhagic lesion.

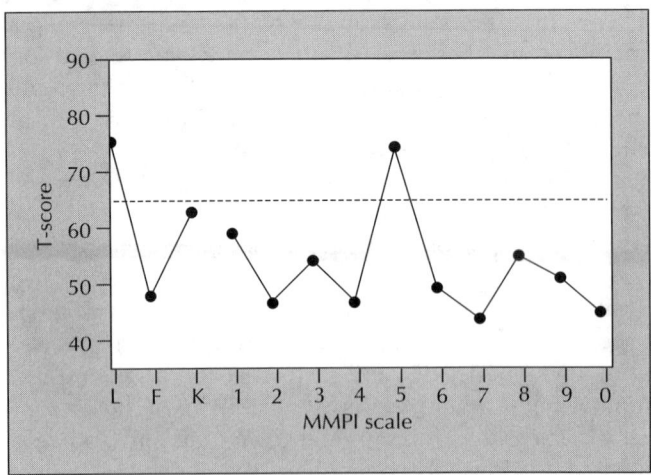

Figure 10. Minnesota Multiphasic Personality Inventory (MMPI)-2 profile 6 months poststroke (case 1).

and removal of a ventricular shunt. Despite the degree of despair she had obviously been experiencing, the patient verbalized only a minimal amount of emotional distress and produced a similar MMPI- 2 profile on reevaluation (Fig. 11). Thus, even in the face of crisis, her decreased awareness of her internal emotional experiences remained pervasive. Alternatively, the patient was more preoccupied with when she would be able to regain some of her prestroke freedoms, such as driving and walking alone, and had little understanding of why she was not allowed to engage in these activities. This case provides a good illustration of the lack of insight and unawareness of deficits (anosognosia) that can accompany right (frontal) lesions. Despite this patient's prominent memory, visuospatial, and executive functioning deficits as identified during neuropsychologic evaluation, she had minimal awareness of her limitations, and could not identify the presence of depression, despite acknowledging suicidal intent. Obviously, the potential for depression in this type of patient cannot be ignored, even though they may present with no apparent affective difficulties. Furthermore, anosognosia or decreased awareness of deficits can be equally problematic for patients and even more frustrating for family members.

The second case entails a 41-year-old woman who experienced a left-sided stroke involving the temporoparietal region and deep white matter structures 8 years prior to evaluation (Fig. 12). Initially she experienced right hemiparesis and impaired memory and language functioning. While her motor deficits had significantly improved over time, she continued to demonstrate right-sided weakness and neurocognitive impairments in memory, language, and executive functioning. At the time of neuropsychologic evaluation, the patient was also experiencing a severe degree of psychologic distress, as can be seen by her MMPI-2 profile (Fig. 13), with pronounced symptoms of depression and anxiety. During clinical interview, she expressed depressed mood, panic attacks, neurovegetative symptoms of decreased appetite and energy, and frequent tearfulness. These symptoms were present to some degree immediately following her stroke, but increased in severity despite a supportive home environment and treatment with antidepressant medication.

It should be noted that this patient's history consists of several potentially mitigating factors that may have predisposed her to developing emotional problems after her

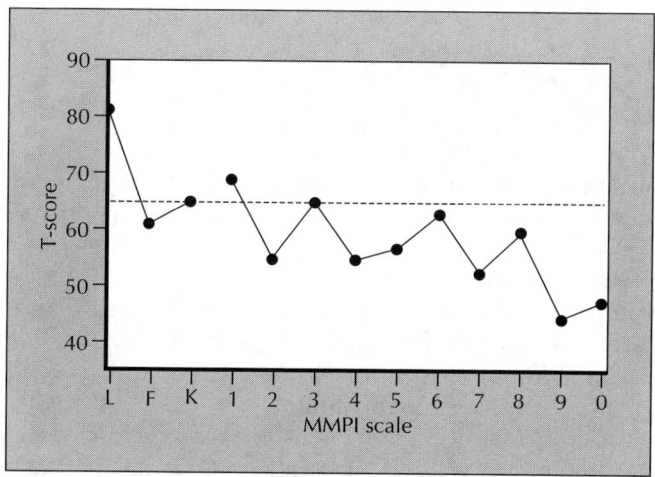

Figure 11. Minnesota Multiphasic Personality Inventory (MMPI)-2 profile 11 months poststroke (case 1).

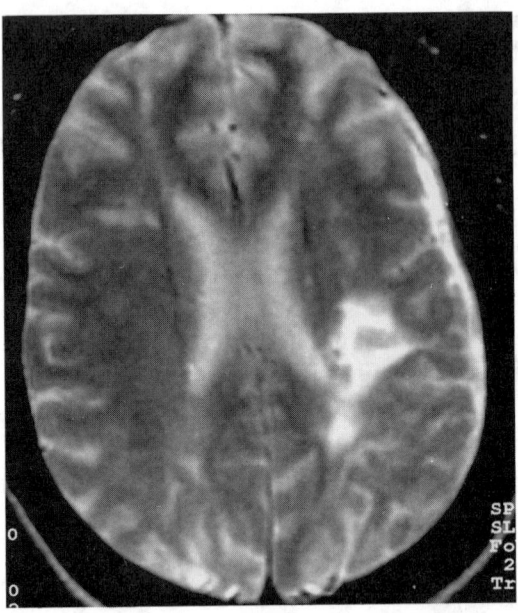

Figure 12. Magnetic resonance imaging scan revealing a remote left-sided lesion involving the temporoparietal region and deep white matter structures.

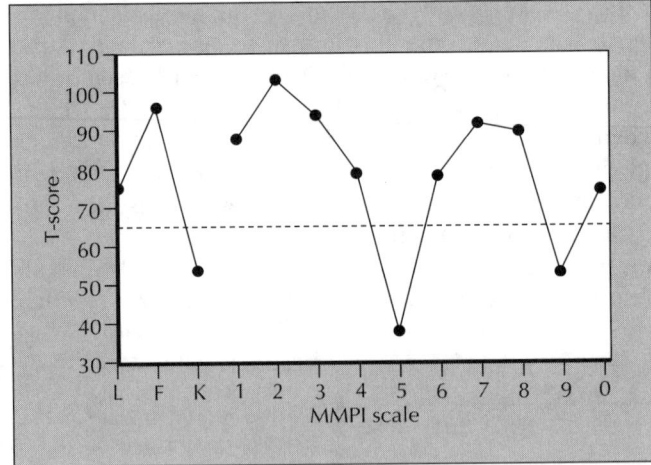

Figure 13. Minnesota Multiphasic Personality Inventory (MMPI)-2 profile for case 2.

stroke. These risk factors include a preexisting history of depression (although never as severe as is currently the case), prior mild traumatic brain injury, and poor support system initially after her stroke. This case provides a good illustration of how premorbid variables combined with clinical factors (*eg*, left-sided lesion, time since stroke) may have made the patient more vulnerable to development of affective difficulties following stroke. Furthermore, her case may be an example of how depression and anxiety following stroke can negatively impact the rate of physical and cognitive recovery. While treatment with antidepressant medication had been minimally effective when this patient was seen, this treatment had only been in place for a short time, and therefore, the ultimate benefit of this intervention had yet to be determined. Given the patient's predisposition for depression and other risk factors for emotional problems, one wonders if this is a case in which early intervention, using a multimodal approach (*eg*, antidepressant medication and psychotherapy), could have protected her from developing a more severe depressive reaction to her situation. While there is no empiric research as yet to sort out this issue, it would benefit clinicians to be sensitive to aspects of a patient's history that may make them more likely to have emotional problems following brain injury, so that proper interventions or preventative measures can be initiated. Even though the two case studies presented were relatively young in the context of stroke patients, their affective problems are typical of the kinds of emotional sequelae that are commonly seen in right- and left-sided stroke, respectively.

Conclusions

The study of PSD is complex and can be influenced by many factors, including neurostructural, temporal, and psychosocial variables. PSD clearly exists as an identifiable entity that closely resembles primary MDD in its presentation and response to treatment. Affective sequelae of stroke can vary depending on lesion location and individual differences, and may include symptoms such as anxiety, mania, apathy, tearfulness, and indifference, in addition to more classical or overt depressive symptomatology. In addition to the need for more systematic research into the neuroanatomy of mood, there is a great need for physicians and family members to be educated about the potential emotional consequences that may occur following stroke (whether neurobiologically based or reactive) so that patients can be treated as swiftly and effectively as possible.

Acknowledgment

We thank Dr. Mark Bauer for his helpful comments on this chapter.

References and Recommended Reading

Papers of particular interest, published recently, have been highlighted as:
- •   Of special interest
- ••   Of outstanding interest

1.   Papez JW: A proposed mechanism of emotion. *Arch Neurol Psychiatry* 1937, 38:725–743.
2.   Cummings JL: The neuroanatomy of depression. *J Clin Psychiatry* 1993, 54(11, suppl):4–20.
3.•• Mayberg, HS: Frontal lobe dysfunction in secondary depression. *J Neuropsychiatry* 1994, 6:428–442.
This paper describes a compilation of studies that examine the relationship between regional brain functioning via PET and depression in patients with Parkinson's disease, Huntington's disease, caudate stroke, and primary depression, implicating the involvement of paralimbic pathways in the development of depression.
4.   Robinson RG, Starkstein SE: Current research in affective disorders following stroke. *J Neuropsychiatry Clin Neurosci* 1990, 2:1–14.
5.   Ross ED, Rush AJ: Diagnosis and neuroanatomical correlates of depression in brain- damaged patients. *Arch Gen Psychiatry* 1981, 38:1344–1354.
6.   Cullum CM, Bigler ED: Short- and long-term psychological status following stroke: short form MMPI results. *J Nerv Ment Disord* 1991, 179:274–278.
7.   Morris PLP, Robinson RG, Raphael B: Prevalence and course of depressive disorders in hospitalized stroke patients. *Int J Psychiatry Med* 1990, 20:349–364.

8. Robinson RG, Starr LB, Price TR: A two year longitudinal study of mood disorders following stroke: prevalence and duration of six months follow-up. *Br J Psychiatry* 1984, 144:256–262.

9. Andersen G, Vestergaard K, Riis JO, *et al.*: Incidence of post-stroke depression during the first year in a large unselected stroke population determined using a valid standardized rating scale. *Acta Psychiatrica Scand* 1994, 90:190–195.

10. American Psychiatric Association: *Diagnostic and Statistical Manual of Mental Disorders*, edn 4. Washington, DC: American Psychiatric Association; 1994.

11. Robinson RG, Morris PLP, Fedoroff JP: Depression and cerebrovascular disease. *J Clin Psychiatry* 1990, 51(7 suppl):26–31.

12. Morris PLP, Shields RB, Hopwood MJ, *et al.*: Are there two depressive syndromes after stroke? *J Nerv Ment Dis* 1994, 182:230–234.

13. *International Statistical Classification of Diseases and Related Health Problems*, edn 10. Geneva: World Health Organization; 1992.

14. Wade DT, Legh-Smith J, Hewer RA: Depressed mood after stroke: a community study of its frequency. *Br J Psychiatry* 1987, 151:200–205.

15. Thompson SC, Sobolew-Shubin A, Graham MA, *et al.*: Psychosocial adjustment following a stroke. *Soc Sci Med* 1989, 28:239–247.

16. Hosking SG, Marsh NV, Friedman PJ: Poststroke depression: prevalence, course, and associated factors. *Neuropsychol Rev* 1996, 6:107–133.

17. Yesavage JA, Brink TL, Rose TL, *et al.*: Development and validation of a geriatric depression screening scale: a preliminary report. *J Psych Res* 1983, 17:37–49.

18. Zung WWK: A self-rating depression scale. *Arch Gen Psychiatry* 1965, 12:63–70.

19. Robinson RG, Bolduc PL, Price TR: Two-year longitudinal study of poststroke mood disorders: diagnosis and outcome at one and two years. *Stroke* 1987, 18:837–843.

20. Robinson RG, Price TR: Post-stroke depressive disorders: a follow-up study of 103 patients. *Stroke* 1982, 13:635–641.

21. Beck AT, Ward CH, Mendelson M, *et al.*: An inventory for measuring depression. *Arch Gen Psychiatry* 1961, 4:561.

22. Wing JK, Cooper JE, Sartorius N: Measurement and classification of psychiatric symptoms. In *Instruction Manual for the PSE*. New York: Cambridge University Press; 1974.

23. House A, Dennis M, Mogridge L, *et al.*: Mood disorders in the first year after first stroke. *Br J Psychiatry* 1991, 158:83–92.

24. Robinson RG, Bolla-Wilson K, Kaplan E, *et al.*: Depression influences intellectual impairment in stroke patients. *Br J Psychiatry* 1986, 148:541–547.

25. Starkstein SE, Robinson RG, Price TR: Comparison of cortical and subcortical lesions in the production of post-stroke mood disorders. *Brain* 1987, 110:1045–1059.

26. Herrmann M, Bartels C, Schumacher M, *et al.*: Post-stroke depression: is there a pathoanatomic correlate for depression in the postacute stage of stroke? *Stroke* 1995, 26:850–856.

27. Morris PLP, Robinson RG, Raphael B, *et al.*: Lesion location and post-stroke depression. *J Neuropsychiatry Clin Neurosci* 1996, 8:399–403.

28. Cullum CM, Bigler ER: Short-form MMPI findings in patients with predominantly lateralized cerebral dysfunction: neuropsychological and computerized axial tomography– derived parameters. *J Nerv Ment Dis* 1988, 176:332–342.

29. Starkstein SE, Robinson RG, Price TR: Comparison of patients with and without poststroke major depression matched for size and location of lesion. *Arch Gen Psychiatry* 1988, 45:247–252.

30. Eastwood MR, Rifat SL, Nobbs H, *et al.*: Mood disorder following cerebrovascular accident. *Br J Psychiatry* 1989, 154:195–200.

31. Morris PLP, Robinson RG, Raphael B, *et al.*: The relationship between the perception of social support and post-stroke depression in hospitalized patients. *Psychiatry* 1991, 54:306–315.

32. Sharpe M, Hawton K, Seagroatt V: Depressive disorders in long-term survivors of stroke: associations with demographic and social factors, functional status, and brain lesion volume. *Br J Psychiatry* 1994, 164:380–386.

33. Robinson RG, Kubos KL, Starr LB, *et al.*: Mood disorders in stroke patients: importance of location of lesion. *Brain* 1984, 107:81–93.

34. Lipsey JR, Spencer WC, Rabins PV, *et al.*: Phenomenological comparison of post-stroke depression and functional depression. *Am J Psychiatry* 1986, 143:527–529.

35. Hamilton M: Development of a rating scale for primary depressive illness. *Br J Soc Clin Psychology* 1967, 6:278–296.

36. Robinson RG, Starkstein SE: Heterogeneity in clinical presentation following stroke neuropathological correlates. *Neuropsychiatry, Neuropsychol Behav Neurol* 1991, 4:4–11.

37. Cullum MC: Cerebral imaging and emotional correlates. In *Neuroimaging in Neuropsychological Functioning.* Edited by Bigler ED, Turkheimer E, Yeo R. New York: Plenum Press; 1989:269–293.

38. Sinyor D, Jacques P, Kaloupek DG, et al.: Poststroke depression and lesion location: an attempted replication. *Brain* 1986, 109:537–546.

39. Starkstein SE, Robinson RG, Berthier ML, et al.: Differential mood changes following basal ganglia versus thalamic lesions. *Arch Neurol* 1988, 45:725–730.

40. Huber SJ, Freidenberg DL, Paulson GW, et al.: The pattern of depressive symptoms varies with progression of Parkinson's disease. *J Neurol Neurosurg Psychiatry* 1990, 53:275–278.

41. Minden SL, Schiffer RB: Affective disorders in multiple sclerosis: review and recommendations for clinical research. *Arch Neurol* 1990, 47:98–104.

42. Rao SM, Huber SJ, Bornstein RA: Emotional changes with multiple sclerosis and Parkinson's disease. *J Consult Clin Psychol* 1992, 60:369–378.

43. Nelson LD, Cicchetti D, Satz P, et al.: Emotional sequelae of stroke: a longitudinal perspective. *J Clin and Exp Neuropsychol* 1994, 16:796–806.

44. Ross ED, Homan RW, Buck R: Differential hemispheric lateralization of primary and social emotions. *Neuropsychiatry Neuropsychol Behav Neurol* 1994, 7:1–19.

45. Agrell B, Dehlin O: Depression in stroke patients with left and right hemisphere lesions: a study in geriatric rehabilitation inpatients. *Aging* 1994, 6:49–56.

46. Starkstein SE, Fedoroff JP, Price TR, et al.: Anosognosia in patients with cerebrovascular lesions: a study of causative factors. *Stroke* 1992, 23:1446–1453.

47. Starkstein SE, Cohen BS, Fedoroff P, et al.: Relationship between anxiety disorders and depressive disorders in patients with cerebrovascular injury. *Arch Gen Psychiatry* 1990, 47:246–251.

48. Finset A: Depressed mood and reduced emotionality after right hemisphere brain damage. In *Cerebral Hemisphere Function in Depression.* Edited by Kinsbourne M. Washington, DC: American Psychiatric Press; 1988:51-64.

49. Lipsey JR, Robinson RG, Pearlson GD, et al.: Nortriptyline treatment for poststroke depression: a double-blind study. *Lancet* 1984, 1:297–300.

50. Starkstein SE, Robinson RG: Affective disorders and cerebral vascular disease. *Br J Psychiatry* 1989, 154:170–182.

51. Dupont RM, Cullum CM, Jeste DV: Poststroke depression and psychosis. *Psychiatric Clin North Am* 1988, 11:133–149.

52. Castillo CS, Starkstein SE, Fedoroff JP, et al.: Generalized anxiety disorder after stroke. *J Nerv Ment Dis* 1993, 181:100–106.

53. Folstein SE: *Huntington's Disease.* Baltimore: The Johns Hopkins University Press; 1989.

54. Grasso MG, Pantano P, Ricci M, et al.: Mesial temporal cortex hypoperfusion is associated with depression in subcortical stroke. *Stroke* 1994, 25:980–985.

55. Mayberg HS, Robinson RG, Wong DF, et al.: PET imaging of cortical S2 serotonin receptors after stroke: lateralized changes and relationship to depression. *Am J Psychiatry* 1988, 145:937–943.

56. Bolla-Wilson K, Robinson RG, Starkstein SE, et al.: Lateralization of dementia of depression in stroke patients. *Am J Psychiatry* 1989, 146:627–634.

57. Robinson RG, Szetela B: Mood change following left hemisphere brain injury. *Ann Neurol* 1981, 9:447–453.

58. Parikh RM, Robinson RG, Lipsey JR, et al.: The impact of post-stroke depression on recovery in activities of daily living over a 2-year follow-up. *Arch Neurol* 1990, 47:785–789.

59. Morris PLP, Robinson RG, Andrzejewski P, et al.: Association of depression with 10-year post-stroke mortality. *Am J Psychiatry* 1993, 150:124–129.

60. Lipsey JR, Robinson RG: Depression: a frequently untreated complication of stroke. *Med Asp Hum Sexual* 1987, 21:57–69.

61. Robinson RG, Lipsey JR, Price TR: Diagnosis and clinical management of post-stroke depression. *Psychosomatics* 1985, 26:769–778.

62. Reding MJ, Orto LA, Winter SW, et al.: Antidepressant therapy after stroke. *Arch Neurol* 1986, 43:763–765.

63.   Lane RM, Sweeney M: Pharmacotherapy of the depressed patient with cardiovascular and/or cerebrovascular illness. *Br J Clin Pract* 1994, 48:256–262.

64.•   Andersen G, Vestergaard K, Lauritzen L: Effective treatment of post-stroke depression with the selective serotonin reuptake inhibitor citalopram. *Stroke* 1994, 25:1099–1104.
This paper presents a well-done, double blind, placebo-controlled investigation of the effectiveness of SSRIs in treating PSD.

65.   Dam M, Tonin P, De Boni A, *et al.*: Effects of fluoxetine and maprotiline on functional recovery in post-stroke hemiplegic patients undergoing rehabilitation therapy. *Stroke* 1996, 27:1211–1214.

66.   Murray GB, Shea V, Conn DK: Electroconvulsive therapy for post-stroke depression. *J Clin Psychiatry* 1986, 47:258–260.

67.   Gustafson Y, Nilsson I, Mattsson M, *et al.*: Epidemiology and treatment of post-stroke depression. *Drugs Aging* 1995, 7:298–309.

68.   Jarrett RB: Comparing and combining short-term psychotherapy and pharmacotherapy for depression. In *Handbook of Depression: Treatment, Assessment, and Research*, edn 2. Edited by Beckham EE, Leber WR. New York: Guilford Press; 1995:435–464.

69.   Bucher J, Smith E, Gillespie C: Short-term group therapy for stroke patients in a rehabilitation center. *Br J Med Psychol* 1984, 57:283–290.

70.   Astrom M, Adolfsson R, Asplund K: Major depression in stroke patients: a 3-year longitudinal study. *Stroke* 1993, 24:976–982.

Index

a

Activities of daily living, in poststroke depression, 351, 352f

Adjunctive treatment, in bipolar disorder, 90

Adjustment disorder with anxiety, diagnosis of, 207t

Adolescents *see* Children and adolescents

α_1-Adrenergic receptor antagonism, drugs causing, 148t

α_2-Adrenergic receptor antagonism, drugs causing, 148t

Adrenergic system, premenstrual dysphoric disorder and, 169

Agoraphobia, diagnosis of, 207t

Akinetic mutism, in basal ganglia-thalamo-frontal loop dysfunction, 5, 6f

Alprazolam
in anxiety disorders, 218
in children and adolescents, 301, 302t, 308t–309t
in obsessive-compulsive disorder, 257
in premenstrual dysphoric disorder, 183, 186t–187t

Alzheimer's disease, depression with, treatment of, 136, 137t

Amantadine, in antidepressant augmentation, 74t, 75

Amitriptyline
in anxiety disorders, in children and adolescents, 310t–311t
in borderline personality disorder, 240t
in depression, in geriatric patients, 125, 126t
in eating disorders with mood disorders, 281
in major depressive disorder, 67t, 69t
mechanism of action of, 69t
in personality disorder with mood disorder, 330t–331t
pharmacology of, 67t, 214t
side effects of, 213t

Amoxapine
in major depressive disorder, 67t
pharmacology of, 67t, 214t
side effects of, 213t

Amphetamines, in antidepressant augmentation, 74t, 75–76

Amygdala
activity of, 13, 14f
seizure kindling in *see* Kindling model

Analgesics, mood symptoms from, 201t

Anorexia nervosa
definition of, 273
mood disorders with
causes of, 274
diagnosis of, 274–277, 275t
familial factors in, 279–280
primary vs secondary depression, 278–279
prognosis for, 287–288
treatment of, 280–281
weight relationship to, 277–278
personality disorders with, 276–277, 276t

Anosognosia, after right hemispheric stroke, 348

Anterior cingulate orbitofrontal basal ganglia-thalamo-frontal loops, dysfunction of, 5, 6f

Antibiotics, mood symptoms from, 201t

Anticonvulsants *see also specific drugs, eg,* Carbamazepine; Valproate
in borderline personality disorder, 239, 240t
in mania, in geriatric patients, 133–134, 133t, 134f

Antidepressants, 211–212 *see also* Tricyclic antidepressants; *specific drugs*
in anxiety disorders, 216
in children and adolescents, 307, 310t–311t
atypical, in major depressive disorder, 69–71, 71t
augmentation strategies for, 72–76, 74t
combined, in treatment-resistant depression, 76–77
in eating disorders with mood disorders, 281
for geriatric patients *see* Geriatric mood disorders, treatment of
high-dose, in treatment-resistant depression, 76
in obsessive-compulsive disorder, 262, 262t
pharmacology of, 214t
prefrontal lobe changes from, 11
side effects of, 213t
switching of, in treatment-resistant depression, 77

Antihypertensive drugs, mood symptoms from, 201t

Anxiety, after stroke, 348

Anxiety disorders *see also* Obsessive-compulsive disorder

m

n

O

q

r

drug interactions of, 153f, 310t
in eating disorders with mood disorders, 281
high-dose, in treatment-resistant depression, 76
mechanism of action of, 65
in mood disorders, 211
overdose of, 66
pharmacology of, 67t, 214t
side effects of, 65–66
switching to/from, in treatment-resistant depression, 77
Triiodothyronine, in obsessive-compulsive disorder, 263t
Trimipramine
in major depressive disorder, 67t
pharmacology of, 214t
side effects of, 213t
Triune brain concept, 3–5
Tryptophan
in obsessive-compulsive disorder, 264
in premenstrual dysphoric disorder, 183, 185, 188t–189t
Tumors, brain, electroconvulsive therapy in, 106
Tyramine-containing foods, monoamine oxidase inhibitor interactions with, 67

u

Ultrarapid cycling, in mood disorders, 23–24, 31–32, 32f, 33f
Ultra-ultrarapid cycling, in mood disorders, 23–24, 31–32, 32f, 33f

v

Valence theory of mood, 6–7
Valproate *see also* Divalproex
in anxiety disorders, in children and adolescents, 314t–315t

in bipolar disorder
in drug combinations, 96
maintenance phase, 94
in secondary mania, 88
in borderline personality disorder, 239, 240t
in mania, in geriatric patients, 133–134, 133t, 134f
side effects of, 97
Venlafaxine
in anxiety disorders, in children and adolescents, 312t–313t
in depression, in geriatric patients, 128, 129t
in major depressive disorder, 68–69, 69t
mechanism of action of, 68–69, 69t
in obsessive-compulsive disorder, 264
pharmacology of, 70t, 214t
side effects of, 129t, 213t
Ventricular-brain ratios, in depression, 349
Verapamil, in bipolar disorder, 86–87
Vitamin B6, supplementation with, in premenstrual dysphoric disorder, 175, 178t–179t

w

Washers, in obsessive-compulsive disorder, 251–252
Weight
loss of, in depression, in frail geriatric patients, 135
mood disorder relationship to, 277–278

y

Yale-Brown Obsessive-Compulsive Scale, 254, 254t, 255t
Yohimbine, drug interactions of, 153f